PoStmodErNism

A Reader

*edited and
introduced by*

THOMAS DOCHERTY

HARVESTER
WHEATSHEAF

New York   London   Toronto   Sydney   Tokyo   Singapore

First published 1993 by
Harvester Wheatsheaf
Campus 400, Maylands Avenue
Hemel Hempstead
Hertfordshire, HP2 7EZ
A division of
Simon & Schuster International Group

Typeset in 10/12 pt Sabon by
Mathematical Composition Setters Ltd, Salisbury

Printed and bound in Great Britain by
·Biddles Ltd, Guildford and King's Lynn

British Library Cataloguing in Publication Data

A catalogue record for this book is available
from the British Library

ISBN 0-7450-1242-6 (hbk)
ISBN 0-7450-1243-4 (pbk)

5 6 7 8 9 01 00 99 98

This one's for the Wee Barra'
and *in memoriam* J.J.D.

Contents

List of Illustrations

Preface

Recent announcements regarding the end of history have been much exaggerated. History is not only continuing, it is also proliferating: the recovery of histories and of local traditions is proceeding in such a way and to such an extent that a disconcerting range of possible futures – some comforting, others distressing – is becoming apparent. The debates over which direction to follow, over which roads to take in these generative narratives, take their place within an extensive set of arguments over what constitutes 'the contemporary'. Another name for the focus of these debates is 'the postmodern question'. We are not at the end of history; we are rather at the beginning of a rethinking of modernity, a rethinking of the world under the sign of postmodernism.

Yet although the term 'postmodern' has become one of the most insistently used terms in the cultural debates of recent years, it is a term which has often been used with a great deal of imprecision. For some, postmodern equates with 'nihilistic' or 'anarchic'; for others, it refers to a culture dominated by the banality of televisual representations and Las Vegas-style neon-signs whose presence everywhere reminds us of the McDonaldisation of an otherwise vegetarian world; yet others think of that explosion of poststructuralist theory which arose in the 1960s and 1970s as a postmodern manner of thinking. The prevalence of such populist, rather superficial and essentially misleading characterisations of the postmodern is troubling for anyone who would take the issues of contemporary culture seriously.

The central rationale for this anthology is to indicate the enormous and eclectic body of interests upon which the postmodern debate has made a significant mark. The gathering of pieces will also reveal how philosophically serious and difficult much of the argument is – and therefore, how necessary is the production of the present *Reader*.

It is thus a good moment to gather together in one volume a diverse and extensive body of writings on the subject which have shaped the varied debates. Critics who are profoundly aware of the arguments within architecture, for instance, will find here that there is some overlap between papers they may already know and papers taken from the field of politics or feminism; readers well versed in literary history will find the possibility of cross-referencing their knowledge in this area with the area of photography or dance or philosophy; people interested in Subaltern studies will discover the ways in which that area enables a possible interface with the avant-garde; and so on.

I have constructed this anthology of pieces with several aims in mind. First, the specific articles collected together constitute a combination of the most influential and the most substantial essays which have shaped the postmodern question. Secondly, I have included articles which are antipathetic to postmodernism as well as some which are more favourably disposed; but the reader will realise fairly quickly that most of the pieces here make a genuine engagement with key cultural issues rather than a simple polemical attack on or defence of a simple position.

Most important is my third aim. I have organised these pieces into eight categories to allow a reader to orientate herself or himself to the book as a whole and to plot her or his own trajectory through it. Each section has its own internal logic and can be – though it need not be – read separately. The whole might be thought of as a 'map of postmodernism', in which each section determines its own 'order of things' internally, while yet retaining the possibility and eventually the necessity of referring to other, different 'orders' to substantiate its significance. The sequential arrangement of these sections hints at my own orientation to the questions, starting from philosophy, moving into cultural questions, and on into overtly political issues. My section introductions, however, are meant to alert the reader more or less covertly to possible lines which will enable a reading 'between' or across the demarcated section boundaries: the reader of this *Reader* will find it possible in time to be transgressive, and will eventually start to draw her or his own different lines across the terrain. Such a redrawing of boundaries, with the concomitant reorganisation of my chronological or temporal sequencing of the articles, is of the essence of a postmodern history whose abiding questions address the rethinking of the temporal and spatial categories within which social and political being is possible.

Many people – apart from the people who actually wrote it – have contributed to the shaping of this book. My colleagues and students in University College Dublin and, more recently, in Trinity College Dublin, gave me the time and energy to undertake the project. It would not have been possible without the extensive and much-appreciated help of the library staff in UCD and in the Bodleian Library, Oxford. As always, Bridie May Sullivan sustained me while the project was in progress, enabling it in the most fundamental ways. Geraldine Mangan gave much-needed secretarial and administrative help at a crucial stage. The project was initially suggested to me by Jackie Jones of Harvester Wheatsheaf, who has shepherded the volume through its entire production, and without whose expert assistance the book simply would not have been made. It would not have been possible to have had a more careful – and caring – editor, whose vision and encouragement have been more than I could have asked for, and more than I deserved. My thanks to all these people does not implicate them in any infelicities in the arrangement of materials here, which remain my fault.

Postmodernism: An Introduction

A spectre is haunting Europe – the spectre of communism.
MARX, *Communist Manifesto*, 1848

'A spectre is roaming through Europe: the Postmodern.'
PORTOGHESI, citing *Le Monde*, 1983

Un spectre hante la pensée contemporaine: le spectre du sujet.
FERRY, 1990

There is hardly a single field of intellectual endeavour which has not been touched by the spectre of 'the postmodern'. It leaves its traces in every cultural discipline from architecture to zoology, taking in on the way biology, forestry, geography, history, law, literature and the arts in general, medicine, politics, philosophy, sexuality, and so on.[1] Yet this amorphous thing remains ghostly – and for some, ghastly – for the simple reason that the debate around the postmodern has never properly been engaged. The term itself hovers uncertainly in most current writings between – on the one hand – extremely complex and difficult philosophical senses, and – on the other – an extremely simplistic mediation as a nihilistic, cynical tendency in contemporary culture.

What is at issue in the postmodern? It would be a futile and pointless exercise to offer any simple definition of the term itself; indeed, much argument arises over the question of precisely how the postmodern should be defined. The term was probably first used by Arnold Toynbee in 1939, and prefigured by him in 1934. In his massive *A Study of History*, Toynbee proposed in a footnote on the first page of the first volume that the period referred to by historians as the 'modern' period ends more or less in the third quarter of the nineteenth century – that is, sometime between 1850 and 1875. This suggests that there is from that moment a kind of break into a period 'after modernism', a postmodernity located not in the twentieth century but rather in the nineteenth. As Toynbee proceeded with his work, he consolidated this notion of an end of the modern period, and in Volume 5 of the study, published in 1939, he used the term 'post-modern', complete with scare quotes, for the first time. At this point he had shifted the chronology slightly, suggesting that the modern now comes to an end during the First World War, 1914–18, and that the postmodern begins to articulate and shape itself in the years between the two wars, between 1918 and 1939.[2]

Toynbee was a product of the late-nineteenth-century desire to found a synoptic and universal history, believing in the possibility of a totalised human history. This demand was answered in Toynbee's work by the fact that his own historiography is, in fact, a Christian theodicy. His task was, in a sense, to write a history which would redeem humanity, by discovering the trajectory of universal history to be a movement of divergence from an original theocentric moment – a sundering from God – driven subsequently by the impulse of return to that same origin: a narrative, like the *Odyssey*, of adventure and return, in which secularity itself is seen as an enormous digression in what is fundamentally a circular narrative structure. The facts of history would make sense, according to Toynbee, in relation to a presiding, governing narrative structure which, if not necessarily always explicit, would none the less be given and legitimated in advance.

This notion of history is one indebted to a certain conflict in the Enlightenment. As Hayden White points out, the Enlightenment broadly agreed with Leibniz's monadology in the sense that the philosophers of the Enlightenment subscribed to the view that there was an underlying unity or direction to human history. But the difference between Leibniz and the Enlightenment is that Leibniz thinks that this essential unity of the human race is simply immanent, whereas the philosophers of Enlightenment view it as an ideal which lies in the future, an ideal which is:

> *yet to be realized* in historical time. They could not take it as a *presupposition* of their historical writing, not merely because the data did not bear it out, but because it did not accord with their own experience of their own social worlds. For them the unity of humanity was an *ideal* which they could *project* into the future ...[3]

Toynbee's invocation of a postmodern moment can thus be seen to be consonant with the idealist drive of Leibniz, but one which acknowledges this necessarily futurist orientation of history itself. Like the critic Erich Auerbach, who also wanted to validate the idea of a shared humanity in which 'below the surface conflicts', 'the elementary things which our lives have in common come to light',[4] Toynbee sees that the 'modern' moment is not one of such universal harmony: both writers were writing under the sign of the Second World War. But Toynbee's answer is to hypothesise a moment in the future, a postmodern moment, when history and humanity can be redeemed.

The word 'postmodern' is thus, characterised, from its very inception, by an ambiguity. On the one hand it is seen as a historical period; on the other it is simply a desire, a mood which looks to the future to redeem the present. The word, with this ambivalence, then hovers around the edges of sociological arguments and the 'end of ideology' debates in the 1950s. But it is in the theories of architecture and in the discourses of literary criticism that the peculiar tension in the term begins to articulate itself more pointedly. In both, there is a tension between, on the one hand, thinking of the postmodern as a chiliastic historical period which, 'after modernity', we either have entered or are about to enter, while on the other realising that we are condemned to live in a present, and adopting a specific – some have said 'schizophrenic' – mood as a result of acknowledging that this present is characterised by struggle or contradiction and incoherence.[5] In this latter case, the mood in question is in the first instance seemingly determined by a quasi-Nietzschean 'active forgetting' of the past-historical conditioning of the present, in the drive to a futurity.[6]

This tension is one which also lays bare the underlying tension between an attitude to postmodernism as an aesthetic style and postmodernity as a political and cultural reality; that is, it opens a question which had been debated before, on the proper relation between aesthetics and politics. The particular intimacy of the relation between the aesthetic and the political under the rubric of the postmodern is apparent even from the earliest engagements. Fiedler, for instance, characterises the emergence of a new artistic priority in the novels of the mid-1960s as a 'critical point' in which we are peculiarly aware 'of the sense in which literature if not invents, at least collaborates in the invention of time'. He goes on:

> At any rate, we have long been aware (in the last decades uncomfortably aware) that a chief function of literature is to express and in part to create not only theories of time but also attitudes toward time. Such attitudes constitute, however, a politics as well as an esthetics ...[7]

Such reconsiderations of culture in terms of the relation between the aesthetic and the political come to their fullest development in the more recent work of Jameson and Lyotard. But it should immediately be noted that a deep formative influence lying behind much of the contemporary debate is the legacy of the Frankfurt School, perhaps most especially the work of Adorno, to which I shall return in more detail below. For present purposes, the salient fact is that aesthetic postmodernism is always intimately imbricated with the issue of a political postmodernity.

As a result of this legacy inherited from Frankfurt, the issue of the postmodern is also – tangentially, at least – an issue of Marxism. Marxism, in placing the labouring body at the interface between consciousness and material history, is the necessary explanatory and critical correlative of a modern culture whose technology (in the form of an industrial revolution) divides human knowledge or consciousness from human power or material history. But the continuing revolutionary shifts within capitalism itself have necessitated in recent years a marked and vigorous self-reflection on the part of Marxism. In Habermas, for instance, Marxism has taken 'the linguistic turn', in arguments for a continuation of the emancipatory goals of Marxist theory and practice under a slightly revised rubric of 'communicative action'.[8] Habermas's faith in the continuing viability of a vigorously self-revising Marxism is shared by a thinker such as Jameson, who models his version of 'Late Marxism' to correspond to Mandel's descriptions of 'Late Capitalism'.[9]

A key date here is, of course, 1968. The seeming availability of a revolution which brought workers and intellectuals together all across Europe represented a high point for a specific kind of Marxist theoretical practice. But when these revolutions failed, many began, at precisely that moment, to rethink their commitment to the fundamental premisses of Marxist theory. Rudolph Bahro and André Gorz began, from an economistic perspective, to rethink issues of growth and sustainable development. Their emergent ecologism coincided nicely with the 'imaginative' aspects of 1968, and Cohn-Bendit began his own movement from red to green. These all joined neatly with the growing awareness of questions of colonialism and imperialism; and the developed countries began to question not only the desire of the underdeveloped countries for the same levels of consumerist technology as those enjoyed by the First World, but also the reliance of that First World upon exhaustible planetary resources. For many, Marxism now began to appear as part of the problem, especially in its assumption of the desirability of human mastery over nature. The emerging Green movement in this period moved closely towards a 'post-Marxism' of sorts, sharing the emancipatory ideals and the desire for the fullest possible enjoyment of human capacities, but tempering that with the idea of a necessary cohabitation between humanity and the rest of nature.[10] Gramsci began to assume a prominent position in this kind of thinking, and his ideas on 'hegemony' began to replace questions of class in importance for some political theorists. Laclau and Mouffe can thus propose a socialist strategy which is, strictly speaking, not Marxist but 'post-Marxist'.[11]

Perhaps the most extreme rethinking of Marx began with the so-called 'philosophy of desire' in texts such as Lyotard's *Economie libidinale*, or in the work of Deleuze and Guattari in the two volumes of their *Capitalisme et schizophrénie*. This work led Lyotard and Deleuze to the position where they seem to favour the supervention of a micropolitics which will attend to the local and the specific without recourse to some grand programme or macropolitical theory such as Marxism, or psychoanalysis, or evolutionary progress. The most explicit attack on the fundamental Marxist category of production is fully developed in Baudrillard's *Le Miroir de la production*. This work set Baudrillard firmly on a trajectory away from any form of classical Marxism. His work since that time has increasingly sustained a case against the oppositional impetus inscribed in Marxist theory. For Baudrillard, opposition is itself always accounted for in any governing ideological formation. Marxism acts as a kind of inoculation, inserted within the body of capitalism the better to sustain it: 'critical' or 'oppositional' thinking is, so to speak, the last refuge of the bourgeois.[12]

Theory – by which I here mean any critical practice which makes a philosophically foundational claim – now enters into crisis itself. Not only has knowledge become uncertain, but more importantly the whole question of how to legitimise certain forms of knowledge and certain contents of knowledge is firmly on the agenda: no single satisfactory mode of epistemological legitimation is available. Even if one were, the very Subject of consciousness has, as a result of deconstruction and psychoanalysis, also been thrown into doubt, provoking Badiou into the proposition of an entirely new and post-Lacanian theory of the Subject. In the postmodern, it has become difficult to make the proposition 'I know the meaning of postmodernism' – not only because the postmodern is a fraught topic, but also because the 'I' who supposedly knows is itself the site of a postmodern problematic. [13]

I propose to introduce the nature of the debate under three main headings. First, I shall address the issue of the Enlightenment and its legacy. This leads into a necessary reconsideration of the conceptions and constructions of the Kantian categories of time and space. Thirdly, I shall raise directly the question of politics, specifically under the rubric of a theory of justice.

I Enlightenment's Legacies

A major source for the contemporary debates around the postmodern is to be found in the work of the Frankfurt School, most specifically in the text proposed by Adorno and Horkheimer in 1944, *Dialectic of Enlightenment*, a work 'written when the end of the Nazi terror was within sight'. This work prefigures some of Lyotard's later questioning of Enlightenment, and seriously engages the issue of mass culture in a way which influences Gorz's thoughts on the 'leisure merchants' of contemporary capitalist societies. It is worth indicating in passing that it is Adorno and Horkheimer, not Lyotard, who propose that 'Enlightenment is totalitarian'. [14] The vulgar characterisation of the German philosophical tradition as pro-Enlightenment and the French as anti-Enlightenment is simplistic and false.

The Enlightenment aimed at human emancipation from myth, superstition and enthralled enchantment to mysterious powers and forces of nature through the progressive operations of a critical reason. According to Gay, 'The Enlightenment may be summed up in two words: criticism and power': criticism would become creative precisely by its capacity for empowering the individual and enabling her or his freedom. [15] Why do Adorno and Horkheimer set themselves in opposition to this ostensibly admirable programme? Why do they argue that 'The fully enlightened earth radiates disaster triumphant'? [16]

The problem lies not so much in the theoretical principle of Enlightenment as in its practice. In the desire to contest any form of animistic enchantment by nature, Enlightenment set out to think the natural world in an abstract form. As a result, the material content of the world becomes a merely formal conceptual set of categories. As Adorno and Horkheimer put it:

> From now on, matter would at last be mastered without any illusion of ruling or inherent powers, of hidden qualities. For the Enlightenment, whatever does not conform to the rule of computation and utility is suspect. [17]

In a word, reason has been reduced to *mathesis*: that is, it has been reduced to a specific *form* of reason. More importantly, this specific inflection of reason is also now presented as if it were reason-as-such, as if it were the only valid or legitimate form of rational thinking. But Adorno and Horkheimer share a fear that, in this procedure, reason has itself simply become a formal category, which reduces or translates the specific contents of material realities into rational concepts, or into a form amenable to mathematisation. Reason becomes no more than a discourse, a language of reason (mathematics), which deals with the 'foreign' matter of reality by translating it into reason's own terms; and something – non-conceptual reality itself – gets lost in the translation. As Adorno and Horkheimer put it: 'The multiplicity of forms is reduced to position and arrangement, history to fact, things to matter.'[18] A mathematical consciousness thus produces the world, not surprisingly, as mathematics. So a desired knowledge of the world is reduced to the merest *anamnesis*, in which the consciousness never cognises the world as it is, but rather *recognises* the world as its own proper image and correlate.[19]

Enlightenment's 'emancipatory' knowledge turns out to involve itself with a question of power, which complicates and perhaps even restricts its emancipatory quality. Knowledge, conceived as abstract and utilitarian, as a mastery over recalcitrant nature, becomes characterised by power; as a result, 'Enlightenment behaves toward things as a dictator toward man. He knows them in so far as he can manipulate them. The man of science knows things in so far as he can make them.'[20] Knowledge is reduced to technology, a technology which enables the *illusion* of power and of domination over nature. It is important to stress that this is an illusion. This kind of knowledge does not give actual power over nature, for that in nature which is unamenable to its formal or conceptual categories simply escapes consciousness entirely. What it does give in the way of power is, of course, a power over the consciousness of others who may be less fluent in the language of reason. Knowledge thus becomes caught up in a dialectic of mastery and slavery in which the mastered or overcome is not nature but rather other human individuals; it is therefore not purely characterised by disenchantment and emancipation. From now on, to know is to be in a position to enslave.

The very myths from which Enlightenment claims the capacity to disenchant humanity are themselves the products of Enlightenment, constructed and produced in order to be unmasked by Enlightenment, and hence to legitimise the utilitarian activity of an Enlightenment epistemology. But we can no longer claim that Enlightenment simply produces a knowledge of the contents of the material world; rather, it produces a formally empowered Subject of consciousness. As Lyotard would later put it: 'what was and is at issue is the introduction of the will into reason'.[21]

Another way of putting this would be to suggest that what is at issue is a confusion between the operations of a pure reason on the one hand and a practical reason on the other. That is, the confusion is between theory and practice, or – as that opposition has most often articulated itself – between *gnosis* and *praxis*. This is an old Aristotelian distinction known for modern times to literary theory via Philip Sidney's mediation of Aristotle and Horace in the Renaissance. Sidney considers a quarrel between the faculties of poetry and philosophy, regarding their respective claims to legislative priority. Poetry, he claims, is 'philophilosophical', philosophy raised to the second power, because it combines epistemology with emotion – combines the *utile* with the *dulce*:

> And that moving is of a higher degree than teaching, it may by this appear, that it is wellnigh the cause and the effect of teaching. For who will be taught, if he be not moved with desire to be taught, and what so much good doth that teaching bring forth (I speak still of moral doctrine) as that it moveth one to do that which it doth teach? For, as Aristotle saith, it is not Gnosis but Praxis must be the fruit. And how Praxis cannot be, without being moved to practise, it is no hard matter to consider. [22]

This prefigures many controversial and pertinent twentieth-century issues, from J. L. Austin's performative linguistics, through Kenneth Burke's advocacy of 'language as symbolic action', to the resurgence of the 'New Pragmatism' in Fish, Rorty and others, all of which might properly by characterised as attempts to bring together the epistemological function of language with the ontological. [23] The idea is most widely known through the practices of Stanley Fish, who once argued that criticism should be attending not to what a text 'means' but to what it 'does'; and, more precisely, that the meaning of a text is, in fact, what it does to its reader. Meaning is located here in an activity of reading; it becomes a practice rather than a merely epistemological listing of verbal senses.

All of this is striving to deal with the same fundamental problem: the relation between the realm of language and the realm of Being. More precisely, it is an attempt to deal with the perceived rupture between these two different orders – a rupture articulated most influentially for our times by Saussurean linguistics, which proposed the arbitrariness of the relation between the linguistic signifier and the conceptual signified. By inserting the cognitive activity of a real historical reader between the text and its epistemological content, critics such as Fish tried to circumvent the threatened split between, on the one hand, the structure of consciousness (i.e. the conceptual forms in which a consciousness appropriates the world for meaning) and, on the other, history (the material content of a text which may – indeed, in Fish's arguments, *must* – disturb such formal or aesthetic structures). [24]

Twentieth-century European criticism has been profoundly aware of the problem here, which can also be formulated in terms of a political question. What is at stake is an old Kantian question regarding the proper 'fit' between the noumenal and the phenomenal. Kant was aware that the world outside of consciousness does not necessarily match precisely our perceptual cognitions of that world; and in the *Critique of Pure Reason* he argued that it was an error to confuse the two. The two elements of signification being confused were distinguished by Frege as 'sense' and 'reference'; and it is a distinction similar to this which is maintained by Paul de Man, who argued that such a confusion is precisely what we know as 'ideology': 'What we call ideology is precisely the confusion of linguistic with natural reality, of reference with phenomenalism.' [25]

De Man's concern was to try to ensure that literary criticism made no premature assumptions of the absolute validity of reference; in this he simply followed the deconstructive practice of maintaining a vigilant scepticism about the legitimacy or truth-contents of any linguistic proposition made about those aspects of the real world that could properly be called 'non-linguistic'. He was aware that the premature assumption that the real was amenable to precise, 'accurate' or truthful linguistic formulation was itself an assumption not only grounded in but precisely demonstrative of ideology. But this, of course, is a reiteration of Adorno and Horkheimer in their complaint about the assumption made by (mathematical) reason that the world is available for a rational comprehension. If we subscribe to de Man's warning, a warning which rehearses the arguments of Adorno and Horkheimer, we can see that the fundamental burden of the *Dialectic of Enlightenment* is that Enlightenment itself is not the great demystifying force which will reveal and unmask ideology; rather, it is precisely the locus of ideology, thoroughly contaminated internally by the ideological assumption that the world can match – indeed, can be encompassed by – our reasoning about it, or that the human is not alienated by the very processes of consciousness itself from the material world of which it desires knowledge in the first place. Enlightenment, postulated upon reason, is – potentially, at least – undone by the form that such reason takes.

For Adorno and Horkheimer, this argument assumed a specific shape recognisable as an abiding question in German philosophy from Kant to Heidegger. What worried Adorno and Horkheimer was that under the sign of Enlightenment, the Subject was capable of an engagement with the world in a manner which would be 'rational' only in the most purely formal sense of the word. That is, they were anxious that what should be a properly political engagement which involves the Subject in a process called intellection or thinking could be reduced to a ritual of thinking, to a merely formal appearance of thinking which would manifest itself as a legitimation not of a perception of the world but of the analytical modes of mathematical reason itself. The political disturbance of the Subject proposed by an engagement with a materially different Other would be reduced to a confirmation of the aesthetic beauty and validity of the process of mathematical reason itself, a reason whose object would thus be not the world in all its alterity but rather the process of reason which confirms the identity of the Subject, an identity untrammelled by the disturbance of politics. In short, the Subject would be reduced to an engagement with and a confirmation of its own rational processes rather than being committed to an engagement with the material alterity of an objective world.

The 'aesthetic engagement' with the world might be characterised as follows: the structure of consciousness determines what can be perceived, and processes it in accordance with its own internal logic, its own internal, formal or ritualistic operations of reason. There is thus a ritual or appearance of engagement with the material world only. 'Political engagement' would be characterised by the rupture of such ritual, the eruption of history into the consciousness in such a way that the aesthetic or formal structures of consciousness must be disturbed. Enlightenment's commitment to abstraction is seen as a mode of disengagement of the ideological, opinionated self: abstraction is itself meant to address precisely this problem. But it leads, according to Adorno and Horkheimer, not to a practice of thinking but rather to the ritualistic form of thought: it offers a form without content. Adorno and Horkheimer's fear is that Enlightenment evades the political precisely when it addresses the political.

One twentieth-century legacy of the Enlightenment is the so-called 'Copernican revolution' proposed initially by structuralism and semiotics. In the wake of Barthes, the world became an extremely 'noisy' place: signs everywhere announced their presence and demanded to be decoded. Such decoding was often done under the aegis of a presiding formal structure, such as myth in anthropology, desire in psychoanalysis, or grammar in literature. In semiotics, it is always important to be able to discover a kind of equivalence between ostensibly different signs: this is, in fact, the principle of decoding or translation itself. But as Adorno and Horkheimer indicate: 'Bourgeois society is ruled by equivalence. It makes the dissimilar comparable by reducing it to abstract qualities.'[26] Such abstraction must wilfully disregard the specificity of the material objects under its consideration: 'Abstraction, the tool of enlightenment, treats its objects as did fate, the notion of which it rejects: it liquidates them.'[27] The semiotic revolution – a revolution which frequently masqueraded as a political, emancipatory heir of Enlightenment – is, like Enlightenment, irredeemably bourgeois, irredeemably caught up in a philosophy of Identity which negates material and historical reality, in the interests of constructing a recognisable Subject of consciousness as a self-identical entity.

The *Dialectic* was written in a profound awareness of the material and historical realities of fascism and the Nazi atrocities. It is a text which inserts itself into a specific tradition of philosophical and ethical tracts which ask for an explanation of the presence of evil in the world. In the eighteenth century, this tradition was properly inaugurated by the debates around Leibniz and Optimism. Optimism is based upon the idea that nature is a Leibnizian monad – that there is a great unifying chain in nature which links together, in a necessary conjunction, all the ostensibly random and diverse elements of a seemingly heterogeneous and pluralistic world. More importantly, Optimism is based upon a specific idea of progressive time which changes the meaning of events. It argues that what appears 'now' to be a local evil will be revealed 'in the fullness of time' to serve the realisation of a greater good. As Voltaire's Pangloss has it in *Candide*, 'all is for the best in the best of all possible worlds'.[28] History would reveal the immanent goodness in the most apparently evil acts; under the sign of a homogeneous and monadic eternity, the heterogeneous and secular would be redeemed.

In a sense, this philosophy is a precursor of some contemporary theoretical principles. According to Optimistic philosophy, the meaning of an event is not immediately apparent, as if it were never present-to-itself: its final sense – to be revealed as the necessity of goodness – is always deferred (to be revealed under the sign of eternity) and thus always different (or not what it may appear to the local eye caught up in the event itself). The major difference between deconstruction and

Optimism is that Optimism believes that the final sense lies *immanently* within an event, whereas deconstruction consistently warns against such metaphysical notions.

Optimism, as a means of explaining away the fact of evil, came under great pressure in the eighteenth century, and was explicitly attacked by Johnson and Voltaire, among others. But one specific event was so catastrophic that the philosophy became incredible. On the morning of Sunday 1 November 1755, an earthquake struck Lisbon and destroyed the city, killing between thirty thousand and forty thousand people. This single event was the final nail in the coffin of a moribund Optimistic philosophy in Europe. But now a different idea of progress in history arises. After 1755, progress is characterised as a gradual emancipation from the demands of the sign of eternity. The secularisation of consciousness becomes a necessary precondition for the possibility of an ethics: that is to say, the ethical is increasingly determined by the philosophically rational, or the good is determined by the true. Blumenberg is eloquent testimony to the inflection that this gives to philosophy and to truth. Traditionally, the pursuit of truth had been considered as pleasurable, eudaemonic; from now on, the absoluteness of truth, and correspondingly its ascetic harshness, becomes a measure of its validity: 'Lack of consideration for happiness becomes the stigma of truth itself, a homage to its absolutism.'[29]

Henceforth, there arises the possibility – and Kant would say the necessity – of separating the realm of facts from the realm of values. Optimism proceeded on the grounds that these were intimately conjoined; and it followed that the progressive movement from evil to good was seen as inevitable. But once epistemology is separated from ethics, the whole idea of historical progress is itself called into question. No longer do we know with any certainty the point towards which history is supposedly progressing. In the wake of this, humanity becomes enslaved not to the enchantments of myth, but rather to the necessities of narrative, for humanity has embarked upon a secular movement whose teleology is uncertain, whose plot is not inherently predetermined by values or by an ethical end.[30]

The critique of progress which becomes available once Kant makes the separation between pure and practical reason makes a resurgence in the twentieth century, specifically around the idea of the postmodern. In architecture, to take a paradigmatic example, there has grown a resistance to the 'modernist' idea that all building must be innovative in its aims and design; rather as Jencks and Portoghesi suggest, it is possible to relearn from the past, to develop a 'new classicism' or simply to engage with an abiding 'presence of the past'. The result is – in principle, if not in fact – a heterogeneous juxtaposing of different styles from different architectural epochs as a putative response to the homogenising tendency of the so-called 'International Style'. This argument leads to the possibility of an awareness in architecture and urban planning in general that the local traditions of a place should be respected in all their specificity, while at the same time those local traditions should be opened to a kind of criticism by their juxtaposition with styles from other localities, different traditions. This is a localism without parochial insularity, in principle.

Much the same arises in some contemporary philosophy. Lyotard has argued that it is becoming increasingly difficult to subscribe to the great – and therapeutically Optimistic – metanarratives which once organised our lives.[31] What he has in his sights are totalising metanarratives, great codes which in their abstraction necessarily deny the specificity of the local and traduce it in the interests of a global homogeneity, a universal history. Such master narratives would include the great narrative of emancipation proposed by Marx; the narrative of the possibility of psychoanalytic therapy and redemption proposed by Freud; or the story of constant development and adaptation proposed under the rubric of evolution by Darwin. Such narratives operate like Enlightenment reason: in order to accommodate widely diverging local histories and traditions, they abstract the meaning of those traditions in a 'translation' into the terms of a master code, a translation which leaves the specific traditions simply unrecognisable. As metanarratives, they also become coercive and normative: Lyotard argues that they effectively control and misshape the local under the sign of the universal. Such a drive to totality cannot respect the historical specificities of the genuinely heterogeneous. Lyotard's debt to the thinking of Critical Theory is obvious here.

Adorno and Horkheimer's pessimism with regard to the difficulty of explaining evil and its place in a supposedly progressive history was foreseen in another important source for the postmodern controversy. In his famous seventh thesis on the philosophy of history, Benjamin indicates the problems of historicism. Historicism is like a critical formalism: it actively forgets the historical effects and consequences flowing from the moment it wishes to investigate, the better to 'empathise' with the moment 'as in itself it really is', so to speak. It formally 'brackets off' its object from history to explore it in itself. The empathy in question is, of course, an empathy with the victors in the struggles inherent in any historical conjuncture; hence historicism benefits and is complicit with the ruling class at the moment of the historian's own writing. The victors in history thus proceed in triumphal procession, bearing with them the spoils of their victory, including those documents which record, legitimise and corroborate the necessity of their victory. Such documents the victors call 'culture'. The historical materialist, unlike the historicist, is profoundly aware of what is being trampled underfoot in this process: the historical materialist remembers what the historicist ignores. Hence historical materialism knows that – in the words of the famous passage – 'There is no document of civilization which is not at the same time a document of barbarism.'[32]

'Modernity' is increasingly being considered as just such a 'document of civilization'. There is, certainly, an enormous amount of good, emancipatory thinking and practice associated with it, and the development of history over the last two hundred years has not been an inexorable progress towards evil. A better attitude to modernity than unmitigated adulation, however, might be one which was analogous to Marx's attitude to the bourgeoisie: on the one hand full of admiration for its civilising energies; on the other critical of its incipient barbarous tendencies.

In his consideration of the implications of modernity, Zygmunt Bauman proceeds on these Benjaminian lines. He cites research into the experiences of the victims of terrorism: people involved in hijacks, people taken hostage. Such people are often apparently fundamentally 'changed' by their experience: their entire personality after the event is different from what it was before. But sociology has contested this notion of a personality change. The person after the event is, in fact, fundamentally the same as the person before; simply certain aspects of the personality which lay dormant in the life before appear now, because the historical conditions are more propitious for their foregrounding. A different aspect of the personality assumes the normative position, repressing certain aspects which were perceived to constitute the essence of the personality before the trauma. It is not the individual who has changed but the historical situation of the individual which demands the appearance of certain aspects of the personality that had always been immanently there.

Bauman then allegorises this, using it as a paradigm to explain the eruption of evil in the Holocaust in the midst of modernity:

> The unspoken terror permeating our collective memory of the Holocaust ... is the gnawing suspicion that the Holocaust could be more than an aberration, more than a deviation from an otherwise straight path of progress, more than a cancerous growth on the otherwise healthy body of the civilized society; that, in short, the Holocaust was not an antithesis of modern civilization and everything (or so we like to think) it stands for. We suspect (even if we refuse to admit it) that the Holocaust could merely have uncovered another face of the same modern society whose other, so familiar, face we so admire. And that the two faces are perfectly comfortably attached to the same body. [33]

So it is not that modernity leads inexorably to the Holocaust. Rather, the civilised face of modernity is attended constantly by a barbarism which is its other side. The historical situation of Germany in the 1930s and 1940s was inhospitable to the civilised priority of modernity, and provided a propitious breeding ground in which the dark and carceral barbarity of modernity could – and did – flourish.

The horror at the evil of the Holocaust is, for Bauman, actually a horror at the rationality of the Holocaust. The Enlightenment project, which was to some extent conditioned by humanity's desire to master nature in the process of disenchantment, enabled the development of an extremely rationally ordered and self-sustaining social process. Part of the legacy of this is the development of efficiency in industry, and the ongoing development – often a self-serving development – of technology. The truth of the matter, according to Bauman, is that:

> every 'ingredient' of the Holocaust ... was normal, 'normal' not in the sense of the familiar ... but in the sense of being fully in keeping with everything we know about our civilization, its guiding spirit, its priorities, its immanent vision of the world. [34]

Structurally, the gas chambers are driven by the same presiding principles that were taken for granted as the positive aspects of modernity: the principles of rational efficiency. The structure of thought which facilitates the possibility of the Holocaust is inscribed in the philosophical structure of Enlightenment itself, for the drive towards a rational society has been controverted into a drive towards rationalism itself, a rationalism which can be used for fascist as well as emancipatory ends. For Bauman, it becomes difficult to disintricate the 'rationality of evil' from 'the evil of rationality'.[35] In the world of the death camps, everything was rationalised:

> Each step on the road to death was carefully shaped so as to be calculable in terms of gains and losses, rewards and punishments. Fresh air and music rewarded the long, unremitting suffocation in the cattle carriage. A bath, complete with cloakrooms and barbers, towel and soap, was a welcome liberation from lice, dirt, and the stench of human sweat and excrement.[36]

The SS also knew that in a perversion of Enlightenment, rationality was their best and most efficient single ally in ensuring that their victims would become complicit in the atrocities. In some situations in the death camps it was perfectly reasonable to betray one's fellow-victims, in the hope of prolonging one's own life:

> to found their order on fear alone, the SS would have needed more troops, arms and money. Rationality was more effective, easier to obtain, and cheaper. And thus to destroy them, the SS men carefully cultivated the rationality of their victims.[37]

Clearly, modernist reason is not inherently good: it can be used for foul purposes, and can be an ally of evil.

Deconstruction provides a philosophical ground for some of this. Derrida places certain strictures upon reason in his famous 'White mythology' essay. In that piece, Derrida characterises metaphysics not in terms of reason as such but rather in terms of a heavily circumscribed reason. He considers metaphysics as:

> the white mythology which reassembles and reflects the culture of the West: the white man takes his own mythology, Indo-European mythology, his own *logos*, that is, the *mythos* of his idiom, for the universal form of what he must still wish to call Reason. Which does not go uncontested.[38]

The Subject of reason, the 'he' who identifies himself here as reasonable, is called into question as a specific historical, cultural and – in a corroboration of Bauman's argument – even racial Subject. To just the same extent (no more, no less) that Enlightenment is totalitarian, Reason is racist and imperialist, taking a specific inflection of consciousness for a universal and necessary form of consciousness. Here Derrida exposes the West's tendency to legitimise itself: the West is reasonable because it says so, and, since it is the definer and bearer of reason, it must be universally reasonable to accede to this proposition. This, as Derrida argues, is clearly a false and troubling logic.

Reason, which was supposed to legitimise the neo-pagan and emancipatory activities of Enlightenment, is now itself in need of legitimation.[39] It can no longer assume the capacity for self-legitimation without assuming an exclusivity; and henceforth its claims upon universality are sullied by its inherent tendency to fall into rationalism. It produces an administered society, not a rational society: reason is replaced by efficiency and by the aesthetic and formal vacuities of rationa*lism*. In *Folie et déraison* Foucault points out that the production of reason is itself dependent upon a primary act of exclusion and incarceration: what reason identifies as its Other – madness – has to be identified and imprisoned in order to enable reason to legitimise itself. Enlightenment reason is in fact a potent weapon in the production of social normativity, driving people towards a conformity with a dominant and centred 'norm' of behaviour. Reason, in short, has to produce the 'scandal' of its Other to keep itself going.[40] Baudrillard has argued that in the present century, this has an extremely important corollary effect. In our time, it is not so much reason itself which requires legitimation as the very principle of reality (which, it is assumed, is founded upon reasonable, rational principles). Society thus produces the Other of the real – fantasy – to legitimise the normativity of its own practices. As Baudrillard puts it in 'The precession of simulacra':

> Disneyland is there to conceal the fact that it is the 'real' country, all of 'real' America, which *is* Disneyland (just as prisons are there to conceal the fact that it is the social in its entirety, in its banal omnipresence, which is carceral).[41]

The emancipation proposed by Enlightenment brings with it its own incarcerating impetus: its 'freedom' turns out to be simply the form of a freedom, an aesthetics rather than a politics of freedom. The name for this aestheticisation of the political is *representation*. In the postmodern, representation, as both a political and an aesthetic category, has come under increasing pressure; and it is to this that we can now turn.

2 The Time is out of Joint

When Deleuze summarises Kantian philosophy, he does so in four 'poetic formulas', the first of which is Hamlet's great proposition that 'The time is out of joint'. Time comes 'unhinged' in Kant, says Deleuze, with the effect of a revolution in the relation between time and space, and time and movement:

> Time is no longer defined by succession because succession concerns only things and movements which are in time. If time itself were succession, it would need to succeed in another time, and on to infinity. Things succeed each other in various times, but they are also simultaneous in the same time, and they remain in an indefinite time. It is no longer a question of defining time by succession, nor space by simultaneity, nor permanence by eternity.[42]

The reconsiderations of time and space in relation to aesthetics were on the German philosophical agenda even before Kant's major *Critiques*, for G. E. Lessing, in *Laoköon* (1766) provoked a debate on the relative priorities of time and space in the different fields of the poetic and the plastic arts.[43]

That the present time is also out of joint is part of my contention in these pages. It is increasingly apparent that many of the debates around the issue of the postmodern not only have their sources in eighteenth-century controversies, but also recapitulate those earlier debates and reconsider them: the late twentieth century is contaminated by the late eighteenth. As Lyotard has recently put it, the whole idea of 'postmodernism' is perhaps better rethought under the rubric of 'rewriting modernity'.[44] But the present day's 'unhinged' time is measured structurally as well in its aesthetic production: the twentieth century is the great moment of an aesthetic which proclaims itself explicitly as 'untimely', the moment of the avant-garde. This avant-garde has put the issue of taste and contemporaneity back on the critical agenda just as firmly as Baumgarten and Kant problematised it in the eighteenth century.[45]

The question of taste is intimately linked to the questions of time and knowledge. Bourdieu indicates that the soi-disant 'aristocracy of culture' disparages 'knowledge' about art, favouring instead an intuitive sense of refinement in the 'connoisseur'. Good taste, which develops for this 'aristocracy' through an aesthetic experience of art at first hand and thus necessarily develops in the time which such a class can afford to devote to aesthetic experience, despises 'education' in questions of taste, which it stigmatises as a time-saving short cut, as superficial, and as a form of *askesis* rather than *aesthesis*.[46] For Kant, such aesthetic experience had always to be formal if it were to have any serious claims to validity in the matter of taste. Unlike Sidney, Kant disparaged as 'barbaric' that kind of taste 'which needs a mixture of *charms* and *emotions* in order that there may be satisfaction'.[47]

The avant-garde made formal experiments whose 'barbaric' effect was carefully contrived, and was often nearly guaranteed because the works proposed themselves as being inappropriate to their present moment, preferring the stance of prolepsis. But this has become problematic as a strategy in the twentieth century. The problem of the avant-garde is that its scurrilous practices themselves, in time, become normative. That is, when they first explode upon the scene, they propose an eruption which shocks thought out of the forms of thought and into the practices of thinking: they critique the 'aristocracy of culture'. There is a movement from gnosis to praxis, from aesthetics to politics – a movement that makes thought as material and real as 'the smell of thyme and the taste of potatoes'.[48] The avant-garde has traditionally served this function of attacking the idealist and formalist sensibility. But the troublesome word in this formulation is, of course, 'traditionally': the avant-garde has entered crisis because it has become a tradition.

Luc Ferry quotes Luciano Berio's scathing comment on the avant-garde: 'Anyone who calls himself avant-garde is an idiot ... the avant-garde is a vacuum.' And Ferry then models an interrogation of the avant-garde on Octavio Paz's astute comments:

Modern art is beginning to lose its powers of negation. For some time now, its negations have been ritual repetitions: rebellion has become method, criticism has become rhetoric, transgression has become ceremony. Negation has ceased to be creative.[49]

By becoming pure criticism, the modernism of the avant-garde has – in a manner akin to the dialectic of Enlightenment – turned back against its own informing principle and subverted it. The search for novelty and innovation has degenerated into its opposite: simple repetition of the formal gestures of innovation for its own sake. As Ferry succinctly puts it, 'The break with tradition itself becomes tradition.'[50] The arising 'dialectic of the avant-garde' results in an enormous speculative and critical pressure upon the avant-garde to justify itself.

The avant-garde used to legitimise itself precisely by being untimely and incomprehensible: a challenge to history and to reason. The work of the avant-garde had to be proposed by one who was somehow in advance of her or his own historical moment. The work produced defies comprehension, in the sense that it defies the possibility of being assimilated into or under the governing philosophical rubric or ideology of its moment of production. It cannot be easily 'translated' into the terms and categories of the already known, and thus challenges the structure of *anamnesis*. The avant-garde necessarily implies that a merely 'conventional' art cannot offer a moment of cognition, but instead indulges in a superficial recognition; and the name for this is representation. For the avant-garde, conventional art was thus an art built entirely upon *anagnorisis*, upon the structure of recognition in which the Subject of consciousness finds the comfort of Identity and self-sameness: the world as it is represented as it is, *tel quel*.[51] Philosophically, therefore, the perceived 'conservatism' of conventional art is also akin to the structure of pragmatism, which is also concerned to engage in practice with the world as it is.[52]

By contrast, the avant-garde presents the world as it is not; more precisely, it has to present a world which is, strictly speaking, unrepresentable. The Subject of consciousness is here going to be refused what Lyotard calls 'the solace of good forms';[53] and, most importantly, what is refused is the solace of the form of Identity. The 'shock of the new' shocks its audience or spectator out of the forms of Identity and into the anxieties of alterity and heterogeneity, into the perception of a world and a Subject of consciousness which is always radically Other.[54] The rationale behind the project of the avant-garde, therefore, is the refusal of gnosis and its replacement with praxis – a shift from epistemology to ontology.

Such a 'practical art' involves the artist in what appears to be a temporal or chronological impossibility. She or he re-presents, in a work or an event, something which cannot yet ever have been present: re-presenting comes before presence in this state of affairs. For the *avant-gardiste*, it is no longer the case that art re-presents an already existing essential world; rather, this relation is reversed and the fact or practice of re-presentation itself produces a world. However, such a production proposes a world which is unrecognisable – or, perhaps more strictly, non-cognisable: a world is presented which is 'essentially' different from the world which we had 'consensually' known before the avant-garde production. Both consensus as such and the identity of the Subject who is implicated in this consensually agreed 'knowledge' are thereby challenged.

Structurally, in the avant-garde, aesthetics precedes politics. Yet it is also argued that the aesthetic precisely *is* politics in this, because of what McHale calls this 'change of dominant',[55] for as a result of the prioritisation of praxis over gnosis there is a corresponding attack upon the philosophy of Identity ('Know thyself') and its replacement with a philosophy of alterity ('Acknowledge the unknowability of the Other'). This proposes a political shift based upon the complication, for the Subject of consciousness, of locating itself always 'elsewhere'. Bakhtin would have thought of this in terms of a 'dialogical' construction of the world in language; Habermas thinks of it in terms of an intersubjective idea of communicative action; Lacanian psychoanalysis would underpin these and other inherently political attacks on the philosophy of Identity. Lacan argued that:

> The Other is ... the locus in which is constituted the I who speaks to him who hears, that which is said by the one being already the reply, the other deciding to hear it whether the one has or has not spoken.[56]

Alterity such as this is fundamental to the avant-garde, which must always be in the time of the other. Ferry points out that the avant-garde project, at least since Kandinsky, is predicated upon – and that it necessarily (even if unwittingly) subscribes to – three central forces, all of them politically charged: elitism, historicism, individualism. The avant-garde is elitist because the artist is the hero who has seen the future in advance of everyone else, and whose task is to risk her or his own greater powers on behalf of the tardy common masses. The avant-garde is historicist because its artists are necessarily historically out of step with the masses around them; but also because this has to be acknowledged as a merely provisional state of affairs. The masses, once history progresses, will see that the artist was always-already right in any case; and, in acknowledging their own tardiness, the masses have to subscribe to a version of history as the site of an inevitable linear *progress*.

This relates back to Lukács's thinking on the avant-garde. Paradoxically, the genuinely avant-garde, for Lukács, was always profoundly realist: in order to qualify as avant-garde, it had to be not merely prophetic but accurately prophetic, anticipatory. This means that the avant-garde can never by identified as such until time has passed to allow for the verification of its propositions: one can only ever 'have been' avant-garde:

> Whether a writer really belongs to the ranks of the avant-garde is something that only history can reveal, for only after the passage of time will it become apparent whether he has perceived significant qualities, trends, and the social functions of individual types, and has given them effective and lasting form ... only the major realists are capable of forming a genuine avant-garde.[57]

It should be noted, in passing, that this is not very far removed from Lyotard's notions of the future anteriority of the postmodern.[58] The same temporal *décalage* is involved in both Lukács and Lyotard.

Finally, and most explicitly, for Ferry the ideology of the avant-garde has to be individualist, for its whole practice is based on the 'expression du Moi':

> ou, pour reprendre la formule même de Kandinsky, 'expression pure de la vie intérieure'
> de celui qui, par son originalité, se trouve tout à la fois au sommet du triangle (élitisme)
> et en avance sur son temps (historicisme) et qui, par suite, constitue seul une véritable
> *individualité* ...[59]
>
> [or, to pick up the very formulation of Kandinsky, 'pure expression of the interior life'
> of she or he who, by virtue of originality, finds herself or himself all at once at the apex
> of the triangle (elitism) and in advance of her or his time (historicism) and who, in
> consequence, constitutes alone a true *individuality*.]

The 'expression du Moi' necessarily distinguishes the avant-garde Self from its
Others, and in fact thereby produces its Other. Alternatively, one could say that it
is precisely such an individuation of the avant-garde artist which produces all other
individuals as a 'mass', a mass culture in the form of a despised culture industry.
So the avant-garde constructs and attacks its own enemy. Structurally, this parallels
the manner in which Enlightenment reduces reason to rationalism: in the case of the
avant-garde, what we see is the reduction of political activity to the ritual form of
such activity – or, in a phrase, the aestheticisation of politics. This is why both the
avant-garde and the notion of a mass culture enter into crisis in the middle of the
twentieth century.

The question of the avant-garde is therefore, fundamentally, a question of the
intimate relations between speed and politics. In some ways, of course, this is also
the question of Enlightenment. In political terms, Enlightenment proposed a
demarcation between the 'advanced' and the 'underdeveloped'; and in this
distinction the advanced feels itself to be legitimised in its activities of mastering,
controlling, dominating and colonising what it stigmatises as the underdeveloped.[60]
It is also important to Enlightenment and its legacy to maintain a structural sense
of development (in accordance with the Whiggish idea of a historical linear
progress). But what Enlightenment mistakes about this process is that there may be
a number of historical lineages, a number of 'progressions' or directions in which
history is flowing simultaneously: that history is not a singular line, but a network
of forces which all proceed in their own directions, heterogeneously. That is,
Enlightenment fails to see that instead of the rubric 'advanced/underdeveloped'
(more recognisably characterised by the terms 'First World' and 'Third World'), it
is better to think that the world is simply lived at different speeds, in different times,
in different places. In short, there is not one world (nor even three), but rather many;
all being lived at different rhythms, none of which need ever converge into
harmony.[61]

There is thus a political dimension to the 'untimely meditation' of the avant-garde:
a politics to speed. It is, of course, Paul Virilio who has considered this most fully.
Virilio's work on urbanism and on the theory and strategy of war offers a different
angle on the question of the Optimism of the avant-garde. The avant-garde is in
conflict with what we might call the dominant aesthetic of its time: it is also,

however, in conflict with time itself, being out of its proper moment: it is always necessarily *anachronistic*. This collocation of time and conflict is of the essence of the political for Virilio.

Virilio returns to Clausewitz, who shared with Marx an interest in the dialectical process of history, and whose conception of the structure of war found echoes in Lenin. Yet there are certain fundamental differences between the Marxist–Leninist tradition and Clausewitz. Clausewitz thought of history as a dialectical process of struggles not between specific classes, but formally between the impulse to attack and the impulse to defend. The resulting dialectic of defence and attack would eventually lead to a state of pure war.[62] This dialectic – this war – is the foundation of the political for Virilio, because it is through war that there arises the need for and the maintenance of those geographical organisations that delimit the space of city or state. But the formation of these boundaries is neither simply nor primarily spatial; on the contrary, the city, the *polis* itself, is formed from a particular relation to time; and its boundaries are grounded in a specific internal historicity, a 'progress' which is relatively autonomous from the time 'outside'. So the city is not a stable point in space but rather a historical 'event': it is not punctual, but eventual.

This requires some explanation. How does a political space develop and consolidate itself as a recognisable entity? Virilio cites, for an explanatory instance, the development of the elevated observation post in the history of war struggles. Because it enables surveillance, such an elevated post gives a group of fighters or a community the time in which to decide among a number of possible military attitudes available to it in a specific given situation. It is in this time – that is, *in the production of time or of a temporal difference between two communities* – that a war mentality becomes genuinely possible, replacing the immediacy which is integral to more 'primitive' conditions of struggle. With this production of time:

> il ne suffira plus d'être rapidement informé sur son milieu, *il faudra aussi l'informer*, c'est-à-dire tenter de conserver *sur place* son *avance* sur l'ennemi, d'où la construction autour du tertre, d'enclaves protégées, d'enceintes, de palisades, destinées à *ralentir* l'aggresseur.[63]

> [it will no longer be enough to be informed about one's milieu, *one must also form it*, that's to say try to maintain *there and then* one's *advance* over the enemy, whence arises the construction, around the hillock, of protected enclaves, of surrounding walls, of stockades, whose purpose is to *slow down* the aggressor.]

This dialectic of speed and slowness, maintaining one's progress away from the enemy while also slowing that enemy's pursuit as much as possible, produces a difference in time between aggressor and victim. The result is the production of the origin of the city built upon the rampart. This space of the *polis* is thus conditional upon a logically prior temporal dialectic between the speed of the settler in claiming her or his ground and the slowness which she or he can impose upon the new, slightly more tardy, aggressor. Such a dialectic of speed and slowness is of the essence of war itself. The tension between the relative speeds of the 'First' world (which establishes the rampart) and its tardy Others (whose political stabilities are less assured) is endemic to what we might call 'significant space', by which I mean any space to which we can assign a mark of identity, be it a name, a history or a culture: in short, a political entity. That which appears to be a stable point in space, the political city, is in fact an event in time, and an event whose very essence is that it is fraught with an internal historicity or mutability. It is therefore not a point, but an event. [64]

This politics is not devoid of aesthetics; on the contrary, questions specifically relating to the perception of beauty enter into the war mentality itself, long before Marinetti and the Futurists laid such questions bare in their adulation of the beauty of the machinery of war. [65] War strategy is profoundly 'aesthetic', in the strict sense of the term which relates it to perception; for war is about the control of appearance and disappearance, a control resting upon a logistics of perception. Virilio considers the paradigmatic example of the *maquisard*, who had to melt into the surrounding topography and even into the vacuous and immaterial atmosphere: 'he lives then under the cover of grass and trees, in atmospheric vibrations, darkness'. [66] War depends upon a mode of subterfuge in which, by making oneself less visible, one can bring the enemy into one's sight and then make her or him disappear in the kill. Virilio charts this in a logical sequence. First there is the hunt for food, whose victim is the animal. This gives way to a second stage of hunting: a hunt whose victim is woman. The domestication of woman enables a third stage of the hunt, which Virilio identifies as the fundamentally homosexual hunt: war as we commonly know it. The homosexuality of the resulting duel is the basis of the beautiful in its more conventional sense, a beauty carved in the semiotics of the body:

> L'homme fatal est le modèle de la femme, le maquillage des préliminaires de la mise à mort précède celui des amours, la séduction du guerrier travesti est comme pour toute l'espèce animal la caractéristique du mâle, l'homosexualité du duel est à l'origine du beau, ce beau qui n'est que le premier degré d'une torture infligée aux corps, par les traits, les scarifications, les cicatrices, en attendant les mutilations, la mort. Le beau est peut-être le premier *uniforme*. [67]

> [The deadly male [*l'homme fatal*] is the model for the woman [*la femme fatale*], make-up for the preliminaries to the killing precedes that for loving, the seduction of the warrior in drag is, as for the whole animal species, the characteristic of the male, the homosexuality of the duel is at the origin of the beautiful, that beautiful which is but the first degree of a torture inflicted upon bodies, by strokes, scarifications, scars, all the way through to multilations and death. The beautiful is, perhaps, the first *uniform*.]

Such a violence in the foundation of the aesthetic might usefully be considered alongside Baudrillard's comments, in which he argues:

> Le déni de l'anatomie et du corps comme destin ne date pas d'hier. Il fut bien plus virulent dans toutes les sociétés antérieures à la nôtre. Ritualiser, cérémonialiser,

affubler, masquer, mutiler, dessiner, torturer – pour séduire: séduire les dieux, séduire les esprits, séduire les morts. Le corps est le premier grand support de cette gigantesque entreprise de la séduction. [68]

[The denial of anatomy and of the body as destiny does not date just from yesterday. It was much more widespread in all societies anterior to our own. Ritualising, ceremonialising, getting decked out, masking, disfiguring, marking, torturing – to seduce: to seduce the gods, to seduce the spirits, to seduce the dead. The body is the first great prop for the gigantic venture of seduction.]

Seduction, in Baudrillard, is much more than simply a sexual activity; he proposes it as a challenge to the logical primacy of the Marxist category of *production* as a primary determinant of the condition of history. Given the political nature of such seduction, then, these statements from Virilio and Baudrillard turn out (perhaps surprisingly) to be much closer to Eagleton's recent work than we might have expected. In *The Ideology of the Aesthetic*, Eagleton proposes an argument which, grounded in the labouring body of Marxism, will aim to restore to the body its plundered powers via the aesthetic: in short, Eagleton – like Baudrillard, Lyotard, Virilio and many others who have challenged Marxism – wishes to restore to the aesthetic its full capacity for the political. The site for such a restoration is the human body.

When Hamlet suggests that 'the time is out of joint', he might well also have indicated that – in this play, at least – the body is also and equally 'out of joint', or disjunctive. The human body in *Hamlet* is itself a central site of the play's peculiar status as a 'modern' drama. First, there are a series of deliberations about the material status of the body, in the figure of the Ghost; this then gives way to reflections on the body as the site of theatrical enactment and representation when Hamlet considers the effects of the Player King's speech, a speech which has a physical effect on the Player, bringing tears to his eyes; then Hamlet, with the gravediggers, ponders the location of the human spirit in a specific corporal location when he fictionalises the downfall of Alexander:

> Alexander died, Alexander was buried. Alexander returneth into dust, the dust is earth, of earth we make loam, and why of that loam whereto he was converted might they not stop a beer-barrel? [69]

Thus begins a series of more or less comic reflections on the 'disjunctive' human body in literature, perhaps culminating in Beckett, whose Murphy becomes precisely the ashes and dust mixed with the detritus of Alexander's beer-barrel. [70] Such a disjunctive body determines the necessity for the modern and postmodern aesthetic obsession with the body – a body now firmly in time, but in a disjunctive time, producing what Kroker characterises as a specifically postmodern 'panic':

> What is postmodernism? It is what is playing at your local theatre, TV studio, office tower, doctor's office, or sex outlet. Not the beginning of anything new or the end of

anything old, but the catastrophic, because fun, implosion of contemporary culture into a whole series of panic scenes at the *fin-de-millennium*.[71]

3 Just Politics

As Foucault indicated in *Discipline and Punish*, the human body is the site for the inscription of justice. Yet at the beginning of 'modernity', in the late eighteenth century, this body undergoes a significant change. In the immediately preceding period, the body was extremely visible in the moment of the exacting of justice: it enabled justice to be seen in the physical torments of punishment for crime, exhibited as public spectacle. But then a fundamental displacement takes place within the judicial system, whose effect is to change the significance – even the experience – of the physical body. Foucault points out that between roughly 1770 and 1840 in Europe, the spectacle of public physical torture disappears; but it is replaced by a supplementary judicial code:

> The body now serves as an instrument or intermediary: if one intervenes upon it to imprison it, or to make it work, it is in order to deprive the individual of a liberty that is regarded both as a right and as property. The body, according to this penality, is caught up in a system of constraints and privations, obligations and prohibitions. Physical pain, the pain of the body itself, is no longer the constituent element of the penalty. From being an art of unbearable sensations punishment has become an economy of suspended rights. If it is still necessary for the law to reach and manipulate the body of the convict, it will be at a distance, in the proper way, according to strict rules, and with a much 'higher' aim. As a result of this new restraint, a whole army of technicians took over from the executioner, the immediate anatomist of pain: warders, doctors, chaplains, psychiatrists, psychologists, educationalists.[72]

This shift in the judicial system is reflected in the development of aesthetics as well. In the late-seventeenth-century English theatre, for instance, a character's response to her or his perception is marked by and on the body, which is extremely expressive. Style comes to the forefront of everything: Restoration theatre in England and Molièresque comedy in France feature characters who lack substantive psychological content and have only the form of style – a style expressed in manners, costume, corporeal decorum. By the late eighteenth century, however, in a text such as Mackenzie's *The Man of Feeling* (1771), this has become almost parodic. This novel looks backwards to a moment when a sociological norm of a specific 'sensibility' was a marker of class, and of sociocultural legitimacy and validation. If one's response to the world was so refined that it was *immediately* visible, legible in the tears or the general deportment of the individual, then that individual, and her or his social values, were validated. Here, a matter of aesthetics or taste determines social and political law. Those whose refinement was of a lesser order (i.e. those who were less 'fashionable') were also thereby stigmatised as the victims – the objects – of the law of the aesthete. As Bourdieu argued, taste becomes law in a situation such as this; and, as in Foucault's horrific tales of punishment and torture, the body becomes the site of an inscription of sense as well as of sensibility.[73]

A mere thirty years later, however, the entire sensibility tradition is being thoroughly satirised in Austen and others. The body is more 'distanced' from the public display of emotion: the beginnings of a specifically 'English' sang-froid or phlegmatic nature are being developed, at a moment when, as Deane has shown, the idea of a 'national character' is gaining ground.[74] That phlegmatic nature, however, is one which distances – or, better, alienates – the human body from art – indeed, even from perception. The history of that alienation, and of its consequent political effect, is charted in Eagleton's *Ideology of the Aesthetic* and in Ferry's *Homo Aestheticus*.

So the modern might be charted in terms of an attitude to the human body and, more importantly, to its appearance and disappearance. For Foucault, the developing history of punishment is one which eradicates the traces of the body as such: even the condemned prisoner's last pain is denied her or him under the anaesthetising needle of the doctor, so that the human body as a material entity almost entirely disappears, even for the human Subject itself. This process, which begins in the eighteenth century, finds its culmination in another attitude to the body in the Nazi atrocities which were also concerned to make certain human bodies disappear in the interests of maintaining a mythic, purely formal body.

What happens to justice in all this? What is the proper relation, in this modernism, between the aesthetic and the political insertion of the body in human space? The just has always been intimately linked to the true; and justice depends upon a revelation of truth. There is a clear structural similarity between this and a Marxist hermeneutic. The project of an ideological demystification starts from the presupposition that a text (or the object of any criticism) is always informed by a specific historical and political nexus, and that the text is the site for the covering over (the disappearance) of the contradictions implicit in this historical conjuncture. The task of criticism here is one which is in the first instance epistemological: it involves the necessary revelation of a truth lying concealed behind an appearance. But it is precisely this opposition – between ideological appearance on the one hand and true reality on the other – which has come under strong speculative pressure. As a result, the question of justice has also required fundamental reconsideration.

This can be explained further. I have already argued for a consideration of the city not as a point in space but rather as an event in time. In general, that which we had assumed to be a relatively stable essence whose true shape can be revealed in analysis turns out to be unstable, traversed by an internal historicity. By extension now, justice cannot be indicated by a series of specific legal 'cases', presented as 'factual', for instance; rather, justice itself can exist only as an event, not as the repetition of a formula or as a judgment made in conformity with a pre-given rule. The real, as modernism already knew, is always in flux. But it now follows that the real is itself not something which can be determined according to a dialectic of appearance and reality; rather, the real depends upon the dialectical – and political – speed regulating appearance and disappearance.

The essence of the political in our time is formulated upon precisely this relation between appearance and disappearance. Since we live in what Debord characterised as a 'society of the spectacle',[75] our politics – and our justice – have become increasingly 'spectacular', a matter of 'show trials' and 'live' TV courtroom drama. A poignant icon of this state of affairs is to be found in the example often cited by Virilio of the women of the Plaza de Maya, who congregate in silence at regular intervals simply to bear witness to their relatives who have been made to 'disappear'. Political systems – including soi-disant 'democratic' systems – increasingly deal with dissident thought by controlling and regulating its appearances; and, on occasion, dissident thinkers themselves are entirely 'disappeared' – or, as Orwell characterised this in *Nineteen Eighty-Four*, 'vaporized'.[76]

To know the real is no longer to know something stable: epistemology is contaminated by history. As a result, knowledge itself – predicated upon a stable relation between Subject and Object of knowledge, a moment of anagnorisis or recognition producing the Identity of the Subject – has entered into crisis. This crisis was foreseen, long before Lacan and Derrida, by Kant. In the *Critique of Pure Reason*, Kant faced up to the question of the scientificity – by which he meant verifiability – of knowledge about the world. He argued for the necessity of *a priori* judgement in such matters. But more than this, he argued that an *a priori* knowledge gleaned simply from analytic methodology would simply tell us a great deal about the methodology, and not necessarily anything new about the world: it would provide only anamnesis. That is to say, to perceive the world at all, consciousness needs a form in which to comprehend it; that form – the analytic method of perception – serves primarily the function of self-legitimation. Kant wanted the world to be able to shock us into new knowledge; he wanted the reality of the world to serve the function of an avant-garde: that is, to be able to shock us out of the ideological conditioning of our mental structures – those structures which, according to the Romanticism of Kant's time, shape the world. He wanted, thus, what he called a *synthetic a priori*, which would exceed the *analytic a priori*. This would not only confirm the method of epistemological analysis of the world, it would also allow for the structural modification of the very analytic method itself to account for and encompass a new given, the new and therefore unpredictable data of the world. It would thus provide not just anamnesis, but the actual event of knowledge.

In the *Critique of Judgement*, this distinction between analytic and synthetic *a priori* more or less maps on to a distinction between determining and reflective judgement. In a determining judgement, the Subject of consciousness is not implicated in the act or event of judging at all: a method, a structure, determines the result of the judgement. In reflection, we have a state of affairs akin to that when we consider the aesthetically beautiful: we judge – in what has become the famous and controversial phrase – 'without criteria'.[77] In short, all this means is that we judge without a predetermining theory. Judgements are then replaced by judging;

and the *form* of justice (a justice which is 'seen to be done', and is legitimised *simply because* it is 'seen', televised, disseminated and distributed 'democratically') by the *event* of justice.

In this state of affairs, the operation of reason is extending itself beyond its own internally coherent framework, and attempting to grasp the new. This extension is one in which we begin to see a shift in emphasis away from what we could call scientific knowledge towards what should properly be considered as a form of narrative knowledge. Rather than knowing the stable essence of a thing, we begin to tell the story of the event of judging it, and to enact the narrative of how it changes consciousness and thus produces a new knowledge. Barthes once advocated a shift 'from work to text'; the postmodern advocates a shift 'from text to event'.[78]

Lyotard understands this in terms of a movement away from any subscription to totality. A scientistic knowledge would be one which is grounded in the totality of a governing theory; and whose formulations and propositions are tested 'internally', by reference to that theory itself. This is also what Lyotard describes as a modern mood; the postmodern, by contrast, is characterised by an 'incredulity towards metanarratives'[79] or, more simply put, by a suspicion of the scientistic nature of much theory. The postmodern prefers the event of knowing to the fact of knowledge, so to speak.

An old problem now returns: how can one legitimise an 'event' of judging? With respect to what can one validate what must effectively be a singular act? For Lyotard, credulity towards metanarratives (i.e. subscription to a prevailing theory against whose norms single events of judging might themselves be judged and validated) is tantamount to a concession to systems theory. Even Habermas, who is opposed to Lyotard on many counts, opposes this. Habermas attacks Luhmann, for instance, after whom there is a danger that 'belief in legitimacy ... shrinks to a belief in legality'.[80] For Habermas, the corrective to this lies in a discursively organised social rationality. Habermas accepts (*pace* the received wisdom) in large measure the basis of Lyotard's critique of Enlightenment reason. He is profoundly aware that there is a potential inequality in a system which claims reason for itself and stigmatises all those with whom it will communicate as being inherently unreasonable. That is, Habermas is aware that the consciousness which pronounces itself reasonable is in danger of imposing its norms, in imperious manner, upon all and every other possible consciousness. The counter to this lies in a 'theory of communicative action'; but here Habermas and Lyotard diverge once more.

For Habermas, it is not only desirable but also possible to establish a consensus among the participants in the event of communication: and it is logically possible to organise a social formation on more rational terms, through a discursively agreed consensus. Lyotard associates such consensus with the end of thinking, and (rather like Adorno, in fact) suggests that such consensus would be merely formal, a means of covering up injustice under a veneer of justice. In a debate with Rorty – who shares with Habermas a faith in some kind of 'conversation' – Lyotard indicates that there is a 'soft imperialism', a 'conversational imperialism' at work in the drive to establish consensus between participants in a dialogue.[81] Only if we respect – and stress – the heterogeneity of language-games will we save the possibility of thinking. In short, this means that it is only in the refusal of consensus and in the search for 'dissensus' that we will be able to extend thinking, to allow it to be shocked into the new, the (chronological) postmodern. Consensus is a means of arresting the flow of events, a mode whereby eventuality can be reduced to punctuality; it is a way of reducing the philosophy of Becoming to a philosophy of Being. The modernist assumes that it is possible to pass from Becoming to Being; the postmodernist believes that any such move is always necessarily premature and unwarranted.

Politics, as we usually think it, depends upon consensus; most often, of course, such consensus articulates itself under the rubric of 'representation' (a category which has already come under pressure in its aesthetic formulation), in which there is first an assumed consensus between representative and represented, and secondly the possibility of consensus among representatives. This is bourgeois democracy, hardly a democracy at all. In place of such a politics, it might be wiser to look for a justice. Justice cannot happen under bourgeois democracy, which is always grounded in the tyranny of the many (and even, of course, in many 'democractic' systems, on the tyranny of the few – on the hegemonic control of thought exercised by a few who mediate the norms of a social formation). We can no longer legislate comfortably between opposing or competing political systems, for we no longer subscribe to any such totalising forms; but we can address the instance, the events, of justice.

Here lies the basis of an ethical demand in the postmodern, a demand whose philosophical roots lie in the work of a thinker such as Levinas. We must judge: there is no escape from the necessity of judging in any specific case. Yet we have no grounds upon which to base our judging. This is akin to Levinas:

> I have spoken a lot about the face of the Other as being the original site of the sensible. ... The proximity of the Other is the face's meaning, and it means in a way that goes beyond those plastic forms which forever try to cover the face like a mask of their presence to perception. But always the face shows through these forms. Prior to any particular expression and beneath all particular expressions, which cover over and protect with an immediately adopted face or countenance, there is the nakedness and destitution of the expression as such, that is to say extreme exposure, defencelessness, vulnerability itself. ... In its expression, in its mortality, the face before me summons me, calls for me, begs for me, as if the invisible death that must be faced by the Other, pure otherness, separated, in some way, from any whole, were my business.[82]

The face-to-face implicates us in a response, in the necessity of sociality. We must behave justly towards the face of the Other; but we cannot do that according to a predetermined system of justice, a predetermined political theory. The Other is itself always other than itself: it is not simply a displaced Identity in which we may once more recognise and reconstitute ourself. The demand is for a just relating to alterity, and for a cognition of the event of heterogeneity. In short, therefore, we must discover – produce – justice. It is here that the real political burden and trajectory of the postmodern is to be found: the search for a just politics, or the search for just a politics.

Notes

Where full details are available in the Bibliography, references contain only essential information.

1. The areas in which postmodernism is already well known can be found in the bibliography, but I draw attention here to some random articles which demonstrate how postmodernism has begun to infiltrate unexpected areas: D. R. Griffin (ed.), *The Reenchantment of Science: Postmodern proposals*, 1988; Harvey Cox, *Religion in the Secular City: Toward a postmodern theology*, 1984; David Harvey, *The Condition of Postmodernity* (on geography), 1989; Edward Soja, *Postmodern Geographies*, 1990; David Platten, 'Postmodern engineering', 1986, 84–6; David Widgery, 'Postmodern medicine', 1989, 897; J. H. Wikstrom, 'Moving into the post-modern world', (on forestry) 1987, 65.

2. See Arnold Toynbee, *A Study of History*, vol. 1. (1934; 2nd edn, Oxford University Press, Oxford, 1935), p. 1, n2; vol. 5 (Oxford University Press, Oxford, 1939), p. 43.

3. Hayden White, *Metahistory* (Johns Hopkins University Press, Baltimore, 1973; repr. 1987, pp. 61–2.

4. Erich Auerbach, *Mimesis*, 1946; transl. Willard R. Trask; repr. Princeton University Press, Princeton, NJ, 1974, p. 552; cf. my comments on this in Docherty, *After Theory*, 1990, pp. 122–3.

5. On schizophrenia and its relation to the postmodern, see e.g., Fredric Jameson, *Postmodernism*, 1991, pp. 25 ff. The larger debates around schizophrenia and culture began largely in the 1960s, most especially in the work of the 'anti-psychiatrists' such as R. D. Laing, Rollo May, David Cooper, Norman O. Brown; and it was related directly to political culture in the writings of Felix Guattari. This movement fed directly into the 'philosophy of desire', and led Gilles Deleuze and Felix Guattari to collaborate on what they called 'schizanalysis' in their two-volume *Capitalism and Schizophrenia*: see Deleuze and Guattari, *Anti-Oedipus*, 1972; transl. 1984, especially ch. 4; and *A Thousand Plateaus*, 1980, transl. 1987.

6. For an explanation of this in terms of active and reactive forces in Nietzsche, see Gilles Deleuze, *Nietzsche and Philosophy*, 1962; transl. Hugh Tomlinson, Athlone Press, 1983, pp. 39 ff.

7. Leslie A. Fiedler, 'The new mutants', 1965, 505–6.

8. See, e.g., Jürgen Habermas, *The Theory of Communicative Action*, vol. 1, 1981; transl. 1984, esp. section III, 'Intermediate Reflections: Social action, purposive activity, and communication'.

9. Ernest Mandel, *Late Capitalism*, 1978; Fredric Jameson, *Late Marxism*, 1990.

10. For a full account of this, see Andrew Dobson, *Green Political Thought*, 1990.

11. Ernesto Laclau and Chantal Mouffe, *Hegemony and Socialist Strategy*, 1985. Gramsci and Foucault, in general, began to be read in ways which offered more purchase for an 'oppositional' political criticism than did the concept of class. It would probably be accurate, if a little oversimplified, to indicate that it is largely British cultural theorists who have retained and wish to rehabilitate the concept of class.

12. See Jean-François Lyotard, *L'Economie libidinale*, 1974; Deleuze and Guattari, op. cit.; Jean Baudrillard, *The Mirror of Production*, 1973; transl. 1975; cf. my comments on this in *After Theory*, pp. 207–13.

13. See Alain Badiou, *Théorie du sujet*, 1982. This problematisation of the status of the Subject is fairly central to the work of critics such as Catherine Belsey in, e.g., *The Subject of Tragedy*, Methuen, London, 1985; and *Critical Practice*, Methuen, London 1980; or in that of Antony Easthope, *Poetry and Phantasy*, Cambridge University Press, Cambridge, 1989. For a different, extremely productive and suggestive argumentation relating the questioning of the subject to postmodernism, and especially to popular cultural forms, see Slavoj Žižek, *Looking Awry*, 1991.

14. Theodor Adorno and Max Horkheimer, *Dialectic of Enlightenment*, 1944; transl. 1986, p. 6.

15. Peter Gay, *The Enlightenment*, vol. 1, 1966, p. xiii. This collocation of criticism and creativity prefigures the twentieth-century avant-garde; see Section 2 below.

16. Adorno and Horkheimer, *Dialectic*, p. 3.

17. *Ibid.*, p. 6.

18. *Ibid.*, p. 7.

19. See Plato, 'The Meno' in *Five Dialogues Bearing on Poetic Inspiration*, Dent, London, 1913, p. 91: 'all our knowledge is reminiscence'. The reduction of cognition to recognition is particularly pertinent to English Romanticism, perhaps most especially in Wordsworth, whose poetry typically celebrates the repetition of an emotion, the recognition of a place or of a state of affairs. There is thus a neo-Romantic hangover in this tendency to mathesis in reason.

20. Adorno and Horkheimer, *Dialectic*, p. 9.

21. J.-F. Lyotard, 'Svelte appendix to the postmodern question' (transl. Thomas Docherty) in Richard Kearney (ed.), *Across the Frontiers*, Wolfhound Press, Dublin, 1988, p. 265.

22. Philip Sidney, 'Apology for poetry', in Edmund D. Jones (ed.), *English Critical Essays: Sixteenth, seventeenth and eighteenth centuries*, Oxford University Press, Oxford, 1922; repr. 1975, pp. 20–1.

23. See, e.g., J. L. Austin, *How to Do Things with Words*, 2nd edn, Oxford University Press, Oxford, 1975; Kenneth Burke, *Language as Symbolic Action*, University of California Press, Berkeley, 1966; Stanley Fish, *Self-Consuming Artifacts*, University of California Press, Berkeley, 1972; and *Is There a Text in this Class?* Harvard University Press, Cambridge, MA, 1980; W. J. T. Mitchell, ed., *Against Theory*, 1985, which includes a 'more-pragmatist-than-thou' statement by Richard Rorty, the most explicitly 'New Pragmatist' of current 'pragmatic' theorists.

24. See Fish, *Self-Consuming Artifacts*. But cf. Jonathan Culler, *On Deconstruction*, Routledge & Kegan Paul, 1983, p. 66: 'What distinguishes Fish's reader is this propensity to fall into the same traps over and over again. Each time it is possible to interpret the end of a line of verse as completing a thought, he does so, only to find, in numerous cases, that the beginning of the next line brings a change of sense. One would expect any real reader, especially one striving to be informed, to notice that premature guesses often prove wrong and to anticipate this possibility as he reads. Stanley E. Fish, after all, not only notices this possibility but writes books about it.' In Fish's work, this has become increasingly accepted. Fish's answer to this is to adopt a pragmatist position in which he is, as Culler suggests here, precisely enabled to predict the response of a reader. For example, given a reader's predisposition for deconstruction, say, it is entirely

predictable that her or his engagement with a text will be a deconstructive one, and her or his reading is entirely predictable.

25. Paul de Man, *The Resistance to Theory*, Manchester University Press, Manchester, 1986, p. 11. See also Gottlob Frege, 'On sense and meaning', in Max Black and P. T. Geach (eds), *Translations from the Philosophical Writings of Gottlob Frege*, 1952.

26. Adorno and Horkheimer, *Dialectic*, p. 7.

27. *Ibid.*, p. 13.

28. Voltaire, *Candide*, Oxford University Press, Oxford, 1968, *passim*.

29. Hans Blumenberg, *The Legitimacy of the Modern Age*, 1966; transl. 1983, p. 404.

30. The indebtedness of this mode of thinking to Kierkegaard should be clear. The sense that one is always 'embarked' and that the grounds upon which one makes judgements are constantly shifting was always close to the centre of Kierkegaardian thinking. Consider, for example, a typical passage in *Either/Or*, in R. Bretall (ed.), *A Kierkegaardian Anthology*, Princeton University Press, Princeton, NJ, 1946, pp. 102–3: 'Think of the captain on board his ship at the instant when it has to come about. He will perhaps be able to say, "I can do either this or that"; but in case he is not a pretty poor navigator, he will be aware that at the same time his ship is all the while making its usual headway, and that therefore it is only an instant when there is no longer any question of an either/or, not because he has chosen but because he has neglected to choose, which is equivalent to saying, because others have chosen for him, because he has lost his self.'

31. See J.-F. Lyotard, *The Postmodern Condition*, 1979; transl. 1984, p. xxiv.

32. Walter Benjamin, *Illuminations*, ed. Hannah Arendt, 1973, p. 258.

33. Zygmunt Bauman, *Modernity and the Holocaust*, 1989, p. 7.

34. *Ibid.*, p. 8.

35. *Ibid.*, p. 202.

36. *Ibid.*, pp. 202–3.

37. *Ibid.*, p. 203.

38. Jacques Derrida, *Margins: Of philosophy*, 1972; transl. Alan Bass, Harvester, Brighton, 1982, p. 213.

39. Gay, *Enlightenment*, vol. 1, p. 24, argues that Enlightenment thought was itself contaminated by the very religiosity it hoped to circumscribe. Cf. Lyotard on contemporary paganism in his *Rudiments païens* (Union générale d'éditions, Paris, 1977), and *Instructions païennes*, 1977. See also Jürgen Habermas, *Legitimation Crisis*, 1973; transl. 1976.

40. Michel Foucault, *Folie et déraison*, Plon, Paris, 1961, *passim*.

41. Jean Baudrillard, *Simulations*, transl. Paul Foss, Paul Patton and Philip Beitchman; Semiotext(e), New York, 1983, p. 25.

42. Gilles Deleuze, *Kant's Critical Philosophy*, 1963; transl. 1984, pp. vii–viii.

43. G. E. Lessing, *Laoköon*, 1766; transl. William A. Steel, Dent, London, 1930.

44. J.-F. Lyotard, 'Reécrire la modernité', in *L'Inhumain*, Galilée, Paris, 1988, pp. 33–44.

45. See, e.g., Alexander Baumgarten, *Reflections on Poetry*, transl. K. Aschenbrenner and W. B. Holther, University of California Press, Berkeley, 1954; Immanuel Kant, *Critique of Judgement*, Oxford University Press, Oxford, 1952.

46. Pierre Bourdieu, *Distinction*, 1979; transl. 1984, pp. 66–72.

47. Kant, *Critique of Judgement*, para. 1, sect. 13, p. 72.

48. Terry Eagleton, *The Ideology of the Aesthetic*, 1990, p. 14. The sentiment expressed at this and similar moments in the book are oddly reminiscent of Eliot's complaints at the

'dissociation of sensibility': see T. S. Eliot, 'The Metaphysical poets', in *Selected Essays*, 3rd edn, Faber & Faber, London 1951; repr. 1980, pp. 281–91, esp. 286–8.

49. Luc Ferry, *Homo Aestheticus*, 1990, pp. 256n, 259; my translation.

50. *Ibid.*, p. 260; my translation.

51. The reference here is to the journal *Tel Quel*, which, it might be argued, continued the work of surrealism via a prolonged engagement with structuralism, whose burden was the importance of political debate over the values of identifiable cultural practices.

52. 'Recognition' has had a specific place in the structure of tragedy at least since Aristotle's *Poetics* (esp. ch. 16). An art based upon the kind of *anagnorisis* I describe here might thus be aligned with tragedy. Given that I am now also suggesting that it links not only to a specific tradition of 'realism' but also to pragmatism, one might intercalate at this point a comment on Kenneth Burke, in whose *Language as Symbolic Action*, University of California Press, Berkeley, CA, 1966, there is a terse footnote, p. 20, n2:

> In his *Parts of Animals*, Chapter X, Aristotle mentions the definition of man as the 'laughing animal,' but he does not consider it adequate. Though I would hasten to agree, I obviously have a big investment in it, owing to my conviction that mankind's only hope is a cult of comedy. (The cult of tragedy is too eager to help out with the holocaust ...).

Such a comedy, as part of the 'risibility' which Burke aligns in the same footnote with 'symbolicity', is germane to the kinds of incongruity which are an important structural feature of the effect of the avant-garde.

53. Lyotard, *Postmodern Condition*, p. 81.

54. See Robert Hughes, *The Shock of the New*; but cf. Peter Bürger on 'The new' in his *Theory of the Avant-Garde*, 1974; transl. Manchester University Press, Manchester, 1984, pp. 59–63.

55. Brian McHale, *Postmodernist Fiction*, 1987, Part 1.

56. Jacques Lacan, *Ecrits: A selection*, 1966; transl. Alan Sheridan; Tavistock, London, 1977, p. 141. See also M. M. Bakhtin, *The Dialogical Imagination*, ed. Michael Holquist, transl. Caryl Emerson and Michael Holquist, University of Texas Press, Austin, 1981; Jürgen Habermas, *Theory of Communicative Action*.

57. Georg Lukács, 'Realism in the balance', in Ernst Bloch *et al.*, *Aesthetics and Politics*, 1977; Verso, London, 1980, p. 48.

58. Lyotard, *Postmodern Condition*, p. 81.

59. Ferry, *Homo Aestheticus*, p. 264; my translation.

60. See, e.g., Samir Amin, *Le Développement inégal*. There is, of course, and especially in English studies, a whole new growth area in Subaltern Studies and the logic of cultural imperialisms. But for a different view of the bases of such imperialist problematics, see Alfred Crosby, *Ecological Imperialism*, 1986.

61. Interestingly, this corresponds historically with the popular development in music of crisscross rhythms, especially in freestyle jazz and in the odd musical tempo frequently adopted by bands such as Soft Machine or Osibisa in the 1970s. Cf. Jacques Attali, *Noise*, 1977; transl. 1985, for a different inflection of the political economy of music.

62. See Carl von Clausewitz, *On War*, ed. Anatol Rapoport, 1832; Penguin Classics, Harmondsworth, 1982; Paul Virilio, *Défense populaire et luttes écologiques*, 1978, pp. 14–15.

63. Virilio, *Défense populaire*, p. 17; my translation.

64. The event, as I describe it here, is necessarily conditioned by mutability. It is important to note in passing, moreover, that the English term 'static', which is ostensibly the opposite of such mutability, in fact contains within its etymology precisely the same kind of mutability. It derives from *stasis* which means in modern Greek a bus stop, but in Ancient Greek a civil war: that is, a state in which there is a great deal of internal dissent and struggle, but where the external boundaries of such a state are not themselves called into question. For a perhaps more conventional way of expressing the basic idea here, see Lewis Mumford, *The City in History*, 1961; Penguin, Hamondsworth, 1979, p. 13: 'Human life swings between two poles: movement and settlement.'

65. See Umbro Appolonio (ed)., *Futurist Manifestoes*, Thames & Hudson, London, 1973, *passim*.

66. Paul Virilio, *L'Horizon négatif*, 1984, p. 100.

67. *Ibid*., pp. 101–2; my translation.

68. Jean Baudrillard, *De la séduction*, 1979, p. 123; my translation.

69. William Shakespeare, *Hamlet*, Act 5, scene i.

70. Samuel Beckett, *Murphy*, Routledge, London, 1938.

71. Arthur Kroker and David Cook, *The Postmodern Scene*, 1988, pp. ii–iii.

72. Michel Foucault, *Discipline and Punish*, 1975; transl. Alan Sheridan, Penguin, Harmondsworth, 1977; repr. 1985, p. 11.

73. In relation to this, one might add Malcolm McLaren: 'Fashion is always right', in discussion on BBC2, 'Did you see?'

74. Seamus Deane, *The French Revolution and Enlightenment in England 1789–1832*, 1988, esp. chs 1 and 2.

75. Guy Debord, *La Société du spectacle*, 1968; cf. Debord, *Comments on the Society of the Spectacle*, 1990.

76. George Orwell, *Nineteen Eighty-Four*, 1949; Penguin, Harmondsworth, 1954; repr. 1982, p. 19. and *passim*.

77. See J.-F. Lyotard and Jean-Loup Thébaud, *Just Gaming*, 1979; transl. 1985, for the most pressing debate on the 'criterion' question.

78. See Roland Barthes, *Image – Music – Text*, ed. Stephen Heath, Fontana, Glasgow, 1977.

79. Lyotard, *Postmodern Condition*, p. xxiv; see especially sections 9 and 10.

80. Habermas, *Legitimation Crisis*, p. 98.

81. J.-F. Lyotard and Richard Rorty, 'Discussion', *Critique*, 41, 581–4.

82. Emmanuel Levinas, *The Levinas Reader*, ed. Séan Hand, 1989, pp. 82, 83.

Part One

Founding Propositions

Introduction

The debate around postmodernism has a long history. Yet it would be true to say that the contemporary interest in the question dates from 1968, that *annus mirabilis* which is the great '1848' of modern Europe. After the perceived failures of certain 'revolutionary' movements in 1968, a substantial rethinking of the question of cultural politics became not only necessary but also – through a questioning of the 'modern' itself – available in new, interesting and challenging, ways. If the logic of a structuralist Marxism was, for whatever reasons, unsuccessful when put into practice, then how might a left-wing politics advance its cause? How can the critic of culture *know* or *predict* the political effects of her or his discourse? In short, if a political theory had failed on the occasion of May 1968 to produce the requisite practice, then from now on, how does one safely ground an emancipatory cultural politics? In philosophy, there arises a whole series of 'anti-foundational' modes of thinking, already foreshadowed in the early deconstruction of Derrida in his three great 1967 texts. In more general terms, one might say that the critique of a foundational – or, perhaps, 'totalising' – theory begins from within theory itself. The general culture faces what Habermas diagnosed in 1973 as a 'legitimation crisis'.

In the arena of science, there was the beginning of the same problem, though mediated in a slightly different manner. So-called 'rogue scientists', such as Paul Feyerabend and Fritjof Capra, had begun to question what we might call the 'theoreticist' basis of contemporary science. In the anarchist science of Feyerabend, more attention is paid to the ways in which empirical practice actually deviates from the theoretically reasoned scientific theorem, for instance; and the theorem itself begins to be considered as something carceral, as a 'form' which polices the actual 'content' of scientific experiment. Knowledge, for Feyerabend and his like, should not be thus 'imprisoned' within the bounds of a series of Western rationalist models whose sole purpose is to bolster Western modes of thinking and of representing the 'truth' about the world.

In 1962, Thomas Kuhn had proposed a specific way of understanding the procedures through which our scientific 'models' for explaining the world change across history. There were, he argued, certain 'paradigms' according to which the world could be satisfactorily explained. But, given an expanding scientific research and increasingly exacting testing of specific problems within science, the paradigms always begin to come under pressure, producing less satisfactory, less predictable results. After a long time, when the existing paradigm is seen as increasingly useless, a new paradigmatic model for explaining the world begins to gain sway. This shift between paradigms constitutes the 'structure of scientific revolutions'. The book bearing this title had enormous influence across all fields of knowledge. It is itself a symptom precisely of a paradigm shift in the field of knowledge and philosophy, away from a model which proclaimed the availability of 'truth' towards one which proclaims instead the much more modest 'pragmatic usefulness'.

Cultural criticism at this moment has begun to go 'relativist', so to speak. Since the eighteenth century in Europe, it had been taken more or less for granted that knowledge gave an entitlement to legislation. That is, social and political formations were grounded upon a truthful knowledge about the ways of the world. But after 1968, all such knowledges begin to be deemed 'local' and specific to the pragmatic necessities of the specific culture from which the knowledges emanate and whose interests they serve. Now, knowledge does not give power; rather, it is utterly imbricated with power from the outset, and is thus not a pure knowledge at all but a practical knowledge, a knowledge whose *raison d'être* is power itself. From 1968, the leftist intellectual begins to be suspicious of a knowledge which will legislate for any culture other than the very culture which produced that knowledge in the first place.

Increasingly, the possibility of criticism itself enters into crisis. It seemed that there was a basic alternative. On the one hand, one could retain the idea of a 'foundational' criticism, according to which the critic, **working** from a 'rational' ground, might legislate for any and every eventuality and might make all the necessary and determined judgements regarding any cultural practice. On the other hand, this mode of criticism begins to be rejected as a symptom of an imperialist cast of mind, according to which one culture arrogates to itself the right to legislate for all other cultures whose foundations might be radically different.

Once the legitimation crisis becomes articulated in these terms, it becomes more and more obvious to refer to the first model as a European and 'Enlightenment' model of criticism. Further, given the fact that the eighteenth-century Enlightenment philosophers saw themselves as 'progressive' and 'modernising', the foundationalist mode of criticism became increasingly stigmatised as specifically 'modernist'. The anti-foundationalist criticism, by dint of the very fact that it subjects modernist thought to speculative pressure, postulates thereby the possibility of an 'outside' of modernist thinking.

The word 'postmodern' was increasingly used to describe this 'outside' of modernist thought; but its meaning was somewhat obfuscated by the prefix 'post-', which carried too much the weight of a simple chronological tardiness. The articles here address this situation. Lyotard's 'Answering the Question: What Is Postmodernism?' not only begins to offer a serious definition of the term, but alludes directly in the title to the history of the question. Lyotard's title is meant explicitly to call to mind Kant's famous piece 'What is Enlightenment?'. To begin to address the postmodern, one has also to address an entire trajectory of European philosophy dating from the Enlightenment. The more immediate 'local' reason for this allusion to Kant, of course, is that in the French philosophical institution attention had begun to turn to Kant, swerving away from the extremely influential version of Hegel proposed by Kojève in the 1930s. In his letter of 1985 to Jessamyn Blau, Lyotard maintains a rigorous sense for the troublesome prefix 'post-', in the face of its increasingly sloppy chronological usage.

The proper sense in which 'postmodern' describes an 'after' of the modern really derives from a sociological discourse referring not to modernism but to modernity. Here, Habermas and Jameson share something of the same terrain, in the sense that they both discern the beginning of a shift in consciousness which is appropriate to the contemporary moment. Habermas is much troubled by such a shift, and has maintained a vigilant regard for the serious and continuing elucidation of modernity, in the face of what he sees as a neo-Nietzschean tendency to nihilism in the contemporary validations of relativism. The fragment included here dates from his 1985 lectures, and is a succinct formulation of what Habermas sees as the main dangers for the building of a rational society – dangers which are exacerbated by the postmodern tendency in contemporary culture. Jameson's piece is the famous, much reworked and much discussed 'Postmodernism, or The Cultural Logic of Late Capitalism', first published in this extended form in *New Left Review* in 1984 (and subsequently further revised in his book *Postmodernism*). Jameson seems much more ambivalent about the postmodern: on the one hand, he is deeply suspicious of it as the articulation of a continued capitalism which is branded by covert exploitation and oppression; yet on the other hand he is, by his own admission, more than half in love with the very practices and objects of a postmodern culture which he wishes to expose as politically disreputable. The four pieces together offer a broad survey of a variety of 'postmodern' concerns apparent in the work of the three most influential figures in the field of the contemporary debate. They are founding – if sometimes anti-foundational – propositions for all the work which follows.

1 □ *Answering the Question: What Is Postmodernism?*

Jean-François Lyotard

A Demand

This is a period of slackening – I refer to the color of the times. From every direction we are being urged to put an end to experimentation, in the arts and elsewhere. I have read an art historian who extols realism and is militant for the advent of a new subjectivity. I have read an art critic who packages and sells 'Transavantgardism' in the marketplace of painting. I have read that under the name of postmodernism, architects are getting rid of the Bauhaus project, throwing out the baby of experimentation with the bathwater of functionalism. I have read that a new philosopher is discovering what he drolly calls Judaeo-Christianism, and intends by it to put an end to the impiety which we are supposed to have spread. I have read in a French weekly that some are displeased with *Mille Plateaux* [by Deleuze and Guattari] because they expect, especially when reading a work of philosophy, to be gratified with a little sense. I have read from the pen of a reputable historian that writers and thinkers of the 1960 and 1970 avant-gardes spread a reign of terror in the use of language, and that the conditions for a fruitful exchange must be restored by imposing on the intellectuals a common way of speaking, that of the historians. I have been reading a young philosopher of language who complains that Continental thinking, under the challenge of speaking machines, has surrendered to the machines the concern for reality, that it has substituted for the referential paradigm that of 'adlinguisticity' (one speaks about speech, writes about writing, intertextuality), and who thinks that the time has now come to restore a solid anchorage of language in the referent. I have read a talented theatrologist for whom postmodernism, with its games and fantasies, carries very little weight in front of political authority, especially when a worried public opinion encourages authority to a politics of totalitarian surveillance in the face of nuclear warfare threats.

I have read a thinker of repute who defends modernity against those he calls the

From Hassan, I. and Hassan, S. (eds), *Innovation/Renovation*, University of Wisconsin Press, Madison, WI, 1983, pp. 71–82.

neoconservatives. Under the banner of postmodernism, the latter would like, he believes, to get rid of the uncompleted project of modernism, that of the Enlightenment. Even the last advocates of *Aufklärung*, such as Popper or Adorno, were only able, according to him, to defend the project in a few particular spheres of life – that of politics for the author of *The Open Society*, and that of art for the author of *Ästhetische Theorie*. Jürgen Habermas (everyone had recognized him) thinks that if modernity has failed, it is in allowing the totality of life to be splintered into independent specialties which are left to the narrow competence of experts, while the concrete individual experiences 'desublimated meaning' and 'destructured form', not as a liberation but in the mode of that immense *ennui* which Baudelaire described over a century ago.

Following a prescription of Albrecht Wellmer, Habermas considers that the remedy for this splintering of culture and its separation from life can only come from 'changing the status of aesthetic experience when it is no longer primarily expressed in judgments of taste', but when it is 'used to explore a living historical situation', that is, when 'it is put in relation with problems of existence'. For this experience then 'becomes a part of a language game which is no longer that of aesthetic criticism'; it takes part 'in cognitive processes and normative expectations'; 'it alters the manner in which those different moments *refer* to one another'. What Habermas requires from the arts and the experiences they provide is, in short, to bridge the gap between cognitive, ethical, and political discourses, thus opening the way to a unity of experience.

My question is to determine what sort of unity Habermas has in mind. Is the aim of the project of modernity the constitution of sociocultural unity within which all the elements of daily life and of thought would take their places as in an organic whole? Or does the passage that has to be charted between heterogeneous language-games – those of cognition, of ethics, of politics – belong to a different order from that? And if so, would it be capable of effecting a real synthesis between them?

The first hypothesis, of a Hegelian inspiration, does not challenge the notion of a dialectically totalizing *experience*; the second is closer to the spirit of Kant's *Critique of Judgement*; but must be submitted, like the *Critique*, to that severe reexamination which postmodernity imposes on the thought of the Enlightenment, on the idea of a unitary end of history and of a subject. It is this critique which not only Wittgenstein and Adorno have initiated, but also a few other thinkers (French or other) who do not have the honor to be read by Professor Habermas – which at least saves them from getting a poor grade for their neoconservatism.

Realism

The demands I began by citing are not all equivalent. They can even be contradictory. Some are made in the name of postmodernism, others in order to combat it. It is not necessarily the same thing to formulate a demand for some referent (and objective reality), for some sense (and credible transcendence), for an addressee (and audience), or an addressor (and subjective expressiveness) or for some communicational consensus (and a general code of exchanges, such as the genre of historical discourse). But in the diverse invitations to suspend artistic experimentation, there is an identical call for order, a desire for unity, for identity, for security, or popularity (in the sense of *Öffentlichkeit*, of 'finding a public'). Artists and writers must be brought back into the bosom of the community, or at least, if the latter is considered to be ill, they must be assigned the task of healing it.

There is an irrefutable sign of this common disposition: it is that for all those writers nothing is more urgent than to liquidate the heritage of the avant-gardes. Such is the case, in particular, of the so-called transavantgardism. The answers given by Achille Bonito Oliva to the questions asked by Bernard Lamarche-Vadel and Michel Enric leave no room for doubt about this. By putting the avant-gardes through a mixing process, the artist and critic feel more confident that they can suppress them than by launching a frontal attack. For they can pass off the most cynical eclecticism as a way of going beyond the fragmentary character of the preceding experiments; whereas if they openly turned their backs on them, they would run the risk of appearing ridiculously neoacademic. The *Salons* and the *Académies*, at the time when the bourgeoisie was establishing itself in history, were able to function as purgation and to grant awards for good plastic and literary conduct under the cover of realism. But capitalism inherently possesses the power to derealize familiar objects, social roles, and institutions to such a degree that the so-called realistic representations can no longer evoke reality except as nostalgia or mockery, as an occasion for suffering rather than for satisfaction. Classicism seems to be ruled out in a world in which reality is so destabilized that it offers no occasion for experience but one for ratings and experimentation.

This theme is familiar to all readers of Walter Benjamin. But it is necessary to assess its exact reach. Photography did not appear as a challenge to painting from the outside, any more than industrial cinema did to narrative literature. The former was only putting the final touch to the program of ordering the visible elaborated by the quattrocento; while the latter was the last step in rounding off diachronies as organic wholes, which had been the ideal of the great novels of education since the eighteenth century. That the mechanical and the industrial should appear as substitutes for hand or craft was not in itself a disaster – except if one believes that art is in its essence the expression of an individuality of genius assisted by an elite craftsmanship.

The challenge lay essentially in that photographic and cinematographic processes can accomplish better, faster, and with a circulation a hundred thousand times larger than narrative or pictorial realism, the task which academicism had assigned to realism: to preserve various consciousnesses from doubt. Industrial photography and cinema will be superior to painting and the novel whenever the objective is to stabilize the referent, to arrange it according to a point of view which endows it with a recognizable meaning, to reproduce the syntax and vocabulary which enable the addressee to decipher images and sequences quickly, and so to arrive easily at the consciousness of his own identity as well as the approval which he thereby receives from others – since such structures of images and sequences constitute a communication code among all of them. This is the way the effects of reality, or if one prefers, the fantasies of realism, multiply.

If they too do not wish to become supporters (of minor importance at that) of what exists, the painter and novelist must refuse to lend themselves to such therapeutic uses. They must question the rules of the art of painting or of narrative as they have learned and received them from their predecessors. Soon those rules must appear to them as a means to deceive, to seduce, and to reassure, which makes it impossible for them to be 'true'. Under the common name of painting and literature, an unprecedented split is taking place. Those who refuse to reexamine the rules of art pursue successful careers in mass conformism by communicating, by means of the 'correct rules', the endemic desire for reality with objects and situations capable of gratifying it. Pornography is the use of photography and film to such an end. It is becoming a general model for the visual or narrative arts which have not met the challenge of the mass media.

As for the artists and writers who question the rules of plastic and narrative arts and possibly share their suspicions by circulating their work, they are destined to have little credibility in the eyes of those concerned with 'reality' and 'identity'; they have no guarantee of an audience. Thus it is possible to ascribe the dialectics of the avant-gardes to the challenge posed by the realisms of industry and mass communication to painting and the narrative arts. Duchamp's 'ready-made' does nothing but actively and parodistically signify this constant process of dispossession of the craft of painting or even of being an artist. As Thierry de Duve penetratingly observes, the modern aesthetic question is not 'What is beautiful?' but 'What can be said to be art (and literature)?'

Realism, whose only definition is that it intends to avoid the question of reality implicated in that of art, always stands somewhere between academicism and kitsch. When power assumes the name of a party, realism and its neoclassical complement triumph over the experimental avant-garde by slandering and banning it – that is, provided the 'correct' images, the 'correct' narratives, the 'correct' forms which the party requests, selects, and propagates can find a public to desire them as the appropriate remedy for the anxiety and depression that public experiences. The demand for reality – that is, for unity, simplicity, communicability, etc. – did not have the same intensity nor the same continuity in German society between the two world wars and in Russian society after the Revolution: this provides a basis for a distinction between Nazi and Stalinist realism.

What is clear, however, is that when it is launched by the political apparatus, the attack on artistic experimentation is specifically reactionary: aesthetic judgment would only be required to decide whether such or such work is in conformity with the established rules of the beautiful. Instead of the work of art having to investigate what makes it an art object and whether it will be able to find an audience, political academicism possesses and imposes *a priori* criteria of the beautiful, which designate some works and a public at a stroke and forever. The use of categories in aesthetic judgment would thus be of the same nature as in cognitive judgment.

To speak like Kant, both would be determining judgments: the expression is 'well formed' first in the understanding, then the only cases retained in experience are those which can be subsumed under this expression.

When power is that of capital and not that of a party, the 'transavantgardist' or 'postmodern' (in Jencks's sense) solution proves to be better adapted than the anti-modern solution. Eclecticism is the degree zero of contemporary general culture: one listens to reggae, watches a western, eats McDonald's food for lunch and local cuisine for dinner, wears Paris perfume in Tokyo and 'retro' clothes in Hong Kong; knowledge is a matter for TV games. It is easy to find a public for eclectic works. By becoming kitsch, art panders to the confusion which reigns in the 'taste' of the patrons. Artists, gallery owners, critics, and public wallow together in the 'anything goes', and the epoch is one of slackening. But this realism of the 'anything goes' is in fact that of money; in the absence of aesthetic criteria, it remains possible and useful to assess the value of works of art according to the profits they yield. Such realism accommodates all tendencies, just as capital accommodates all 'needs', providing that the tendencies and needs have purchasing power. As for taste, there is no need to be delicate when one speculates or entertains oneself.

Artistic and literary research is doubly threatened, once by the 'cultural policy' and once by the art and book market. What is advised, sometimes through one channel, sometimes through the other, is to offer works which, first, are relative to subjects which exist in the eyes of the public they address, and second, works so made ('well made') that the public will recognize what they are about, will understand what is signified, will be able to give or refuse its approval knowingly, and if possible, even to derive from such work a certain amount of comfort.

The interpretation which has just been given of the contact between the industrial and mechanical arts, and literature and the fine arts, is correct in its outline, but it remains narrowly sociologizing and historicizing – in other words, one-sided. Stepping over Benjamin's and Adorno's reticences, it must be recalled that science and industry are no more free of the suspicion which concerns reality than are art and writing. To believe otherwise would be to entertain an excessively humanistic notion of the Mephistophelian functionalism of sciences and technologies. There is no denying the dominant existence today of techno-science, that is, the massive subordination of cognitive statements to the finality of the best possible performance, which is the technological criterion. But the mechanical and the industrial, especially when they enter fields traditionally reserved for artists, are carrying with them much more than power effects. The objects and the thoughts which originate in scientific knowledge and the capitalist economy convey with them one of the rules which supports their possibility: the rule that there is no reality unless testified by a consensus between partners over a certain knowledge and certain commitments.

This rule is of no little consequence. It is the imprint left on the politics of the scientist and the trustee of capital by a kind of flight of reality out of the metaphysical, religious, and political certainties that the mind believed it held. This withdrawal is absolutely necessary to the emergence of science and capitalism. No industry is possible without a suspicion of the Aristotelian theory of motion, no industry without a refutation of corporatism, of mercantilism, and of physiocracy. Modernity, in whatever age it appears, cannot exist without a shattering of belief and without discovery of the 'lack of reality' of reality, together with the invention of other realities.

What does this 'lack of reality' signify if one tries to free it from a narrowly historicized interpretation? The phrase is of course akin to what Nietzsche calls nihilism. But I see a much earlier modulation of Nietzschean perspectivism in the Kantian theme of the sublime. I think in particular that it is in the aesthetic of the sublime that modern art (including literature) finds its impetus and the logic of avant-gardes finds its axioms.

The sublime sentiment, which is also the sentiment of the sublime, is, according to Kant, a strong and equivocal emotion: it carries with it both pleasure and pain. Better still, in it pleasure derives from pain. Within the tradition of the subject, which comes from Augustine and Descartes and which Kant does not radically challenge, this contradiction, which some would call neurosis or masochism, develops as a conflict between the faculties of a subject, the faculty to conceive of something and the faculty to 'present' something. Knowledge exists if, first, the statement is intelligible, and second, if 'cases' can be derived from the experience which 'corresponds' to it. Beauty exists if a certain 'case' (the work of art), given first by the sensibility without any conceptual determination, the sentiment of pleasure independent of any interest the work may elicit, appeals to the principle of a universal consensus (which may never be attained).

Taste, therefore, testifies that between the capacity to conceive and the capacity to present an object corresponding to the concept, an undetermined agreement, without rules, giving rise to a judgment which Kant calls reflective, may be experienced as pleasure. The sublime is a different sentiment. It takes place, on the contrary, when the imagination fails to present an object which might, if only in principle, come to match a concept. We have the Idea of the world (the totality of what is), but we do not have the capacity to show an example of it. We have the Idea of the simple (that which cannot be broken down, decomposed), but we cannot illustrate it with a sensible object which would be a 'case' of it. We can conceive the infinitely great, the infinitely powerful, but every presentation of an object destined to 'make visible' this absolute greatness or power appears to us painfully inadequate. Those are Ideas of which no presentation is possible. Therefore, they impart no knowledge about reality (experience); they also prevent the free union of the faculties which gives rise to the sentiment of the beautiful; and they prevent the formation and the stabilization of taste. They can be said to be unpresentable.

I shall call modern the art which devotes its 'little technical expertise' [*son 'petit technique'*], as Diderot used to say, to present the fact that the unpresentable exists. To make visible that there is something which can be conceived and which can neither be seen nor made visible: this is what is at stake in modern painting. But how to make visible that there is something which cannot be seen? Kant himself shows the way when he names 'formlessness, the absence of form', as a possible index to the unpresentable. He also says of the empty 'abstraction' which the imagination experiences when in search for a presentation of the infinite (another unpresentable): this abstraction itself is like a presentation of the infinite, its 'negative presentation'. He cites the commandment 'Thou shalt not make graven images' (Exodus) as the most sublime passage in the Bible in that it forbids all presentation of the Absolute. Little needs to be added to those observations to outline an aesthetic of sublime paintings. As painting, it will of course 'present' something, though negatively; it will therefore avoid figuration or representation. It will be 'white' like one of Malevich's squares; it will enable us to see only by making it impossible to see; it will please only by causing pain. One recognizes in those instructions the axioms of avant-gardes in painting, inasmuch as they devote themselves to making an allusion to the unpresentable by means of visible presentations. The systems in the name of which, or with which, this task has been able to support or to justify itself deserve the greatest attention; but they can originate only in the vocation of the sublime in order to legitimize it, that is, to conceal it. They remain inexplicable without the incommensurability of reality to concept which is implied in the Kantian philosophy of the sublime.

It is not my intention to analyze here in detail the manner in which the various avant-gardes have, so to speak, humbled and disqualified reality by examining the pictorial techniques which are so many devices to make us believe in it. Local tone, drawing, the mixing of colors, linear perspective, the nature of the support and that of the instrument, the treatment, the display, the museum: the avant-gardes are perpetually flushing out artifices of presentation which make it possible to subordinate thought to the gaze and to turn it away from the unpresentable. If Habermas, like Marcuse, understands this task of derealization as an aspect of the (repressive) 'desublimation' which characterizes the avant-garde, it is because he confuses the Kantian sublime with Freudian sublimation, and because aesthetics has remained for him that of the beautiful.

The Postmodern

What, then, is the postmodern? What place does it or does it not occupy in the vertiginous work of the questions hurled at the rules of image and narration? It is undoubtedly a part of the modern. All that has been received, if only yesterday (*modo, modo*, Petronius used to say), must be suspected. What space does Cézanne challenge? The Impressionists'. What object do Picasso and Braque attack? Cézanne's. What presupposition does Duchamp break with in 1912? That which says one must make a painting, be it cubist. And Buren questions that other presupposition which he believes had survived untouched by the work of Duchamp: the place of presentation of the work. In an amazing acceleration, the generations precipitate themselves. A work can become modern only if it is first postmodern. Postmodernism thus understood is not modernism at its end but in the nascent state, and this state is constant.

Yet I would like not to remain with this slightly mechanistic meaning of the word. If it is true that modernity takes place in the withdrawal of the real and according to the sublime relation between the presentable and the conceivable, it is possible, within this relation, to distinguish two modes (to use the musician's language). The emphasis can be placed on the powerlessness of the faculty of presentation, on the nostalgia for presence felt by the human subject, on the obscure and futile will which inhabits him in spite of everything. The emphasis can be placed, rather, on the power of the faculty to conceive, on its 'inhumanity' so to speak (it was the quality Apollinaire demanded of modern artists), since it is not the business of our understanding whether or not human sensibility or imagination can match what it conceives. The emphasis can also be placed on the increase of being and the jubilation which result from the invention of new rules of the game, be it pictorial, artistic, or any other. What I have in mind will become clear if we dispose very schematically a few names on the chessboard of the history of avant-gardes: on the side of melancholia, the German Expressionists, and on the side of *novatio*, Braque and Picasso, on the former Malevich and on the latter Lissitsky, on the one Chirico and on the other Duchamp. The nuance which distinguishes these two modes may be infinitesimal; they often coexist in the same piece, are almost indistinguishable; and yet they testify to a difference [*un différend*] on which the fate of thought depends and will depend for a long time, between regret and assay.

The work of Proust and that of Joyce both allude to something which does not allow itself to be made present. Allusion, to which Paolo Fabbri recently called my attention, is perhaps a form of expression indispensable to the works which belong to an aesthetic of the sublime. In Proust, what is being eluded as the price to pay for this allusion is the identity of consciousness, a victim to the excess of time [*au trop de temps*]. But in Joyce, it is the identity of writing which is the victim of an excess of the book [*au trop de livre*] or of literature.

Proust calls forth the unpresentable by means of a language unaltered in its syntax and vocabulary and of a writing which in many of its operators still belongs to the genre of novelistic narration. The literary institution, as Proust inherits it from Balzac and Flaubert, is admittedly subverted in that the hero is no longer a character but the inner consciousness of time, and in that the diegetic diachrony, already damaged by Flaubert, is here put in question because of the narrative voice. Nevertheless, the unity of the book, the odyssey of that consciousness, even if it is deferred from chapter to chapter, is not seriously challenged: the identity of the writing with itself throughout the labyrinth of the interminable narration is enough to connote such unity, which has been compared to that of *The Phenomenology of Mind*.

Joyce allows the unpresentable to become perceptible in his writing itself, in the signifier. The whole range of available narrative and even stylistic operators is put into play without concern for the unity of the whole, and new operators are tried. The grammar and vocabulary of literary language are no longer accepted as given; rather they appear as academic forms, as rituals originating in piety (as Nietzsche said) which prevent the unpresentable from being put forward.

Here, then, lies the difference: modern aesthetics is an aesthetic of the sublime, though a nostalgic one. It allows the unpresentable to be put forward only as the missing contents; but the form, because of its recognizable consistency, continues to offer to the reader or viewer matter for solace and pleasure. Yet these sentiments do not constitute the real sublime sentiment, which is in an intrinsic combination of pleasure and pain: the pleasure that reason should exceed all presentation, the pain that imagination or sensibility should not be equal to the concept.

The postmodern would be that which, in the modern, puts forward the unpresentable in presentation itself; that which denies itself the solace of good forms, the consensus of a taste which would make it possible to share collectively the nostalgia for the unattainable; that which searches for new presentations, not in order to enjoy them but in order to impart a stronger sense of the unpresentable. A postmodern artist or writer is in the position of a philosopher: the text he writes, the work he produces are not in principle governed by preestablished rules, and they cannot be judged according to a determining judgment, by applying familiar categories to the text or to the work. Those rules and categories are what the work of art itself is looking for. The artist and the writer, then, are working without rules in order to formulate the rules of what *will have been done*. Hence the fact that work and text have the characters of an *event*; hence also, they always come too late for their author, or, what amounts to the same thing, their being put into work, their realization [*mise en oeuvre*] always begin too soon. *Post modern* would have to be understood according to the paradox of the future [*post*] anterior [*modo*].

It seems to me that the essay (Montaigne) is postmodern, while the fragment (*The Athaeneum*) is modern.

Finally, it must be clear that it is our business not to supply reality but to invent allusions to the conceivable which cannot be presented. And it is not to be expected that this task will effect the last reconciliation between language-games (which, under the name of faculties, Kant knew to be separated by a chasm), and that only the transcendental illusion (that of Hegel) can hope to totalize them into a real unity. But Kant also knew that the price to pay for such an illusion is terror. The nineteenth and twentieth centuries have given us as much terror as we can take. We have paid a high enough price for the nostalgia of the whole and the one, for the reconciliation of the concept and the sensible, of the transparent and the communicable experience. Under the general demand for slackening and for appeasement, we can hear the mutterings of the desire for a return of terror, for the realization of the fantasy to seize reality. The answer is: Let us wage a war on totality; let us be witnesses to the unpresentable; let us activate the differences and save the honor of the name.

2 □ *Note on the Meaning of 'Post-'*

Jean-François Lyotard

To Jessamyn Blau
Milwaukee, May 1, 1985

I would like to pass on to you a few thoughts that are merely intended to raise certain problems concerning the term 'postmodern', without wanting to resolve them. By doing this, I do not want to close the debate but rather to situate it, in order to avoid confusion and ambiguity. I have just three points to make.

First, the opposition between postmodernism and modernism, or the modern movement (1910–45) in architecture. According to Portoghesi, the rupture of postmodernism consists in an abrogation of the hegemony of Euclidean geometry (its sublimation in the plastic poetics of de Stijl, for example). To follow Gregotti, the difference between modernism and postmodernism would be better characterized by the following feature: the disappearance of the close bond that once linked the project of modern architecture to an ideal of the progressive realization of social and individual emancipation encompassing all humanity. Postmodern architecture finds itself condemned to undertake a series of minor modifications in a space inherited from modernity, condemned to abandon a global reconstruction of the space of human habitation. The perspective then opens onto a vast landscape, in the sense that there is no longer any horizon of universality, universalization, or general emancipation to greet the eye of postmodern man, least of all the eye of the architect. The disappearance of the Idea that rationality and freedom are progressing would explain a 'tone', style, or mode specific to postmodern architecture. I would say it is a sort of 'bricolage': the multiple quotation of elements taken from earlier styles or periods, classical and modern; disregard for the environment; and so on.

One point about this perspective is that the 'post-' of postmodernism has the sense of a simple succession, a diachronic sequence of periods in which each one is clearly

From Lyotard, J., *The Postmodern Explained: Correspondence 1982–1985*, University of Minnesota Press, Minneapolis, MN/Power Publications, Sydney, 1992, pp. 64–8.

identifiable. The 'post-' indicates something like a conversion: a new direction from the previous one.

Now this idea of a linear chronology is itself perfectly 'modern'. It is at once part of Christianity, Cartesianism, and Jacobinism: since we are inaugurating something completely new, the hands of the clock should be put back to zero. The very idea of modernity is closely correlated with the principle that it is both possible and necessary to break with tradition and institute absolutely new ways of living and thinking.

We now suspect that this 'rupture' is in fact a way of forgetting or repressing the past, that is, repeating it and not surpassing it.

I would say that, in the 'new' architecture, the quotation of motifs taken from earlier architectures relies on a procedure analogous to the way dream work uses diurnal residues left over from life past, as outlined by Freud in *The Interpretation of Dreams* [*Traumdeutung*]. This destiny of repetition and quotation – whether it is taken up ironically, cynically, or naively – is in any event obvious if we think of the tendencies that at present dominate painting, under the names of transavantgardism, neoexpressionism, and so forth. I will return to this a bit later.

This departure from architectural 'postmodernism' leads me to a second connotation of the term 'postmodern' (and I have to admit that I am no stranger to its misunderstanding).

The general idea is a trivial one. We can observe and establish a kind of decline in the confidence that, for two centuries, the West invested in the principle of a general progress in humanity. This idea of a possible, probable, or necessary progress is rooted in the belief that developments made in the arts, technology, knowledge, and freedoms would benefit humanity as a whole. It is true that ascertaining the identity of the subject who suffered most from a lack of development – the poor, the worker, or the illiterate – continued to be an issue throughout the nineteenth and twentieth centuries. As you know, there was controversy and even war between liberals, conservatives, and 'leftists' over the true name to be given to the subject whose emancipation required assistance. Yet all these tendencies were united in the belief that initiatives, discoveries, and institutions only had legitimacy in so far as they contributed to the emancipation of humanity.

After two centuries we have become more alert to signs that would indicate an opposing movement. Neither liberalism (economic and political) nor the various Marxisms have emerged from these bloodstained centuries without attracting accusations of having perpetrated crimes against humanity. We could make a list of proper names – places, people, dates – capable of illustrating or substantiating our suspicions. Following Theodor Adorno, I have used the name 'Auschwitz' to signify just how impoverished recent Western history seems from the point of view of the 'modern' project of the emancipation of humanity. What kind of thought is capable of 'relieving' Auschwitz – relieving [*relever*] in the sense of *aufheben* – capable of situating it in a general, empirical, or even speculative process directed toward universal emancipation? There is a sort of grief in the *Zeitgeist*. It can find expression in reactive, even reactionary, attitudes or in utopias – but not in a positive orientation that would open up a new perspective.

Technoscientific development has become a means of deepening the malaise rather than allaying it. It is no longer possible to call development progress. It seems to proceed of its own accord, with a force, an autonomous motoricity that is independent of us. It does not answer to demands issuing from human needs. On the contrary, human entities – whether social or individual – always seem destabilized by the results and implications of development. I am thinking of its intellectual and mental results as well as its material results. We could say that humanity's condition has become one of chasing after the process of the accumulation of new objects (both of practice and of thought).

As you might imagine, understanding the reason for this process of complexification is an important question for me – an obscure question. We could say there exists a sort of destiny, or involuntary destination toward a condition that is increasingly complex. The needs for security, identity, and happiness springing from our immediate condition as living beings, as social beings, now seem irrelevant next to this sort of constraint to complexify, mediatize, quantify, synthesize, and modify the size of each and every object. We are like Gullivers in the world of technoscience: sometimes too big, sometimes too small, but never the right size. From this perspective, the insistence on simplicity generally seems today like a pledge to barbarism.

On this same point, the following issue also has to be elaborated. Humanity is divided into two parts. One faces the challenge of complexity, the other that ancient and terrible challenge of its own survival. This is perhaps the most important aspect of the failure of the modern project – a project that, need I remind you, once applied in principle to the whole of humanity.

I will give my third point – the most complex – the shortest treatment. The question of postmodernity is also, or first of all, a question of expressions of thought: in art, literature, philosophy, politics.

We know that in the domain of art, for example, or more precisely in the visual and plastic arts, the dominant view today is that the great movement of the avant-gardes is over and done with. It has, as it were, become the done thing to indulge or deride the avant-gardes – to regard them as the expression of an outdated modernity.

I do not like the term avant-garde, with its military connotations, any more than anyone else. But I do observe that the true process of avant-gardism was in reality a kind of work, a long, obstinate, and highly responsible work concerned with investigating the assumptions implicit in modernity. I mean that for a proper understanding of the work of modern painters from, say, Manet to Duchamp or Barnett Newman, we would have to compare their work with *anamnesis*, in the sense of a psychoanalytic therapy. Just as patients try to elaborate their current problems by freely associating apparently inconsequential details with past situations – allowing them to uncover hidden meanings in their lives and their behavior – so we can think of the work of Cézanne, Picasso, Delaunay, Kandinsky, Klee, Mondrian, Malevich, and finally Duchamp as a working through [*durcharbeiten*] performed by modernity on its own meaning.

If we abandon that responsibility, we will surely be condemned to repeat, without any displacement, the West's 'modern neurosis' – its schizophrenia, paranoia, and so on, the source of the misfortunes we have known for two centuries.

You can see that when it is understood in this way, the 'post-' of 'postmodern' does not signify a movement of *comeback*, *flashback*, or *feedback* – that is, not a movement of repetition but a procedure in 'ana-': a procedure of analysis, anamnesis, anagogy, and anamorphosis that elaborates an 'initial forgetting.'

3 □ The Entry into Postmodernity: Nietzsche as a turning point

Jürgen Habermas

I

Neither Hegel nor his direct disciples on the Left or Right ever wanted to call into question the achievements of modernity from which the modern age drew its pride and self-consciousness. Above all the modern age stood under the sign of subjective freedom. This was realized in society as the space secured by civil law for the rational pursuit of one's own interests; in the state, as the in principle equal rights to participation in the formation of political will; in the private sphere, as ethical autonomy and self-realization; finally, in the public sphere related to this private realm, as the formative process that takes place by means of the appropriation of a culture that has become reflective. Even the forms of the absolute and of the objective spirit, looked at from the perspective of the individual, had assumed a structure in which the subjective spirit could emancipate itself from the naturelike spontaneity of the traditional way of life. In the process, the spheres in which the individual led his life as *bourgeois*, *citoyen*, and *homme* thereby grew ever further apart from one another and became self-sufficient. This separation and self-sufficiency, which, considered from the standpoint of philosophy of history, paved the way for emancipation from age-old dependencies, were experienced at the same time as abstraction, as alienation from the totality of an ethical context of life. Once religion had been the unbreakable seal upon this totality; it is not by chance that this seal has been broken.

The religious forces of social integration grew weaker in the wake of a process of enlightenment that is just as little susceptible of being revoked as it was arbitrarily brought about in the first place. One feature of this enlightenment is the irreversibility of learning processes, which is based on the fact that insights cannot be forgotten at will; they can only be repressed or corrected by better insights. Hence, enlightenment can only make good its deficits by radicalized enlightenment;

From Habermas, J., *Philosophical Discourse of Modernity*, MIT Press, Cambridge, MA, 1987, pp. 83–8, 97–105.

this is why Hegel and his disciples had to place their hope in a dialectic of enlightenment in which reason was validated as an equivalent for the unifying power of religion. They worked out concepts of reason that were supposed to fulfill such a program. We have seen how and why these attempts failed.

Hegel conceived of reason as the reconciling self-knowledge of an absolute spirit; the Hegelian Left, as the liberating appropriation of productively externalized, but withheld, essential powers; the Hegelian Right, as the rememorative compensation for the pain of inevitable diremptions. Hegel's concept proved too strong; the absolute spirit was posited unperturbed, beyond the process of a history open to the future and beyond the unreconciled character of the present. Against the quietistic withdrawal of the priestly caste of philosophers from an unreconciled reality, therefore, the Young Hegelians invoked the profane right of a present that still awaited the realization of philosophical thought. In doing so, they brought to bear a concept of praxis that fell short. This concept only enhanced the force of the absolutized purposive rationality that it was supposed to overcome. Neoconservatives could spell out for praxis philosophy the social complexity that stubbornly asserted itself in the face of all revolutionary hopes. They in turn altered Hegel's concept of reason in such a way that modern society's need for compensation was brought to the fore at the same time as its rationality. But this concept did not reach far enough to make intelligible the compensatory function of a historicism that was supposed to bring traditional forces back to life through the medium of the *Geisteswissenschaften*.

Against this contemporary culture fed from the springs of an antiquarian historiography, Nietzsche brought the modern time-consciousness to bear in a way similar to that in which the Young Hegelians once did against the objectivism of the Hegelian philosophy of history. In the second of his *Untimely Observations*, *On the Advantage and Disadvantage of History for Life*, Nietzsche analyzes the fruitlessness of cultural tradition uncoupled from action and shoved into the sphere of interiority. 'Knowledge, taken in excess without hunger, even contrary to need, no longer acts as a transforming motive impelling to action and remains hidden in a certain chaotic inner world ... and so the whole of modern culture is essentially internal ... a "Handbook of Inner Culture for External Barbarians".'[1] Modern consciousness, overburdened with historical knowledge, has lost 'the plastic power of life' that makes human beings able, with their gaze toward the future, to 'interpret the past from the standpoint of the highest strength of the present'.[2] Because the methodically proceeding *Geisteswissenschaften* are dependent on a false, which is to say unattainable, ideal of objectivity, they neutralize the standards necessary for life and make way for a paralyzing relativism: 'Things were different in all ages; it does not matter who you are.'[3] They block the capacity 'to shatter and dissolve something [past]' from time to time, in order 'to enable [us] to live [in the present]'.[4] Like the Young Hegelians, Nietzsche senses in the historicist admiration of the 'power of history' a tendency that all too easily turns into an admiration of naked success in the style of *Realpolitik*.

With Nietzsche's entrance into the discourse of modernity, the argument shifts, from the ground up. To begin with, reason was conceived as a reconciling self-knowledge, then as a liberating appropriation, and finally as a compensatory remembrance, so that it could emerge as the equivalent for the unifying power of religion and overcome the diremptions of modernity by means of its own driving forces. Three times this attempt to tailor the concept of reason to the program of an intrinsic dialectic of enlightenment miscarried. In the context of this constellation, Nietzsche had no choice but to submit subject-centered reason yet again to an immanent critique – or to give up the program entirely. Nietzsche opts for the second alternative: He renounces a renewed revision of the concept of reason and *bids farewell* to the dialectic of enlightenment. In particular, the historicist deformation of modern consciousness, in which it is flooded with arbitrary contents and emptied of everything essential, makes him doubt that modernity could still fashion its criteria out of itself – 'for from ourselves we moderns have nothing at all'.[5] Indeed Nietzsche turns the thought-figure of the dialectic of enlightenment upon the historicist enlightenment as well, but this time with the goal of exploding modernity's husk of reason as such.

Nietzsche uses the ladder of historical reason in order to cast it away at the end and to gain a foothold in myth as the other of reason: 'for the origin of historical education – and its inner, quite radical contradiction with the spirit of a "new age", a "modern consciousness" – this origin *must* itself in turn be historically understood, history *must* itself dissolve the problem of history, knowledge *must* turn its sting against itself – this threefold *must* is the imperative of the new spirit of the "new age" if it really does contain something new, mighty, original and a promise of life'.[6] Nietzsche is thinking here of his *Birth of Tragedy*, an investigation, carried out with historical-philological means, that led him beyond the Alexandrian world and beyond the Roman-Christian world back to the beginnings, back to the 'ancient Greek world of the great, the natural and human'. On this path, the antiquarian-thinking 'latecomers' of modernity are to be transformed into 'firstlings' of a postmodern age – a program that Heidegger will take up again in *Being and Time*. For Nietzsche, the starting situation is clear. On the one hand, historical enlightenment only strengthens the now palpable diremptions in the achievements of modernity; reason as manifested in the form of a religion of culture no longer develops any synthetic forces that could renew the unifying power of traditional religion. On the other hand, the path of restoration is barred to modernity. The religious-metaphysical world-views of ancient civilizations are themselves already a product of enlightenment; they are *too rational*, therefore, to be able to provide opposition to the radicalized enlightenment of modernity.

Like all who leap out of the dialectic of enlightenment, Nietzsche undertakes a conspicuous leveling. Modernity loses its singular status; it constitutes only a last epoch in the far-reaching history of a rationalization initiated by the dissolution of archaic life and the collapse of myth.[7] In Europe, Socrates and Christ, the founders of philosophical thought and of ecclesiastical monotheism, mark this turning point: 'The tremendous historical need of our unsatisfied historical culture, the assembling around one of the countless other cultures, the consuming desire for knowledge –

what does all this point to, if not to the loss of myth, the loss of the mythical home?'[8] The modern time-consciousness, of course, prohibits any thoughts of regression, of an unmediated return to mythical origins. Only the future constitutes the horizon for the arousal of mythical pasts: 'The past always speaks as an oracle: Only as masterbuilders of the future who know the present will you understand it.'[9] This *utopian* attitude, directed to the god *who is coming*, distinguishes Nietzsche's undertaking from the reactionary call of 'Back to the origins!' Teleological thought that contrasts origin and goal with each other loses its power completely. And because Nietzsche does not negate the modern time-consciousness, but heightens it, he can imagine modern art, which in its most subjective forms of expression drives this time-consciousness to its summit, as the medium in which modernity makes contact with the archaic. Whereas historicism presents us with the world as an exhibition and transforms the contemporaries enjoying it into blasé spectators, only the suprahistorical power of an art consuming itself in actuality can bring salvation for 'the true neediness and inner poverty of man'.[10]

Here the young Nietzsche has in mind the program of Richard Wagner, who opened his 'Essay on religion and art' with the statement: 'One could say that wherever religion has become artistic, it is left to art to save the core of religion, in that it grasps the mythic symbols (which religion wants to believe are true in a real sense) in terms of their symbolic values, so that the profound truth hidden in them can be recognized through their ideal representation.'[11] The religious festival become work of art is supposed, with a culturally revived public sphere, to overcome the inwardness of privately appropriated historical culture. An aesthetically renewed mythology is supposed to relax the forces of social integration consolidated by competitive society. It will decenter modern consciousness and open it to archaic experiences. This art of the future denies that it is the product of an individual artist and establishes 'the people itself as the artist of the future'.[12] This is why Nietzsche celebrates Wagner as the 'Revolutionary of Society' and as the one who overcomes Alexandrian culture. He expects the effect of Dionysian tragedy to go forth from Bayreuth – 'that the state and society and, quite generally, the gulfs between man and man give way to an overwhelming feeling of unity leading back to the very heart of nature'.[13]

As we know, later on Nietzsche turned away in disgust from the world of the Wagnerian opera. What is more interesting than the personal, political, and aesthetic reasons for this aversion is the philosophical motive that stands behind the question, 'What would a music have to be like that would no longer be of Romantic origin (like Wagner's) – but Dionysian?'[14] The idea of a new mythology is of Romantic provenance, and so also is the recourse to Dionysus as the god who is coming. Nietzsche likewise distances himself from the Romantic use of these ideas and proclaims a manifestly more radical version pointing far beyond Wagner. But wherein does the Dionysian differ from the Romantic?

[. . .]

IV

Heidegger wants to take over the essential motifs of Nietzsche's Dionysian messianism while avoiding the aporias of a self-enclosed critique of reason. Nietzsche, operating in a 'scholarly' mode, wanted to catapult modern thinking beyond itself by way of a genealogy of the belief in truth and of the ascetic ideal; Heidegger, who espies an uncleansed remnant of enlightenment in this power-theoretical strategy of unmasking, would rather stick with Nietzsche the 'philosopher'. The goal that Nietzsche pursued with a totalized, self-consuming critique of ideology, Heidegger wants to reach through a destruction of Western metaphysics that proceeds immanently. Nietzsche had spanned the arch of the Dionysian event between Greek tragedy and a new mythology. Heidegger's later philosophy can be understood as an attempt to displace this even from the area of an aesthetically revitalized mythology to that of philosophy.[15] Heidegger is faced first of all with the task of putting philosophy in the place that art occupies in Nietzsche (as a countermovement to nihilism), in order then to transform philosophical thinking in such a way that it can become the area for the ossification and renewal of the Dionysian forces – he wants to describe the emergence and overcoming of nihilism as the beginning and end of metaphysics.

Heidegger's first Nietzsche lecture is entitled 'The will to power as art'. It is based above all on the posthumous fragments, which in their compilation by Elisabeth Foerster-Nietzsche were puffed up into an unwritten magnum opus, *The Will to Power*.[16] Heidegger attempts to substantiate the thesis that 'Nietzsche moves in the orbit of Western philosophy'.[17] He does call the thinker who 'in his metaphysics ... reverts to the beginnings of Western philosophy'[18] and leads the countermovement to nihilism an 'artist-philosopher'. However, Nietzsche's ideas about the saving power of art are supposed to be 'aesthetic' only 'at first glance' but 'metaphysical ... according to [their] innermost will'.[19] Heidegger's classicist understanding of art requires this interpretation. Like Hegel, he is convinced that art reached its essential end with Romanticism. A comparison with Walter Benjamin would show how little Heidegger was influenced by genuine experiences of avant-garde art. And so he was also unable to grasp why it is that only a subjectivistically heightened and radically differentiated art, which consistently develops the meaning proper to the aesthetic dimension out of the self-experience of a decentered subjectivity, recommends itself as the inaugurator of a new mythology.[20] Thus, he has little difficulty in imagining the leveling of the 'aesthetic phenomenon' and the assimilation of art to metaphysics. The beautiful allows Being to show forth: 'Both beauty and truth are related to Being, indeed by way of unveiling the Being of beings.'[21]

Later on this will read: 'The poet proclaims the holy, which reveals itself to the thinker. Poetry and thinking are of course interdependent, but in the end it is poetry that stems from thinking in its initial stages'.[22]

Once art has been ontologized in this way,[23] philosophy must again take on the task that it had handed over to art in Romanticism, namely, creating an equivalent for the unifying power of religion, in order effectively to counter the diremptions of modernity. Nietzsche had entrusted the overcoming of nihilism to the aesthetically revived Dionysian myth. Heidegger projects this Dionysian happening onto the screen of a critique of metaphysics, which thereby takes on world-historical significance.

Now it is Being that has withdrawn itself from beings and announces its indeterminate arrival by an absence made palpable and by the mounting pain of deprival. Thinking, which stalks Being through the destiny of the forgetfulness of Being to which Western philosophy has been doomed, has a catalytic function. The thinking that simultaneously emerges out of metaphysics, inquires into the origins of metaphysics, and transcends the limits of metaphysics from inside no longer shares in the self-confidence of a reason boasting of its own autonomy. To be sure, the different strata within which Being is buried have to be excavated. But the work of destruction, in contrast with the power of reflection, serves to train one in a new heteronomy. It focuses its energy singlemindedly on the self-overcoming and the self-renunciation of a subjectivity that has to learn perseverance and is supposed to dissolve in humility. As for reason itself, it can only be exercised in the baleful activity of forgetting and expelling. Even memory lacks the power to promote the return of what has been exiled. As a result, Being can only come about as a fateful dispensation; those who are in need can at most hold themselves open and prepared for it. Heidegger's critique of reason ends in the distancing radicality of a change in orientation that is all-pervasive but empty of content – away from autonomy and toward a self-surrender to Being, which supposedly leaves behind the opposition between autonomy and heteronomy.

Bataille's Nietzsche-inspired critique of reason takes another tack. It too employs the concept of the sacred for those decentering experiences of ambivalent rapture in which a hardened subjectivity transgresses its boundaries. The actions of religious sacrifice and of erotic fusion, in which the subject seeks to be 'loosed from its relatedness to the I' and to make room for a reestablished 'continuity of Being', are exemplary for him.[24] Bataille, too, pursues the traces of a primordial force that could heal the discontinuity or rift between the rationally disciplined world of work and the outlawed other of reason. He imagines this overpowering return to a lost continuity as the eruption of elements opposed to reason, as a breathtaking act of self-de-limiting. In this process of dissolution, the monadically closed-off subjectivity of self-assertive and mutually objectifying individuals is dispossessed and cast down into the abyss.

Bataille does not approach this Dionysian violence directed against the principle of individuation by way of the restrained path of a self-overcoming of knowledge that is caught up in metaphysics, but by way of an empirical and analytic grasp of phenomena associated with the self-transgression and self-extinction of the purposive-rational subject. He is obviously interested in the Bacchanalian traits of an orgiastic will to power – the creative and exuberant activity of a mighty will manifested as much in play, dance, rapture, and giddiness as in the kinds of stimulation aroused by destruction, by viewing pain that incites cruelty and pleasure, by witnessing violent death. The curious gaze with which Bataille patiently dissects the limit experiences of ritual sacrifice and sexual love is guided and informed by an aesthetics of terror. The years-long follower and later opponent of André Breton does not, like Heidegger, pass by the foundational aesthetic experience of Nietzsche, but follows out the radicalization of this experience into surrealism. Like one possessed, Bataille investigates those ambivalent, offputting emotional reactions of shame, loathing, shock; he analyzes the sadistic satisfaction released by sudden, injurious, intrusive, violently intervening impressions. In these explosive stimuli are joined the countervailing tendencies of longing and of horrified withdrawal into paralyzing fascination. Loathing, disgust, and horror fuse with lust, attraction, and craving. The consciousness exposed to these rending ambivalences enters a sphere beyond comprehension. The Surrealists wanted to arouse this state of shock with aggressively employed aesthetic means. Bataille pursues the traces of this 'profane illumination' (Benjamin) right back to the taboos regarding the human corpse, cannibalism, naked bodies, menstrual bleeding, incest, and so on.

These anthropological investigations, which we shall consider below, provide the starting point for a theory of sovereignty. Just as Nietzsche did in the *Genealogy of Morals*, so Bataille studies the demarcating and ever fuller extirpating of everything heterogeneous by which the modern world of purposively rational labor, consumption, and domination is constituted. He does not avoid constructing a history of Western reason which, like Heidegger's critique of metaphysics, portrays modernity as an epoch of depletion. But in Bataille's account the heterogeneous, extraneous elements appear not in the guise of an apocalyptically fateful dispensation, mystically tacked on, but as subversive forces that can only be convulsively released if they are unfettered within a libertarian socialistic society.

Paradoxically, Bataille fights for the rights of this renewal of the sacral with the tools of scientific analysis. By no means does he regard methodical thought as suspect. 'No one [can] pose the problem of religion if he starts out from arbitrary solutions not allowed by the present *climate of exactitude*. Insofar as I talk about internal experience and not about objects, I am not a man of science; but the moment I talk about objects, I do so with the unavoidable rigor of the scientist.'[25]

Bataille is separated from Heidegger both by his access to a genuinely aesthetic experience (from which he draws the concept of the sacred) and by his respect for the scientific character of the knowledge that he would like to enlist in the service of his analysis of the sacred. At the same time, if one considers their respective contributions to the philosophical discourse of modernity, there are parallels between the two thinkers. The structural similarities can be explained by the fact that Heidegger and Bataille want to meet the same challenge in the wake of Nietzsche. They both want to carry out a radical critique of reason – one that attacks the roots of the critique itself. Similar constraints on argumentation result from this agreement about the posing of the problem.

To begin with, the object of the critique has to be determined sharply enough so that we can recognize in it subject-centered reason as the principle of modernity. Heidegger picks the objectifying thought of the modern sciences as his point of departure; Bataille, the purposively rational behavior of the capitalist enterprise and of the bureaucratized state apparatus as his. The one, Heidegger, investigates the basic ontological concepts of the philosophy of consciousness in order to lay bare the will to technical control of objectified processes as the underlying impulse governing the train of thought from Descartes to Nietzsche. Subjectivity and reification distort our view of the unmanipulable. The other, Bataille, investigates the imperatives to utility and efficiency, to which work and consumption have been ever more exclusively subordinated, in order to identify within industrial production an inherent tendency toward self-destruction in all modern societies. Rationalized societies hinder the unproductive spending and generous squandering of accumulated wealth.

Since such totalizing critique of reason has given up all hope of a dialectic of enlightenment, what falls under this totalizing critique is so comprehensive that the other of reason, the counterforce of *Being* or of *sovereignty*, can no longer be conceived of only as repressed and split-off moments of reason itself. Consequently, like Nietzsche, Heidegger and Bataille must reach beyond the origins of Western history back to archaic times in order to rediscover the traces of the Dionysian, whether in the thought of the pre-Socratics or in the state of excitement surrounding sacred rites of sacrifice. It is here that they have to identify those buried, rationalized-away experiences that are to fill the abstract terms 'Being' and 'sovereignty' with life. Both are just names to start with. They have to be introduced as concepts contrasting with reason in such a way that they remain resistant to any attempts at rational incorporation. 'Being' is defined as that which has *withdrawn* itself from the totality of beings that can be grasped and known as something in the objective world; 'sovereignty' as that which has been *excluded* from the world of the useful and calculable. These primordial forces appear in images of a plenitude that is to be bestowed but is now withheld, missing – of a wealth that awaits expending. Whereas reason is characterized by calculating manipulation and valorization, its counterpart can only be portrayed negatively, as what is simply unmanipulable and not valorizable – as a medium into which the subject can plunge if it gives itself up and transcends itself *as* subject.

The two moments – that of reason and that of its other – stand not in opposition pointing to a dialectical *Aufhebung*, but in a relationship of tension characterized by mutual repugnance and exclusion. Their relationship is not constituted by the dynamics of repression that could be reversed by countervailing processes of self-reflection or of enlightened practice. Instead, reason is delivered over to the dynamics of withdrawal and of retreat, of expulsion and proscription, with such impotence that narrow-minded subjectivity can never, by its own powers of anamnesis and of analysis, reach what escapes it or holds itself at a remove from it. Self-reflection is sealed off from the other of reason. There reigns a play of forces of a metahistorical or cosmic sort, which calls for an effort of a *different* observance altogether. In Heidegger, the paradoxical effort of a reason transcending itself takes on the chiliastic form of an urgent meditation conjuring up the dispensation of Being, whereas, with his heterological sociology of the sacred, Bataille promises himself enlightenment about, but ultimately no influence over, the transcendent play of forces.

Both authors develop their theory by way of a narrative reconstruction of the history of Western reason. Heidegger, who interprets reason as self-consciousness in line with motifs from the philosophy of the subject, conceives of nihilism as the expression of a technical world-mastery loosed in totalitarian fashion. The ill fate of metaphysical thought is supposed to culminate in this way – a thought that was set in motion by the question about Being, but that more and more loses sight of what is essential in view of the totality of reified entities. Bataille, who interprets reason as labor in line with motifs from praxis philosophy, conceives of nihilism as the consequence of a compulsive accumulation process. The ill fate of surplus production that at first still served celebratory and sovereign exuberance, but then uses up ever more resources for the purpose of just raising the level of productivity, culminates in this way: Extravagance changes into productive consumption and removes the basis for creative, self-transcending sovereignty.

Forgetfulness of Being and the expulsion of the outlawed part are the two dialectical images that have till now inspired all those attempts to dissociate the critique of reason from the pattern of a dialectic of enlightenment and to raise the other of reason to a court of appeal before which modernity can be called to order. In what follows, I will examine whether Heidegger's later philosophy (and the productive continuation of his philosophical mysticism by Derrida), on the one hand, and Bataille's general economy (and Foucault's genealogy of knowledge grounded on a theory of power), on the other – these two ways suggested by Nietzsche – really lead us out of the philosophy of the subject.

Heidegger has resolutely ontologized art and bet everything on the one card: a movement of thought that liberates by destroying, that is supposed to overcome metaphysics on its own ground. He thereby evades the aporias of a self-referential critique of reason that is bound to undermine its own foundations. He gives an ontological turn to Dionysian messianism; with this he ties himself to the style of thought and the mode of reasoning of *Ursprungsphilosophie* in such a way that he can only overcome the foundationalism of Husserlian phenomenology at the price of a foundationalizing of history, which leads into a void. Heidegger tries to break out of the enchanted circle of the philosophy of the subject by setting its foundations aflow temporally. The superfoundationalism of a history of Being abstracted from all concrete history shows that he remains fixated on the thinking he negates. By contrast, Bataille remains faithful to an authentic aesthetic experience and opens himself to a realm of phenomena in which subject-centered reason can be opened up to its other. To be sure, he cannot admit the modern provenance of this experience out of surrealism; he has to transplant it into an archaic context with the help of anthropological theories. Thus, Bataille pursues the project of a scientific analysis of the sacred and of a general economy, which are supposed to illuminate the world-historical process of rationalization and the possibility of a final reversal. In this way, he gets into the same dilemma as Nietzsche: His theory of power cannot satisfy the claim to scientific objectivity and, at the same time, put into effect the program of a total and hence self-referential critique of reason that also affects the truth of theoretical propositions.

Notes

1. Friedrich Nietzsche, *On the Advantage and Disadvantage of History for Life*, Cambridge, 1980, pp. 24–5.
2. *Ibid.*, pp. 62, 37.
3. *Ibid.*, p. 41.
4. *Ibid.*, p. 21.
5. *Ibid.*, p. 24.
6. *Ibid.*, p. 45.
7. This is true of Horkheimer and Adorno as well; in this respect they are close to Nietzsche, Bataille, and Heidegger.
8. Friedrich Nietzsche, *The Birth of Tragedy and the Case of Wagner*, New York, 1967, p. 136.
9. Nietzsche, *Advantage and Disadvantage*, p. 38.
10. *Ibid.*, pp. 32, 64.
11. Richard Wagner, *Sämtlich Schriften und Dichtungen*, vol. 10, p. 211.
12. *Ibid.*, p. 172.
13. Nietzsche, *The Birth of Tragedy*, p. 59.
14. Nietzsche, 'Attempt at self-criticism', in *The Birth of Tragedy*, p. 25. See the *Nachlass*, vol. 12 of Nietzsche's *Sämtliche Werke*, ed. G. Colli and M. Montinari, Berlin, 1967 ff., p. 117.
15. Between 1936 and 1946 (that is, between the *Introduction to Metaphysics*, which still shows traces of the fascist Heidegger, and the 'Letter on Humanism', which introduces the postwar philosophy), Heidegger was continually occupied with Nietzsche. The idea of the history of Being was formed in an intensive dialogue with Nietzsche. Heidegger explicitly acknowledges this in the 1961 foreword to the two volumes that document this segment of his path of thought. See Martin Heidegger, *Nietzsche*, Pfullingen, 1961, pp. 9 ff.
16. This fiction has been demolished without remainder by the edition of Giorgio Colli and Mazzino Montinar; see their commentary to the late work, in Nietzsche's *Sämtliche Werke*, vol. 14, pp. 383 ff., and the chronology of Nietzsche's life, in vol. 15, p. 1.
17. Martin Heidegger, *Nietzsche*, vol. 1: *The Will to Power as Art*, New York, 1979, p. 4.
18. *Ibid.*, p. 19.
19. *Ibid.*, p. 131.
20. In this respect, Oskar Becker demonstrates an incomparably greater sensibility with his dualistic counterproposal to Heidegger's fundamental ontology; see Oskar Becker, 'Von der Hinfälligkeit des Schönen und der Abenteuerlichkeit des Künstlers' and 'Von der Abenteuerlichkeit des Künstlers und der vorsichtigen Verwegenheit des Philosophen', in *Dasein und Dawesen. Gesammelte philosophische Aufsätze*, Pfullingen, 1963, pp. 11 ff., 103 ff.
21. Heidegger, *Nietzsche*, vol. 1, p. 200.
22. Martin Heidegger, 'Nachwort zu Was *ist metaphysik?*' in *Wegmarken*, Frankfurt, 1978, p. 309.

23. Heidegger sums up his first Nietzsche lectures with the words: 'From the perspective of the essence of Being, art has to be conceived of as the basic happening of beings, as the authentically creative moment.'
24. Georges Bataille, introduction to *Der heilige Eros*, Frankfurt, 1982, pp. 10 ff.
25. *Ibid.*, p. 29.

4 □ *Postmodernism, or The Cultural Logic of Late Capitalism*

Fredric Jameson

The last few years have been marked by an inverted millenarianism, in which premonitions of the future, catastrophic or redemptive, have been replaced by senses of the end of this or that (the end of ideology, art, or social class; the 'crisis' of Leninism, social democracy, or the welfare state, etc., etc.): taken together, all of these perhaps constitute what is increasingly called postmodernism. The case for its existence depends on the hypothesis of some radical break or *coupure*, generally traced back to the end of the 1950s or the early 1960s. As the word itself suggests, this break is most often related to notions of the waning or extinction of the hundred-year-old modern movement (or to its ideological or aesthetic repudiation). Thus, abstract expressionism in painting, existentialism in philosophy, the final forms of representation in the novel, the films of the great *auteurs*, or the modernist school of poetry (as institutionalized and canonized in the works of Wallace Stevens): all these are now seen as the final, extraordinary flowering of a high-modernist impulse which is spent and exhausted with them. The enumeration of what follows then at once becomes empirical, chaotic, and heterogeneous: Andy Warhol and pop art, but also photorealism, and beyond it, the 'new expressionism'; the moment, in music, of John Cage, but also the synthesis of classical and 'popular' styles found in composers like Phil Glass and Terry Riley, and also punk and new wave rock (the Beatles and the Stones now standing as the high-modernist moment of that more recent and rapidly evolving tradition); in film, Godard, post-Godard and experimental cinema and video, but also a whole new type of commercial film (about which more below); Burroughs, Pynchon, or Ishmael Reed, on the one hand, and the French *nouveau roman* and its succession on the other, along with alarming new kinds of literary criticism, based on some new aesthetic of textuality or *écriture*. ... The list might be extended indefinitely; but does it imply any more fundamental change or break than the periodic style- and fashion-changes determined by an older high-modernist imperative of stylistic innovation?

From Jameson, F., *Postmodernism, or The Cultural Logic of Late Capitalism*, Verso, London/Duke University Press, Durham, NC, 1991, pp. 53–7, 58–71, 80–92.

The Rise of Aesthetic Populism

It is in the realm of architecture, however, that modifications in aesthetic production are most dramatically visible, and that their theoretical problems have been most centrally raised and articulated; it was indeed from architectural debates that my own conception of postmodernism – as it will be outlined in the following pages – initially began to emerge. More decisively than in the other arts or media, postmodernist positions in architecture have been inseparable from an implacable critique of architectural high modernism and of the so-called International Style (Frank Lloyd Wright, Le Corbusier, Mies), where formal criticism and analysis (of the high-modernist transformation of the building into a virtual sculpture, or monumental 'duck', as Robert Venturi puts it) are at one with reconsiderations on the level of urbanism and of the aesthetic institution. High modernism is thus credited with the destruction of the fabric of the traditional city and of its older neighbourhood culture (by way of the radical disjunction of the new Utopian high-modernist building from its surrounding context); while the prophetic elitism and authoritarianism of the modern movement are remorselessly denounced in the imperious gesture of the charismatic Master.

Postmodernism in architecture will then logically enough stage itself as a kind of aesthetic populism, as the very title of Venturi's influential manifesto, *Learning from Las Vegas*, suggests. However we may ultimately wish to evaluate this populist rhetoric, it has at least the merit of drawing our attention to one fundamental feature of all the postmodernisms enumerated above: namely, the effacement in them of the older (essentially high-modernist) frontier between high culture and so-called mass or commercial culture, and the emergence of new kinds of texts infused with the forms, categories and contents of that very Culture Industry so passionately denounced by all the ideologues of the modern, from Leavis and the American New Criticism all the way to Adorno and the Frankfurt School. The postmodernisms have in fact been fascinated precisely by this whole 'degraded' landscape of schlock and kitsch, of TV series and *Reader's Digest* culture, of advertising and motels, of the late show and the grade-B Hollywood film, of so-called paraliterature with its airport paperback categories of the gothic and the romance, the popular biography, the murder mystery and science-fiction or fantasy novel: materials they no longer simply 'quote', as a Joyce or a Mahler might have done, but incorporate into their very substance.

Nor should the break in question be thought of as a purely cultural affair: indeed, theories of the postmodern – whether celebratory or couched in the language of moral revulsion and denunciation – bear a strong family resemblance to all those more ambitious sociological generalizations which, at much the same time, bring us the news of the arrival and inauguration of a whole new type of society, most famously baptized 'post-industrial society' (Daniel Bell), but often also designated consumer society, media society, information society, electronic society or 'high tech', and the like. Such theories have the obvious ideological mission of demonstrating, to their own relief, that the new social formation in question no longer obeys the laws of classical capitalism, namely the primacy of industrial production and the omnipresence of class struggle. The Marxist tradition has therefore resisted them with vehemence, with the signal exception of the economist Ernest Mandel, whose book *Late Capitalism* sets out not merely to anatomize the historic originality of this new society (which he sees as a third stage or moment in the evolution of capital), but also to demonstrate that it is, if anything, a *purer* stage of capitalism than any of the moments that preceded it. I will return to this argument later; suffice it for the moment to emphasize a point I have defended in greater detail elsewhere,[1] namely that every position on postmodernism in culture – whether apologia or stigmatization – is also at one and the same time, and *necessarily*, an implicitly or explicitly political stance on the nature of multinational capitalism today.

Postmodernism as Cultural Dominant

A last preliminary word on method: what follows is not to be read as stylistic description, as the account of one cultural style or movement among others. I have rather meant to offer a periodizing hypothesis, and that at a moment in which the very conception of historical periodization has come to seem most problematical indeed. I have argued elsewhere that all isolated or discrete cultural analysis always involves a buried or repressed theory of historical periodization; in any case, the conception of the 'genealogy' largely lays to rest traditional theoretical worries about so-called linear history, theories of 'stages', and teleological historiography. In the present context, however, lengthier theoretical discussion of such (very real) issues can perhaps be replaced by a few substantive remarks.

One of the concerns frequently aroused by periodizing hypotheses is that these tend to obliterate difference, and to project an idea of the historical period as massive homogeneity (bounded on either side by inexplicable 'chronological' metamorphoses and punctuation marks). This is, however, precisely why it seems to me essential to grasp 'postmodernism' not as a style, but rather as a cultural dominant: a conception which allows for the presence and coexistence of a range of very different, yet subordinate features.

Consider, for example, the powerful alternative position that postmodernism is itself little more than one more stage of modernism proper (if not, indeed, of the even older romanticism); it may indeed be conceded that all of the features of postmodernism I am about to enumerate can be detected, full-blown, in this or that preceding modernism (including such astonishing genealogical precursors as Gertrude Stein, Raymond Roussel, or Marcel Duchamp, who may be considered outright postmodernists, *avant la lettre*). What has not been taken into account by this view is, however, the social position of the older modernism, or better still, its passionate repudiation by an older Victorian and post-Victorian bourgeoisie, for whom its forms and ethos are received as being variously ugly, dissonant, obscure, scandalous, immoral, subversive and generally 'anti-social'. It will be argued here that a mutation in the sphere of culture has rendered such attitudes archaic. Not only are Picasso and Joyce no longer ugly; they now strike us, on the whole, as rather 'realistic'; and this is the result of canonization and an academic institutionalization of the modern movement generally, which can be traced to the late 1950s. This is indeed surely one of the most plausible explanations for the emergence of postmodernism itself, since the younger generation of the 1960s will now confront the formerly oppositional modern movement as a set of dead classics, which 'weigh like a nightmare on the brains of the living', as Marx once said in a different context.

As for the postmodern revolt against all that, however, it must equally be stressed that its own offensive features – from obscurity and sexually explicit material to psychological squalor and overt expressions of social and political defiance, which transcend anything that might have been imagined at the most extreme moments of high modernism – no longer scandalize anyone and are not only received with the greatest complacency but have themselves become institutionalized and are at one with the official culture of Western society.

What has happened is that aesthetic production today has become integrated into commodity production generally: the frantic economic urgency of producing fresh waves of ever more novel-seeming goods (from clothing to airplanes), at ever greater rates of turnover, now assigns an increasingly essential structural function and position to aesthetic innovation and experimentation. Such economic necessities then find recognition in the institutional support of all kinds available for the newer art, from foundations and grants to museums and other forms of patronage. Architecture is, however, of all the arts that closest constitutively to the economic, with which, in the form of commissions and land values, it has a virtually unmediated relationship: it will therefore not be surprising to find the extraordinary flowering of the new postmodern architecture grounded in the patronage of multinational business, whose expansion and development is strictly contemporaneous with it. That these two new phenomena have an even deeper dialectical interrelationship than the simple one-to-one financing of this or that individual project we will try to suggest later on. Yet this is the point at which we must remind the reader of the obvious, namely that this whole global, yet American, postmodern culture is the internal and superstructural expression of a whole new wave of American military and economic domination throughout the world: in this sense, as throughout class history, the underside of culture is blood, torture, death and horror.

The first point to be made about the conception of periodization in dominance, therefore, is that even if all the constitutive features of postmodernism were identical and continuous with those of an older modernism – a position I feel to be demonstrably erroneous but which only an even lengthier analysis of modernism proper could dispel – the two phenomena would still remain utterly distinct in their meaning and social function, owing to the very different positioning of postmodernism in the economic system of late capital, and beyond that, to the transformation of the very sphere of culture in contemporary society.

More on this point at the conclusion of the present essay. I must now briefly address a different kind of objection to periodization, a different kind of concern about its possible obliteration of heterogeneity, which one finds most often on the Left. And it is certain that there is a strange quasi-Sartrean irony – a 'winner loses' logic – which tends to surround any effort to describe a 'system', a totalizing dynamic, as these are detected in the movement of contemporary society. What happens is that the more powerful the vision of some increasingly total system or logic – the Foucault of the prisons book is the obvious example – the more powerless the reader comes to feel. Insofar as the theorist wins, therefore, by constructing an increasingly closed and terrifying machine, to that very degree he loses, since the critical capacity of his work is thereby paralysed, and the impulses of negation and revolt, not to speak of those of social transformation, are increasingly perceived as vain and trivial in the face of the model itself.

I have felt, however, that it was only in the light of some conception of a dominant cultural logic or hegemonic norm that genuine difference could be measured and assessed. I am very far from feeling that all cultural production today is 'postmodern' in the broad sense I will be conferring on this term. The postmodern is, however, the force field in which very different kinds of cultural impulses – what Raymond Williams has usefully termed 'residual' and 'emergent' forms of cultural production – must make their way. If we do not achieve some general sense of a cultural dominant, then we fall back into a view of present history as sheer heterogeneity, random difference, a coexistence of a host of distinct forces whose effectivity is undecidable. This has been at any rate the political spirit in which the following analysis was devised: to project some conception of a new systemic cultural norm and its reproduction, in order to reflect more adequately on the most effective forms of any radical cultural politics today.

[. . .]

I The Deconstruction of Expression

'Peasant Shoes'

We will begin with one of the canonical works of high modernism in visual art, Van Gogh's well-known painting of the peasant shoes, an example which, as you can imagine, has not been innocently or randomly chosen. I want to propose two ways of reading this painting, both of which in some fashion reconstruct the reception of the work in a two-stage or double-level process.

I first want to suggest that if this copiously reproduced image is not to sink to the level of sheer decoration, it requires us to reconstruct some initial situation out of which the finished work emerges. Unless that situation – which has vanished into the past – is somehow mentally restored, the painting will remain an inert object, a reified end-product, and be unable to be grasped as a symbolic act in its own right, as praxis and as production.

This last term suggests that one way of reconstructing the initial situation to which the work is somehow a response is by stressing the raw materials, the initial content, which it confronts and which it reworks, transforms, and appropriates. In Van Gogh, that content, those initial raw materials, are, I will suggest, to be grasped simply as the whole object world of agricultural misery, of stark rural poverty, and the whole rudimentary human world of backbreaking peasant toil, a world reduced to its most brutal and menaced, primitive and marginalized state.

Fruit trees in this world are ancient and exhausted sticks coming out of poor soil; the people of the village are worn down to their skulls, caricatures of some ultimate grotesque typology of basic human feature types. How is it, then, that in Van Gogh such things as apple trees explode into a hallucinatory surface of colour, while his village stereotypes are suddenly and garishly overlaid with hues of red and green? I will briefly suggest, in this first interpretative opinion, that the willed and violent transformation of a drab peasant object world into the most glorious materialization of pure colour in oil paint is to be seen as a Utopian gesture: as an act of compensation which ends up producing a whole new Utopian realm of the senses, or at least of that supreme sense – sight, the visual, the eye – which it now reconstitutes for us as a semi-autonomous space in its own right – part of some new division of labour in the body of capital, some new fragmentation of the emergent sensorium which replicates the specializations and divisions of capitalist life at the same time that it seeks in precisely such fragmentation a desperate Utopian compensation for them.

There is, to be sure, a second reading of Van Gogh which can hardly be ignored when we gaze at this particular painting, and that is Heidegger's central analysis in *Der Ursprung des Kunstwerkes*, which is organized around the idea that the work of art emerges within the gap between Earth and World, or what I would prefer to translate as the meaningless materiality of the body and nature and the meaning-endowment of history and of the social. We will return to that particular gap or rift later on; suffice it here to recall some of the famous phrases, which model the process whereby these henceforth illustrious peasant shoes slowly re-create about themselves the whole missing object world which was once their lived context. 'In them,' says Heidegger, 'there vibrates the silent call of the earth, its quiet gift of ripening corn and its enigmatic self-refusal in the fallow desolation of the wintry field.' 'This equipment,' he goes on, 'belongs to the *earth* and it is protected in the *world* of the peasant woman ... Van Gogh's painting is the disclosure of what the equipment, the pair of peasant shoes, *is* in truth. ... This entity emerges into the unconcealment of its being', by way of the mediation of the work of art, which draws the whole absent world and earth into revelation around itself, along with the heavy tread of the peasant woman, the loneliness of the field path, the hut in the clearing, the worn and broken instruments of labour in the furrows and at the hearth. Heidegger's account needs to be completed by insistence on the renewed materiality of the work, on the transformation of one form of materiality – the earth itself and its paths and physical objects – into that other materiality of oil paint affirmed and foregrounded in its own right and for its own visual pleasures; but has none the less a satisfying plausibility.

'Diamond Dust Shoes'

At any rate, both of these readings may be described as *hermeneutical*, in the sense in which the work, in its inert, objectal form, is taken as a clue or a symptom for some vaster reality which replaces it as its ultimate truth. Now we need to look at some shoes of a different kind, and it is pleasant to be able to draw for such an image on the recent work of the central figure in contemporary visual art. Andy Warhol's 'Diamond Dust Shoes' evidently no longer speaks to us with any of the immediacy of Van Gogh's footgear: indeed, I am tempted to say that it does not really speak to us at all. Nothing in this painting organizes even a minimal place for the viewer, who confronts it at the turning of a museum corridor or gallery with all the contingency of some inexplicable natural object. On the level of the content, we have to do with what are now far more clearly fetishes, both in the Freudian and in the Marxian sense (Derrida remarks, somewhere, about the Heideggerian *Paar Bauernschuhe*, that the Van Gogh footgear are a heterosexual pair, which allows neither for perversion nor for fetishization). Here, however, we have a random collection of dead objects, hanging together on the canvas like so many turnips, as shown of their earlier life-world as the pile of shoes left over from Auschwitz, or the remainders and tokens of some incomprehensible and tragic fire in a packed dance hall. There is therefore in Warhol no way to complete the hermeneutic gesture, and to restore to these oddments that whole larger lived context of the dance hall or the ball, the world of jetset fashion or of glamour magazines. Yet this is even more paradoxical in the light of biographical information. Warhol began his artistic career as a commercial illustrator for shoe fashions and a designer of display windows in which various pumps and slippers figured prominently. Indeed, one is tempted to raise here – far too prematurely – one of the central issues about postmodernism itself and its possible political dimensions: Andy Warhol's work in fact turns centrally around commodification, and the great billboard images of the Coca-Cola bottle or the Campbell's Soup Can, which explicitly foreground the commodity fetishism of a transition to late capital, *ought* to be powerful and critical political statements. If they are not that, then one would surely want to know why, and one would want to begin to wonder a little more seriously about the possibilities of political or critical art in the postmodern period of late capital.

But there are some other significant differences between the high-modernist and the postmodernist moment, between the shoes of Van Gogh and the shoes of Andy Warhol, on which we must now very briefly dwell. The first and most evident is the emergence of a new kind of flatness or depthlessness, a new kind of superficiality in the most literal sense – perhaps the supreme formal feature of all the postmodernisms to which we will have occasion to return in a number of other contexts.

Then we must surely come to terms with the role of photography and the photographic/negative in contemporary art of this kind: and it is this indeed which confers its deathly quality on the Warhol image, whose glacéd X-ray elegance mortifies the reified eye of the viewer in a way that would seem to have nothing to do with death or the death obsession or the death anxiety on the level of content. It is indeed as though we had here to do with the inversion of Van Gogh's Utopian gesture: in the earlier work, a stricken world is by some Nietzschean fiat and act of the will transformed into the stridency of Utopian colour. Here, on the contrary, it is as though the external and coloured surface of things – debased and contaminated in advance by their assimilation to glossy advertising images – has been stripped away to reveal the deathly black-and-white substratum of the photographic negative which subtends them. Although this kind of death of the world of appearance becomes thematized in certain of Warhol's pieces – most notably, the traffic accidents or the electric chair series – this is not, I think, a matter of content any longer but of some more fundamental mutation both in the object world itself – now become a set of texts or simulacra – and in the disposition of the subject.

The Waning of Affect

All of which brings me to the third feature I had in mind to develop here briefly, namely what I will call the waning of affect in postmodern culture. Of course, it would be inaccurate to suggest that all affect, all feeling or emotion, all subjectivity, has vanished from the newer image. Indeed, there is a kind of return of the repressed in 'Diamond Dust Shoes', a strange compensatory decorative exhilaration, explicitly designated by the title itself although perhaps more difficult to observe in the reproduction. This is the glitter of gold dust, the spangling of gilt sand, which seals the surface of the painting and yet continues to glint at us. Think, however, of Rimbaud's magical flowers 'that look back at you', or of the august premonitory eye-flashes of Rilke's archaic Greek torso which warn the bourgeois subject to change his life: nothing of that sort here, in the gratuitous frivolity of this final decorative overlay.

The waning of affect is, however, perhaps best initially approached by way of the human figure, and it is obvious that what we have said about the commodification of objects holds as strongly for Warhol's human subjects, stars – like Marilyn Monroe – who are themselves commodified and transformed into their own images. And here too a certain brutal return to the older period of high modernism offers a dramatic shorthand parable of the transformation in question. Edvard Munch's painting 'The Scream' is of course a canonical expression of the great modernist thematics of alienation, anomie, solitude and social fragmentation and isolation, a virtually programmatic emblem of what used to be called the age of anxiety. It will here be read not merely as an embodiment of the expression of that kind of affect, but even more as a virtual deconstruction of the very aesthetic of expression itself, which seems to have dominated much of what we call high modernism, but to have vanished away – for both practical and theoretical reasons – in the world of the postmodern. The very concept of expression presupposes indeed some separation within the subject, and along with that a whole metaphysics of the inside and the outside, of the wordless pain within the monad and the moment in which, often carthartically, that 'emotion' is then projected out and externalized, as gesture or cry, as desperate communication and the outward dramatization of inward feeling. And this is perhaps the moment to say something about contemporary theory, which has among other things been committed to the mission of criticizing and discrediting this very hermeneutic model of the inside and the outside and of stigmatizing such models as ideological and metaphysical. But what is today called contemporary theory – or, better still, theoretical discourse – is also, I would want to argue, itself very precisely a postmodernist phenomenon. It would therefore be inconsistent to defend the truth of its theoretical insights in a situation in which the very concept of 'truth' itself is part of the metaphysical baggage which poststructuralism seeks to abandon. What we can at least suggest is that the poststructuralist critique of the hermeneutic, of what I will shortly call the depth model, is useful for us as a very significant symptom of the very postmodernist culture which is our subject here.

Overhastily, we can say that besides the hermeneutic model of inside and outside which Munch's painting develops, there are at least four other fundamental depth models which have generally been repudiated in contemporary theory: the dialectical one of essence and appearance (along with a whole range of concepts of ideology or false consciousness which tend to accompany it); the Freudian model of latent and manifest, or of repression (which is of course the target of Michel Foucault's programmatic and symptomatic pamphlet *La Volonté de savoir*); the existential model of authenticity and inauthenticity, whose heroic or tragic thematics are closely related to that of the great opposition between alienation and disalienation, itself equally a casualty of the poststructural or postmodern period; and finally, latest in time, the great semiotic opposition between signifier and signified, which was itself rapidly unravelled and deconstructed during its brief heyday in the 1960s and 1970s. What replaces these various depth models is for the most part a conception of practices, discourses and textual play, whose new syntagmatic structures we will examine later on: suffice it merely to observe that here too depth is replaced by surface, or by multiple surfaces (what is often called intertextuality is in that sense no longer a matter of depth).

Nor is this depthlessness merely metaphorical: it can be experienced physically and literally by anyone who, mounting what used to be Raymond Chandler's Beacon Hill from the great Chicano markets on Broadway and 4th Street in downtown Los Angeles, suddenly confronts the great free-standing wall of the Crocker Bank Center (Skidmore, Owings and Merrill) – a surface which seems to be unsupported by any volume, or whose putative volume (rectangular, trapezoidal?) is ocularly quite undecidable. This great sheet of windows, with its gravity-defying two-dimensionality, momentarily transforms the solid ground on which we climb into the contents of a stereopticon, pasteboard shapes profiling themselves here and there around us. From all sides, the visual effect is the same: as fateful as the great monolith in Kubrick's *2001* which confronts its viewers like an enigmatic destiny, a call to evolutionary mutation. If this new multinational downtown (to which we will return later in another context) effectively abolished the older ruined city fabric which it violently replaced, cannot something similar be said about the way in which this strange new surface, in its own peremptory way, renders our older systems of perception of the city somehow archaic and aimless, without offering another in their place?

Euphoria and Self-annihilation

Returning now for one last moment to Munch's painting, it seems evident that 'The Scream' subtly but elaborately deconstructs its own aesthetic of expression, all the while remaining imprisoned within it. Its gestural content already underscores its own failure, since the realm of the sonorous, the cry, the raw vibrations of the human throat, are incompatible with its medium (something underscored within the work by the homunculus's lack of ears). Yet the absent scream returns more closely towards that even more absent experience of atrocious solitude and anxiety which the scream was itself to 'express'. Such loops inscribe themselves on the painted surface in the form of those great concentric circles in which sonorous vibration becomes ultimately visible, as on the surface of a sheet of water – in an infinite regress which fans out from the sufferer to become the very geography of a universe in which pain itself now speaks and vibrates through the material sunset and the landscape. The visible world now becomes the wall of the monad on which this 'scream running through nature' (Munch's words) is recorded and transcribed: one thinks of that character of Lautréamont who, growing up inside a sealed and silent membrane, on sight of the monstrousness of the deity, ruptures it with his own scream and thereby rejoins the world of sound and suffering.

All of which suggests some more general historical hypothesis: namely, that concepts such as anxiety and alienation (and the experiences to which they correspond, as in 'The Scream') are no longer appropriate in the world of the postmodern. The great Warhol figures – Marilyn herself, or Edie Sedgwick – the notorious burn-out and self-destruction cases of the ending 1960s and the great dominant experiences of drugs and schizophrenia – these would seem to have little enough in common any more, either with the hysterics and neurotics of Freud's own day, or with those canonical experiences of radical isolation and solitude, anomie, private revolt, Van Gogh-type madness, which dominated the period of high modernism. This shift in the dynamics of culture pathology can be characterized as one in which the alienation of the subject is displaced by the fragmentation of the subject.

Such terms inevitably recall one of the more fashionable themes in contemporary theory – that of the 'death' of the subject itself = the end of the autonomous bourgeois monad or ego or individual – and the accompanying stress, whether as some new moral ideal or as empirical description, on the *decentring* of that formerly centred subject or psyche. (Of the two possible formulations of this notion – the historicist one, that a once-existing centred subject, in the period of classical capitalism and the nuclear family, has today in the world of organizational bureaucracy dissolved; and the more radical poststructuralist position for which such a subject never existed in the first place but constituted something like an ideological mirage – I obviously incline towards the former; the latter must in any case take into account something like a 'reality of the appearance'.)

We must add that the problem of expression is itself closely linked to some conception of the subject as a monad-like container, within which things are felt which are then expressed by projection outwards. What we must now stress, however, is the degree to which the high-modernist conception of a unique *style*, along with the accompanying collective ideals of an artistic or political vanguard or *avant-garde*, themselves stand or fall along with that older notion (or experience) of the so-called centred subject.

Here too Munch's painting stands as a complex reflexion on this complicated situation: it shows us that expression requires the category of the individual monad, but it also shows us the heavy price to be paid for that precondition, dramatizing the unhappy paradox that when you constitute your individual subjectivity as a self-sufficient field and a closed realm in its own right, you thereby also shut yourself off from everything else and condemn yourself to the windless solitude of the monad, buried alive and condemned to a prison-cell without egress.

Postmodernism will presumably signal the end of this dilemma, which it replaces with a new one. The end of the bourgeois ego or monad no doubt brings with it the end of the psychopathologies of that ego as well – what I have generally here been calling the waning of affect. But it means the end of much more – the end, for example, of style, in the sense of the unique and the personal, the end of the distinctive individual brushstroke (as symbolized by the emergent primacy of mechanical reproduction). As for expression and feelings or emotions, the liberation, in contemporary society, from the older *anomie* of the centred subject may also mean, not merely a liberation from anxiety, but a liberation from every other kind of feeling as well, since there is no longer a self present to do the feeling. This is not to say that the cultural products of the postmodern era are utterly devoid of feeling, but rather that such feelings – which it may be better and more accurate to call 'intensities' – are now free-floating and impersonal, and tend to be dominated by a peculiar kind of euphoria to which I will want to return at the end of this essay.

The waning of affect, however, might also have been characterized, in the narrower context of literary criticism, as the waning of the great high-modernist thematics of time and temporality, the elegiac mysteries of *durée* and of memory (something to be understood fully as a category of literary criticism associated as much with high modernism as with the works themselves). We have often been told, however, that we now inhabit the synchronic rather than the diachronic, and I think it is at least empirically arguable that our daily life, our psychic experience, our cultural languages, are today dominated by categories of space rather than by categories of time, as in the preceding period of high modernism proper.

2 The Postmodern and the Past

Pastiche Eclipses Parody

The disappearance of the individual subject, along with its formal consequence, the increasing unavailability of the personal *style*, engender the well-nigh universal practice today of what may be called pastiche. This concept, which we owe to Thomas Mann (in *Doktor Faustus*), who owed it in turn to Adorno's great work on the two paths of advanced musical experimentation (Schoenberg's innovative planification, Stravinsky's irrational eclecticism), is to be sharply distinguished from the more readily received idea of parody.

This last found, to be sure, a fertile area in the idiosyncrasies of the moderns and their 'inimitable' styles: the Faulknerian long sentence with its breathless gerundives, Lawrentian nature imagery punctuated by testy colloquialism, Wallace Stevens's inveterate hypostasis of non-substantive parts of speech ('the intricate evasions of as'), the fateful, but finally predictable, swoops in Mahler from high orchestral pathos into village accordion sentiment, Heidegger's meditative-solemn practice of the false etymology as a mode of 'proof'. ... All these strike one as somehow 'characteristic', insofar as they ostentatiously deviate from a norm which then reasserts itself, in a not necessarily unfriendly way, by a systematic mimicry of their deliberate eccentricities.

Yet, in the dialectical leap from quantity to quality, the explosion of modern literature into a host of distinct private styles and mannerisms has been followed by a linguistic fragmentation of social life itself to the point where the norm itself is eclipsed: reduced to a neutral and reified media speech (far enough from the Utopian aspirations of the inventors of Esperanto or Basic English), which itself then becomes but one more idiolect among many. Modernist styles thereby become postmodernist codes: and that the stupendous proliferation of social codes today into professional and disciplinary jargons, but also into the badges of affirmation of ethnic, gender, race, religious, and class-fraction adhesion, is also a political phenomenon, the problem of micropolitics sufficiently demonstrates. If the ideas of a ruling class were once the dominant (or hegemonic) ideology of bourgeois society, the advanced capitalist countries today are now a field of stylistic and discursive heterogeneity without a norm. Faceless masters continue to inflect the economic strategies which constrain our existences, but no longer need to impose their speech (or are henceforth unable to); and the postliteracy of the late capitalist world reflects not only the absence of any great collective project, but also the unavailability of the older national language itself.

In this situation, parody finds itself without a vocation; it has lived, and that strange new thing pastiche slowly comes to take its place. Pastiche is, like parody, the imitation of a peculiar mask, speech in a dead language: but it is a neutral practice of such mimicry, without any of parody's ulterior motives, amputated of the satiric impulse, devoid of laughter and of any conviction that alongside the abnormal tongue you have momentarily borrowed, some healthy linguistic normality still exists. Pastiche is thus blank parody, a statue with blind eyeballs: it is to parody what that other interesting and historically original modern thing, the practice of a kind of blank irony, is to what Wayne Booth calls the 'stable ironies' of eighteenth century.

It would therefore begin to seem that Adorno's prophetic diagnosis has been realized, albeit in a negative way: not Schoenberg (the sterility of whose achieved system he already glimpsed) but Stravinsky is the true precursor of the postmodern cultural production. For with the collapse of the high-modernist ideology of style – what is as unique and unmistakable as your own fingerprints, as incomparable as your own body (the very source, for an early Roland Barthes, of stylistic invention and innovation) – the producers of culture have nowhere to turn but to the past: the imitation of dead styles, speech through all the masks and voices stored up in the imaginary museum of a now global culture.

'Historicism' Effaces History

This situation evidently determines what the architecture historians call 'historicism', namely the random cannibalization of all the styles of the past, the play of random stylistic allusion, and in general what Henri Lefebvre has called the increasing primacy of the 'neo'. This omnipresence of pastiche is, however, not incompatible with a certain humour (nor is it innocent of all passion) or at least with addiction – with a whole historically original consumers' appetite for a world transformed into sheer images of itself and for pseudo-events and 'spectacles' (the term of the Situationists). It is for such objects that we may reserve Plato's conception of the 'simulacrum' – the identical copy for which no original has ever existed. Appropriately enough, the culture of the simulacrum comes to *life* in a society where exchange-value has been generalized to the point at which the very memory of use-value is effaced, a society of which Guy Debord has observed, in an extraordinary phrase, that in it 'the image has become the final form of commodity reification' (*The Society of the Spectacle*).

The new spatial logic of the simulacrum can now be expected to have a momentous effect on what used to be historical time.

The past is thereby itself modified: what was once, in the historical novel as Lukács defines it, the organic genealogy of the bourgeois collective project – what is still, for the redemptive historiography of an E. P. Thompson or of American 'oral history', for the resurrection of the dead of anonymous and silenced generations, the retrospective dimension indispensable to any vital reorientation of our collective future – has meanwhile itself become a vast collection of images, a multitudinous photographic simulacrum. Guy Debord's powerful slogan is now even more apt for the 'prehistory' of a society bereft of all historicity, whose own putative past is little more than a set of dusty spectacles. In faithful conformity to poststructuralist linguistic theory, the past as 'referent' finds itself gradually bracketed, and then effaced altogether, leaving us with nothing but texts.

The Nostalgia Mode

Yet it should not be thought that this process is accompanied by indifference: on the contrary, the remarkable current intensification of an addiction to the photographic image is itself a tangible symptom of an omnipresent, omnivorous and well-nigh libidinal historicism. The architects use this (exceedingly polysemous) word for the complacent eclecticism of postmodern architecture, which randomly and without principle but with gusto cannibalizes all the architectural styles of the past and combines them in overstimulating ensembles. Nostalgia does not strike one as an altogether satisfactory word for such fascination (particularly when one thinks of the pain of a properly modernist nostalgia with a past beyond all but aesthetic retrieval), yet it directs our attention to what is a culturally far more generalized manifestation of the process in commercial art and taste, namely the so-called 'nostalgia film' (or what the French call 'la mode rétro').

These restructure the whole issue of pastiche and project it onto a collective and social level, where the desperate attempt to appropriate a missing past is now refracted through the iron law of fashion change and the emergent ideology of the 'generation'. *American Graffiti* (1973) set out to recapture, as so many films have attempted since, the henceforth mesmerizing lost reality of the Eisenhower era: and one tends to feel that for Americans at least, the 1950s remain the privileged lost object of desire – not merely the stability and prosperity of a *pax Americana*, but also the first naive innocence of the countercultural impulses of early rock-and-roll and youth gangs (Coppola's *Rumble Fish* will then be the contemporary dirge that laments their passing, itself, however, still contradictorily filmed in genuine 'nostalgia film' style). With this initial breakthrough, other generational periods open up for aesthetic colonization: as witness the stylistic recuperation of the American and the Italian 1930s, in Polanski's *Chinatown* and Bertolucci's *Il Conformista* respectively. What is more interesting, and more problematical, are the ultimate attempts, through this new discourse, to lay siege either to our own present and immediate past, or to a more distant history that escapes individual existential memory.

Faced with these ultimate objects – our social, historical and existential present, and the past as 'referent' – the incompatibility of a postmodernist 'nostalgia' art language with genuine historicity becomes dramatically apparent. The contradiction propels this model, however, into complex and interesting new formal inventiveness: it being understood that the nostalgia film was never a matter of some old-fashioned 'representation' of historical content, but approached the 'past' through stylistic connotation, conveying 'pastness' by the glossy qualities of the image, and '1930s-ness' or '1950s-ness' by the attributes of fashion (therein following the prescription of the Barthes of *Mythologies*, who saw connotation as the purveying of imaginary and stereotypical idealities, 'Sinité', for example, as some Disney-EPCOT 'concept' of China).

The insensible colonization of the present by the nostalgia mode can be observed in Lawrence Kasdan's elegant film *Body Heat*, a distant 'affluent society' remake of James M. Cain's *The Postman Always Rings Twice*, set in a contemporary Florida small town not far from Miami. The word 'remake' is, however, anachronistic to the degree to which our awareness of the pre-existence of other versions, previous films of the novel as well as the novel itself, is now a constitutive and essential part of the film's structure: we are now, in other words, in 'intertextuality' as a deliberate, built-in feature of the aesthetic effect, and as the operator of a new connotation of 'pastness' and pseudo-historical depth, in which the history of aesthetic styles displaces 'real' history.

Yet from the outset a whole battery of aesthetic signs begin to distance the officially contemporary image from us in time: the Art Deco scripting of the credits, for example, serves at once to programme the spectator for the appropriate 'nostalgia' mode of reception (Art Deco quotation has much the same function in contemporary architecture, as in Toronto's remarkable Eaton Centre). Meanwhile, a somewhat different play of connotations is activated by complex (but purely formal) allusions to the institutions of the star system itself. The protagonist, William Hurt, is one of a new generation of film 'stars' whose status is markedly distinct from that of the preceding generation of male superstars, such as Steve McQueen or Jack Nicholson (or even, more distantly, Brando), let alone of earlier moments in the evolution of the institutions of the star. The immediately preceding generation projected its various roles through, and by way of, well-known 'off-screen' personalities, who often connoted rebellion and non-conformism. The latest generation of starring actors continues to assure the conventional functions of stardom (most notably, sexuality) but in the utter absence of 'personality' in the older sense, and with something of the anonymity of character acting (which in actors like Hurt reaches virtuoso proportions, yet of a very different kind from the virtuosity of the older Brando or Olivier). This 'death of the subject' in the institution of the star, however, opens up the possibility of a play of historical allusions to much older roles – in this case to those associated with Clark Gable – so that the very style of the acting can now also serve as a 'connotator' of the past.

Finally, the setting has been strategically framed, with great ingenuity, to eschew most of the signals that normally convey the contemporaneity of the United States in its multinational era: the small-town setting allows the camera to elude the high-rise landscape of the 1970s and 1980s (even though a key episode in the narrative involves the fatal destruction of older buildings by land speculators); while the object world of the present-day – artifacts and appliances, even automobiles, whose styling would at once serve to date the image – is elaborately edited out. Everything in the film, therefore, conspires to blur its official contemporaneity and to make it possible for you to receive the narrative as though it were set in some eternal Thirties, beyond real historical time. The approach to the present by way of the art language of the simulacrum, or of the pastiche of the stereotypical past, endows present reality and the openness of present history with the spell and distance of a glossy mirage. But this mesmerizing new aesthetic mode itself emerged as an elaborated symptom of the waning of our historicity, of our lived possibility of experiencing history in some active way: it cannot therefore be said to produce this strange occultation of the present by its own formal power, but merely to demonstrate, through these inner contradictions, the enormity of a situation in which we seem increasingly incapable of fashioning representations of our own current experience.

The Fate of 'Real History'

As for 'real history' itself – the traditional object, however it may be defined, of what used to be the historical novel – it will be more revealing now to turn back to that older form and medium and to read its postmodern fate in the work of one of the few serious and innovative Left novelists at work in the United States today, whose books are nourished with history in the more traditional sense, and seem, so far, to stake out successive generational moments in the 'epic' of American history. E. L. Doctorow's *Ragtime* gives itself officially as a panorama of the first two decades of the century; his most recent novel, *Loon Lake*, addresses the Thirties and the Great Depression, while *The Book of Daniel* holds up before us, in painful juxtaposition, the two great moments of the Old Left and the New Left, of Thirties and Forties Communism and the radicalism of the 1960s (even his early western may be said to fit into this scheme and to designate in a less articulated and formally self-conscious way the end of the frontier of the late nineteenth century).

The Book of Daniel is not the only one of these three major historical novels to establish an explicit narrative link between the reader's and the writer's present and the older historical reality which is the subject of the work; the astonishing last page of *Loon Lake*, which I will not disclose, also does this in a very different way; while it is a matter of some interest to note that the first sentence of the first version of *Ragtime* positions us explicitly in our own present, in the novelist's house in New Rochelle, New York, which will then at once become the scene of its own (imaginary) past in the 1900s. This detail has been suppressed from the published text, symbolically cutting its moorings and freeing the novel to float in some new world of past historical time whose relationship to us is problematical indeed. The authenticity of the gesture, however, may be measured by the evident existential fact of life that there no longer does seem to be any organic relationship between the American history we learn from the schoolbooks and the lived experience of the current multinational, high-rise, stagflated city of the newspapers and of our own daily life.

A crisis in historicity, however, inscribes itself symptomally in several other curious formal features within this text. Its official subject is the transition from a pre-World-War I radical and working-class politics (the great strikes) to the technological invention and new commodity production of the 1920s (the rise of Hollywood and the image as commodity): the interpolated version of Kleist's

Michael Kohlhaas, the strange tragic episode of the Black protagonist's revolt, may be thought to be a moment related to this process. My point, however, is not some hypothesis as to the thematic coherence of this decentred narrative; but rather just the opposite, namely the way in which the kind of reading this novel imposes makes it virtually impossible for us to reach and to thematize those official 'subjects' which float above the text but cannot be integrated into our reading of the sentences. In that sense, not only does the novel resist interpretation, it is organized systematically and formally to short-circuit an older type of social and historical interpretation which it perpetually holds out and withdraws. When we remember that the theoretical critique and repudiation of interpretation as such is a fundamental component of poststructuralist theory, it is difficult not to conclude that Doctorow has somehow deliberately built this very tension, this very contradiction, into the flow of his sentences.

As is well known, the book is crowded with real historical figures – from Teddy Roosevelt to Emma Goldman, from Harry K. Thaw and Sandford White to J. Pierpont Morgan and Henry Ford, not to speak of the more central role of Houdini – who interact with a fictive family, simply designated as Father, Mother, Older Brother, and so forth. All historical novels, beginning with Scott himself, no doubt in one way or another involve a mobilization of previous historical knowledge, generally acquired through the schoolbook history manuals devised for whatever legitimizing purpose by this or that national tradition – thereafter instituting a narrative dialectic between what we already 'know' about The Pretender, say, and what he is then seen to be concretely in the pages of the novel. But Doctorow's procedure seems much more extreme than this; and I would argue that the designation of both types of characters – historical names or capitalized family roles – operates powerfully and systematically to reify all these characters and to make it impossible for us to receive their representation without the prior interception of already acquired knowledge or doxa – something which lends the text an extraordinary sense of *déjà vu* and a peculiar familiarity one is tempted to associate with Freud's 'return of the repressed' in 'The Uncanny', rather than with any solid historiographic formation on the reader's part.

Loss of the Radical Past

Meanwhile, the sentences in which all this is happening have their own specificity, which will allow us a little more concretely to distinguish the moderns' elaboration of a personal style from this new kind of linguistic innovation, which is no longer personal at all but has its family kinship rather with what Barthes long ago called 'white writing'. In this particular novel, Doctorow has imposed upon himself a rigorous principle of selection in which only simple declarative sentences (predominantly mobilized by the verb 'to be') are received. The effect is, however, not really one of the condescending simplification and symbolic carefulness of children's literature, but rather something more disturbing, the sense of some profound subterranean violence done to American English which cannot, however, be detected empirically in any of the perfectly grammatical sentences with which this work is formed. Yet other more visible technical 'innovations' may supply a clue to what is happening in the language of *Ragtime*: it is, for example, well known that the source of many of the characteristic effects of Camus's novel *L'Etranger* can be traced back to that author's wilful decision to substitute, throughout, the French tense of the *passé composé* for the other past tenses more normally employed in narration in that language. I will suggest that it is *as if* something of that sort were at work here (without committing myself further to what is obviously an outrageous leap): it is, I say, *as though* Doctorow had set out systematically to produce the effect or the equivalent, in his language, of a verbal past tense we do not possess in English, namely the French preterite (or *passé simple*), whose 'perfective' movement, as Emile Benveniste taught us, serves to separate events from the present of enunciation and to transform the stream of time and action into so many finished, complete, and isolated punctual event-objects which find themselves sundered from any present situation (even that of the act of storytelling or enunciation).

E. L. Doctorow is the epic poet of the disappearance of the American radical past, of the suppression of older traditions and moments of the American radical tradition: no one with Left sympathies can read these splendid novels without a poignant distress which is an authentic way of confronting our own current political dilemmas in the present. What is culturally interesting, however, is that he has had to convey this great theme formally (since the waning of the content is very precisely his subject), and, more than that, has had to elaborate his work by way of that very cultural logic of the postmodern which is itself the mark and symptom of his dilemma. *Loon Lake* much more obviously deploys the strategies of the pastiche (most notably in its reinvention of Dos Passos); but *Ragtime* remains the most peculiar and stunning monument to the aesthetic situation engendered by the disappearance of the historical referent. This historical novel can no longer set out to represent the historical past; it can only 'represent' our ideas and stereotypes about that past (which thereby at once becomes 'pop history'). Cultural production is thereby driven back inside a mental space which is no longer that of the old monadic subject, but rather that of some degraded collective 'objective spirit': it can no longer gaze directly on some putative real world, at some reconstruction of a past history which was once itself a present; rather, as in Plato's cave, it must trace our mental images of that past upon its confining walls. If there is any realism left here, therefore, it is a 'realism' which is meant to derive from the shock of grasping that confinement, and of slowly becoming aware of a new and original historical situation in which we are condemned to seek History by way of our own pop images and simulacra of that history, which itself remains forever out of reach.

[. . .]

5 Postmodernism and the City

Now, before I try to offer a somewhat more positive conclusion, I want to sketch the analysis of a full-blown postmodern building – a work which is in many ways uncharacteristic of that postmodern architecture whose principal names are Robert Venturi, Charles Moore, Michael Graves, and more recently Frank Gehry, but which to my mind offers some very striking lessons about the originality of postmodernist space. Let me amplify the figure which has run through the preceding remarks, and make it even more explicit: I am proposing the motion that we are here in the presence of something like a mutation in built space itself. My implication is that we ourselves, the human subjects who happen into this new space, have not kept pace with that evolution; there has been a mutation in the object, unaccompanied as yet by any equivalent mutation in the subject; we do not yet possess the perceptual equipment to match this new hyperspace, as I will call it, in part because our perceptual habits were formed in that older kind of space I have called the space of high modernism. The newer architecture therefore – like many of the other cultural products I have evoked in the preceding remarks – stands as something like an imperative to grow new organs, to expand our sensorium and our body to some new, as yet unimaginable, perhaps ultimately impossible, dimensions.

The Bonaventura Hotel

The building whose features I will very rapidly enumerate in the next few moments is the Bonaventura Hotel, built in the new Los Angeles downtown by the architect and developer John Portman, whose other works include the various Hyatt Regencies, the Peachtree Center in Atlanta, and the Renaissance Center in Detroit. I have mentioned the populist aspect of the rhetorical defence of postmodernism against the elite (and Utopian) austerities of the great architectural modernisms: it is generally affirmed, in other words, that these newer buildings are popular works on the one hand; and that they respect the vernacular of the American city fabric on the other – that is to say, that they no longer attempt, as did the masterworks and monuments of high modernism, to insert a different, a distinct, an elevated, a new Utopian language into the tawdry and commercial sign-system of the surrounding city, but rather, on the contrary, seek to speak that very language, using its lexicon and syntax as that has been emblematically 'learned from Las Vegas'.

On the first of these counts, Portman's Bonaventura fully confirms the claim: it is a popular building, visited with enthusiasm by locals and tourists alike (although Portman's other buildings are even more successful in this respect). The populist insertion into the city fabric is, however, another matter, and it is with this that we will begin. There are three entrances to the Bonaventura, one from Figueroa, and the other two by way of elevated gardens on the other side of the hotel, which is built into the remaining slope of the former Beacon Hill. None of these is anything like the old hotel marquee, or the monumental portecochère with which the sumptuous buildings of yesteryear were wont to stage your passage from city street to the older interior. The entryways of the Bonaventura are as it were lateral and rather backdoor affairs: the gardens in the back admit you to the sixth floor of the towers, and even there you must walk down one flight to find the elevator by which you gain access to the lobby. Meanwhile, what one is still tempted to think of as the front entry, on Figueroa, admits you, baggage and all, onto the second-storey shopping balcony, from which you must take an escalator down to the main registration desk. More about these elevators and escalators in a moment. What I first want to suggest about these curiously unmarked ways-in is that they seem to have been imposed by some new category of closure governing the inner space of the hotel itself (and this over and above the material constraints under which Portman had to work). I believe that, with a certain number of other characteristic postmodern buildings, such as the Beaubourg in Paris, or the Eaton Centre in Toronto, the Bonaventura aspires to being a total space, a complete world, a kind of miniature city (and I would want to add that to this new total space corresponds a new collective practice, a new mode in which individuals move and congregate, something like the practice of a new and historically original kind of hyper-crowd). In this sense, then, ideally the mini-city of Portman's Bonaventura ought not to have entrances at all, since the entryway is always the seam that links the building to the rest of the city that surrounds it: for it does not wish to be a part of the city, but rather its equivalent and its replacement or substitute. That is, however, obviously not possible or practical, whence the deliberate downplaying and reduction of the entrance function to its bare minimum. But this disjunction from the surrounding city is very different from that of the great monuments of the International Style: there, the act of disjunction was violent, visible, and had a very real symbolic significance – as in Le Corbusier's great *pilotis* whose gesture radically separates the new Utopian space of the modern from the degraded and fallen city fabric which it thereby explicitly repudiates (although the gamble of the modern was that this new Utopian space, in the virulence of its Novum, would fan out and transform that eventually by the very power of its new spatial language). The Bonaventura, however, is content to 'let the fallen city fabric continue to be in its being' (to parody Heidegger); no further effects, no larger protopolitical Utopian transformation, is either expected or desired.

This diagnosis is to my mind confirmed by the great reflective glass skin of the Bonaventura, whose function I will now interpret rather differently than I did a moment ago when I saw the phenomenon of reflexion generally as developing a thematics of reproductive technology (the two readings are, however, not incompatible). Now one would want rather to stress the way in which the glass skin repels the city outside; a repulsion for which we have analogies in those reflector sunglasses which make it impossible for your interlocutor to see your own eyes and thereby achieve a certain aggressivity towards and power over the Other. In a similar way, the glass skin achieves a peculiar and placeless dissociation of the Bonaventura from its neighbourhood: it is not even an exterior, inasmuch as when you seek to look at the hotel's outer walls you cannot see the hotel itself, but only the distorted images of everything that surrounds it.

Now I want to say a few words about escalators and elevators: given their very real pleasures in Portman, particularly these last, which the artist has termed 'gigantic kinetic sculptures' and which certainly account for much of the spectacle and the excitement of the hotel interior, particularly in the Hyatts, where like great Japanese lanterns or gondolas they ceaselessly rise and fall – given such a deliberate marking and foregrounding in their own right, I believe one has to see such 'people movers' (Portman's own term, adapted from Disney) as something a little more than mere functions and engineering components. We know in any case that recent architectural theory has begun to borrow from narrative analysis in other fields, and to attempt to see our physical trajectories through such buildings as virtual narratives or stories, as dynamic paths and narrative paradigms which we as visitors are asked to fulfil and to complete with our own bodies and movements. In the Bonaventura, however, we find a dialectical heightening of this process: it seems to me that the escalators and elevators here henceforth replace movement but also and above all designate themselves as new reflexive signs and emblems of movement proper (something which will become evident when we come to the whole question of what remains of older forms of movement in this building, most notably walking itself). Here the narrative stroll has been underscored, symbolized, reified and replaced by a transportation machine which becomes the allegorical signifier of that older promenade we are no longer allowed to conduct on our own: and this is a dialectical intensification of the autoreferentiality of all modern culture, which tends to turn upon itself and designate its own cultural production as its content.

I am more at a loss when it comes to conveying the thing itself, the experience of space you undergo when you step off such allegorical devices into the lobby or atrium, with its great central column, surrounded by a miniature lake, the whole positioned between the four symmetrical residential towers with their elevators, and surrounded by rising balconies capped by a kind of greenhouse roof at the sixth level. I am tempted to say that such space makes it impossible for us to use the language of volume or volumes any longer, since these last are impossible to seize. Hanging streamers indeed suffuse this empty space in such a way as to distract systematically and deliberately from whatever form it might be supposed to have; while a constant busyness gives the feeling that emptiness is here absolutely packed, that it is an element within which you yourself are immersed, without any of that distance that formerly enabled the perception of perspective or volume. You are in this hyperspace up to your eyes and your body; and if it seemed to you before that that suppression of depth I spoke of in postmodern painting or literature would necessarily be difficult to achieve in architecture itself, perhaps you may now be willing to see this bewildering immersion as the formal equivalent in the new medium.

Yet escalator and elevator are also in this context dialectical opposites; and we may suggest that the glorious movement of the elevator gondolas is also a dialectical compensation for this filled space of the atrium – it gives us the chance at a radically different, but complementary, spatial experience, that of rapidly shooting up through the ceiling and outside, along one of the four symmetrical towers, with the referent, Los Angeles itself, spread out breathtakingly and even alarmingly before us. But even this vertical movement is contained: the elevator lifts you to one of those revolving cocktail lounges, in which you, seated, are again passively rotated about and offered a contemplative spectacle of the city itself, now transformed into its own images by the glass windows through which you view it.

Let me quickly conclude all this by returning to the central space of the lobby itself (with the passing observation that the hotel rooms are visibly marginalized: the corridors in the residential sections are low-ceilinged and dark, most depressingly functional indeed; while one understands that the rooms are in the worst of taste). The descent is dramatic enough, plummeting back down through the roof to splash down in the lake; what happens when you get there is something else, which I can only try to characterize as milling confusion, something like the vengeance this space takes on those who still seek to walk through it. Given the absolute symmetry of the four towers, it is quite impossible to get your bearings in this lobby; recently, colour coding and directional signals have been added in a pitiful and revealing, rather desperate attempt to restore the coordinates of an older space. I will take as the most dramatic practical result of this spatial mutation the notorious dilemma of the shopkeepers on the various balconies: it has been obvious, since the very opening of the hotel in 1977, that nobody could ever find any of these stores, and even if you located the appropriate boutique, you would be most unlikely to be as fortunate a second time; as a consequence, the commercial tenants are in despair and all the merchandise is marked down to bargain prices. When you recall that Portman is a businessman as well as an architect, and a millionaire developer, an artist who is at one and the same time a capitalist in his own right, one cannot but feel that here too something of a 'return of the repressed' is involved.

So I come finally to my principal point here, that this latest mutation in space – postmodern hyperspace – has finally succeeded in transcending the capacities of the individual human body to locate itself, to organize its immediate surroundings perceptually, and cognitively to map its position in a mappable external world. And I have already suggested that this alarming disjunction point between the body and its built environment – which is to the initial bewilderment of the older modernism as the velocities of space craft are to those of the automobile – can itself stand as the symbol and analogue of that even sharper dilemma which is the incapacity of our minds, at least at present, to map the great global multinational and decentred communicational network in which we find ourselves caught as individual subjects.

The New Machine

But as I am anxious that Portman's space not be perceived as something either exceptional or seemingly marginalized and leisure-specialized on the order of Disneyland, I would like in passing to juxtapose this complacent and entertaining (although bewildering) leisure-time space with its analogue in a very different area, namely the space of postmodern warfare, in particular as Michael Herr evokes it in his great book on the experience of Vietnam, called *Dispatches*. The extraordinary linguistic innovations of this work may still be considered postmodern, in the eclectic way in which its language impersonally fuses a whole range of contemporary collective idiolects, most notably rock language and Black language: but the fusion is dictated by problems of content. This first terrible postmodernist war cannot be told in any of the traditional paradigms of the war novel or movie – indeed that breakdown of all previous narrative paradigms is, along with the breakdown of any shared language through which a veteran might convey such experience, among the principal subjects of the book and may be said to open up the place of a whole new reflexivity. Benjamin's account of Baudelaire, and of the emergence of modernism from a new experience of city technology which transcends all the older habits of bodily perception, is both singularly relevant here, and singularly antiquated, in the light of this new and virtually unimaginable quantum leap in technological alienation:

> He was a moving-target-survivor subscriber, a true child of war, because except for the rare times when you were pinned or stranded the system was geared to keep you mobile, if that was what you thought you wanted. As a technique for staying alive it seemed to make as much sense as anything, given naturally that you were there to begin with and wanted to see it close; it started out sound and straight but it formed a cone as it progressed, because the more you moved the more you saw, the more you saw the more besides death and mutilation you risked, and the more you risked of that the more you would have to let go of one day as a 'survivor'. Some of us moved around the war like crazy people until we couldn't see which way the run was taking us anymore, only the war all over its surface with occasional, unexpected penetration. As long as we could have choppers like taxis it took real exhaustion or depression near shock or a dozen pipes of opium to keep us even apparently quiet, we'd still be running around inside our skins like something was after us, ha ha, La Vida Loca. In the months after I got back the hundreds of helicopters I'd flown in began to draw together until they'd formed a collective meta-chopper, and in my mind it was the sexiest thing going; saver-destroyer, provider-waster, right hand-left hand, nimble, fluent, canny and human; hot steel, grease, jungle-saturated canvas webbing, sweat cooling and warming up again, cassette rock and roll in one ear and door-gun fire in the other, fuel, heat, vitality and death, death itself, hardly an intruder.[2]

In this new machine, which does not, like the older modernist machinery of the locomotive or the airplane, represent motion, but which can only be represented *in motion*, something of the mystery of the new postmodernist space is concentrated.

6 The Abolition of Critical Distance

The conception of postmodernism outlined here is a historical rather than a merely stylistic one. I cannot stress too greatly the radical distinction between a view for which the postmodern is one (optional) style among many others available, and one which seeks to grasp it as the cultural dominant of the logic of late capitalism: the two approaches in fact generate two very different ways of conceptualizing the phenomenon as a whole, on the one hand moral judgements (about which it is indifferent whether they are positive or negative), and on the other a genuinely dialectical attempt to think our present of time in History.

Of some positive moral evaluation of postmodernism little needs to be said: the complacent (yet delirious) camp-following celebration of this aesthetic new world (including its social and economic dimension, greeted with equal enthusiasm under the slogan of 'post-industrial society') is surely unacceptable – although it may be somewhat less obvious the degree to which current fantasies about the salvational nature of high technology, from chips to robots – fantasies entertained not only by Left as well as Right governments in distress, but also by many intellectuals – are essentially of a piece with more vulgar apologies for postmodernism.

But in that case it is also logical to reject moralizing condemnations of the postmodern and of its essential triviality, when juxtaposed against the Utopian 'high seriousness' of the great modernisms: these are also judgements one finds both on the Left and on the radical Right. And no doubt the logic of the simulacrum, with its transformation of older realities into television images, does more than merely replicate the logic of late capitalism; it reinforces and intensifies it. Meanwhile, for political groups which seek actively to intervene in history and to modify its otherwise passive momentum (whether with a view towards channelling it into a socialist transformation of society or diverting it into the regressive reestablishment of some simpler fantasy past), there cannot but be much that is deplorable and reprehensible in a cultural form of image addiction which, by transforming the past visual mirages, stereotypes or texts, effectively abolishes any practical sense of the future and of the collective project, thereby abandoning the thinking of future change to fantasies of sheer catastrophe and inexplicable cataclysm – from visions of 'terrorism' on the social level to those of cancer on the personal. Yet if postmodernism is a historical phenomenon, then the attempt to conceptualize it in terms of moral or moralizing judgements must finally be identified as a category-mistake. All of which becomes more obvious when we interrogate the position of the cultural critic and moralist: this last, along with all the rest of us, is now so deeply immersed in postmodernist space, so deeply suffused and infected by its new cultural categories, that the luxury of the old-fashioned ideological critique, the indignant moral denunciation of the other, becomes unavailable.

The distinction I am proposing here knows one canonical form in Hegel's differentiation of the thinking of individual morality or moralizing [*Moralität*] from that whole very different realm of collective social values and practices [*Sittlichkeit*]. But it finds its definitive form in Marx's demonstration of the materialist dialectic, most notably in those classic pages of the *Manifesto* which teach the hard lesson of some more genuinely dialectical way to think historical development and change. The topic of the lesson is, of course, the historical development of capitalism itself and the deployment of a specific bourgeois culture. In a well-known passage, Marx powerfully urges us to do the impossible, namely to think this development positively *and* negatively all at once; to achieve, in other words, a type of thinking that would be capable of grasping the demonstrably baleful features of capitalism along with its extraordinary and liberating dynamism simultaneously, within a single thought, and without attenuating any of the force of either judgement. We are, somehow, to lift our minds to a point at which it is possible to understand that capitalism is at one and the same time the best thing that has ever happened to the human race, and the worst. The lapse from this austere dialectical imperative into the more comfortable stance of the taking of moral positions is inveterate and all too human: still, the urgency of the subject demands that we make at least some effort to think the cultural evolution of late capitalism dialectically, as catastrophe and progress all together.

Such an effort suggests two immediate questions, with which we will conclude these reflexions. Can we in fact identify some 'moment of truth' within the more evident 'moments of falsehood' of postmodern culture? And, even if we can do so, is there not something ultimately paralysing in the dialectical view of historical development proposed above; does it not tend to demobilize us and to surrender us to passivity and helplessness, by systematically obliterating possibilities of action under the impenetrable fog of historical inevitability? It will be appropriate to discuss these two (related) issues in terms of current possibilities for some effective contemporary cultural politics and for the construction of a genuine political culture.

To focus the problem in this way is of course immediately to raise the more genuine issue of the fate of culture generally, and of the function of culture specifically, as one social level or instance, in the postmodern era. Everything in the previous discussion suggests that what we have been calling postmodernism is inseparable from, and unthinkable without the hypothesis of, some fundamental mutation of the sphere of culture in the world of late capitalism, which includes a momentous modification of its social function. Older discussions of the space, function or sphere of culture (most notably Herbert Marcuse's classic essay on 'The affirmative character of culture') have insisted on what a different language would call the 'semi-autonomy' of the cultural realm: its ghostly, yet Utopian, existence, for good or ill, above the practical world of the existent, whose mirror image it throws back in forms which vary from the legitimations of flattering resemblance to the contestatory indictments of critical satire or Utopian pain.

What we must now ask ourselves is whether it is not precisely this 'semi-autonomy' of the cultural sphere which has been destroyed by the logic of late capitalism. Yet to argue that culture is today no longer endowed with the relative autonomy it once enjoyed as one level among others in earlier moments of capitalism (let alone in pre-capitalist societies) is not necessarily to imply its disappearance or extinction. On the contrary: we must go on to affirm that the dissolution of an autonomous sphere of culture is rather to be imagined in terms of an explosion: a prodigious expansion of culture throughout the social realm, to the point at which everything in our social life – from economic value and state power to practices and to the very structure of the psyche itself – can be said to have become 'cultural' in some original and as yet untheorized sense. This perhaps startling proposition is, however, substantively quite consistent with the previous diagnosis of a society of the image or the simulacrum, and a transformation of the 'real' into so many pseudo-events.

It also suggests that some of our most cherished and time-honoured radical conceptions about the nature of cultural politics may thereby find themselves outmoded. However distinct those conceptions may have been – which range from slogans of negativity, opposition, and subversion to critique and reflexivity – they all shared a single, fundamentally spatial, presupposition, which may be resumed in the equally time-honoured formula of 'critical distance'. No theory of cultural politics current on the Left today has been able to do without one notion or another of a certain minimal aesthetic distance, of the possibility of the positioning of the cultural act outside the massive Being of capital, which then serves as an Archimedean point from which to assault this last. What the burden of our preceding demonstration suggests, however, is that distance in general (including 'critical distance' in particular) has very precisely been abolished in the new space of postmodernism. We are submerged in its henceforth filled and suffused volumes to the point where our now postmodern bodies are bereft of spatial coordinates and practically (let alone theoretically) incapable of distantiation; meanwhile, it has already been observed how the prodigious new expansion of multinational capital ends up penetrating and colonizing those very pre-capitalist enclaves (Nature and the Unconscious) which offered extraterritorial and Archimedean footholds for critical effectivity. The shorthand language of 'cooptation' is for this reason omnipresent on the Left; but offers a most inadequate theoretical basis for understanding a situation in which we all, in one way or another, dimly feel that not only punctual and local countercultural forms of cultural resistance and guerrilla warfare, but also even overtly political interventions like those of The Clash, are all somehow secretly disarmed and reabsorbed by a system of which they themselves might well be considered a part, since they can achieve no distance from it.

What we must now affirm is that it is precisely this whole extraordinarily demoralizing and depressing original new global space which is the 'moment of truth' of postmodernism. What has been called the postmodernist 'sublime' is only the moment in which this content has become most explicit, has moved the closest to the surface of consciousness, as a coherent new type of space in its own right – even though a certain figural concealment or disguise is still at work here, most notably in the high-technological thematics in which the new spatial content is still dramatized and articulated. Yet the earlier features of the postmodern which were enumerated above can all now be seen as themselves partial (yet constitutive) aspects of the same general spatial object.

The argument for a certain authenticity in these otherwise patently ideological productions depends on the prior proposition that what we have now been calling postmodern (or multinational) space is not merely a cultural ideology or fantasy, but has genuine historical (and socio-economic) reality as a third great original expansion of capitalism around the globe (after the earlier expansions of the national market and the older imperialist system, which each had their own cultural specificity and generated new types of space appropriate to their dynamics). The distorted and unreflexive attempts of newer cultural production to explore and to express this new space must then also, in their own fashion, be considered as so many approaches to the representation of (a new) reality (to use a more antiquated language). As paradoxical as the terms may seem, they may thus, following a classic interpretative option, be read as peculiar new forms of realism (or at least of the mimesis of reality), at the same time that they can equally well be analysed as so many attempts to distract and to divert us from that reality or to disguise its contradictions and resolve them in the guise of various formal mystifications.

As for that reality itself, however – the as yet untheorized original space of some new 'world system' of multinational or late capitalism (a space whose negative or baleful aspects are only too obvious), the dialectic requires us to hold equally to a positive or 'progressive' evaluation of its emergence, as Marx did for the newly unified space of the national markets, or as Lenin did for the older imperialist global network. For neither Marx nor Lenin was socialism a matter of returning to small (and thereby less repressive and comprehensive) systems of social organization; rather, the dimensions attained by capital in their own times were grasped as the promise, the framework, and the precondition for the achievement of some new and more comprehensive socialism. How much the more is this not the case with the even more global and totalizing space of the new world system, which demands the invention and elaboration of an internationalism of a radically new type? The disastrous realignment of socialist revolution with the older nationalisms (not only in South East Asia), whose results have necessarily aroused much serious recent Left reflexion, can be adduced in support of this position.

The Need for Maps

But if all this is so, then at least one possible form of a new radical cultural politics becomes evident: with a final aesthetic proviso that must quickly be noted. Left cultural producers and theorists – particularly those formed by bourgeois cultural traditions issuing from Romanticism and valorizing spontaneous, instinctive or unconscious forms of 'genius' – but also for very obvious historical reasons such as Zhdanovism and the sorry consequences of political and party interventions in the arts – have often by reaction allowed themselves to be unduly intimidated by the repudiation, in bourgeois aesthetics and most notably in high modernism, of one of the age-old functions of art – namely the pedagogical and the didactic. The teaching function of art was, however, always stressed in classical times (even though it there mainly took the form of *moral* lessons); while the prodigious and still imperfectly understood work of Brecht reaffirms, in a new and formally innovative and original way, for the moment of modernism proper, a complex new conception of the relationship between culture and pedagogy. The cultural model I will propose similarly foregrounds the cognitive and pedagogical dimensions of political art and culture, dimensions stressed in very different ways by *both* Lukács *and* Brecht (for the distinct moments of realism and modernism, respectively).

We cannot, however, return to aesthetic practices elaborated on the basis of historical situations and dilemmas which are no longer ours. Meanwhile, the conception of space that has been developed here suggests that a model of political culture appropriate to our own situation will necessarily have to raise spatial issues as its fundamental organizing concern. I will therefore provisionally define the aesthetic of such new (and hypothetical) cultural form as an aesthetic of *cognitive mapping*.

In a classic work, *The Image of the City*, Kevin Lynch taught us that the alienated city is above all a space in which people are unable to map (in their minds) either their own positions or the urban totality in which they find themselves: grids such as those of Jersey City, in which none of the traditional markers (monuments, nodes, natural boundaries, built perspectives) obtain, are the most obvious examples. Disalienation in the traditional city, then, involves the practical reconquest of a sense of place, and the construction or reconstruction of an articulated ensemble which can be retained in memory and which the individual subject can map and remap along the moments of mobile, alternative trajectories. Lynch's own work is limited by the deliberate restriction of his topic to the problems of the city form as such; yet it becomes extraordinarily suggestive when projected outwards onto some of the larger national and global spaces we have touched on here. Nor should it be too hastily assumed that his model – while it clearly raises very central issues of representation as such – is in any way easily vitiated by the conventional poststructuralist critiques of the 'ideology of representation' or mimesis. The cognitive map is not exactly mimetic, in that older sense; indeed the theoretical issues it poses allow us to renew the analysis of representation on a higher and much more complex level.

There is, for one thing, a most interesting convergence between the empirical problems studied by Lynch in terms of city space and the great Althusserian (and Lacanian) redefinition of ideology as 'the representation of the subject's *Imaginary* relationship to his or her *Real* conditions of existence'. Surely this is exactly what the cognitive map is called upon to do, in the narrower framework of daily life in the physical city: to enable a situational representation on the part of the individual subject to that vaster and properly unrepresentable totality which is the ensemble of the city's structure as a whole.

Yet Lynch's work also suggests a further line of development insofar as cartography itself constitutes its key mediatory instance. A return to the history of this science (which is also an art) shows us that Lynch's model does not yet in fact really correspond to what will become map-making. Rather, Lynch's subjects are clearly involved in pre-cartographic operations whose results traditionally are described as itineraries rather than as maps; diagrams organized around the still subject-centred or existential journey of the traveller, along which various significant key features are marked – oases, mountain ranges, rivers, monuments and the like. The most highly developed form of such diagrams is the nautical itinerary, the sea chart or *portulans*, where coastal features are noted for the use of Mediterranean navigators who rarely venture out into the open sea.

Yet the compass at once introduces a new dimension into sea charts, a dimension that will utterly transform the problematic of the itinerary and allow us to pose the problem of a genuine cognitive mapping in a far more complex way. For the new instruments – compass, sextant and theodolite – do not merely correspond to new geographic and navigational problems (the difficult matter of determining longitude, particularly on the curving surface of the planet, as opposed to the simpler matter of latitude, which European navigators can still empirically determine by ocular inspection of the African coast); they also introduce a whole new coordinate – that of relationship to the totality, particularly as it is mediated by the stars and by new operations like that of triangulation. At this point, cognitive mapping in the broader sense comes to require the coordination of existential data (the empirical position of the subject) with unlived, abstract conceptions of the geographic totality.

Finally, with the first globe (1490) and the invention of the Mercator projection around the same period, yet a third dimension of cartography emerges, which at once involves what we would today call the nature of representational codes, the intrinsic structures of the various media, the intervention, into more naive mimetic conceptions of mapping, of the whole new fundamental question of the languages of representation itself: and in particular the unresolvable (well-nigh Heisenbergian) dilemma of the transfer of curved space to flat charts; at which point it becomes clear that there can be no true maps (at the same time in which it also becomes clear that there can be scientific progress, or better still, a dialectical advance, in the various historical moments of map-making).

Social Cartography and Symbol

Transcoding all this now into the very different problematic of the Althusserian definition of ideology, we would want to make two points. The first is that the Althusserian concept now allows us to rethink these specialized geographical and cartographic issues in terms of social space, in terms, for example, of social class and national or international context, in terms of the ways in which we all necessarily *also* cognitively map our individual social relationship to local, national and international class realities. Yet to reformulate the problem in this way is also to come starkly up against those very difficulties in mapping which are posed in heightened and original ways by that very global space of the postmodernist or multinational moment which has been under discussion here. There are not merely theoretical issues, but have urgent practical political consequences: as is evident from the conventional feelings of First World subjects that existentially (or 'empirically') they really do inhabit a 'post-industrial society', from which traditional production has disappeared and in which social classes of the classical type no longer exist – a conviction which has immediate effects on political praxis.

The second observation to be proposed is that a return to the Lacanian underpinnings of Althusser's theory can afford some useful and suggestive methodological enrichments. Althusser's formulation remobilizes an older and henceforth classical Marxian distinction between science and ideology, which is still not without value for us. The existential – the positioning of the individual subject, the experience of daily life, the monadic 'point of view' on the world to which we are necessarily, as biological subjects, restricted – is in Althusser's formula implicitly opposed to the realm of abstract knowledge, a realm which, as Lacan reminds us, is never positioned in or actualized by any concrete subject but rather by that structural void called 'le sujet supposé savoir', 'the subject supposed to know', a subject-place of knowledge: what is affirmed is not that we cannot know the world and its totality in some abstract or 'scientific' way – Marxian 'science' provides just such a way of knowing and conceptualizing the world abstractly, in the sense in which, e.g. Mandel's great book offers a rich and elaborated *knowledge* of that global world system, of which it has never been said here that it was unknowable, but merely that it was unrepresentable, which is a very different matter. The Althusserian formula, in other words, designates a gap, a rift, between existential experience and scientific knowledge: ideology has then the function of somehow inventing a way of articulating those two distinct dimensions with each other. What a historicist view of this 'definition' would want to add is that such coordination, the production of functioning and living ideologies, is distinct in different historical situations, but above all, that there may be historical situations in which it is not possible at all – and this would seem to be our situation in the current crisis.

But the Lacanian system is threefold and not dualistic. To the Marxian–Althusserian opposition of ideology and science correspond only two of Lacan's tripartite functions, the Imaginary and the Real, respectively. Our digression on cartography, however, with its final relevation of a properly representational dialectic of the codes and capacities of individual languages or media, reminds us that what has until now been omitted was the dimension of the Lacanian Symbolic itself.

An aesthetic of cognitive mapping – a pedagogical political culture which seeks to endow the individual subject with some new heightened sense of its place in the global system – will necessarily have to respect this now enormously complex representational dialectic and to invent radically new forms in order to do it justice. This is not, then, clearly a call for a return to some older kind of machinery, some older and more transparent national space, or some more traditional and reassuring perspectival or mimetic enclave: the new political art – if it is indeed possible at all – will have to hold to the truth of postmodernism, that is to say, to its fundamental object – the world space of multinational capital – at the same time at which it achieves a breakthrough to some as yet unimaginable new mode of representing this last, in which we may again begin to grasp our positioning as individual and collective subjects and regain a capacity to act and struggle which is at present neutralized by our spatial as well as our social confusion. The political form of postmodernism, if there ever is any, will have as its vocation the invention and projection of a global cognitive mapping, on a social as well as a spatial scale.

Notes

1. In 'The politics of theory', *New German Critique*, 32 (Spring/Summer 1984).
2. Michael Herr, *Dispatches*, New York, 1978, pp. 8–9.

Part Two

Modernity Complete and Incomplete

Introduction

Is the postmodern most satisfactorily characterised by a chronological demand? Should we abandon the cultural and historical project originating in Enlightenment and identified as 'modernity'; and if so, should we abandon it in the name of 'progress' or advancement, themselves terms clearly identified with the ideology of an enlightened 'modernisation'? These vibrant questions in the debate were brought sharply into focus in Habermas's polemical essay, given initially in the form of an address upon receipt of the Adorno Prize in 1980, 'Modernity – An Incomplete Project'. The occasion of the essay aligns Habermas with Adorno; yet the content of the lecture aligns him with precisely that rationalist tradition in Enlightenment of which Adorno was enormously sceptical. Here, as in his later work of the 1980s, Habermas sees the possibility of salvaging Enlightenment rationality. The project of modernity begun by eighteenth-century philosophers 'consisted in their efforts to develop objective science, universal morality and law, and autonomous art according to their inner logic', their aim being, according to Habermas here, 'the rational organization of everyday social life'. Habermas accepts that errors have been made in the attempt to attain such a rational society; but this should not negate the project of modernity as such. Later, Habermas will argue that the problem lies in the individuation of the rational Subject of consciousness, and for a 'theory of communicative action' which will relocate the Subject as the agent of an intersubjectively agreed reason, a reason whose basis lies in communication or discourse and in the social consensus produced by such discourse. In the early 1980s, however, it was not so much the question of the Subject of reason as reason itself which began to come under pressure.

Reason, as the basis for action, faces the danger of becoming purely 'instrumental', and hence of degenerating into a pursuit of rationalism for its own sake, regardless of the effects produced by such a 'practical reason'. But a reason produced in the name of a social practice is, of course, at the root of any cultural politics. Without it, the 'engaged' intellectual of the European tradition, who culminates perhaps in Sartre, simply could not exist. It is Gianni Vattimo who begins to entertain this possibility in all seriousness for the first time. In 1983 he began to explore, in collaboration with Pier Aldo Rovati, what they called *il pensiero debole*, a weak or 'disengaged' thinking. In this, reason's *raison d'être* is no longer to be instrumental; and 'weak thinking', precisely to the extent that it eschews 'engagement', can be more genuinely 'reasonable'. A few years later, Vattimo investigates this more fully in *La fine della modernità*, a passage from which is included here. Vattimo works most often in the field of hermeneutic philosophy, and is thus already favourably disposed to the reduction of truth to interpretation alluded to earlier. Adopting the Kuhnian notion of paradigm shifts, Vattimo here explains 'the structure of artistic revolutions', and specifically the structure of the shift from modern to postmodern. Modernity he defines as 'that era in which being modern becomes a value, or rather, it becomes *the* fundamental value to which all other values refer', and this 'value' is itself defined in modernity with 'the new', a new seen as a symptom of secular progress. It is precisely this covert sense of 'the new' from which the postmodern will ('weakly') disengage itself: 'the postmodern displays ... an effort to free itself from the logic of overcoming, development, and innovation'. Such an art is itself proleptic of a postmodern social formation, yielding a formation – a society – which is at best 'weakly' articulated. The consensual agreement as to what constitutes the 'value' of the 'new' (i.e. the consensus called 'modernity') is no longer so readily available.

A similar kind of argument is advanced by David Cook, whose 'The Last Days of Liberalism', reprinted here, is part of a larger study written in collaboration with Arthur Kroker, *The Postmodern Scene*. Cook locates in Kantian philosophy not only a politics of liberalism but also an inbuilt obsolescence of such liberalism. The argument hinges on the special relation in Kant between power and judgement: power is predicated upon judgement. This Kantian position is open to two possible political orientations: one leading to political liberalism (ostensibly favoured by Kant), the other leading to the exercise of power against the foundation of the social itself. Modern thought, argues Cook, has taken this second orientation, producing not only the possibility of the 'social contract' but also a corresponding ideology of 'obedience'. The conceptual isolation of power enables power to disengage itself from the political and to insert itself into the aesthetic, as a matter of judgement in the realm of taste. The result, argues Cook, is the graduated self-liquidation of an individual who is deprived of a body, a will and an imagination, a self-liquidation carried out 'in the name of good taste'.

A more directly political line of argument is adopted by Bauman, who has pondered deeply the great Adornian questions regarding the possibility of 'enlightenment', art and culture after Auschwitz. In the piece included here, he argues that the modern period is characterised by the possibility of a legislative knowledge. Knowledge, in modernity, is sufficiently self-assured to feel itself capable of prescriptive legislation for a culture. In most of his writing on the postmodern, Bauman has seen such an attitude as the arrogance of a masterful instrumental reason: the arrogance of a reason – or, indeed of a consciousness – whose entire aim is, in fact, the mastery, domination and control of nature or of the unconscious. Like Vattimo, he does not put in place of this a kind of 'counter-arrogance'; rather, he argues for a more modest and circumscribed role for the contemporary consciousness. If an instrumental reason can lead to the 'economy' of Auschwitz, via the degradation of reason to rationalism, then it might be wiser to restrict the 'legislator'. Instead of legislation, the intellectual will now be characterised by her or his 'interpretative' activity.

Modernity, characterised by the progress of reason towards a social end, is now thoroughly in question. The great initiation of this debate in Habermas is joined here by a number of sceptical positions which, broadly, share the desire for a humbler attitude to reason, an attitude which itself causes enormous difficulties, which are taken up later in the political discourse around postmodernism.

5 □ Modernity – An Incomplete Project

Jürgen Habermas

In 1980, architects were admitted to the Biennial in Venice, following painters and filmmakers. The note sounded at this first Architecture Biennial was one of disappointment. I would describe it by saying that those who exhibited in Venice formed an avant-garde of reversed fronts. I mean that they sacrificed the tradition of modernity in order to make room for a new historicism. Upon this occasion, a critic of the German newspaper *Frankfurter Allgemeine Zeitung* advanced a thesis whose significance reaches beyond this particular event; it is a diagnosis of our times: 'Postmodernity definitely presents itself as Antimodernity.' This statement describes an emotional current of our times which has penetrated all spheres of intellectual life. It has placed on the agenda theories of post-enlightenment, postmodernity, even of post-history.

From history we know the phrase 'The Ancients and the Moderns'. Let me begin by defining these concepts. The term 'modern' has a long history, one which has been investigated by Hans Robert Jauss.[1] The word 'modern' in its Latin form 'modernus' was used for the first time in the late fifth century in order to distinguish the present, which had become officially Christian, from the Roman and pagan past. With varying content, the term 'modern' again and again expresses the consciousness of an epoch that relates itself to the past of antiquity, in order to view itself as the result of a transition from the old to the new.

Some writers restrict this concept of 'modernity' to the Renaissance, but this is historically too narrow. People considered themselves modern during the period of Charles the Great in the twelfth century, as well as in France of the late seventeenth century at the time of the famous 'Querelle des Anciens et des Modernes'. That is to say, the term 'modern' appeared and reappeared exactly during those periods in Europe when the consciousness of a new epoch formed itself through a renewed relationship to the ancients – whenever, moreover, antiquity was considered a model to be recovered through some kind of imitation.

The spell which the classics of the ancient world cast upon the spirit of later times

From *New German Critique*, 22 (Winter 1981), 3–15.

was first dissolved with the ideals of the French Enlightenment. Specifically, the idea of being 'modern' by looking back to the ancients changed with the belief, inspired by modern science, in the infinite progress of knowledge and in the infinite advance towards social and moral betterment. Another form of modernist consciousness was formed in the wake of this change. The romantic modernist sought to oppose the antique ideals of the classicists; he looked for a new historical epoch and found it in the idealized Middle Ages. However, this new ideal age, established early in the nineteenth century, did not remain a fixed ideal. In the course of the nineteenth century, there emerged out of this romantic spirit that radicalized consciousness of modernity which freed itself from all specific historical ties. This most recent modernism simply makes an abstract opposition between tradition and the present; and we are, in a way, still the contemporaries of that kind of aesthetic modernity which first appeared in the midst of the nineteenth century. Since then, the distinguishing mark of works which count as modern is 'the new' which will be overcome and made obsolete through the novelty of the next style. But while that which is merely 'stylish' will soon become outmoded, that which is modern preserves a secret tie to the classical. Of course, whatever can survive time has always been considered to be a classic. But the emphatically modern document no longer borrows this power of being a classic from the authority of a past epoch; instead, a modern work becomes a classic because it has once been authentically modern. Our sense of modernity creates its own self-enclosed canons of being classic. In this sense we speak, e.g., in view of the history of modern art, of classical modernity. The relation between 'modern' and 'classical' has definitely lost a fixed historical reference.

The Discipline of Aesthetic Modernity

The spirit and discipline of aesthetic modernity assumed clear contours in the work of Baudelaire. Modernity then unfolded in various avant-garde movements and finally reached its climax in the Café Voltaire of the dadaists and in surrealism. Aesthetic modernity is characterized by attitudes which find a common focus in a changed consciousness of time. This time consciousness expresses itself through metaphors of the vanguard and the avant-garde. The avant-garde understands itself as invading unknown territory, exposing itself to the dangers of sudden, shocking encounters, conquering an as yet unoccupied future. The avant-garde must find a direction in a landscape into which no one seems to have yet ventured.

But these forward gropings, this anticipation of an undefined future and the cult of the new, mean in fact the exaltation of the present. The new time consciousness, which enters philosophy in the writings of Bergson, does more than express the experience of mobility in society, of acceleration in history, of discontinuity in everyday life. The new value placed on the transitory, the elusive and the ephemeral, the very celebration of dynamism, discloses a longing for an undefiled, immaculate and stable present.

This explains the rather abstract language in which the modernist temper has spoken of the 'past'. Individual epochs lose their distinct forces. Historical memory is replaced by the heroic affinity of the present with the extremes of history – a sense of time wherein decadence immediately recognizes itself in the barbaric, the wild and the primitive. We observe the anarchistic intention of blowing up the continuum of history, and we can account for it in terms of the subversive force of this new aesthetic consciousness. Modernity revolts against the normalizing functions of tradition; modernity lives on the experience of rebelling against all that is normative. This revolt is one way to neutralize the standards of both morality and utility. This aesthetic consciousness continuously stages a dialectical play between secrecy and public scandal; it is addicted to a fascination with that horror which accompanies the act of profaning, and yet is always in flight from the trivial results of profanation.

On the other hand, the time consciousness articulated in avant-garde art is not simply ahistorical; it is directed against what might be called a false normativity in history. The modern, avant-garde spirit has sought to use the past in a different way; it disposes those pasts which have been made available by the objectifying scholarship of historicism, but it opposes at the same time a neutralized history which is locked up in the museum of historicism.

Drawing upon the spirit of surrealism, Walter Benjamin constructs the relationship of modernity to history in what I would call a post-historicist attitude. He reminds us of the self-understanding of the French Revolution: 'The Revolution cited ancient Rome, just as fashion cites an antiquated dress. Fashion has a scent for what is current, whenever this moves within the thicket of what was once.' This is Benjamin's concept of the *Jetztzeit*, of the present as a moment of revelation; a time in which splinters of a messianic presence are enmeshed. In this sense, for Robespierre, the antique Rome was a past laden with momentary revelations.[2]

Now, this spirit of aesthetic modernity has recently begun to age. It has been recited once more in the 1960s; after the 1970s, however, we must admit to ourselves that this modernism arouses a much fainter response today than it did fifteen years ago. Octavio Paz, a fellow-traveller of modernity, noted already in the middle of the 1960s that 'the avant-garde of 1967 repeats the deeds and gestures of those of 1917. We are experiencing the end of the idea of modern art.' The work of Peter Bürger has since taught us to speak of 'post-avant-garde' art; this term is chosen to indicate the failure of the surrealist rebellion.[3] But what is the meaning of this failure? Does it signal a farewell to modernity? Thinking more generally, does the existence of a post-avant-garde mean there is a transition to that broader phenomenon called postmodernity?

This is in fact how Daniel Bell, the most brilliant of the American neoconservatives, interprets matters. In his book *The Cultural Contradictions of Capitalism*, Bell argues that the crises of the developed societies of the West are to be traced back to a split between culture and society. Modernist culture has come to penetrate the values of everyday life; the life-world is infected by modernism. Because of the forces of modernism, the principle of unlimited self-realization, the demand for authentic self-experience and the subjectivism of a hyperstimulated sensitivity have come to be dominant. This temperament unleashes hedonistic motives irreconcilable with the discipline of professional life in society, Bell says. Moreover, modernist culture is altogether incompatible with the moral basis of a purposive, rational conduct of life. In this manner, Bell places the burden of responsibility for the dissolution of the Protestant ethic (a phenomenon which had already disturbed Max Weber) on the 'adversary culture'. Culture in its modern form stirs up hatred against the conventions and virtues of everyday life, which has become rationalized under the pressures of economic and administrative imperatives.

I would call your attention to a complex wrinkle in this view. The impulse of modernity, we are told on the other hand, is exhausted; anyone who considers himself avant-garde can read his own death warrant. Although the avant-garde is still considered to be expanding, it is supposedly no longer creative. Modernism is dominant but dead. For the neoconservative the question then arises: how can norms arise in society which will limit libertinism, reestablish the ethic of discipline and work? What new norms will put a brake on the levelling caused by the social welfare state so that the virtues of individual competition for achievement can again dominate? Bell sees a religious revival to be the only solution. Religious faith tied to a faith in tradition will provide individuals with clearly defined identities and existential security.

Cultural Modernity and Societal Modernization

One can certainly not conjure up by magic the compelling beliefs which command authority. Analyses like Bell's, therefore, only result in an attitude which is spreading in Germany no less than in the States: an intellectual and political confrontation with the carriers of cultural modernity. I cite Peter Steinfels, an observer of the new style which the neoconservatives have imposed upon the intellectual scene in the 1970s:

> The struggle takes the form of exposing every manifestation of what could be considered an oppositionist mentality and tracing its 'logic' so as to link it to various forms of extremism: drawing the connection between modernism and nihilism ... between government regulation and totalitarianism, between criticism of arms expenditures and subservience to communism, between Women's liberation or homosexual rights and the destruction of the family ... between the Left generally and terrorism, anti-semitism, and fascism ...[4]

The *ad hominem* approach and the bitterness of these intellectual accusations have also been trumpeted loudly in Germany. They should not be explained so much in terms of the psychology of neoconservative writers; rather, they are rooted in the analytical weaknesses of neoconservative doctrine itself.

Neoconservatism shifts onto cultural modernism the uncomfortable burdens of a more or less successful capitalist modernization of the economy and society. The neoconservative doctrine blurs the relationship between the welcomed process of societal modernization on the one hand, and the lamented cultural development on the other. The neoconservative does not uncover the economic and social causes for the altered attitudes towards work, consumption, achievement and leisure. Consequently, he attributes all of the following – hedonism, the lack of social identification, the lack of obedience, narcissism, the withdrawal from status and achievement competition – to the domain of 'culture'. In fact, however, culture is intervening in the creation of all these problems in only a very indirect and mediated fashion.

In the neoconservative view, those intellectuals who still feel themselves committed to the project of modernity are then presented as taking the place of those unanalyzed causes. The mood which feeds neoconservatism today in no way originates from discontent about the antinomian consequences of a culture breaking from the museums into the stream of ordinary life. This discontent has not been called into life by modernist intellectuals. It is rooted in deep-seated reactions against the process of *societal* modernization. Under the pressures of the dynamics of economic growth and the organizational accomplishments of the state, this social modernization penetrates deeper and deeper into previous forms of human existence. I would describe this subordination of the life-worlds under the system's imperatives as a matter of disturbing the communicative infrastructure of everyday life.

Thus, for example, neopopulist protests only express in pointed fashion a widespread fear regarding the destruction of the urban and natural environment and of forms of human sociability. There is a certain irony about these protests in terms of neoconservatism. The tasks of passing on a cultural tradition, of social integration and of socialization require adherence to what I call communicative rationality. But the occasions for protest and discontent originate precisely when spheres of communicative action, centered on the reproduction and transmission of values and norms, are penetrated by a form of modernization guided by standards of economic and administrative rationality – in other words, by standards of rationalization quite different from those of communicative rationality on which those spheres depend. But neoconservative doctrines turn our attention precisely away from such societal processes: they project the causes, which they do not bring to light, onto the plane of a subversive culture and its advocates.

To be sure, cultural modernity generates its own aporias as well. Independently from the consequences of *societal* modernization and within the perspective of *cultural* development itself, there originate motives for doubting the project of modernity. Having dealt with a feeble kind of criticism of modernity – that of neoconservatism – let me now move our discussion of modernity and its discontents into a different domain that touches on these aporias of cultural modernity – issues that often serve only as a pretense for those positions which either call for a postmodernity, recommend a return to some form of premodernity, or throw modernity radically overboard.

The Project of Enlightenment

The idea of modernity is intimately tied to the development of European art, but what I call 'the project of modernity' comes into focus only when we dispense with the usual concentration upon art. Let me start a different analysis by recalling an idea from Max Weber. He characterized cultural modernity as the separation of the substantive reason expressed in religion and metaphysics into three autonomous spheres. They are: science, morality and art. These came to be differentiated because the unified world-views of religion and metaphysics fell apart. Since the eighteenth century, the problems inherited from these older world-views could be arranged so as to fall under specific aspects of validity: truth, normative rightness, authenticity and beauty. They could then be handled as questions of knowledge, or of justice and morality, or of taste. Scientific discourse, theories of morality, jurisprudence, and the production and criticism of art could in turn be institutionalized. Each domain of culture could be made to correspond to cultural professions in which problems could be dealt with as the concern of special experts. This professionalized treatment of the cultural tradition brings to the fore the intrinsic structures of each of the three dimensions of culture. There appear the structures of cognitive-instrumental, of moral-practical and of aesthetic-expressive rationality, each of these under the control of specialists who seem more adept at being logical in these particular ways than other people are. As a result, the distance grows between the culture of the experts and that of the larger public. What accrues to culture through specialized treatment and reflection does not immediately and necessarily become the property of everyday praxis. With cultural rationalization of this sort, the threat increases that the life-world, whose traditional substance has already been devalued, will become more and more impoverished.

The project of modernity formulated in the eighteenth century by the philosophers of the Enlightenment consisted in their efforts to develop objective science, universal morality and law, and autonomous art according to their inner logic. At the same time, this project intended to release the cognitive potentials of each of these domains from their esoteric forms. The Enlightenment philosophers wanted to utilize this accumulation of specialized culture for the enrichment of everyday life – that is to say, for the rational organization of everyday social life.

Enlightenment thinkers of the cast of mind of Condorcet still had the extravagant expectation that the arts and sciences would promote not only the control of natural forces but also the understanding of the world and of the self, moral progress, the justice of institutions and even the happiness of human beings. The twentieth century has shattered this optimism. The differentiation of science, morality and art has come to mean the automony of the segments treated by the specialist and their separation from the hermeneutics of everyday communication. This splitting off is the problem that has given rise to efforts to 'negate' the culture of expertise. But the problem won't go away: should we try to hold on to the *intentions* of the Enlightenment, feeble as they may be, or should we declare the entire project of modernity a lost cause? I now want to return to the problem of artistic culture, having explained why, historically, aesthetic modernity is only a part of cultural modernity in general.

The False Programs of the Negation of Culture

Greatly oversimplifying, I would say that in the history of modern art one can detect a trend towards ever greater autonomy in the definition and practice of art. The category of 'beauty' and the domain of beautiful objects were first constituted in the Renaissance. In the course of the eighteenth century, literature, the fine arts and music were institutionalized as activities independent from sacred and courtly life. Finally, around the middle of the nineteenth century an aestheticist conception of art emerged, which encouraged the artist to produce his work according to the distinct consciousness of art for art's sake. The autonomy of the aesthetic sphere could then become a deliberate project: the talented artist could lend authentic expression to those experiences he had in encountering his own decentered subjectivity, detached from the constraints of routinized cognition and everyday action.

In the mid-nineteenth century, in painting and literature, a movement began which Octavio Paz finds epitomized already in the art criticism of Baudelaire. Color, lines, sounds and movement ceased to serve primarily the cause of representation; the media of expression and the techniques of production themselves became the aesthetic object. Theodor W. Adorno could therefore begin his *Aesthetic Theory* with the following sentence: 'It is now taken for granted that nothing which concerns art can be taken for granted any more: neither art itself, nor art in its relationship to the whole, nor even the right of art to exist.' And this is what surrealism then denied: *das Existenzrecht der Kunst als Kunst*. To be sure, surrealism would not have challenged the right of art to exist, if modern art had no longer advanced a promise of happiness concerning its own relationship 'to the whole' of life. For Schiller, such a promise was delivered by aesthetic intuition, but not fulfilled by it. Schiller's *Letters on the Aesthetic Education of Man* speaks to us of a utopia reaching beyond art itself. But by the time of Baudelaire, who repeated this *promesse de bonheur* via art, the utopia of reconciliation with society had gone sour. A relation of opposites had come into being; art had become a critical mirror, showing the irreconcilable nature of the aesthetic and the social worlds. This modernist transformation was all the more painfully realized, the more art alienated itself from life and withdrew into the untouchableness of complete autonomy. Out of such emotional currents finally gathered those explosive energies which unloaded in the surrealist attempt to blow up the autarkical sphere of art and to force a reconciliation of art and life.

But all those attempts to level art and life, fiction and praxis, appearance and reality to one plane; the attempts to remove the distinction between conscious staging and spontaneous excitement; the attempts to declare everything to be art and everyone to be an artist, to retract all criteria and to equate aesthetic judgment with the expression of subjective experiences – all these undertakings have proved themselves to be sort of nonsense experiments. These experiments have served to bring back to life, and to illuminate all the more glaringly, exactly those structures of art which they were meant to dissolve. They gave a new legitimacy, as ends in themselves, to appearance as the medium of fiction, to the transcendence of the artwork over society, to the concentrated and planned character of artistic production as well as to the special cognitive status of judgments of taste. The radical attempt to negate art has ended up ironically by giving due exactly to these categories through which Enlightenment aesthetics had circumscribed its object domain. The surrealists waged the most extreme warfare, but two mistakes in particular destroyed their revolt. First, when the containers of an autonomously developed cultural sphere are shattered, the contents get dispersed. Nothing remains from a desublimated meaning or a destructured form; an emancipatory effect does not follow.

Their second mistake has more important consequences. In everyday communication, cognitive meanings, moral expectations, subjective expressions and evaluations must relate to one another. Communication processes need a cultural tradition covering all spheres – cognitive, moral-practical and expressive. A rationalized everyday life, therefore, could hardly be saved from cultural impoverishment through breaking open a single cultural sphere – art – and so providing access to just one of the specialized knowledge complexes. The surrealist revolt would have replaced only one abstraction.

In the spheres of theoretical knowledge and morality, there are parallels to this failed attempt of what we might call the false negation of culture, only they are less pronounced. Since the days of the Young Hegelians, there has been talk about the negation of philosophy. Since Marx, the question of the relationship of theory and practice has been posed. However, Marxist intellectuals joined a social movement; and only at its peripheries were there sectarian attempts to carry out a program of the negation of philosophy similar to the surrealist program to negate art. A parallel to the surrealist mistakes becomes visible in these programs when one observes the consequences of dogmatism and of moral rigorism.

A reified everyday praxis can be cured only by creating unconstrained interaction of the cognitive with the moral-practical and the aesthetic-expressive elements. Reification cannot be overcome by forcing just one of those highly stylized cultural spheres to open up and become more accessible. Instead, we see under certain circumstances a relationship emerge between terroristic activities and the over-extension of any one of these spheres into other domains: examples would be tendencies to aestheticize politics, or to replace politics by moral rigorism or to submit it to the dogmatism of a doctrine. These phenomena should not lead us, however, into denouncing the intentions of the surviving Enlightenment tradition as intentions rooted in a 'terroristic reason'.[5] Those who lump together the very project of modernity with the state of consciousness and the spectacular action of the individual terrorist are no less short-sighted than those who would claim that the incomparably more persistent and extensive bureaucratic terror practiced in the dark, in the cellars of the military and secret police, and in camps and institutions, is the *raison d'être* of the modern state, only because this kind of administrative terror makes use of the coercive means of modern bureaucracies.

Alternatives

I think that instead of giving up modernity and its project as a lost cause, we should learn from the mistakes of those extravagant programs which have tried to negate modernity. Perhaps the types of reception of art may offer an example which at least indicates the direction of a way out.

Bourgeois art had two expectations at once from its audiences. On the one hand, the layman who enjoyed art should educate himself to become an expert. On the other hand, he should also behave as a competent consumer who uses art and relates aesthetic experiences to his own life problems. This second, and seemingly harmless, manner of experiencing art has lost its radical implications exactly because it had a confused relation to the attitude of being expert and professional.

To be sure, artistic production would dry up, if it were not carried out in the form of specialized treatment of autonomous problems and if it were to cease to be the concern of experts who do not pay so much attention to exoteric questions. Both artists and critics accept thereby the fact that such problems fall under the spell of what I earlier called the 'inner logic' of a cultural domain. But this sharp delineation, this exclusive concentration on one aspect of validity alone and the exclusion of aspects of truth and justice, break down as soon as aesthetic experience is drawn into an individual life history and is absorbed into ordinary life. The reception of art by the layman, or by the 'everyday expert', goes in a rather different direction than the reception of art by the professional critic.

Albrecht Wellmer has drawn my attention to one way that an aesthetic experience which is not framed around the experts' critical judgments of taste can have its significance altered: as soon as such an experience is used to illuminate a life-historical situation and is related to life problems, it enters into a language game which is no longer that of the aesthetic critic. The aesthetic experience then not only renews the interpretation of our needs in whose light we perceive the world. It permeates as well our cognitive signification and our normative expectations and changes the manner in which all these moments refer to one another. Let me give an example of this process.

This manner of receiving and relating to art is suggested in the first volume of the work *The Aesthetics of Resistance* by the German-Swedish writer Peter Weiss. Weiss describes the process of reappropriating art by presenting a group of politically motivated, knowledge-hungry workers in 1937 in Berlin.[6] These were young people who, through an evening high-school education, acquired the intellectual means to fathom the general and social history of European art. Out of the resilient edifice of this objective mind, embodied in works of art which they saw again and again in museums in Berlin, they started removing their own chips of stone, which they gathered together and reassembled in the context of their own milieu. This milieu was far removed from that of traditional education as well as from the then existing regime. These young workers went back and forth between the edifice of European art and their own milieu until they were able to illuminate both.

In examples like this which illustrate the reappropriation of the expert's culture from the standpoint of the life-world, we can discern an element which does justice to the intentions of the hopeless surrealist revolts, perhaps even more to Brecht's and Benjamin's interests in how art works, which having lost their aura, could yet be received in illuminating ways. In sum, the project of modernity has not yet been fulfilled. And the reception of art is only one of at least three of its aspects. The project aims at a differentiated relinking of modern culture with an everyday praxis that still depends on vital heritages, but would be impoverished through mere traditionalism. This new connection, however, can only be established under the condition that societal modernization will also be steered in a different direction. The life-world has to become able to develop institutions out of itself which set limits to the internal dynamics and imperatives of an almost autonomous economic system and its administrative complements.

If I am not mistaken, the chances for this today are not very good. More or less in the entire Western world a climate has developed that furthers capitalist modernization processes as well as trends critical of cultural modernism. The disillusionment with the very failures of those programs that called for the negation of art and philosophy has come to serve as a pretense for conservative positions. Let me briefly distinguish the antimodernism of the 'young conservatives' from the premodernism of the 'old conservatives' and from the postmodernism of the neoconservatives.

The 'young conservatives' recapitulate the basic experience of aesthetic modernity. They claim as their own the revelations of a decentered subjectivity, emancipated from the imperatives of work and usefulness, and with this experience they step outside the modern world. On the basis of modernistic attitudes they justify an irreconcilable antimodernism. They remove into the sphere of the far-away and the archaic the spontaneous powers of imagination, self-experience and emotion. To instrumental reason they juxtapose in Manichean fashion a principle only accessible through evocation, be it the will to power or sovereignty, Being or the Dionysiac force of the poetical. In France this line leads from Georges Bataille via Michel Foucault to Jacques Derrida.

The 'old conservatives' do not allow themselves to be contaminated by cultural modernism. They observe the decline of substantive reason, the differentiation of science, morality and art, the modern world-view and its merely procedural rationality, with sadness and recommend a withdrawal to a position *anterior* to modernity. Neo-Aristotelianism, in particular, enjoys a certain success today. In view of the problematic of ecology, it allows itself to call for a cosmological ethic. (As belonging to this school, which originates with Leo Strauss, one can count the interesting works of Hans Jonas and Robert Spaemann.)

Finally, the neoconservatives welcome the development of modern science, as long as this only goes beyond its sphere to carry forward technical progress, capitalist growth and rational administration. Moreover, they recommend a politics of defusing the explosive content of cultural modernity. According to one thesis, science, when properly understood, has become irrevocably meaningless for the orientation of the life-world. A further thesis is that politics must be kept as far aloof as possible from the demands of moral-practical justification. And a third thesis asserts the pure immanence of art, disputes that it has a utopian content, and points to its illusory character in order to limit the aesthetic experience to privacy. (One could name here the early Wittgenstein, Carl Schmitt of the middle period, and Gottfried Benn of the late period.) But with the decisive confinement of science, morality and art to autonomous spheres separated from the life-world and administered by experts, what remains from the project of modernity is only what we would have if we were to give up the project of modernity altogether. As a replacement one points to traditions which, however, are held to be immune to demands of (normative) justification and validation.

This typology is like any other, of course, a simplification, but it may not prove totally useless for the analysis of contemporary intellectual and political confrontations. I fear that the ideas of antimodernity, together with an additional touch of premodernity, are becoming popular in the circles of alternative culture. When one observes the transformations of consciousness within political parties in Germany, a new ideological shift [*Tendenzwende*] becomes visible. And this is the alliance of postmodernists with premodernists. It seems to me that there is no party in particular that monopolizes the abuse of intellectuals and the position of neoconservatism. I therefore have good reason to be thankful for the liberal spirit in which the city of Frankfurt offers me a prize bearing the name of Theodor Adorno, a most significant son of this city, who as philosopher and writer has stamped the image of the intellectual in our country in incomparable fashion, who, even more, has become the very image of emulation for the intellectual.

Notes

1. Jauss is a prominent German literary historian and critic involved in the 'aesthetics of reception', a type of criticism related to reader-response criticism in this country. For a discussion of 'modern' see Jauss, *Asthetische Normen und geschichtliche Reflexion in der Querelle des Anciens et des Modernes*, Munich, 1964. For a reference in English see Jauss, 'History of art and pragmatic history', in *Toward an Aesthetic of Reception*, transl. Timothy Bahti, University of Minnesota Press, Minneapolis, 1982, pp. 46–8.

2. See Benjamin, 'Theses on the philosophy of history', in *Illuminations*, transl. Harry Zohn, Schocken, New York, 1969, p. 261.

3. For Paz on the avant-garde see in particular *Children of the Mire: Modern poetry from Romanticism to the avant-garde*, Harvard University Press, Cambridge, MA, 1974, pp. 148–64. For Bürger see *Theory of the Avant-Garde*, University of Minnesota Press, Minneapolis, Fall 1983.

4. Peter Steinfels, *The Neoconservatives*, Simon & Schuster, New York, 1979, p. 65.

5. The phrase 'to aestheticize politics' echoes Benjamin's famous formulation of the false social program of the fascists in 'The work of art in the age of mechanical reproduction'. Habermas's criticism here of Enlightenment critics seems directed less at Adorno and Max Horkheimer than at the contemporary *nouveaux philosophes* (Bernard-Henri Lévy, etc.) and their German and American counterparts.

6. The reference is to the novel *Die Ästhetik des Widerstands* (1975–8) by the author perhaps best known here for his 1965 play *Marat/Sade*. The work of art 'reappropriated' by the workers is the Pergamon altar, emblem of power, classicism and rationality.

6 □ *The Structure of Artistic Revolutions*

Gianni Vattimo

[. . .]

II

All this seems to me to signal the emergence in contemporary epistemology of an aesthetic model of historicity opposed to the notion of a process of cumulative development; furthermore, it leads also the the acknowledgement of a particular 'responsibility' for the aesthetic itself. This responsibility belongs not so much, nor only, to aesthetics as a philosophical discipline, but rather to the aesthetic as a domain of experience and as a dimension of existence that assumes exemplary value as a model for thinking about historicity in general.

The aestheticization of the history of science – if it may, with all due caution, be referred to in this way – which takes place in Kuhn's work is not a strange or exceptional event. It corresponds in fact to a much wider phenomenon, of which it is at once a symptom and a decisive instance: namely, it corresponds to what may be called the centrality of the aesthetic (aesthetic experience, art and other related phenomena) in modernity. This apparent centrality of the aesthetic could not possibly be due solely to the prejudiced point of view of philosophers and historians of art. Schelling's notion of art as the organ of philosophy, for instance, is but one of the more extreme expressions of a thematic which is found throughout modernity and which characterizes the latter. Nietzsche, in making the expression 'The will to power as art' the projected title of a section of his final theoretical work (which he never finished, and which was published in fragmentary form as *Der Wille zur Macht*), summarizes in perhaps the clearest and most demythified terms this profound current of the modern spirit. Beginning with Nietzsche, it becomes possible to recognize theoretically the meaning of aesthetics in modernity. This centrality affirms itself first of all at a practical level, in the process of the social promotion of the artist and his products starting with the Renaissance,[1] a process

From Vattimo, G., *The End of Modernity*, Polity Press, Oxford, 1988, pp. 95–107.

which gradually confers on the artist a certain dignity and superiority, along with both civil and quasi-religious functions. In a parallel fashion, this same centrality first emerges at a theoretical level in the works of Vico and the Romantics, which consider the origin of civilization and culture to be 'aesthetic'. Finally, with the advent of modern mass society, we see this same centrality in the ever greater importance which aesthetic models of behaviour (such as the various types of 'stars') and the organization of social consensus (since the strength of the mass media is above all an aesthetic and rhetorical kind of strength) continue to acquire. This process is an extremely far-ranging one; yet perhaps only in Nietzsche do we find an awareness of the authentic meaning of the function of *anticipation* that the aesthetic possesses in relation to the global development of modern civilization. In the notes at the beginning of the part of *Der Wille zur Macht* entitled 'The will to power as art' (sections 794–7), which were by a stroke of good fortune placed there by the first editors of the text, Nietzsche explicitly points out the foundation of this function of anticipation and of modelling which art assumes in regard to a world which ever more openly appears as the world of the will to power. Once denied any faith in the *Grund* and in the course of events as a development toward an ultimate point, the world appears as a work of art which makes itself: '*ein sich selbst gebärendes Kunstwerk*', an expression that Nietzsche takes from F. W. Schlegel. The artist is a *Vorstufe* or a place in which the will to power can make itself known and be set in motion on a small scale (section 795); and, with the revelation of the technological organization of the world (it might be added, without betraying Nietzsche's thought), this will to power can unveil itself as the very essence of the world. The relation with technology has assumed a central importance in the arts in the twentieth century, not only in terms of the specific techniques of the different arts, which can be seen everywhere at close range, but also in terms of technology as a more general socio-historical fact involving the technological organization of production and social life (here I refer the reader to the work of Hans Sedlmayr, even if I do not agree with his own evaluation of the issue).[2] This in turn displays in a concrete manner the function – as prelude, anticipation, and model – that Nietzsche assigns to art and to artists in relation to the world as will to power. The long struggle of the aesthetics and poetics of modernity against the Aristotelian definition of art as imitation attains here its full meaning, which can only be called an ontological one ('imitation' can be understood to mean either of nature or of classical models, although the latter are still legitimated by their supposed proximity to nature and its perfect proportions). Hans Blumenberg,[3] and Edgar Zilsel before him (in his reconstruction of the origins of the notion of genius in Humanism and in the Renaissance), have shown to precisely what degree *technicity* is to be found at the basis of the concept of the artist as a creative genius. The determination of the will to power as art in Nietzsche expresses this idea and draws out all the consequences implicit in the nineteenth-century destruction of the deep roots that for Kant still link 'genius' to nature.[4] In the work of Kant, the rooting of genius in nature corresponds to the rooting of scientific knowledge in an 'objectivity' of the world of nature that impedes the identification of the scientist with the artist. From the point of view at which Nietzsche arrives, though, all these roots appear instead to be torn up: nor, for him, can a genius legitimate his own creations simply because he is inspired by nature, any more than a scientist can make progress in the knowledge of the true by discovering 'something already extant but not yet known, like America was before Columbus'.[5] In theoretical consciousness and in modern social practice, art constantly reasserts itself as a 'dense' site. This is the case in regard both to the social figure of the artist and to the special dignity (Benjamin's 'aura') assigned to artistic works from a point of view – such as Nietzsche's – which sees the notion of the will to power as the basis for a true ontology of modernity. Art thus assumes the sense of an anticipation of the essence of modernity – of its authentic nature, that is, and of the way in which its essence arises in the modern era – prior to its being completely displayed in the technological organization of today's world. The theoretical and practical centrality attributed, more or less explicitly, to art since the Renaissance reaches an extreme degree in the emergence of aesthetic models as well in the version of the history of science proposed by Kuhn. This centrality is not to be understood as a sign of a general aestheticizing tendency in the culture of the last few centuries; rather, it is an anticipation of and a prelude to the emergence of the will to power as the essence of Being in modernity. If, however, Nietzsche supplies the most radical and theoretically explicit point of view (at least in terms of the hypothesis that we are exploring here) for understanding the meaning of the centrality of art in modern consciousness, it is at the same time undeniable that he himself does not possess a perfectly clear awareness of the typically modern nature of this phenomenon. For Nietzsche, the appearance of the will to power as the essence of Being or (what amounts to the same thing) as the death of God is a historical event, and not the discovery of a 'true' metaphysical structure. It is therefore, to some extent, linked to modernity. Yet it would be difficult to argue that for Nietzsche the concept of the 'modern' is typically defined in relation to these events. It is more likely that he offers an extreme example of the consciousness of modernity in the subjective meaning of the genitive, not in the objective one: the numerous texts in which Nietzsche discusses modernity as a phenomenon of decadence cannot be easily reconciled to those in which he instead speaks of the necessity of fulfilling nihilism (and therefore decadence) through a passage from the reactive stage of nihilism to the active and affirmative stage. Even the central function of art, as the principle of a *Gegenbewegung* against the various forms of reactive nihilism (religion, morality, and philosophy: cf. section 794 of *Der Wille zur Macht*), is not thought of by Nietzsche in terms of a specific relation to modernity, but rather in far more general terms. This difference between our point of view today, which is nonetheless linked to Nietzsche's and Nietzsche's own is far more theoretically charged than it would appear to be at first glance. If this difference means that in Nietzsche's work we find the culmination of the consciousness of modernity only in the subjective meaning of the genitive, then this also means that we can never simply reuse his arguments, but must instead situate ourselves – or recognize that we find ourselves – in terms of a different displacement. This 'displacement' not only distances us from Nietzsche, but also places us in a position distinct from his as regards the significance of the centrality of art in modernity.

Passing over a few passages and a more detailed analysis of the difference between the subjective and objective meanings of the genitive in the phrase 'Nietzsche, philosopher of modernity', while at the same time keeping this difference firmly in mind, it is necessary to recognize that the particular connection between the centrality of art and modernity may appear more clearly to us than it does to Nietzsche, thanks to the light cast on it by a concept that Nietzsche never thematizes (perhaps because it is still too close to him). This concept is the value of the new, or the new as value. Here we need to introduce explicitly a definition of modernity, which, even if not formulated in exactly the terms that we aim to use in the present work, can still be considered widely present in the work of many theoreticians of the modern, from Weber to Gehlen, Blumenberg, and Koselleck.[6] This definition, which certainly reflects a Nietzschean thematics as well, goes as follows: modernity is that era in which being modern becomes a value, or rather, it becomes *the* fundamental value to which all other values refer. This formula may be corroborated if we see that it coincides with the other, and more widely disseminated, definition of the modern in terms of secularization. Secularization, as the modern, is a term that describes not only what happens in a certain era and what nature it assumes, but also the 'value' that dominates and guides consciousness in the era in question, primarily as faith in progress – which is both a secularized faith and a faith in secularization.[7] But faith in progress, understood as a kind of faith in the historical process that is ever more devoid of providential and meta-historical elements, is purely and simply identified with faith in the value of the new. Against this background we must see, first of all, the grandiosity invested in the concept of genius, and, secondarily, the centrality that art and artists acquire in modern culture. Modernity is primarily the era in which the increased circulation of goods (Simmel)[8] and ideas, and increased social mobility (Gehlen)[9], bring into focus the value of the new and predispose the conditions for the identification of value (the value of Being itself) with the new. A good deal of twentieth-century philosophy describes the future in a way deeply tinged with the grandiose. Such descriptions range from the early Heidegger's definition of existence as project and transcendence to Sartre's notion of transcendence, to Ernst Bloch's utopianism (which is emblematic of all Hegelian/Marxist philosophy), and to the various ethics which seem ever more insistently to locate the value of an action in the fact of its making possible other choices and other actions, thus opening up a future. This same grandiose vision is the faithful mirror of an era that in general may legitimately be called 'futuristic', to borrow an expression from an essay by Kryzstof Pomian to which I will refer again later.[10] The same may naturally be said of the twentieth-century artistic avant-garde movements, whose radically anti-historicist inspiration is most authentically expressed by Futurism and Dadaism. Both in philosophy and in avant-garde poetics, the pathos of the future is still accompanied by an appeal to the authentic, according to a model of thought characteristic of all *modern* 'futurism': the tension towards the future is seen as a tension aimed towards a renewal and return to a condition of originary authenticity.

A visible link between modernity, secularization and the value of the new can therefore be discovered when the following points are brought into focus. (a) Modernity is characterized as the era of *Diesseitigkeit*, namely the abandonment of the sacred vision of existence and the affirmation of the realm of profane value instead, that is, of secularization. (b) The key point of secularization, at the conceptual level, is faith in progress (or the ideology of progress), which takes shape through a resumption of the Judeo-Christian vision of history, from which all references to transcendence are 'progressively' eliminated.[11] This occurs because progress depicts itself ever more insistently as a value in and of itself, in order to escape from the risk of theorizing the end of history (which is a risk when there is no longer a belief in the afterlife as defined by Christianity). Progress is just that process which leads toward a state of things in which further progress is possible, and nothing else. (c) This extreme secularization of the providential vision of history is simply the equivalent of affirming the new as the fundamental value.

In this process of secularization and the affirmation of the value of the new – a process which, historically speaking, is not at all as linear as it appears when its theoretically essential traits are retrospectively reassembled – art functions as an anticipation or emblem. This is the same as saying that, while for much of the modern age the discoveries made by 'mechanical heads' have still been limited and directed – at the level of science and technology – by the value of 'truth' or by the value of 'usefulness for life', for art these limitations and forms of metaphysical founding have long since been abandoned. Thus from the beginning of the modern era or thereabouts, art (although there are of course differences in the development of the individual arts) has found itself in the same ungrounded condition that science and technology only today explicitly recognize themselves to be in.

In his 1967 essay on 'Die Säkularisierung des Fortschritts', Arnold Gehlen describes this process in rather different terms, which by and large, however, fit in with the argument that we have put forward here. He sees the secularization of progress to be articulated in different ways, depending upon whether it occurs in the field of science and technology (more precisely, what he calls the operative connection – *Zusammenarbeit* – of 'exact sciences, technological development and industrial application),[12] or in the field of culture as constituted by the arts, literature, and the *schöne Wissenschaften* in general. In the former, progress represents a kind of fatalism, for it becomes 'routine': in science, technology and industry what is new simply signifies survival of these domains of activity (as economics reasons solely in terms of the rate of development, not in terms of the satisfaction of vital basic needs). The transformation of progress into a routine in these fields, Gehlen argues, discharges all the pathos of the new onto the other field, that is, that of the arts and literature. Here, though, in a way and for reasons that Gehlen's text does not seem to explain clearly, the value of the new and the pathos of development undergo a still more radical secularization than that which occurs in the passage from faith in the history of redemption to the profane ideology of progress. For different reasons, both in the becoming 'routine' of scientific/ technological/industrial progress and in the displacement of the pathos of the new towards the territory of art, there occurs a true dissolution of progress itself. This dissolution is linked on the one hand to the very process of secularization itself. Gehlen writes that secularization:

> consists in general in this – that the specific laws of the new world suffocate faith, or rather, not faith as much as its triumphalistic certitude [*die siegesbeglückte Gewissheit*]. At the same time, the overall project following an objective impulse of things fans out [*fächert auf*] in divergent processes that develop their own internal legality ever further, and slowly progress (since in the meantime we want to keep on believing in it) is displaced towards the periphery of facts and consciousness, and there is totally emptied out.[13]

Secularization itself, in short, contains a tendency toward dissolution which is accentuated with the passage of the pathos of the new toward the field of art. This is in itself a peripheral field, according to Gehlen, in which the need for the new – and its progressively becoming inessential – is intensified.[14] Secularization, as the establishment of laws proper to each of many different fields and domains of experience, thus appears as a menace to the notion of progress inasmuch as it can eventually thwart that very notion. This can be seen in the work of Bloch, for instance, who wants to remain faithful to a vision of the progressive and emancipatory movement of history, but who examines with concern the 'differentiations in the concept of progress'[15] and seeks to find in them a unitary design, in spite of the multiplicity of historical time (which is linked to the nature of class conflict). The discovery of this same design is also the objective of Benjamin's critique in his 'Theses on the philosophy of history'.

III

Gehlen is the first to use the term *post-histoire* in regard to late modernity. He claims to take this from the mathematician Antoine Augustin Cournot, who, however, never seems to have employed exactly this term; Gehlen probably borrows it from Hendrik de Man instead.[16] The *extreme secularization* which Gehlen describes offers us the opportunity to go one step further and to try to answer the question (already apparent in my earlier allusion to Nietzsche) that asks for the difference between a consciousness of modernity in the subjective meaning of the genitive, on the one hand, and in the objective meaning of the genitive, on the other. The definition of modernity as the era in which being modern is the base-value is not a definition which modernity could give of itself. The essence of the modern becomes truly visible only from the moment in which – in a way that needs to be examined more carefully – the mechanism of modernity distances itself from us. Gehlen, in speaking of the dissolution and emptying-out of the notion of progress both in the domain of science/technology/industry and of the arts, supplies a clue to understanding this distancing of modernity. The fact (noted by Gehlen) that the final condition sought by the radically 'future-oriented' utopias, like the great revolutionary ideologies themselves, reveals noticeable traits of ahistoricity, can perhaps be placed together with this same tendency to dissolution. 'Where we effectively try to make the new man, our relationship with history also changes. ... The French revolutionaries called 1793 the year One of a new era.'[17] Gehlen detects this trait of ahistoricity in a typical eighteenth-century utopia, Sebastien Mercier's *L'an 2240* (published in 1770). In the future world described by Mercier, which is governed by Rousseauian sobriety and virtue, all forms of credit have been abolished, everyone pays for everything in cash, and classical languages are no longer studied, since they are not needed in order for men to be virtuous.[18] The suppression of all credit and classical languages emblematically embodies a reduction of existence to the naked present, that is, the elimination of any historical dimension.

Progress seems to show a tendency to dissolve itself, and with it the value of the new as well, not only in the effective process of secularization, but even in the most extremely futuristic utopias. This dissolution is the event that enables us to distance ourselves from the mechanism of modernity, much more than Gehlen ever acknowledges. Krzysztof Pomian's essay on 'The crisis of the future', although it does not refer directly to Gehlen's work, takes up the line of reflection developed by the latter. Pomian adds some useful ideas for the present discourse, for he thematizes more openly the crisis of the value of the new which seems to characterize the present-day situation (it might be added that it is on this basis that it is defined as *post-histoire*, in a more precise sense of the term than Gehlen's). In his discussion of the characterization of modernity as a 'futuristic' era, Pomian makes explicit the nexus between the emergence of the value of the new and the constitution of the modern state. We have already seen that Mercier's utopia calls for the end of all credit arrangements: Pomian writes that 'the future is, literally, injected into the very texture of the present in the form of paper money. ... The history of more than two thousand years of monetarization of the economy is also the history of a growing dependence of the present on the future' (102). Even if this dependence already exists in principle in every agricultural society in which there is an interval between planting and harvest-time, it becomes a decisive dimension only in modern society. 'Only large-scale commerce, in the form that first appears in the twelfth century in Italian, Flemish and Hanseatic cities, together with the concomitant development of credit and maritime insurance, granted the future the role of a constitutive dimension' (103). The value assigned to the reproductive role of the family as a secularized form of eternity, and the consequent recognition of childhood and youth as conditions possessed of specific values which are entirely future-related, are connected to this basic mechanism of the modern form of society. More clearly than Gehlen, Pomian recognizes the crisis of the value of the future in contemporary culture that runs parallel to the crisis – with its tendencies to dissolution – that plagues the very institutions that conditioned the emergence of that value, in particular the modern state. The institutions which embody the futuristic orientation of the modern world 'appear to be plagued by serious malfunctions' (112), ranging from inflation (which destabilizes the purchasing power of money) to the complexity and uncontrolled growth of the state apparatus, etc. If we leave aside Pomian and matters of macrosociology, and turn instead to the field of the arts, here too we are struck by the dissolution of the value of the new. This is the meaning of the postmodern, to the degree in which it cannot be reduced to a mere fact of cultural fashion. From architecture to the novel to poetry to the figurative arts, the postmodern displays, as its most common and most imposing trait, an effort to free itself from the logic of overcoming, development, and innovation. From this point of view, the postmodern corresponds to Heidegger's attempt to prepare a post-metaphysical kind of thought which would not be an *Überwindung* but rather a *Verwindung* of metaphysics. This latter term, despite all its ambiguities, deserves to be placed alongside those of 'secularization' and (Nietzschean) 'nihilism' in any consideration of modernity that is philosophical and not merely *historisch*. Seen in the light not only of Nietzsche's 'Wille zur Macht als Kunst', but also especially of Heidegger's post-metaphysical ontology, the postmodern experience of art appears as the way in which art occurs in the era of the end of metaphysics. This holds good not only for what we today call 'postmodern' figurative art, literature, and architecture, but also for the dissolutive tendencies already apparent in the great early-twentieth-century avant-garde movements, such as, for instance, Joyce's transition from *Ulysses* to *Finnegans Wake*, which Ihab Hassan correctly sees as a key event for the definition of the postmodern.[19]

IV

Postmodern art appears as the most advanced point at which the process of secularization described by Gehlen has arrived. It is also a preparatory phase for the conditions in which the consciousness of modernity may become such, even in the objective meaning of the genitive. In the phantasmagoric (as Adorno calls it) play of a society built around the marketplace and technological mass media, the arts have experienced without any further metaphysical mask (such as the search for a supposedly authentic foundation of existence) the experience of the value of the new as such. This experience occurs in a purer and more visible way than it does for science and technology, which are still to a degree tied to truth-value or use-value. For the arts, the value of the new, once it has been radically unveiled, loses all possibility of foundation or value. The crisis of the future which permeates all late-modern culture and social life finds in the experience of art a privileged locus of expression. Such a crisis, obviously, implies a radical change in our way of experiencing history and time, as is somewhat obscurely anticipated by Nietzsche in his 'doctrine' of the eternal return of the Same. It is not perhaps an insignificant coincidence that certain 'epoch-making' works of the twentieth century – from

Proust's *Remembrance of Things Past* to Musil's *The Man without Qualities* to Joyce's *Ulysses* and *Finnegans Wake* – concentrate, even at the level of content itself, on the problem of time and on ways of experiencing temporality outside its supposedly natural linearity.[20] This suggests a positive direction for Gehlen's *post-histoire*, not just a purely dissolutive one, while at the same time avoiding all Spenglerian nostalgia for 'decline'. If in this way the very notion of artistic revolution, caught up in this game of ungrounding, loses some of its meaning, at the same time it perhaps supplies a means of establishing a dialogue between philosophical thought and poetry, in view of that which in contemporary philosophy continually reasserts itself as the possible – though problematical – overcoming of metaphysics.

Notes

1. On this point, cf. Mario Perniola, *L'alienazione artistica*, Mursia, Milan, 1971.
2. See especially Sedlmayr's *Art in Crisis, the Lost Center*, 1948, transl. Brian Battershaw, H. Regnery Co., Chicago, 1958; and *The Revolution of Modern Art*, 1955.
3. Cf. Hans Blumenberg, *Wirklichkeiten in denen wir leben*, Reclam, Stuttgart, 1981, especially the essay 'Nachahmung der Natur'; and, more generally, *Die Legitimät der Neuzeit*, Suhrkamp, Frankfurt, 1966.
4. On this point, see the first part of H.-G. Gadamer, *Truth and Method*, transl. Garrett Barden and John Cummings, 2nd edn, 1975; repr. Crossroads, New York, 1984.
5. Kant, *Anthropology from a Pragmatic Point of View*, transl. Gregor, para. 57.
6. See Max Weber, *The Sociology of Religion*, transl. Ephraim Fischoff, Beacon, Boston, MA, 1964. For Arnold Gehlen, see his *Man in the Age of Technology* (1957), transl. Patricia Lipscomb, Columbia University Press, New York, 1980; and his 1967 essay on 'Die Säkularisierung des Fortschritts', in vol. VII of his collected works, entitled *Einblicke*, ed. K. S. Rehberg, Klostermann, Frankfurt, 1978. For R. Koselleck, see esp. *Vergangene Zukunft. Zur Semantik geschichtlicher Zeiten*, Suhrkamp, Frankfurt, 1979.
7. The best overall history of the concept of secularization is H. Lübbe's *Säkularisierung. Geschichte eines ideenpolitischen Begriffs*, Alber, Freiburg, 1965.
8. Cf. Georg Simmel's essay on 'Fashion' (1895), in *On Individuality and Social Forms*, ed. Donald N. Levine, Chicago University Press, Chicago, 1971, pp. 294–323.
9. Cf. above all Gehlen's essay on 'Die Säkularisierung des Fortschritts'.
10. K. Pomian, 'The crisis of the future', published in Italian ('La crisi dell'avvenire') in *Le frontiere del tempo*, ed. R. Romano, Il Saggiatore, Milan, 1981.
11. The classic argument concerning modern historicism as the secularization of the theology of Judeo-Christian history is found in Löwith's *Meaning in History*, 1949; repr. Chicago University Press, 1957.
12. Gehlen, 'Die Säkularisierung des Fortschritts', p. 410.
13. *Ibid.*, p. 409.
14. *Ibid.*, p. 411.
15. Ernst Bloch, 'Differenzierungen im Begriff Fortschritt', in *Tübinger Einleitung in die Philosophie*, Suhrkamp, Frankfurt, 1964, vol. I, pp. 160–202. On Bloch's notion of

history, specifically in regard to a 'plurality' of historical times, cf. R. Bodel, *Multiversum. Tempo e storia in Ernst Bloch*, Bibliopolis, Naples, 1979.

16. Gehlen, 'Die Säkularisierung des Fortschritts', note for pp. 468–70.
17. *Ibid.*, p. 408.
18. *Ibid.*, p. 409.
19. Cf. Ihab Hassan, *Paracriticisms*, Illinois University Press, Urbana, 1975.
20. See Alberto Asor Rosa's essay, 'Tempo e nuovo nell'avanguardia ovvero: l'infinita manipolazione del tempo', in *Le frontiere del tempo*, ed. Romano.

7 □ The Last Days of Liberalism

David Cook

Aesthetic Liberalism

As late capitalism moves from the commodity relation based on wage/labour exploitation to the simulated economy of excess, it plays out the logic of liberalism. The turn to 'justice and values', nominally identified with conservatism, becomes the rallying point for a society that has accomplished by definition the main tenets of liberalism, freedom and equality. In the last days of liberalism, we are presented with a culturally refined model of behaviour that has left behind the crudity of Bentham's quip that 'pushpin is as good as poetry'. The 'last men' of Nietzsche's herd are content in actively seeking the role of a passive spectator in the democratic process as Nietzsche predicted. They have all become critics whose main task is to sit in judgement.

It is our thesis that Immanuel Kant, in his last days, reverses the field of liberalism creating the topology of the postmodern society of the spectacle under the sign of the aesthetic. All of this may be found in the *Critique of Judgement*,[1] the definitive text of the dead power of aesthetic liberalism:

- no longer critical theory's 'What is Enlightenment', but rather 'The End of All things' as instrumental reason becomes a culture text;
- no longer Lyotard's nostalgia for a sublime transcendent, but rather the nauseous allegory;
- no longer Deleuze's harmony of the faculties, but rather the nihilism of the will-not-to-will;
- no longer Arendt's citizen, but rather the disembodied eye of the voyeur;
- no longer Marcuse's play, but rather spectator sports;

From Kroker, A. and Cook, D., *The Postmodern Scene*, Macmillan Education, Basingstoke/New World Perspectives, Quebec/St Martin's Press, New York, 1988, pp. 159–67.

• no longer liberalism, but rather aesthetic liberalism and the society of the
  spectacle.

We begin by moving to the site of aesthetic liberalism – the imagination.

As Heidegger points out in his study of Kant's metaphysics, the *Critique of
Judgement* establishes the central role of the transcendental imagination.[2] This, in
turn, reestablishes liberal theory as the unity of wills under the concept of an end
which has a subjective claim to universality based on the transcendental
imagination. The imagination founds the individual and the state on the basis of the
aesthetic informing the judgement of the 'kingdom of ends'. Thus the *Critique*
stands as the founding text of aesthetic liberalism.

The importance attached to the aesthetic imagination sends one back to the
origins of the aesthetic in the 'sensibility' of the natural world. For Kant, this
sensibility expresses itself in the desires which share with the imagination the
structure of calling to 'life' what is not there. The senses are determined by the
'natural' causality of fulfilling desires. This is sometimes portrayed as amoral, for
example, the eating of food for survival, or at other times as immoral, as greed, but
in the long run as part of the antagonism that leads to the moral end of perpetual
peace. The will which is determined by these natural causes is claimed by Kant to
be free *a priori* as a transcendental moral agent whose chief characteristic is its
disinterestedness.[3]

This gives rise to the familiar Hobbesian view of politics: an antagonistic desiring
individual needing, to quote the sixth proposition of the *Idea for a Universal
History*, 'a master to break his self-will and force him to obey a universally valid
will is the categorical imperative, or the principle of political right, which establishes
the form of the state as an authoritative agent to administer justice universally'[4]
leaving the end of the state under the sign of cosmopolitan purpose.

Three observations may be drawn. First, economics becomes the realm of the
unfettered will in the competition of all against all. It is an amoral activity which
appears in the catalogue of technical skills under practical reason. As an unfettered
will economics is the site reflecting Kant's possessive individualism with the
privileged position of the infinite appropriator, yet, with a long run moral aim, the
underlying calculus of pleasure/pain, or sensibility, contributes to the Idea of
perpetual peace.

Second, the state under the Idea of perpetual peace is given no practical end, only
form, in accord with the moral law, yet, as a sensible entity it has an end.
Determining the particular end from the general is the function of judgement in
Kant's system. This returns one again to the sensible realm as a question of pleasure
and pain, but now beyond economics as culture.

Third, judgement works by breaking the self-will. This is fundamentally a power
relation predicated on a will-not-to-will which includes all individuals as sensible
entities, but excludes the supersensible Master. Thus, the Kantian will has implicit
in it a nihilism which Nietzsche later identifies as the will-to-will.

'Good Taste'

The problem of liberal theory rests on how one arrives at aesthetic judgements in reference to the calculus of the senses, and how one arrives at the teleological judgement of ends. Kant begins with the proposition of pleasure and pain, which he has earlier rejected as a transcendental principle of reason. He is bound by this rejection, yet the sensible as principle will be given a form of universality having a space not unlike that of the supersensible Ideas, which are not known-in-themselves, but are necessary. What must be overcome is the subjectiveness of pleasure and pain, that is their interested aspect, so that one is given over to the paradoxical notion of disinterested interestedness. A similar shift occurs in teleological judgements with respect to the idea of purposiveless purposiveness.

In each case the starting-point is from 'taste', which was central to the eighteenth-century view of culture. While taste rests on the pleasurable as it is experienced sensually, it is apprehended in a separate exercise of judgement. This judgement becomes an aesthetic judgement in its pure form as a subjective judgement, and not an objective determinate judgement, as there is no corresponding concept. Yet the universal aspect of the judgement is asserted by Kant's arguing that the perspective outside of the self employed by the judge is, in principle, common to all rational individuals. Thus taste has its roots in the realm of common sense, and as 'good taste' defines higher culture and a higher faculty. Thus it shares both aspects of disinterestedness and purposiveness in Kant's schema.

A number of conclusions can be drawn from this. In _Truth and Method_[5] Gadamer sees in common sense the link to the _sensus communis_ of the Roman antiquity, and the medieval period. Politics and morality are brought together to form a community on the basis of the 'moral feeling' of taste. By shifting the foundation of politics to the sensual realm from the strictly rational capacity of the understanding, Kant's argument presents a more plausible version of how individuals under liberal mythology leave the state of nature. However, the cost is to move the central principle of the political towards the aesthetic from the understanding. Gadamer's resistance to this sends his thought back to Aristotle, although this is itself a dead-end, for Aristotle's citizen would hardly find life in the modern world possible.

The aesthetic is further emphasized by Kant's use of 'good taste'. This continues the rupture of politics from reason, and extends the rupture towards the moral. Kant maintained the relation of the aesthetic to the moral by arguing in the _Critique_ that the relation was by analogy, but Kant is opening up the way for the split of morals from a politics that rests on aesthetics. The schema is played out today.

Neurotic Liberalism

Kant would find this schism unacceptable, yet a similar situation is present in taking the argument from moral feeling. Following Heidegger's analysis in _The Basic_

Problems of Phenomenology[6] the moral feeling in Kant is described as arising from the sensibility of the individual to oneself as a person. It is the way the self reveals itself to itself through the feeling of the self. Thus it is at once existential, and aesthetic. Heidegger distinguishes this feeling in Kant's empirical ego, from the thinking and knowing ego. This feeling, when brought in line, or in conformity with the moral law, establishes the person as a person, and the unity of the thinking, moral and aesthetic egos. This, Heidegger notes, is called 'respect' in Kant's schema, which is at the basis of the Kantian theory of personality: that is the respect for the individual as a self-determining end. From the perspective of Heidegger's ontology the analysis remains on the ontical level, but a level suited to the political uses for respect. For example, in the *Groundwork of the Metaphysics of Morals*, the concept of duty requires acting out of reverence, or respect for the laws.[7] A respect, Kant adds, that comes from a rational concept, and hence is self-produced, and not a fear induced from the outside. Kant here is not Hobbes, but he is not far off. Indeed, Kant and Hobbes are mirror-images because fear is internalized with the production of the subject, thereby re-creating the antagonism of the 'unsocial social' world – a form of inner check.

The shifting of the paradox of fear/respect to the level of pure practical reason may solve the problem for the perfectly rational individual by making him or her neurotic, but willing. But more fundamentally it drives the argument back to the problem of the unknowability of either the end or the means of reverence. This is analogous to the problem of why individuals joined together, and why they obey the law referred to earlier as the problem of common sense. For Kant, common sense allows individuals to judge disinterestedly their interest, hence allowing them to sensibly form political collectivities. It also allows individuals to judge the pleasing and displeasing aspect of works of art when taste becomes 'good taste'. In other words, individuals can make judgements on objects as beautiful or sublime. These judgements are paradigmatic of what it means to be civilized in the Kantian schema, thereby establishing the political role of law.

The Citizen as Voyeur

While the distinctions drawn in eighteenth-century aesthetics between the beautiful and sublime are often arbitrary, beauty may refer to the site where individuals encounter themselves as an end either in nature, or in the social world. To phrase it differently, the beautiful object tells us something of the essence of individuals. The sublime, on the other hand, treats of the incomprehensible, of the transcendental to humans, hence the ability to instill fear. It is more the area of the existential. Kant was most comfortable with the beautiful or the sublime in the natural world. In politics these ideas appear most forcibly in the initial proposition of the *Idea for a Universal History with a Cosmopolitan Purpose* when natural capacities 'sooner or later [will] be developed completely and in conformity with their end' in accordance with the 'teleological theory of nature …'.[8] Here the design of nature is outside of individuals giving rise to the 'two will' problem. In pursuing enlightenment, the individual is given the task of 'emerging from his self-induced immaturity'[9] through freedom and the exercise of the will. However, the design is only perceived from the position of the spectator by observing the beauty and terror of God's works, or by observing human works reflecting God's will. From the position of the spectator, the individual assumes the role of the passive individual willing-not-to-will.

Hannah Arendt's interpretation of Kant rests on the role of the spectator in witnessing the public event of politics. She references Kant's attitude to the French Revolution, where meaning is attributed to the event precisely because of 'his disinterestedness, his non-participation, his non-involvement'.[10] Kant's aversion to revolution on *a priori* grounds vanishes once the event becomes that of a natural phenomenon to be observed. The causal chain of the natural world, in this case the necessity of revolution, is respected along with the freedom of the pen now placed safely in the intelligible realm. We are very close at this point to the 'dead power' at the heart of liberalism where the events are assigned meaning, and controlled solely by the judge's eye.

The Ideology of Genius

In the ideological schema related here, the 'passivity' of the citizen as voyeur is contrasted to the 'activity' in the realm of free beauty created by the 'genius'. Kant's genius is no product of history, being a gift of nature, but as a part of nature genius may express the design of nature. This expression of design by the genius, as Hans Saner points out in *Kant's Political Philosophy*, 'as a whole lies in time'.[11] The artistic vision of the creative imagination by existing in time directly challenges the claims of the supersensible ideas to the regulation of human conduct. Further, the description of genius in terms of the unregulated, or unlawful, 'play' of the faculties contrasts sharply with the rule of the moral personality. The creative genius also challenges the disinterested stance of the judging spectator in the very creation of the object or end for which judgements are to be formed. The unlawful lawfulness of play differs, then, from other Kantian paradoxes to the extent that the claims of universality attached to the sensible realm are made known through the judgement of the work of art. This element of finality is lacking in the Ideas themselves. Finality only exists in the realm of power.

The political implications of the creative genius, and the concept of play have, then, full impact in reformulating the ideology at the basis of aesthetics in postmodern thought. This can be seen in Marcuse's use of play in a Freudian-Marxian sense, and Gadamer's use in a hermeneutical sense; each tearing apart Kant, yet remaining with him. Genius acts to 'valorize' both the left and right under the nihilism of artistic codes.

The Aesthetic Contract

Kant was caught in the spider's web of the realm of aesthetics and the role of the creative imagination in politics. The foundation and end of government expressed through the image of the state of nature is more fundamentally a myth than an idea of reason. It is the product of the creative imagination which supplies not only the beginning and end, but the fear upon which the will is brought to obedience. This fear or reverence falls under the category of the sublime. The sublime creates fear, but fear at a distance which checks the will by bringing it under the transcendental authority of the Idea of Nature. A similar awe is present in the Hobbesian sovereign, and by delegation in the judges of the state. This type of fear remains passive as long as the citizen is passive in internalizing the higher authority. Once active the fear gives way to violence and rebellion which directly threatens the state and the individual, and hence is not countenanced by Kant. To express this in a different fashion, the sublime rests on the existential and, in particular, on the fear of death or nihilation. The imagination, in making present what is not, is precisely the vehicle for communicating this fear.

Thus Kantian liberal politics rests on two basic myths. The first, expressed in the analogy of beauty, is the moral good will which creates the idea of the harmony of all based on the individual as an end. This is the ideological basis of the social contract. The second, expressed in the analogy of the sublime, threatens the individual and society with annihilation. This is the ideological basis of obedience. Both myths are present and rely on the concept of judgement. Though Kant favours the myth of the good, modern thought has used both ideologies in the control of the dying social by the coercive culture created by this aesthetic.

Nauseous Allegories

The last days of liberalism are mirrored in Kant's depiction of the 'Last Day of Judgement'. The last judgement, in its apocalyptic form, represents final justice as well as the end of time. Kant treats of this Idea in the short article entitled 'The end of all things', written in 1794. The end of time corresponds for Kant to the end of the sensible world which we know from Kant's earlier critique represents the bounds of knowledge. Thus the end of all time, as the cessation of time, cannot be thought of except as a supersensible Idea within time. Kant reiterates that the individual's end, in a supersensible sense, is the moral end of pure practical reason which by its very nature is never obtained in time though it regulates existence in time. Because we cannot know of eternity, and hence know of the Last Judgement, Kant carries the judgement into the sensible world as an everyday event in the long run progress of morality towards perpetual peace. Hence the necessity in the political realm of the judge to the long run moral progress.

But to the extent that the individual is a sensible creature who lives in time, the thought of annihilation or death occurs to her or him.

> In point of fact, men, not without reason, feel the burden of their existence even though they themselves are the cause of it. The reason for this seems to me to lie in the fact that in the progress of the human race the cultivation of talents, art, and taste (with their consequence, luxury) naturally precedes the development of morality ...[12]

These are two conclusions. The first is to see in the progress of culture the progress of the individual as a basis for the moral state. This is the basis of postmodern liberalism's claim to the moral and just, but it is sublated by the second element of this ideology. The second conclusion is to see in the desires and their satisfaction the process of nihilation at the root of sensibility. Individuals as creatures in time live through successive nihilations, and as members of the human community reach their own nihilation. We enter here the self-liquidation in the nihilism of Kant's aesthetic liberalism.

At this point, we meet Kant's reluctance to think through this nihilation which he calls a 'purely negative [concept]'. Kant admits that 'The thought is sublime in its terror ... it is even required to be interwoven in a wondrous way with common human reason, because this notion of eternity is encountered in all reasoning peoples in all times ...' Yet faced with the implications of this nihilism, he retreats. This is how he expresses it in 'The end of all things': 'There is something appalling in this thought because it leads, as it were, to the brink of an abyss, and for him who sinks into it, no return is possible.'

Kant identifies how the nihilism at the core of aesthetic liberalism gives rise to a vision of the postmodern world that has lived out the 'logic' of the *Critique*. Part of this future is sketched in Kant's footnote commenting on the implications of the negative. This he describes as giving rise to 'inimical, partly nauseous allegories'. These are the 'allegory' of 'life' as an inn where we are soon to be replaced by a new traveller, a penitentiary, a lunatic asylum and as a privy. Taking these 'allegories' in turn, the inn is a symbol of mortality, the penitentiary of the judged individual, the lunatic asylum of the use of unreason or the imagination, and the privy of the body. Each is a logical implication of the ideology at the heart of the 'good will'. Each is denied by Kant under the heading of the 'perverse end of all things'. Each depicts an aspect of existence forced back into the 'obscurity' where the transcendental imagination had found it. Each places existence outside the good taste of society in the writings of authors like the Marquis de Sade or in the vision of poets like Blake. Each illustrates the aesthetic code of post-liberal politics in the postmodern condition.

Kant has enucleated the fundamental abstraction inherent in the liberal concept of power. Being predicated on judgement, power is able to remove itself from the living force of the society to assume the masque of the spectator. Removed from the body, power is set against the body; removed from the will, it is directed against the will; removed from the imagination, it is hostile to the imagination. The citizen is caught up within this absence, for in following common sense the individual self-liquidates – all in the name of good taste: not an unreasonable description of the last days of liberalism.

Notes

1. Immanuel Kant, *The Critique of Judgement*, transl. J. C. Meredith, Oxford University Press, London, 1952.
2. Martin Heidegger, *Kant and the Problem of Metaphysics*, Indiana University Press, Bloomington, 1962.
3. Immanuel Kant, *Kant's Political Writings*, ed. H. Reiss, Cambridge University Press, Cambridge, 1977, p. 46.
4. *Ibid.*, p. 45.
5. Hans-Georg Gadamer, *Truth and Method*, The Seabury Press, New York, 1975. For a very interesting study of Gadamer, Arendt and Kant, see Ronald Beiner, *Political Judgement*, University of Chicago Press, Chicago, 1983.
6. Martin Heidegger, *The Basic Problems of Phenomenology*, Indiana University Press, Bloomington, 1982, pp. 131–2.
7. Immanuel Kant, *Groundwork for the Metaphysics of Morals*, Harper Torch, New York, 1964, p. 68.
8. Reiss, *Kant's Political Writings*, p. 42.
9. *Ibid.*, p. 54.
10. Hannah Arendt, *Lectures on Kant's Political Philosophy*, ed. Ronald Beiner, University of Chicago Press, Chicago, 1982, p. 54.
11. Hans Saner, *Kant's Political Philosophy*, University of Chicago Press, Chicago, 1978, p. 298.
12. Immanuael Kant, *On History*, Bobbs-Merrill, Indianapolis, IN, 1963, pp. 74–86.

8 □ *The Fall of the Legislator*

Zygmunt Bauman

From at least the seventeenth century and well into the twentieth, the writing elite of Western Europe and its footholds on other continents considered its own way of life as a radical break in universal history. Virtually unchallenged faith in the superiority of its own mode over all alternative forms of life – contemporaneous or past – allowed it to take itself as the reference point for the interpretation of the *telos* of history. This was a novelty in the experience of objective time; for most of the history of Christian Europe, time-reckoning was organized around a fixed point in the slowly receding past. Now, while rendering the thus far local, Christian calendar, well nigh universal, Europe set the reference point of objective time in motion, attaching it firmly to its own thrust towards colonizing the future in the same way as it had colonized the surrounding space.

The self-confidence of the enlightened elite of Europe was projected on adjacent categories of mankind, in measures strictly proportional to the perceived closeness of kinship. Thus the group distinguished by an enlightened way of life was seen as decidedly superior in relation to their own ignorant and superstitious working classes or villagers. Together, educated and uneducated Europeans constituted a race which had already situated itself on the side of history that other races were – at best – only struggling to reach. Rather than deriving its own self-confidence from its belief in progress, the educated elite forged the idea of progress from the untarnished experience of its own superiority. Rather than drawing its missionary, proselytizing zeal from an uncritical belief in the infinite perfectibility of man, the educated elite coined the idea of the pliability of human nature, its capacity for being moulded and improved by society, out of the experience of its own role in the disciplining, training, educating, healing, punishing and reforming aimed at categories other than itself. Collective experience of a category cast in a 'gardener' role in relation to all other categories, was recast as a theory of history.

As if following Marx's methodological precept about using the anatomy of man as the key to the anatomy of ape, the educated elite used its own mode of life, or

From Bauman, Z., *Legislators and Interpreters*, Basil Blackwell, Oxford, 1987, pp. 110–26.

the mode of life of that part of the world over which it presided (or thought it presided), as the benchmark against which to measure and classify other forms of life – past or present – as retarded, underdeveloped, immature, incomplete or deformed, maimed, distorted and otherwise inferior stages or versions of itself. Its own form of life, ever more often called 'modernity', came to denote the restless, constantly moving pointer of history; from its vantage point, all the other known or guessed forms appeared as past stages, side-shoots or culs-de-sac. The many competing conceptualizations of modernity, invariably associated with a theory of history, agreed on one point: they all took the form of life developed in parts of the Western world as the 'given', 'unmarked' unit of the binary opposition which relativized the rest of the world and the rest of historical times as the problematic, 'marked' side, understandable only in terms of its distinction from the Western pattern of development, taken as normal. The distinction was seen first and foremost as a set of absences – as a lack of the attributes deemed indispensable for the identity of most advanced age.

One such conceptualization is the vision of history as the unstoppable march of *les Lumières*; a difficult, but eventually victorious struggle of Reason against emotions or animal instincts, science against religion and magic, truth against prejudice, correct knowledge against superstition, reflection against uncritical existence, rationality against affectivity and the rule of custom. Within such a conceptualization, the modern age defined itself as, above all, the kingdom of Reason and rationality; the other forms of life were seen, accordingly, as wanting in both respects. This was the first and most basic of the conceptualizations providing modernity with its self-definition. It was also the most persistent and clearly the most favoured by those whose job it was to conceptualize. It posited, after all, the conceptualizers themselves as in charge of the levers of history and presented them, strategically, as the most important and powerful agents of change. This conceptualization, as we remember, was already implicit in the thinking of *les philosophes*; it found its full expression in the writings of Condorcet and other ideologists; it was codified by Comte and since then taken as a canon and obligatory framework of the Whig version of history; it reached its culminating point and fullest elaboration in Weber's vision of history as progressive rationalization, and of modern society as a radical break which disclosed its own past as, above all, the long dominion of irrational conduct.

To Marx, as Marshall Berman recently reminded us in his beautiful and profound analysis of modernity, ours was the age in which 'everything solid melts into air, everything sacred is profaned'; an age of the breathtaking pace of development, of the multiplication of material wealth, of the ever increasing mastery of humankind over its natural environment, of the universal emancipation from all, real or imaginary, restrictions which constrained and hampered human creative potential for an interminably long part of history. This, to Marx, was the effect of the sudden eruption of the material means of mastery over nature, together with the ability and the will to use them; that, in its turn, was the outcome of a new organization of the productive effort of humanity – one in which the productive activities of individuals had been rhythmicized, routinized, co-ordinated, subjected to a purposeful design, supervised and put to the task of operating the tools, the power of which was no longer restricted by the limited capacity (and so the horizon) of their petty owners. To Marx, the modern age would eventually discard the few remaining limits to practical mastery over nature; the means of production, he insisted, were already 'social' in their character, and the private character of ownership, however grand in scale yet short of universal, will be the last 'solidity' to melt into air. 'Human freedom' (identified with freedom from necessity, identified in its turn with Nature) would then be complete.

Not all conceptualizations, of course, sang such unqualified praise of modernity. Towards the end of the nineteenth century, in particular, the modern age appeared to many a mixed blessing. The great achievement of humanity, no doubt, but at a price; a heavy price, perhaps. It became increasingly clear to the educated elite that the anticipated kingdom of Reason had been slow to materialize. More importantly, it was somewhat less clear that it ever would. The kingdom of Reason was always at bottom the rule of its spokesmen. Such a rule was now a remote and receding probability. Humanities failed to humanize, that is, the designs of social order and the strategies for their implementation were produced and administered by categories other than the humanizers themselves, and the unity between the growing power of the 'civilized' part of mankind and the growing centrality of its civilizers had been broken. Conceptualization had acquired a dramatic tinge; the images of historical progress became more and more reminiscent of a Greek tragedy, where nothing is ever achieved without a sacrifice, and the sacrifice may be as painful as the achievement is enjoyable.

The Faustian man of Nietzsche and his followers was carved in the image of the modern age, proud of its power and its superiority, considering all other human forms as inferior to itself. But the Faustian man could no longer – unlike his philosophic or entrepreneurial predecessors – casually refer his own self-confidence to the inexorable and omnipotent powers of spiritual or material progress; he had to carry modernity, this greatest achievement of the human race, on his own shoulders. The Faustian man was a romantic, not a classicist or positivist. He was the maker of history, not its product; he had to make history against all odds, forcing it to submit to his will and not necessarily counting on its willingness to surrender. History remained what it was to its Whig courtiers: the triumph of the daring, the courageous, the insightful, the profound, the clear-headed over the slavish, cowardly, superstitious, muddled and ignorant. But the triumph was not now guaranteed – particularly not by forces other than the wilful effort of prospective victors. This struggle will be costly, as all struggles are. In all conquests, there are victims as well as victors. The Faustian man must reconcile himself to the need for marching over the bodies of the weak. And he is a Faustian man because he does.

Another dramatic vision of modernity has been inspired by Freud. This one depicts modernity as a time when the 'reality principle' attains domination over the 'pleasure principle', and when people, as a result, trade off part of their freedom (and happiness) for a degree of security, grounded in a hygienically safe, clean and peaceful environment. The trade-off may be profitable, but it comes about as a product of the suppression of 'natural' drives and the imposition of patterns of behaviour which ill fit human predispositions and offer only oblique outlets for instincts and passions. Suppression is painful, it leaves psychological wounds which are difficult to heal. The price of modernity is the high incidence of psychotic and neurotic ailments; civilization breeds its own discontents and sets the individual in a permanent – potential or overt – conflict with society.

Shortly after *Civilization and its Discontents* appeared, sending waves of shock and admiration far and wide, young Norbert Elias decided to subject Freud's hypotheses, presented as they were in intuitive and ideal–typical form, to the test of historical research. Elias's decision resulted in the remarkable *Civilizing Process*, which opened new horizons for socio-historical study by reaching a heretofore unexplored and neglected kind of historical source and bringing 'daily life' into the focus of historical investigation. Elias demonstrated that the 'suppression of instincts' which Freud deduced from the nature of mature modernity was in fact a historical process which could be pinned down to specific time, place and socio-cultural figurations. One of the many brilliant observations of Elias's study was the idea that the successful culmination of the process consists of the historical episode of suppression being forgotten, pseudo-rational legitimations being supplied for newly introduced patterns and the whole historical form of life being 'naturalized'. A radical interpretation of Elias's study would see it as a direct attack upon Weber's Whiggish vision of modernity as an era of rationality. The powers which brought about modern society and preside over its reproduction have been denied the sanction of Reason. The essentially progressive character of their accomplishment has not, however, been put in question.

A complex hate–love attitude towards modernity saturates Simmel's vision of urban society, closely related to the somewhat later interpretation Benjamin gave to Baudelaire's seminal insights. The combined image is one of tragedy – of twisted dialectics of inextricable contradictions: the absolute manifesting itself only in the particularity of individuals and their encounters; the permanent hiding behind fleeting episodes, the normal behind the unique. Above all, the drama of modernity derives from the 'tragedy of culture', the human inability to assimilate cultural products, over-abundant because of the unbound creativity of the human spirit. Once set in motion, cultural processes acquire their own momentum, develop their own logic, and spawn new multiple realities confronting individuals as an outside, objective world, too powerful and distant to be 'resubjectivized'. The richness of objective culture results therefore in the cultural poverty of individual human beings, who now act according to a principle *omnia habentes, nihil possidentes* (as Günther S. Stent inverted the famous principle of St Francis).[1] A frantic search for objects to be appropriated vainly seeks to replace the repossession of lost meanings. Simmel bewails the advent of 'partial intellectuals' (a term later coined by Foucault) and the passing of a time when the erudite *Principles of Political Economy* were the common property of all enlightened contemporaries and extensively reviewed by such 'non-specialists' as Dickens or Ruskin. This is a vision of modernity as seen through the eyes of a capital city intellectual, dreaming of a continuation of the role bequeathed by *les philosophes* under conditions which render it all but impossible; conditions brought about by nothing else but the tremendous success of the philosophers' legacy.

The above is a very sketchy, simplified and in no way complete list of the visions of modernity which summoned enough following and made enough impact on the public consciousness to be recognized as traditional or classic. They differ from each other; sometimes they stand in sharp opposition to each other. For many decades the differences and oppositions overshadowed any common features and dominated social scientific debate. Only quite recently, owing to a new cognitive perspective, have the differences begun to look considerably less important – as no more than family quarrels. What the new perspective made salient, on the other hand, was exactly that close kinship bond between the apparently antagonistic views, which at the present stage of the debate would tend to overshadow the differences.

The family bond seems to have been constituted by at least three shared characteristics.

First, all listed visions and most of their contemporary alternatives or variants assumed, whether explicitly or implicitly, the irreversible character of the changes modernity signified or brought in its wake. They might have been enthusiastic, caustic or downright critical regarding the balance between good and evil within the form of life associated with modern society, but they hardly ever questioned the 'superiority' of modernity in the sense of subordinating, marginalizing, evicting or annihilating its pre-modern alternatives. None of the visions entailed (at least not organically) doubts as to the eventual ascendancy of modernity; most assumed the inevitability of such ascendancy. (Although this was not necessarily in the deterministic sense; it was not in the sense that the advent of modernity was historically inescapable, but in the sense that – once it has emerged in one part of the world – its domination, or perhaps universalization, would be unstoppable.) Seeing modernity as the highest point of development encouraged the interpretation of preceding social forms as describing or measuring their distance from modernity, as manifest in the idea of developing countries.

Secondly, all the listed visions conceived of modernity in processual terms: as an essentially unfinished project. Modernity was open-ended, and inevitably so; indeed, the open-endedness was seen as the paramount, perhaps defining, attribute of modernity. Against the intrinsic mobility of modernity, the pre-modern forms appeared stagnant, organized around the mechanism of equilibration and stability, almost devoid of history. This optical effect resulted from choosing modernity as the vantage point from which to contemplate features of alternative societies; and choosing to consider modernity as the historically, or logically, later form. This choice enclosed and objectified other social forms, and prompted them to be perceived as finished, complete objects – a perception which had been articulated as their intrinsic timelessness. To return to the visions of modernity: they all tried to capture the process of ongoing transformations *in statu nascendi*; they were, in a sense, mid-career reports, conscious of describing a movement with a destination not yet fully known, one that could only be anticipated. In the vision of modernity, only the starting-point was more or less firmly fixed. The rest, precisely because of its underdetermined character, appeared as a field of design, action and struggle.

Thirdly, all visions were 'inside' views of modernity. Modernity was a phenomenon with a rich pre-history but with nothing visible beyond it, nothing which could relativize or objectivize the phenomenon itself, enclose it as a finished episode of − by the same token − confined, limited significance. As such, the way this 'insider' experience of modernity had been articulated supplied the frame of reference for the perception of non-modern forms of life. At the same time, however, no outside vantage point was available as a frame of reference for the perception of modernity itself. In a sense, modernity was − in those visions − self-referential and self-validating.

It is precisely this last circumstance which has recently changed; its change could not but affect the rest of the family resemblances which united the traditional, or classic, visions of modernity. To put it correctly, the change brought to the surface the very presence of the family traits, and their limiting role, now seen as responsible for the historical relativity of the classic visions. What has happened in recent years could be articulated as the appearance of a vantage point which allows the view of modernity itself as an enclosed object, an essentially complete product, an episode of history, with an end as much as a beginning.

Such a vantage point has been supplied by the postmodernist debate. On the face of it, this debate is just another name for the discourse organized around a family of notions, of which the most popular and widely commented upon are the concepts of post-industrial or post-capitalist societies. Whatever the connections and similarities, the differences, however, are formidable. The idea of post-industrial society does not necessarily constitute a break with the way in which modernity was traditionally conceived. More often than not, this idea refers simply to internal transformations within the Western type of civilization, allegedly reconstituting its continuing superiority in a novel fashion and on a changing socio-economic basis. Far from undermining such a superiority, the transformations pointed out as symptomatic of the post-industrial or post-capitalist stage reinforce the image of the Western socio-cultural system as a pinnacle of development or a most advanced form of human society which other forms either approach or are bound to recognize as superior. The post-industrial discourse emphasizes also the continuity of development; the post-industrial is seen as a natural product of industrial development, as a next phase following the success of the preceding one − and, in a sense, fulfilling the promise and the potential contained in its own past.

It is, on the other hand, the postmodernist discourse that looks back at its immediate past as a closed episode, as a movement in a direction unlikely to be followed, as perhaps even an aberration, the pursuit of a false track, a historical error now to be rectified. In doing so, the postmodernist debate does not necessarily oppose itself to the factual propositions construed within the post-industrial discourse; the frequent confusion notwithstanding, the two debates do not share their respective subject-matters. The post-industrial discourse is about the changes in the socio-economic system of a society which recognizes itself as 'modern' in the sense spelled out above: the changes discussed do not imply that society needs to stop identifying itself in such a way. The postmodernist discourse, on the other hand, is about the credibility of 'modernity' itself as a self-designation of Western civilization, whether industrial or post-industrial, capitalist or post-capitalist. It implies that the self-ascribed attributes contained in the idea of modernity do not hold today, perhaps did not hold yesterday either. The postmodernist debate is about the self-consciousness of Western society, and the grounds (or the absence of grounds) for such consciousness.

The concept of postmodernism was coined first; introduced as a designation of the rebellion against functionalist, scientifically grounded, rational architecture, it was soon taken over and extended to assimilate the profound changes of direction visible all over the territory of Western art. It proclaimed the end of the exploration of the ultimate truth of the human world or human experience, the end of the political or missionary ambitions of art, the end of dominant style, of artistic canons, of interest in the aesthetic grounds of artistic self-confidence and objective boundaries of art. The absence of grounds, the futility of all attempts to draw the limits of artistic phenomena in an objective fashion, the impossibility of legislating the rules of a true art as distinct from non-art or bad art, were the ideas which gestated first within the discourse of artistic culture (much as two hundred years earlier the conquest of the cultural field preceded the expansion of *les sociétés de pensée* on to the area of political and social philosophy). Only later did the notion of postmodernism, originally confined to the history of arts, begin to expand. It had opened the eyes of intellectual observers to those features shared by the transformations in contemporary arts and the fascinating shifts of attention, anti-traditionalist rebellion, and strikingly heretical new paradigms competing for domination in philosophy and the philosophically informed social sciences. Eyes were opened to the similarity between the erosion of 'objective grounds' in art and the sudden popularity of post-Wittgensteinian and post-Gadamerian hermeneutics in social sciences, or the vitriolic attacks of the 'new pragmatists' against Cartesian–Lockean–Kantian tradition in modern philosophy. It became increasingly plausible that these apparently disparate phenomena were manifestations of the same process.

It was this process, or rather the conditions under which it was taking place, that has been called here postmodernity (as distinct from postmodernism, which refers to the collection of works of art or intellectual products created under the conditions, or within the period, of postmodernity). Unlike the notion of a post-industrial society, the concept of postmodernity refers to a distinct quality of intellectual climate, to a distinctly new meta-cultural stance, to a distinct self-awareness of the era. One of the basic, if not *the* basic, elements of this self-awareness is the realization that modernity is over; that modernity is a closed chapter of history, which can now be contemplated in its entirety, with retrospective knowledge of its practical accomplishments as much as its theoretical hopes.

Thanks to this element of the new self-awareness called postmodernity, modernity, serving thus far as the Marxian 'anatomy of man', has been for the first time relegated to the position of 'the ape', which discloses the unsuspected, or unduly neglected aspects of its anatomy when examined with the *ex post facto* wisdom of postmodernity. This wisdom rearranges our knowledge of modernity and redistributes the importance assigned to its various characteristics. It also brings into relief such aspects of modernity as went unnoticed when looked upon from the inside of the modern era simply because of their then uncontested status and consequent taken-for-grantedness; which, however, suddenly burst into vision precisely because their absence in the later, postmodern, period makes them problematic. Such aspects, first and foremost, are those which bear relation to modernity's self-confidence; its conviction of its own superiority over alternative forms of life, seen as historically or logically 'primitive'; and its belief that its pragmatic advantage over pre-modern societies and cultures, far from being a historic coincidence, can be shown to have objective, absolute foundations and universal validity.

Indeed, this is exactly the kind of belief which the consciousness of the postmodern era is most conspicuously lacking; all the more striking is the solid presence of such a belief in the self-consciousness of modernity. From the postmodern perspective the episode of modernity appears to have been, more than anything else, the era of certainty.

It is so because the most poignant of the postmodern experiences is the *lack* of self-confidence. It is perhaps debatable whether the philosophers of the modern era ever articulated to everybody's satisfaction the foundations of the objective superiority of Western rationality, logic, morality, aesthetics, cultural precepts, rules of civilized life, etc. The fact is, however, that they never stopped looking for such an articulation and hardly ever ceased to believe that the search would bring – must bring – success. The postmodern period is distinguished by abandoning the search itself, having convinced itself of its futility. Instead, it tries to reconcile itself to a life under conditions of permanent and incurable uncertainty; a life in the presence of an unlimited quantity of competing forms of life, unable to prove their claims to be grounded in anything more solid and binding than their own historically shaped conventions.

Modernity, by comparison, seems never to have entertained similar doubts as to the universal grounding of its status. The hierarchy of values imposed upon the world administered by the north-western tip of the European peninsula was so firm, and supported by powers so enormously overwhelming, that for a couple of centuries it remained the baseline of the world vision, rather than an overtly debated problem. Seldom brought to the level of consciousness, it remained the all-powerful 'taken-for-granted' of the era. It was evident to everybody except the blind and the ignorant that the West was superior to the East, white to black, civilized to crude, cultured to uneducated, sane to insane, healthy to sick, man to woman, normal to criminal, more to less, riches to austerity, high productivity to low productivity, high culture to low culture. All these 'evidences' are now gone. Not a single one remains unchallenged. What is more, we can see now that they did not hold in separation from each other; they made sense together, as manifestations of the same power complex, the same power structure of the world, which retained credibility as long as the structure remained intact, but were unlikely to survive its demise.

The structure has been, moreover, increasingly sapped by the resistance and the struggle of categories cast (practically by the power structure, theoretically by the associated value hierarchy) as inferior. It is the measure of the effectiveness of such resistance that no power today feels able to claim an objective superiority for the form of life it represents; the most it can do is to demand, following Ronald Reagan's example, the right to 'defend our way of life'. All absolute superiorities met a fate similar to the one perceptively observed by Ian Miles and John Irvine regarding the West over East domination: as far as the objections of the 'underdeveloped' part of the world go, 'with increasing global instability, this claim may become more than a moral plea: it may be enforceable through political or economic action'.[2] Indeed it may, if it has not been already, and in view of this possibility the philosophical pursuit of the absolute foundations of Western superiority must sound increasingly hollow: the fact which was to be explained has disappeared.

How different this situation appears when compared with the intellectual and moral comfort of uncontested domination, which, as Richard L. Rubenstein recently observed, made the self-consciousness of the modern era, from Calvin to Darwin, so confident in professing its moral evaluations masquerading as statements of objective truth:

> Darwin's vision resembles a Biblical theology of history: the plight of those who suffer must be viewed from the larger perspective of the Great Plan. In the Bible, God is the Author of the Plan; in Darwin it is 'Nature'. In both, history derives its meaning from the fate of the fortunate few. Of greatest importance is the fact that both Calvinism and Darwinism provide a cosmic justification for the felicity of the few and the misery of the many.[3]

With the many no longer accepting obediently their misery, even the felicitous few do not seem to have much demand for cosmic justification of their felicity. Practical and effective means of defending their felicity against rising threats seem to possess more urgency and promise more benefit.

The 'shrinking' of Europe, and the humbling of the values with which it grew used to identifying itself, is not, of course, a phenomenon reducible solely to changes in the world's balance of power. The changes are real enough (and large enough at least to problematize the previously taken-for-granted European superiority), but by themselves they would not generate a crisis of confidence in the 'absolute foundations', if it were not for the dwindling confidence of those who once theorized European superiority. Those who once scanned the world as the field to be cultivated by Europe, armed as it was with Reason, tend to speak today of the 'failed' or 'yet unfulfilled' project of modernity. (Modernity, once the 'background' one does not reflect upon, has suddenly been perceived as a project now that its attributes have begun to disappear one by one.) In the same way as the intellectual climates which preceded it, the contemporary crisis of confidence is an intellectual construction; it reflects, as before, the collective experience of those who articulate the self-identities of their times and societies; the only category of people which describes and defines itself, and which cannot describe or define itself in any other fashion but through describing and defining societies of which it is a part.

The pessimistic and defensive mood of the intellectuals, which presents itself as the crisis of European civilization, becomes understandable if seen against the difficulties the intellectuals encounter whenever attempting to fulfil their traditional role; to wit, the role which, with the advent of the modern era, they were trained – and trained themselves – to perform. The contemporary world is ill fitted for intellectuals as legislators; what appears to our consciousness as the crisis of civilization, or the failure of a certain historical project, is a genuine crisis of a particular role, and the corresponding experience of the collective redundancy of the category which specialized in playing this role.

One aspect of this crisis is the absence of sites from which authoritative statements of the kind the function of intellectual legislators involves could be made. The external limitations of European (or Western) power form only a part of the story. Another part, arguably more consequential still, comes from the growing independence of societal powers, within Western societies themselves, from the services intellectuals were able, eager and hoping to supply. This process has been well captured by Michel de Certeau:

> The old powers cleverly managed their 'authority' and thus compensated for the inadequacy of their technical and administrative apparatus; they were systems of clienteles, allegiances, 'legitimacies' etc. They sought, however, to make themselves more independent of the fluctuations of these fidelities through rationalization, the control and organization of space. As the result of this labour, the powers in our developed societies have at their disposal rather subtly and closely-knit procedures for the control of all social networks; these are the administrative and 'panoptic' systems of the police, the schools, health services, security etc. But they are slowly losing all credibility. They have more power and less authority.[4]

The point is that the state is not necessarily weaker from this demise of authority; it simply has found better, more efficient ways of reproducing and reinforcing its power; authority has become redundant, and the category specializing in servicing the reproduction of authority has become superfluous. Whoever insists on continuing to supply such services just because he or she is well qualified and efficient in producing them, must perceive the situation as critical.

The new technology of power and control also needs experts, of course; but the traditional intellectuals–legislators would hardly recognize this new demand as geared to their skills and ambitions. A witty but profound description of new power routines is contained in a recent study by Stanley Cohen:

> Orwell's terrible image of totalitarianism was the boot eternally trampling a human face. My vision of social control is much more mundane and assuring. It is the eternal case conference, diagnostic and allocation board or pre-sentence investigation unit. Serious-looking PhDs are sitting around a table. Each is studying the same computerized records, psychological profiles, case histories, neat files punched out on the word processor. The atmosphere is calm. Everyone present knows that no amount of criticism of individual treatment methods, no empirical research, no dodo-bird verdicts can slow the work down. The reverse is true. The more negative the results, the more manic and baroque the enterprise of selection becomes: more psychological tests, more investigation units, more pre-sentence reports, more post-sentence allocation centres, more contract forms, more case summaries, more referral notations, more prediction devices.[5]

There is hardly any way left leading from this self-propelling, self-perpetuating, self-divisive, autonomous and self-sufficient mechanism of expert knowledge, back to the kind of generalized expertise entailed by the traditional role of the legislators. From the vantage point of memory (or the 'unfulfilled project of modernity') realities of modern power routines may be seen, as they indeed are, as a bureaucratic displacement of the educated experts, as an act of expropriation – intellectuals having been deprived of the functions and entitlements they grew to see as their own.

There is also another factor exacerbating the intellectual lack of self-confidence. The hope that the modern, that is, the rationally administered, highly and increasingly productive, science-based world would eventually generate patterns of social organization fit to be universalized is fading, as the disenchantments accumulate: none of the patterns so far produced inside the modern world is likely ever to respond to the expectations born of intellectual practice. To put it a different way, no pattern so far produced, or likely to be produced as things go at the moment, promises to render the social world hospitable to intellectuals in their traditional role. This realization finds its outlet in the widespread feeling, admirably captured by Agnes Heller and her colleagues from the post-Lukácsian school, that the modern world faces a situation without good choices. The choice is, indeed, between the 'dictatorship over needs' in the Soviet-type system, and the consumer society of the West – one that has taken all the lids off human desires, and has left no space for the limiting role of values, breeding instead an incessantly growing volume of dissatisfaction parallel to the unstoppably swelling volume of commodities. In the system of the first type, the intellectuals have been, so to speak, liquidated as a class, that is, they have been collectively expropriated of their shared function of generating and promoting the values the state and its subjects are expected to implement and observe. Values are now articulated by the state itself, but above all they are (in practice, if not in theory) by-passed as the means of societal reproduction and all but replaced by techniques of coercion, manipulation and panoptic control. In a system of the second type, the practical effects on the position of the intellectuals are virtually the same, once all the obvious differences between the two systems are granted: values have been turned into attributes of commodities, and otherwise rendered irrelevant. It is therefore the mechanism of the market which now takes upon itself the role of the judge, the opinion-maker, the verifier of values. Intellectuals have been expropriated again. They have been displaced even in the area which for several centuries seemed to remain uncontestably their own monopolistic domain of authority – in the area of culture in general, 'high culture' in particular. In David Carrier's realistic assessment, 'aesthetic judgments directly imply economic judgments. To persuade us that a work [of art] is good, and so convince the art world [i.e. the sellers and buyers of art] that it is valuable, are two descriptions of one and the same action. Truth of criticism is relative to what art-world people believe ... theory becoming true when enough of these people believe it.'[6] The power of adjudication passing away from their hands, the intellectuals cannot but experience the world as one without values 'worthy of the name'. They would, on the whole, agree with the sombre premonition of Georg Simmel, jotted down on the eve of the First World War: 'unlike men in all these earlier epochs, we have been for some time now living without any shared ideal, even perhaps without any ideals at all'.[7] In such a mood, it takes a lot of courage to persist in presenting the values of one's choice as absolutely binding. Some would undoubtedly do just that, bracing themselves for the noble, yet not evidently effective, role of the voice crying in the wilderness. Many others would consider pragmatic modesty a more reasonable choice.

This has been a very preliminary list of hypotheses which may possibly account for the crisis of the traditional legislator's role (the crisis which seems to stand behind the current postmodernist discourse). Social reality hiding behind the notion of postmodernism, and, more importantly, the generic name of postmodernity, requires of course a much more thorough analysis.

Analysis of postmodernity, however conscientious, must bear the same 'until further notice', incomplete character, as the traditional theories of modernity once did; constructed from within modernity, they perceived the latter as a yet unfinished, and hence organically open-ended, process. Analysis of postmodernity cannot be anything more than a mid-career report. Its propositions must be tentative, particularly in view of the fact that the only solid and indubitable accomplishment of the postmodernist debate has been thus far the proclamation of the end of modernism; as to the rest, it is far from clear which among the many topics of the discourse signal lasting and irreversible tendencies, and which will soon find their place among the passing fads of a century notorious for its love of fashions. This uncertainty extends to the issue most crucial to our topic: the changing social location, and hence the role, of the intellectuals. There are many signs that the traditional role (performed or aspired to), portrayed by the metaphor of 'legislators', is being gradually replaced by the role best captured by the metaphor of 'interpreters'. Is this, however, an irrevocable transformation, or a momentary loss of nerve?

In the century or so immediately preceding the advent of modernity, Europe went through a similar period of uncertainty, and the proto-pragmatism of Mercenne or

Gassendi was its response. That period did not last long. Soon the philosophers joined forces in exorcizing the ghost of relativism that the proto-pragmatists tried to accommodate. The exorcism has gone on ever since, never fully successful. Descartes's *malin génie* has always been with us, in one disguise or another, his presence confirmed by ever renewed desperate attempts to annihilate the threat of relativism, as if no such attempts had ever been undertaken in the past. Modernity was lived in a haunted house. Modernity was an age of certainty, but it had its inner demons; its was the security of a besieged fortress, confidence of a commander of a so far, thank God, stronger army. Unlike the medieval certainty of the schoolmen, the certainty of modern philosophers constantly entailed the poignant awareness of the *problem* of relativism. It had to be an embattled, militant certainty. A momentary loss of vigilance could cost dearly. It did, occasionally.

Is the time we live in another such occasion? Or does it differ from the previous ones? Is the current crisis of certainty the effect of a temporary loss of vigilance? Is it a typical interim period which follows, and precedes, successive forms of societal organization? Or is it the first sighting of the shape of things to come?

None of these three possibilities can be accepted, or rejected, with confidence. At this stage, the best one can do is try to take stock of possible scenarios and their socially grounded probabilities.

Notes

Where full details are available in the Bibliography, references contain only essential information.

1. Cf. Günther S. Stent, *The Coming of the Golden Age: A view of the end of progress*, National History Press, New York, 1969.
2. Ian Miles and John Irvine, *The Poverty of Progress: Changing ways of life in industrial societies*, Pergamon Press, 1982, p. 2.
3. Richard L. Rubenstein, 'The elect and the preterite', in *Modernisation: The Humanist response to its promise and problems*, ed. Richard L. Rubenstein, Paragon House, Washington, DC, 1982, p. 183.
4. Michel de Certeau, *The Practice of Everyday Life*, 1984, p. 179.
5. Stanley Cohen, *Visions of Social Control: Crime, punishment and classification*, Polity Press, Oxford, 1985, p. 185.
6. David Carrier, 'Art and its market', in Richard Hertz, *Theories of Contemporary Art*, Prentice Hall, Englewood Cliffs, NJ, 1985, pp. 202, 204.
7. Georg Simmel, 'The conflict in modern culture', in *The Conflict in Modern Culture and Other Essays*, transl. K. Peter Etzkorn, Teachers College Press, New York, 1968, p. 15.

Part Three

Aesthetic and Cultural Practices

Introduction

In recent years, talk about the arts has become explicitly more interdisciplinary and eclectic. The most dedicated site for such talk is, of course, the academic institutions, the universities and the museums. Yet this is itself countered somewhat by the – often covert – appearance, within 'popular' or mass-mediatic forms, of so-called 'high' cultural matters: for instance, the cinema-going audience for Coppola's *Apocalypse Now* would certainly not all have been aware of Conrad's *Heart of Darkness* (a text read almost exclusively these days within the framework of a university syllabus), which the film extensively and randomly plundered for much of its symbolic substance. This dislocation and re-engagement between 'high art' and 'popular culture' is of central importance to aesthetic and cultural practices within the postmodern.

The great self-conscious moment of experimentalism in all the arts is found between the late nineteenth century and the early twentieth century; yet the great identification of this moment as a moment of cultural 'modernism' comes significantly later. Artists, in their diverse fields at the turn of the century, were doing what they had always done in those fields: working within traditions and looking for ways to extend them. Often (though clearly not always) such pursuits went on entirely independently of each other. Later, however, instead of the development of a discourse called 'the history of dance' and a separate one called 'the history of literature' and a further one designated as 'the history of music', and so on, we witness the development of a discourse which eventually became known in the 1970s as 'Cultural Studies'. This new university discourse is eclectic, and feels itself capable of addressing the separate aesthetic and cultural fields together. The basis for the establishment of Cultural Studies lies in an earlier moment in twentieth-century intellectual life when comparative and historical work in various fields began to relate the diverse aesthetic experiments of the early twentieth century to each other, thereby beginning the identification of a cultural practice known as 'modernism', a term which, prior to this moment, had a theological rather than an aesthetic significance.

The identification of modernism in this way goes hand in hand with the identification of a means for its analysis: semiotics. It is semiotics which, by translating all cultural practices into signifying practices and by considering all aesthetic events as 'signs', inaugurates the possibility, eagerly embraced, of Cultural Studies as a 'foundational philosophy'. Under this there lies a would-be 'democratising' impetus: to comment on dance, for instance, one no longer needs a

143

specialised knowledge of choreography, for the dance is a practice of signs, open to decoding and deciphering according to some basic semiotic procedures. The intellectual, previously locked in an esoteric and elitist engagement with the texts of high culture, is now, in this framework, just as competent to comment upon a war in the South Atlantic in the 1980s as she or he is to comment upon Milton's 1644 text *Areopagitica*, for everything is equally a war over meanings, a war carried out by the various strategies of signifying practices.

The position I have just described is modernist through and through. The semiotic discourse not only produces its proper object of analysis – the entity called 'modernism', which describes the artistic experiments of the period 1850–1939 in Europe; it also produces and legitimises itself *in exactly the same vein* as an 'experimental' mode of analysis, scornful of great divisions between high and popular art forms, arrogant in its encyclopaedic pretensions (just as *Ulysses* – to take a random example – was ambitious in its mythopoeic intent), and assured of its mastery over a world-history which has been reduced to the merest grammar of events. Accordingly, this modernism is a self-serving act of mere self-legitimation.

What has the postmodern to say to this? Made aware, at least institutionally, of the grand successes of modernist aesthetic experiment, the belated artist faces a huge Bloomian anxiety of influence. After *Finnegans Wake*, what might one do with the novel?; after Mallarmé, what is to become of poetry?; after Stravinsky or the Second Viennese School, how can music continue to develop?; after Diaghilev and Nijinsky, what happens to the dance?; and so on. Clearly, the wealth of artistic work in all these and other fields is testimony to the fact that artists have indeed found some way of continuing their work. Broadly, it seems apparent that two main trajectories become available. On the one hand, faced with the huge successes of formal 'modernist' experimentation, the artist might *revert* from experiment. This way lies a resurgence of content, which has adapted itself to the various demands of the twentieth century from socialist realism through to the new figurative art of Campbell or Conroy, Rego or Ballagh, and so on. On the other hand, one might indeed continue to *extend* the experimentalism of the early twentieth century, moving into severe forms of abstraction, say, and culminating in the problematic status of work by artists as diverse as Beuys or Warhol, to take random examples.

What is shared among artists of the contemporary moment is a specific set of critical problems regarding *representation*. The essays included here by Crimp, Crowther, Baudrillard and Eco are all focused on the crisis in representation which affects and sometimes effects contemporary aesthetic and cultural practices. I have 'encompassed' these essays with two pieces, one by Banes and one by Nyman, which share a suspicion regarding the exclusivity of certain aesthetic practices in dance and music. The general problem of modernism as at once elitist and contaminated by popular forms is being addressed vigorously by some contemporary artists, as these articles show. The crisis in representation which is so central to postmodernism is not only a crisis in the perception of art; it is also a crisis in its production.

Ihab Hassan's piece tabulates the differences between the modern and the postmodern. While this is admittedly epistemologically useful, it is itself somewhat symptomatic of a modernist tendency in criticism: the tendency to master by giving aesthetic form (in this case the form of a dialectical opposition) to diverse and random materials. There is, clearly, no simple evasion of the modern in the postmodern, as Hassan's procedure of tabulation and synthesis shows; but this itself is a crucial part of the postmodern tendency in cultural and aesthetic practices. The modern is not so much avoided as reconsidered, reconstellated.

9 □ *Toward a Concept of Postmodernism*

Ihab Hassan

The strains of silence in literature, from Sade to Beckett, convey complexities of language, culture, and consciousness as these contest themselves and one another. Such eerie music may yield an experience, an intuition, of postmodernism but no concept or definition of it. Perhaps I can move here toward such a concept by putting forth certain queries. I begin with the most obvious: can we really perceive a phenomenon, in Western societies generally and in their literatures particularly, that needs to be distinguished from modernism, needs to be named? If so, will the provisional rubric 'postmodernism' serve? Can we then – or even should we at this time – construct of this phenomenon some probative scheme, both chronological and typological, that may account for its various trends and counter-trends, its artistic, epistemic, and social character? And how would this phenomenon – let us call it postmodernism – relate itself to such earlier modes of change as turn-of-the-century avant-gardes or the high modernism of the twenties? Finally, what difficulties would inhere in any such act of definition, such a tentative heuristic scheme?

I am not certain that I can wholly satisfy my own questions, though I can assay some answers that may help to focus the larger problem. History, I take it, moves in measures both continuous and discontinuous. Thus the prevalence of postmodernism today, if indeed it prevails, does not suggest that ideas or institutions of the past cease to shape the present. Rather, traditions develop, and even types suffer a seachange. Certainly, the powerful cultural assumptions generated by, say, Darwin, Marx, Baudelaire, Nietzsche, Cézanne, Debussy, Freud, and Einstein still pervade the Western mind. Certainly those assumptions have been reconceived, not once but many times – else history would repeat itself, forever the same. In this perspective postmodernism may appear as a significant revision, if not an original *épistémè*, of twentieth-century Western societies.

Some names, piled here pell-mell, may serve to adumbrate postmodernism, or at

From Hassan, I., *The Postmodern Turn*, Ohio State University Press, Columbus, 1987, pp. 84–96.

least suggest its range of assumptions: Jacques Derrida, Jean-François Lyotard (philosophy), Michel Foucault, Hayden White (history), Jacques Lacan, Gilles Deleuze, R. D. Laing, Norman O. Brown (psychoanalysis), Herbert Marcuse, Jean Baudrillard, Jürgen Habermas (political philosophy), Thomas Kuhn, Paul Feyerabend (philosophy of science), Roland Barthes, Julia Kristeva, Wolfgang Iser, the 'Yale Critics' (literary theory), Merce Cunningham, Alwin Nikolais, Meredith Monk (dance), John Cage, Karlheinz Stockhausen, Pierre Boulez (music), Robert Rauschenberg, Jean Tinguely, Joseph Beuys (art), Robert Venturi, Charles Jencks, Brent Bolin (architecture), and various authors from Samuel Beckett, Eugène Ionesco, Jorge Luis Borges, Max Bense, and Vladimir Nabokov to Harold Pinter, B. S. Johnson, Rayner Heppenstall, Christine Brooke-Rose, Helmut Heissenbüttel, Jürgen Becker, Peter Handke, Thomas Bernhardt, Ernst Jandl, Gabriel García Márquez, Julio Cortázar, Alain Robbe-Grillet, Michel Butor, Maurice Roche, Philippe Sollers, and in America, John Barth, William Burroughs, Thomas Pynchon, Donald Barthelme, Walter Abish, John Ashbery, David Antin, Sam Shepard, and Robert Wilson. Indubitably, these names are far too heterogeneous to form a movement, paradigm, or school. Still, they may evoke a number of related cultural tendencies, a constellation of values, a repertoire of procedures and attitudes. These we call *postmodernism*.

Whence this term? Its origin remains uncertain, though we know that Federico de Onís used the word *postmodernismo* in his *Antología de la poesía española e hispanoamericana* (1882–1932), published in Madrid in 1934; and Dudley Fitts picked it up again in his *Anthology of Contemporary Latin-American Poetry* of 1942.[1] Both meant thus to indicate a minor reaction to modernism already latent within it, reverting to the early twentieth century. The term also appeared in Arnold Toynbee's *A Study of History* as early as D. C. Somervell's first-volume abridgement in 1947. For Toynbee, Post-Modernism designated a new historical cycle in Western civilization, starting around 1875, which we now scarcely begin to discern. Somewhat later, during the fifties, Charles Olson often spoke of postmodernism with more sweep than lapidary definition.

But prophets and poets enjoy an ample sense of time, which few literary scholars seem to afford. In 1959 and 1960, Irving Howe and Harry Levin wrote of postmodernism rather disconsolately as a falling off from the great modernist movement.[2] It remained for Leslie Fiedler and myself, among others, to employ the term during the sixties with premature approbation, and even with a touch of bravado.[3] Fiedler had it in mind to challenge the elitism of the high-modernist tradition in the name of popular culture. I wanted to explore the impulse of self-unmaking which is part of the literary tradition of silence. Pop and silence, or mass culture and deconstructing, or Superman and Godot – or as I shall later argue, immanence and indeterminacy – may all be aspects of the postmodern universe. But all this must wait upon more patient analysis, longer history.

Yet the history of literary terms serves only to confirm the irrational genius of language. We come closer to the question of postmodernism itself by acknowledging the psychopolitics, if not the psychopathology, of academic life. Let us admit it:

there is a will to power in nomenclature, as well as in people or texts. A new term opens for its proponents a space in language. A critical concept or system is a 'poor' poem of the intellectual imagination. The battle of the books is also an ontic battle against death. That may be why Max Planck believed that one never manages to convince one's opponents – not even in theoretical physics – one simply tries to outlive them. William James described the process in less morbid terms: novelties are first repudiated as nonsense, then declared obvious, then appropriated by former adversaries as their own discoveries.

I do not mean to take my stand with the postmoderns against the (ancient) moderns. In an age of frantic intellectual fashions, values can be too recklessly voided, and tomorrow can quickly preempt today or yesteryear. Nor is it merely a matter of fashions; for the sense of supervention may express some cultural urgency that partakes less of hope than fear. This much we recall: Lionel Trilling entitled one of his most thoughtful works *Beyond Culture* (1965); Kenneth Boulding argued that 'postcivilization' is an essential part of *The Meaning of the 20th Century* (1964); and George Steiner could have subtitled his essay *In Bluebeard's Castle* (1971) 'Notes toward the definition of postculture'. Before them, Roderick Seidenberg published his *Post-Historic Man* exactly in mid-century; and most recently, I have myself speculated, in *The Right Promethean Fire* (1980), about the advent of a posthumanist era. As Daniel Bell put it: 'It used to be that the great literary modifier was the word *beyond*. ... But we seem to have exhausted the beyond, and today the sociological modifier is *post*.'[4]

My point here is double: in the question of postmodernism, there is a will and counter-will to intellectual power, an imperial desire of the mind, but this will and desire are themselves caught in a historical moment of supervention, if not exactly of obsolescence. The reception or denial of postmodernism thus remains contingent on the psychopolitics of academic life – including the various dispositions of people and power in our universities, of critical factions and personal frictions, of boundaries that arbitrarily include or exclude – no less than on the imperatives of the culture at large. This much, reflexivity seems to demand from us at the start.

But reflection demands also that we address a number of conceptual problems that both conceal and constitute postmodernism itself. I shall try to isolate ten of these, commencing with the simpler, moving toward the more intractable.

1. The word postmodernism sounds not only awkward, uncouth; it evokes what it wishes to surpass or suppress, modernism itself. The term thus contains its enemy within, as the terms romanticism and classicism, baroque and rococo, do not. Moreover, it denotes temporal linearity and connotes belatedness, even decadence, to which no postmodernist would admit. But what better name have we to give this curious age? The Atomic, or Space, or Television, Age? These technological tags lack theoretical definition. Or shall we call it the Age of Indetermanence (indeterminacy + immanence) as I have half-antically proposed?[5] Or better still, shall we simply live and let others live to call us what they may?

2. Like other categorical terms – say poststructuralism, or modernism, or romanticism for that matter – postmodernism suffers from a certain *semantic instability*: that is, no clear consensus about its meaning exists among scholars. The general difficulty is compounded in this case by two factors: (a) the relative youth, indeed brash adolescence, of the term postmodernism and (b) its semantic kinship to more current terms, themselves equally unstable. Thus some critics mean by postmodernism what others call avant-gardism or even neo-avant-gardism, while still others would call the same phenomenon simply modernism. This can make for inspired debates.[6]

3. A related difficulty concerns the *historical* instability of many literary concepts, their openness to change. Who, in this epoch of fierce misprisions, would dare to claim that romanticism is apprehended by Coleridge, Pater, Lovejoy, Abrams, Peckham, and Bloom in quite the same way? There is already some evidence that postmodernism, and modernism even more, are beginning to slip and slide in time, threatening to make any diacritical distinction between them desperate.[7] But perhaps the phenomenon, akin to Hubble's 'red shift' in astronomy, may someday serve to measure the historical velocity of literary concepts.

4. Modernism and postmodernism are not separated by an Iron Curtain or a Chinese Wall; for history is a palimpsest, and culture is permeable to time past, time present, and time future. We are all, I suspect, a little Victorian, Modern, and Postmodern, at once. And an author may, in his or her own lifetime, easily write both a modernist and postmodernist work. (Contrast Joyce's *Portrait of the Artist as a Young Man* with his *Finnegans Wake*.) More generally, on a certain level of narrative abstraction, modernism itself may be rightly assimilated to romanticism, romanticism related to the Enlightenment, the latter to the Renaissance, and so back, if not to the Olduvai Gorge, then certainly to ancient Greece.

5. This means that a 'period', as I have already intimated, must be perceived in terms of *both* continuity *and* discontinuity, the two perspectives being complementary and partial. The Apollonian view, rangy and abstract, discerns only historical conjunctions; the Dionysian feeling, sensuous though nearly purblind, touches only the disjunctive moment. Thus postmodernism, by invoking two divinities at once, engages a double view. Sameness and difference, unity and rupture, filiation and revolt, all must be honored if we are to attend to history, apprehend (perceive, understand) change both as a spatial, mental structure and as a temporal, physical process, both as pattern and as unique event.

6. Thus a 'period' is generally not a period at all; it is rather both a diachronic and synchronic construct. Postmodernism, again like modernism or romanticism, is no exception; it requires *both* historical *and* theoretical definition. We would not seriously claim an inaugural 'date' for it as Virginia Woolf pertly did for modernism,

through we may sometimes woefully imagine that postmodernism began 'in or about September 1939'. Thus we continually discover 'antecedents' of postmodernism – in Sterne, Sade, Blake, Lautréamont, Rimbaud, Jarry, Tzara, Hofmannsthal, Gertrude Stein, the later Joyce, the later Pound, Duchamp, Artaud, Roussel, Bataille, Broch, Queneau, and Kafka. What this really indicates is that we have created in our mind a model of postmodernism, a particular typology of culture and imagination, and have proceeded to 'rediscover' the affinities of various authors and different moments with that model. We have, that is, reinvented our ancestors – and always shall. Consequently, 'older' authors can be postmodern – Kafka, Beckett, Borges, Nabokov, Gombrowicz – while 'younger' authors need not be so – Styron, Updike, Capote, Irving, Doctorow, Gardner.

7. As we have seen, any definition of postmodernism calls upon a fourfold vision of complementarities, embracing continuity and discontinuity, diachrony and synchrony. But a definition of the concept also requires a dialectical vision, for defining traits are often antithetical, and to ignore this tendency of historical reality is to lapse into single vision and Newton's sleep. Defining traits are dialectical and also plural; to elect a single trait as an absolute criterion of postmodern grace is to make of all other writers preterites.[8] Thus we can not simply rest – as I have sometimes done – on the assumption that postmodernism is antiformal, anarchic, or decreative; for though it is indeed all these, and despite its fanatic will to unmaking, it also contains the need to discover a 'unitary sensibility' (Sontag), to 'cross the border and close the gap' (Fiedler), and to attain, as I have suggested, an immanence of discourse, an expanded noetic intervention, a 'neo-gnostic immediacy of mind'.[9]

8. All this leads to the prior problem of periodization itself, which is also that of literary history conceived as a particular apprehension of change. Indeed, the concept of postmodernism implies some theory of innovation, renovation, novation, or simply change. But which one? Heraclitean? Viconian? Darwinian? Marxist? Freudian? Kuhnian? Derridean? Eclectic?[10] Or is a 'theory of change' itself an oxymoron best suited to ideologues intolerant of the ambiguities of time? Should postmodernism, then, be left – at least for the moment – unconceptualized, a kind of literary-historical 'difference' or 'trace'?[11]

9. Postmodernism can expand into a still larger problem: is it only an artistic tendency or also a social phenomenon, perhaps even a mutation in Western humanism? If so, how are the various aspects of this phenomenon – psychological, philosophical, economic, political – joined or disjoined? In short, can we understand postmodernism in literature without some attempt to perceive the lineaments of a postmodern society, a Toynbeean postmodernity, or future Foucauldian *episteme*, of which the literary tendency I have been discussing is but a single, elitist strain?[12]

10. Finally, though not least vexing, is postmodernism an honorific term, used insidiously to valorize writers, however disparate, whom we otherwise esteem, to hail trends, however discordant, which we somehow approve? Or is it, on the contrary, a term of opprobrium and objurgation? In short, is postmodernism a descriptive as well as evaluative or normative category of literary thought? Or does it belong, as Charles Altieri notes, to that category of 'essentially contested concepts' in philosophy that never wholly exhaust their constitutive confusions? [13]

No doubt, other conceptual problems lurk in the matter of postmodernism. Such problems, however, cannot finally inhibit the intellectual imagination, the desire to apprehend our historical presence in noetic constructs that reveal our being to ourselves. I move, therefore, to propose a provisional scheme that the literature of silence, from Sade to Beckett, seems to envisage, and do so by distinguishing, tentatively, between three modes of artistic change in the last hundred years. I call these avant-garde, modern, and postmodern, though I realize that all three have conspired together to create that 'tradition of the new' that since Baudelaire, brought 'into being an art whose history, regardless of the credos of its practitioners, has consisted of leaps from vanguard to vanguard, and political mass movements whose aim has been the total renovation not only of social institutions but of man himself'. [14]

By avant-garde, I mean those movements that agitated the earlier part of our century, including 'Pataphysics, Cubism, Futurism, Dadaism, Surrealism, Suprematism, Constructivism, Merzism, de Stijl. Anarchic, these assaulted the bourgeoisie with their art, their manifestoes, their antics. But their activism could also turn inward, becoming suicidal – as happened later to some postmodernists like Rudolf Schwartzkogler. Once full of brio and bravura, these movements have all but vanished now, leaving only their story, at once fugacious and exemplary. Modernism, however, proved more stable, aloof, hieratic, like the French Symbolism from which it derived; even its experiments now seen Olympian. Enacted by such 'individual talents' as Valéry, Proust, and Gide, the early Joyce, Yeats, and Lawrence, Rilke, Mann, and Musil, the early Pound, Eliot, and Faulkner, it commanded high authority, leading Delmore Schwartz to chant in *Shenandoah*: 'Let us consider where the great men are/Who will obsess the child when he can read...'. But if much of modernism appears hieratic, hypotactical, and formalist, postmodernism strikes us by contrast as playful, paratactical, and deconstructionist. In this it recalls the irreverent spirit of the avant-garde, and so carries sometimes the label of neo-avant-garde. Yet postmodernism remains 'cooler', in McLuhan's sense, than older vanguards – cooler, less cliquish, and far less aversive to the pop, electronic society of which it is a part, and so hospitable to kitsch.

Can we distinguish postmodernism further? Perhaps certain schematic differences from modernism will provide a start.

↕	↔
Modernism	Postmodernism
Romanticism/Symbolism	'Pataphysics/Dadaism
Form (conjunctive, closed)	Antiform (disjunctive, open)
Purpose	Play
Design	Chance
Hierarchy	Anarchy
Mastery/Logos	Exhaustion/Silence
Art Object/Finished Work	Process/Performance/Happening
Distance	Participation
Creation/Totalization	Decreation/Deconstruction
Synthesis	Antithesis
Presence	Absence
Centering	Dispersal
Genre/Boundary	Text/Intertext
Semantics	Rhetoric
Paradigm	Syntagm
Hypotaxis	Parataxis
Metaphor	Metonymy
Selection	Combination
Root/Depth	Rhizome/Surface
Interpretation/Reading	Against Interpretation/Misreading
Signified	Signifier
Lisible (Readerly)	*Scriptible* (Writerly)
Narrative/*Grande Histoire*	Anti-narrative/*Petite Histoire*
Master Code	Idiolect
Symptom	Desire
Type	Mutant
Genital/Phallic	Polymorphous/Androgynous
Paranoia	Schizophrenia
Origin/Cause	Difference-Differance/Trace
God the Father	The Holy Ghost
Metaphysics	Irony
Determinacy	Indeterminacy
Transcendence	Immanence

The preceding table draws on ideas in many fields – rhetoric, linguistics, literary theory, philosophy, anthropology, psychoanalysis, political science, even theology – and draws on many authors – European and American – aligned with diverse movements, groups, and views. Yet the dichotomies this table represents remain insecure, equivocal. For differences shift, defer, even collapse; concepts in any one vertical column are not all equivalent; and inversions and exceptions, in both modernism and postmodernism, abound. Still, I would submit that rubrics in the right column point to the postmodern tendency, the tendency of indetermanence, and so may bring us closer to its historical and theoretical definition.

The time has come, however, to explain a little that neologism: 'indetermanence'. I have used that term to designate two central, constitutive tendencies in postmodernism: one of indeterminacy, the other of immanence. The two tendencies are not dialectical; for they are not exactly antithetical; nor do they lead to a synthesis. Each contains its own contradictions, and alludes to elements of the other. Their interplay suggests the action of a 'polylectic', pervading postmodernism. Since I have discussed this topic at some length earlier, I can advert to it here briefly. [15]

By indeterminacy, or better still, *indeterminacies*, I mean a complex referent that these diverse concepts help to delineate: ambiguity, discontinuity, heterodoxy, pluralism, randomness, revolt, perversion, deformation. The latter alone subsumes a dozen current terms of unmaking: decreation, disintegration, deconstruction, decenterment, displacement, difference, discontinuity, disjunction, disappearance, decomposition, de-definition, demystification, detotalization, delegitimization – let alone more technical terms referring to the rhetoric of irony, rupture, silence. Through all these signs moves a vast will to unmaking, affecting the body politic, the body cognitive, the erotic body, the individual psyche – the entire realm of discourse in the West. In literature alone our ideas of author, audience, reading, writing, book, genre, critical theory, and of literature itself, have all suddenly become questionable. And in criticism? Roland Barthes speaks of literature as 'loss', 'perversion', 'dissolution'; Wolfgang Iser formulates a theory of reading based on textual 'blanks'; Paul de Man conceives rhetoric – that is, literature – as a force that 'radically suspends logic and opens up vertiginous possibilities of referential aberration'; and Geoffrey Hartman affirms that 'contemporary criticism aims at the hermeneutics of indeterminacy'. [16]

Such uncertain diffractions make for vast dispersals. Thus I call the second major tendency of postmodernism *immanences*, a term that I employ without religious echo to designate the capacity of mind to generalize itself in symbols, intervene more and more into nature, act upon itself through its own abstractions and so become, increasingly, im-mediately, its own environment. This noetic tendency may be evoked further by such sundry concepts as diffusion, dissemination, pulsion, interplay, communication, interdependence, which all derive from the emergence of human beings as language animals, *Homo pictor* or *Homo significans*, gnostic creatures constituting themselves, and determinedly their universe, by symbols of their own making. Is 'this not the sign that the whole of this configuration is about to topple, and that man is in the process of perishing as the being of language continues to shine ever brighter upon our horizon?' Foucault famously asks. [17] Meanwhile, the public world dissolves as fact and fiction blend, history becomes derealized by media into a happening, science takes its own models as the only accessible reality, cybernetics confronts us with the enigma of artificial intelligence, and technologies project our perceptions to the edge of the receding universe or into the ghostly interstices of matter. [18] Everywhere – even deep in Lacan's 'lettered unconscious', more dense than a black hole in space – everywhere we encounter that immanence called Language, with all its literary ambiguities, epistemic conundrums, and political distractions. [19]

No doubt these tendencies may seem less rife in England, say, than in America or France, where the term postmodernism, reversing the recent direction of poststructuralist flow, has now come into use.[20] But the fact in most developed societies remains: as an artistic, philosophical, and social phenomenon, postmodernism veers toward open, playful, optative, provisional (open in time as well as in structure or space), disjunctive, or indeterminate forms, a discourse of ironies and fragments, a 'white ideology' of absences and fractures, a desire of diffractions, an invocation of complex, articulate silences. Postmodernism veers toward all these yet implies a different, if not antithetical, movement toward pervasive procedures, ubiquitous interactions, immanent codes, media, languages. Thus our earth seems caught in the process of planetization, transhumanization, even as it breaks up into sects, tribes, factions of every kind. Thus, too, terrorism and totalitarianism, schism and ecumenicism, summon one another, and authorities decreate themselves even as societies search for new grounds of authority. One may well wonder: is some decisive historical mutation – involving art and science, high and low culture, the male and female principles, parts and wholes, involving the One and the Many, as pre-Socratics used to say – active in our midst? Or does the dismemberment of Orpheus prove no more than the mind's need to make but one more construction of life's mutabilities and human mortality?

And what construction lies beyond, behind, within, that construction?

Notes

Where full details are available in the Bibliography, references contain only essential information.

1. For the best history of the term *postmodernism* see Michael Köhler, "Postmodernismus": Ein begriffsgeschichtlicher Überblick', 1977, 8–18. That same issue contains other excellent discussions and bibliographies on the term; see particularly Gerhard Hoffmann, Alfred Hornung, and Rüdiger Kunow, '"Modern", "postmodern", and "contemporary" as criteria for the analysis of 20th century literature'.

2. Irving Howe, 'Mass society and postmodern fiction', 1959, 420–36, reprinted in his *Decline of the New*, New York, 1970, pp. 190–207; and Harry Levin, 'What was modernism?', *Massachusetts Review*, 1, 4 (1960), reprinted in *Refractions*, New York, 1966, pp. 271–95.

3. Leslie Fiedler, 'The new mutants', 1965, reprinted in his *Collected Essays*, vol. 2, New York, 1971, pp. 379–400; and Ihab Hassan, 'Frontiers of criticism: Metaphors of silence', *Virginia Quarterly*, 46, 1 (1970). In earlier essays I had also used the term 'anti-literature' and 'the literature of silence' in a proximate sense; see, for instance, Ihab Hassan, 'The literature of silence', *Encounter*, 28, 1 (1967).

4. Daniel Bell, *The Coming of Post-Industrial Society*, 1973, p. 53.

5. See I. Hassan, *The Postmodern Turn*, 1987, pp. 46–83.

6. Matei Calinescu, for instance, tends to assimilate 'postmodern' to 'neo-avant-garde' and sometimes to 'avant-garde', in *Faces of Modernity: Avant-garde, decadence, kitsch*, 1977, though later he discriminates between these terms thoughtfully, in 'Avant-garde,

neo-avant-garde, and post-modernism', unpublished manuscript. Miklos Szabolcsi would identify 'modern' with 'avant-garde' and call 'postmodern' the 'neo-avant-garde', in 'Avant-garde, neo-avant-garde, modernism: Questions and suggestions', *New Literary History*, 3, 1 (1971); while Paul de Man would call 'modern' the innovative element, the perpetual 'moment of crisis' in the literature of every period, in 'Literary history and literary modernity', in *Blindness and Insight*, New York, 1971, ch. 8; in a similar vein, William V. Spanos employs the term 'postmodernism' to indicate 'not fundamentally a chronological event, but rather a permanent mode of human understanding', in 'De-struction and the question of postmodern literature: Towards a definition', *Par Rapport*, 2, 2 (1979), 107. And even John Barth, as inward as any writer with postmodernism, now argues that postmodernism is a synthesis yet to come, and what we had assumed to be postmodernism all along was only late modernism, in 'The literature of replenishment: Postmodernist fiction', 1980, 65–71.

7. In my own earlier and later essays on the subject I can discern such a slight shift. See 'POSTmodernISM', *New Literary History*, 3, 1 (1971), 5–30, 'Joyce, Beckett, and the Post-modern imagination', *TriQuarterly*, 34 (1975), and 'Culture, indeterminacy, and immanence', in *The Postmodern Turn*, pp. 46–83.

8. Though some critics have argued that postmodernism is primarily 'temporal' and others that it is mainly 'spatial', it is in the particular relation between these single categories that postmodernism probably reveals itself. See the two seemingly contradictory views of William V. Spanos, 'The detective at the boundary', in *Existentialism* 2, ed. William V. Spanos (New York, 1976), pp. 163–89; and Jürgen Peper, 'Postmodernismus: Unitary sensibility', 1977, 65–89.

9. Susan Sontag, 'One culture and the new sensibility', in *Against Interpretation*, 1967, pp. 293–304; Leslie Fiedler, 'Cross the border – close that gap', in *Collected Essays*, vol. 2, New York, 1971, pp. 461–85; and Ihab Hassan, 'The new gnosticism', *Paracriticisms: Seven speculations of the times*, Urbana, IL, 1975, ch. 6.

10. For some views of this, see Ihab Hassan and Sally Hassan, eds, *Innovation/Renovation: Recent trends and reconceptions in Western culture*, 1983.

11. At stake here is the idea of literary periodicity, challenged by current French thought. For other views of literacy and historical change, including 'hierarchic organization' of time, see Leonard Meyer, *Music, the Arts, and Ideas*, Chicago, 1967, pp. 93, 102; Calinescu, *Faces of Modernity*, pp. 147 ff; Ralph Cohen, 'Innovation and variation: Literary change and Georgic poetry', in Ralph Cohen and Murray Krieger, *Literature and History*, Los Angeles, 1974; and my *Paracriticisms*, ch. 7. A harder question is one Geoffrey Hartman asks: 'With so much historical knowledge, how can we avoid historicism, or the staging of history as a drama in which epiphanic raptures are replaced by epistemic ruptures?' Or, again, how can we 'formulate a theory of reading that would be historical rather than historicist'? *Saving the Text: Literature/Derrida/philosophy*, Baltimore, MD, 1981, p. xx.

12. Writers as different as Marshall McLuhan and Leslie Fiedler have explored the media and pop aspects of postmodernism for two decades, though their efforts are now out of fashion in some critical circles. The difference between postmodernism, as a contemporary artistic tendency, and postmodernity, as a cultural phenomenon, perhaps even an era of history, is discussed by Richard E. Palmer in 'Postmodernity and hermeneutics', 1977, 363–93.

13. Charles Altieri, 'Postmodernism: A question of definition', *Par Rapport*, 2, (1979), 90.

This leads Altieri to conclude: 'The best one can do who believes himself post-modern ... is to articulate spaces of mind in which the confusions can not paralyze because one enjoys the energies and glimpses of our condition which they produce', p. 99.

14. Harold Rosenberg, *The Tradition of the New*, New York, 1961, p. 9.

15. See I. Hassan, *The Postmodern Turn*, pp. 65–72. Also, my 'Innovation/renovation: Toward a cultural theory of change', *Innovation/Renovation*, ch. 1.

16. See, for instance, Roland Barthes and Maurice Nadeau, *Sur la littérature*, Paris, 1980, pp. 7, 16, 19f., 41; Wolfgang Iser, *The Act of Reading*, Baltimore, MD, 1978, *passim*; Paul de Man, *Allegories of Reading*, New Haven, CT, 1979, p. 10; and Geoffrey H. Hartman, *Criticism in the Wilderness*, New Haven, CT, 1980, p. 41.

17. Michel Foucault, *The Order of Things*, New York, 1970, p. 386.

18. 'Just as Pascal sought to throw dice with God ... so do the decisions theorists, and the new intellectual technology, seek their own *tableau entier* – the compass of rationality itself,' Daniel Bell remarks in 'Technology, nature, and society', in *Technology and the Frontiers of Knowledge*, Garden City, NY, 1975, p. 53. See also the more acute analysis of '*l'informatique*' by Jean-François Lyotard, *La Condition postmoderne*, 1979, *passim*.

19. This tendency also makes for the abstract, conceptual, and irrealist character of so much postmodern art. See Suzi Gablik, *Progress in Art*, New York, 1977, whose argument was prefigured by Ortega y Gasset, *The Dehumanization of Art*, Princeton, NJ, 1968. Note also that Ortega presaged the gnostic or noetic tendency to which I refer here in 1925: 'Man humanizes the world, injects it, impregnates it with his own ideal substance and is finally entitled to imagine that one day or another, in the far depths of time, this terrible outer world will become so saturated with man that our descendants will be able to travel through it as today we mentally travel through our own inmost selves – he finally imagines that the world, without ceasing to be like the world, will one day be changed into something like a materialized soul, and, as in Shakespeare's *Tempest*, the winds will blow at the bidding of Ariel, the spirit of ideas', p. 184.

20. Though postmodernism and poststructuralism can not be identified, they clearly reveal many affinities. Thus in the course of one brief essay, Julia Kristeva comments on both immanence and indeterminacy in terms of her own: 'postmodernism is that literature which writes itself with the more or less conscious intention of expanding the signifiable, and thus human, realm', and again: 'At this degree of singularity, we are faced with ideolects, proliferating uncontrollably.' Julia Kristeva, 'Postmodernism?', in *Romanticism, Modernism, Postmodernism*, ed. Harry R. Garvin, 1980, pp. 137, 141.

10 □ *Introduction to* Terpsichore in Sneakers

Sally Banes

[. . .]

The aspirations of modern dance, anti-academic from the first, were simultaneously primitivist and modernist. Gravity, dissonance, and a potent horizontality of the body were means to describe the stridency of modern life, as choreographers kept one eye on the future while casting the other to the ritual dances of non-Western culture.[1] Though they were especially conscious of their oppositional role to modern dance, the early postmodern choreographers, possessed of an acute awareness of a historical crisis in dance as well as in the other arts, recognized that they were both bearers and critics of two separate dance traditions. One was the uniquely twentieth-century phenomenon of modern dance; the other was the balletic, academic *danse de l'école*, with its strict canons of beauty, grace, harmony, and the equally potent, regal verticality of the body extending back to the Renaissance courts of Europe. Rainer, Simone Forti, Steve Paxton, and other postmodern choreographers of the sixties were not united in terms of their aesthetic. Rather, they were united by their radical approach to choreography, their urge to reconceive the medium of dance.

By the early 1970s, a new style with its own aesthetic canons seems to have emerged. In 1975, Michael Kirby published an issue of *The Drama Review* devoted to postmodern dance, using the term in print for one of the first times in regard to dance and proposing a definition of the new genre:

> In the theory of post-modern dance, the choreographer does not apply visual standards to the work. The view is an interior one: movement is not pre-selected for its characteristics but results from certain decisions, goals, plans, schemes, rules, concepts, or problems. Whatever actual movement occurs during the performance is acceptable as long as the limiting and controlling principles are adhered to.[2]

From Banes, S., *Terpsichore in Sneakers: Postmodern dance*, Wesleyan University Press, Wesleyan, CT, 1987, pp. xiii–xvi, xix–xxxiv, xxxvii–xxxviii.

According to Kirby, postmodern dance rejects musicality, meaning, characterization, mood, and atmosphere; it uses costume, lighting, and objects in purely functional ways. At present, Kirby's definition seems far too limited. It refers to only one of several stages – analytic postmodern dance – in the development of postmodern dance, which I intend to trace here.

The term 'postmodern' means something different in every art form, as well as in culture in general. In 1975, the same year the postmodern dance issue of *The Drama Review* appeared, Charles Jencks used the term to refer to a new trend in architecture that had also begun to emerge in the early sixties. According to Jencks, postmodernism in architecture is a doubly-coded aesthetic that has popular appeal, on the one hand, and esoteric historical significance for the cognoscenti, on the other.[3] In the dance world, perhaps only Twyla Tharp could have fit such a definition at the time, but her work was not commonly considered postmodern dance. (Much 'new dance' of the eighties could also fit such a definition, but at this point it would be revisionist to call only eighties dance postmodern. It is, rather, as I discuss below, postmodern*ist*.) In the visual-art world and theatre, a number of critics have used the term to refer to artworks that are copies of or comments on other artworks, challenging values of originality, authenticity, and the masterpiece and provoking Derridean theories of simulacra. This notion fits some postmodern dances, but not all.

In dance, the confusion the term 'postmodern' creates is further complicated by the fact that historical modern dance was never really *modernist*. Often it has been precisely in the arena of postmodern dance that issues of modernism in the other arts have arisen: the acknowledgement of the medium's materials, the revealing of dance's essential qualities as an art form, the separation of formal elements, the abstraction of forms, and the elimination of external references as subjects. Thus in many respects it is postmodern dance that functions as *modernist* art. That is, postmodern dance came after modern dance (hence, post-) and, like the postmodernism of the other arts, was anti-modern dance. But since 'modern' in dance did not mean modernist, to be anti-modern dance was not at all to be anti-modernist. In fact, quite the opposite. The analytic postmodern dance of the seventies in particular displayed these modernist preoccupations, and it aligned itself with that consummately modernist visual art, minimalist sculpture.[4] And yet, there are also aspects of postmodern dance that do fit with postmodernist notions (in the other arts) of pastiche, irony, playfulness, historical reference, the use of vernacular materials, the continuity of cultures, an interest in process over product, breakdowns of boundaries between art forms and between art and life, and new relationships between artist and audience.[5] Some of the new directions of dance in the eighties are even more closely allied to the concerns and techniques, especially that of pastiche, of postmodernism in the other arts. But if we were to call sixties and seventies postmodern dance *postmodern* and dub eighties new dance *postmodernist*, the confusion would probably not be worth the scrupulous accuracy. Further, as I argue in the section on the eighties below, I believe the avant-garde dance of all three decades is united and can be embraced by a single term. And

I continue to recommend the term 'postmodern'. The use of the word, however, deserves yet another caveat. Although in dance postmodern began as a choreographer's term, it has since become a critic's term that most choreographers now find either constricting or inexact. By now, many writers on dance use the term so loosely it can mean anything or nothing. However, since the term has been used widely for almost a decade, it seems to me that, rather than avoid it, we should define it and use it discriminately.

The 1960s: Breakaway Postmodern Dance

The early postmodern choreographers saw as their task the purging and melioration of historical modern dance, which had made certain promises in respect to the use of the body and the social artistic function of dance that had not been fulfilled. Rather than freeing the body and making dance accessible even to the smallest children, rather than bringing about social and spiritual change, the institution of modern dance had developed into an esoteric art form for the intelligentsia, more remote from the masses than ballet. The bodily configurations modern dance drew on had ossified into various stylized vocabularies; dances had become bloated with dramatic, literary, and emotional significance; dance companies were often structured as hierarchies; young choreographers were rarely accepted into an implicit, closed guild of masters. (Ballet, for obvious reasons, was not acceptable as an alternative to modern dance. So something new had to be created.) Although Merce Cunningham had made radical departures from classical modern dance, his work remained within certain technical and contextual restraints – that is, his vocabulary remained a specialized, technical one, and he presented his dances in theaters for the most part. Cunningham is a figure who stands on the border between modern and postmodern dance. His vertical, vigorous movement style and his use of chance (which segments not only such elements as stage space, timing, and body parts, but also meaning in dance) seem to create a bodily image of a modern intellect. In his emphasis on the formal elements of choreography, the separation of elements such as décor and music from the dancing, and the body as the sensuous medium of the art form, Cunningham's practice is modernist; his work and the theories of John Cage, his collaborator, formed an important base from which many of the ideas and actions of the postmodern choreographers sprang, either in opposition or in a spirit of extension. In a sense, Cunningham moved away from modern dance by synthesizing it with certain aspects of ballet. Those who came after him rejected synthesis altogether.[6]

By breaking the rules of historical modern dance, and even those of the avant-garde of the fifties (including not only Cunningham, but also such choreographers as Ann Halprin, James Waring, Merle Marsicano, Aileen Passloff, and others),[7] the postmodern choreographers found new ways to foreground the medium of dance rather than its meaning.

[. . .]

The problem of defining dance for the early postmodern choreographers was related
to the inquiries into time, space, and the body, but extended beyond them,
embracing the other arts and asserting propositions about the nature of dance.
Games, sports, contests, the simple acts of walking and running, the gestures
involved in playing music and giving a lecture, and even the motion of film and the
mental action of language were presented as dances. In effect, the postmodern
choreographers proposed that a dance was a dance not because of its content but
because of its context – i.e., simply because it was framed as a dance. This opening
of the borders of dance was a break from the modern dance that was qualitatively
different than issues of time, space, and the body. To be nude was more extreme
than to be barefoot, but it was still an action of the same sort. To call a dance a
dance because of its functional relation to its *context* (rather than because of its
internal movement qualities, or *content*) was to shift the terms of dance theory,
aligning it with the contemporary 'institutional' theory of art.[8]

The years 1968 to 1973 were a transitional period in which at least three more
themes were developed: politics, audience engagement, and non-Western influence.
Political themes of participation, democracy, cooperation, and ecology, although
often implicit in the early sixties, were now made explicit. As theater and dance
became more political, the political movements of the late sixties – anti-war, black
power, student, feminist, and gay groups – used theatrical means to stage their
battles. A number of choreographers mobilized large groups in their dances.
Rainer's pieces of this period included *WAR*, a version of *Trio A* for the Judson Flag
Show, and a street protest (all 1970). Her *Continuous Project – Altered Daily*
(1970) examined not only the stages and modes of performance, but also issues of
leadership and control. Paxton's *Untitled Lecture, Beautiful Lecture, Audience
Performances* (all 1968), *Intravenous Lecture* (1970), *Collaboration with
Wintersoldier* (1971), and *Air* (1973) were didactic works that dealt more or less
overtly with issues of censorship, war, personal intervention, and civic
responsibility. The Grand Union, a collective for improvisation, formed in 1970 and
the following year gave a benefit performance for the Black Panthers. A women's
improvisation collective, the Natural History of the American Dancer, was formed
in 1971. In 1972, Paxton and others began Contact Improvisation, which has
evolved not only as an alternative technique, but also as an alternative social
network. Contact Improvisation is concerned with physical techniques of falling,
with duet situations, and with physical improvisation, but its forms have social and
political connotations. Its performance seems to project a lifestyle, a model for a
possible world, in which improvisation stands for freedom and adaptation, and
support stands for trust and cooperation.

The influence of non-Western forms and movement philosophies, although
present from the beginnings of postmodern dance through the influence of John
Cage and Zen Buddhism, became more pronounced in the late sixties, as dancers
forsook regular dance classes for training in such forms as Tai Chi Chuan and

Aikido and, in Rainer's case, found new sources for narrative in the epic mythological dramas of India. The American fascination with the Third World, expressed not only in postmodern dance and in a resurgent black dance movement, but also in cultural forms as diverse as kung-fu films, Hindu religious cults, Maoist political sects, and Oriental and African fashions in clothing, reflected the changing power relations of African and Far Eastern nations and the impact of the war in Vietnam. These political crises sparked conflicts between Eastern and Western values as basic as attitudes toward time and the body. New directions in political change suggested new models for dance forms – for instance, the prospect of millions of Chinese people rising early to practice Tai Chi Chuan for health and communal spirit. For complex historical and political reasons, the aesthetic and social functions of the black dance movement of the sixties diverged sharply from the predominantly white postmodern dance movement; although African dance became an important source for black choreographers in the sixties and seventies, several postmodern choreographers were drawn to Eastern forms.[9]

The 1970s: Analytic Postmodern Dance

By 1973, a wide range of basic questions about dance had been raised in the arena of postmodern choreography. A new phase of consolidation and analysis began, building on the issues that the experiments of the sixties had unearthed. A recognizable style had emerged, one that was reductive, factual, objective, and down-to-earth. It is this style to which Kirby refers. Expressive elements such as music, special lighting, costumes, props, et cetera, were stripped away from the dancing. Performers wore functional clothing – sweatpants and T-shirts or casual everyday dress – and danced in silence in plain, well-lit rooms. Structural devices such as repetition and reversal, mathematical systems, geometric forms, and comparison and contrast allowed for the perusal of pure, often simple movement. If the dances of the first phase of postmodern dance were primarily polemical in their theoretical thrust – an assortment of all kinds of rejections of the then prevailing, constraining definition of dance – then the works of analytic postmodern dance were programmatic in their theoretical thrust. That is, the analytic postmoderns were committed to the goal of redefining dance in the wake of the polemics of the sixties. And, further, they had an idea of how such a definition should be pursued, that is, in terms of emphasizing choreographic structure and in terms of foregrounding movement *per se*. Their program was to make dance as such the locus of audience attention by making dances in which all the audience was given to see was structure and movement *per se*, i.e., movement without overtly expressive or illusionistic effects or reference.

[. . .]

The analytic dances called attention to the workings of the body in an almost scientific way. One noted the workings of the muscles in Batya Zamir's body, for instance, as she traversed her aerial sculptures. One scrutinized the particular configuration of a lift or a hold in a Contact Improvisation encounter. The anti-illusionist approach demanded close viewing and clarified the smallest unit of dance, shifting the emphasis from the phrase to the step or gesture. It combined low-key presentation and physical intelligence in a way that seemed to define a new virtuosity – a heroism of the ordinary. As I have noted, analytic postmodern dance was a style and approach that was consistent with the values of minimalist sculpture. It was also consistent with the values of bearing the facts and conserving means that were the legacy of a post-Watergate, post-oil-crisis society. The energy of postmodern dance was literally reduced. One of the most obvious divergences from modern dance, ballet, and the black dance movement was the rejection of musicality and rhythmic organization. But also, the analytic choreographers dispensed with principles of dramatic phrasing, contrast, and resolution. The bodies of their dancers were relaxed but ready, without the pulled-up, stretched muscle tone of the ballet or classical modern dancer.[10] The analytic postmodern dances pulled the spectator into the process of choreography, either by direct participation or by baring devices. And although these dances were not meant to have expressive meaning – e.g., the psychological or literary significance of historical modern dance – they did, of course, mean something: the discovery and understanding of their forms and processes was one aspect of that meaning, and the striving toward objectivity, the down-to-earth style, the casual or cool attitude, the sense that 'it is what it is' did not excise meaning, but rather, constituted a crucial aspect of the dance's import.[11]

[. . .]

The 1970s: Metaphor and the Metaphysical

Although the analytic mode of postmodern dance dominated the early seventies, another strand developed out of related sources. The spiritual aspect of the same asceticism that led to the clarification of simple movements led in its way to devotional expression. The appreciation of non-Western dance led to an interest in the spiritual, religious, healing, and social functions of dancing in other cultures. The disciplines of martial-arts forms led to new metaphysical attitudes. Experiences of communal living gave rise to dance forms that expressed or even caused social bonds. Dance became a vehicle for spiritual expression.

[. . .]

Where analytic postmodern dance is exclusive of such elements, metaphoric postmodern dance is inclusive of theatrical elements of all kinds, such as costume, lighting, music, props, character, and mood. In this way, and in its making of expressive metaphors and representations, this strand of avant-garde dance resembles historical modern dance. But it also differs from historical modern dance in such important, basic ways that it seems more useful to include it as another category of postmodern dance than to consider it modern dance. These dances draw on postmodern processes and techniques. The key postmodern choreographic technique is radical juxtaposition. But also, these dances often use ordinary movements and objects; they propose new relationships between performer and spectator; articulate new experiences of space, time, and the body; incorporate language and film; employ structures of stillness and repetition. Metaphoric postmodern dance also counts as postmodern because it participates in the distribution system – the lofts, galleries, and other venues – that has become the arena for postmodern dance. That is, it presents itself as postmodern dance.

The 1980s: The Rebirth of Content

Since 1978 or so, avant-garde dance has taken a number of new directions. Some of these directions stand apparently in direct opposition to the values of analytic postmodern dance, making the very use of the term 'postmodern' problematic for current dancing. Perhaps we should reserve the term for use only in reference to the analytic mode of the 1970s, just as the strictest definition of modern dance restricts us to the late 1920s through the 1950s. Then the breakaway choreographers of the 1960s could be called the forerunners of postmodern dance, just as Isadora Duncan, Loïe Fuller, and Ruth St Denis are sometimes called the forerunners of modern dance. And the new dance of the 1980s could be called postmodern*ist*. But as I have already made clear, I want to argue for an inclusive use of the term 'postmodern', one that applies to the breakaway dances of the sixties, the analytic and metaphoric dances of the seventies, and the new dances of the eighties, because all of these currents are related, principally because they set themselves apart from mainstream theatrical dance in ways that are not simply chronological.

The current generation of postmodern choreographers (and the current work of the older generation) reopens some of the issues that concerned historical modern dance. Thus it seems to depart from the concerns of its immediate predecessors. But it would be ahistorical to call the current generation modern dance; we would intuitively recoil, I think, from placing the modern dance choreographers Jennifer Muller and Norman Walker in the same camp as postmoderns Wendy Perron, Johanna Boyce, or Bill T. Jones. The views and practices of the current generation are not simply a return to an older style or method. They build on and, in their turn, depart from the redefinitions and analyses, as well as the techniques and anti-techniques, of the postmodern inquiry into the nature and function of dance. The shift is an obvious reaction by a new generation of choreographers to the concerns of their elders; by the end of the 1970s, the clarity and simplicity of analytic postmodern dance had served its purpose and threatened to become an exercise in empty formalism. Dance had become so shorn of meaning (other than reflexive) that for a younger generation of choreographers and spectators it was beginning to be regarded as almost meaningless. The response was to look for ways to reinstall meaning in dance.

The postmodern choreographers of the 1960s and 1970s saw their work as part of a continuing debate about the nature and function of theatrical dance. From the breakaway years of the early sixties, especially during the time of the Judson Dance Theater, when every rule was questioned, to the consolidation of the analytic and metaphoric streams of postmodern dance in the late sixties and seventies, when earlier experiments grew into recognizable styles, choreographers have been asking, 'What is dance?' and 'Where, when, and how should it be performed?' and even 'Who should perform it?'[12] While the 'new dance' choreographers of the eighties still enthusiastically enter into that mediumistic debate, one of the most striking features that sets them off from their postmodern forebears (which sometimes even includes themselves at an earlier time) is the question 'What does it mean?' For reasons that have to do with both the history of the avant-garde and the temper of our times, the eighties are witnessing an urgent search to reopen the question of content in all the arts, and dance is no exception. But beyond the question of emphasis on form and function versus content, the two 'generations' diverge on such fundamental issues as technical virtuosity, permanence of repertory, elements of theatricality, the use of other media, the relationship between dance and music, the influence of mass culture, and even on such seemingly external features as venue.

A noticeable shift in the style of postmodern dance, which in retrospect marked the beginning of new dance in the 1980s, took place in 1979 with a number of key works by established postmodern choreographers. For Trisha Brown's *Glacial Decoy*, Robert Rauschenberg designed the elegant costumes and décor, adding layers of translucent nondance material to the liquidity of the choreography. Lucinda Childs's *Dance*, a collaboration with composer Philip Glass and visual artist Sol LeWitt, both extended Childs's analytic rigor – LeWitt's décor included a series of stringent geometric backdrops, each one lit in turn in a primary color, alternating with films of the dance that invited contrast and comparison between the larger-than-life images of the performers and their live actions, and Glass's music was built upon repetitive phrasing – and simultaneously added an element of celestial expressivity, as both the film and the music buoyed the dancers with a sense of monumentality and harmony. Laura Dean, whose use of folk dance style and structure had for some time depended on strictly patterned musical accompaniment, presented *Music*, in which, as a choreographer and composer, dancer and pianist, she made herself a human emblem of the fusion of music and dancing. Steve Paxton, who for years had worked, in a down-to-earth style, primarily with either Contact Improvisation formats and techniques or in solo performance improvising with percussionist David Moss, in the same year presented a collaboration with Lisa Nelson, *PA RT*, in which both took on humorous, vague character roles to the recorded music of Robert Ashley's mantralike, chanted, Midwestern inner monologues, *Private Parts*. In *Foot Rules*, Douglas Dunn explored the conventions of the *pas de deux* and changed brightly colored costumes with a vengeance. In *An Audience with the Pope, or This is Where I Came In*, David Gordon introduced a unified narrative conceit.

[. . .]

One kind of meaning in dance has always been the skills and complexities of sheer virtuosity. In the sixties, the impulse of the postmodern choreographers was to deny virtuosity and to relinquish technical polish, literally to let go of bodily constraints and inhibitions, to act freely, and also, in a spirit of democracy, to refuse to differentiate the dancer's body from an ordinary body. The level of dance technique in both ballet and modern dance had steadily risen (and continues to rise) in the United States since the 1930s. As in other periods in Euro-American dance history when technique seemed all-important, the choreographers of the 1960s protested. But unlike, for instance, the Romantic choreographers of the 1830s and 1840s, their response was not to emphasize expression over technique; rather, they dropped out of the technical arena altogether. The notion of letting go also manifested itself metaphorically in the 'one-night stand' – a refusal to hang on to dances and to store them in a repertory, an acknowledgment of dance's ephemeral nature – and, further, in the method of improvisation, in which the dance is created for the moment and instantaneously disappears. In the 1980s, this impulse has reversed. The spirit is one of survival. Dances are preserved on film and videotape. One of Trisha Brown's recent works (*Opal Loop*) includes material improvised in performance by Steve Paxton that Brown's dancers Lisa Kraus and Stephen Petronio learned by watching a videotape of Paxton's performance. Now postmodern choreographers have companies – for instance, the David Gordon Pick-Up Company, the Trisha Brown Company, the Lucinda Childs Dance Company, Kenneth King and Dancers – and their companies perform works from the repertory. I suspect that this is partly a response to economic demands set down by touring commitments, producers, and granting agencies; but certainly it is also part of the process of becoming an established choreographer. Now choreography demands strength, skill, and endurance. The more a dance has in it, the more it seems worth – *contra* the 'less is more' philosophy of analytic postmodern dance. Virtuosity becomes the subject in dances by choreographers such as Charles Moulton, whose works build on a vocabulary of athletic moves; Elizabeth Streb, whose dances quote circus acrobatics; and Molissa Fenley, whose pieces are 'walls of dance' that operate at top speed, and whose dancers rehearse wearing weights. These dances border on the physical feats of the athlete/gymnast, while in the world of gymnastics, figure skating, and other sports, the form has become more dancerly. Ironically, as more and more Americans take up athletic pastimes, from jogging to weight-lifting, what it means to have an ordinary body has changed over the past decade. Now everyone is an athlete, and sports are no longer fun to do, but, for some, a daily grind and even a source of injury. In social dancing (beginning with the disco routines of the seventies but continuing with forms such as new wave, robot dancing, break dancing, and electric boogie), 'doing your own thing', as in the sixties, was gradually replaced by actions of physical dexterity, complicated timing and partnering, and acrobatic embellishment. The ante has been upped for postmodern choreographers. In the virtuosic works of the eighties, the significance of the dance is the refinement of bodily skills, and yet, in light of the previous generation's renunciation of bravura, the current dances also seem to establish themselves as another installment of the debate on the subject.

If in the sixties and seventies we were content to let artworks simply be, rather than mean, and to let criticism describe, rather than interpret, in the eighties we want to find substance and order in an increasingly recalcitrant world. We can no longer afford the permissiveness of the sixties. The modest thriftiness of seventies retrenchment has given way to values in every aspect of American life more suited to the drastic economic cutbacks of Reaganism. Ours is an age of artifice, specialization, conservation, and competition. As in the 1930s, the contradictions between rich and poor are great, but even those with less money to spend are willing to spend it with a vengeance on elegant clothing and entertainment, immediate pleasures that will partly compensate for inflation, debt, and unemployment. In this milieu, the current values in postmodern dance of virtuosity, elegance, and ornament are not surprising.

Perhaps the most striking overall shift in new dance since the seventies is what Noël Carroll has called 'the return of the repressed' – i.e., expression. [13] The search for meaning in art finds a parallel in current critical writing, just as the artists' refusal to manufacture specific meaning in an earlier generation was accompanied by a spate of descriptive criticism, of the kind Susan Sontag called for in 'Against interpretation'. The recent intellectual infatuation with structuralism and poststructuralism, symptomatic of our present rage for meaning and order, is in turn perhaps a symptom of our national, indeed global, sense of insecurity and doom. Scholars in every field turn to linguistic analysis and the new jargon of literary criticism and French psychoanalysis in attempts to make tidy sense of the messiness of experience. Artists, at times following the theorists, incorporate ready-made sign systems and arch commentaries on other artworks in their works.

While the critical community in dance has not rushed to embrace semiotics and poststructuralism with the fervor found in other fields, choreographers (though not necessarily motivated by deeply theoretical concerns) have been exploring some of the implications of this perspective. There are many kinds of meaning in current dancing, and many ways of making meaning as well. To eschew content beyond the dancing *per se* is in itself a kind of expression, but much of the new dance choreography seeks content external to the dance medium. One method of installing meaning in dance, the most nonverbal of the arts, is in fact to appropriate language and languagelike systems. A number of choreographers make dances based on the hand gesture, an emphasis unusual for Euro-American dance. Dana Reitz, for instance, makes improvisations in which the movements and static shapes of the hands are foregrounded; the open palms or wavelike gestures, rooted in movements of Tai Chi Chuan, remind us of the powerfully emblematic use of the hands in daily life, but in the dance they do not serve as signals. The 'language' of gesture emerges in a different form in Wendy Perron's highly personal system of arm and hand movements. Remy Charlip uses the conventional gestures of American Sign

Language for the deaf, often juxtaposed to verbal texts – dreams and stories and, notably, the song 'Every Little Movement (Has a Meaning All Its Own)'. Jane Comfort and other younger choreographers have also used sign-language translations of spoken texts as movement vocabularies in their dances, much like closed-caption television. David Gordon since the late seventies has elucidated the mysteriously shifting correspondences between verbal behaviour (often embellished with puns) and gesture as illustration, as emblem, as feedback, and simply as an abstract movement pattern.

Not surprisingly, the interest in verbal language has been accompanied by a rekindling of interest in narrative structures. Where the previous generation of postmodern dancers either repudiated literary devices altogether, preferring the radical juxtaposition of movement over logical connections, or, in the case of Meredith Monk, whose works might be said to add up to some kind of story, made fragmented, rather than linear, tales, in yet another cyclical development so typical of dance history, the narrative, whose death seemed a certainty in the sixties and seventies, has been reborn in the eighties. Yet this development is not simply a return to older values or even techniques, for the new narrative finds exposition in ways that take into account the entire history of the postmodern choreographers' deliberate dismantling of literary devices.[14]

One important way the new narrative departs from the stories of classical modern dance is in its use of verbal language, rather than movement, to tell the story. As in *Peter and the Wolf*, the narration takes place on two simultaneous levels – oral (or, occasionally, written) commentary and dancing. (Arnie Zane in fact choreographed a punk version of *Peter and the Wolf* in 1985 that raised questions of gender and linguistic confusion and sexual extremes.) It is striking that the folktale, an exemplary case of literary narrative structure, has attracted several younger new dance choreographers (as it did, for different reasons, the Romantic choreographers of the 1830s and 1840s), for instance, Ralph Lemon in his *FolkTales* and Hope Gillerman in *The Princess Story* (both 1985). The renewed fascination with the workings of narrative and with language as the domain of the choreographer parallels the revival of a new orientation toward the verbal in the avant-garde generally, after the previous generation's mistrust of the word. And this also fits with the rise of semiotic theory.

One outgrowth of the revival of the narrative is an emphasis on the genre of autobiography, a result, perhaps, of the synthesis of new narrative concerns with the personal, intimate mode of performance that emerged in the work of Grand Union and other early postmodern choreographers, as boundaries between performer and spectator, art and life were challenged. The public display of the personal was partly a political gesture in the style of the New Left, and thus it is not surprising that several of the choreographers who work in the genre of autobiography often work in the arena of political dance as well: Boyce, Muller, Jones and Zane, Perron, Bernd, Ishmael Houston-Jones and Fred Holland, among others. They use the intimate revelation of personal details as occasions to meditate on larger issues: war, racism, sexual politics. But even where their dances remain specifically private, that very act of confessional revelation seems to take on political meaning. Autobiography also provides an anti-sentimental twist on the practice of narrative; it imbues a plot with tension by mixing the suspense structure of a story with the direct, factual quality of intimacy that relates to earlier postmodern dance.

Beyond narrative meaning, the new dance strives to express other features that the analytic dancers tried to purge from their work, such as character, mood, emotion, situation.

[. . .]

These dances are different from modern dance, however, because in important ways they *present* the nondance information (i.e., plot, character, situation), rather than *represent* it. They are not seamless theatrical illusions, productions of fictional worlds (*à la* Martha Graham or Doris Humphrey). The movement vocabulary is only partially expressive; it also remains partly abstract and it resists definitive interpretation. The emotional or narrative content remains elusive and fragmented, and the meaning of dance is played out in several, not always corresponding, dimensions.

One of the devices for bearing the new expression, as may be seen from some of these examples, is the use of popular genres and allusions to popular performance styles, including vernacular dance. This interest in itself constitutes an entire stream of new direction in new dance (although it has roots in the Pop Art sensibility of the early sixties).

[. . .]

The merging of 'high art' and popular traditions is one of the characteristics of postmodernism, and yet in the history of the avant-garde arts it is nothing new; vanguard artists have perennially turned to folk, popular, and exotic art as sources for breaking with mainstream values as well as for 'new' materials and techniques. Perhaps what makes the current version of this practice particularly postmodern is that it is enveloped in an acute historical self-consciousness, making quotation a laminating process across both historical periods and current geographical, social, and stylistic divisions.

Another way of installing expression in dance is the use of multiple channels of communication, the proliferation of media that the analytic choreographers of the seventies staunchly renounced. The rigor of Childs's work of the seventies has softened into an elegant expressiveness in her recent collaborative works: *Dance* (1979; LeWitt/Glass), *Relative Calm* (1981; Wilson/Gibson), *Formal Abandon* (1982; Riesman), and *Available Light* (1983; Gehry/Adams). At the same time, she has embellished her earlier, austere choreography with dips, rises, hops, and pirouettes that recall the pulsing musicality of Baroque style. Similarly, Trisha Brown's collaborations *Glacial Decoy* (1979, Rauschenberg), *Opal Loop/Cloud Installation #72503* (1980; Nakaya), *Son of Gone Fishin'* (1981; Judd/Ashley), *Set and Reset* (1983; Rauschenberg/Anderson), and *Lateral Pass* (1985; Graves/Zummo) assert the liquidity of her recent choreography on many levels: the slipperiness of the movement as well as the transparent or even watery imagery of the décor and costumes. A number of choreographers have set their dancers changing costumes throughout a work, as though they were using a manual for the semiotic analysis of clothing. New dance once again opens itself to music, special lighting, film, and new technologies such as video and computers.[15]

Perhaps the key means for bearing expression in dance, as choreographers have always known, and the major, most obvious shift from the previous generation's values, is the use of music. The evocative use of music can instantly create an entire mood; for example, the nostalgia of rock-and-roll 'oldies' or the currency of punk music, as suggested above, and the recent rise of MTV shows a general cultural fascination with visualizing music through dance. But, more generally, the association of new dance with music – often, the very closest correspondence, 'dancing to the music' – signals a radical shift in the history of twentieth-century avant-garde dance, which until the eighties had been systematically separating itself from music. The new musicality is more closely related to social dance practice than to the development of modern dance in the twentieth century. Where Isadora Duncan and Ruth St Denis made their dances visualizations of symphonic music, Mary Wigman, a generation later, preferred to use simple percussion; Cunningham makes dances that do not correspond structurally to the music at all (except by accident); the analytic postmodern choreographers often danced in silence. Meredith Monk's 'operas', Laura Dean's collaborations with Steve Reich (inspired by various non-Western traditions), and Twyla Tharp's use of Afro-American social dance style were early examples of the new fusion of music and dance. Fenley intensified this trend, making dances to the polyrhythms of Afro-Caribbean music that were inspired, in part, by the ritual and social dancing of West Africa and the high energy of new wave music, but that also reflect a commitment to a search for an original movement vocabulary. The interest in popular entertainment clearly reinforces this direction, both in new dance and in new music. But an equally powerful recent interest by postmodern choreographers in choreographing for the ballet also reinforces the new musicality.[16] This new relationship between music and dance has practical results: where in the sixties and seventies postmodern dance became part of the visual-art world, sharing its theories and structures as well as its venues, in the eighties dance has moved into the music world, taking place in clubs and cabarets, rather than galleries and museums. In the eighties, the worlds of avant-garde music, avant-garde visual art, performance, and popular music have begun to merge, and the postmodern choreographers have joined them, and the music scene in New York has replaced the visual-art world in providing a new context for postmodern dance. For reasons of its own, the visual-art world is less conducive to providing that context. Visual artists have returned to making commodities that will last, and the gallery system is no longer inclined to deal in live performance. The underlying impulse of Conceptual Art – to undermine the status of the art object as a means of investment – is obviously spent; in times of economic distress, people want to buy objects rather than finance ideas or actions. The changing social life of the avant-garde also reflects the next context. In the sixties, artists and dancers went out social dancing after concerts; the avant-garde of the eighties programs performance into the social scene, selling beer at intermissions or presenting art dance at discotheques and clubs in late-night performances, especially on the Lower East Side, where a cabaret scene has joined the new gallery scene. Thus, on the one hand, postmodern dance has built its own special audiences and circuits, and on the other hand, it seeks new audiences in the wider network of popular music and dance culture.

The downtown dance world has by now established its own institutions for showing new dance. In the eighties, one can place oneself in the postmodern camp simply by choosing (or being chosen) to perform in a postmodern venue.

Notes

1. For an explication of traditional modern dance structures, see the three bibles of modern dance composition: Louis Horst, *Pre-Classic Dance Forms*, The Dance Observer, New York 1937; repr. Dance Horizons, 1972; Louis Horst and Carroll Russell, *Modern Dance Forms*, Impulse Publications, San Francisco, 1961; and Doris Humphrey, *The Art of Making Dances*, Rinehart, New York, 1959; repr. Grove Press, 1962; see also the many reviews and histories of modern dance.
2. Michael Kirby, 'Introduction', *The Drama Review*, 19 (T-65; March 1975), 3.
3. Charles Jencks, *The Language of Post-Modern Architecture*, Rizzoli, New York, 1977.
4. Noël Carroll unraveled some of these complexities with particular clarity in his lecture on postmodernism in the arts and in culture generally at Jacob's Pillow, Becket, Massachusetts, 16 July 1985.
5. Jerome Rothenberg discusses some of these aspects of postmodernism in 'New models, new visions: Some notes toward a poetics of performance', in Michel Bénamou and Charles Caramello, eds, *Performance in Postmodern Culture*, Coda Press, Madison, WI, 1977. In 'Postmodern dance and the repudiation of primitivism', *Partisan Review*, 50 (1983), 101–21, Roger Copeland argues that modern dance strove for synthesis in terms of form and unity in terms of the audience's experience of the work. A mistrust of language underlies the primitivist longings of the modern dancers. Here and in a second article, 'Postmodern dance/postmodern architecture/postmodernism', *Performing Arts Journal*, 19 (1983), 27–43, Copeland makes some useful observations about postmodern dance. However, his definition is much more narrow than the one I propose here, although he does suggest the possibility of two different camps of postmodern dance (in 'Postmodern dance/postmodern architecture/postmodernism', p. 33).
6. For descriptions and analyses of Cunningham's work, see Merce Cunningham, *Changes: Notes on choreography*, ed. Frances Starr, Something Else Press, New York, 1968; Sally Banes and Noël Carroll, 'Cunningham and Duchamp', *Ballet Review*, 11 (1983), 73–9; Roger Copeland, 'The politics of perception', *The New Republic*, 17 November 1979.
7. On the avant-garde of the 1950s, see Jill Johnston, 'The new American modern dance', in *The New American Arts*, ed. Richard Kostelanetz, Collier Books, New York, 1967, pp. 162–93; and Selma Jeanne Cohen, 'Avant-garde choreography', *Criticism* 3 (1961), 16–35, reprinted in three parts in *Dance Magazine*, 36 (June 1962), 22–4, 57; (July 1962), 29, 31, 58; (August 1962), 45, 54–6.

8. On the institutional theory of art, see George Dickie, *Art and the Aesthetic*, Cornell University Press, Ithaca, NY, 1974.

9. On black dance in the sixties, see Lynne Fauley Emery, *Black Dance in the United States from 1619 to 1970*, National Press Books, Palo Alto, CA, 1972; repr. Dance Horizons, Brooklyn, NY, 1980.

10. Two short films exist that show these stylistic features very clearly: Childs's *Calico Mingling* and Rainer's *Trio A*.

11. On meaning and expressiveness in postmodern dance, see Nöel Carroll and Sally Banes, 'Working and dancing: A response to Monroe Beardsley's "What Is Going On in a Dance?"', *Dance Research Journal*, 15 (1982), 37–41, and Noël Carroll, 'Post-modern dance and expression', in *Philosophical Essays in Dance*, ed. Gordon Fancher and Gerald Myers, Dance Horizons, New York, 1981, pp. 95–104.

12. In addition to the various books and articles about postmodern dance cited above, the films *Making Dances* (Michael Blackwood) and *Beyond the Mainstream* (Merrill Brockway for Dance in America), show works in both the analytic and metaphoric veins of 1970s postmodern dance.

13. Noël Carroll, 'The return of the repressed: The re-emergence of expression in contemporary American dance', *Dance Theatre Journal*, 2, 1 (1984), 16–19, 27. Deborah Jowitt writes differently about the same phenomenon in 'The return of drama', *Dance Theatre Journal*, 2, 2 (1984), 28–31.

14. See, for instance, Marcia Pally, 'The rediscovery of narrative: dance in the 1980s', *Next Wave* Festival Catalogue, 1984.

15. See Noël Carroll, review of The Public Theater's FilmDance Festival, *Dance Magazine*, 58 (1984), 52–4, 90–1, and his review of The Moving Camera: A Series of Performance and Video Collaborations, *Dance Magazine*, 59 (1985), 93–4, 98, for specific descriptions of cinedances and live dances using video, and for analyses of this trend. Also, see the various essays by artists and critics in the catalogue (ed. Amy Greenfield) for the FilmDance Festival, a project of the Experimental Intermedia Foundation, 1983.

16. The appeal of ballet to the new generation of postmodern choreographers (as well as to the older ones) is a complex phenomenon that deserves closer study. In certain ways, the formalist values of contemporary ballet have more in common with postmodern dance than with modern dance. But also, many postmodern dancers began to use the study of ballet technique as an antidote to the personal style of teaching in modern dance; others had first studied ballet as children and found in its vocabulary yet more material for their pluralistic view of dance. If anything can be used in a dance, why not the Western high-art-dance tradition as well as social dance, non-Western dance, and nondance moves?

11 □ *The Photographic Activity of Postmodernism*

Douglas Crimp

It is a fetishistic, fundamentally anti-technical notion of art with which theorists of photography have tussled for almost a century, without, of course, achieving the slightest result. For they sought nothing beyond acquiring credentials for the photographer from the judgment-seat which he had already overturned.

WALTER BENJAMIN, 'A short history of photography'

That photography had overturned the judgment-seat of art is a fact which the discourse of modernism found it necessary to repress, and so it seems that we may accurately say of postmodernism that it constitutes precisely the return of the repressed. Postmodernism can only be understood as a specific breach with modernism, with those institutions which are the preconditions for and which shape the discourse of modernism. These institutions can be named at the outset: first, the museum; then, art history; and finally, in a more complex sense, because modernism depends both upon its presence and upon its absence, photography. Postmodernism is about art's dispersal, its plurality, by which I certainly do not mean pluralism. Pluralism is, as we know, that fantasy that art is free, free of other discourses, institutions, free, above all, of history. And this fantasy of freedom can be maintained because every work of art is held to be absolutely unique and original. Against this pluralism of originals, I want to speak of the plurality of copies.

  Nearly two years ago in an essay called 'Pictures', in which I first found it useful to employ the term *postmodernism*, I attempted to sketch in a background to the work of a group of younger artists who were just beginning to exhibit in New York.[1] I traced the genesis of their concerns to what had pejoratively been labeled the theatricality of minimal sculpture and the extensions of that theatrical position into the art of the seventies. I wrote at that time that the aesthetic mode that was exemplary during the seventies was performance, all those works that were constituted in a specific situation and for a specific duration; works for which it

From *October*, 15 (1980), 91–101.

could be said literally that you had to be there; works, that is, which assumed the presence of a spectator in front of the work as the work took place, thereby privileging the spectator instead of the artist.

In my attempt to continue the logic of the development I was outlining, I came eventually to a stumbling block. What I wanted to explain was how to get from this condition of presence – the *being there* necessitated by performance – to that kind of presence that is possible only through the absence that we know to be the condition of representation. For what I was writing about was work which had taken on, after nearly a century of its repression, the question of representation. I effected that transition with a kind of fudge, an epigraph quotation suspended between two sections of the text. The quotation, taken from one of the ghost tales of Henry James, was a false tautology, which played on the double, indeed antithetical meaning of the word *presence*: 'The presence before him was a presence.'

What I just said was a fudge was perhaps not really that, but rather the hint of something really crucial about the work I was describing, which I would like now to elaborate. In order to do so, I want to add a third definition to the word *presence*. To that notion of presence which is about *being there*, being in front of, and that notion of presence that Henry James uses in his ghost stories, the presence which is a ghost and therefore really an absence, the presence which is *not there*, I want to add the notion of presence as a kind of increment to being there, a ghostly aspect of presence that is its excess, its supplement. This notion of presence is what we mean when we say, for example, that Laurie Anderson is a performer with presence. We mean by such a statement not simply that she is there, in front of us, but that she is more than there, that in addition to being there, she has presence. And if we think of Laurie Anderson in this way, it may seem a bit odd, because Laurie Anderson's particular presence is effected through the use of reproductive technologies which really make her quite absent, or only there as the kind of presence that Henry James meant when he said, 'The presence before him was a presence.'

This is precisely the kind of presence that I attributed to the performances of Jack Goldstein, such as *Two Fencers*, and to which I would now add the performances of Robert Longo, such as *Surrender*. These performances were little else than presences, performed tableaux that were there in the spectator's space but which appeared ethereal, absent. They had that odd quality of holograms, very vivid and detailed and present and at the same time ghostly, absent. Goldstein and Longo are artists whose work, together with that of a great number of their contemporaries, approaches the question of representation through photographic modes, particularly all those aspects of photography that have to do with reproduction, with copies, and copies of copies. The extraordinary presence of their work is effected through absence, through its unbridgeable distance from the original, from even the possibility of an original. Such presence is what I attribute to the kind of photographic activity I call postmodernist.

This quality of presence would seem to be just the opposite of what Walter

Benjamin had in mind when he introduced into the language of criticism the notion of the aura. For the aura has to do with the presence of the original, with authenticity, with the unique existence of the work of art in the place in which it happens to be. It is that aspect of the work that can be put to the test of chemical analysis or of connoisseurship, that aspect which the discipline of art history, at least in its guise as *Kunstwissenschaft*, is able to prove or disprove, and that aspect, therefore, which either admits the work of art into, or banishes it from, the museum. For the museum has no truck with fakes or copies or reproductions. The presence of the artist in the work must be detectable; that is how the museum knows it has something authentic.

But it is this very authenticity, Benjamin tells us, that is inevitably depreciated through mechanical reproduction, diminished through the proliferation of copies. 'That which withers in the age of mechanical reproduction is the aura of the work of art,' is the way Benjamin put it.[2] But, of course, the aura is not a mechanistic concept as employed by Benjamin, but rather a historical one. It is not something a handmade work has that a mechanically-made work does not have. In Benjamin's view, certain photographs had an aura, while even a painting by Rembrandt loses its aura in the age of mechanical reproduction. The withering away of the aura, the dissociation of the work from the fabric of tradition, is an *inevitable* outcome of mechanical reproduction. This is something we have all experienced. We know, for example, the impossibility of experiencing the aura of such a picture as the 'Mona Lisa' as we stand before it at the Louvre. Its aura has been utterly depleted by the thousands of times we've seen its reproduction, and no degree of concentration will restore its uniqueness for us.

It would seem, though, that if the withering away of the aura is an inevitable fact of our time, then equally inevitable are all those projects to recuperate it, to pretend that the original and the unique are still possible and desirable. And this is nowhere more apparent than in the field of photography itself, the very culprit of mechanical reproduction.

Benjamin granted a presence or aura to only a very limited number of photographs. These were photographs of the so-called primitive phase, the period prior to photography's commercialization after the 1850s. He said, for example, that the people in these early photographs 'had an aura about them, a medium which mingled with their manner of looking and gave them a plenitude and security'.[3] This aura seemed to Benjamin to be a product of two things: the long exposure time during which the subjects grew, as it were, into the images; and the unique, unmediated relationship between the photographer who was 'a technician of the latest school', and his sitter, who was 'a member of a class on the ascendant, replete with an aura which penetrated to the very folds of his bourgeois overcoat or bow-tie'.[4] The aura in these photographs, then, is not to be found in the presence of the photographer in the photograph in the way that the aura of a painting is determined by the presence of the painter's unmistakable hand in his picture. Rather it is the presence of the subject, of what is photographed, 'the tiny spark of chance, of the here and now, with which reality has, as it were, seared the character of the picture'.[5] For Benjamin, then, the connoisseurship of photography is an activity diametrically opposed to the connoisseurship of a painting: it means looking not for the hand of the artist but for the uncontrolled and uncontrollable intrusion of reality, the absolutely unique and even magical quality not of the artist but of his subject. And that is perhaps why it seemed to him so misguided that photographers began, after the commercialization of the medium, to stimulate the lost aura through the application techniques imitative of those of a painting. His example was the gum bichromate process used in pictorial photography.

Although it may at first seem that Benjamin lamented the loss of the aura, the contrary is in fact true. Reproduction's 'social significance, particularly in its most positive form, is inconceivable', wrote Benjamin, 'without its destructive, cathartic aspect, its liquidation of the traditional value of the cultural heritage'.[6] That was for him the greatness of Atget: 'He initiated the liberation of the object from the aura, which is the most incontestable achievement of the recent school of photography.'[7] 'The remarkable thing about [Atget's] pictures ... is their emptiness.'[8]

This emptying operation, the depletion of the aura, the contestation of the uniqueness of the work of art, has been accelerated and intensified in the art of the past two decades. From the multiplication of silkscreened photographic images in the works of Rauschenberg and Warhol to the industrially manufactured, repetitively structured works of the minimal sculptors, everything in radical artistic practice seemed to conspire in that liquidation of traditional cultural values that Benjamin spoke of. And because the museum is that institution which was founded upon just those values, whose job it is to sustain those values, it has faced a crisis of considerable proportions. One symptom of that crisis is the way in which our museums, one after another, around 1970, abdicated their responsibility toward contemporary artistic practice and turned with nostalgia to the art that had previously been relegated to their storerooms. Revisionist art history soon began to be vindicated by 'revelations' of the achievements of academic artists and minor figures of all kinds.

By the mid-1970s another, more serious symptom of the museum's crisis appeared, the one I have already mentioned: the various attempts to recuperate the auratic. These attempts are manifest in two, contradictory phenomena: the resurgence of expressionist painting and the triumph of photography-as-art. The museum has embraced both of these phenomena with equal enthusiasm, not to say voraciousness.

Little, I think, needs to be said about the return to a painting of personal expression. We see it everywhere we turn. The marketplace is glutted with it. It comes in all guises – pattern painting, new-image painting, neoconstructivism, neoexpressionism; it is pluralist to be sure. But within its individualism, this painting is utterly conformist on one point: its hatred of photography. Writing a manifesto-like text for the catalogue of her *American Painting: The eighties* – that oracular exhibition staged in the fall of 1979 to demonstrate the miraculous resurrection of painting – Barbara Rose told us:

> The serious painters of the eighties are an extremely heterogeneous group – some
> abstract, some representational. But they are united on a sufficient number of critical
> issues that it is possible to isolate them as a group. They are, in the first place, dedicated
> to the preservation of painting as a transcendental high art, and an art of universal as
> opposed to local or topical significance. Their aesthetic, which synthesizes tactile with
> optical qualities, defines itself in conscious opposition to photography and all forms of
> mechanical reproduction which seek to deprive the art work of its unique 'aura'. It is,
> in fact, the enhancement of this aura, through a variety of means, that painting now
> self-consciously intends – either by emphasizing the artist's hand, or by creating highly
> individual visionary images that cannot be confused either with reality itself or with one
> another.[9]

That this kind of painting should so clearly see mechanical reproduction as the
enemy is symptomatic of the profound threat to inherited ideas (the only ideas
known to this painting) posed by the photographic activity of postmodernism. But
in this case it is also symptomatic of a more limited and internecine threat: the one
posed to painting when photography itself suddenly acquires an aura. Now it's not
only a question of ideology; now it's a real competition for the acquisition budget
and wall space of the museum.

But how is it that photography has suddenly had conferred upon it an aura? How
has the plenitude of copies been reduced to the scarcity of originals? And how do
we know the authentic from its reproduction?[10]

Enter the connoisseur. But not the connoisseur of photography, of whom the type
is Walter Benjamin, or closer to us, Roland Barthes. Neither Benjamin's 'spark of
chance' nor Barthes's 'third meaning' would guarantee photography's place in the
museum. The connoisseur needed for this job is the old-fashioned art historian with
his chemical analyses and, more importantly, his stylistic analyses. To authenticate
photography requires all the machinery of art history and museology, with a few
additions, and more than a few sleights of hand. To begin, there is, of course, the
incontestable rarity of age, the vintage print. Certain techniques, paper types, and
chemicals have passed out of use and thus the age of a print can easily be established.
But this kind of certifiable rarity is not what interests me, nor its parallel in
contemporary photographic practice, the limited edition. What interests me is the
subjectivization of photography, the ways in which the connoisseurship of the photograph's 'spark of chance' is converted into a connoisseurship of the photograph's
style. For now, it seems, we can detect the photographer's hand after all, except of
course that it is his eye, his unique vision. (Although it can also be his hand; one
need only listen to the partisans of photographic subjectivity describe the mystical
ritual performed by the photographer in his darkroom.)

I realize of course that in raising the question of subjectivity I am reviving the
central debate in photography's aesthetic history, that between the straight and
the manipulated print, or the many variations on that theme. But I do so here in
order to point out that the recuperation of the aura for photography would in fact

subsume under the banner of subjectivity *all* of photography, the photography whose source is the human mind and the photography whose source is the world around us, the most thoroughly manipulated photographic fictions and the most faithful transcriptions of the real, the directorial and the documentary, the mirrors and the windows, *Camera Work* in its infancy, *Life* in its heyday. But these are only the terms of style and mode of the agreed-upon spectrum of photography-as-art. The restoration of the aura, the consequent collecting and exhibiting, does not stop there. It is extended to the carte-de-visite, the fashion plate, the advertising shot, the anonymous snap or polaroid. At the origin of every one there is an Artist and therefore each can find its place on the spectrum of subjectivity. For it has long been a commonplace of art history that realism and expressionism are only matters of degree, matters, that is, of style.

The photographic activity of postmodernism operates, as we might expect, in complicity with these modes of photography-as-art, but it does so only in order to subvert and exceed them. And it does so precisely in relation to the aura, not, however, to recuperate it, but to displace it, to show that it too is now only an aspect of the copy, not the original. A group of young artists working with photography have addressed photography's claims to originality, showing those claims for the fiction they are, showing photography to be always a *re*presentation, always-already-seen. Their images are purloined, confiscated, appropriated, *stolen*. In their work, the original cannot be located, is always deferred; even the self which might have generated an original is shown to be itself a copy.

In a characteristic gesture, Sherrie Levine begins a statement about her work with an anecdote that is very familiar:

> Since the door was only half closed, I got a jumbled view of my mother and father on the bed, one on top of the other. Mortified, hurt, horror-struck, I had the hateful sensation of having placed myself blindly and completely in unworthy hands. Instinctively and without effort, I divided myself, so to speak, into two persons, of whom one, the real, the genuine one, continued on her own account, while the other, a successful imitation of the first, was delegated to have relations with the world. My first self remains at a distance, impassive, ironical, and watching.[11]

Not only do we recognize this as a description of something we already know – the primal scene – but our recognition might extend even further to the Moravia novel from which it has been lifted. For Levine's autobiographical statement is only a string of quotations pilfered from others; and if we might think this a strange way of writing about one's own working methods, then perhaps we should turn to the work it describes.

At a recent exhibition, Levine showed six photographs of a nude youth. They were simply rephotographed from the famous series by Edward Weston of his young son Neil, available to Levine as a poster published by the Witkin Gallery. According to the copyright law, the images belong to Weston, or now to the Weston estate. I think, to be fair, however, we might just as well give them to Praxiteles, for if it is the *image* that can be owned, then surely these belong to classical sculpture, which would put them in the public domain. Levine has said that, when she showed her photographs to a friend, he remarked that they only made him want to see the originals. 'Of course,' she replied, 'and the originals make you want to see that little boy, but when you see the boy, the art is gone.' For the desire that is initiated by that representation does not come to closure around that little boy, is not at all satisfied by him. The desire of representation exists only insofar as it never be fulfilled, insofar as the original always be deferred. It is only in the absence of the original that representation may take place. And representation takes place because it is always already there in the world *as* representation. It was, of course, Weston himself who said that 'the photograph must be visualized in full before the exposure is made'. Levine has taken the master at his word and in so doing has shown him what he really meant. The *a priori* Weston had in mind was not really in his mind at all; it was in the world, and Weston only copied it.

This fact is perhaps even more crucial in those series by Levine where that *a priori* image is not so obviously confiscated from high culture – by which I intend both Weston and Praxiteles – but from the world itself, where nature poses as the antithesis of representation. Thus the images which Levine has cut out of books of photographs by Andreas Feininger and Elliot Porter show scenes of nature that are utterly familiar. They suggest that Roland Barthes's description of the tense of photography as the 'having been there' be interpreted in a new way. The presence that such photographs have for us is the presence of *déjà vu*, nature as already having been seen, nature as representation.

If Levine's photographs occupy a place on that spectrum of photography-as-art, it would be at the farthest reaches of straight photography, not only because the photographs she appropriates operate within that mode but because she does not manipulate her photographs in any way; she merely, and literally, *takes* photographs. At the opposite end of that spectrum is the photography which is self-consciously composed, manipulated, fictionalized, the so-called directorial mode, in which we find such *auteurs* of photography as Duane Michaels and Les Krims. The strategy of this mode is to use the apparent veracity of photography against itself, creating one's fictions through the appearance of a seamless reality into which has been woven a narrative dimension. Cindy Sherman's photographs function within this mode, but only in order to expose an unwanted dimension of that fiction, for the fiction Sherman discloses is the fiction of the self. Her photographs show that the supposed autonomous and unitary self out of which those other 'directors' would create their fictions is itself nothing other than a discontinuous series of representations, copies, fakes.

Sherman's photographs are all self-portraits in which she appears in disguise enacting a drama whose particulars are withheld. This ambiguity of narrative parallels the ambiguity of the self that is both actor in the narrative and creator of it. For though Sherman is literally self-created in these works, she is created in the image of already-known feminine stereotypes; her self is therefore understood as contingent upon the possibilities provided by the culture in which Sherman participates, not by some inner impulse. As such, her photographs reverse the terms of art and autobiography. They use art not to reveal the artist's true self, but to show the self as an imaginary construct. There is no real Cindy Sherman in these photographs; there are only the guises she assumes. And she does not create these guises; she simply chooses them in the way that any of us do. The pose of authorship is dispensed with not only through the mechanical means of making the image, but through the effacement of any continuous, essential persona or even recognizable visage in the scenes depicted.

That aspect of our culture which is most thoroughly manipulative of the roles we play is, of course, mass advertising, whose photographic strategy is to disguise the directorial mode as a form of documentary. Richard Prince steals the most frank and banal of these images, which register, in the context of photography-as-art, as a kind of shock. But ultimately their rather brutal familiarity gives way to strangeness, as an unintended and unwanted dimension of fiction reinvades them. By isolating, enlarging, and juxtaposing fragments of commercial images, Prince points to their invasion by these ghosts of fiction. Focusing directly on the commodity fetish, using the master tool of commodity fetishism of our time, Prince's rephotographed photographs take on a Hitchcockian dimension: the commodity becomes a clue. It has, we might say, acquired an aura, only now it is a function not of presence but of absence, severed from an origin, from an originator, from authenticity. In our time, the aura has become only a presence, which is to say, a ghost.

Notes

1. Douglas Crimp, 'Pictures', *October*, 8 (1979), 75–88.
2. Walter Benjamin, 'The work of art in the age of mechanical reproduction', in *Illuminations*, transl. Harry Zohn, Schocken Books, New York, 1969, p. 221.
3. Walter Benjamin, 'A short history of photography', transl. Stanley Mitchell, *Screen*, 13, 1 (1972), 18.
4. *Ibid.*, 19.
5. *Ibid.*, 7.
6. Benjamin, 'Work of art', p. 221.
7. Benjamin, 'Short history', 20.
8. *Ibid.*, 21.
9. Barbara Rose. *American Painting: The eighties*, Thoren-Sidney Press, Buffalo, New York, 1979, n.p.
10. The urgency of these questions first became clear to me as I read the editorial prepared by Annette Michelson for *October*, 5, A Special Issue on Photography (1978), 3–5.
11. Sherrie Levine, unpublished statement, 1980.

12 □ *Postmodernism in the Visual Arts: A question of ends*

Paul Crowther

Introduction

The question of postmodernism in the visual arts has been dominated by a number of themes, notably the idea that art, its history, and its theory, have come to an end; and that postmodernism is largely the product of a force external to art – namely, the market. It might be argued that, for the most part, these themes have been set forth and received with rather more enthusiasm than understanding (the works of Victor Burgin are perhaps a case in point here). However, in the writings of the philosopher and art critic Arthur Danto, the themes are linked in a more coherent and incisive way as part of an interesting discourse concerning the end of modernity in the visual arts. In this chapter, therefore, I shall use a critique of Danto's theory as a means of answering the question of postmodernism in the visual arts. Specifically, in Part I, I will outline Danto's theory at length, and will argue that it is not philosophically decisive. In Parts II and III, I will go on to offer a more plausible alternative reading of modernity and postmodernity; and in Part IV, will offer a final refutation of Danto's claim that (through being rendered post-historical in the postmodern era) art has come to an end.

I

The premise of Danto's argument concerning the end of art is that the advent of cinematography precipitated a traumatic crisis in the art world. This crisis consisted in the fact that, whilst art had always taken itself to be essentially bound with imitating the world, it was now recognised that cinematography could achieve this in a more total way. Twentieth-century modernist art, therefore, turned towards a

From Boyne, R. and Rattansi, A. (eds), *Postmodernism and Society*, Macmillan Education, Basingstoke/St Martin's Press, New York, 1990, pp. 237–59.

kind of self-interrogation. As Danto puts it,

> In its great philosophical phase, from about 1905 to about 1964, modern art undertook a massive investigation into its own nature and essence. It set out to seek a form of itself so pure as art that nothing like what caused it to undertake this investigation in the first place could ever happen to it again. (Danto, 1987, p. 217)

This interpretation is, according to Danto, confirmed by the fact that modernist movements seem to be in perpetual conflict with each other. Again, in his words,

> There have been more projected definitions of art, each identified with a different movement in art, in the six or seven decades of this modern era, than in the six or seven centuries that preceded it. Each definition was accompanied by a severe condemnation of everything else, as *not* art. (Danto, 1987, p. 217)

On these terms, then, the discontinuity and conflict between modern movements should be taken as signifying the fact that all were involved in a search for art's essence, and that all were offering different, mutually exclusive, answers.

Now for Danto, this search ends at a quite specific point – namely in Warhol's Pop Art, and in particular the exhibition at the Stable Gallery in 1964 where the infamous 'Brillo Boxes' were shown for the first time. Since Warhol's Boxes were ostensibly indistinguishable from real Brillo cartons, the question of what differentiates artworks from real things was posed in the most naked and unambiguous fashion, or, as Danto has it, 'its true philosophical form'. And the answer emerged as follows. It is only an atmosphere of theory which differentiates artworks from other things. The essence of art does not consist in some perceptible property or set of properties, but rather in art's institutional setting. Broadly speaking, the artwork is what the artist designates as such, on the basis of some theory about art.

Now, this answer – and its reiteration in minimal and (one presumes) conceptual art – effectively brought the internal logic of modernist art's quasi-philosophical questioning to fulfilment. But this created a hiatus. As Danto puts it, 'the institutions of the art world continued to believe in – indeed to expect – breakthroughs, and the galleries, the collectors, the art magazines, the museums and finally the corporations that had become the major patrons of the age were also awaiting prophets and revelations' (Danto, 1987, p. 205). Danto's point, then, is that the radical improvements of modernist work had by the late 1960s and 1970s found a market, and thence created a *demand* for art that was innovative and new. But what came next was a mere pluralism – a repetition or refinement of proceeding styles (be they representational or abstract) and a willingness to accept these on their own terms, rather than on a partisan basis of mutual exclusivity. Indeed, in the terms of Danto's argument this is an entirely logical development, in so far as once modernist art has worked through to and declared art's essence, there is nothing new for art to do. It can only rework old ground. The advent and triumph of Neo-Expressionism in the 1980s is simply a special case of this. According to Danto, 'Neo-Expressionism raised, as art, no philosophical question at all, and indeed it could raise none that would not be some variant on the one raised in its perfected form by Warhol' (Danto, 1987, p. 209).

Neo-Expressionism, then, is to be seen as an exaggerated and empty response to the art market's demand for innovation. It provides, as it were, a show of newness, but in terms of strict artistic criteria, can only be an inflated repetition of what has gone before.

The central substantive claims of Danto's position, then, are these. In response to the usurping of its mimetic functions by cinematography, modernist art became energised by an internal 'logic' necessarily progressing towards the revelation of art's real essence – an essence that would not be assimilable in terms of other forms of communication. In Warhol's Pop Art, this progression issues in its logical culmination. The essence of art is, in effect, declared as institutional. This self-congruence of art with its own essence is the culmination of art history. After it there can be nothing new in a distinctively artistic sense. On these terms, in other words, postmodern art is essentially *post-historical*. Art, in effect, has come to an end.

Having outlined Danto's theory, I shall now make some observations concerning its strengths, and some philosophical points concerning its weaknesses. Its strength lies in two basic achievements. First, Danto has pinpointed a crucial fact – namely that in the modern epoch, art practice has been taken to its *logical* limit. For once what counts as art is determined by artistic intention alone – rather than by possession of specifiable phenomenal characteristics – then we have reached a point beyond which there can be no *new kinds* of artwork. Anything and everything is admissible in the context of artistic theory and intention. The second strength of Danto's theory is that this first point enables him to explain exactly why postmodern art is fundamentally empty and a product of market forces. Rather than simply declaring it as regressive or the result of a general cultural 'slackening' (Lyotard), he provides a model wherein the origins of the slackening can be traced to art's progression towards logical exhaustion at the end of the modernist era. Postmodern art is empty because it is post-historical. However, whilst Danto thence offers a superficially plausible explanation of the origins and nature of postmodernism, it is not, I think, an ultimately satisfying one. For even if we allow Danto's claim that twentieth-century modernism consists fundamentally in a necessary progression towards the logical limit of art, there is no reason why the attainment of this limit should be regarded – as Danto clearly does – as a restriction upon the creativity and historical development of art. What is lacking here is an argument to establish that creativity and artistic advancement are necessarily connected to the having of new ideas about what counts as the essence of art. For example, we might not count something as creative and quality art unless it does embody some new and novel feature, but this feature does not *have* to take the form of an embodiment of new ideas about what kind of item should be counted as art. It could, rather, take the form of a new style of handling, or the refinement of an existing style to an optimum degree. Indeed, it is the pattern and structure of just these sorts of developments which are the key elements in the history of art. The fact that, on Danto's reading, modernist art fixes on a particular sort of innovation bound up with quasi-philosophical questioning, could simply be regarded as the kind of extended detour from the standard preoccupations of art. Indeed the fact that this detour leads to the logical limits of art acts only as a restriction on the scope of art which is explicitly orientated towards the question of what counts as art. On these terms, in other words, the logical limit reached by modernist art does not exhaust the possibilities of artistic creativity and advancement as such. Hence, we do not *have* on philosophical grounds to regard postmodern art as essentially post-historical.

The second major area of difficulty raised by Danto's approach concerns his very reading of twentieth-century modernism as a kind of quasi-philosophical endeavour. For one must ask whether there is anything which *compels* such a reading? As I interpret him, Danto might offer us two putatively compelling reasons. First, the fact that modernist movements offer, in effect, different and mutually exclusive definitions of what counts as art – and hence embody rival philosophical viewpoints. Now in relation to this, whilst it is true that the twentieth century has seen more conflicting philosophical theories of art than any other, these have generally been put forward by philosophers rather than artists. Indeed, whilst many modernist artists have rejected the *worth* of traditional art in relation to modern experience, very few have claimed that it – or the work of rival modern movements – should not be regarded as art at all. What we find, rather, is a willingness to expand the field of art, rather than to restrict it to one style or one kind of artifact. Danto, in other words, wholly ignores the crucial bonds of practical and theoretical *continuity* which link modern movements. Now, the second reason which Danto might argue as justifying his reading of modernism concerns the traditional supposed function of art. He claims that because the advent of cinematography finally vanquished art's mimetic function, art was led to a necessary progression towards the discovery of its essence. This, however, makes some pretty simplistic assumptions about the life which art traditionally plays in our culture. It is certainly true – as Aristotle noted – that mimesis seems to have an intrinsic fascination for human beings, but one might argue that the fascination with mimesis for its own sake has rarely been regarded as art's *definitive* function. Mimesis, has, rather, been seen as a means to the end of various salutary effects – such as moral improvement, or the expression of feeling. Hence, one might see the impact of photography and cinema not as precipitating a crisis of philosophical questioning, but rather as a liberation. Artists were now free to orientate their work towards salutary effects that eluded more conventional techniques of representation.

I am arguing, then, that Danto's approach to the question of twentieth-century modernism and postmodernism is not philosophically decisive. In particular, he overlooks possible dimensions of practical and theoretical continuity and salutary effects which might link modernist and, indeed, postmodern movements together. In the following section of this chapter, therefore, I shall continue my critique of Danto by constructing an alternative historical interpretation which takes full account of the dimension of continuity.

II

Modernist art in the twentieth century has moved in two dominant directions. On the one hand in, say, Fauvism, Futurism, Expressionism and Surrealism, we find a *revisionary* approach towards representation which seeks to reappropriate it for the needs of modern experience. On the other hand, in, say, Suprematism, Neo-Plasticism, and Abstract Expressionism, we find a *tendency* towards purely abstract form. Now, these two tendencies are linked in two crucial respects. First, virtually all of them embody to greater or lesser degree a debt to Cézannesque and Cubist form or space. That is to say, they employ a formal vocabulary which tends to reduce form to more basic geometric shape, and/or which distributes such forms in a hyper-pictorial space – i.e. one which accentuates the two-dimensionality of the picture plane, and diminishes the sense of three-dimensional illusion. Hence, whilst modernist movements tend in different stylistic directions, they do so on the basis of a root vocabulary derived from Cézanne and Cubism. Now although this vocabulary is one that departs from, and to some degree subverts, conventional forms of representation, it is not one which radically subverts the notion of high art, as such. Picasso and Braque's Cubism, for example, reappropriates and relegitimises traditional genres such as the still life, the nude, and the portrait, in terms of an aggressive subjectivity. Indeed, even in Cubist collage – where alien physical material is incorporated into the work – such material is thoroughly mediated. Any oppositional sense of its physical reality is lost within the totality of the overall artistic composition. Again, in the case of Surrealism's dislocations of form, these do not subvert art as such, but rather draw on the precedent of Romantic and Symbolist Fantasy, in order to evoke repressed depths of subjectivity. The function of Cubist space, in other words, is not to posit an antithesis to high art, but rather to refocus it in terms of a liberating affirmation of the subject. It is this affirmative dimension which provides the second and most important bond between twentieth-century modernists. It even encompasses those American Abstract Expressionists who radically break with Cubist space after 1945. Barnett Newman, for example, declared that 'Instead of making *cathedrals* out of Christ, man, or "life", we are making it out of ourselves, out of our own feelings' (Newman in Chipp, 1968, p. 553). Compare this with the following set of statements:

> When we invented Cubism, we had no intention of inventing Cubism. We simply wanted to express what was in us. (Picasso in Chipp, 1968, p. 210)

> Without much intention, knowledge, or thought, I had followed an irresistible desire to represent profound spirituality, religion and tenderness. (Emil Nolde in Chipp, 1968, p. 146)

> We ... create a sort of emotive ambience, seeking by intuition the sympathies and the links which exist between the exterior (concrete) scene and the interior (abstract) emotion. (Umberto Bocciono in Chipp, 1968, p. 297)

> The truly modern artist is aware of abstraction in an emotion of beauty. (Piet Mondrian in Chipp, 1968, p. 321)

what interests me is the intensity of a personality transposed directly into the work; the
man and his vitality; ... what manner he knows how to gather sensation, emotion, into
a lacework of words and sentiments. (Tristan Tzara in Chipp, 1968, p. 387)

On these terms, then, Newman's declaration that he and his contemporaries are
making 'cathedrals' of 'our own feelings' is a statement that captures a profound
theme running throughout modernist art – namely, that the artwork receives its
ultimate authentification as a vehicle for expression of *feeling*. What *sort* of feeling
is expressed here varies (as the foregoing statements show) from artist to artist. In
some, it is bound up with aesthetic experience and religious sentiments; in others,
it is linked to the artist's affective response to technological change and Utopian
political ideals. But what all these have in common is the view that what legitimises
modern art, and gives it its worth, is some kind of *elevating* expressive effect
embodied in its creation and reception. I shall hereafter call this view the
'legitimising discourse' of art.

There are now two crucial points to be made. First (*contra* Danto) far from
modernist art movements being engaged in a kind of war between mutually
exclusive definitions of art, there exists a surprising degree of continuity between
them at the level of both phenomenal appearance and theoretical justification.
Second, the legitimising discourse of modernist art also gives it continuity with more
traditional idioms. For since the Renaissance at least, the *raison d'être* of art in
Western culture has been insistently tied to its elevating effects. As J.-J. David puts
it somewhere, 'the purpose of the arts is to serve morality and elevate the soul'.

What demarcates modernist art from such sentiments as these is the different
readings of morality and elevation which it involves, and the different pictorial
means with which it operates. But the fundamental point is the same – art has its
justification as a vehicle of – in the broadest terms – ethical and aesthetic
improvement and elevation. If, therefore, we are to talk of a 'logic' of modernity
in the visual arts at all, it can only be in the loose sense of a *radical transformation
of the existing legitimising discourse of art*. This, however, should not be seen as
a logic of 'necessary' progression; neither must it be viewed as a matter wholly
internal to art itself. For, in modernist art, the different senses of elevation operative
in the works of different artists and the means by which they are achieved are
frequently enmeshed in complex responses to broader societal changes. Danto, then,
is led astray in historical terms by his failure to look at the continuity of modernist
art in its sociological context.

There is, however, one point in the growth of modernism which does seem more
amenable to Danto's narrative. This is to be located in certain aspects of Pop Art
– such as Warhol's 'Brillo Boxes' – and in the development of minimal and
conceptual art in the 1960s and 1970s. The former tendency seems to insist on
collapsing the distinction between art and life, whilst the latter tendencies
(respectively) seem to declare – in the most strident terms – that the minimum
conditions for something being an artwork are mere objecthood, or embodying
an 'idea' about what counts as art. Now even if (with Danto) we view these as

quasi-philosophical statements about the definition of art, they point in a rather
different direction from that which Danto's interpretation would lead us to expect.
For if, as I have argued, the central feature of modernism is a radical transformation
of the legitimising discourse, then the fact that certain movements after 1960 seem
to *break* with this carries with it the implication that we have here the beginnings
of a break with modernity *itself*. What Danto's narrative of quasi-philosophical
questioning *really* signifies, in other words, is not the underlying 'logic' of
modernity, but the transitional point at which modernity begins to pass into
postmodernity. In the next section of this chapter, therefore, I will develop this
interpretation by showing how the critique of the legitimising discourse can be
construed as a definitive feature of postmodernism in the visual arts.

III

The key artist in understanding the transition from modern to postmodern is
Malcolm Morley. In the late 1950s and early 1960s, Morley was working in an
abstract expressionist idiom much indebted to Barnett Newman. However, around
1965 he began producing works such as '*S.S. Amsterdam* at Rotterdam'. Now at
first sight, in utilising imagery derived from the mass media – in this case a
commonplace postcard – it might seem that Morley is linking himself to those
aspects of Pop Art which overtly celebrate the virtues of mass culture. This,
however, would be a very superficial reading. For Morley's 'Super Realism' lacks
any sense of the hedonism, humour, or gentle irony which generally characterises
Pop Art's relation to its sources. The internal resources of an image such as '*S.S.
Amsterdam*', rather, declare it as more serious and critical through the very
insistency with which it manifests its own origin in an image derived from
mechanical reproduction. (Even the margin of the postcard is, in fact, worked into
Morley's image.) This impression is consolidated by knowledge of how the work is
created. In this (and kindred works of the late 1960s) Morley has small-scale
photographic-based material blown up into poster size. He then inverts the image,
divides it up into a series of grid squares, and transcribes it – one square at a time
(with the rest covered up) – in acrylic paint on to a canvas. Thus the process of
making the work is reduced to the level of a quasi-mechanical reproduction. We
have a framed picture offered in the 'big' format characteristic of 'high art', but
whose status as high art is subverted by the image's banal content. Other levels of
negation are also operative. For here, a mechanically reproduced image (the postcard)
is the original, whereas the high-art format painting is only a *copy* of this original.
Indeed, whilst the common prejudices of the general public equate 'good' painting
with verisimilitude ('it could almost be a photograph'), here the 'good' painting is
achieved by quasi-mechanical reproduction, rather than the virtuoso fluency of the
skilled hand. Morley's Super Realism, in other words, is a critical practice which
highlights, questions and thwarts our expectations of art as a 'high' cultural activity.
It addresses not so much the minimalist and conceptualist preoccupation with the

minimum conditions for something to be counted as art, but rather the legitimising discourse whereby art is justified as a vehicle of elevation and improvement. To some degree, this is anticipated in the blatant parodies of Duchamp, but in Morley's case the critical dimension is, as it were, painted into the image. We have not so much a kind of external 'anti-art', as art which internalises and displays the problematics of its own socio-cultural status. Now, in the work of a number of other Super Realist artists in the late 1960s and early 1970s – such as the paintings of Audrey Flack and Chuck Close or the sculptures of Duane Hanson – a broadly similar critical dimension is operative. However, the great bulk of work in this idiom has a much more superficial orientation. For, as the Super Realist tendency spread, it began to address itself to more traditional concerns and became simply a *style*. In the work of John Salt or Richard Estes, for example, we find close-up images of such things as cars or flashy shop frontages, which, whilst being derived from photographs, present themselves as ostensibly *virtuoso* performances. Super Realism becomes the means for intricate, aesthetically dazzling compositions on the grand scale. The work of Morley and the other innovators, in other words, is reappropriated within the legitimising discourse. Indeed, Super Realism of this sort has overwhelming market appeal through its combining both the traditional and modernist exemplifications of this discourse. On the one hand, its flashy verisimilitude appeals to the traditional prejudices that art should uplift through its complexity and virtuosity; on the other hand, because such works look *so* much like photographs, they still seem odd – vaguely outrageous even – thus feeding on the demand for fashionable novelty and unexpectedness that is created by modernism.

One might trace a similar pattern in relation to the development and consumption of the tendency that began to displace Super Realism in the late 1970s – namely, 'Neo-Expressionism'. Again, the case of Malcolm Morley proves decisive here. Around 1970, he began to ruffle the surfaces of his photographic-derived works, by working them in more broken brushstrokes. Of especial interest here is 'School of Athens' (1972). This work is a copy of a photographic reproduction of Raphael's original. Raphael's work – in both content and handling – affirms art's status as a dignified and uplifting activity akin to the pursuit of those timeless essential truths which are the vocation of the great philosophers depicted in the painting. It is the quintessential icon of the very notion of high art itself. Morley's treatment of Raphael's work, however, makes the artistic enterprise look earthy and contingent. This is achieved not only through the disruptions effected by the loose handling, but through the fact that Morley leaves a transcriptional *mistake* intact in the 'finished' work (namely a horizontal line of grid squares, that is manifestly asynchronous with the rest of the composition). Indeed, it becomes acutely difficult to locate Morley's 'School of Athens' within the customary discourse of art history itself. Is it a copy; is it expressionist; is it a parody; is it surrealist; is it classicist? Perhaps all – yet none of these. Such dislocational effects are even more manifest in Morley's more recent works. In 'Day of the Locust' (1977), for example, Morley not only completely mixes up such categories as expressionist and surrealist, but blatantly parodies that notion of 'stylistic development' which is so central to art history. Morley injects motifs drawn from his earlier work, but malforms them and screws them up. One must also note a further crucial dimension to this and kindred works. Morley does not simply overload us with images of breakdown and catastrophe, but rather tangles these up in a way that makes difficult to disentangle strands of depicted reality from strands of fiction. He does not offer an illusion of real space, but neither does he open up a surreal space of pure fantasy. We are left, rather, in a state of insecurity that seems to bear witness to painting's *inadequacy* in relation to articulating the complexity and/or horrors of contemporary existence. This felt inadequacy, in other words, arises from a pictorial *compromisation* of the legitimising discourse. A critical dimension of this sort is to be found in other innovative 'Neo-Expressionist' artists of the 1970s and 1980s, notably Anselm Kiefer, Georg Baselitz, and Philip Guston. Kiefer, for example, moves from large claustrophobic interiors that hint at unseen powers and violence, to devastated landscapes linked with symbols or inscriptions that allude more directly to catastrophe, and, in particular, the disasters of German history. In these works, the very overload of scale, catastrophic excess, and an insistence on the physical means of the medium itself, expressly thematises painting's inadequacy in relation to life. Now, whilst Morley, Kiefer, and others make Neo-Expressionism into a critical practice, their work created a stylistic precedent and climate which enabled less incisive, more market-orientated Neo-Expressionisms to flourish. In relation to the work of Julian Schnabel, Sandro Chia, and Francisco Clemente, for example, the term 'Neo-Expressionism' is a catch-all phrase that picks out a discourse of painterly excess, and unbridled eclecticism. The overload of paint and imagery connects with its audiences fundamentally at the level of private and arbitrary association. If a dimension of public or collective significance is lacking in these works, it is taken as a signifier of the artist's profundity or depth of being. The viewer is invited to compensate for his or her own lack of experience by vicarious identification with the complex signs borne by the canvas. By engaging with the work, in other words, the viewer is elevated and improved.

I am arguing, then, that there are two fundamentally different aspects to postmodernism in the visual arts. First, in the late 1960s and 1970s there developed a kind of art which is sceptical about the legitimising discourse of art as a vehicle of elevation and improvement. Now, whereas radical modern movements such as Cubism and Surrealism redeploy traditional genres such as still life and fantasy as a means of elevating subjectivity, artists such as Morley and Kiefer radically question the affirmative discourse of high art, as such. They do so either by incorporating (in an *apparently* unmediated fashion) that which is most *directly* antithetical to high art – namely, mechanically reproduced imagery; or by thematising (within the particular work) the inadequacy of artistic categories, and, indeed, art's inability to express the complexities and catastrophes of concrete historical experience. We have, in other words, a new form of art whose very pictorial means embody a scepticism as to the possibility of high art. By internalising this scepticism and making it thematic within art practice, *Critical* Super Realism and *Critical* Neo-Expressionism give art a *deconstructive* dimension. Such work embodies the same kinds of strategy which inform contemporary poststructuralist approaches to discourse in general. They can, therefore, be defined as the definitive postmodern tendency. However, this deconstructive approach also created a market demand which was rapidly met by *Secondary* (uncritical) Super Realisms and Neo-Expressionisms. These works served directly to reinvigorate the legitimising discourse of art by tapping the traditional expectation of virtuoso performances and 'profundity' and the modernist appetite for the odd and the outrageous. Now in the latter half of the 1980s the Critical aspect of postmodern art has reached a crisis point. It is to a consideration of this phenomenon and some broader questions, that I now turn in the final section of this chapter.

IV

Much art practice of the late 1980s involves a kind of ironic deconstruction that recognises and internalises its own inevitable assimilation by the market. In the Neo-Geo abstractions of Phillip Taffe, for example, we find parodies and subversions of modernist colour-field painting and 'op' art. Barnett Newman's high-modernist 'Who's Afraid of Red, Yellow, and Blue?' finds its riposte in Taffe's send-up '"We Are Not Afraid"'. Likewise Peter Halley's Neo-Geo electric cell and conduit paintings parody the high-falutin claims of Rothko-style colour-field painting by stating it and containing it in terms of banal imagery drawn from the technological base of postmodern culture. Again, the 'sculpture' of Jeff Koons and David Mach questions conventional notions of taste and representation, through creating assemblages of quirky and comical ingenuity. Mach's '101 Dalmations', for example, turns Disney's hounds loose on the domestic environment. The disturbing sense of gravitational precariousness created by Barnett Newman's 'Broken Obelisk' or Richard Serra's 'Delineator' is here achieved through a Dalmatian balancing a washing-machine on its nose. Now, in all these Neo-Geo paintings and sculptures, a dimension of deconstruction is present, in so far as art's pretensions to elevation or improvement are called into question or shifted to the level of the humorous. But the very good humour of this strategy and the ludicrousness of its means bespeaks an overtly self-ironical and self-negating level of insight. We can deconstruct, but the legitimising discourse and the market will still have us – so let's have fun with the whole situation while we can. This comic fatalism is of some broader significance, in so far as it marks the point where critical postmodernism recognises its own limits. Any art objects set forth with internal critical intent will be assimilated by the legitimising discourse and market forces, and redistributed in the form of a *style*. This fate is promised as soon as the attempt to criticise the legitimising discourse of art is made internal to art itself. For here, the deconstructive tendency succeeds in fulfilling the legitimising discourse *despite* itself. To see why this is so, one must invoke the experience of the sublime, in terms of its two main expositors – Kant and Burke. In the Kantian version, when we encounter some phenomenon which overwhelms, or threatens to overwhelm, our imagination or emotions, this can sometimes issue in a kind of rational counterthrust. In such a case, we recognise and comprehend that which overwhelms or threatens to overwhelm us. Indeed, the very fact that a phenomenon which so manifestly defeats our sensible capacities can nevertheless be articulated and thence, in a sense, contained by reason, serves to vividly affirm the extraordinary scope and resilience of rational selfhood. I would suggest that an affirmative response on something like these lines is embodied in our engagement with certain aspects of Critical postmodernist art. Consider, for example, the overwhelming disaster motifs and dislocational effects of Critical Neo-Expressionism. These signify art's essential inadequacy in relation to expressing the complexity and immensity of the real world and its problems. However, the very fact that such a profound insight can be articulated within the idioms of art serves, paradoxically, to *vivify* the extraordinary scope of art itself as a mode of rational artifice. The disaster of failure to signify is, as it were, contained and redeemed by the achieved signification of this failure within the visual means of art. The artist offers an affirmative and elevating experience of a kind of artistic sublimity. Now there is another – somewhat cruder – experience of the sublime which can also be related to Critical postmodernism (and, indeed, to any avant-garde art). One might call it the *protosublime*. Burke is its most effective expositor. According to him, prolonged states of inactivity and monotony are deleterious to our organic constitution. In order to counter this, we need to experience mild shocks – which will stimulate our sensibilities, but without involving any real sense of pain or danger. Experiences of this sort are provided by such things as vast or destructive objects encountered from a position of safety, or by human artifacts which outrage or thrill us in some way. Now, Burke's argument can be transposed into contemporary terms, on the basis of our response to patterns of work and social existence in a society characterised by the division of labour. In such a society, the rectified and monotonous pattern of life demands a compensating substitute for real experience. The shocks and thrills provided by media news items, or such things as violent adventure films and the like, fulfil this function. It is this vein of compensatory affective response, I would suggest, which is tapped by Critical postmodernism. In the case of Critical Super Realism and Neo-Geo, for example, we have works which engage us fundamentally in terms of affective jolts – through thwarting or parodying expectations based on our intercourse with high art of the traditional or modernist kinds. They have a shock or surprise value which rejuvenates and heightens our very sense of being alive. The means may be banal or ludicrous, but in the midst of social monotony and accelerating standardisation, the 'whatever-will-they-do-next' aspect of artistic innovation is a life-enhancing force. Its affective jolt, indeed, may even thematise the notion that the individual creator *can* resist the forces of reification to some degree – however trivial.

I am arguing, then, both that the Critical dimension of postmodern art has ended up in a kind of comical recognition of its own limits; and that this kind of result was implicit in the very attempt to deconstruct art from within. Such a practice tends towards elevating experiences of the sublime in either the Kantian or Burkean modes. This interpretation raises two questions. First, is there any way in which

Critical postmodernism in the visual arts can avoid assimilation by the legitimising discourse and market forces; and second, if it cannot, does this not mean that Danto is at least right in his claim that postmodernism is post-historical? Let me address the former question. First, as I have already argued, internalised deconstruction is assimilated by the legitimising discourse in terms of the sublime. But what about those cases where the critique is conducted from a more external viewpoint? A good example here is the work of the feminist artist Mary Kelly. In her *Post-Partum Document*, Kelly seeks to break out of the patriarchal power structures which have regulated what is admissible as art and what is not. The work consists of a series of largely documentary displays charting biographical facts about, and theoretical interpretations of, her relationship with her son – from earliest infancy to earliest childhood. Now the problem with this work (and, indeed, the problem faced by 'conceptual art' in general) is that the level of sensuous, essentially visual meaning is almost entirely eliminated. It might, of course, be argued that the removal of this dimension is an extremely positive feature, in so far as it is art's sensuousness which appeals to the market and which provides the essential spectacle for the male gaze. However, on these terms, Kelly's work merely throws out the baby with the bathwater. For to remove the appeal to distinctively visual meaning is to render the notion of visual art itself superfluous. Collapsing the boundary between art and documentation in this way simply eliminates art. Interestingly, however, Kelly – as is the case with most conceptual artists – is not willing to allow her *Post-Partum* work to be judged *as* a series of theoretical statements, for its units are mounted so as to be hung in accordance with the presentational formats of conventional art. Thus the work takes on its deconstructive edge through the play-off between its primarily non-artistic content, and its conventional art format of presentation. Again, however, whilst this thwarts our normal expectations as to what should be counted as art, the fact that it is mounted *as* an-object-for-contemplation serves to contain the shock response. We feel that this is just the avant-garde thrilling us with the outrageous and extending our horizons once more. Our sensibility is, once more, elevated and improved. That the legitimising discourse should exert so profound a pull in relation to even the most (superficially) antithetical works is hardly surprising. For whilst the concept 'art' is a social construct of Western culture, it is not *merely* a construct. The reason why it *needs* to be constructed is to pick out the fact that certain kinds of artifact bring about certain positive effects *through the mere contemplation of them*. It is the fact that certain artifacts *can* be valued in this way that necessitates the concept 'art'. The legitimising discourse, in other words, legitimises not just this art and that, but the very concept of 'art' as such.

I shall now finally return to Danto's implicit equation between postmodern art and post-historicality. It will be remembered that, for Danto, the reason why this equation is justified is that modernist art – in the form of Warhol's 'Brillo Boxes' – brings about a congruence between art and the statement of its essence. Thereafter, there cannot be anything artistically new – only a rehash of old forms. Now, whilst I rehearsed the philosophical objections to this claim in Part I, it is worth looking at again in the light of my alternative historical account of modernity and postmodernity. First, I have tried to show that there is some continuity between the late modernism of Warhol, minimal art, and conceptual art, and the Critical varieties of postmodern Super Realism and Neo-Expressionism. All these tendencies are energised by the philosophical implications of art. The difference between them consists in the fact that whereas the late modernists question the logical scope of art and take it to and beyond its limits, the Critical postmodernists question the social reality of art (i.e. the status of the legitimising discourse) from within. This latter fact is itself a concrete illustration of how postmodern art − working within and loosening up the limits of already established idioms (i.e. 'Realism' and 'Expressionism') − is authentically critical and historically innovative, rather than the mere product of market demands. Now, of course, I also argued that whilst Critical postmodernism shakes up and questions the legitimising discourse, it does not escape it; but this fact in no way restricts its historical possibilities. For, as I further suggested, the legitimising discourse is the very basis of our having a concept of art at all − indeed, it is the very basis of our interest in art's historical development. To escape the legitimising discourse, in other words, would involve giving up art. One might expect, therefore, that future postmodern art will become less obsessed with criticising the legitimising discourse, and will instead orientate itself towards new ways of exemplifying it. To some degree, this process is already under way. Therese Oulton's paintings, for example, draw on tradition in a way that redirects rather than criticises it. She articulates primeval experiences of place and presence through a collectively accessible vocabulary of form, texture, and colour. Ross Blechner's sinister memorial paintings referring to Aids victims likewise state private experience in a way that is collectively moving and enlightening. Here, in other words, we have the beginnings of a postmodern art that is profoundly creative, and which involves an elevating reappropriation of the *life-world*, rather than criticism or eclecticism alone.

In conclusion, then, one must concede only one major point to Danto − namely, that all future art will have to work within the logical limits that were set out by late modernism, and this will involve operating with genres and categories already defined. Even this, however, would only rule out the possibility of future authentic artistic innovation on the assumption that such innovation is sufficiently definable in *negative* terms, i.e. as *simply* creating something the like of which has not been created before. But, of course, this assumption is false. Historical innovation in art has always been determined in the context of *creative* breaks with, *or* refinements of, what has already been given. We do not want new artifacts that are simply unprecedented − but rather ones whose unprecedentedness casts new light on the traditions of art or on our broader relation to the life-world. Artistic innovation, in other words, is a complex relation between art and its past, rather than the kind of absolute philosophical break which Danto's reading makes of it. The moral is clear. Art lives ... and will continue to do so whilstsoever artists see their world and, in particular, their discipline's history, from different viewpoints.

Note

For a much fuller discussion of the general relation between art and Kant's theory of the sublime, see Crowther, 1989, ch. 7.

Bibliography

Danto, A. *The State of the Art*, Prentice Hall, New York, 1987.
Chipp, H. *Theories of Modern Art*, University of California Press, Los Angeles, 1968.
Crowther, P. *The Kantian Sublime: From morality to art*, Oxford University Press, Oxford, 1989.

13 □ *The Evil Demon of Images and The Precession of Simulacra*

Jean Baudrillard

The Evil Demon of Images

There is a kind of primal pleasure, of anthropological joy in images, a kind of brute fascination unencumbered by aesthetic, moral, social or political judgements. It is because of this that I suggest they are immoral, and that their fundamental power lies in this immorality.

This brute fascination for images, above and beyond all moral or social determination, is also not that of dreaming or the imaginary, understood in the traditional sense. Other images, such as those in painting, drawing, theatre or architecture, have been better able to make us dream or imagine; other modes of expression as well (undoubtedly language makes us dream better than the image). So there is something more than that which is peculiar to our modern media images; if they fascinate us so much it is not because they are sites of the production of meaning and representation – this would not be new – it is on the contrary because they are sites of the *disappearance* of meaning and representation, sites in which we are caught quite apart from any judgement of reality, thus sites of a fatal strategy of denegation of the real and of the reality principle.

We have arrived at a paradox regarding the image, our images, those which unfurl upon and invade our daily life – images whose proliferation, it should be noted, is potentially infinite, whereas the extension of meaning is always limited precisely by its end, by its finality; from the fact that images ultimately have no finality and proceed by total contiguity, infinitely multiplying themselves according to an irresistible epidemic process which no one today can control, our world has become truly infinite, or rather exponential by means of images. It is caught up in a mad pursuit of images, in an ever greater fascination which is only accentuated by video and digital images. We have thus come to the paradox that these images describe the equal impossibility of the real and of the imaginary.

For us the medium, the image medium, has imposed itself between the real and

From Baudrillard, J., *The Evil Demon of Images*, The Power Institute of Fine Arts, Sydney, 1987, pp. 28–31, 33; and Baudrillard, J., *Simulations*, Semiotext(e) Inc., New York, 1983, pp. 10–13, 38–44.

the imaginary, upsetting the balance between the two, with a kind of fatality which has its own logic. I call this a fatal process in the sense that there is a definitive immanence of the image, without any possible transcendent meaning, without any possible dialectic of history – fatal also in the sense not merely of an exponential, linear unfolding of images and messages but of an exponential enfolding of the medium around itself. The fatality lies in this endless enwrapping of images (literally: without end, without destination) which leaves images no other destiny than images. The same thing happens everywhere today, when production has no destiny apart from production – overdetermination of production by itself – when sex has no destiny other than sex – sexual overdetermination of sexuality. This process may be found everywhere today, for better and for worse. In the absence of rules of the game, things become caught up in their own game; images become more real than the real; cinema itself becomes more cinema than cinema, in a kind of vertigo in which (to return to our initial problem, that of resemblance) it does no more than resemble itself and escape in its own logic, in the very perfection of its own model.

I am thinking of those exact, scrupulous set-pieces such as *Chinatown*, *The Day of the Condor*, *Barry Lyndon*, *1900*, *All the President's Men*, the very perfection of which is disturbing. It is as if we were dealing with perfect remakes, with extraordinary montages which belong more to a combinatory process (or mosaic in the McLuhanesque sense), with large photo, kino or historio-synthetic machines, rather than with real films. Let us be clear: their quality is not in question. The problem is rather that they leave us somehow totally indifferent.

Take *The Last Picture Show*. You need only be sufficiently distracted, as I was, to see it as a 1950s original production; a good film of manners and the ambience of small-town America, etc. A slight suspicion: it was a little too good, better adjusted, better than the others, without the sentimental, moral and psychological tics of the films of that period. Astonishment at the discovery that it is a 1970s film, perfectly nostalgic, brand new, retouched, a hyperrealist restitution of a 1950s film. There is talk of remaking silent films, doubtless better than those of the period. A whole generation of films is appearing which will be to those we have known what the android is to man: marvellous, flawless artifacts, dazzling simulacra which lack only an imaginary and that particular hallucination which makes cinema what it is. Most of those that we see today (the best) are already of this order. *Barry Lyndon* is the best example: no better has been made, no better will be made, but *what* exactly? Evocation? No, not even evocation but *simulation*. All the toxic radiation has been filtered out, all the ingredients are present in precise doses, not a single mistake.

[. . .]

In its present endeavours cinema increasingly approaches, with ever-increasing perfection, absolute reality: in its banality, in its veracity, in its starkness, in its tedium, and at the same time in its pretentiousness, in its pretension to be the real, the immediate, the unsignified, which is the maddest of enterprises (in the same way that the pretension of functionalist design to designate, as the highest degree of the object, the form in which it coincides with its function, its use-value, is properly an insane enterprise). No culture has ever had this naive and paranoiac, this puritanical and terrorist vision of signs. Terrorism is always of the real. Simultaneous with this attempt at absolute coincidence with the real, cinema also approaches an absolute coincidence with itself. This is not contradictory: it is the very definition of the hyperreal. Hypotyposis and specularity. Cinema plagiarises and copies itself, remakes its classics, retroactivates its original myths, remakes silent films more perfect than the originals, etc. All this is logical. *Cinema is fascinated by itself as a lost object just as it (and we) are fascinated by the real as a referential in perdition.*

The Precession of Simulacra

Thus perhaps at stake has always been the murderous capacity of images, murderers of the real, murderers of their own model as the Byzantine icons could murder the divine identity. To this murderous capacity is opposed the dialectical capacity of representations as a visible and intelligible mediation of the Real. All of Western faith and good faith was engaged in this wager on representation: that a sign could refer to the depth of meaning, that a sign could *exchange* for meaning, and that something could guarantee this exchange – God, of course. But what if God himself can be simulated, that is to say, reduced to the signs which attest his existence? Then the whole system becomes weightless, it is no longer anything but a gigantic simulacrum – not unreal, but a simulacrum, never again exchanging for what is real, but exchanging in itself, in an uninterrupted circuit without reference or circumference.

So it is with simulation, insofar as it is opposed to representation. The latter starts from the principle that the sign and the real are equivalent (even if this equivalence is utopian, it is a fundamental axiom). Conversely, simulation starts from the *utopia* of this principle of equivalence, *from the radical negation of the sign as value*, from the sign as reversion and death sentence of every reference. Whereas representation tries to absorb simulation by interpreting it as false representation, simulation envelops the whole edifice of representation as itself a simulacrum.

This would be the successive phases of the image:

● it is the reflection of a basic reality
● it masks and perverts a basic reality
● it masks the *absence* of a basic reality
● it bears no relation to any reality whatever: it is its own pure simulacrum.

In the first case, the image is a *good* appearance – the representation is of the order of sacrament. In the second, it is an *evil* appearance – of the order of malefice. In the third, it *plays at being* an appearance – it is of the order of sorcery. In the fourth, it is no longer in the order of appearance at all, but of simulation.

The transition from signs which dissimulate something to signs which dissimulate that there is nothing marks the decisive turning point. The first implies a theology of truth and secrecy (to which the notion of ideology still belongs). The second inaugurates an age of simulacra and simulation, in which there is no longer any God to recognise his own, nor any last judgement to separate true from false, the real from its artificial resurrection, since everything is already dead and risen in advance. When the real is no longer what it used to be, nostalgia assumes its full meaning. There is a proliferation of myths of origin and signs of reality; of second-hand truth, objectivity and authenticity. There is an escalation of the true, of the lived experience; a resurrection of the figurative where the object and substance have disappeared. And there is a panic-stricken production of the real and the referential, above and parallel to the panic of material production: this is how simulation appears in the phase that concerns us – a strategy of the real, neo-real and hyperreal whose universal double is a strategy of deterrence.

[. . .]

Strategy of the Real

Of the same order as the impossibility of rediscovering an absolute level of the real is the impossibility of staging an illusion. Illusion is no longer possible, because the real is no longer possible. It is the whole *political* problem of the parody, of hypersimulation or offensive simulation, which is posed here.

For example: it would be interesting to see whether the repressive apparatus would not react more violently to a simulated hold-up than to a real one? For the latter only upsets the order of things, the right of property, whereas the other interferes with the very principle of reality. Transgression and violence are less serious, for they only contest the *distribution* of the real. Simulation is infinitely more dangerous, however, since it always suggests, over and above its object, that *law and order themselves might really be nothing more than a simulation.*

But the difficulty is in proportion to the peril. How to feign a violation and put it to the test? Go and simulate a theft in a large department store: how do you convince the security guards that it is a simulated theft? There is no 'objective' difference: the same gestures and the same signs exist as for a real theft; in fact the signs incline neither to one side nor the other. As far as the established order is concerned, they are always of the order of the real.

Go and organise a fake hold-up. Be sure to check that your weapons are harmless, and take the most trustworthy hostage, so that no life is in danger (otherwise you risk committing an offence). Demand ransom, and arrange it so that the operation creates the greatest commotion possible – in brief, stay close to the 'truth', so as to test the reaction of the apparatus to a perfect simulation. But you won't succeed: the web of artificial signs will be inextricably mixed up with real elements (a police officer will really shoot on sight; a bank customer will faint and die of a heart attack; they will really turn the phoney ransom over to you) – in brief, you will unwittingly find yourself immediately in the real, one of whose functions is precisely to devour every attempt at simulation, to reduce everything to some reality – that's exactly how the established order is, well before institutions and justice come into play.

In this impossibility of isolating the process of simulation must be seen the whole thrust of an order than can only see and understand in terms of some reality, because it can function nowhere else. The simulation of an offence, if it is patent, will either be punished more lightly (because it has no 'consequences') or be punished as an offence to public office (for example, if one triggered off a police operation 'for nothing') – but *never as simulation*, since it is precisely as such that no equivalence with the real is possible, and hence no repression either. The challenge of simulation is irreceivable by power. How can you punish the simulation of virtue? Yet as such it is as serious as the simulation of crime. Parody makes obedience and transgression equivalent, and that is the most serious crime, since it *cancels out the difference upon which the law is based.* The established order can do nothing against it, for the law is a second-order simulacrum whereas simulation is third-order, beyond true and false, beyond equivalences, beyond the rational distinctions upon which function all power and the entire social. Hence, *failing the real*, it is here that we must aim at order.

This is why order always opts for the real. In a state of uncertainty, it always prefers this assumption (thus in the army they would rather take the simulator as a true madman). But this becomes more and more difficult, for if it is practically impossible to isolate the process of simulation, through the force of inertia of the real which surrounds us, the inverse is also true (and this very reversibility forms part of the apparatus of simulation and of power's impotency): namely, *it is now impossible to isolate the process of the real*, or to prove the real.

Thus all hold-ups, hijacks and the like are now as it were simulation hold-ups, in the sense that they are inscribed in advance in the decoding and orchestration rituals of the media, anticipated in their mode of presentation and possible consequences. In brief, they function as a set of signs dedicated exclusively to their recurrence as signs, and no longer to their 'real' goal at all. But this does not make them inoffensive. On the contrary, it is as hyperreal events, no longer having any particular contents or aims, but indefinitely refracted by each other (for that matter like so-called historical events: strikes, demonstrations, crises, etc.), that they are precisely unverifiable by an order which can only exert itself on the real and the rational, on ends and means: a referential order which can only dominate referentials, a determinate power which can only dominate a determined world, but which can do nothing about that indefinite recurrence of simulation, about that weightless nebula no longer obeying the law of gravitation of the real – power itself eventually breaking apart in this space and becoming a simulation of power (disconnected from its aims and objectives, and dedicated to *power effects* and mass simulation).

The only weapon of power, its only strategy against this defection, is to reinject realness and referentiality everywhere, in order to convince us of the reality of the social, of the gravity of the economy and the finalities of production. For that purpose it prefers the discourse of crisis, but also – why not? – the discourse of desire. 'Take your desires for reality!' can be understood as the ultimate slogan of power, for in a non-referential world even the confusion of the reality principle with the desire principle is less dangerous than contagious hyperreality. One remains among principles, and there power is always right.

Hyperreality and simulation are deterrents of every principle and of every objective; they turn against power this deterrence which was itself so well utilised for a long time. For, finally, it was capital which was the first to feed throughout its history on the destruction of every referential, of every human goal, which shattered every ideal distinction between true and false, good and evil, in order to establish a radical law of equivalence and exchange, the iron law of its power. It was the first to practise deterrence, abstraction, disconnection, deterritorialisation, etc.; and if it was capital which fostered reality, the reality principle, it was also the first to liquidate it in the extermination of every use-value, of every real equivalence, of production and wealth, in the very sensation we have of the unreality of the stakes and the omnipotence of manipulation. Now, it is this very logic which is today hardened even more *against* it. And when it wants to fight this catastrophic spiral by secreting one last glimmer of reality, on which to found one last glimmer of power, it only multiplies the *signs* and accelerates the play of simulation.

As long as it was historically threatened by the real, power risked deterrence and simulation, disintegrating every contradiction by means of the production of equivalent signs. When it is threatened today by simulation (the threat of vanishing in the play of signs), power risks the real, risks crisis, it gambles on remanufacturing artificial, social, economic, political stakes. This is a question of life or death for it. But it is too late.

Whence the characteristic hysteria of our time: the hysteria of production and reproduction of the real. The other production, that of goods and commodities, that of *la belle époque* of political economy, no longer makes any sense of its own, and has not for some time. What society seeks through production, and overproduction, is the restoration of the real which escapes it.

[. . .]

14 □ *The City of Robots*

Umberto Eco

In Europe, when people want to be amused, they go to a 'house' of amusement (whether a cinema, theatre, or casino); sometimes a 'park' is created, which may seem a 'city', but only metaphorically. In the United States, on the contrary, as everyone knows, there exist amusement cities. Las Vegas is one example; it is focused on gambling and entertainment, its architecture is totally artificial, and it has been studied by Robert Venturi as a completely new phenomenon in city planning, a 'message' city, entirely made up of signs, not a city like the others, which communicate in order to function, but rather a city that functions in order to communicate. But Las Vegas is still a 'real' city, and in a recent essay on Las Vegas, Giovanni Brino showed how, though born as a place for gambling, it is gradually being transformed into a residential city, a place of business, industry, conventions. The theme of our trip – on the contrary – is the Absolute Fake; and therefore we are interested only in absolutely fake cities. Disneyland (California) and Disney World (Florida) are obviously the chief examples, but if they existed alone they would represent a negligible exception. The fact is that the United States is filled with cities that imitate a city, just as wax museums imitate painting and the Venetian palazzos or Pompeiian villas imitate architecture. In particular there are the 'ghost towns', the Western cities of a century and more ago. Some are reasonably authentic, and the restoration or preservation has been carried out on an extant, 'archeological' urban complex; but more interesting are those born from nothing, out of pure imitative determination. They are 'the real thing'.

There is an embarrassment of riches to choose from: You can have fragments of cities, as at Stone Mountain near Atlanta, where you take a trip on a nineteenth-century train, witness an Indian raid, and see sheriffs at work, against the background of a fake Mount Rushmore. The Six Guns Territory, in Silver Springs, also has train and sheriffs, a shoot-out in the streets and French cancan in the saloon. There is a series of ranches and Mexican missions in Arizona; Tombstone with its

From Eco, U., *Travels in Hyperreality*, Harcourt Brace Jovanovich, Orlando, FL, 1986, pp. 39–48.

OK Corral, Old Tucson, Legend City near Phoenix. There is the Old South Bar-b-Q Ranch at Clewison, Florida, and so on. If you venture beyond the myth of the West, you have cities like the Magic Mountain in Valencia, California, or Santa Claus Village, Polynesian gardens, pirate islands, Astroworlds like the one in Kirby, Texas, and the 'wild' territories of the various Marinelands, as well as ecological cities.

There are also the ship imitations. In Florida, for example, between Tampa and St Petersburg, you can board the *Bounty*, anchored at the edge of a Tahitian village, faithfully reconstructed according to the drawings preserved by the Royal Society in London, but with an eye also on the old film with Charles Laughton and Clark Gable. Many of the nautical instruments are of the period, some of the sailors are waxworks, one officer's shoes are those worn by the actor who played the part, the historical information on the various panels is credible, the voices that pervade the atmosphere come from the sound track of the movie. But we'll stick to the Western myth and take as a sample city the Knott's Berry Farm of Buena Park, Los Angeles.

Here the whole trick seems to be exposed; the surrounding city context and the iron fencing (as well as the admission ticket) warn us that we are entering not a real city but a toy city. But as we begin walking down the first streets, the studied illusion takes over. First of all, there is the realism of the reconstruction: the dusty stables, the sagging shops, the offices of the sheriff and the telegraph agent, the jail, the saloon are life size and executed with absolute fidelity; the old carriages are covered with dust, the Chinese laundry is dimly lit, all the buildings are more or less practical, and the shops are open, because Berry Farm, like Disneyland, blends the reality of trade with the play of fiction. And if the dry-goods store is fake nineteenth-century and the shopgirl is dressed like a John Ford heroine, the candies, the peanuts, the pseudo-Indian handicrafts are real and are sold for real dollars, just as the soft drinks, advertised with antique posters, are real, and the customer finds himself participating in the fantasy because of his own authenticity as a consumer; in other words, he is in the role of the cowboy or the gold-prospector who comes into town to be fleeced of all he has accumulated while out in the wilds.

Furthermore the levels of illusion are numerous, and this increases the hallucination – that is to say, the Chinese in the laundry or the prisoner in the jail are wax dummies, who exist, in realistic attitudes, in settings that are equally realistic, though you can't actually enter them; but you don't realize that the room in question is a glass display case, because it looks as if you could, if you chose, open the door or climb through the window; and then the next room, say, which is both the general store and the justice of the peace's office, looks like a display case but is actually practical, and the justice of the peace, with his black alpaca jacket and his pistols at his hips, is an actual person who sells you his merchandise. It should be added that extras walk about the streets and periodically stage a furious gun battle, and when you realize that the average American visitor is wearing blue jeans not very different from the cowboy's, many of the visitors become confused with the extras, increasing the theatricality of the whole. For example, the village school, reconstructed with hyperrealistic detail, has behind the desk a schoolmarm wearing a bonnet and an ample checked skirt, but the children on the benches are little passing visitors, and I heard one tourist ask his wife if the children were real or 'fake' (and you could sense his psychological readiness to consider them, at will, extras, dummies, or moving robots of the sort we will see in Disneyland).

Apparently ghost towns involve a different approach from that of wax museums or museums for copies of works of art. In the first nobody expects the wax Napoleon to be taken for real, but the hallucination serves to level the various historical periods and erase the distinction between historical reality and fantasy; in the case of the works of art what is culturally, if not psychologically, hallucinatory is the confusion between copy and original, and the fetishization of art as a sequence of famous subjects. In the ghost town, on the contrary, since the theatricality is explicit, the hallucination operates in making the visitors take part in the scene and thus become participants in that commercial fair that is apparently an element of the fiction but in fact represents the substantial aim of the whole imitative machine.

In an excellent essay on Disneyland as 'degenerate utopia' ('a degenerate utopia is an ideology realized in the form of myth'), Louis Marin analyzed the structure of that nineteenth-century frontier city street that receives entering visitors and distributes them through the various sectors of the magic city. Disneyland's Main Street seems the first scene of the fiction, whereas it is an extremely shrewd commercial reality. Main Street – like the whole city, for that matter – is presented as at once absolutely realistic and absolutely fantastic, and this is the advantage (in terms of artistic conception) of Disneyland over the other toy cities. The houses of Disneyland are full-size on the ground floor, and on a two-thirds scale on the floor above, so they give the impression of being inhabitable (and they are) but also of belonging to a fantastic past that we can grasp with our imagination. The Main Street façades are presented to us as toy houses and invite us to enter them, but their interior is always a disguised supermarket, where you buy obsessively, believing that you are still playing.

In this sense Disneyland is more hyperrealistic than the wax museum, precisely because the latter still tries to make us believe that what we are seeing reproduces reality absolutely, whereas Disneyland makes it clear that within its magic enclosure it is fantasy that is absolutely reproduced. The Palace of Living Arts presents its Venus de Milo as almost real, whereas Disneyland can permit itself to present its reconstructions as masterpieces of falsification, for what it sells is, indeed, goods, but genuine merchandise, not reproductions. What is falsified is our will to buy, which we take as real, and in this sense Disneyland is really the quintessence of consumer ideology.

But once the 'total fake' is admitted, in order to be enjoyed it must seem totally real. So the Polynesian restaurant will have, in addition to a fairly authentic menu, Tahitian waitresses in costume, appropriate vegetation, rock walls with little cascades, and once you are inside nothing must lead you to suspect that outside there is anything but Polynesia. If, between two trees, there appears a stretch of river that belongs to another sector, Adventureland, then that section of stream is so designed that it would not be unrealistic to see in Tahiti, beyond the garden hedge, a river like this. And if in the wax museums wax is not flesh, in Disneyland, when rocks are involved, they are rock, and water is water, and a baobab a baobab. When there is a fake – hippopotamus, dinosaur, sea serpent – it is not so much because it wouldn't be possible to have the real equivalent but because the public is meant to admire the perfection of the fake and its obedience to the program. In this sense Disneyland not only produces illusion, but – in confessing it – stimulates the desire for it: A real crocodile can be found in the zoo, and as a rule it is dozing or hiding, but Disneyland tells us that faked nature corresponds much more to our daydream demands. When, in the space of twenty-four hours, you go (as I did deliberately) from the fake New Orleans of Disneyland to the real one, and from the wild river of Adventureland to a trip on the Mississippi, where the captain of the paddle-wheel steamer says it is possible to see alligators on the banks of the river, and then you don't see any, you risk feeling homesick for Disneyland, where the wild animals don't have to be coaxed. Disneyland tells us that technology can give us more reality than nature can.

In this sense I believe the most typical phenomenon of this universe is not the more famous Fantasyland – an amusing carousel of fantastic journeys that take the visitor into the world of Peter Pan or Snow White, a wondrous machine whose fascination and lucid legitimacy it would be foolish to deny – but the Caribbean Pirates and the Haunted Mansion. The pirate show lasts a quarter of an hour (but you lose any sense of time, it could be ten minutes or thirty); you enter a series of caves, carried in boats over the surface of the water, you see first abandoned treasures, a captain's skeleton in a sumptuous bed of moldy brocade, pendent cobwebs, bodies of executed men devoured by ravens, while the skeleton addresses menacing admonitions to you. Then you navigate an inlet, passing through the crossfire of a galleon and the cannon of a fort, while the chief corsair shouts taunting challenges at the beleaguered garrison; then, as if along a river, you go by an invaded city which is being sacked, with the rape of the women, theft of jewels, torture of the mayor; the city burns like a match, drunken pirates sprawled on piles of kegs sing obscene songs; some, completely out of their heads, shoot at the visitors; the scene degenerates, everything collapses in flames, slowly the last songs die away, you emerge into the sunlight. Everything you have seen was on human scale, the vault of the caves became confused with that of the sky, the boundary of this underground world was that of the universe and it was impossible to glimpse its limits. The pirates moved, danced, slept, popped their eyes, sniggered, drank – really. You realize that they are robots, but you remain dumbfounded by their verisimilitude. And, in fact, the 'Audio-Animatronic' technique represented a great source of pride for Walt Disney, who had finally managed to achieve his own dream and reconstruct a fantasy world more real than reality, breaking down the wall of the second dimension, creating not a movie, which is illusion, but total theatre, and not with anthropomorphized animals, but with human beings. In fact, Disney's robots are masterpieces of electronics; each was devised by observing the expressions of a real actor, then building models, then developing skeletons of absolute precision, authentic computers in human form, to be dressed in 'flesh' and 'skin' made by craftsmen, whose command of realism is incredible. Each robot obeys a program, can synchronize the movements of mouth and eyes with the words and sounds of the audio, repeating *ad infinitum* all day long his established part (a sentence, one or two gestures) and the visitor, caught off guard by the succession of events, obliged to see several things at once, to left and right and straight ahead, has not time to look back and observe that the robot he has just seen is already repeating his eternal scenario.

The 'Audio-Animatronic' technique is used in many other parts of Disneyland and also enlivens a review of presidents of the United States, but in the pirates' cave, more than anywhere else, it demonstrates all its miraculous efficacy. Humans could do no better, and would cost more, but the important thing is precisely the fact that these are not humans and we know they're not. The pleasure of imitation, as the ancients knew, is one of the most innate in the human spirit; but here we not only enjoy a perfect imitation, we also enjoy the conviction that imitation has reached its apex and afterwards reality will always be inferior to it.

Similar criteria underlie the journey through the cellars of the Haunted Mansion, which looks at first like a rundown country house, somewhere between Edgar Allan Poe and the cartoons of Charles Addams; but inside, it conceals the most complete array of witchcraft surprises that anyone could desire. You pass through an abandoned graveyard, where skeletal hands raise gravestones from below, you cross a hill enlivened by a witches' sabbath complete with spirits and beldams; then you move through a room with a table all laid and a group of transparent ghosts in nineteenth-century costume dancing while diaphanous guests, occasionally vanishing into thin air, enjoy the banquet of a barbaric sovereign. You are grazed by cobwebs, reflected in crystals on whose surface a greenish figure appears, behind your back; you encounter moving candelabra. ... In no instance are these the cheap tricks of some tunnel of love; the involvement (always tempered by the humor of the inventions) is total. As in certain horror films, detachment is impossible, you are not witnessing another's horror, you are inside the horror through complete synesthesia; and if there is an earthquake the movie theater must also tremble.

I would say that these two attractions sum up the Disneyland philosophy more than the equally perfect models of the pirate ship, the river boat, and the sailing ship *Columbia*, all obviously in working order. And more than the Future section, with the science-fiction emotions it arouses (such as a flight to Mars experienced from inside a spacecraft, with all the effects of deceleration, loss of gravity, dizzying movement away from the earth, and so on). More than the models of rockets and atomic submarines, which prompted Marin to observe that whereas the fake Western cities, the fake New Orleans, the fake jungle provide life-size duplicates of organic but historical or fantastic events, these are reduced-scale models of mechanical realities of today, and so, where something is incredible, the full-scale model prevails, and where it is credible, the reduction serves to make it attractive to the imagination. The Pirates and the Ghosts sum up all Disneyland, at least from the point of view of our trip, because they transform the whole city into an immense robot, the final realization of the dreams of the eighteenth-century mechanics who gave life to the Writer of Neuchâtel and the Chess-playing Turk of Baron von Kempelen.

Disneyland's precision and coherence are to some extent disturbed by the ambitions of Disney World in Florida. Built later, Disney World is a hundred fifty times larger than Disneyland, and proudly presents itself not as a toy city but as the model of an urban agglomerate of the future. The structures that make up California's Disneyland form here only a marginal part of an immense complex of construction covering an area twice the size of Manhattan. The great monorail that takes you from the entrance to the Magic Kingdom (the Disneyland part proper) passes artificial bays and lagoons, a Swiss village, a Polynesian village, golf courses and tennis courts, an immense hotel: an area dedicated, in other words, to organized vacationing. So you reach the Magic Kingdom, your eyes already dazzled by so much science fiction that the sight of the high medieval castle (far more Gothic than Disneyland: a Strasbourg Cathedral, let's say, compared to a San Miniato) no longer stirs the imagination. Tomorrow, with its violence, has made the colors fade from the stories of Yesterday. In this respect Disneyland is much shrewder; it must be visited without anything to remind us of the future surrounding it. Marin has observed that, to enter it, the essential condition is to abandon your car in an endless parking lot and reach the boundary of the dream city by special little trains. And for a Californian, leaving his car means leaving his own humanity, consigning himself to another power, abandoning his own will.

An allegory of the consumer society, a place of absolute iconism, Disneyland is also a place of total passivity. Its visitors must agree to behave like its robots. Access to each attraction is regulated by a maze of metal railings which discourages any individual initiative. The number of visitors obviously sets the pace of the line; the officials of the dream, properly dressed in the uniforms suited to each specific attraction, not only admit the visitor to the threshold of the chosen sector, but, in successive phases, regulate his every move ('Now wait here please, go up now, sit down please, wait before standing up', always in a polite tone, impersonal, imperious, over the microphone). If the visitor pays this price, he can have not only 'the real thing' but the abundance of the reconstructed truth. Like the Hearst Castle, Disneyland also has no transitional spaces; there is always something to see, the great voids of modern architecture and city planning are unknown here. If America is the country of the Guggenheim Museum or the new skyscrapers of Manhattan, then Disneyland is a curious exception and American intellectuals are quite right to refuse to go there. But if America is what we have seen in the course of our trip, then Disneyland is its Sistine Chapel, and the hyperrealists of the art galleries are only the timid voyeurs of an immense and continuous 'found object'.

15 □ *Against Intellectual Complexity in Music*

Michael Nyman

Stockhausen's notoriously arrogant aside to Morton Feldman – '[I] once told Feldman that one of his pieces could be a moment in my music, but never the other way around'[1] – is indicative of an attitude that cannot comprehend true simplicity in music. A simple 'moment' can be recognized as such only when posited against another, more complex moment. In Stockhausen's music *simplified* moments are either set against other moments of greater complexity, or they fulfill a complex role in the total structure of the work; whereas Feldman's *simple* work is a complete field in which moments of greater and/or lesser simplicity, if they occur at all, have no intended relational significance in the traditional sense. In what we call experimental music – loosely speaking, the music of the Cage 'tradition' – simplicity is something approaching a constant, an absolute, although there are obviously degrees of simplicity, just as there are degrees of complexity. Still, simplicity is not one alternative to be selected from the vast reservoir of means of expression or techniques upon which the avant-garde composer can draw as occasion, instrumentation, or compositional situation demands. The straightforwardness of most experimental music, which usually finds the most direct route to the effective presentation of the chosen sound material, might be interpreted by an outsider as a reaction to traditional and modernist intellectual complexity. But it has not *simplified* the complex technical paraphernalia which makes European art music respectable; it has quite bluntly ignored that paraphernalia, since the aesthetic, structural, and expressive requirements of the so-called New Simplicity demand the development of a totally different, independent (some might say naive, innocent, and simple-minded) compositional methodology.

Reaction against complexity is, in fact, a characteristic of intellectually complex music itself, as Stockhausen himself noted when he observed that in the early days of total serialism in the fifties:

> all elements had equal rights in the forming process and constantly renewed *all* their characteristics from one sound to the next. ... If from one sound to the next, pitch,

From *October*, 13 (1980), 81–9.

duration, timbre, and intensity change, then the music finally becomes static: it changes extremely quickly, one is constantly traversing the entire realm of experience in a very short time and thus one finds oneself in a state of suspended animation, the music 'stands still'. If one wanted to articulate larger time-phases, the only way of doing this was to let one sound-characteristic predominate over all others for some time. However, under the circumstances then prevalent, this would have radically contradicted the sound-characteristics. And a solution was found to distribute in space, among different groups of loudspeakers, or instruments, variously long time-phases of this kind of homogeneous sound-structure.[2]

In the revolving brass chords in *Gruppen*, for instance, this simplification, a demonstrable reaction against a complex statistical rather than musical process, bears absolutely no relation to the simplicity described by John Cage in 1961 when discussing the music of La Monte Young:

> Young is doing something quite different from what I am doing, and it strikes me as being very important. Through the few pieces of his I've heard [presumably such minimal classics as *X for Henry Flint* and *Composition 1960 No. 7*], I've had, actually, utterly different experiences of listening than I've had with any other music. He is able either through the repetition of a single sound or through the continued performance of a single sound for a period like twenty minutes, to bring it about that after, say, five minutes, I discover that what I have all along been thinking was the same thing is not the same thing after all, but full of variety. I find his work remarkable almost in the same sense that the change of experience of seeing is when you look through a microscope. You see that there is something other than what you thought was there.
> On the other hand, La Monte Young's music can be heard by Europeans as being European. For example, take the repetition of a tone cluster or a single sound at a seemingly constant amplitude over, say, a ten-minute period. The European listener is able to think, 'Well, that is what we've always had, minus all the elements of variation.' So they imagine, you see, that something is being done to them, namely a simplification of what they're familiar with. My response is not that he is doing something to me, but that I am able to hear differently than I ever heard.[3]

Consider Young's chord of B and F sharp in *Composition 1960 No. 7*, or the dominant eleventh extended from one beat to over 200 beats by Steve Reich in his *Four Organs*. If we take these 'primitive' musical materials as reductions or concentrations of traditional tonal occurrences, then we are indeed talking of simplification. It is possible, of course, to analyze (rather than to hear) them in this way, especially if yours is a symbolic or metaphoric view of music. Reich, for instance, employs the dominant eleventh in such a way that it 'contains' both tonic and dominant chords, and could therefore be said to 'represent', in digest form, the tensions of the tonal system. As the dominant eleventh extends itself, we may perceive the tonic/dominant pull, that is, the dominant in the chord appears to 'resolve' onto its tonic element. It would, however, be incorrect to believe that when Reich sat down to compose *Four Organs* he had anything more in mind than the material itself (a 'preferred fragment' taken not from traditional music but more likely from Dizzy Gillespie) and the most suitable process for articulating this fragment over a comparatively long period of time.[4]

In the instance of the dominant eleventh, it should be remembered that one of the most fundamental lessons of Cage's aesthetic is the principle of not reducing the whole of music – or culture – to a single set, but the opposite: beginning from nothing, building from zero or, as 4′ 33″ shows, from silence. This is perhaps the fundamental difference between, on the one hand, an avant-garde whose intellectually complex music builds on, grows from, develops, and extends traditional compositional techniques and concepts and, on the other, experimental music, in which apparent straightforwardness and lack of *notated* complexity derives from principles alien to European music, at least since 1600.[5]

While the material of a work – the open fifth or the dominant eleventh – appears to arise from zero, this new compositional attitude actually arose out of serialism. In Reich and Young, specific, if unconventional, musical attitudes revealed themselves to be at work *within* serialism, rather than as a blanket reaction *against* serialism. Writing serial music for Berio at Mills College, Reich avoided transposing his rows in order to retain some sort of tonal feeling. And he approached the row itself as a repeating constant to be regrouped each time it recurred.

A totally new attitude towards duration arose out of Young's serial writing in the fifties; individual pitches began to extend themselves from within the serial context, so that in his *Octet for Brass* (1957) long notes would often be held for three or four minutes. Nothing else would happen, apart from the overlapping of other occasional long notes, and rests which lasted for a minute or more. From the viewpoint of traditional composition, we may justifiably speak of simplification, since there has been a significant reduction in pitch information and rhythmic complexity. This is emphasized even more in Young's subsequent *Trio for Strings*, where according to the composer there is a greater emphasis on harmony than in any other music, 'to the exclusion of almost any semblance of what had been generally known as melody'.[6] But once this new emphasis on extended duration as the *subject* of the composition emerged out of the old serial organism – leading naturally to the exclusive use of sustained notes, the melodyless harmony which Young continued to explore in his temporally all-embracing *The Tortoise, His Journeys and Dreams* – we can no longer speak of reduction, reaction, or even rejection, but of entirely new musical concerns and materials demanding entirely new methods of structuring and articulation.

In sketching this background to the so-called New Simplicity, it is also useful to distinguish two different reactions to one of the main exponents of intellectually complex music – Anton Webern. Both Reich and Young (as well as Christian Wolff in the 'first generation' of experimental composers in the early fifties) heard the results of Webern's serial manipulations in an entirely selective way. Reich has spoken of the 'intervallic consistency' of the *Orchestral Variations*, which 'give[s] a kind of harmonic sound to his music'.[7] And Young, noting Webern's practice of repeating the same pitches in the same octave positions whatever their position in the different forms and transpositions of the row, remarked that while on the surface this represented 'constant variation', it could also be heard as stasis, 'because it uses the same form throughout the piece. ... We have the same information repeated over and over and over again.'[8] This kind of selective hearing, which depends, of course, on the hearer's individual musical interests and perceptions, is the obverse of the situation outlined by Cage. In Webern one perceives sameness out of (apparent) variety, while in Young's, Glass's, or Reich's music one perceives variety out of (apparent) sameness – a variety of a different order, demanding a different mode of listening and of experiencing musical time.

At times the question of variety-in-sameness poses problems for the performer as well, as Cornelius Cardew indicated in his analysis of Young's seminal *X for Henry Flint*. Young's work exists only in oral form and concerns a single, dense, heavy, decaying sound repeated as uniformly and regularly as possible. Cardew asks:

> What is the model for this uniformity? The first sound? Or does each sound become the model for the one succeeding it? If the former, the first sound has to be fixed in the mind as a mental ideal which all the remaining sounds are to approach as closely as possible. (In practice the first sound too is an attempt to approach a mental image that exists before the piece began.) If the latter method is chosen, constant care has to be taken to assimilate the various accidental variations as they occur. David Tudor has approached the piece in this way and tells how, on noticing that certain keys in the centre of the keyboard were not being depressed, it became his task to make sure that these particular keys continued to be silent. The task of assimilating and maintaining accidental variations, if logically pursued, requires superhuman powers of concentration and technique. ... It must be remembered that although uniformity is demanded ('as far as possible'), what is *desired* is variation. It is simply this: that the variation that is desired is that which results from the human (not the superhuman) attempt at uniformity.[9]

Written in 1963, such minutely detailed analytical sophistry may be somewhat outdated in terms of contemporary musical practice; yet it does show that there are forms of complexity other than the intellectual at work in experimental music, which, generally speaking, reveal creative and perceptual areas neglected in traditional and avant-garde music, and which have changed the accepted emphases in the conception–composition–performance–perception chain.

To return to the experimental composers' response to Webern: How are we to judge the reaction to Webern's intellectual complexity as it manifests itself in the work of Morton Feldman, for example? It was through Webern that Feldman first met Cage – after a performance of the *Symphony*, which both found 'beautiful'. Feldman's interest in the early fifties was, he claims, in sound rather than structure. Abstract-expressionist painting suggested a sound world 'more direct, more immediate, more physical than anything that had existed before'. Varèse, he felt, had searched after this ideal, 'but he was too "Varèse"'; Webern also glimpsed it, 'but his work was too involved with the disciplines of the 12-tone system'.[10] It is well known that Feldman's first 'experimental' pieces had certain improvisational or free elements, since 'the new structure required a concentration more demanding than if the technique were that of still photography', which is what precise notation had become for him. In a piece like *Projection No. 2* for flute, trumpet, and cello, he said that his desire was not to 'compose' but to 'project sounds into time, free from a compositional rhetoric that had no place here. In order not to involve the performer [Feldman himself] in memory [relationships], and because sounds no longer had an inherent shape',[11] he allowed for certain indeterminacies in pitch. This was certainly a heretical idea in the face of a serial system which was then, as it is now, more or less exclusively pitch oriented. In a later statement, Feldman made his attitude towards serialism startlingly clear:

> It appears to me that the subject of music, from Machaut to Boulez, has always been its construction. Melodies of 12-tone rows just don't happen. They must be constructed. ... To demonstrate any formal idea in music, whether structure or stricture, is a matter of construction, in which the methodology is the controlling metaphor of the composition. ... Only by 'unfixing' the elements traditionally used to construct a piece of music could the sounds exist in themselves – not as symbols, or memories which were the memories of other music to begin with.

The radical concept is, of course, that of *unfixing relationships*, since all post-Renaissance music has been concerned with fixing with increasing exactitude the relationships between sounds. Cage's attitude towards unfixing relationships was – and unfortunately remains – as rigorous and strict as the serialist's towards fixing relationships. It might be useful to recall Cage's approach, even though it might appear to be only indirectly related to the so-called New Simplicity. In 1970 he remarked that he would assume:

> that relations would exist between sounds as they would exist between people and that those relationships are more complex than any I would be able to prescribe. So by simply dropping that responsibility of making relationships I don't lose the relationship. I keep the situation in what you might call a natural complexity that can be observed in one way or another. Now it used to be thought that the function of the artist was to express himself and therefore he had to set up particular relationships. I think that this whole question of art is a question of changing our minds and that the function of the artist is not self-expression but rather self-alteration, and the thing being altered is clearly not his hands or his eyes but rather his mind. ...
>
> Given a particular situation, one person will observe certain relationships, another will observe others. If we have the view we used to have, that there was only one right way of observing the relationships of things, then we have a situation that really doesn't appeal to me. We have, in other words, one thing that's right and all the rest are wrong. I would like to have a multiplicity of rights.[12]

Compared with the music of La Monte Young, Cage's music appears, at its most characteristic (and he would say its best), to be 'complex'; but this non- or even anti-intellectual complexity is only apparent, since any relationships that emerge are only skin deep, like the relationships between strangers who happen to pass on the street.

This, then, is just one extreme of the New Simplicity, where all musical events, devoid of intentional relationships, are of equal importance (or, in Cage, of equal unimportance). The opposite extreme, represented in America by the music of Terry Riley, Reich, Glass, Young, and Jon Gibson, and in England by Gavin Bryars, John White, Christopher Hobbs, and myself, is closely related conceptually, methodologically, and structurally to Cage, even when its purposes and methods appear to contradict this relation. Cage himself perceived the similarity; his own music may be antistructure, yet if one of these younger composers 'maintains in his work aspects of structure, they are symmetrical in character, canonic or enjoying an equal importance of parts, either those that are present at one instant, or those that succeed one another in time'.[13] Once Cage had attempted – and succeeded – in removing the glue from musical relationships by resorting to chance methods of articulating a multiplicity of sounds in combination and sequence, younger composers found themselves free to explore and to realize the potential of extending *single* sounds or limited sets of sounds and to create relationships between different aspects of these restricted sets.

The equality of vertical and horizontal compositional aspects is fundamental to experimental music. Simplicity is an absolute, a constant, not part of a scale of values, textures, techniques, dramatic structure, or whatever, spanning the entire gamut from absolute simplicity to frightening (and usually self-defeating) complexity. Nor are there moments of greater or lesser simplicity during a work, unless they result naturally from the chosen process, as for example in Reich's *Pendulum Music*, at the conclusion of which all the microphones come to rest – reach unison, so to speak – after the more 'complex' interaction of independent and gradually elongated feedback pulses. Similarly, simplicity is not a dualistic or multiple quality (in the end, the apparent complexity of Cage's multiplicity is simple, since no structural relations are established between successive parts); only in rare cases, such as Gavin Bryars's *Jesus' Blood Never Failed Me Yet*, are melody/harmony polarizations aimed for or achieved. When they are – in my own music, for instance – repetition guarantees that such overt background/foreground focus is destroyed, negated, or reassessed in some way. Similarly, the parts of a sectional work, such as Reich's *Drumming*, relate to each other in a $1:1$, or $1:1+1$ ... relationship.

In this new, simple experimental music the given material of a piece is its *only* material and relates only to itself; there are no contrasting, complementary, or secondary ideas. The single, unitary musical idea, usually of immense and deliberate simplicity, is extended through the composition by means of repetition, augmentation, phrase shifting, imitation, accumulation, rotation, number permutation, vertical stacking, addition, layering, etc. These basic techniques are not used, as they are in 'complex' music, to transform, disguise, transubstantiate, or intermodulate either themselves or the initial musical idea; where change is an important part of a work (in the old terminology, when the work is more 'developed'), the systems, procedures, and processes guarantee that the identity of the material is always audibly retained.

Perhaps the reaction of experimental composers to the so-called intellectual complexity of avant-garde music is a reaction not against intellectual complexity itself, but against what brings about the need for such complexity, as well as its audible result. We should perhaps speak of the qualities that serial music denied and which have resurfaced in experimental music: symmetrical rhythms (i.e. regular beat); euphony; consonant, diatonic, or modal materials; absence of theatricality and grandiloquence, of drama, of sound used as symbol.

In discussing experimental music as a whole, we should perhaps read 'New Objectivity' for 'New Simplicity', since composer-publisher-publicist Dick Higgins found Cage's emphasis on chance procedures significant as a means of distancing oneself from one's materials; the composer no longer feels the necessity of consciously influencing the creative process at every moment. According to Higgins, 'What Cage did was to place the material at one remove from the composer, by allowing it to be determined by a system which he determined. And the real innovation lies in the emphasis on the creation of a system.'[14] This 'emphasis on the creation of a system' applies both to the mechanical acceptance of a system (in the percussion music of Hobbs and White, for example) and to the music of Steve Reich, who has increasingly sought to make personal 'aesthetic' interventions which seem to contradict the principles laid down in the 1968 statement *Music as a Gradual Process*. Despite the intervention of personal decisions which to some extent override the abstract mechanics of the system, Reich's music still retains the basic nontraditional characteristics shared by all experimental music: that of stasis and a nondirectional, nondramatic, nondynamic approach to musical structure; there are no hierarchies, no transitions, no tension, no relaxation, and change is quantitative rather than qualitative.

In 1948 Cage wrote: 'We may recognize what may be called perhaps a new contemporary awareness of form: it is static, rather than progressive in character.'[15] This was unconsciously echoed some twenty years later by La Monte Young when he distinguished his music from that of the Western tradition: 'Climax and directionality have been among the most important guiding factors [in music since the thirteenth century], whereas music before that time, from the chants through organum and Machaut, used stasis as a point of structure a little bit more the way certain Eastern musical systems have.'[16] And just as pre-thirteenth-century and non-Western music often present surprisingly complex perceptual problems for the listener reared on European classical music, so too does this 'simple' music that I have chosen to call experimental.

Notes

1. Jonathan Cott, 'Talking (whew!) to Karlheinz Stockhausen', *Rolling Stone*, 8 July 1971.
2. Karlheinz Stockhausen, 'Music in space', 'Two lectures', *Die Reihe*, 5, Theodore Presser, Bryn Mawr, 1961, p. 69.
3. Roger Reynolds, 'Interview with John Cage', in *John Cage*, Henmar Press, New York, 1962, p. 52.

4. Two points of clarification are necessary: first, twenty or so minutes may not be a long duration for a piece of 'new music', yet it may (or may not) be a long period for the gradual augmentation of a single chord; second, 'sitting down to compose' is a metaphor taken from traditional composition. It usually has little to do with the process of producing experimental music, which effectively bypasses the traditional idea of the 'craft of musical composition' and all that it involves.

5. My own music, which I consider to fall into the experimental category as defined in my book *Experimental Music, Cage and Beyond* (Schirmer Books, New York, 1974), is, however, related to seventeenth- and eighteenth-century variation forms, while systems music in general is related, however distantly, to serialism.

6. Richard Kostelanetz, 'Conversation with La Monte Young', in La Monte Young and Maria Zazeela, *Selected Writings*, Heiner Friedrich, Munich, 1969.

7. Personal communication to the author.

8. Kostelanetz, 'Conversation with La Monte Young'.

9. Cornelius Cardew, *Treatise Handbook*, Peters Editions, London, 1971.

10. Cited in Michael Nyman, *Experimental Music*, p. 44.

11. *Ibid.*

12. Frank Kermode, 'Is an elite necessary?' (interview with Cage), *The Listener* (London), 5 November 1970.

13. John Cage, *A Year from Monday*, Wesleyan University Press, Middletown, CT, 1967, p. 31.

14. Dick Higgins, *foew & ombwhnw*, Something Else Press, New York, 1969.

15. Richard Kostelanetz (ed.), *John Cage*, Praeger, New York, 1970, p. 81.

16. Kostelanetz, 'Conversation with La Monte Young'.

Part Four

Crisis in the Avant-Garde

Introduction

Paradoxically, tradition is revolutionary. A tradition is always older than the immediate past; hence the endorsement of tradition always implies a rejection of that immediate past in the interests of something purer, and such rejection is always experienced as revolutionary, an overturning of the values of an immediate past which have outlived their usefulness. This makes sense of the great modernist paradox in which T. S. Eliot claimed 'tradition' as his own in what was perceived as an overtly revolutionary form of poetry. By extension, the endorsement of tradition, in the rejection of the immediate past, also always presupposes the possibility of a different future; and the adoption of tradition can thus (though this is not always *necessarily* the case) put an artist in the position of being avant-garde, the originator of a different future, the liberator of a number of proleptic possibilities. A second level of paradox arises, however, whenever this strategy is repeated. Once it becomes possible to repeat the avant-garde procedure of the 'revolutionary' adoption of 'tradition', one has begun the process whereby the avant-garde strategy is in danger of becoming itself 'traditional' in a weak sense of the term. An inbuilt crisis of obsolescence is necessarily inscribed in the logic of the avant-garde. The avant-garde artist is an emancipatory 'hero' whose very individuation and status as a leading figure or exemplary artist is necessarily worthless, for such individuation is characterised by the necessity of her or his self-sacrifice in the interests of the arrière-garde.

If we are in a moment when modernism is no longer adequate to our condition, and if we have the emergence of something which can be characterised as 'postmodern' in the weak, chronological sense of the term, then it seems obvious to identify the postmodern with a contemporary avant-garde. But such an allegiance between the postmodern and the avant-garde is, at best, rather uneasy. Huyssen indicates in the piece included here that two crucial aspects of the avant-garde are, first, the constitution of an intimate relation between art and the everyday lived-world and, secondly, the vibrant production of a sense of the future. In a comparison between the cultural conditions of Europe and the United States of America in the twentieth century, Huyssen manages to identify the historical European avant-garde (Dada, surrealism, Constructivism, etc.) as 'the most fascinating component of modernity', with whose 'progressive' project it is complicit. Many sectors of the contemporary – postmodern – culture 'would reject the avant-garde's universalizing and totalizing gesture as much as its ambiguous espousal of technology and modernization'. Yet this does not necessarily put the

217

postmodern in the camp of those who reject the revolutionary credentials of the historical avant-garde. This historical avant-garde itself may now occupy the position of an immediate past which is to be rejected in the name of a postmodern gesture.

This does not deal with the whole of the problem. As Bürger shows, 'the protest of the historical avant-garde against art as institution is accepted as *art*', which makes it rather difficult for a contemporary avant-garde to continue this process, a process which is central to the point of the avant-garde's project of eliminating the idea of an autonomous art, divorced from the everyday political and lived world. In the contemporary situation, we do indeed have works which break down the division between autonomous aesthetic realm   and lived-historical political realm; but they can be populist works which make art merely consumable, producing a commodity aesthetics which is hardly conducive to revolutionary activity. It seems that the avant-garde, if it is to continue its project, must be 'difficult'.

The avant-garde artwork is, in a strict sense of the word, 'untimely'; by definition, it must be out of its 'proper' historical moment, more appropriately located in the future which it envisages and towards which it beckons. It thereby problematises, in the manner of Hegel at the start of *The Phenomenology of Spirit*, the great deictics 'here' and 'now'. It is this terrain on which Lyotard exercises his thought on the avant-garde in the piece included here. The avant-garde is caught in an 'event', a term which has a very specific sense in Lyotard's lexicon. There is an 'it happens' which cannot be assimilated to consciousness, or does not take its place within consciousness. That is to say, as Lyotard puts it here, the 'it happens' rather 'dismantles' consciousness, and is not mastered by it. We might put it in other words by saying that the 'it happens' refuses to be assimilated into a system according to which consciousness orientates itself to the world. The 'it happens' is thus the moment of a dislocation, the moment when a 'now' or a 'here' gives a momentary glimpse of a 'then' and a 'there'. The function of an avant-garde is to go a stage further and to enable the posing of the question: 'Does it happen?' With such a question, the consciousness implicitly acknowledges its deprivation of a specific mastery, the mastery of time. The mastery of time is that which allows consciousness to insert a random 'it happens' into a sequence or narrative which will 'make sense' of the 'it happens' and thereby evacuate it of force. That meaningful sequence is itself given by the structure of consciousness itself. But the avant-garde disrupts and denies such mastery, dislocating consciousness with respect to time, depriving it of its 'mastery', but enabling the possibility of a contemporary 'sublime'.

Lyotard's postmodern, thus, has its own tradition, deriving from – among others – Kant and Burke on the sublime. Oliva adopts an ostensibly more radical position than this in 'The International Trans-avant-garde', included here. This piece is influenced by debates in anthropological linguistics and in the 'evolution' of specific languages in specific cultures. Rather than adopting the idea that one universal language slowly evolves into variant linguistic programmes with a resulting linear view of historical development, Oliva approaches contemporary art history from what he characterises as a more 'nomadic' viewpoint. In this respect, he is at one with the nomadism advanced by Deleuze and Guattari in their critique of totalising and universalising systems or in theory itself. The 'tradition' according to which the trans-avant-garde defines itself is not singular, but rather eclectic; the result is that the trans-avant-garde is, in a strict sense of the term, 'directionless' or amorphous. We have here the validation of an art that 'does not entail identification with the styles of the past, but the ability to pick and choose from their surface, in the conviction that, in a society in transition toward an undefinable end, the only option open is that afforded by a nomadic and transitory mentality'. The international trans-avant-garde will thus avoid the confrontational 'revolutionary' stance of the historical avant-gardes, and will prefer to operate 'laterally', making affiliations which do not presuppose the arrogation to themselves of a proleptic status. The temporal linearity implicit in the revolutionary stance of all historical avant-gardes gives way here to a spatial horizon across which affiliations and disaffiliations may occur; fragmentariness, mutability, inconstancy are the results.

The articles gathered here focus the crisis of the avant-garde in ways which are relevant to the entire postmodern debate. What we witness is the graduated shifts between a consciousness determined by time on the one hand, and a consciousness determined by the horizontality of space on the other: the 'here, now' which is called into question in postmodernism.

16 □ *The Search for Tradition: Avant-garde and post-modernism in the 1970s*

Andreas Huyssen

Imagine Walter Benjamin in Berlin, the city of his childhood, walking through the international avant-garde exhibit *Tendenzen der zwanziger Jahre*, on display in 1977 in the new Nationalgalerie built by Bauhaus architect Mies van der Rohe in the 1960s. Imagine Walter Benjamin as a *flaneur* in the city of boulevards and arcades he so admirably described, happening upon the Centre Georges Pompidou and its multi-media show *Paris–Berlin 1900–1933*, which was a major cultural event in 1978. Or imagine the theorist of media and image reproduction in 1981 in front of a television set watching Robert Hughes's BBC-produced eight-part series on avant-garde art, 'The Shock of the New'.[1] Would this major critic and aesthetician of the avant-garde have rejoiced in its success – manifest even in the architecture of the museums housing the exhibits – or would shadows of melancholy have clouded his eyes? Would he, perhaps, have been shocked by 'The Shock of the New', or would he have felt called upon to revise the theory of post-auratic art? Or would he simply have argued that the administered culture of late capitalism had finally succeeded in imposing the phony spell of commodity fetishism even on that art which more than any other had challenged the values and traditions of bourgeois culture? Maybe after another penetrating gaze at that architectural monument to wholesale technological progress in the heart of Paris, Benjamin would have quoted himself: 'In every era the attempt must be made to wrest tradition away from a conformism that is about to overpower it.'[2] Thus might he acknowledge not only that the avant-garde – embodiment of anti-tradition – has itself become tradition, but, moreover, that its inventions and its imagination have become integral even to Western culture's most official manifestations.

Of course, there is nothing new in such observations. Already in the early 1960s Hans Magnus Enzensberger had analyzed the aporias of the avant-garde,[3] and Max Frisch had attributed to Brecht 'the striking ineffectualness of a classic'.[4] The use of visual montage, one of the major inventions of the avant-garde, had already become

From Huyssen, A., *After the Great Divide*, Macmillan, London/Indiana University Press, Bloomington, 1986, pp. 160–77.

standard procedure in commercial advertising, and reminders of literary modernism popped up in Volkswagen's beetle ads: 'Und läuft und läuft und läuft'. In fact, obituaries on modernism and the avant-garde abounded in the 1960s, in both Western Europe and the United States.

Avant-garde and modernism had not only been accepted as major cultural expressions of the twentieth century. They were fast becoming history. This then raised questions about the status of that art and literature which was produced after World War II, after the exhaustion of surrealism and abstraction, after the death of Musil and Thomas Mann, Valéry and Gide, Joyce and T. S. Eliot. One of the first critics to theorize about a shift from modernism to postmodernism was Irving Howe in his 1959 essay 'Mass society and postmodern fiction'.[5] And only a year later, Harry Levin used the same concept of the postmodern to designate what he saw as an 'anti-intellectual undercurrent' which threatened the humanism and enlightenment so characteristic of the culture of modernism.[6] Writers such as Enzensberger and Frisch clearly continued in the tradition of modernism (and this is true for Enzensberger's poetry of the early 1960s as well as for Frisch's plays and novels), and critics such as Howe and Levin sided with modernism against the newer developments, which they could only see as symptoms of decline. But postmodernism[7] took off with a vengeance in the early to mid-1960s, most visibly in Pop art, in experimental fiction, and in the criticism of Leslie Fiedler and Susan Sontag. Since then the notion of postmodernism has become the key to almost any attempt to capture the specific and unique qualities of contemporary activities in art and architecture, in dance and music, in literature and theory. Debates in the late 1960s and early 1970s in the United States were increasingly oblivious to modernism and to the historical avant-garde. Postmodernism reigned supreme, and a sense of novelty and cultural change was pervasive.

How then do we explain the striking fascination of the late 1970s with the avant-garde of the first three to four decades of this century? What is the meaning of this energetic comeback, in the age of postmodernism, of Dada, constructivism, futurism, surrealism, and the New Objectivity of the Weimar Republic? Exhibits of the classical avant-garde in France, Germany, England and the United States turned into major cultural events. Substantial studies of the avant-garde were published in the United States and in West Germany, initiating lively debates.[8] Conferences were held on various aspects of modernism and the avant-garde.[9] All of this has happened at a time when there seems to be little doubt that the classical avant-garde has exhausted its creative potential and when the waning of the avant-garde is widely acknowledged as a *fait accompli*. Is this a case, then, of Hegel's owl of Minerva beginning its flight after the shades of night have fallen? Or are we dealing with a nostalgia for the 'good years' of twentieth-century culture? And if nostalgia it is, does it point to the exhaustion of cultural resources and creativity in our own time or does it hold the promise of a revitalization in contemporary culture? What, after all, is the place of postmodernism in all this? Can we perhaps compare this phenomenon with that other obnoxious nostalgia of the 1970s, the nostalgia for Egyptian mummies (Tut exhibit in United States), medieval emperors (Stauffer exhibit in Stuttgart), or, most recently, Vikings (Minneapolis)? A search for traditions seems to be involved in all these instances. Is this search for tradition perhaps just another sign of the conservatism of the 1970s, the cultural equivalent, as it were, of the political backlash or the so-called *Tendenzwende*? Or, alternatively, can we interpret the museum and TV revival of the classical avant-garde as a defense against the neo-conservative attacks on the culture of modernism and avant-gardism, attacks which have intensified in these last years in Germany, France and the United States?

In order to answer some of these questions it may be useful to compare the status of art, literature, and criticism in the late 1970s with that of the 1960s. Paradoxically, the 1960s, for all their attacks on modernism and the avant-garde, still stand closer to the traditional notion of the avant-garde than the archeology of modernity so characteristic of the late 1970s. Much confusion could have been avoided if critics had paid closer attention to distinctions that need to be made between avant-garde and modernism as well as to the different relationship of each one to mass culture in the United States and Europe respectively. American critics especially tended to use the terms avant-garde and modernism interchangeably. To give just two examples, Renato Poggioli's *Theory of the Avant-Garde*, translated from the Italian in 1968, was reviewed in the United States as if it were a book about modernism,[10] and John Weightman's *The Concept of the Avant-Garde* of 1973 is subtitled *Explorations in Modernism*.[11] Both avant-garde and modernism may legitimately be understood as representing artistic emanations from the sensibility of modernity, but from a European perspective it makes little sense to lump Thomas Mann together with Dada, Proust with André Breton, or Rilke with Russian constructivism. While there are areas of overlap between the tradition of the avant-garde and that of modernism (e.g. vorticism and Ezra Pound, radical language experimentation and James Joyce, expressionism and Gottfried Benn), the overall aesthetic and political differences are too pervasive to be ignored. Thus Matei Calinescu makes the following point:

> In France, Italy, Spain and other European countries the avantgarde, despite its various and often contradictory claims, tends to be regarded as the most extreme form of artistic negativism – art itself being the first victim. As for modernism, whatever its specific meaning in different languages and for different authors, it never conveys that sense of universal and hysterical negation so characteristic of the avantgarde. The anti-traditionalism of modernism is often subtly traditional.[12]

As to the political differences, the historical avant-garde tended predominantly to the left, the major exception being Italian futurism, while the right could claim a surprising number of modernists among its supporters, Ezra Pound, Knut Hamsun, Gottfried Benn, Ernst Jünger among others.

Whereas Calinescu makes much of the negativistic, anti-aesthetic and self-destructive aspects of the avant-garde as opposed to the reconstructive art of the modernists, the aesthetic and political project of the avant-garde might be approached in more positive terms. In modernism art and literature retained their traditional nineteenth-century autonomy from everyday life, an autonomy which had first been articulated by Kant and Schiller in the late eighteenth century; the 'institution art' (Peter Bürger),[13] i.e. the traditional way in which art and literature were produced, disseminated, and received, is never challenged by modernism but maintained intact. Modernists such as T. S. Eliot and Ortega y Gasset emphasized time and again that it was their mission to salvage the purity of high art from the encroachments of urbanization, massification, technological modernization – in short, of modern mass culture. The avant-garde of the first three decades of this century, however, attempted to subvert art's autonomy, its artificial separation from life, and its institutionalization as 'high art' that was perceived to feed right into the legitimation needs of the nineteenth-century forms of bourgeois society. The avant-garde posited the reintegration of art and life as its major project at a time when that traditional society, especially in Italy, Russia, and Germany, was undergoing a major transformation towards a qualitatively new stage of modernity. Social and political ferment of the 1910s and 1920s was the breeding ground for avant-garde radicalism in art and literature as well as in politics.[14] When Enzensberger wrote about the aporias of the avant-garde several decades later, he did not just have the co-option of the avant-garde by the culture industry in mind, as is sometimes surmised; he fully understood the political dimension of the problem and pointed out how the historical avant-garde had failed to deliver what it had always promised: to sever political, social and aesthetic chains, explode cultural reifications, throw off traditional forms of domination, liberate repressed energies.[15]

If with these distinctions in mind we look at United States culture of the 1960s it becomes clear that the 1960s can be regarded as the closing chapter in the tradition of avant-gardism. Like all avant-gardes since Saint-Simon and the utopian socialists and anarchists up through Dada, surrealism, and the post-revolutionary art of Soviet Russia in the early 1920s, the 1960s fought tradition, and this revolt took place at a time of political and social turmoil. The promise of unlimited abundance, political stability, and new technological frontiers of the Kennedy years was shattered fast, and social conflict emerged dominant in the civil rights movement, in the urban riots, and in the anti-war movement. It certainly is more than coincidental that the protest culture of the period adopted the label 'counter-culture', thus projecting an image of an avant-garde leading the way to an alternative kind of society. In the field of art, Pop revolted against abstract expressionism and sparked off a series of art movements from Op to Fluxus, Concept, and Minimalism which made the art scene of the 1960s as lively and vibrating as it was commercially profitable and fashionable.[16] Peter Brook and the Living Theatre exploded the endless entrapments of absurdism and created a new style of theatrical performance. The theater attempted to bridge the gap between stage and audience and experimented with new forms of immediacy and spontaneity in performance. There was a participatory ethos in the theater and in the arts which can easily be linked to the teach-ins and sit-ins of the protest movement. Exponents of a new sensibility rebelled against the complexities and ambiguities of modernism, embracing camp and pop culture instead, and literary critics rejected the congealed canon and interpretive practices of the New Criticism, claiming for their own writing the creativity, autonomy and presence of original creation.

When Leslie Fiedler declared the 'Death of avant-garde literature' in 1964,[17] he was really attacking modernism, and he himself embodied the ethos of the classical avant-garde, American style. I say 'American style' because Fiedler's major concern was not to democratize 'high art'; his goal was rather to validate popular culture and to challenge the increasing institutionalization of high art. Thus when a few years later he wanted to 'Cross the border – close that gap' (1968)[18] between high culture and popular culture, he reaffirmed precisely the classical avant-garde's project to reunite these artificially separated realms of culture. For a moment in the 1960s it seemed the Phoenix avant-garde had risen from the ashes, fancying a flight toward the new frontier of the postmodern. Or was American postmodernism rather a Baudelairean albatross trying in vain to lift off the deck of the culture industry? Was postmodernism plagued from its very inception by the same aporias Enzensberger had already analyzed so eloquently in 1962? It seems that even in the United States the uncritical embracing of Western and camp, porno and rock, pop and counter-culture as genuine popular culture points to an amnesia which may have been the result of Cold War politics as much as of the postmodernists' relentless fight against tradition. American analyses of mass culture did have a critical edge in the late 1940s and 1950s[19] which went all but unacknowledged in the 1960s' uncritical enthusiasm for camp, pop, and the media.

A major difference between the United States and Europe in the 1960s is that European writers, artists, and intellectuals then were much more aware of the increasing co-option of all modernist and avant-garde art by the culture industry. Enzensberger, after all, had not only written about the aporias of the avant-garde, but about the pervasiveness of the 'consciousness industry' as well.[20] Since the tradition of the avant-garde in Europe did not seem to offer what, for historical reasons, it could still offer in the United States, one politically feasible way to react to the classical avant-garde and to cultural tradition in general was to declare the death of all art and literature and to call for cultural revolution. But even this rhetorical gesture, articulated most emphatically in Enzensberger's *Kursbuch* in 1968 and in the Parisian graffiti of May '68, was part of the traditional anti-aesthetic, anti-elitist, and anti-bourgeois strategies of the avant-garde. And by no means all writers and artists heeded the call. Peter Handke, for instance, denounced as infantile the attack on all high art and literature and he continued to write experimental plays, poetry, and prose. And the cultural left in West Germany, which agreed with Enzensberger's funeral for art and literature as long as it buried 'bourgeois' art only, undertook the task of unearthing an alternative cultural tradition, especially that of the left avant-gardes of the Weimar Republic. But the reappropriation of the left tradition of the Weimar Republic did not revitalize contemporary art and literature in Germany the way the undercurrent of Dada had revitalized the American art scene of the 1960s. Important exceptions to this general observation can be found in the work of Klaus Staeck, Günter Wallraff, and Alexander Kluge, but they remain isolated cases.

It soon became clear that the European attempt to escape from the 'ghetto' of art and to break the bondage of the culture industry also had ended in failure and frustration. Whether in the Geman protest movement or in May '68 in France, the illusion that cultural revolution was imminent foundered on the hard realities of the status quo. Art was not reintegrated into everyday life. The imagination did not come to power. The Centre Georges Pompidou was built instead, and the SPD came to power in West Germany. The vanguard thrust of group movements developing and asserting the newest style seemed to be broken after 1968. In Europe, 1968 marks not the breakthrough then hoped for, but rather the replayed end of the traditional avant-garde. Symptomatic of the 1970s were loners like Peter Handke, whose work defies the notion of a unitary style; cult figures like Joseph Beuys, who conjures up an archaic past; or film-makers like Herzog, Wenders, and Fassbinder, whose films – despite their critique of contemporary Germany – lack one of the basic prerequisites of avant-garde art, a sense of the future.

In the United States, however, the sense of the future, which had asserted itself so powerfully in the 1960s, is still alive today in the postmodernist scene, even though its breathing space is shrinking fast as a result of recent economic and political changes (e.g. the cutting of the NEA budget). There also seems to be a major shift of postmodernist interest from the earlier two-pronged concern with popular culture and with experimental art and literature, to a new focus on cultural theory, a shift which certainly reflects the academic institutionalization of postmodernism, but is not fully explained by it. More on this later. What concerns me here is the temporal imagination of postmodernism, the unshaken confidence of being at the edge of history which characterizes the whole trajectory of American postmodernism since the 1960s and of which the notion of a *post-histoire* is only one of the sillier manifestations. A possible explanation of this resilience to the shifting mood of the culture at large, which certainly since the mid-1970s has all but lost its confidence in the future, may lie precisely in the subterranean proximity of postmodernism to those movements, figures and intentions of the classical European avant-garde which were hardly ever acknowledged by the Anglo-Saxon notion of modernism. Despite the importance of Man Ray and the activities of Picabia and Duchamp in New York, New York Dada remained at best a marginal phenomenon in American culture, and neither Dada nor surrealism ever met with much public success in the United States. Precisely this fact made Pop, happenings, Concept, experimental music, surfiction, and performance art of the 1960s and 1970s look more novel than they really were. The audience's expectation horizon in the United States was fundamentally different from what it was in Europe. Where Europeans might react with a sense of *déjà vu*, Americans could legitimately sustain a sense of novelty, excitement, and breakthrough.

A second major factor comes into play here. If we want to understand fully the power the dadaist subcurrent assumed in the United States in the 1960s, the absence of an American Dada or surrealist movement in the earlier twentieth century also needs to be explained. As Peter Bürger has argued, the major goal of the European avant-gardes was to undermine, attack, and transform the bourgeois 'institution art'. Such an iconoclastic attack on cultural institutions and traditional modes of representation, narrative structure, perspective, and poetic sensibility only made sense in countries where 'high art' had an essential role to play in legitimizing bourgeois political and social domination, e.g. in the museum and salon culture, in the theaters, concert halls and opera houses and in the socialization and education process in general. The cultural politics of twentieth-century avant-gardism would have been meaningless (if not regressive) in the United States, where 'high art' was still struggling hard to gain wider legitimacy and to be taken seriously by the public. Thus it is not surprising that major American writers since Henry James, such as T. S. Eliot, Faulkner and Hemingway, Pound and Stevens, felt drawn to the constructive sensibility of modernism, which insisted on the dignity and autonomy of literature, rather than to the iconoclastic and anti-aesthetic ethos of the European avant-garde, which attempted to break the political bondage of high culture through a fusion with popular culture, and to integrate art into life.

I would suggest that it was not only the absence of an indigenous American avant-garde in the classical European sense, say in the 1920s, which, forty years later, benefited the postmodernists' claim to novelty in their struggle against the entrenched traditions of modernism, abstract expressionism, and New Criticism. There is more to it than that. A European-style avant-gardist revolt against tradition made eminent sense in the United States at a time when high art had become institutionalized in the burgeoning museum, concert, and paperback culture of the 1950s, when modernism itself had entered the mainstream via the culture industry, and later, during the Kennedy years, when high culture began to take on functions of political representation (Robert Frost and Pablo Casals at the White House).

All of this, then, is not at all to say that postmodernism is merely a pastiche of an earlier continental avant-garde. It rather serves to point to the similarity and continuity between American postmodernism and certain segments of an earlier European avant-garde, a similarity on the levels of formal experimentation and of a critique of the 'institution art'. This continuity was already marginally acknowledged in some postmodernist criticism, e.g., by Fiedler and Ihab Hassan,[21] but it emerged in full clarity with the recent retrospectives of and writings on the classical European avant-garde. From the perspective of today, American art of the 1960s – precisely because of its successful attack on abstract expressionism – shines as the colorful death mask of a classical avant-garde which in Europe had already been liquidated culturally and politically by Stalin and Hitler. Despite its radical and legitimate critique of the gospel of modernism, postmodernism, which in its artistic practices and its theory was a product of the 1960s, must be seen as the endgame of the avant-garde and not as the radical breakthrough it often claimed to be.[22]

At the same time it goes without saying that the postmodernist revolt against the institution art in the United States was up against bigger odds than futurism, Dada, or surrealism were in their time. The earlier avant-garde was confronted with the culture industry in its stage of inception, while postmodernism had to face a technologically and economically fully developed media culture which had mastered the high art of integrating, diffusing, and marketing even the most serious challenges. This factor, combined with the altered constitution of audiences, accounts for the fact that, compared with the earlier twentieth century, the shock of the new was much harder, perhaps even impossible, to sustain. Furthermore, when Dada erupted in 1916 in the placid nineteenth-century culture of bourgeois Zurich, there were no ancestors to contend with. Even the formally much less radical avant-gardes of the nineteenth century had not yet had a measurable impact on Swiss culture at large. The happenings at the Cabaret Voltaire could not but scandalize the public. When Rauschenberg, Jasper Johns, and the Madison Avenue pop artists began their assault on abstract expressionism, drawing their inspiration as they did from the everyday life of American consumerism, they soon had to face serious competition: the work of dadaist father figure Marcel Duchamp was presented to the American public in major museum and gallery retrospectives, e.g. in Pasadena (1963) and New York (1965). The ghost of the father was not only out of the closet of art history, but Duchamp himself was always already there in flesh and blood saying, like the hedgehog to the hare: 'Ich bin schon da.'

All of this goes to show that the mammoth avant-garde spectacles of the late 1970s can be interpreted as the flip side of postmodernism, which now appears much more traditional than it did in the 1960s. Not only do the avant-garde shows of the late 1970s in Paris and Berlin, London, New York, and Chicago help us come to terms with the tradition of the earlier twentieth century, but postmodernism itself can now be described as a search for a viable modern tradition apart from, say, the Proust–Joyce–Mann triad and outside the canon of classical modernism. The search for tradition combined with an attempt at recuperation seems more basic to postmodernism than innovation and breakthrough. The cultural paradox of the 1970s is not so much the side-by-side coexistence of a future-happy postmodernism with avant-garde museum retrospectives. Nor is it the inherent contradiction of the postmodernist avant-garde itself, i.e. the paradox of an art that simultaneously wants to be art and anti-art and of a criticism that pretends to be criticism and anti-criticism. The paradox of the 1970s is rather that the postmodernist search for cultural tradition and continuity, which underlies all the radical rhetoric of rupture, discontinuity, and epistemological breaks, has turned to that tradition which fundamentally and on principle despised and denied all traditions.

Seeing the avant-garde exhibits of the 1970s in the light of postmodernism may also help focus attention on some important differences between American postmodernism and the historical avant-garde. In post-World War II America, the historical realities of massive technological, social, and political change, which had given the myth of avant-gardism and innovation its power, persuasiveness, and utopian drive in the earlier twentieth century, had all but vanished. During the 1940s and 1950s American art and intellectual life had gone through a period of depoliticization in which avant-gardism and modernism actually had been realigned with the conservative liberalism of the times.[23] While postmodernism rebelled against the culture and politics of the 1950s, it nevertheless lacked a radical vision of social and political transformation that had been so essential to the historical avant-garde. Time and again the future was incanted rhetorically, but it never became clear how and in what forms postmodernism would help implement that alternative culture of the coming age. Despite this ostentatious orientation toward the future, postmodernism may well have been an expression of the contemporary crisis of culture rather than the promised transcendence toward cultural rejuvenation. Much more than the historical avant-garde, which was surreptitiously connected to the dominant modernizing and anti-traditionalist trends of nineteenth- and twentieth-century Western civilization, postmodernism was in danger of becoming affirmative culture right from the start. Most of the gestures which had sustained the shock value of the historical avant-garde were no longer and could no longer be effective. The historical avant-garde's appropriation of technology for high art (e.g. film, photography, montage principle) could produce shock, since it broke with the aestheticism and the doctrine of art's autonomy from 'real' life which were dominant in the late nineteenth century. The postmodernist espousal of space-age technology and electronic media in the wake of McLuhan, however, could scarcely shock an audience which had been inculturated to modernism via the very same media. Nor did Leslie Fiedler's dive into popular culture cause outrage in a country where the pleasures of popular culture have always been acknowledged (except perhaps in academia) with more ease and less secrecy than in Europe. And most postmodernist experiments in visual perspective, narrative structure, and temporal logic, which all attacked the dogma of mimetic referentiality, were already known from the modernist tradition. The problem was compounded by the fact that experimental strategies and popular culture were no longer connected in a critical aesthetic and political project, as they had been in the historical avant-garde. Popular culture was accepted uncritically (Leslie Fiedler) and postmodernist experimentation had lost the avant-gardist consciousness that social change and the transformation of everyday life were at stake in every artistic experiment. Rather than aiming at a mediation between art and life, postmodernist experiments soon came to be valued for typically modernist features such as self-reflexivity, immanence, and indeterminacy (Ihab Hassan). The American postmodernist avant-garde, therefore, is not only the endgame of avant-gardism. It also represents the fragmentation and the decline of the avant-garde as a genuinely critical and adversary culture.

My hypothesis that postmodernism always has been in search of tradition while pretending to innovation is also borne out by the recent shift toward cultural theory which distinguishes the postmodernism of the 1970s from that of the 1960s. On one level, of course, the American appropriation of structuralist and especially poststructuralist theory from France reflects the extent to which postmodernism itself has been academicized since it won its battle against modernism and the New Criticism.[24] It is also tempting to speculate that the shift toward theory actually points to the falling rate of artistic and literary creativity in the 1970s, a proposition which would help explain the resurgence of historical retrospectives in the museums.

To put it simply, if the contemporary art scene does not generate enough movements, figures, and trends to sustain the ethos of avant-gardism, then museum directors have to turn to the past to satisfy the demand for cultural events. However, the artistic and literary superiority of the 1960s over the 1970s should not be taken for granted, and quantity is no appropriate criterion anyway. Perhaps the culture of the 1970s is just more amorphous and diffuse, richer in difference and variation than that of the 1960s, when trends and movements evolved in a more or less 'orderly' sequence. Beneath the surface of continuously changing trends, there was indeed a unifying drive behind the culture of the 1960s which was inherited precisely from the tradition of avant-gardism. Since the cultural diversity of the 1970s no longer sustained this sense of unity – even if it was the unity of experimentation, fragmentation, *Verfremdung*, and indeterminacy – postmodernism withdrew into a kind of theory which, with its key notions of decentering and deconstruction, seemed to guarantee the lost center of avant-gardism. Suspicion is in order that the postmodernist critics' shift to continental theory is the last desperate attempt of the postmodernist avant-garde to hold on to a notion of avant-gardism which had already been refuted by certain cultural practices of the 1970s. The irony is that in this peculiarly American appropriation of recent French theory the postmodernist search for tradition comes full circle; for several major exponents of French poststructuralism such as Foucault, Deleuze, Guattari, and Derrida are more concerned with the archeology of modernity than with breakthrough and innovation, with history and the past more than with the year 2001.

Two concluding questions can be posed at this juncture. Why was there this intense search for viable traditions in the 1970s and what, if anything, is historically specific about it? And, secondly, what can the identification with the classical avant-garde contribute to our sense of cultural identity, and to what extent is such an identification desirable? The Western industrialized countries are currently experiencing a fundamental cultural and political identity crisis. The 1970s' search for roots, for history and traditions, was an inevitable and in many ways productive offshoot of this crisis; apart from the nostalgia for mummies and emperors, we are confronted with a multifaceted and diverse search for the past (often for an alternative past) which, in many of its more radical manifestations, questions the fundamental orientation of Western societies toward future growth and toward unlimited progress. This questioning of history and tradition – as it informs, for instance, the feminist interest in women's history and the ecological search for alternatives in our relationship with nature – should not be confused with the simple-minded rearguard assertion of traditional norms and values, although both phenomena reflect, with diametrically opposed political intentions, the same disposition toward tradition and history. The problem with postmodernism is that it relegates history to the dustbin of an obsolete *épistémè*, arguing gleefully that history does not exist except as text, i.e. as historiography.[25] Of course, if the 'referent' of historiography, that which historians write *about*, is eliminated, then history is indeed up for grabs – or, to put it in more trendy words, up for 'strong misreadings'. When Hayden White lamented the 'burden of history' in 1966 and suggested, perfectly in line with the early phase of postmodernism, that we accept our lot of discontinuity, disruption, and chaos,[26] he replayed the Nietzschean impetus of the classical avant-garde, but his suggestion is less than helpful in dealing with the new cultural constellations of the 1970s. Cultural practices of the 1970s – postmodernist theory notwithstanding – actually point to the vital need not to abandon history and the past to tradition-mongering neo-conservatives bent on reestablishing the norms of earlier industrial capitalism: discipline, authority, the work ethic, and the traditional family. There is indeed an alternative search for tradition and history going on today which manifests itself in the concern with cultural formations not dominated by logocentric and technocratic thought, in the decentering of traditional notions of identity, in the search for women's history, in the rejection of centralisms, mainstreams and melting pots of all kinds, and in the great value put on difference and otherness. This search for history is of course also a search for cultural identities today, and as such it clearly points to the exhaustion of the tradition of the avant-garde, including postmodernism. The search for tradition, to be sure, is not peculiar to the 1970s alone. Ever since Western civilization entered the throes of modernization, the nostalgic lament for a lost past has accompanied it like a shadow that held the promise of a better future. But in all the battles between ancients and moderns since the seventeenth and eighteenth centuries, from Herder and Schlegel to Benjamin and the American postmodernists, the moderns tended to embrace modernity, convinced that they had to pass through it before the lost unity of life and art could be reconstructed on a higher level. This conviction was the basis for avant-gardism. Today, when modernism looks increasingly like a dead end, it is this foundation itself which is being challenged. The universalizing drive inherent in the tradition of modernity no longer holds that *promesse de bonheur* as it used to.

Which brings me to the second question: whether an identification with the historical avant-garde – and, by extension, with postmodernism – can contribute to our sense of cultural identity in the 1980s. I do not want to give a definitive answer, but I suggest that an attitude of skepticism is called for. In traditional bourgeois culture the avant-garde was successful in sustaining difference. Within the project of modernity it launched a successful assault on nineteenth-century aestheticism, which insisted on the absolute autonomy of art, and on traditional realism, which remained locked into the dogma of mimetic representation and referentiality. Postmodernism has lost that capacity to gain shock value from difference, except perhaps in relation to forms of a very traditional aesthetic conservatism. The counter-measures the historical avant-garde proposed to break the grip of bourgeois institutionalized culture are no longer effective. The reasons that avant-gardism is no longer viable today can be located not only in the culture industry's capacity to co-opt, reproduce, and commodify, but, more interestingly, in the avant-garde itself. Despite the power and integrity of its attacks against traditional bourgeois culture and against the deprivations of capitalism, there are moments in the historical avant-garde which show how deeply avant-gardism itself is implicated in the Western tradition of growth and progress. The futurist and constructivist confidence in technology and modernization, the relentless assaults on the past and on tradition which went hand in hand with a quasi-metaphysical glorification of a present on the edge of the future, the universalizing, totalizing, and centralizing impetus inherent in the very concept of avant-garde (not to speak of its metaphoric militarism), the elevation to dogma of an initially legitimate critique of traditional artistic forms rooted in mimesis and representation, the unmitigated media and computer enthusiasm of the 1960s – all these phenomena reveal the secret bond between avant-garde and official culture in advanced industrial societies. Certainly the avant-gardists' use of technology was mostly *verfremdend* and critical rather than affirmative. And yet, from today's perspective the classical avant-garde's belief in technological solutions for culture appears more a symptom of the disease than a cure. Similarly one might ask whether the uncompromising attack on tradition, narration, and memory which characterizes large segments of the historical avant-garde is not just the other side of Henry Ford's notorious statement that 'history is bunk'. Perhaps both are expressions of the same spirit of cultural modernity in capitalism, a dismantling of story and perspective indeed paralleling, even if only subterraneously, the destruction of history.

At the same time, the tradition of avant-gardism, if stripped of its universalizing and normative claims, leaves us with a precious heritage of artistic and literary materials, practices, and strategies which still inform many of today's most interesting writers and artists. Preserving elements of the avant-gardist tradition is not at all incompatible with the recuperation and reconstitution of history and of story which we have witnessed in the 1970s. Good examples of this kind of coexistence of seemingly opposite literary strategies can be found in the post-experimental prose works of Peter Handke from *The Goalie's Anxiety at the Penalty Kick* through *Short Letter, Long Farewell* and *A Sorrow Beyond Dreams* to *The Left-Handed Woman* or, quite differently, in the work of women writers such as Christa Wolf from *The Quest for Christa T.* through *Self-Experiment* to *No Place on Earth*. The recuperation of history and the reemergence of story in the 1970s are not part of a leap back into a pre-modern, pre-avant-garde past, as some postmodernists seem to suggest. They can be better described as attempts to shift into reverse in order to get out of a dead-end street where the vehicles of avant-gardism and postmodernism have come to a standstill. At the same time, the contemporary concern for history will keep us from lapsing back into the avant-gardist gesture of totally rejecting the past – this time the avant-garde itself. Especially in the face of recent wholesale neo-conservative attacks on the culture of modernism, avant-gardism and postmodernism, it remains politically important to defend this tradition against neo-conservative insinuations that modernist and postmodernist culture is to be held responsible for the current crisis of capitalism. Emphasizing the subterranean links between avant-gardism and the development of capitalism in the twentieth century can effectively counteract Daniel Bell's propositions which separate an 'adversary culture' from the realm of social norms in order to blame the former for the disintegration of the latter.

In my view, however, the problem in contemporary culture is not so much the struggle between modernity and postmodernity, between avant-gardism and conservatism, as Jürgen Habermas has argued in his Adorno-prize speech.[27] Of course, the old conservatives, who reject the culture of modernism and the avant-garde, and the neo-conservatives, who advocate the immanence of art and its separateness from the *Lebenswelt*, must be fought and refuted. In that debate, especially, the cultural practices of avant-gardism have not yet lost their vigor. But this struggle may well turn out to be a rearguard skirmish between two dated modes of thought, two cultural dispositions which relate to each other like the two sides of one coin: the universalists of tradition pitted against the universalists of a modernist enlightenment. While I stand with Habermas against old conservatives and neo-conservatives, I find his call for the completion of the project of modernity, which is the political core of his argument, deeply problematic. As I hope to have shown in my discussion of avant-garde and postmodernism, too many aspects of the trajectory of modernity have became suspect and unviable today. Even the aesthetically and politically most fascinating component of modernity, the historical avant-garde, no longer offers solutions for major sectors of contemporary culture, which would reject the avant-garde's universalizing and totalizing gesture as much as its ambiguous espousal of technology and modernization. What Habermas as a theoretician shares with the aesthetic tradition of avant-gardism is precisely this universalizing gesture, which is rooted in the bourgeois enlightenment, pervades Marxism, and ultimately aims at a holistic notion of modernity. Significantly, the original title of Habermas's text, as it was printed in *Die Zeit* in September 1980, was 'Modernity – An Incomplete Project'. The title points to the problem – the teleological unfolding of a history of modernity – and it raises a question: to what extent is the assumption of a *telos* of history compatible with 'histories'? And this question is legitimate. For not only does Habermas smooth over contradictions and discontinuities in the trajectory of modernity itself, as Peter Bürger has poignantly pointed out.[28] Habermas ignores the fact that the very idea of a holistic modernity and of a totalizing view of history has become anathema in the 1970s, and precisely not on the conservative right. The critical deconstruction of enlightenment rationalism and logocentrism by theoreticians of culture, the decentering of traditional notions of identity, the fight of women and gays for a legitimate social and sexual identity outside of the parameters of male, heterosexual vision, the search for alternatives in our relationship with nature, including the nature of our own bodies – all these phenomena, which are key to the culture of the 1970s, make Habermas's proposition to complete the project of modernity questionable, if not undesirable.

Given Habermas's indebtedness to the tradition of critical enlightenment, which in German political history – and this should be mentioned in Habermas's defense – always was the adversary and underdog current rather than the mainstream, it comes as no surprise that Bataille, Foucault, and Derrida are lumped with the conservatives in the camp of postmodernity. There is no doubt in my mind that much of the postmodernist appropriation of Foucault and especially Derrida in the United States is indeed politically conservative, but that, after all, is only *one* line of reception and response. Habermas himself could be accused of constructing a Manichean dualism in his essay where he pits the dark forces of anti-modern conservatism against the enlightened and enlightening forces of modernity. This Manichean view manifests itself again in the way Habermas tends to reduce the project of modernity to its rational enlightenment components and to dismiss other, equally important parts of modernity as mistakes. Just as Bataille, Foucault, and Derrida are said to have stepped outside the modern world by removing the imagination, emotionality, and self-experience into the sphere of the archaic (a proposition which is itself debatable), surrealism is described by Habermas as modernity gone astray. Relying on Adorno's critique of surrealism, Habermas reproaches the surrealist avant-garde for having advocated a false sublation [*Aufhebung*] of the art/life dichotomy. While I agree with Habermas that a total sublation of art is indeed a false project fraught with contradictions, I would defend surrealism on three counts. More than any other avant-garde movement, surrealism dismantled false notions of identity and artistic creativity; it attempted to explode the reifications of rationality in capitalist culture and, by focusing on psychic processes, it exposed the vulnerability of all rationality, not only that of instrumental rationality; and, finally, it included the concrete human subject and his/her desires in its artistic practices and in its notion that the reception of art should systematically disrupt perception and senses.[29]

Although Habermas, in the section entitled 'Alternatives', seems to retain the surrealist gesture when he speculates about the possibility of relinking art and literature with everyday life, everyday life itself – contrary to surrealism – is defined in exclusively rational, cognitive and normative terms. Significantly, Habermas's example about an alternative reception of art in which the experts' culture is reappropriated from the standpoint of the *Lebenswelt* involves young male workers, 'politically motivated' and 'knowledge hungry'; the time is 1937, Berlin; the artwork reappropriated by the workers is the Pergamon altar, symbol of classicism, power, and rationality; and the status of this reappropriation is fiction, a passage in Peter Weiss's novel *Die Ästhetik des Widerstands*. The one concrete example Habermas gives is several times removed from the *Lebenswelt* of the 1970s and its cultural practices, which, in such major manifestations as the women's movement, the gay movement, and the ecology movement, seem to point beyond the culture of modernity, beyond avant-garde and postmodernism, and most certainly beyond neo-conservatism.

Habermas is right in arguing that a relinking of modern culture with everyday praxis can only be successful if the *Lebenswelt* is able 'to develop institutions out of itself which set limits to the internal dynamics and to the imperatives of an almost autonomous economic system and its administrative complements'. As a result of the conservative backlash the chances for this may indeed not be very good at the present time. But to suggest, as Habermas implicitly does, that there are as yet no such attempts to steer modernity in different and alternative directions, is a view which results from the blind spot of the European enlightenment, its tendency to homogenize heterogeneity, otherness, and difference.

P.S.: Some time ago, avant-garde/postmodernist artist Christo planned to wrap the
Berlin Reichstag, an event which, according to Berlin mayor Stobbe, could have led
to a stimulating political discussion. Conservative Bundestagspräsident Karl
Carstens, however, feared spectacle and scandal, so instead Stobbe suggested the
organization of a major historical exhibition about Prussia. When the great Preußen-
Ausstellung opens in Berlin in August 1981, the avant-garde will truly be dead. Time
for Heiner Müller's *Germania Death in Berlin*.

Notes

Where full details are available in the Bibliography, references contain only essential
information.

1. Catalogues: *Tendenzen der Zwanziger Jahre: 15. Europäische Kunstausstellung* (Berlin,
   1977); *Wem gehört die Welt: Kunst und Gesellschaft in der Weimarer Republik*, Neue
   Gesellschaft für bildende Kunst (Berlin, 1977); *Paris–Berlin 1900–1933*, Centre
   Georges Pompidou (Paris, 1978). Robert Hughes's television series has also been
   published in book form as *The Shock of the New*, 1981. See also *Paris–Moscow
   1900–1930*, Centre Georges Pompidou (Paris, 1979).
2. Walter Benjamin, 'Theses on the philosophy of history', in *Illuminations*, ed. Hannah
   Arendt, Schocken Books, New York, 1969.
3. Hans Magnus Enzensberger, 'Die Aporien der Avantgarde', in *Einzelheiten: Poesie und
   Politik*, Suhrkamp, Frankfurt am Main, 1962. In this essay Enzensberger analyzes the
   contradictions in the temporal sensibility of avant-gardism, the relationship of artistic
   and political avant-gardes, and certain post-1945 avant-garde phenomena such as *art
   informel*, action painting, and the literature of the beat generation. His major thesis is
   that the historical avant-garde is dead and that the revival of avant-gardism after 1945
   is fraudulent and regressive.
4. Max Frisch, 'Der Autor und das Theater', 1964, in *Gesammelte Werke in zeitlicher
   Folge*, vol. 5,2, Suhrkamp, Frankfurt am Main, 1976, p. 342.
5. *Partisan Review*, 1959, 420–36. Reprinted in Irving Howe, *The Decline of the New*,
   Harcourt, Brace and World, New York, 1970, pp. 190–207.
6. Harry Levin, 'What was modernism?', 1960, in *Refractions*, Oxford University Press,
   New York, 1966, p. 271.
7. It is not my purpose in this essay to define and delimit the term 'postmodernism'
   conceptually. Since the 1960s the term has accumulated several layers of meaning which
   should not be forced into the straitjacket of a systematic definition. In this essay the term
   'postmodernism' will variously refer to American art movements from pop to
   performance, to recent experimentalism in dance, theater and fiction, and to certain
   avant-gardist trends in literary criticism from the work of Leslie Fiedler and Susan Sontag
   in the 1960s to the more recent appropriation of French cultural theory by American
   critics who may or may not call themselves postmodernists. Some useful discussions of
   postmodernism can be found in Matei Calinescu, *Faces of Modernity: Avant-garde,
   decadence, kitsch*, Indiana University Press, Bloomington and London, 1977, especially
   pp. 132–43; and in a special issue on postmodernism of *Amerikastudien*, 2, (1977); this
   issue also contains a substantive bibliography on postmodernism, *ibid.*, 40–6.

8. Calinescu (see note 7); Peter Bürger, *Theorie der Avantgarde*, Suhrkamp, Frankfurt am Main, 1974; Engl. translation: *Theory of the Avant-Garde*, 1984; '*Theorie der Avantgarde': Antworten auf Peter Bürgers Bestimmung von Kunst und bürgerlicher Gesellschaft*, ed. W. Martin Lüdke, Suhrkamp, Frankfurt am Main, 1976, Bürger's reply to his critics is contained in the introduction to his *Vermittlung-Rezeption-Funktion*, Suhrkamp, Frankfurt am Main, 1979; special issue on *Montage/Avantgarde* of the Berlin journal *Alternative*, 122–3 (1978). See also the essays by Jürgen Habermas, Hans Platscheck and Karl Heinz Bohrer in *Stichworte zur 'Geistigen Situation der Zeit'*, 2 vols, ed. Jürgen Habermas, Suhrkamp, Frankfurt am Main, 1979.

9. E.g. the 1979 conference on fascism and the avant-garde in Madison, Wisconsin: *Faschismus und Avantgarde*, ed. Reinhold Grimm and Jost Hermand, Athenäum, Königstein/Ts, 1980.

10. References in Calinescu, *Faces of Modernity*, p. 140 and p. 287, fn 40.

11. John Weightman, *The Concept of the Advant-Garde*, Library Press, La Salle, IL, 1973.

12. Calinescu, *Faces of Modernity*, p. 140.

13. Peter Bürger, *Theory of the Avant-Garde*, 1984.

14. On the political aspects of the left avant-garde, see David Bathrick, 'Affirmative and negative culture: Technology and the left avant-garde', in *The Technological Imagination*, ed. Teresa de Lauretis, Andreas Huyssen, and Kathleen Woodward, Coda Press, Madison, WI, 1980, pp. 107–22.

15. See Enzensberger, 'Aporien', pp. 66 f.

16. On Pop Art see Andreas Huyssen, 'The cultural politics of pop', in *After the Great Divide*.

17. Leslie Fiedler, *The Collected Essays of Leslie Fiedler*, vol. II, Stein & Day, New York, 1971, pp. 454–61.

18. Reprinted in Leslie Fiedler, *A Fiedler Reader*, Stein & Day, New York, 1977, pp. 270–94.

19. Cf. many essays in the anthology *Mass Culture: The popular arts in America*, eds Bernard Rosenberg and David Manning White, The Free Press, New York, 1957.

20. Hans Magnus Enzensberger, *Einzelheiten I: Bewußtseinsindustrie*, Suhrkamp, Frankfurt am Main, 1962.

21. Ihab Hassan, *Paracriticsms: Seven speculations of the times*, 1975. See also Ihab Hassan, *The Right Promethean Fire: Imagination, science, and cultural change*, 1980.

22. For an incisive critique of postmodernism from an aesthetically rather conservative position, see Gerald Graff, 'The myth of the postmodernist breakthrough', 1973, 383–417. The essay also appeared in Graff, *Literature Against Itself: Literary ideas on modern society*, 1979, pp. 31–62.

23. See Serge Guilbaut, 'The new adventures of the avant-garde in America', 1980, 61–78. Cf. also Eva Cockroft, 'Abstract Expressionism: Weapon of the Cold War', *Artforum*, XII (1974).

24. I am not identifying poststructuralism with postmodernism, even though the concept of postmodernism has recently been incorporated into French poststructuralist writing in the works of Jean-François Lyotard. All I am saying is that there are definite links between the ethos of postmodernism and the American appropriation of poststructuralism as the latest avant-garde in theory. For more on the postmodernism–poststructuralism constellation, see Andreas Huyssen, 'Mapping the postmodern', in *After the Great Divide*.

25. For a sustained critique of the denial of history in contemporary American literary

criticsm, see Fredric Jameson, *The Political Unconscious: Narrative as a socially symbolic act*, Cornell University Press, Ithaca, NY, 1981, especially ch. 1.

26. Hayden White, 'The burden of history', reprinted in *Tropics of Discourse: Essays in cultural criticism*, 1978, pp. 27–50.
27. Jürgen Habermas, 'Modernity vs. postmodernity', *New German Critique*, 22 (1981), 3–14; see pp. 98–109 of the present volume.
28. Peter Bürger, 'Avantgarde and contemporary aesthetics: a reply to Jürgen Habermas', *New German Critique*, 22 (1981), 19–22.
29. See Peter Bürger, *Der französische Surrealismus*, Athenäum, Frankfurt am Main, 1971.

17 □ *The Negation of the Autonomy of Art by the Avant-Garde*

Peter Bürger

In scholarly discussion up to now, the category 'autonomy' has suffered from the imprecision of the various subcategories thought of as constituting a unity in the concept of the autonomous work of art. Since the development of the individual subcategories is not synchronous, it may happen that sometimes courtly art seems already autonomous, while at other times only bourgeois art appears to have that characteristic. To make clear that the contradictions between the various interpretations result from the nature of the case, we will sketch a historical typology that is deliberately reduced to three elements (purpose or function, production, reception), because the point here is to have the nonsynchronism in the development of individual categories emerge with clarity.

  A. Sacral Art (example: the art of the High Middle Ages) serves as cult object. It is wholly integrated into the social institution 'religion'. It is produced collectively, as a craft. The mode of reception also is institutionalized as collective.[1]

  B. Courtly Art (example: the art at the court of Louis XIV) also has a precisely defined function. It is representational and serves the glory of the prince and the self-portrayal of courtly society. Courtly art is part of the life praxis of courtly society, just as sacral art is part of the life praxis of the faithful. Yet the detachment from the sacral tie is a first step in the emancipation of art. ('Emancipation' is being used here as a descriptive term, as referring to the process by which art constitutes itself as a distinct social subsystem.) The difference from sacral art becomes particularly apparent in the realm of production: the artist produces as an individual and develops a consciousness of the uniqueness of his activity. Reception, on the other hand, remains collective. But the content of the collective performance is no longer sacral, it is sociability.

  C. Only to the extent that the bourgeoisie adopts concepts of value held by the

From Bürger, P., *Theory of the Avant-Garde*, Manchester University Press, Manchester/ University of Minnesota Press, Minneapolis, MN, 1984, pp. 47–54.

aristocracy does bourgeois art have a representational function. When it is genuinely bourgeois, this art is the objectification of the self-understanding of the bourgeois class. Production and reception of the self-understanding as articulated in art are no longer tied to the praxis of life. Habermas calls this the satisfaction of residual needs, that is, of needs that have become submerged in the life praxis of bourgeois society. Not only production but reception also are now individual acts. The solitary absorption in the work is the adequate mode of appropriation of creations removed from the life praxis of the bourgeois, even though they still claim to interpret that praxis. In Aestheticism, finally, where bourgeois art reaches the stage of self-reflection, this claim is no longer made. Apartness from the praxis of life, which had always been the condition that characterized the way art functioned in bourgeois society, now becomes its content. The typology we have sketched here can be represented in the accompanying tabulation (the vertical lines in boldface refer to a decisive change in the development, the broken ones to a less decisive one).

	Sacral Art	Courtly Art	Bourgeois Art
Purpose or function	cult object	representational object	portrayal of bourgeois self-understanding
Production	collective craft	individual	individual
Reception	collective (sacral)	collective (sociable)	individual

The tabulation allows one to notice that the development of the categories was not synchronous. Production by the individual that characterizes art in bourgeois society has its origins as far back as courtly patronage. But courtly art still remains integral to the praxis of life, although as compared with the cult function, the representational function constitutes a step toward a mitigation of claims that art plays a direct social role. The reception of courtly art also remains collective, although the content of the collective performance has changed. As regards reception, it is only with bourgeois art that a decisive change sets in: its reception is one by isolated individuals. The novel is that literary genre in which the new mode of reception finds the form appropriate to it.[2] The advent of bourgeois art is also the decisive turning point as regards use or function. Although in different ways, both sacral and courtly art are integral to the life praxis of the recipient. As cult and representational objects, works of art are put to a specific use. This requirement no longer applies to the same extent to bourgeois art. In bourgeois art, the portrayal of bourgeois self-understanding occurs in a sphere that lies outside the praxis of life. The citizen who, in everyday life, has been reduced to a partial function (means–ends activity) can be discovered in art as 'human being'. Here, one can unfold the abundance of one's talents, though with the proviso that this sphere remain strictly separate from the praxis of life. Seen in this fashion, the separation of art from the praxis of life becomes the decisive characteristic of the autonomy of bourgeois art (a fact that the tabulation does not bring out adequately). To avoid misunderstandings, it must be emphasized once again that autonomy in this sense defines the status of art in bourgeois society, but that no assertions concerning the contents of works are involved. Although art as an institution may be considered fully formed toward the end of the eighteenth century, the development of the contents of works is subject to a historical dynamics, whose terminal point is reached in Aestheticism, where art becomes the content of art.

The European avant-garde movements can be defined as an attack on the status of art in bourgeois society. What is negated is not an earlier form of art (a style) but art as an institution that is unassociated with the life praxis of men. When the avant-gardists demand that art become practical once again, they do not mean that the contents of works of art should be socially significant. The demand is not raised at the level of the contents of individual works. Rather, it directs itself to the way art functions in society, a process that does as much to determine the effect that works have as does the particular content.

The avant-gardists view its dissociation from the praxis of life as the dominant characteristic of art in bourgeois society. One of the reasons this dissociation was possible is that Aestheticism had made the element that defines art as an institution the essential content of works. Institution and work contents had to coincide to make it logically possible for the avant-garde to call art into question. The avant-gardists proposed the sublation of art – sublation in the Hegelian sense of the term: art was not to be simply destroyed, but transferred to the praxis of life where it would be preserved, albeit in a changed form. The avant-gardists thus adopted an essential element of Aestheticism. Aestheticism had made the distance from the praxis of life the content of works. The praxis of life to which Aestheticism refers and which it negates is the means–ends rationality of the bourgeois everyday. Now, it is not the aim of the avant-gardists to integrate art into *this* praxis. On the contrary, they assent to the aestheticists' rejection of the world and its means–ends rationality. What distinguishes them from the latter is the attempt to organize a new life praxis from a basis in art. In this respect also, Aestheticism turns out to have been the necessary precondition of the avant-gardist intent. Only an art the contents of whose individual works is wholly distinct from the (bad) praxis of the existing society can be the center that can be the starting point for the organization of a new life praxis.

With the help of Herbert Marcuse's theoretical formulation concerning the twofold character of art in bourgeois society [in 'The affirmative character of culture'], the avant-gardist intent can be understood with particular clarity. All those needs that cannot be satisfied in everyday life, because the principle of competition pervades all spheres, can find a home in art, because art is removed from the praxis of life. Values such as humanity, joy, truth, solidarity are extruded from life, as it were, and preserved in art. In bourgeois society, art has a contradictory role: it projects the image of a better order and to that extent protests against the bad order that prevails. But by realizing the image of a better order in fiction, which is semblance [*Schein*] only, it relieves the existing society of the pressure of those forces that make for change. They are assigned to confinement in an ideal sphere. Where art accomplishes this, it is 'affirmative' in Marcuse's sense of the term. If the twofold character of art in bourgeois society consists in the fact that the distance from the social production and reproduction process contains an element of freedom and an element of the noncommittal and an absence of any consequences, it can be seen that the avant-gardists' attempt to reintegrate art into the life process is itself a profoundly contradictory endeavor. For the (relative) freedom of art *vis-à-vis* the praxis of life is at the same time the condition that must be fulfilled if there is to be a critical cognition of reality. An art no longer distinct from the praxis of life but wholly absorbed in it will lose the capacity to criticize it, along with its distance. During the time of the historical avant-garde movements, the attempt to do away with the distance between art and life still had all the pathos of historical progressiveness on its side. But in the meantime, the culture industry has brought about the false elimination of the distance between art and life, and this also allows one to recognize the contradictoriness of the avant-gardist undertaking.[3]

In what follows, we will outline how the intent to eliminate art as an institution found expression in the three areas that we used above to characterize autonomous art: purpose or function, production, reception. Instead of speaking of the avant-gardist work, we will speak of avant-gardist manifestation. A dadaist manifestation does not have work character but is nonetheless an authentic manifestation of the artistic avant-garde. This is not to imply that the avant-gardists produced no works whatever and replaced them by ephemeral events. We will see that whereas they did not destroy it, the avant-gardists profoundly modified the category of the work of art.

Of the three areas, the *intended purpose or function* of the avant-gardist manifestation is most difficult to define. In the aestheticist work of art, the disjointure of the work and the praxis of life characteristic of the status of art in bourgeois society has become the work's essential content. It is only as a consequence of this fact that the work of art becomes its own end in the full meaning of the term. In Aestheticism, the social functionlessness of art becomes manifest. The avant-gardist artists counter such functionlessness not by an art that would have consequences within the existing society, but rather by the principle of the sublation of art in the praxis of life. But such a conception makes it impossible to define the intended purpose of art. For an art that has been reintegrated into the praxis of life, not even the absence of a social purpose can be indicated, as was still possible in Aestheticism. When art and the praxis of life are one, when the praxis is aesthetic and art is practical, art's purpose can no longer be discovered, because the existence of two distinct spheres (art and the praxis of life) that is constitutive of the concept of purpose or intended use has come to an end.

We have seen that the *production* of the autonomous work of art is the act of an individual. The artist produces as individual, individuality not being understood as the expression of something but as radically different. The concept of genius testifies to this. The quasi-technical consciousness of the makeability of works of art that Aestheticism attains seems only to contradict this. Valéry, for example, demystifies artistic genius by reducing it to psychological motivations on the one hand, and the availability to it of artistic means on the other. While pseudo-romantic doctrines of inspiration thus come to be seen as the self-deception of producers, the view of art for which the individual is the creative subject is let stand. Indeed, Valéry's theorem concerning the force of pride [*orgueil*] that sets off and propels the creative process renews once again the notion of the individual character of artistic production central to art in bourgeois society.[4] In its most extreme manifestations, the avant-garde's reply to this is not the collective as the subject of production but the radical negation of the category of individual creation. When Duchamp signs mass-produced objects (a urinal, a bottle drier) and sends them to art exhibits, he negates the category of individual production. The signature, whose very purpose it is to mark what is individual in the work, that it owes its existence to this particular artist, is inscribed on an arbitrarily chosen mass product, because all claims to individual creativity are to be mocked. Duchamp's provocation not only unmasks the art market where the signature means more than the quality of the work; it radically questions the very principle of art in bourgeois society according to which the individual is considered the creator of the work of art. Duchamp's Ready-Mades are not works of art but manifestations. Not from the form–content totality of the individual object Duchamp signs can one infer the meaning, but only from the contrast between mass-produced object on the one hand, and signature and art exhibit on the other. It is obvious that this kind of provocation cannot be repeated indefinitely. The provocation depends on what it turns against: here, it is the idea that the individual is the subject of artistic creation. Once the signed bottle drier has been accepted as an object that deserves a place in a museum, the provocation no longer provokes; it turns into its opposite. If an artist today signs a stove pipe and exhibits it, that artist certainly does not denounce the art market but adapts to it. Such adaptation does not eradicate the idea of individual creativity, it affirms it, and the reason is the failure of the avant-gardist intent to sublate art. Since now the protest of the historical avant-garde against art as institution is accepted as *art*, the gesture of protest of the neo-avant-garde becomes inauthentic. Having been shown to be irredeemable, the claim to be protest can no longer be maintained. This fact accounts for the arts-and-crafts impression that works of the avant-garde not infrequently convey.[5]

The avant-garde negates not only the category of individual production but also that of individual *reception*. The reactions of the public during a dada manifestation where it has been mobilized by provocation, which can range from shouting to fisticuffs, are certainly collective in nature. True, these remain reactions, responses to a preceding provocation. Producer and recipient remain clearly distinct, however active the public may become. Given the avant-gardist intention to do away with art as a sphere that is separate from the praxis of life, it is logical to eliminate the antithesis between producer and recipient. It is no accident that both Tzara's instructions for the making of a dadaist poem and Breton's for the writing of automatic texts have the character of recipes.[6] This represents not only a polemical attack on the individual creativity of the artist; the recipe is to be taken quite literally as suggesting a possible activity on the part of the recipient. The automatic texts also should be read as guides to individual production. However, production is to be understood not as artistic production, but as part of a liberating life praxis. This is what is meant by Breton's demand that poetry be practiced [*pratiquer la poésie*]. Beyond the coincidence of producer and recipient that this demand implies, there is the fact that these concepts lose their meaning: producers and recipients no longer exist. All that remains is the individual who uses poetry as an instrument for living one's life as best one can. There is also a danger here to which Surrealism at least partly succumbed, and that is solipsism, the retreat to the problems of the isolated subject. Breton himself saw this danger and envisaged different ways of dealing with it. One of them was the glorification of the spontaneity of the erotic relationship. Perhaps the strict group discipline was also an attempt to exorcize the danger of solipsism that surrealism harbors.[7]

In summary, we note that the historical avant-garde movements negate those determinations that are essential in autonomous art: the disjunction of art and the praxis of life, individual production, and individual reception as distinct from the former. The avant-garde intends the abolition of autonomous art, by which it means that art is to be integrated into the praxis of life. This has not occurred, and presumably cannot occur, in bourgeois society unless it be as a false sublation of autonomous art.[8] Pulp fiction and commodity aesthetics prove that such a false sublation exists. A literature whose primary aim is to impose a particular kind of consumer behavior on the reader is in fact practical, though not in the sense the avant-gardists intended. Here, literature ceases to be an instrument of emancipation and becomes one of subjection.[9] Similar comments could be made about commodity aesthetics that treat form as mere enticement, designed to prompt purchasers to buy what they do not need. Here also, art becomes practical, but it is an art that enthralls.[10] This brief allusion will show that the theory of the avant-garde can also serve to make us understand popular literature and commodity aesthetics as forms of a false sublation of art as institution. In late capitalist society, intentions of the historical avant-garde are being realized, but the result has been a disvalue. Given the experience of the false sublation of autonomy, one will need to ask whether a sublation of the autonomy status can be desirable at all, whether the distance between art and the praxis of life is not requisite for that free space within which alternatives to what exists become conceivable.

Notes

1. On this, see the essay by R. Warning, 'Ritus, Mythos und geistliches Spiel', in *Terror*

und Spiel. Probleme der Mythenrezeption, ed. Fuhrmann, Wilhelm Fink Verlag, Munich, 1971, pp. 211–39.

2. Hegel already referred to the novel as 'the modern middle-class epic' (*Ästhetik*, ed. F. Bassenge, 2 vols [Berlin/Weimar, 1965], vol. II, p. 452). [In his translation of the *Aesthetics*, T. M. Knox renders this passage as follows: 'But it is quite different with romance, the modern popular epic' (vol. II, p. 1092), but this seems wrong. Translator's note.]

3. On the problem of the false sublation of art in the praxis of life, see J. Habermas, *Strukturwandel der Öffentlichkeit. Untersuchungen zu einer Kategorie der bürgerlichen Gesellschaft*, Neuwied/Berlin, 1968, § 18, pp. 176 ff.

4. See P. Bürger, 'Funktion und Bedeutung des *orgueil* bei Paul Valéry', *Romanistisches Jahrbuch*, 16 (1965), 149–68.

5. Examples of neo-avant-gardist paintings and sculptures to be found in the catalog of the exhibit *Sammlung Cremer. Europäische Avantgarde 1950–1970*, ed. G. Adriani, Tübingen, 1973.

6. T. Tzara, 'Pour faire un Poème dadaiste', in Tzara, *Lampisteries précédées des sept manifestes dada*, place of publication not given, 1963, p. 64. A. Breton, 'Manifeste du surréalisme' (1924), in Breton, *Manifestes du surréalisme*, Coll. Idées 23, Paris, 1963, pp. 42 f.

7. On the Surrealists' conception of groups and the collective experiences they sought and partially realized, see Elisabeth Lenk, *Der springende Narziss. André Bretons poetischer Materialismus*, Munich, 1971, pp. 57 ff., 73 f.

8. One would have to investigate to what extent, after the October revolution, the Russian avant-gardists succeeded to a degree, because social conditions had changed, in realizing their intent to reintegrate art in the praxis of life. Both B. Arvatov and S. Tretjakov turn the concept of art as developed in bourgeois society around and define art quite straightforwardly as socially useful activity: 'The pleasure of transforming the raw material into a particular, socially useful form, connected to the skill and the intensive search for the suitable form – those are the things the slogan "art for all" should mean' (S. Tretjakov, 'Die Kunst in der Revolution und die Revolution in der Kunst', in Tretjakov, *Die Arbeit des Schriftstellers*, ed. H. Boehncke, Rowohlt, Reinbek bei Hamburg, 1971, p. 13). 'Basing himself on the technique which is common to all spheres of life, the artist is imbued with the idea of suitability. It is not by subjective taste that he will allow himself to be guided as he works on his material but by the objective tasks of production' (B. Arvatov, 'Die Kunst im System der proletarischen Kultur', in Arvatov, *Kunst und Produktion*, p. 15). With the theory of the avant-garde as a point of departure, and with concrete investigations as guide, one should also discuss the problem of the extent (and of the kinds of consequences for the artistic subjects) to which art as an institution occupies a place in the society of the socialist countries that differs from its place in bourgeois society.

9. See Christa Bürger, *Textanalyse als Ideologiekritik. Zur Rezeption zeitgenössischer Unterhaltungsliteratur*, Athenäum, Frankfurt, 1973.

10. See W. F. Haug, *Kritik der Warenästhetik*, Suhrkamp, Frankfurt, 1971.

18 □ *The Sublime and the Avant-Garde*

Jean-François Lyotard

I

In 1950–1, Barnett Baruch Newman painted a canvas measuring 2.42 m by 5.42 m which he called 'Vir Heroicus Sublimis'. In the early sixties he entitled his first three sculptures 'Here I', 'Here II', 'Here III'. Another painting was called 'Not Over There, Here', two paintings were called 'Now', and two others were entitled 'Be'. In December 1948, Newman wrote an essay entitled 'The sublime is now'.

How is one to understand the sublime, or let us say provisionally, the object of a sublime experience, as a 'here and now'? Quite to the contrary, isn't it essential to this feeling that it alludes to something which can't be shown, or presented (as Kant said, *dargestellt*)? In a short unfinished text dating from late 1949, *Prologue for a New Aesthetic*, Newman wrote that in his painting, he was not concerned with a 'manipulation of space nor with the image, but with a sensation of time'. He added that by this he did not mean time laden with feelings of nostalgia, or drama, or references and history, the usual subjects of painting. After this denial [*dénégation*] the text stops short.

So, what kind of time was Newman concerned with, what 'now' did he have in mind? Thomas Hess, his friend and commentator, felt justified in writing that Newman's time was the *Makom* or the *Hamakom* of Hebraic tradition – the *there*, the site, the place, which is one of the names given by the Torah to the Lord, the Unnameable. I do not know enough about *Makom* to know whether this was what Newman had in mind. But then again, who does know enough about *Now*? Newman can certainly not have been thinking of the 'present instant', the one that tries to hold itself between the future and the past, and gets devoured by them. This 'now' is one of the temporal 'ecstasies' that has been analysed since Augustine's day and since Edmund Husserl, according to a line of thought that has attempted to constitute time on the basis of consciousness. Newman's *now* which is no more than *now* is a stranger to consciousness and cannot be constituted by it. Rather,

From Benjamin, A. (ed.), *The Lyotard Reader*, Basil Blackwell, Oxford, 1989, pp. 196–211.

it is what dismantles consciousness, what deposes consciousness, it is what consciousness cannot formulate, and even what consciousness forgets in order to constitute itself. What we do not manage to formulate is that something happens, *dass etwas geschieht*. Or rather, and more simply, that it happens ... *dass es geschieht*. Not a major event in the media sense, not even a small event. Just an occurrence.

This isn't a matter of sense or reality bearing upon *what* happens or *what* this might mean. Before asking questions about what it is and about its significance, before the *quid*, it must 'first' so to speak 'happen', *quod*. That it happens 'precedes', so to speak, the question pertaining to what happens. Or rather, the question precedes itself, because 'that it happens' is the question relevant as event, and it 'then' pertains to the event that has just happened. The event happens as a question mark 'before' happening as a question. *It happens* is rather 'in the first place' *is it happening, is this it, is it possible*? Only 'then' is any mark determined by the questioning: is this or that happening, is it this or something else, is it possible that this or that?

An event, an occurrence – what Martin Heidegger called *ein Ereignis* – is infinitely simple, but this simplicity can only be approached through a state of privation. That which we call thought must be disarmed. There is a tradition and an institution of philosophy, of painting, of politics, of literature. These 'disciplines' also have a future in the form of Schools, of programmes, projects, and 'trends'. Thought works over what is received, it seeks to reflect on it and overcome it. It seeks to determine what has already been thought, written, painted, or socialized in order to determine what hasn't been. We know this process well, it is our daily bread. It is the bread of war, soldiers' biscuit. But this agitation, in the most noble sense of the word (agitation is the word Kant gives to the activity of the mind that has judgement and exercises it), this agitation is only possible if something remains to be determined, something that hasn't yet been determined. One can strive to determine this something by setting up a system, a theory, a programme or a project – and indeed one has to, all the while anticipating that something. One can also inquire about the remainder, and allow the indeterminate to appear as a question mark.

What all intellectual disciplines and institutions presuppose is that not everything has been said, written down or recorded, that words already heard or pronounced are not the last words. 'After' a sentence, 'after' a colour, comes another sentence, another colour. One doesn't know which, but one thinks one knows if one relies on the rules that permit one sentence to link up with another, one colour with another, rules preserved in precisely those institutions of the past and future that I mentioned. The School, the programme, the project – all proclaim that after this sentence comes that sentence, or at least that kind of sentence is mandatory, that one kind of sentence is permitted, while another is forbidden. This holds true for painting as much as for the other activities of thought. After one pictorial work, another is necessary, permitted, or forbidden. After one colour, this other colour; after this line, that one. There isn't an enormous difference between an avant-garde manifesto and a curriculum at the Ecole des Beaux-Arts, if one considers them in the light of this relationship to time. Both are options with respect to what they feel is a good thing to happen subsequently. But both also forget the possibility of nothing happening, of words, colours, forms or sounds not coming; of this sentence being the last, of bread not coming daily. This is the misery that the painter faces with a plastic surface, of the musician with the acoustic surface, the misery the thinker faces with a desert of thought, and so on. Not only faced with the empty canvas or the empty page, at the 'beginning' of the work, but every time something has to be waited for, and thus forms a question at every point of questioning [*point d'interrogation*], at every 'and what now?'

The possibility of nothing happening is often associated with a feeling of anxiety, a term with strong connotations in modern philosophies of existence and of the unconscious. It gives to waiting, if we really mean waiting, a predominantly negative value. But suspense can also be accompanied by pleasure, for instance pleasure in welcoming the unknown, and even by joy, to speak like Baruch Spinoza, the joy obtained by the intensification of being that the event brings with it. This is probably a contradictory feeling. It is at the very least a sign, the question mark itself, the way in which *it happens* is withheld and announced: *Is it happening?* The question can be modulated in any tone. But the mark of the question is 'now', *now* like the feeling that nothing might happen: the nothingness now.

Between the seventeenth and eighteenth centuries in Europe this contradictory feeling – pleasure and pain, joy and anxiety, exaltation and depression – was christened or re-christened by the name of the *sublime*. It is around this name that the destiny of classical poetics was hazarded and lost; it is in this name that aesthetics asserted its critical rights over art, and that romanticism – in other words, modernity – triumphed.

It remains to the art historian to explain how the word sublime reappeared in the language of a Jewish painter from New York during the forties. The word sublime is common currency today in colloquial French to suggest surprise and admiration, somewhat like America's 'great', but the idea connoted by it has belonged (for at least two centuries) to the most rigorous kind of reflection on art. Newman is not unaware of the aesthetic and philosophical stakes with which the word *sublime* is involved. He read Edmund Burke's *Inquiry* and criticized what he saw as Burke's over-'surrealist' description of the sublime work. Which is as much as to say that, conversely, Newman judged surrealism to be over-reliant on a pre-romantic or romantic approach to indeterminacy. Thus, when he seeks sublimity in the here and now he breaks with the eloquence of romantic art but he does not reject its fundamental task, that of bearing pictorial or otherwise expressive witness to the inexpressible. The inexpressible does not reside in an over there, in another world, or another time, but in this: in that (something) happens. In the determination of pictorial art, the indeterminate, the 'it happens' is the paint, the picture. The paint, the picture as occurrence or event, is not expressible, and it is to this that it has to witness.

To be true to this displacement in which consists perhaps the whole of the difference between romanticism and the 'modern' avant-garde, one would have to read 'The sublime is now' not as 'The sublime is now' but as 'Now the sublime is like this'. Not elsewhere, not up there or over there, not earlier or later, not once upon a time. But as here, now, it happens that, ... and it's this painting. Here and now there is this painting, rather than nothing, and that's what is sublime. Letting go of all grasping intelligence and of its power, disarming it, recognizing that this occurrence of painting was not necessary and is scarcely foreseeable, a privation in the face of *Is it happening?* guarding the occurrence 'before' any defence, any illustration, and any commentary, guarding before being on one's guard, before 'looking' [*regarder*] under the aegis of *now*, this is the rigour of the avant-garde. In the determination of literary art this requirement with respect to the *Is it happening?* found one of its most rigorous realizations in Gertrude Stein's *How to Write*. It's still the sublime in the sense that Burke and Kant described, and yet it isn't their sublime any more.

II

I have said that the contradictory feeling with which indeterminacy is both announced and missed was what was at stake in reflection on art from the end of the seventeenth to the end of the eighteenth centuries. The sublime is perhaps the only mode of artistic sensibility to characterize the modern. Paradoxically, it was introduced to literary discussion and vigorously defended by the French writer who has been classified in literary history as one of the most dogged advocates of ancient classicism. In 1674 Boileau published his *Art poétique*, but he also published *Du Sublime*, his translation or transcription from the *Peri tou hupsou*. It is a treatise, or rather an essay, attributed to a certain Longinus, about whose identity there has long been confusion, and whose life we now estimate as having begun towards the end of the first century of our era. The author was a rhetorician. Basically, he taught those oratorical devices with which a speaker can persuade or move (depending on the genre) his audience. The didactics of rhetoric had been traditional since Aristotle, Cicero, and Quintilian. They were linked to the republican institution; one had to know how to speak before assemblies and tribunals.

One might expect that Longinus's text would invoke the maxims and advice transmitted by this tradition by perpetuating the didactic form of *technè rhetorikè*. But surprisingly, the sublime, the indeterminate − were destabilizing the text's didactic intention. I cannot analyse this uncertainty here. Boileau himself and numerous other commentators, especially Fénélon, were aware of it and concluded that the sublime could only be discussed in sublime style. Longinus certainly tried to define sublimity in discourse, writing that it was unforgettable, irresistible, and most important, thought-provoking − '*il y a à partir d'elle beaucoup de réflexion*' [*hou polle anatheoresis*] (from the sublime springs a lot of reflection). He also tried to locate sources for the sublime in the ethos of rhetoric, in its pathos, in its techniques: figures of speech, diction, enunciation, composition. He sought in this way to bend himself to the rules of the genre of the 'treatise' (whether of rhetoric or poetics, or politics) destined to be a model for practitioners.

However, when it comes to the sublime, major obstacles get in the way of a regular exposition of rhetorical or poetic principles. There is, for example, wrote Longinus, a sublimity of thought sometimes recognizable in speech by its extreme simplicity of turn of phrase, at the precise point where the high character of the speaker makes one expect greater solemnity. It sometimes even takes the form of outright silence. I don't mind if this simplicity, this silence, is taken to be yet another rhetorical figure. But it must be granted that it constitutes the most indeterminate of figures. What can remain of rhetoric (or of poetics) when the rhetorician in Boileau's translation announces that to attain the sublime effect 'there is no better figure of speech than one which is completely hidden, that which we do not even recognize as a figure of speech'? Must we admit that there are techniques for hiding figures, that there are figures for the erasure of figures? How do we distinguish between a hidden figure and what is not a figure? And what is it, if it isn't a figure? And what about this, which seems to be a major blow to didactics: when it is sublime, discourse accommodates defects, lack of taste, and formal imperfections. Plato's style, for example, is full of bombast and bloated strained comparisons. Plato, in short, is a mannerist, or a baroque writer, compared to Lysias, and so is Sophocles compared to an Ion or Pindar compared to a Bacchylides. The fact remains that, like those first named, he is sublime, whereas the second ones are merely perfect. Shortcomings in technique are therefore trifling matters if they are the price to be paid for 'true grandeur'. Grandeur in speech is true when it bears witness to the incommensurability between thought and the real world.

Is it Boileau's transcription that suggests this analogy, or is it the influence of early Christianity on Longinus? The fact that grandeur of spirit is not of this world cannot but suggest Pascal's hierarchy of orders. The kind of perfection that can be demanded in the domain of *technè* isn't necessarily a desirable attribute when it comes to sublime feeling. Longinus even goes so far as to propose inversions of reputedly natural and rational syntax as examples of sublime effect. As for Boileau, in the preface he wrote in 1674 for Longinus's text, in still further addenda made in 1683 and 1701 and also in the *Xth Réflexion* published in 1710 after his death, he makes final the previous tentative break with the classical institution of *technè*. The sublime, he says, cannot be taught, and didactics are thus powerless in this respect; the sublime is not linked to rules that can be determined through poetics; the sublime only requires that the reader or listener have conceptual range, taste, and the ability 'to sense what everyone senses first'. Boileau therefore takes the same stand as Père Bouhours, when in 1671 the latter declared that beauty demands more than just a respect for rules, that it requires a further '*je ne sais quoi*', also called *genius* or something 'incomprehensible and inexplicable', a 'gift from God', a fundamentally 'hidden' phenomenon that can be recognized only by its effects on the addressee. And in the polemic that set him against Pierre-Daniel Huet, over the issue of whether the Bible's *Fiat Lux, et Lux fuit* is sublime, as Longinus thought it was, Boileau refers to the opinion of the Messieurs de Port-Royal and in particular to Silvestre de Saci: the Jansenists are masters when it comes to matters of hidden meaning, of eloquent silence, of feeling that transcends all reason and finally of openness to the *Is it happening?*

At stake in these poetic-theological debates is the status of works of art. Are they copies of some ideal model? Can reflection on the more 'perfect' examples yield rules of formation that determine their success in achieving what they want, that is, persuasiveness and pleasure? Can understanding suffice for this kind of reflection? By meditating on the theme of sublimity and of indeterminacy, meditation about works of art imposes a major change on *technè* and the institutions linked to it – Academies, Schools, masters and disciples, taste, the enlightened public made up of princes and courtiers. It is the very destination or destiny of works which is being questioned. The predominance of the idea of *technè* placed works under a multiple regulation, that of the model taught in the studios, Schools, and Academies, that of the taste shared by the aristocratic public, that of a purposiveness of art, which was to illustrate the glory of a name, divine or human, to which was linked the perfection of some cardinal virtue or other. The idea of the sublime disrupts this harmony. Let us magnify the features of – this disruption. Under Diderot's pen, *technè* becomes '*le petit technique*' (mere trivial technique). The artist ceases to be guided by a culture which made of him the sender and master of a message of glory: he becomes, insofar as he is a genius, the involuntary addressee of an inspiration come to him from an 'I know not what'. The public no longer judges according to the criteria of a taste ruled by the tradition of shared pleasure: individuals unknown to the artist (the 'people') read books, go through the galleries of the Salons, crowd into the theatres and the public concerts, they are prey to unforeseeable feelings: they are shocked, admiring, scornful, indifferent. The question is not that of pleasing them by leading them to identify with a name and to participate in the glorification of its virtue, but that of surprising them. 'The sublime', writes Boileau, 'is not strictly speaking something which is proven or demonstrated, but a marvel, which seizes one, strikes one, and makes one feel.' The very imperfections, the distortions of taste, even ugliness, have their share in the shock-effect. Art does not imitate nature, it creates a world apart, *eine Zwischenwelt*, as Paul Klee will say, *eine Nebenwelt*, one might say, in which the monstrous and the formless have their rights because they can be sublime.

You will (I hope) excuse such a simplification of the transformation which takes place with the modern development of the idea of the sublime. The trace of it could be found before modern times, in medieval aesthetics – that of the Victorines, for example. In any case, it explains why reflection on art should no longer bear essentially on the 'sender' instance/agency of works, but on the 'addressee' instance. And under the name 'genius' the latter instance is situated, not only on the side of the public, but also on the side of the artist, a feeling which he does not master. Henceforth it seems right to analyse the ways in which the subject is affected, its ways of receiving and experiencing feelings, its ways of judging works. This is how aesthetics, the analysis of the addressee's feelings, comes to supplant poetics and rhetoric, which are didactic forms, of and by the understanding, intended for the artist as sender. No longer 'How does one make a work of art?', but 'What is it to experience an affect proper to art?' And indeterminacy returns, even within the analysis of this last question.

III

Baumgarten published his *Aesthetica*, the first aesthetics, in 1750. Kant will say of this work simply that it was based on an error. Baumgarten confuses judgement, in its determinant usage, when the understanding organizes phenomena according to categories, with judgement in its reflexive usage when, in the form of feeling, it relates to the indeterminate relationship between the faculties of the judging subject. Baumgarten's aesthetics remains dependent on a conceptually determined relationship to the work of art. The sense of beauty is for Kant, on the contrary, kindled by a free harmony between the function of images and the function of concepts occasioned by an object of art or nature. The aesthetics of the sublime is still more indeterminate: a pleasure mixed with pain, a pleasure that comes from pain. In the event of an absolutely large object – the desert, a mountain, a pyramid – or one that is absolutely powerful – a storm at sea, an erupting volcano – which, like all absolutes, can only be thought, without any sensible/sensory intuition, as an Idea of reason, the faculty of presentation, the imagination, fails to provide a representation corresponding to this Idea. This failure of expression gives rise to a pain, a kind of cleavage within the subject between what can be conceived and what can be imagined or presented. But this pain in turn engenders a pleasure, in fact a double pleasure: the impotence of the imagination attests *a contrario* to an imagination striving to figure even that which cannot be figured, and that imagination thus aims to harmonize its object with that of reason – and that furthermore, the inadequacy of the images is a negative sign of the immense power of ideas. This dislocation of the faculties among themselves gives rise to the extreme tension (Kant calls it agitation) that characterizes the pathos of the sublime, as opposed to the calm feeling of beauty. At the edge of the break, infinity, or the absoluteness of the Idea can be revealed in what Kant calls a negative presentation, or even a non-presentation. He cites the Jewish law banning images as an eminent example of negative presentation: optical pleasure when reduced to near nothingness promotes an infinite contemplation of infinity. Even before romantic art had freed itself from classical and baroque figuration, the door had thus been opened to inquiries pointing towards abstract and Minimal art. Avant-gardism is thus present in germ in the Kantian aesthetic of the sublime. However, the art whose effects are analysed in that aesthetics is, of course, essentially made up of attempts to represent sublime objects. And the question of time, of the *Is it happening?*, does not form part – at least not explicitly – of Kant's problematic.

I do, however, believe that question to be at the centre of Edmund Burke's *Philosophical Inquiry into the Origin of our Ideas of the Sublime and Beautiful*, published in 1757. Kant may well reject Burke's thesis as empiricism and physiologism, he may well borrow from Burke the analysis of the characterizing contradiction of the feeling of the sublime, but he strips Burke's aesthetic of what I consider to be its major stake – to show that the sublime is kindled by the threat of nothing further happening. Beauty gives a positive pleasure. But there is another kind of pleasure that is bound to a passion stronger than satisfaction, and that is pain and impending death. In pain the body affects the soul. But the soul can also affect the body as though it were experiencing some externally induced pain, by the sole means of representations that are unconsciously associated with painful situations. This entirely spiritual passion, in Burke's lexicon, is called terror. Terrors are linked to privation: privation of light, terror of darkness; privation of others, terror of solitude; privation of language, terror of silence; privation of objects, terror of emptiness; privation of life, terror of death. What is terrifying is that the *It happens that* does not happen, that it stops happening.

Burke wrote that for this terror to mingle with pleasure and with it to produce the feeling of the sublime, it is also necessary that the terror-causing threat be suspended, kept at bay, held back. This suspense, this lessening of a threat or a danger, provokes a kind of pleasure that is certainly not that of a positive satisfaction, but is, rather, that of relief. This is still a privation, but it is privation at one remove: the soul is deprived of the threat of being deprived of light, language, life. Burke distinguishes this pleasure of secondary privation from positive pleasures, and he baptizes it with the name *delight*.

Here, then, is an account of the sublime feeling: a very big, very powerful object threatens to deprive the soul of any 'it happens', strikes it with 'astonishment' (at lower intensities the soul is seized with admiration, veneration, respect). The soul is thus dumb, immobilized, as good as dead. Art, by distancing this menace, procures a pleasure of relief, of delight. Thanks to art, the soul is returned to the agitated zone between life and death, and this agitation is its health and its life. For Burke, the sublime was no longer a matter of elevation (the category by which Aristotle defined tragedy), but a matter of intensification.

Another of Burke's observations merits attention because it heralds the possibility of emancipating works of art from the classical rule of imitation. In the long debate over the relative merits of painting and poetry, Burke sides with poetry. Painting is doomed to imitate models, and to figurative representations of them. But if the object of art is to create intense feelings in the addressee of works, figuration by means of images is a limiting constraint on the power of emotive expression, since it works by recognition. In the arts of language, particularly in poetry, and particularly in poetry which Burke considered to be not a genre with rules, but the field where certain researches into language have free rein, the power to move is free from the verisimilitudes of figuration. 'What does one do when one wants to represent an angel in a painting? One paints a beautiful young man with wings: but will painting ever provide anything as great as the addition of this one word – the Angel of the *Lord*? and how does one go about painting, with equal strength of feeling, the words "A universe of death" where ends the journey of the fallen angels in Milton's *Paradise Lost*?'

Words enjoy several privileges when it comes to expressing feelings: they are themselves charged with passionate connotations; they can evoke matters of the soul without having to consider whether they are visible; finally, Burke adds, 'It is in our power to effect with words combinations that would be impossible by any other means.' The arts, whatever their materials, pressed forward by the aesthetics of the sublime in search of intense effects, can and must give up the imitation of models that are merely beautiful, and try out surprising, strange, shocking combinations. Shock is, *par excellence*, the evidence of (something) *happening*, rather than nothing, suspended privation.

Burke's analyses can easily, as you will have guessed, be resumed and elaborated in a Freudian–Lacanian problematic (as Pierre Kaufman and Baldine Saint-Girons have done). But I recall them in a different spirit, the one my subject – the avant-garde – demands. I have tried to suggest that at the dawn of romanticism, *Burke's elaboration of the aesthetics of the sublime, and to a lesser degree Kant's, outlined a world of possibilities for artistic experiments in which the avant-gardes would later trace out their paths.* There are in general no direct influences, no empirically observable connections. Manet, Cézanne, Braque, and Picasso probably did not read Kant or Burke. It is more a matter of an irreversible deviation in the destination of art, a deviation affecting all the valencies of the artistic condition. The artist attempts combinations allowing the event. The art-lover does not experience a simple pleasure, or derive some ethical benefit from his contact with art, but expects an intensification of his conceptual and emotional capacity, an ambivalent enjoyment. Intensity is associated with an ontological dislocation. The art object no longer bends itself to models, but tries to present the fact that there is an unpresentable; it no longer imitates nature, but is, in Burke, the actualization of a figure potentially there in language. The social community no longer recognizes itself in art objects, but ignores them, rejects them as incomprehensible, and only later allows the intellectual avant-garde to preserve them in museums as the traces of offensives that bear witness to the power, and the privation, of the spirit.

IV

With the advent of the aesthetics of the sublime, the stake of art in the nineteenth and twentieth centuries was to be the witness to the fact that there is indeterminacy. For painting, the paradox that Burke signalled in his observations on the power of words is that such testimony can only be achieved in a determined fashion. Support, frame, line, colour, space, the figure – were to remain, in romantic art, subject to the constraint of representation. But this contradiction of end and means had, as early as Manet and Cézanne, the effect of casting doubt on certain rules that had determined, since the Quattrocento, the representation of the figure in space and the organization of colours and values. Reading Cézanne's correspondence, one understands that his *oeuvre* was not that of a talented painter finding his 'style', but that of an artist attempting to respond to the question: what is a painting? His work had at stake to inscribe on the supporting canvas only those 'colouristic sensations', those 'little sensations' that of themselves, according to Cézanne's hypothesis, constitute the entire pictorial existence of objects, fruit, mountain, face, flower, without consideration of either history or 'subject', or line, or space, or even light. These elementary sensations are hidden in ordinary perception, which remains under the hegemony of habitual or classical ways of looking. They are only accessible to the painter, and can therefore only be re-established by him, at the expense of an interior ascesis that rids perceptual and mental fields of prejudices inscribed even in vision itself. If the viewer does not submit to a complementary ascesis, the painting will remain senseless and impenetrable to him. The painter must not hesitate to run the risk of being taken to be a mere dauber. 'One paints for very few people,' writes Cézanne. Recognition from the regulatory institutions of painting – Academy, salons, criticism, taste – is of little importance compared to the judgement made by the painter-researcher and his peers on the success obtained by the work of art in relation to what is really at stake: to make seen what makes one see, and not what is visible.

Maurice Merleau-Ponty elaborated on what he rightly called 'Cézanne's doubt', as though what was at stake for the painter was indeed to grasp and render perception at its birth – perception 'before' perception. I would say: colour in its occurrence, the wonder that 'it happens' ('it', something: colour), at least to the eye. There is some credulity on the part of the phenomenologist in this trust he places in the 'originary' value of Cézanne's 'little sensations'. The painter himself, who often complained of their inadequacy, wrote that they were 'abstractions', that 'they did not suffice for covering the canvas'. But why should it be necessary to cover the canvas? Is it forbidden to be abstract?

The doubt which gnaws at the avant-gardes did not stop with Cézanne's 'colouristic sensations' as though they were indubitable, and, for that matter, no more did it stop with the abstractions they heralded. The task of having to bear witness to the indeterminate carries away, one after another, the barriers set up by the writings of theorists and by the manifestos of the painters themselves. A formalist definition of the pictorial object, such as that proposed in 1961 by Clement Greenberg when confronted with American 'post-plastic' abstraction, was soon overturned by the current of Minimalism. Do we have to have stretchers so that the canvas is taut? No. What about colours? Malevich's black square on white had already answered this question in 1915. Is an object necessary? Body art and happenings went about proving that it is not. A space, at least, a space in which to display, as Duchamp's 'fountain' still suggested? Daniel Buren's work testifies to the fact that even this is subject to doubt.

Whether or not they belong to the current that art history calls Minimalism or Arte Povera, the investigations of the avant-gardes question one by one the constituents one might have thought 'elementary' or at the 'origin' of the art of painting. They operate *ex minimis*. One would have to confront the demand for rigour that animates them with the principle sketched out by Adorno at the end of *Negative Dialectics*, and that controls the writing of his *Aesthetic Theory*: the thought that 'accompanies metaphysics in its fall', he said, can only proceed in terms of 'micrologies'.

Micrology is not just metaphysics in crumbs, any more than Newman's painting is Delacroix in scraps. Micrology inscribes the occurrence of a thought as the unthought that remains to be thought in the decline of 'great' philosophical thought. The avant-gardist attempt inscribes the occurrence of a sensory now as what cannot be presented and remains to be presented in the decline of great representational painting. Like micrology, the avant-garde is not concerned with what happens to the 'subject', but with: 'Does it happen?', with privation. This is the sense in which it still belongs to the aesthetics of the sublime.

In asking questions of the *It happens* that the work of art is, avant-garde art abandons the role of identification that the work previously played in relation to the community of addressees. Even when conceived, as it was by Kant, as a *de jure* horizon or presumption rather than a *de facto* reality, a *sensus communis* (which, moreover, Kant refers to only when writing about beauty, not the sublime) does not manage to achieve stability when it comes to interrogative works of art. It barely coalesces, too late, when these works, deposited in museums, are considered part of the community heritage and are made available for its culture and pleasure. And even here, they must be objects, or they must tolerate objectification, for example through photography.

In this situation of isolation and misunderstanding, avant-garde art is vulnerable and subject to repression. It seems only to aggravate the identity-crisis that communities went through during the long 'depression' that lasted from the thirties until the end of 'reconstruction' in the mid-fifties. It is impossible here even to suggest how the Party-states born of fear faced with the 'Who are we?', and the anxiety of the void, tried to convert this fear or anxiety into hatred of the avant-gardes. Hildegarde Brenner's study of artistic policy under Nazism, or the films of Hans-Jürgen Syberberg, do not merely analyse these repressive manoeuvres. They also explain how neo-romantic, neo-classical and symbolic forms imposed by the cultural commissars and collaborationist artists – painters and musicians especially – had to block the negative dialectic of the 'Is it happening?', by translating and betraying the question as a waiting for some fabulous subject or identity: 'Is the pure people coming?', 'Is the Führer coming?', 'Is Siegfried coming?' The aesthetics of the sublime, thus neutralized and converted into a politics of myth, was able to come and build its architectures of human 'formations' on the Zeppelin Feld in Nürnberg.

Thanks to the 'crisis of overcapitalization' that most of today's so-called highly developed societies are going through, another attack on the avant-gardes is coming to light. The threat exerted against the avant-garde search for the artwork event, against attempts to welcome the *now*, no longer requires Party-states to be effective. It proceeds 'directly' out of market economics. The correlation between this and the aesthetics of the sublime is ambiguous, even perverse. The latter, no doubt, has been and continues to be a reaction against the matter-of-fact positivism and the calculated realism that governs the former, as writers on art such as Stendhal, Baudelaire, Mallarmé, Apollinaire and Breton all emphasize.

Yet there is a kind of collusion between capital and the avant-garde. The force of scepticism and even of destruction that capitalism has brought into play, and that Marx never ceased analysing and identifying, in some way encourages among artists a mistrust of established rules and a willingness to experiment with means of expression, with styles, with ever-new materials. There is something of the sublime in capitalist economy. It is not academic, it is not physiocratic, it admits of no nature. It is, in a sense, an economy regulated by an Idea – infinite wealth or power. It does not manage to present any example from reality to verify this Idea. In making science subordinate to itself through technologies, especially those of language, it only succeeds, on the contrary, in making reality increasingly ungraspable, subject to doubt, unsteady.

The experience of the human subject – individual and collective – and the aura that surrounds this experience, are being dissolved into the calculation of profitability, the satisfaction of needs, self-affirmation through success. Even the virtually theological depth of the worker's condition, and of work, that marked the socialist and union movements for over a century, is becoming devalorized, as work becomes a control and manipulation of information. These observations are banal, but what merits attention is the disappearance of the temporal continuum through which the experience of generations used to be transmitted. The availability of information is becoming the only criterion of social importance. Now information is by definition a short-lived element. As soon as it is transmitted and shared, it ceases to be information, it becomes an environmental given, and 'all is said', we 'know'. It is put into the machine memory. The length of time it occupies is, so to speak, instantaneous. Between two pieces of information, 'nothing happens', by definition. A confusion thereby becomes possible between what is of interest to information and the director, and what is the question of the avant-gardes between what happens – the new – and the 'Is it happening?', the *now*.

It is understandable that the art-market, subject like all markets to the rule of the new, can exert a kind of seduction on artists. This attraction is not due to corruption alone. It exerts itself thanks to a confusion between innovation and the *Ereignis*, a confusion maintained by the temporality specific to contemporary capitalism. 'Strong' information, if one can call it that, exists in inverse proportion to the meaning that can be attributed to it in the code available to its receiver. It is like 'noise'. It is easy for the public and for artists, advised by intermediaries – the diffusers of cultural merchandise – to draw from this observation the principle that a work of art is avant-garde in direct proportion to the extent that it is stripped of meaning. Is it not then like an event?

It is still necessary that its absurdity does not discourage buyers, just as the innovation introduced into a commodity must allow itself to be approached, appreciated and purchased by the consumers. The secret of an artistic success, like that of a commercial success, resides in the balance between what is surprising and what is 'well-known', between information and code. This is how innovation in art operates: one re-uses formulae confirmed by previous success, one throws them off balance by combining them with other, in principle incompatible, formulae, by amalgamations, quotations, ornamentations, pastiche. One can go as far as kitsch or the grotesque. One flatters the 'taste' of a public that can have no taste, and the eclecticism or a sensibility enfeebled by the multiplication of available forms and objects. In this way one thinks that one is expressing the spirit of the times, whereas one is merely reflecting the spirit of the market. Sublimity is no longer in art, but in speculation on art.

The enigma of the 'Is it happening?' is not dissolved for all this, nor is the task of painting: that there is something which is not determinable, the 'There is' [*Il y a*] itself, out of date. The occurrence, the *Ereignis*, has nothing to do with the *petit frisson*, the cheap thrill, the profitable pathos, that accompanies an innovation. Hidden in the cynicism of innovation is certainly the despair that nothing further will happen. But innovating means to behave as though lots of things happened, and to make them happen. Through innovation, the will affirms its hegemony over time. It thus conforms to the metaphysics of capital, which is a technology of time. The innovation 'works'. The question mark of the 'Is it happening?' stops. With the occurrence, the will is defeated. The avant-gardist task remains that of undoing the presumption of the mind with respect to time. The sublime feeling is the name of this privation.

19 □ *The International Trans-Avant-Garde*

Achille Bonito Oliva

The art of the last generation operates in the area of the *trans-avant-garde*, where language is considered an instrument of change, of passage from one work to another and from one style to another. If one accepts the idea that the avant-garde of the last twenty or thirty years developed along the evolutionary lines of linguistic Darwinism, looking for precedents to the accomplishments of the first decades of the century, then one must draw a distinction with respect to the trans-avant-garde, which operates outside these obligatory limits, following a nomadic attitude that has proven capable of reversing the language of the past.

The dematerialization of the work and the impersonality of execution that characterized the art of the seventies (carrying further ideas pioneered by Duchamp) have given way to hand craftsmanship and to a pleasure of execution which reintroduces the tradition of painting into art. The trans-avant-garde rejects the idea of an artistic process aimed entirely at conceptual abstraction. It introduces the possibility of not considering the linear course of earlier art as final, by opting for attitudes that take into account languages that had previously been abandoned.

This recovery does not entail identification with the styles of the past, but the ability to pick and choose from their surface, in the conviction that, in a society in transition toward an undefinable end, the only option open is that afforded by a nomadic and transitory mentality. Just as philosophical positivism (which penetrated and to a great extent determined the development of Western civilization, accelerating social and economic changes in terms of technological experimentation) has recently come under fire, so has its cultural implication, the hysteria for the new typical of the traditional avant-garde. This has caused the historical optimism of the avant-garde – the idea of progress inherent in its experimentation with new techniques and new materials – to collapse. The attention of the artists of the trans-avant-garde is thus polycentric and dispersed over a broad area. These artists no longer seek head-on confrontation. They engage instead in a continuous lateral

From *Flash Art*, 104 (1981), 36–43.

movement whose path crosses every contradiction and every commonplace, including that of technical and operative originality.

In short, the recent avant-gardes espoused the principle of dialectics, regarding art as a means of overcoming and reconciling contradictions and differences. The trans-avant-garde, in contrast, is an indefinite area that groups artists together, not on the basis of trends and linguistic affinities, but in view of an artistic attitude and philosophy which emphasizes their own centrality, and advocates the recovery of an internal reason unbounded by the fetters of the art of the immediate past (the chief asset of which was the coherent development of the linguistic precedents of the major movements of the early twentieth century).

The trans-avant-garde does not boast the privilege of a direct lineage. Its family stock extends fan-like over precedents of diverse descent and provenance, encompassing not only such noble ancestors as the early-twentieth-century avant-garde, but also lesser ones, like crafts and the minor arts. The artists of the trans-avant-garde realize that cultural growth may extend downward as well as upward; that anthropological roots, while independent of each other, all tend to affirm the biology of art, the necessity of a kind of creativity aimed at extending its own experience as an instance of seduction and mutation.

The second half of the seventies and the beginning of the eighties have been deeply affected by this mentality. Art has availed itself of numerous expressive means, especially that of painting, of the tools connected with the language of marks and color. By applying its metaphoric and metonymic capacities (the latter being the ability to transfer or shift meaning between the parts and the whole), and aided by a highly stratified cultural context (which affords a more generally anthropological climate, conducive to the abstract furies of the imagination and to a broad range of linguistic and social implications), the new image has found a natural habitat in the history of art and of styles.

The fabric of the new artistic production is marked by an intertexture of subjectivity which is not an autobiographical or personal phenomenon, but which represents art's response to personal motives purified from the use of a conscious and controlled language. Language is never the gauge of a totally subjective condition; rather, it is the knowing and ironic medium of a vision which contains the pleasure of its own presence and the reasons for its own persistence.

Persistence and emergence are the characteristics of the new image, understood as the possibility, on one hand, to take up again the traditional processes of art and the constant felicity that supports it; and, on the other hand, to reject or differentiate between preceding accomplishments. Here the art of the last generation rediscovers the pleasure of timelessness, which consists in part of the recovery of languages, positions, and methodologies pertaining to the past.

The failure of political discourse and ideological dogma has caused the superstition of art as a progressive attitude to be overcome. Artists have realized that the principles of progressivist thought can be reduced, in the final analysis, to an internal progression or evolution of language along lines of escape which parallel the utopian escape of ideology. The art of the immediate past sought to take part in social change through the expansion of new processes and new materials, moving away from painting and from the static time of the work. Present art tends to discard illustrations of what lies outside itself, and to turn back on its own footsteps.

Naturally, this does not entail enclosure of the painting within the frame. The sensibility of the work calls up echoes of the outside in the field of language. It binds spatial and temporal motives to the reasons of art through installations of painting, collage, and drawing.

This process is favored by the disintegration of the unitary idea of the work, a projection of the disintegration of unitary visions of the world. The totalizing vainglory of ideology was reflected in the stringent arrogance of the work of art, which bore models for the symbolic transformation of the world. Now, that arrogance has died out, and the artist no longer intends pathetically to preserve the myth of an impossible and impracticable integrity.

Working in fragments means preferring the vibrations of sensibility to monolithic ideological content. These vibrations are necessarily discontinuous. They carry the artist toward a project made of numerous linguistic accidents, beyond the logical coherence of poetry. Fragments are symptoms of an ecstasy of dissociation. They are signs of a desire for continuous mutation.

This continuous mutation becomes possible when the artist returns to the centrality of art. The work then becomes the point where the shifts in sensibility flow together. But this sensibility does not exclude the emotion of the mind, nor does it block out the tension of intelligence and culture. In fact, the work solidifies within itself the cultural and visual memory of other works – not as a quotation, but as a mobile and shifting investigation of preceding linguistic modules.

Fragments point to the possibility of constructing images piece by piece, outside the logic of planning, but within the bounds of a conception of art history that is open to reprise. As the ideological imperative has fallen, so has the preclusion of former linguistic models. Taking these models up again implies the possibility of a duet and a duel animated by other collisions of language. Fragments present the option of injecting the work with a healthy dose of inconstancy.

The artist employs the image as the solidification of numerous currents, as the agent of a thousand factors that guide the creative impulse. The latter becomes the new subject of the work; and the artist becomes a vehicle of sensibility which, through its shiftings, leads to the work and to the final result. This, in its ultimate persistence, is the fruit of a work process that rediscovers the ethic of a time of execution that was lost in the processes of conceptual art.

The discontinuity of sensibility leads also to the production of different images bound together by a practice that never repeats itself. These images take the disguise of figuration, of abstract marks, of opulence of material and color, without ever submitting to standardization. The work always responds to the requirements of the unrepeatable chance, because the relationship between the artist and his means of expression is unrepeatable.

This feature, too, makes the work timeless, in the sense that it is never able to represent the artist in the present. If anything, it becomes the symptom of a sensible fragmentation of making art. Description and decoration are the emblems that adorn the work, leading it away from the obligatory position of a one-way function.

Description is the purport of a tension that tends to present itself in the guise of a cordial explicitness aimed at drawing external attention to itself. Decoration is the mark of a style which finds in abstraction and in the repetition of fanciful motifs the way to create a field of fascination and indeterminateness that does not seek to impose its own meaning. In both cases the image is freed from its traditional connotations. It is still the result of a symbolic condensation, the purport of an idea masked behind the visual form it takes on. But, in the work of the last generation, it does not condense a strong meaning within itself – it does not transmit an explicit idea. It is a *bewildered image* which no longer shows in a haughty way the sedimentations derived from a special situation, but reveals the declarative aspect of a minor presence.

Minority is an explicit feature of creative work. It is the fruit of a mentality free from superstition. The work intentionally lacks character, it does not hold heroic attitudes, and it does not recall exemplary situations. Instead, it presents small events related to individual sensibility and circumscribed by adventures laced with irony and subtle detachment.

The new art, then, violates the expectations that derive from its usual function as a vehicle of meaning. It acquires the free will to be whim, to describe internal states of sensibility without implying a psychological condition.

An ironic component is both explicitly and implicitly present in such art. Explicitly, it is given by the miniaturization of the event presented, by placing the work at the service of a microsensibility that dramatized nothing because it lacks the historical energy to do so. A healthy historical breakdown has purified language of all symbolic or ideological valency, in favor of free-flowing and interchangeable usage. Implicitly, the ironic element is given by the use of the work as a logos of continuous shiftings of meaning, an unending chain that follows the journey of the image through great and small adventures. The irony is released in the inversion that a traditionally metaphorical position produces on one that is more specifically metonymical and hence free of symbolic capacity. The image is engaged through a neutralization of its strong meaning, as the occasion for a representation in which the abstract and the figurative are equalized.

Everything is fair game for the mark in a conception which constantly sees language without gradients, horizontally. To deprive language of meaning always means something; in this case it is the symptom of a mentality that no longer shows preferences, but tends to consider the language of painting entirely interchangeable, removing it from fixation and mania and delivering it to a practice which sees value in inconstancy.

If every language has its own internal exemplarity, or capacity for description, then its deprivation produces an ideological destitution that is both consequent and consequential with respect to that deprivation.

The work presents an intentionally heterogeneous result, open to color and material as to figurative and abstract marks. The pleasure principle replaces the reality principle, understood here as the ingratiating economy of artistic activity. The work becomes an opulent show which no longer tends toward economy, but toward waste; and which no longer recognizes a special reserve to draw upon.

The contiguity of different styles produces a chain of images, all of which work on the basis of shifting and progression which is fluid rather than planned, and which moves in sudden leaps and bounds. In every instance the image oscillates between invention and convention. The convention is the moment in which the language is taken up as style, in which the artist recovers the mark rather than the meaning, the surface level. The invention is triggered through the contiguity and unpredictable meeting of linguistic differences and assonances, which do not cause dissonances or lacerations, and do not determine fields of visual disturbance, but establish the possibility of an unexpected outflow, crisscrossed and animated by a light sensibility.

The work is a micro-event that always starts from the inside of the image, the center of radiation of sensibility. Therefore invention is not explicit, obvious, or coarsely linguistic. Its originality consists in bringing forth emotional, cultural and conceptual latencies condensed under these meetings and continuities.

Another level of intuitional conventionality is that of the use of a visual language tied to the use of marks, drawing, color, and pictorial space; and of the consideration of external space as a potential area of extension, in which the fragments of the work are reflected without the presence of preferential points.

But the work is not a mosaic of forms: an image always remains as a consequence. Form, by definition, internalizes idea and visual mark in an inextricable unit; an image is a metamorphosis of a concept which takes on the appearance of figurative representations that may differ greatly from one another.

In order to facilitate this process of unburdening, images avail themselves of a tension entirely based on a vicissitude of pleasure composed of mobility and small gestures. Attention is by no means associated with care or cleverness; rather, it is a capacity to grasp the relations and links between the various characters the work takes on.

In fact, the work possesses an inner inconstancy which arises from a voluble use of language, that is, from the fragments which go to make up the final organic constellation. It combines hot and cold, concrete and abstract, day and night, in a timeless and pervasive intertexture. The work loses its traditional composure as it is freed from the stylized rigidity of art as an ideal whole. Now, in contrast, it is crowded with tensions of diverse provenance that cannot be explained according to the sedateness of its poetics. If it has a meaning, this meaning is one of disseminated attention, of a sensibility that opens out fan-like to aid and encourage numerous inattentions. The use of metonymy permits the image to take on a mobile meaning that arises progressively from the language's internal economy, through visual assonances and passages of marks that establish the work of a field which, by definition, derives its value from the potentiality of mobile relations. The accentuation of the shifting character now makes possible a precarious and unstable meaning, constructed through a continuous chain of marks which do not function according to predictable and rigid mechanics.

In this way meaning is bewildered, attenuated, made relative, and related to other semantic substances which float behind the recovery of the innumerable systems of marks. There results a sort of mildness of the work, which no longer speaks peremptorily, nor bases its appeal on ideological fixity, but dissolves in multi-directional digression. The numerous directions are those of the language and its points of recovery, which at this stage can no longer be circumscribed for they are subjected to an assiduous search, and intense courtship without preferences and preclusions. The new art draws on an endless reserve where abstract and figurative, avant-garde and tradition coexist.

The art of the sixties operated through the presentation of real materials as an image of energy and a reference to nature. That of the seventies was the sum of presentation and representation, an intersection of nature and culture. Now art has finally chosen the area of representation, abolishing concrete reference to the real, or replacing the naturalness of materials directly introduced into art with the artifice of strictly pictorial materials. The reduction of the material physicality of the work and its orientation toward materials more tightly bound to the artistic tradition arise from a historical consideration that does not allow for illusions with regard to the capacity for expansion beyond the frame, beyond its own specific condition, or beyond artistic creation.

The mythic force of art deliberately loses its monolithic tension in favor of an image that is both intense and, at the same time, deconcentrated, sliding across the surface of style and of recovered languages. The new art revives the ambivalency of poetic play as described in Martin Heidegger's definition: 'Poetry appears as play and yet is not play. Play brings men together, but in such a way that each one forgets himself.'

Part Five

Architecture and Urbanicity

Introduction

In 1932 the first 'International Exhibition of Modern Architecture' was held at the Museum of Modern Art in New York, and it exhibited work by Gropius, Mies and Le Corbusier, who were heralded as the leading figures in a new architectural style, the 'International Style' (which was the name of the catalogue prepared for the exhibition by Philip Johnson and Henry-Russell Hitchcock). In the wake of the First World War, there were two important determinants of the new style. First, urban planning on a large scale was called for as devastated economies tried to rehabilitate themselves; and it was of central importance that cities could be rebuilt with a large amount of low-cost materials and standardised units of construction. Secondly, since this first necessity was more or less uniform across Europe, and since international communications were quickly re-established, regional or national variations in architectural design began to disappear. The resulting International Style was characterised by three central factors. First, design was executed according to an economy of 'function', according to which the use of a building was a determinant of its style. Secondly, ferroconcrete and steel, as the main building materials, themselves determined certain possibilities and limitations in design, such as a geometric regularity. Thirdly, applied decoration was out, in favour of a kind of austerity. The result was a homogeneity of urban planning and building design which threatened the idea of a specific located tradition; in short, the 'genius loci', the very foundation of architectural thought, was under threat as a guiding principle for the determination of lived space.

Architecture, as a means of inhabiting space, is also a means of inhabiting time, for – as Heidegger would have had it – building in a place must acknowledge the history of that place, its being in time as well as its being in space. The danger of a homogenising internationalism is precisely that it will reduce criticism to conformism, to commodity aesthetics. The critical consciousness is critical precisely to the extent that it is historical, aware of the possibility that tomorrow might differ from today. Homogeneity in an international style has the potential effect of making the *accident* of style appear to be a matter of *necessity*: in a strict sense of the phrase, 'there is no alternative'. The critical consciousness is one which acknowledges that while there *is* no alternative, there still yet *can be*.

The modernist International project in architecture begins to come under pressure almost as soon as it is established as a dominant style. Technology makes new materials available; and the outbreak of the Second World War brings the return of a consciousness of place, a sense of 'location' evoked by the various dislocations of war itself.

In his piece included here, Kenneth Frampton argues for an architecture which will enable a critical 'resistance', an adversarial stance for consciousness, a stance which will not encourage the historical human Subject to become a mere conformist going along blindly with the socio-cultural organisation of life as determined by the built environment. In his argument, there is no denial of the actuality of a 'universal civilisation'; but Frampton argues that this should be tempered and mediated by the specifics of a particular place. The result is a 'regionalism' which avoids pastoral myth, but retains a sense of the possibilities of heterogeneous traditions. He is thus not sympathetic to a modernist tradition; yet nor is he any more in agreement with the postmodernism of Jencks and others.

The kind of building proposed by Jencks is, according to Frampton, one which encourages precisely the commodity aesthetics and the conformity of consciousness of a media-saturated society. Jencks himself hardly sees it this way, of course. Indeed, in his 'Emergent Rules', reprinted here, he explicitly argues for a postmodernism that is characterised by pluralism, anthropomorphic humanism, multivalence and – probably his most favoured term – 'double-coding'. Double-coding is, in a word, irony; or, as Jencks himself defines it here, 'contradiction'. The purpose of contradiction in architecture and urbanicity for Jencks is that it 'acknowledges the simultaneous validity of opposite approaches and different tastes'. Further, this contradiction is most efficiently considered by Jencks as a kind of historical contradiction, a contradiction set in time. He is keen on the idea of a historical continuum, but one in which, within a specific instance of building, one will be aware simultaneously of the present in the past and of the past in the present. As in Oliva's consideration of a trans-avant-garde, the postmodern here is not confrontational before its tradition; rather, it brings the tradition to bear while shifting it in a gradualist – and, Jencks would argue, *contra* Frampton, 'critical' – manner.

Jencks's 'new classicism' is entertaining, decidely and avowedly upbeat, optimistic about the possibility of new and most frequently unexpected discoveries. Yet some might argue that the postmodern architecture which he favours has become precisely as homogeneous internationally as the very modernist International Style which it exists to challenge. The world has increasingly begun to look the same, it is sometimes argued, for we have all been 'Learning from Las Vegas'. Robert Venturi and his associates (Denise Scott-Brown, John Rauch) take the line that kitsch is good. Against the 'heroic originality' of buildings which they characterise as 'ducks', Venturi and associates set the 'ugly and ordinary' type of building, the 'decorated shed' of their own preferred design. For them, as for Jencks, contradiction is important. The ideal decorated shed is one where 'some form of conventional systems-building shelter that corresponds closely to the space, structure, and program requirements of the architecture' is explicitly contradicted by a 'decoration' which is superimposed upon it. At times, Venturi reads like the Futurist Marinetti, singing the praise of an automobile culture living at high speed in an urban sprawl.

For Frampton (as, to a lesser or less explicit extent, for Portoghesi and Jencks) such a neo-Futurist postmodern architecture is anathema. Portoghesi's notions of the presence of the past, like that of Jencks's historical continuum, are consistent with the postmodern suspicion of progress, or of speed as a cultural value for its own sake.

What is at stake in the debate in postmodern architecture, fundamentally, is the issue of the heterogeneity of lived space and, perhaps paradoxically, of lived time. Postmodern thinking in this area has made it clear that architecture is an art of time every bit as much as it is an art of space. Its significance, as the essays gathered here make clear, is historical as well as spatial; its orientation, as some of the writing here would testify, is towards a cultural heterogeneity in the form of pluralism. Once more, the spirit of place (the 'here') is also the spirit of time (the 'now').

20 □ *Toward a Critical Regionalism: Six points for an architecture of resistance*

Kenneth Frampton

The phenomenon of universalization, while being an advancement of mankind, at the same time constitutes a sort of subtle destruction, not only of traditional cultures, which might not be an irreparable wrong, but also of what I shall call for the time being the creative nucleus of great cultures, that nucleus on the basis of which we interpret life, what I shall call in advance the ethical and mythical nucleus of mankind. The conflict springs up from there. We have the feeling that this single world civilization at the same time exerts a sort of attrition or wearing away at the expense of the cultural resources which have made the great civilizations of the past. This threat is expressed, among other disturbing effects, by the spreading before our eyes of a mediocre civilization which is the absurd counterpart of what I was just calling elementary culture. Everywhere throughout the world, one finds the same bad movie, the same slot machines, the same plastic or aluminium atrocities, the same twisting of language by propaganda, etc. It seems as if mankind, by approaching *en masse* a basic consumer culture, were also stopped *en masse* at a subcultural level. Thus we come to the crucial problem confronting nations just rising from underdevelopment. In order to get on to the road toward modernization, is it necessary to jettison the old cultural past which has been the *raison d'être* of a nation? ... Whence the paradox: on the one hand, it has to root itself in the soil of its past, forge a national spirit, and unfurl this spiritual and cultural revindication before the colonialist's personality. But in order to take part in modern civilization, it is necessary at the same time to take part in scientific, technical, and political rationality, something which

From Foster, H. (ed.), *The Anti-Aesthetic: Essays on postmodern culture*, Bay Press, Port Townsend, WA, 1983, pp. 16–30.

> very often requires the pure and simple abandon of a whole
> cultural past. It is a fact: every culture cannot sustain and
> absorb the shock of modern civilization. There is that para-
> dox: how to become modern and to return to sources; how to
> revive an old, dormant civilization and take part in universal
> civilization.[1]
>
> PAUL RICOEUR, *History and Truth*

1 Culture and Civilization

Modern building is now so universally conditioned by optimized technology that the
possibility of creating significant urban form has become extremely limited. The
restrictions jointly imposed by automotive distribution and the volatile play of land
speculation serve to limit the scope of urban design to such a degree that any
intervention tends to be reduced either to the manipulation of elements
predetermined by the imperatives of production, or to a kind of superficial masking
which modern development requires for the facilitation of marketing and the
maintenance of social control. Today the practice of architecture seems to be
increasingly polarized between, on the one hand, a so-called 'high-tech' approach
predicated exclusively upon production and, on the other, the provision of a
'compensatory façade' to cover up the harsh realities of this universal system.[2]

Twenty years ago the dialectical interplay between civilization and culture still
afforded the possibility of maintaining some general control over the shape and
significance of the urban fabric. The last two decades, however, have radically
transformed the metropolitan centers of the developed world. What were still
essentially nineteenth-century city fabrics in the early 1960s have since become
progressively overlaid by the two symbiotic instruments of Megalopolitan
development – the freestanding high-rise and the serpentine freeway. The former
has finally come into its own as the prime device for realizing the increased land
value brought into being by the latter. The typical downtown which, up to twenty
years ago, still presented a mixture of residential stock with tertiary and secondary
industry has now become little more than a *burolandschaft* city-scape: the victory
of universal civilization over locally inflected culture. The predicament posed by
Ricoeur – namely, 'how to become modern and to return to sources'[3] – now seems
to be circumvented by the apocalyptic thrust of modernization, while the ground in
which the mytho-ethical nucleus of a society might take root has become eroded by
the rapacity of development.[4]

Ever since the beginning of the Enlightenment, *civilization* has been primarily
concerned with instrumental reason, while *culture* has addressed itself to the
specifics of expression – to the realization of the being and the evolution of its
collective psychosocial reality. Today civilization tends to be increasingly embroiled
in a never-ending chain of 'means and ends' wherein, according to Hannah Arendt,

'The "in order to" has become the content of the "for the sake of"; utility established as meaning generates meaninglessness.'[5]

2 The Rise and Fall of the Avant-Garde

The emergence of the avant-garde is inseparable from the modernization of both society and architecture. Over the past century-and-a-half avant-garde culture has assumed different roles, at times facilitating the process of modernization and thereby acting, in part, as a progressive, liberative form, at times being virulently opposed to the positivism of bourgeois culture. By and large, avant-garde architecture has played a positive role with regard to the progressive trajectory of the Enlightenment. Exemplary of this is the role played by Neoclassicism: from the mid-eighteenth century onwards it serves as both a symbol of and an instrument for the propagation of universal civilization. The mid-nineteenth century, however, saw the historical avant-garde assume an adversary stance towards both industrial process and Neoclassical form. This is the first concerted reaction on the part of 'tradition' to the process of modernization as the Gothic Revival and the Arts-and-Crafts movements take up a categorically negative attitude towards both utilitarianism and the division of labor. Despite this critique, modernization continues unabated, and throughout the last half of the nineteenth century bourgeois art distances itself progressively from the harsh realities of colonialism and paleo-technological exploitation. Thus at the end of the century the avant-gardist Art Nouveau takes refuge in the compensatory thesis of 'art for art's sake', retreating to nostalgic or phantasmagoric dream-worlds inspired by the cathartic hermeticism of Wagner's music-drama.

The progressive avant-garde emerges in full force, however, soon after the turn of the century with the advent of Futurism. This unequivocal critique of the *ancien régime* gives rise to the primary positive cultural formations of the 1920s: to Purism, Neoplasticism and Constructivism. These movements are the last occasion on which radical avant-gardism is able to identify itself wholeheartedly with the process of modernization. In the immediate aftermath of World War I – 'the war to end all wars' – the triumphs of science, medicine and industry seemed to confirm the liberative promise of the modern project. In the 1930s, however, the prevailing backwardness and chronic insecurity of the newly urbanized masses, the upheavals caused by war, revolution and economic depression, followed by a sudden and crucial need for psychosocial stability in the face of global political and economic crises, all induce a state of affairs in which the interests of both monopoly and state capitalism are, for the first time in modern history, divorced from the liberative drives of cultural modernization. Universal civilization and world culture cannot be drawn upon to sustain 'the myth of the State', and one reaction-formation succeeds another as the historical avant-garde founders on the rocks of the Spanish Civil War.

Not least among these reactions is the reassertion of Neo-Kantian aesthetics as a substitute for the culturally liberative modern project. Confused by the political and cultural politics of Stalinism, former left-wing protagonists of socio-cultural modernization now recommend a strategic withdrawal from the project of totally transforming the existing reality. This renunciation is predicated on the belief that as long as the struggle between socialism and capitalism persists (with the manipulative mass-culture politics that this conflict necessarily entails), the modern world cannot continue to entertain the prospect of evolving a marginal, liberative, avant-gardist culture which would break (or speak of the break) with the history of bourgeois repression. Close to *l'art pour l'art*, this position was first advanced as a 'holding pattern' in Clement Greenberg's 'Avant-garde and kitsch' of 1939; this essay concludes somewhat ambiguously with the words: 'Today we look to socialism *simply* for the preservation of whatever living culture we have right now.'[6] Greenberg reformulated this position in specifically formalist terms in his essay 'Modernist painting' of 1965, wherein he wrote:

> Having been denied by the Enlightenment of all tasks they could take seriously, they [the arts] looked as though they were going to be assimilated to entertainment pure and simple, and entertainment looked as though it was going to be assimilated, like religion, to therapy. The arts could save themselves from this leveling down only by demonstrating that the kind of experience they provided was valuable in its own right and not to be obtained from any other kind of activity.[7]

Despite this defensive intellectual stance, the arts have nonetheless continued to gravitate, if not towards entertainment, then certainly towards commodity and – in the case of that which Charles Jencks has since classified as Post-Modern Architecture[8] – towards pure technique or pure scenography. In the latter case, the so-called postmodern architects are merely feeding the media society with gratuitous, quietistic images rather than proffering, as they claim, a creative *rappel à l'ordre* after the supposedly proven bankruptcy of the liberative modern project. In this regard, as Andreas Huyssens has written, 'The American postmodernist avant-garde, therefore, is not only the endgame of avant-gardism. It also represents the fragmentation and decline of the avant-garde as a genuinely critical and adversary culture.'[9]

Nevertheless, it is true that modernization can no longer be simplistically identified as liberative *in se*, in part because of the domination of mass culture by the media industry (above all television which, as Jerry Mander reminds us, expanded its persuasive power a thousandfold between 1945 and 1975)[10] and in part because the trajectory of modernization has brought us to the threshold of nuclear war and the annihilation of the entire species. So too, avant-gardism can no longer be sustained as a liberative moment, in part because its initial utopian promise has been overrun by the internal rationality of instrumental reason. This 'closure' was perhaps best formulated by Herbert Marcuse when he wrote:

> The technological *apriori* is a political *apriori* inasmuch as the transformation of nature involves that of man, and inasmuch as the 'man-made creations' issue from and

re-enter the societal ensemble. One may still insist that the machinery of the technological universe is 'as such' indifferent towards political ends – it can revolutionize or retard society. ... However, when technics becomes the universal form of material production, it circumscribes an entire culture, it projects a historical totality – a 'world'.[11]

3 Critical Regionalism and World Culture

Architecture can only be sustained today as a critical practice if it assumes an *arrière-garde* position, that is to say, one which distances itself equally from the Enlightenment myth of progress and from a reactionary, unrealistic impulse to return to the architectonic forms of the preindustrial past. A critical arrière-garde has to remove itself from both the optimization of advanced technology and the ever-present tendency to regress into nostalgic historicism or the glibly decorative. It is my contention that only an arrière-garde has the capacity to cultivate a resistant, identity-giving culture while at the same time having discreet recourse to universal technique.

It is necessary to qualify the term arrière-garde so as to diminish its critical scope from such conservative policies as Populism or sentimental Regionalism with which it has often been associated. In order to ground arrière-gardism in a rooted yet critical strategy, it is helpful to appropriate the term Critical Regionalism as coined by Alex Tzonis and Liliane Lefaivre in 'The grid and the pathway' (1981); in this essay they caution against the ambiguity of regional reformism, as this has become occasionally manifest since the last quarter of the nineteenth century:

> Regionalism has dominated architecture in almost all countries at some time during the past two centuries and a half. By way of general definition we can say that it upholds the individual and local architectonic features against more universal and abstract ones. In addition, however, regionalism bears the hallmark of ambiguity. On the one hand, it has been associated with movements of reform and liberation; ... on the other, it has proved a powerful tool of repression and chauvinism. ... Certainly, critical regionalism has its limitations. The upheaval of the populist movement – a more developed form of regionalism – has brought to light these weak points. No new architecture can emerge without a new kind of relations between designer and user, without new kinds of programs. ... Despite these limitations critical regionalism is a bridge over which any humanistic architecture of the future must pass.[12]

The fundamental strategy of Critical Regionalism is to mediate the impact of universal civilization with elements derived *indirectly* from the peculiarities of a particular place. It is clear from the above that Critical Regionalism depends upon maintaining a high level of critical self-consciousness. It may find its governing inspiration in such things as the range and quality of the local light, or in a *tectonic* derived from a peculiar structural mode, or in the topography of a given site.

But it is necessary, as I have already suggested, to distinguish between Critical Regionalism and simple-minded attempts to revive the hypothetical forms of a lost vernacular. In contradistinction to Critical Regionalism, the primary vehicle of Populism is the *communicative* or *instrumental* sign. Such a sign seeks to evoke not a critical perception of reality, but rather the sublimation of a desire for direct experience through the provision of information. Its tactical aim is to attain, as economically as possible, a preconceived level of gratification in behavioristic terms. In this respect, the strong affinity of Populism for the rhetorical techniques and imagery of advertising is hardly accidental. Unless one guards against such a convergence, one will confuse the resistant capacity of a critical practice with the demagogic tendencies of Populism.

The case can be made that Critical Regionalism as a cultural strategy is as much a bearer of *world culture* as it is a vehicle of *universal civilization*. And while it is obviously misleading to conceive of our inheriting world culture to the same degree as we are all heirs to universal civilization, it is nonetheless evident that since we are, in principle, subject to the impact of both, we have no choice but to take cognizance today of their interaction. In this regard the practice of Critical Regionalism is contingent upon a process of double mediation. In the first place, it has to 'deconstruct' the overall spectrum of world culture which it inevitably inherits; in the second place, it has to achieve, through synthetic contradiction, a manifest critique of universal civilization. To deconstruct world culture is to remove oneself from that eclecticism of the *fin de siècle* which appropriated alien, exotic forms in order to revitalize the expressivity of an enervated society. (One thinks of the 'form-force' aesthetics of Henri van de Velde or the 'whiplash-Arabesques' of Victor Horta.) On the other hand, the mediation of universal technique involves imposing limits on the optimization of industrial and post-industrial technology. The future necessity for resynthesizing principles and elements drawn from diverse origins and quite different ideological sets seems to be alluded to by Ricoeur when he writes:

> No one can say what will become of our civilization when it has really met different civilizations by means other than the shock of conquest and domination. But we have to admit that this encounter has not yet taken place at the level of an authentic dialogue. That is why we are in a kind of lull or interregnum in which we can no longer practice the dogmatism of a single truth and in which we are not yet capable of conquering the skepticism into which we have stepped. [13]

A parallel and complementary sentiment was expressed by the Dutch architect Aldo Van Eyck who, quite coincidentally, wrote at the same time: 'Western civilization habitually identifies itself with civilization as such on the pontifical assumption that what is not like it is a deviation, less advanced, primitive, or, at best, exotically interesting at a safe distance.'[14]

That Critical Regionalism cannot be simply based on the autochthonous forms of a specific region alone was well put by the Californian architect Hamilton

Harwell Harris when he wrote, now nearly thirty years ago:

> Opposed to the Regionalism of Restriction is another type of regionalism, the
> Regionalism of Liberation. This is the manifestation of a region that is especially in tune
> with the emerging thought of the time. We call such a manifestation 'regional' only
> because it has not yet emerged elsewhere. ... A region may develop ideas. A region may
> accept ideas. Imagination and intelligence are necessary for both. In California in the
> late Twenties and Thirties modern European ideas met a still-developing regionalism.
> In New England, on the other hand, European Modernism met a rigid and restrictive
> regionalism that at first resisted and then surrendered. New England accepted
> European Modernism whole because its own regionalism had been reduced to a
> collection of restrictions. [15]

The scope for achieving a self-conscious synthesis between universal civilization and
world-culture may be specifically illustrated by Jørn Utzon's Bagsvaerd Church,
built near Copenhagen in 1976, a work whose complex meaning stems directly from
a revealed conjunction between, on the one hand, the *rationality* of normative
technique and on the other, the *arationality* of idiosyncratic form. Inasmuch as this
building is organized around a regular grid and is comprised of repetitive, in-fill
modules – concrete blocks in the first instance and precast concrete wall units in the
second – we may justly regard it as the outcome of universal civilization. Such a
building system, comprising an *in situ* concrete frame with prefabricated concrete
in-fill elements, has indeed been applied countless times all over the developed
world. However, the universality of this productive method – which includes, in this
instance, patent glazing on the roof – is abruptly mediated when one passes from
the optimal modular skin of the exterior to the far less optimal reinforced concrete
shell vault spanning the nave. The last is obviously a relatively uneconomic mode
of construction, selected and manipulated first for its direct associative capacity –
that is to say, the vault signifies sacred space – and second for its multiple cross-
cultural references. While the reinforced concrete shell vault has long since held an
established place within the received tectonic canon of Western modern architecture,
the highly configured section adopted in this instance is hardly familiar, and
the only precedent for such a form, in a sacred context, is Eastern rather than
Western – namely, the Chinese pagoda roof, cited by Utzon in his seminal essay
of 1963, 'Platforms and plateaus'. [16] Although the main Bagsvaerd vault
spontaneously signifies its religious nature, it does so in such a way as to preclude
an exclusively Occidental or Oriental reading of the code by which the public and
sacred space is constituted. The intent of this expression is, of course, to secularize
the sacred form by precluding the usual set of semantic religious references and
thereby the corresponding range of automatic responses that usually accompany
them. This is arguably a more appropriate way of rendering a church in a highly
secular age, where any symbolic allusion to the ecclesiastic usually degenerates
immediately into the vagaries of kitsch. And yet paradoxically, this desacralization
at Bagsvaerd subtly reconstitutes a renewed basis for the spiritual, one founded,

I would argue, in a regional reaffirmation – grounds, at least, for some form of collective spirituality.

4 The Resistance of the Place-form

The Megalopolis recognized as such in 1961 by the geographer Jean Gottmann[17] continues to proliferate throughout the developed world to such an extent that, with the exception of cities which were laid in place before the turn of the century, we are no longer able to maintain defined urban forms. The last quarter of a century has seen the so-called field of urban design degenerate into a theoretical subject whose discourse bears little relation to the processal realities of modern development. Today even the super-managerial discipline of urban planning has entered into a state of crisis. The ultimate fate of the plan which was officially promulgated for the rebuilding of Rotterdam after World War II is symptomatic in this regard, since it testifies, in terms of its own recently changed status, to the current tendency to reduce all planning to little more than the allocation of land use and the logistics of distribution. Until relatively recently, the Rotterdam master plan was revised and upgraded every decade in the light of buildings which had been realized in the interim. In 1975, however, this progressive urban cultural procedure was unexpectedly abandoned in favor of publishing a nonphysical, infrastructure plan conceived at a regional scale. Such a plan concerns itself almost exclusively with the logistical projection of changes in land use and with the augmentation of existing distribution systems.

In his essay of 1954, 'Building, dwelling, thinking', Martin Heidegger provides us with a critical vantage point from which to behold this phenomenon of universal placelessness. Against the Latin or, rather, the antique *abstract* concept of space as a more or less endless continuum of evenly subdivided spatial components or integers – what he terms *spatium* and *extensio* – Heidegger opposes the German word for space (or, rather, place), which is the term *Raum*. Heidegger argues that the phenomenological essence of such a space/place depends upon the *concrete*, clearly defined nature of its boundary, for, as he puts it, 'A boundary is not that at which something stops, but, as the Greeks recognized, the boundary is that from which something begins its presencing.'[18] Apart from confirming that Western abstract reason has its origins in the antique culture of the Mediterranean, Heidegger shows that etymologically the German gerund *building* is closely linked with the archaic forms of *being*, *cultivating* and *dwelling*, and goes on to state that the condition of 'dwelling', and hence ultimately of 'being', can only take place in a domain that is clearly bounded.

While we may well remain skeptical as to the merit of grounding critical practice in a concept so hermetically metaphysical as Being, we are, when confronted with the ubiquitous placelessness of our modern environment, nonetheless brought to posit, after Heidegger, the absolute precondition of a bounded domain in order to create an architecture of resistance. Only such a defined boundary will permit the built form to stand against – and hence literally to withstand in an institutional sense – the endless processal flux of the Megalopolis.

The bounded place-form, in its public mode, is also essential to what Hannah Arendt has termed 'the space of human appearance', since the evolution of legitimate power has always been predicated upon the existence of the *polis* and upon comparable units of institutional and physical form. While the political life of the Greek *polis* did not stem directly from the physical presence and representation of the city-state, it displayed, in contrast to the Megalopolis, the cantonal attributes of urban density. Thus Arendt writes in *The Human Condition*:

> The only indispensable material factor in the generation of power is the living together of people. Only where men live so close together that the potentialities for action are always present will power remain with them and the foundation of cities, which as city states have remained paradigmatic for all Western political organization, is therefore the most important material prerequisite for power. [19]

Nothing could be more removed from the political essence of the city-state than the rationalizations of positivistic urban planners such as Melvin Webber, whose ideological concepts of *community without propinquity* and the *non-place urban realm* are nothing if not slogans devised to rationalize the absence of any true public realm in the modern motopia. [20] The manipulative bias of such ideologies has never been more openly expressed than in Robert Venturi's *Complexity and Contradiction in Architecture* (1966), wherein the author asserts that Americans do not need piazzas, since they should be at home watching television. [21] Such reactionary attitudes emphasize the impotence of an urbanized populace which has paradoxically lost the object of its urbanization.

While the strategy of Critical Regionalism as outlined above addresses itself mainly to the maintenance of an *expressive density and resonance* in an architecture of resistance (a cultural density which under today's conditions could be said to be potentially liberative in and of itself, since it opens the user to manifold *experiences*), the provision of a place-form is equally essential to critical practice, inasmuch as a resistant architecture, in an institutional sense, is necessarily dependent on a clearly defined domain. Perhaps the most generic example of such an urban form is the perimeter block, although other related, introspective types may be evoked, such as the galleria, the atrium, the forecourt and the labyrinth. And while these types have in many instances today simply become the vehicles for accommodating pseudo-public realms (one thinks of recent megastructures in housing, hotels, shopping centers, etc.), one cannot even in these instances entirely discount the latent political and resistant potential of the place-form.

5 Culture Versus Nature: Topography, Context, Climate, Light and Tectonic Form

Critical Regionalism necessarily involves a more directly dialectical relation with nature than the more abstract, formal traditions of modern avant-garde architecture allow. It is self-event that the *tabula rasa* tendency of modernization favors the optimum use of earth-moving equipment inasmuch as a totally flat datum is regarded as the most economic matrix upon which to predicate the rationalization of construction. Here again, one touches in concrete terms this fundamental opposition between universal civilization and autochthonous culture. The bulldozing of an irregular topography into a flat site is clearly a technocratic gesture which aspires to a condition of absolute *placelessness*, whereas the terracing of the same site to receive the stepped form of a building is an engagement in the act of 'cultivating' the site.

Clearly such a mode of beholding and acting brings one close once again to Heidegger's etymology; at the same time, it evokes the method alluded to by the Swiss architect Mario Botta as 'building the site'. It is possible to argue that in this last instance the specific culture of the region – that is to say, its history in both a geological and agricultural sense – becomes inscribed into the form and realization of the work. This inscription, which arises out of 'in-laying' the building into the site, has many levels of significance, for it has a capacity to embody, in built form, the prehistory of the place, its archeological past and its subsequent cultivation and transformation across time. Through this layering into the site the idiosyncrasies of place find their expression without falling into sentimentality.

What is evident in the case of topography applies to a similar degree in the case of an existing urban fabric, and the same can be claimed for the contingencies of climate and the temporally inflected qualities of local light. Once again, the sensitive modulation and incorporation of such factors must almost by definition be fundamentally opposed to the optimum use of universal technique. This is perhaps most clear in the case of light and climate control. The generic window is obviously the most delicate point at which these two natural forces impinge upon the outer membrane of the building, fenestration having an innate capacity to inscribe architecture with the character of a region and hence to express the place in which the work is situated.

Until recently, the received precepts of modern curatorial practice favored the exclusive use of artificial light in all art galleries. It has perhaps been insufficiently recognized how this encapsulation tends to reduce the artwork to a commodity, since such an environment must conspire to render the work placeless. This is because the local light spectrum is never permitted to play across its surface: here, then, we see how the loss of aura, attributed by Walter Benjamin to the processes of mechanical reproduction, also arises from a relatively static application of universal technology. The converse of this 'placeless' practice would be to provide that art galleries be top-lit through carefully contrived monitors so that, while the injurious effects of direct sunlight are avoided, the ambient light of the exhibition volume changes under the impact of time, season, humidity, etc. Such conditions guarantee the appearance of a place-conscious poetic – a form of filtration compounded out of an interaction between culture and nature, between art and light. Clearly this principle applies to all fenestration, irrespective of size and location. A constant 'regional inflection' of the form arises directly from the fact that in certain climates the glazed aperture is advanced, while in others it is recessed behind the masonry façade (or alternatively, shielded by adjustable sun breakers).

The way in which such openings provide for appropriate ventilation also constitutes an unsentimental element reflecting the nature of local culture. Here, clearly, the main antagonist of rooted culture is the ubiquitous air-conditioner, applied in all times and in all places, irrespective of the local climatic conditions which have a capacity to express the specific place and the seasonal variations of its climate. Wherever they occur, the fixed window and the remote-controlled air-conditioning system are mutually indicative of domination by universal technique.

Despite the critical importance of topography and light, the primary principle of architectural autonomy resides in the *tectonic* rather than the *scenographic*: that is to say, this autonomy is embodied in the revealed ligaments of the construction and in the way in which the syntactical form of the structure explicitly resists the action of gravity. It is obvious that this discourse of the load borne (the beam) and the load-bearing (the column) cannot be brought into being where the structure is masked or otherwise concealed. On the other hand, the tectonic is not to be confused with the purely technical, for it is more than the simple revelation of stereotomy or the expression of skeletal framework. Its essence was first defined by the German aesthetician Karl Bötticher in his book *Die Tektonik der Hellenen* (1852); and it was perhaps best summarized by the architectural historian Stanford Anderson when he wrote:

> '*Tektonik*' referred not just to the activity of making the materially requisite construction ... but rather to the activity that raises this construction to an art form. ... The functionally adequate form must be adapted so as to give expression to its function. The sense of bearing provided by the entasis of Greek columns became the touchstone of this concept of *Tektonik*.[22]

The tectonic remains to us today as a potential means for distilling play between material, craftwork and gravity, so as to yield a component which is in fact a condensation of the entire structure. We may speak here of the presentation of a structural poetic rather than the re-presentation of a façade.

6 The Visual Versus the Tactile

The tactile resilience of the place-form and the capacity of the body to read the environment in terms other than those of sight alone suggest a potential strategy for resisting the domination of universal technology. It is symptomatic of the priority given to sight that we find it necessary to remind ourselves that the tactile is an important dimension in the perception of built form. One has in mind a whole range of complementary sensory perceptions which are registered by the labile body: the intensity of light, darkness, heat and cold; the feeling of humidity; the aroma of material; the almost palpable presence of masonry as the body senses its own confinement; the momentum of an induced gait and the relative inertia of the body as it traverses the floor; the echoing resonance of our own footfall. Luchino Visconti was well aware of these factors when making the film *The Damned*, for he insisted that the main set of the Altona mansion should be paved in real wooden parquet. It was his belief that without a solid floor underfoot the actors would be incapable of assuming appropriate and convincing postures.

A similar tactile sensitivity is evident in the finishing of the public circulation in Alvar Aalto's Säynatsalo Town Hall of 1952. The main route leading to the second-floor council chamber is ultimately orchestrated in terms which are as much tactile as they are visual. Not only is the principal access stair lined in raked brickwork, but the treads and risers are also finished in brick. The kinetic impetus of the body in climbing the stair is thus checked by the friction of the steps, which are 'read' soon after in contrast to the timber floor of the council chamber itself. This chamber asserts its honorific status through sound, smell and texture, not to mention the springy deflection of the floor underfoot (and a noticeable tendency to lose one's balance on its polished surface). From this example it is clear that the liberative importance of the tactile resides in the fact that it can only be decoded in terms of *experience* itself: it cannot be reduced to mere information, to representation or to the simple evocation of a simulacrum substituting for absent presences.

In this way, Critical Regionalism seeks to complement our normative visual experience by readdressing the tactile range of human perceptions. In so doing, it endeavors to balance the priority accorded to the image and to counter the Western tendency to interpret the environment in exclusively perspectival terms. According to its etymology, perspective means rationalized sight or clear seeing, and as such it presupposes a conscious suppression of the senses of smell, hearing and taste, and a consequent distancing from a more direct experience of the environment. This self-imposed limitation relates to that which Heidegger has called a 'loss of nearness'. In attempting to counter this loss, the tactile opposes itself to the scenographic and the drawing of veils over the surface of reality. Its capacity to arouse the impulse to touch returns the architect to the poetics of construction and to the erection of works in which the tectonic value of each component depends upon the density of its objecthood. The tactile and the tectonic jointly have the capacity to transcend the mere appearance of the technical in much the same way as the place-form has the potential to withstand the relentless onslaught of global modernization.

Notes

Where full details are available in the Bibliography, references contain only essential information.

  1. Paul Ricoeur, 'Universal civilization and national cultures' (1961), in *History and Truth*, transl. Chas. A. Kelbley, Northwestern University Press, Evanston, IL, 1965, pp. 276–7.

2. That these are but two sides of the same coin has perhaps been most dramatically demonstrated in the Portland City Annex completed in Portland, Oregon in 1982 to the designs of Michael Graves. The constructional fabric of this building bears no relation whatsoever to the 'representative' scenography that is applied to the building both inside and out.
3. Ricoeur, p. 277.
4. Fernand Braudel informs us that the term 'culture' hardly existed before the beginning of the nineteenth century when, as far as Anglo-Saxon letters are concerned, it already finds itself opposed to 'civilization' in the writings of Samuel Taylor Coleridge – above all in Coleridge's *On the Constitution of Church and State* of 1830. The noun 'civilization' has a somewhat longer history, first appearing in 1766, although its verb and participle forms date to the sixteenth and seventeenth centuries. The use that Ricoeur makes of the opposition between these two terms relates to the work of twentieth-century German thinkers and writers such as Osvald Spengler, Ferdinand Tönnies, Alfred Weber and Thomas Mann.
5. Hannah Arendt, *The Human Condition*, University of Chicago Press, Chicago, 1958, p. 154.
6. Clement Greenberg, 'Avant-garde and kitsch', 1969, p. 126.
7. Greenberg, 'Modernist painting', 1966, pp. 101–2.
8. See Charles Jencks, *The Language of Post-Modern Architecture*, Rizzoli, New York, 1977.
9. See ch. 16 above, p. 228.
10. Jerry Mander, *Four Arguments for the Elimination of Television*, Morrow Quill, New York, 1978, p. 134.
11. Herbert Marcuse, *One-Dimensional Man*, Beacon Press, Boston, MA, 1964, p. 156.
12. Alex Tzonis and Liliane Lefaivre. 'The grid and the pathway. An introduction to the work of Dimitris and Susana Antonakakis', *Architecture in Greece*, 15, Athens, 1981, 178.
13. Ricoeur, p. 283.
14. Aldo Van Eyck, *Forum*, Amsterdam, 1962.
15. Hamilton Harwell Harris, 'Liberative and restrictive regionalism'. Address given to the Northwest Chapter of the AIA in Eugene, Oregon in 1954.
16. Jørn Utzon, 'Platforms and plateaus: Ideas of a Danish architect', *Zodiac*, 10, Milan, Edizioni Communita, 1963, 112–14.
17. Jean Gottmann, *Megalopolis*, MIT Press, Cambridge, MA, 1961.
18. Martin Heidegger, 'Building dwelling, thinking', in *Poetry, Language, Thought*, 1971, p. 154. This essay first appeared in German in 1954.
19. Arendt, p. 201.
20. Melvin Webber, *Explorations in Urban Structure*, University of Pennsylvania Press, Philadelphia, 1964.
21. Robert Venturi, *Complexity and Contradiction in Architecture*, 1966, p. 133.
22. Stanford Anderson, 'Modern architecture and industry, Peter Behrens, the AEG, and industrial design', *Oppositions*, 21, 1980, 83.

21 □ *The Emergent Rules*

Charles Jencks

[. . .]

Postmodern Poetics and the New Rules

Often in history there is a combination of continuity and change which looks perplexing because our view of both the old and the new is altered. Thus, with Postmodern Classicism the meanings, values and forms of modernism and classicism are simultaneously transformed into a hybrid combination. The present mode looks disturbing, partly because it is both strange and yet very familiar. Previous rules of decorum and composition are not so much disregarded, as extended and distorted. Indeed, the very notion of designing within a set of rules, which has been anathema since the Romantic age, takes on new meanings.

Now, rules or canons for production are seen as preconditions for creativity, a situation caused partly by the advent of the computer, which makes us conscious of the assumptions behind a building. Analytical scholarship within the art world has also increased this consciousness, as students are now forced to become aware of the conventions behind such seemingly spontaneous twentieth-century movements as Primitivism and Expressionism. The only escape from rule-governed art is to suppress from consciousness the canons behind one's creativity – hardly a comforting liberation. And it's practically impossible to remain ignorant of these, at least of antecedent ones, in an age of constant communication and theorising. Thus, consciousness of rules, conventions and canons is thrust upon us.

To conclude this survey of Postmodern Classicism we might summarise a few of the more outstanding canons that lie behind the new art and architecture. These canons are not universally held by postmodernists and some are contingent upon the momentary historical situation arising after Modernism. They thus contrast with the older notion of classical rules in being understood as relative rather than absolute,

From Jencks, C., *Postmodernism*, Academy Editions, London/Rizzoli International Publications, Inc., New York, 1987, pp. 329–32, 335–49, 350.

responses to a world of fragmentation, pluralism and inflation rather than formulae to be applied indiscriminately. The following list is a selection of eleven of the most significant.

1. The most obvious new convention concerns beauty and composition. In place of Renaissance harmony and Modernist integration is the new hybrid of *dissonant beauty*, or *disharmonious harmony*. Instead of a perfectly finished totality 'where no part can be added or subtracted except for the worse' (Alberti), we find the 'difficult whole' (Venturi) or the 'fragmented unity' of artists like the Poiriers and architects like Hans Hollein. This new emphasis on complexity and richness parallels the Mannerist emphasis on *difficultà* and skill, but it has a new social and metaphysical basis. From a pluralist society a new sensibility is formed which finds an oversimple harmony either false or unchallenging. Instead, the juxtaposition of tastes and world-views is appreciated as being more real than the integrated languages of both Exclusionist Classicism and High Modernism. The new taste for disjunctions and collisions is apparent in such popular films as *The Gods Must be Crazy*, which alternates frequently between the world-view of a scientist, drop-out journalist, Kalahari Bushman and a revolutionist, yet manages to create from these a coherent drama. Significantly it appeals to different tastes and ages.

'Disharmonious harmony' also finds validity in the present consensus among scientists that the universe is dynamic and evolving. In the past, classical revivals have been associated with a presumed cosmic harmony. Vitruvius equated the 'perfect' human body with the celestial order and then justified the perfected order of the temple on these assumptions. The Renaissance, with its well-proportioned buildings and sculpture, followed these equations between microcosm and macrocosm. Today, however, with our compound and fragmented view of a Newtonian/Einsteinian universe, we have several theories of the macrocosm competing for our acceptance, none of which sounds wholly plausible, complete or harmonious. Any scientist who has listened to the supposed origin of the universe – the noise of the Big Bang that apparently is still reverberating – does not speak only of 'the music of the spheres': the 'violent universe' is as good a description of exploding supernovae as the eternally ordered and calm picture behind classical and Christian art of the past.

Inevitably art and architecture must represent this paradoxical view, the oxymoron of 'disharmonious harmony', and it is therefore not surprising that we find countless formal paradoxes in postmodern work such as 'asymmetrical symmetry', 'syncopated proportion', 'fragmented purity', 'unfinished whole' and 'dissonant unity'. Oxymoron, or quick paradox, is itself a typical postmodern trope and 'disharmonious harmony' recurs as often in its poetics as 'organic whole' recurs in the aesthetics of classicism and Modernism.

[. . .]

2. As strong a rule as 'disharmonious harmony', and one which justifies it, is

pluralism, both cultural and political. As we have seen, the fundamental position of postmodernism in the 1970s was its stylistic variety, its celebration of difference, 'otherness' and irreducible heterogeneity. Feminist art and advocacy planning were two typical unrelated movements which helped form the tolerance of, and taste for, variety. In architecture, the stylistic counterpart of pluralism is *radical eclecticism* – the mixing of different languages to engage different taste cultures and define different functions according to their appropriate mood.

James Stirling's addition to the Tate Gallery is undoubtedly his most divergent creation to date, a building which changes surface as it meets different buildings and defines different uses (21.1). Where it attaches to the classical gallery it continues the cornice line and some of the stonework, but where it approaches a preexisting brick structure it adopts some of this red and white grammar. Its main entrance is different again, a formal grid of green mullioned glass which reappears in another main public area, the reading room. As if these changes were not enough to articulate the changing functions and mood, the grammar becomes Late-Modern to the rear – a style suitable to the service area – and more neutral on the other side so as to be in keeping with the back of the Tate. To pull this heterogeneity together is a grid frame, presented as something analogous to a classical order. A square wall pattern, like the Renaissance application of pilasters, reappears again and again, inside and outside, to form the conceptual ordering system. But it is used in a dissonant, not harmonious way – broken into quarter rhythms around the entrance, hanging in fragments over the reading room, and marching down part of the side façades (21.2). Thus Renaissance harmony is mixed with Modernist collage even in the background structure that is supposed to unify the fragments. While such extreme eclecticism may be questioned for such a small building, it does serve to characterise the heterogeneous functions, such as accommodating groups of schoolchildren, for which this building was specifically designed. Stirling speaks of it as a garden building attached to a big house, and this helps explain the informality, the lily pond, trellis work and pergola. It also underscores why this eclecticism is radical: because unlike weak eclecticism, which is more a matter of whim, it is tied to very specific functions and symbolic intentions. Another motive for the heterogeneity is its communicational role – the idea that an eclectic language speaks to a wide and divergent audience – something of a necessity for a public art gallery.

David Salle is an artist who adopts an analogous approach in his divided canvases. Mixing different styles, as does Stirling, which vary from the popular and banal to the sophisticated and classical, he achieves some of the same wry clashes and mutual cancellations. In 'Midday', 1984, a secretary ambiguously wards off the effigy of her boss as she falls back on to a sleazy office floor. This potential narrative is juxtaposed with a Modernist colour field painting and other signs of abstract art, while the conventions of journalism, TV and graffiti cancel to a degree the classical and Modernist conventions. Although the eclecticism reaches out to various audiences, the message it sends is disturbing and unresolved.

Enigmatic allegory and suggestive narrative are two postmodern genres, as we

21.1, 2 James Stirling and Michael Wilford, 'Clore Gallery', addition to the Tate Gallery, London, 1982–6 (Photographs R. Bryant).

have seen, which try to make a virtue of ambiguity and in this sense reflect an open, plural metaphysics. When several possible readings are presented simultaneously, it is left to the reader to supply the unifying text. This also entails frustration – the postmodern counterpart to the classical canon of 'withheld gratification'. Both Stirling's and Salle's work is frustrating in the sense that it avoids a hierarchy of meanings. One has to look elsewhere to find a clearer expression of a unified view.

3. The most commonly-held aim of postmodern architects is to achieve an *urbane urbanism*. Urban contextualism gains near universal assent. New buildings, according to this doctrine, should both fit into and extend the urban context, reuse such constants as the street, arcade and piazza, yet acknowledge too the new technologies and means of transport. This double injunction amounts to a new rule, as clear and well defined as any tenet of Canonic Classicism. Furthermore, there are those such as Leon Krier who would argue for an optimum relationship between all the parts of a city, what I have called the 'proper balance' between essential elements: public to private, work to living, monument to infill, short blocks to city grid, foreground square to background housing. If one focuses on this balance, rather than any particular set of dualities, then one will achieve the urbane urbanism of the Roman *insulae*, or the traditional eighteenth-century European city, or nineteenth-century American village (21.3). Small block, mixed-use planning thus amounts to an urban absolute for convivial living. In Krier's schemes the physical and functional hierarchies are clear. There's no ambiguity, irony or juxtaposition here, which is why they seem at once so powerful and nostalgic. The urbane way of life is simply better than is the dissociated and overcentralised city.

4. Almost as favoured as contextualism is the postmodern trope of *anthropomorphism*. Almost all of the new classicists incorporate ornament and mouldings suggestive of the human body. Geoffrey Scott, in the *Architecture of Humanism*, 1914, applauded classicism because it 'transcribed in stone the body's favourable states'. Its profiles, as Michelangelo emphasised, could resemble silhouettes of a face; its sculptural mass and chiaroscuro could echo the body's muscles. Such architecture humanises inanimate form as we naturally project our physiognomy and moods on to it. This empathetic response is most welcome on large housing estates, or in a context which is fundamentally alienating or over-built. Jeremy Dixon, Robert Krier, Hans Hollein, Cesar Pelli, Kazumasa Yamashita and Charles Moore among others have developed this anthropomorphism, just as Michael Graves and I have tried to make abstract representations of the face and body in our work (21.4). The explicitness of the image varies from the obvious caryatid, or herm, to the hidden figure, and seems most successful when combining these extremes. At a large scale the figure is best incorporated with other motifs and meanings, so it is not overpowering: in the 'Thematic House', for instance, head, shoulders, arms, belt and legs are as much arches and windows as they are anatomical parts (21.5). The general rule favours a subliminal anthropomorphism, but promotes an explicitness in detail and ornament. In an age when architects and

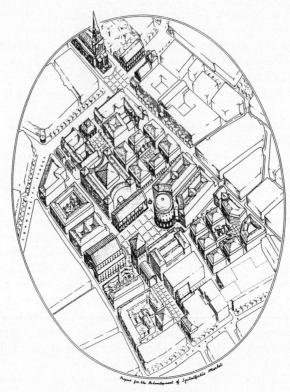

21.3 Leon Krier, 'Spitalfields Market', aerial view of
redevelopment project, London, 1986.

artists are often at a loss for legitimate subject matter, the human presence remains
a valid departure point.

5. Another credible subject is the historical continuum and the relation between the
past and present. This has led to an outbreak of parody, nostalgia and pastiche –
the lesser genres with which postmodernism is equated by its detractors – but has
also resulted in *anamnesis*, or suggested recollection. In a post-Freudian age the
unconscious is often invoked as the source of anamnesis, and it works
characteristically with the juxtaposition of related and opposed fragments. Ann and
Patrick Poirier have captured this logic of dreams in their fragmented constructions
which combine archetypes, half-remembered myths and miniature landscapes. We
search these ruins for possible relations between such things as an arrow, bronze
leaves and black lips: not fully comprehending the ancient story of which they may
be fragments, but nevertheless invited to make a guess as to their significance. The
engimatic allegory makes use of dissociated and partial memories and, at best,
creates a simulacrum of meaning where the overtones combine and harmonise. It
is this harmonious aura which becomes the subject matter of this paradoxical genre

21.5 Charles Jencks and Terry Farrell, 'Thematic House', garden elevation, London, 1978–82 (Photograph C. Jencks).

21.4 Michael Graves, 'Plocek House', detail of rear elevation, Warren, New Jersey, 1978–82 (Photograph C. Jencks).

– a narrative without a plot. Anamnesis is one of the oldest rhetorical tropes and today has become a goal in itself.

6. The well-publicised 'return to painting' of postmodernism has also been accompanied by a 'return to content', and this content is as diverse and divergent as a pluralist society. The Hirschorn Museum exhibition *Content*, 1974–84, showed some of this variety – the subject matter extended from autobiography to high and popular culture, from social commentary to metaphysical speculation, from paintings of nature to portrayals of psychological nature.[1] In addition there was the extension of the traditional genres, such as narrative painting, still-life and landscape painting, summarised in exhibitions on realism.[2] There is clearly no underlying thread, coherence, mythology or emergent rule in this heterogeneity beyond the general 'will to meaning' as it was termed by the Hirschorn. Yet, through pluralism, the overall movement has a *divergent signification* and allows multiple readings through the convention of enigmatic allegory. Many postmodern critics have emphasised intertextuality (the way several discontinuous texts combine to form their own meaning) as both a strategy and contemporary reality. This has led to two precepts, *radical eclecticism* in architecture and *suggestive narrative* in art.

[. . .]

7. This brings us to the most prevalent aspect of postmodernism, its *double-coding*, use of irony, ambiguity and contradiction. Irony and ambiguity were key concepts in modern literature, and postmodernists have continued using these tropes and methods while extending them to painting and architecture. The idea of double meaning and the *coincidentia oppositorum* ultimately goes back to Heraclitus and Nicholas of Cusa. Well before Robert Venturi and Matthias Ungers were formulating their poetics of dualism, a character in a Strindberg play exhorts: 'Don't say "either ... or" but instead "both ... and"!'[3]

This Hegelian injunction has become *the* method for urban infill and is practised as a delicate art by Charles Vandenhove, who stitches several parts of Belgian cities together with fragments of opposite languages. He has renovated the Hors-Château quarter of Liège with a variable order which has the dualism new/old consciously built in as a sign of reconciliation. His renovation of the Hotel Torrentius, a sixteenth-century mansion in the same city, is an exquisite compilation of opposites susceptible to several simultaneous readings: as real archaeological fragment, as secessionist ornament and as the superimposition of abstract geometries (21.6). The ironies and juxtapositions are underplayed in favour of a 'both ... and' harmony. This attitude to the past, more like Renaissance mixing than Modernist collage, implies the historical continuum which is so essential to the postmodern vision. Present style and technology are accepted as valid realities, but not required to overassert themselves; it is a case of peaceful, not antagonistic, coexistence.

When Vandenhove adds a new façade to a museum of decorative arts, he invents a new stylised Ionic Order, with oversize volutes made from concentric circles, but reconciles this with the previous geometry in a way that implies both continuity with

21.6 Charles Vandenhove, 'Hotel Torrentius Renovation', ground floor, Liège, 1981–2, decoration by Olivie Debré (Photograph courtesy the architect).

the past and the separate identity of the present (21.7). This form of double-coding allows us to read the present in the past as much as the past in the present, as if history proceeded by a gradual evolution of permanent forms rather than a succession of revolutionary styles each one of which obliterates its predecessor. Double-coding can, of course, be used in an opposite way to emphasise the disjunctions, as for instance Stirling and Salle employ it; but however the method is articulated it acknowledges the simultaneous validity of opposite approaches and different tastes.

8. When several codes are used coherently to some purpose they produce another quality sought by postmodernists, *multivalence*. A univalent building or Minimalist work of art can have integrity, but only of an exclusive and generally self-referential type. By contrast, a multivalent work reaches out to the rest of the environment, to many adjacent references, and to many different associations. It is inclusive by intent and, when successful, resonant as a symbol. The resonance consists in linking forms, colours and themes. This idea – an old one stemming from the notion of 'organic unity' – is relatively rare in our culture, where art and architecture tend to have gone their separate ways: art to the gallery and architecture to a limited institutional practice. Recently there have been many calls for collaboration, mutual commissions have been promoted, joint organisations formed; but most of these efforts have produced a juxtaposition of the two disciplines, rarely an integration

21.7 Charles Vandenhove, 'Façade of the Museum of
Decorative Arts', renovation, Ghent, 1986
(Photograph courtesy the architect).

of the artwork and its setting.[4] Nevertheless, artists such as Eduardo Paolozzi and
Robert Graham, and architects such as Michael Graves and Cesar Pelli, have sought
a deeper collaboration that starts near the beginning of design, so that their work
can be modified as it progresses. For mutual modification is the key to multivalence;
only where the diverse meanings have been worked through will the art, architecture
and daily activity begin to interact and form a greater unity.

[. . .]

The great advantage and delight of multivalence is the continual reinterpretation it
prompts, a result of the multiple links between the work and its setting. This
unlimited semiosis (the continual discovery of new meaning in works that are rich
in external and internal associations) is characteristic of both postmodernism and
inclusive art in general.

[. . .]

9. A precondition for this resonance is a complex relation to the past: without memories and associations a building is diminished in meaning, while if it is purely revivalist its scope will be equally restricted. Hence the postmodern emphasis on anamnesis, or the historical continuum, and another of its defining rules – the displacement of conventions, or *tradition reinterpreted*. Most discussions of postmodernism focus on one or other of the many 'returns': the 'return to painting', figuration, ornament, monument, comfort, the human body, and so on. The list is virtually endless, but all these returns must to some degree be inventive in order to transcend replication. Terry Farrell, for instance, will reinterpret the syntax and colour of the traditional temple form and use it on a boathouse in Henley. The festive polychromy of the Henley Regatta obviously forms the pretext for strong blues and reds which also relate to the colours of the site and, incidentally, to nineteenth-century investigations into Greek polychromy. The temple columns become paired pilasters, the broken pediment is extended down into the brick base to become a water gate for the boats, and the acroteria become spotlights. The Henley blue is also an obvious sign of both water and sky, as is the waving ornament etched in the stucco frieze. Thus in many ways old forms are given new meanings to justify their existence. The proportions and flatness of detail, not to mention the saturated polychromy, appear strange at first glance (as do all such displacements of tradition) and it is only after we understand their new validity and they become familiar that the aura of pastiche disappears. The reinterpretation of tradition must always carry some overtones of this kind, since conventions are simultaneously affirmed and distorted.

10. Another way of renewing past conventions is by consciously elaborating *new rhetorical figures*. Postmodernists, like the modernists before then, or for that matter any historical movement, are definable by stylistic formulae which they invent or adapt. Fashion and function both play a role in establishing these new figures, and the most prevalent are the ones we have touched on here, paradox, oxymoron, ambiguity, double-coding, disharmonious harmony, amplification, complexity and contradiction, irony, eclectic quotation, anamnesis, anastrophe, chiasmus, ellipsis, elision and erosion. Charles Moore has used the last three rhetorical devices recently to create something of a personal style. Characteristically he will erode a classical arch, or set of them, to create an ambiguous, layered space equivalent to the Baroque. But whereas these traditional forms were built in substantial masonry, Moore constructs them in plywood and stucco because it is both cheaper and lighter. Inevitably this is censored by some critics as scenographic architecture which deteriorates quickly, but the positive aspects of this innovation must not be overlooked. 'Cardboard architecture' allows new spatial experiences, new ways of joining thin surfaces which elide different shapes to create the effect of a run-on sentence, or a homogeneous and continuous structure. In the Sammis Hall (21.8), for instance, cut-out arches are held above by keystones, and on the sides by eroded Venetian windows, to form a magical, diaphanous space through which light pours and bounces. The complex ambiguity and layering are reminiscent of Vittone's

21.8 Moore Grover Harper, 'Sammis Hall',
central light well, Cold Spring
Harbour, 1980–1 (Photograph
courtesy the architect).

Baroque domes, but the airy insubstantiality is very much of our time. Aside from
economic motives, there is a psychological reason for the prevalence of such erosions
– they are symptomatic of the taste for unfinished figures, incomplete classical
shapes, and formality that is also informal. Marking a return to humanism, but
without the full and confident metaphysics which supported it in the Renaissance,
these erosions relate also to that feeling of loss which is a recurring theme within
postmodernism: the 'presence of the absence'.

11. This *return to the absent centre* is one of the most recurring figures of
postmodernism. It is portrayed both consciously by Arata Isozaki as a comment on
the decentred nature of Japanese life, and unselfconsciously by James Stirling at
Stuttgart, Michael Graves at the Humana Building, Ricardo Bofill at Montpellier
and just about every postmodern architect who makes a central plan and then
doesn't know what to put in the honorific place. This paradox is both startling and
revealing: a desire for communal space, a perfectly valid celebration of what we have
in common, and then the admission that there is nothing quite adequate to fill
fill it.

Perhaps this reflects the sense of loss which underlies so many of the departures which can be characterised with the prefix 'post'. For, if we return to the first usage of the term by Arnold Toynbee and others in the 1940s and 1950s, we detect a similar melancholic connotation. Postmodern then meant a culture that was post-Western and post-Christian: a culture that had a strong sense of its departure point, but no clear sense of destination. This ambivalence is worth stressing because, of course, the term also meant still-Modern and still-Christian – suggesting a very clear appreciation of the cultural roots and values embedded in everyday behaviour, law and language, which cannot disappear in one, two, or even five generations. The same is true of other global uses of the term – post-industrial and post-Marxist – they point as much to the very real survivals of preexisting patterns as they do to the transcendence of them. A post-industrial society, for instance, still depends fundamentally on industry, no matter how much its power structure and economy have moved on to the next level of organisation – computers, information exchange and a service economy. The ambivalence accurately reflects this double state of transition, where activity moves away from a well-known point, acknowledges the move and yet keeps a view, or trace, or love of that past location. Sometimes it idealizes the security of this point of departure, with nostalgia and melancholy, but at the same time it may exult in a new-found freedom and sense of adventure. Post-modernism is in this sense schizophrenic about the past: equally as determined to retain and preserve aspects of the past as it is to go forward; excited about revival, yet wanting to escape the dead formulae of the ·past. Fundamentally it mixes the optimism of Renaissance revival with that of the Futurists, but is pessimistic about finding any certain salvation point, be it technology, a classless society, a meritocracy or rational organisation of a world economy (i.e. any of the answers which have momentarily been offered in the last hundred years). The 'grand narratives', as Jean-François Lyotard insists, have lost their certainty even if they remain locally desirable. The mood on board the ship of postmodernism is that of an Italian and Spanish crew looking for India, which may, if it's lucky, accidentally discover America: a crew which necessarily transports its cultural baggage and occasionally gets homesick, but one that is quite excited by the sense of liberation and promise of discoveries.

[. . .]

There are more generative values in postmodern art and architecture than these eleven formulae and they are, inevitably, in a state of evolution. Furthermore, like the values and motives of any large movement, they are partly inconsistent. Nevertheless, these emerging canons are, in the third, classical phase of postmodernism, beginning to develop a discernible shape and direction, and we can say that this year's version of the ornamental building is likely to be more sophisticated than last year's. Urban building codes are evolving in a more enlightened direction as client and architect become more aware of the importance of context, while the many 'returns' in art have, in limited ways, made it richer and more accessible. Rules, however, do not necessarily a masterpiece make, and tend to generate new sets of dead-ends, imbalances and urban problems. Hence the ambivalence of our age to orthodoxy and the romantic impulse to challenge all canons of art and architecture while, at the same time, retaining them as a necessary precondition for creation: simultaneously promoting rules and breaking them. We are still near the beginning of the classical phase, which started in the late 1970s, and although one cannot predict its future, it is likely to deepen as it synthesizes the distant and more recent past, as it sustains more profoundly the Western tradition of humanism. The modern world, which started with the Renaissance as an economic, social and political reality, has itself integrated as a twenty-four-hour market-place on a much more complex level. Modern communications, scholarship and fabrication methods make any and every style equally possible, if not equally plausible. Even more than in the nineteenth century, the age of eclecticism, we have the freedom to choose and perfect our conventions, and this choice forces us to look both inwards and outwards to culture as a whole. For the modernist predicament, often epitomised in Yeats's words – 'Things fall apart: the centre cannot hold' – we have the dialectical answer: 'Things fall together, and there is no centre, but connections.' Or, in E. M. Forster's words: 'connect, only connect'.

Notes

Where full details are given in the Bibliography, many references contain only essential information.

1. *Content, a Contemporary Focus*, 1974–84. Hirschorn Museum, Washington DC, 4–6 Jan 1985; curated by Howard N. Fox: essays by Fox, Miranda McClintic and Phyllis Rosenzweig.
2. For these categories and the best discussion of realist painting today see Frank H. Goodyear Jr, *Contemporary American Realism Since 1960*, exhibition catalogue and book, New York Graphic Society, Boston, MA, 1981.
3. Strindberg's dualism is discussed in James McFarlane's 'The mind of modernism', in *Modernism 1890–1930*, eds, Malcolm Bradbury and James McFarlane, 1976; quote from p. 88.
4. For the recent conferences, exhibitions and commissions involving the collaboration between artists and architects, see *Collaboration*, ed. Barbara Lee Diamonstein, Architectural Press.

22 □ *The Duck and the Decorated Shed*

Robert Venturi

The Duck and the Decorated Shed

Let us elaborate on the decorated shed by comparing Paul Rudolph's Crawford Manor with our Guild House (in association with Cope and Lippincott). These two buildings are comparable in use, size, and date of construction: Both are high-rise apartments for the elderly, consisting of about ninety units, built in the mid-1960s. Their settings vary: Guild House, although freestanding, is a six-story, imitation palazzo, analogous in structure and materials to the surrounding buildings and continuing, through its position and form, the street line of the Philadelphia gridiron plan it sits in. Crawford Manor, on the other hand, is unequivocally a soaring tower, unique in its Modern, Ville Radieuse world along New Haven's limited-access, Oak Street Connector.

But it is the contrast in the *images* of these buildings in relation to their systems of construction that we want to emphasize. The system of construction and program of Guild House are ordinary and conventional and look it; the system of construction and program of Crawford Manor are ordinary and conventional but do not look it.

Let us interject here that we chose Crawford Manor for this comparison not because of any particular antagonism toward that building. It is, in fact, a skillful building by a skillful architect, and we could easily have chosen a much more extreme version of what we are criticizing. But in general we chose it because it can represent establishment architecture now (that is, it represents the great majority of what you see today in any architecture journal), and in particular because it corresponds in fundamental ways with Guild House. On the other hand, our choosing Guild House for comparison involves a disadvantage, because that building is now five years old, and some of our later work can more explicitly and vividly convey our current ideas. Last, please do not criticize us for primarily

From Venturi, R., Scott-Brown, D. and Izenour, S., *Learning from Las Vegas*, Institute of Technology, Cambridge, MA, 1972, pp. 65–8, 70–1, 73–4, 83–4, 86–7, 106.

22.1 'The Long Island Duckling' from *God's Own Junkyard*.

22.2 Duck.

22.3 Road scene from *God's Own Junkyard*.

DECORATED SHED

22.4 Decorated shed.

analyzing image: We are doing so simply because image is pertinent to our argument, not because we wish to deny an interest in or the importance of process, program, and structure or, indeed, social issues in architecture or in these two buildings. Along with most architects, we probably spend 90 percent of our design time on these other important subjects and less than 10 percent on the questions we are addressing here; they are merely not the direct subject of this inquiry.

To continue our comparisons, the construction of Guild House is poured-in-place concrete plate with curtain walls, pierced by double-hung windows and enclosing the interior space to make rooms. The material is common brick – darker than usual to match the smog-smudged brick of the neighborhood. The mechanical systems of Guild House are nowhere manifest in the outside forms. The typical floor plan contains a 1920s-apartment-house variety of units to accommodate particular needs, views, and exposures; this distorts the efficient grid of columns. The structure of Crawford Manor, which is poured-in-place concrete with concrete block faced with a striated pattern, is likewise a conventional frame supporting laid-up masonry walls. But it does not look it. It looks more advanced technologically and more progressive spatially. It looks as if its supports are spatial, perhaps mechanical-harboring shafts made of a continuous plastic material reminiscent of *béton brut* with the striated marks of violently heroic construction process embossed in their form. They articulate the flowing interior space, their structural purity never punctured by holes for windows or distorted by exceptions in the plan. Interior light is 'modulated' by the voids between the structure and the 'floating' cantilevered balconies.

The architectural elements for supplying exterior light in Guild House are frankly windows. We relied on the conventional method of doing windows in a building, and we by no means thought through from the beginning the subject of exterior light modulation but started where someone else had left off before us. The windows look familiar; they *look like*, as well as *are*, windows, and in this respect their use is explicitly symbolic. But like all effective symbolic images, they are intended to look familiar and unfamiliar. They are the conventional element used slightly unconventionally. Like the subject matter of Pop Art, they are commonplace elements made uncommon through distortion in shape (slight), change in scale (they are much bigger than normal double-hung windows), and change in context (double-hung windows in a perhaps high-fashion building).

Ornament: Signs and Symbols, Denotation and Connotation, Heraldry and Physiognomy, Meaning and Expression

A sign on a building carries a denotative meaning in the explicit message of its letters and words. It contrasts with the connotative expression of the other, more architectural elements of the building. A big sign, like that over the entrance of Guild House, big enough to be read from passing cars on Spring Garden Street, is particularly ugly and ordinary in its explicit commercial associations. It is significant that the sign for Crawford Manor is modest, tasteful, and not commercial. It is too small to be seen from fast-moving cars on the Oak Street Connector. But signs as explicit symbols, especially big, commercial-looking signs, are anathema in architecture such as Crawford Manor. Its identification comes, not through explicit, denotative communication, through literally spelling out 'I am Guild House', but through the connotation implicit in the physiognomy of its pure architectural form, which is intended to express in some way housing for the elderly.

We have borrowed the simple literary distinctions between 'denotative' and 'connotative' meanings and applied them to the heraldic and physiognomic element in architecture. To clarify further, the sign saying GUILD HOUSE *denotes* meaning through its words; as such, it is the heraldic element *par excellence*. The character of the graphics, however, *connotes* institutional dignity, while contradictorily, the size of the graphics *connotes* commercialism. The position of the sign perhaps also *connotes* entering. The white-glazed brick *denotes* decoration as a unique and rich appliqué on the normal red brick. Through the location of the white areas and stripes on the façade, we have tried *connotatively* to suggest floor levels associated with palaces and thereby palacelike scale and monumentality. The double-hung windows *denote* their function, but their grouping *connotes* domesticity and ordinary meanings.

Denotation indicates specific meaning; connotation suggests general meanings. The same element can have both denotative and connotative meanings, and these may be mutually contradictory. Generally, to the extent that it is denotative in its meaning, an element depends on its heraldic characteristics; to the extent that it is connotative, an element depends on its physiognomic qualities. Modern architecture, and Crawford Manor as its exemplar, has tended to shun the heraldic and denotative in architecture and to exaggerate the physiognomic and connotative. Modern architecture uses expressive ornament and shuns (explicit) symbolic ornament.

[. . .]

Heroic and Original, or Ugly and Ordinary

The content of Crawford Manor's implicit symbolism is what we call 'heroic and original'. Although the substance is conventional and ordinary, the image is heroic and original. The content of the explicit symbolism of Guild House is what we call 'ugly and ordinary'. The technologically unadvanced brick, the old-fashioned, double-hung windows, the pretty materials around the entrance, and the ugly antenna not hidden behind the parapet in the accepted fashion, all are distinctly conventional in image as well as substance or, rather, ugly and ordinary. (The inevitable plastic flowers at home in these windows are, rather, *pretty* and ordinary; they do not make this architecture look silly as they would, we think, the heroic and original windows of Crawford Manor.)

But in Guild House, the symbolism of the ordinary goes further than this. The pretensions of the 'giant order' on the front, the symmetrical, palazzolike composition with its three monumental stories (as well as its six real stories), topped by a piece of sculpture – or almost sculpture – suggest something of the heroic and original. It is true that in this case the heroic and original façade is somewhat ironical, but it is this juxtaposition of contrasting symbols – the appliqué of one order of symbols on another – that constitutes for us the decorated shed. This is what makes Guild House an architect's decorated shed – not architecture without architects.

The purest decorated shed would be some form of conventional systems-building shelter that corresponds closely to the space, structure, and program requirements of the architecture, and upon which is laid a contrasting – and if in the nature of the circumstances, contradictory – decoration. In Guild House the ornamental-symbolic elements are more or less literally appliqué: The planes and stripes of white brick are appliqué; the street façade through its disengagement at the top corners implies its separation from the bulk of the shed at the front. (This quality also implies continuity, and therefore unity, with the street line of façades of the other older, nonfreestanding buildings on each side.) The symbolism of the decoration happens to be ugly and ordinary with a dash of ironic heroic and original, and the shed is straight ugly and ordinary, though in its brick and windows it is symbolic too. Although there is ample historical precedent for the decorated shed, present-day roadside commercial architecture – the $10,000 stand with the $100,000 sign – was the immediate prototype of our decorated shed. And it is in the sign of Guild House that the purest manifestation of the decorated shed and the most vivid contrast with Crawford Manor lies.

Decoration on the Shed

Guild House has ornament on it; Crawford Manor does not. The ornament on Guild House is explicit. It both reinforces and contradicts the form of the building it adorns. And it is to some extent symbolic. The continuous stripe of white-glazed brick high on the façade, in combination with the plane of white-glazed brick below, divides the building into three uneven stories: basement, principal story, and attic. It contradicts the scale of the six real and equal floors on which it is imposed and suggests the proportions of a Renaissance palace. The central white panel also enhances the focus and scale of the entrance. It extends the ground floor to the top of the balcony of the second floor in the way, and for the same reasons, that the increased elaboration and scale around the door of a Renaissance palace or Gothic portal does. The exceptional and fat column in an otherwise flat wall surface increases the focus of the entrance, and the luxurious granite and glazed brick enhance the amenity there, as does the veined marble that developers apply at street level to make their apartment entrances more classy and rentable. At the same time, the column's position in the middle of the entrance diminishes its importance.

The arched window in Guild House is not structural. Unlike the more purely ornamental elements in this building, it reflects an interior function of the shed, that is, the common activities at the top. But the big common room itself is an exception to the system inside. On the front elevation, an arch sits above a central vertical stripe of balcony voids, whose base is the ornamental entrance. Arch, balconies, and base together unify the façade and, like a giant order (or classic jukebox front), undermine the six stories to increase the scale and monumentality of the front. In turn, the giant order is topped by a flourish, an unconnected, symmetrical television antenna in gold anodized aluminium, which is both an imitation of an abstract Lippold sculpture and a symbol for the elderly. An open-armed, polychromatic, plaster madonna in this position would have been more imageful but unsuitable for a Quaker institution that eschews all outward symbols – as do Crawford Manor and most orthodox modern architecture that reject ornament and association in the perception of forms.

[. . .]

Historical and Other Precedents: Towards an old architecture

Historical Symbolism and Modern Architecture

The forms of modern architecture have been created by architects and analyzed by critics largely in terms of their perceptual qualities and at the expense of their symbolic meanings derived from association. To the extent that the Moderns recognize the systems of symbols that pervade our environment, they often refer to the debasement of our symbols. Although largely forgotten by Modern architects, the historical precedent for symbolism in architecture exists, and the complexities of iconography have continued to be a major part of the discipline of art history. Early Modern architects scorned recollection in architecture. They rejected eclecticism and style as elements of architecture as well as any historicism that minimized the revolutionary over the evolutionary character of their almost exclusively technology-based architecture. A second generation of Modern architects acknowledged only the 'constituent facts' of history, as extracted by Sigfried Giedion,[1] who abstracted the historical building and its piazza as pure form and space in light. These architects' preoccupation with space as *the* architectural quality caused them to read the buildings as forms, the piazzas as space, and the graphics and sculpture as color, texture, and scale. The ensemble became an abstract expression in architecture in the decade of abstract expressionism in painting. The iconographic forms and trappings of medieval and Renaissance architecture were reduced to polychromatic texture at the service of space; the symbolic complexities and contradictions of Mannerist architecture were appreciated for their formal complexities and contradictions; neo-Classical architecture was liked, not for its Romantic use of association, but for its formal simplicity. Architects liked the *backs* of nineteenth-century railroad stations – literally the sheds – and tolerated the fronts as irrelevant, if amusing, aberrations of historical eclecticism. The well-developed symbol systems by the commercial artists of Madison Avenue that constitute the symbolic ambience of urban sprawl, they did not acknowledge.

In the 1950s and 1960s, these 'Abstract Expressionists' of Modern architecture acknowledged one dimension of the hill town–piazza complex: its 'pedestrian scale' and the 'urban life' engendered by its architecture. This view of medieval urbanism encouraged the megastructural (or megasculptural?) fantasies – in this context hill towns with technological trimmings – and reinforced the anti-automobile bias of the modern architect. But the competition of signs and symbols in the medieval city at various levels of perception and meaning in both building and piazza was lost on the space-oriented architect. Perhaps the symbols, besides being foreign in content, were at a scale and a degree of complexity too subtle for today's bruised sensibilities and impatient pace. This explains, perhaps, the ironical fact that the return to iconography for some of us architects of that generation was via the sensibilities of the Pop artists of the early 1960s and via the duck and the decorated shed on Route 66: from Rome to Las Vegas, but also back again from Las Vegas to Rome.

The Cathedral as Duck and Shed

In iconographic terms, the cathedral is a decorated shed *and* a duck. The late Byzantine Metropole Cathedral in Athens is absurd as a piece of architecture. It is 'out of scale': Its small size does not correspond to its complex form – that is, if form must be determined primarily by structure – because the space that the square room encloses could be spanned without the interior supports and the complex roof configuration of dome, drum, and vaults. However, it is not absurd as a duck – as a domed, Greek cross, evolved structurally from large buildings in greater cities, but developed symbolically here to mean cathedral. And this duck is itself decorated with an appliqué collage of *objets trouvés* – bas-reliefs in masonry – more or less explicitly symbolic in content.

Amiens is a billboard with a building behind it. Gothic cathedrals have been considered weak in that they did not achieve an 'organic unity' between front and side. But this disjunction is a natural reflection of an inherent contradiction in a complex building that, toward the cathedral square, is a relatively two-dimensional screen for propaganda and, in back, is a masonry systems building. This is the reflection of a contradiction between image and function that the decorated shed often accommodates. (The shed behind is also a duck because its shape is that of a cross.)

The façades of the great cathedrals of the Île-de-France are two-dimensional planes at the scale of the whole; they were to evolve at the top corners into towers to connect with the surrounding countryside. But in detail these façades are buildings in themselves, simulating an architecture of space in the strongly three-dimensional relief of their sculpture. The niches for statues – as Sir John Summerson has pointed out – are yet another level of architecture within architecture. But the impact of the façade comes from the immensely complex meaning derived from the symbolism and explicit associations of the aedicules and their statues and from their relative positions and sizes in the hierarchic order of the kingdom of heaven on the façades. In this orchestration of messages, connotation as practiced by modern architects is scarcely important. The shape of the façade, in fact, disguises the sihouette of nave and aisles behind, and the doors and the rose windows are the barest reflections of the architectural complex inside.

[. . .]

Urban Sprawl and the Megastructure

The urban manifestations of ugly and ordinary architecture and the decorated shed are closer to urban sprawl than to the megastructure. We have explained how, for us, commercial vernacular architecture was a vivid initial source for symbolism in architecture. We have described in the Las Vegas study the victory of symbols-in-space over forms-in-space in the brutal automobile landscape of great distances and high speed, where the subtleties of pure architectural space can no longer be savored. But the symbolism of urban sprawl lies also in its residential architecture, not only in the strident, roadside communications of the commercial strip (decorated shed or duck). Although the ranch house, split level or otherwise, conforms in its spatial configuration to several set patterns, it is appliquéd with varied though conforming ornament, evoking combinations of Colonial, New Orleans, Regency, Western, French Provincial, Modern, and other styles. Garden apartments – especially those of the Southwest – equally are decorated sheds whose pedestrian courts, like those of motels, are separate from, but close to, the automobile. A comparison of urban sprawl with the megastructure is made in Table 22.1.

Sprawl city's image is a result of process. In this respect it follows the canons of Modern architecture that require form to result from function, structure, and construction methods, that is, from the processes of its making. But for our time the megastructure is a distortion of normal city building process for the sake *inter alia* of image. Modern architects contradict themselves when they support functionalism and the megastructure. They do not recognize the image of the

Table 22.1 Comparison of Urban Sprawl with Megastructure

Urban Sprawl	Megastructure
Ugly and ordinary	Heroic and original
Depends on explicit symbolism	Rejects explicit symbolism
Symbols in space	Forms in space
Image	Form
Mixed media	Pure architecture
Big signs designed by commercial artists	Little signs (and only if absolutely necessary) designed by 'graphic artists'
Auto environment	Post- and pre-auto environment
Cars	Public transportation
Takes the parking lot seriously and pastiches the pedestrian	'Straight' architecture with serious but egocentric aims for the pedestrian; it irresponsibly ignores or tries to 'piazzafy' the parking lot
Disneyland	Piazzas
Promoted by salesmen	Promoted by experts
Feasible and being built	Technologically feasible perhaps, but socially and economically unfeasible
Popular life-style	'Correct' life-style
Historical styles	Modern style
Uses typological models	Uses original creations
Process city	Instant city
Broadacre City	Ville Radieuse
Looks awful	Makes a nice model
Architects don't like	Architects like
Twentieth-century communication technology	Nineteenth-century industrial vision
Social realism	Science fiction
Expedience	Technological indulgence
Expedient	Visionary
Ambiguous urban image	Traditional urban image
Vital mess	'Total Design' (and design review boards)
Building for men (markets)	Building for Man
This year's problems	The old architectural revolution
Heterogeneous images	The image of the middle-class intelligentsia
The difficult image	The easy image
The difficult whole	The easy whole

process city when they see it on the Strip, because it is both too familiar and too different from what they have been trained to accept.

[. . .]

Ugly and Ordinary as Symbol and Style

Artistically, the use of conventional elements in ordinary architecture – be they dumb doorknobs or the familiar forms of existing construction systems – evokes associations from past experience. Such elements may be carefully chosen or thoughtfully adapted from existing vocabularies or standard catalogs rather than uniquely created via original data and artistic intuition. To design a window, for instance, you start not only with the abstract function of modulating diurnal light rays to serve interior space but with the image of window – of all the windows you know plus others you find out about. This approach is symbolically and functionally conventional, but it promotes an architecture of meaning, broader and richer if less dramatic than the architecture of expression.

We have shown how heroic and original (H&O) architecture derives dramatic expression from the connotative meanings of its 'original' elements: It gives off abstract meanings – or rather, expressions – recognizable in the physiognomic character of the architectural elements. The ugly and ordinary (U&O) architecture, on the other hand, includes denotative meanings as well, derived from its familiar elements; that is, it suggests more or less concrete meanings via association and past experience. The 'brutalism' of an H&O fire station comes from its rough texture; its civic monumentality comes from its big scale; the expression of structure and program and 'truth to materials' comes from the particular articulations of its forms. Its total image derives from these purely architectural qualities transmitted through abstract forms, textures, and colors, carefully composed. The total image of our U&O fire house – an image implying civic character as well as specific use – comes from the conventions of roadside architecture that it follows; from the decorated false façade, from the banality through familiarity of the standard aluminum sash and roll-up doors, and from the flagpole in front – not to mention the conspicuous sign that identifies it through spelling, the most denotative of symbols: FIRE STATION NO. 4. These elements act as symbols as well as expressive architectural abstractions. They are not merely ordinary but represent ordinariness symbolically and stylistically; they are enriching as well, because they add a layer of literary meaning.

Richness can come from conventional architecture. For three hundred years European architecture was variations on a Classical norm – a rich conformity. But it can also come through an adjusting of the scale or context of familiar and conventional elements to produce unusual meanings. Pop artists used unusual juxtapositions of everyday objects in tense and vivid plays between old and new associations to flout the everyday interdependence of context and meaning, giving us a new interpretation of twentieth-century cultural artifacts. The familiar that is a little off has a strange and revealing power.

The double-hung window in Guild House is familiar in form but unusually large in size and horizontal in proportion, like the big, distorted Campbell Soup can in Andy Warhol's painting. This typical window is also juxtaposed with a smaller window of the same form and proportion. The exact location of the bigger window on a parallel plane behind the smaller window tends to disturb the habitual perception of distance through perspective; the resultant symbolic and optical tensions are, we maintain, a means of making boring architecture interesting – a more valid means than the irrelevant articulations of today's strident but boring minimegastructures.

Against Ducks, or Ugly and Ordinary over Heroic and Original, or Think Little

We should not emphasize the ironic richness of banality in today's artistic context at the expense of discussing its appropriateness and inevitability on a wider basis. Why do we uphold the symbolism of the ordinary via the decorated shed over the symbolism of the heroic via the sculptural duck? Because this is not the time and ours is not the environment for heroic communication through pure architecture. Each medium has its day, and the rhetorical environmental statements of our time – civic, commercial, or residential – will come from media more purely symbolic, perhaps less static and more adaptable to the scale of our environment. The iconography and mixed media of roadside commercial architecture will point the way, if we will look.

[. . .]

Silent-White-Majority Architecture

Many people like suburbia. This is the compelling reason for learning from Levittown. The ultimate irony is that although Modern architecture from the start has claimed a strong social basis for its philosophy, Modern architects have worked to keep formal and social concerns separate rather than together. In dismissing Levittown, Modern architects, who have characteristically promoted the role of the social sciences in architecture, reject whole sets of dominant social patterns because they do not like the architectural consequences of these patterns. Conversely, by defining Levittown as 'silent-white-majority' architecture, they reject it again because they do not like what they believe to be the silent white majority's political views. These architects reject the very heterogeneity of our society that makes the social sciences relevant to architecture in the first place. As Experts with Ideals, who pay lip service to the social sciences, they build for Man rather than for men – this means, to suit themselves, that is, to suit their own particular upper-middle-class values, which they assign to all mankind. Most suburbanites reject the limited formal vocabularies architects' values promote, or accept them twenty years later modified by the tract builder: The Usonian house becomes the ranch house. Only the very poor, via public housing, are dominated by architects' values. Developers build for markets rather than for Man and probably do less harm than authoritarian architects would do if they had the developers' power.

One does not have to agree with hard-hat politics to support the rights of the middle-middle class to their own architectural aesthetics, and we have found that Levittown-type aesthetics are shared by most members of the middle-middle class, black as well as white, liberal as well as conservative. If analyzing suburbia's architecture implies that one has let the Nixon regime 'penetrate even the field of architectural criticism',[2] then the field of urban planning has been infiltrated by Nixonites for more than ten years – by Abrams, Gans, Webber, Dyckman, and Davidoff. For our critique is nothing new; the social planners have been making it for more than a decade. But in this Nixon-silent-majority critique, especially in its architectural, as opposed to its racial and military, dimensions, there is a fine line between liberalism and old-fashioned class snobbery.

Another obvious point is that 'visual pollution' (usually someone else's house or business) is not the same order of phenomenon as air and water pollution. You can like billboards without approving of strip mining in Appalachia. There is no 'good' way to pollute land, air, or water. Sprawl and strip we can learn to do well. However, *Life* magazine, in an editorial entitled 'Erasing grown-up vandalism', equates suburban sprawl, billboards, wires, and gasoline stations with the strip mining that has despoiled too much of the country.[3] 'Visual pollution' seems to inspire editorial writers and photographers, who view it with alarm, to poetic descriptions of it in the manner of Milton and Doré. Their style is often in direct conflict with their opprobrium. If it is all bad, why is it so inspiring?

Notes

1. Sigfried Giedion, *Space, Time and Architecture*, Harvard University Press, Cambridge, MA, 1944, Part I.
2. Ulrich Franzen, *Progressive Architecture*, Letter to the Editor, April 1970, 8.
3. *Life*, 9 April 1971, 34. *Life*'s own language is more graphic.

23 □ *Postmodern*

Paolo Portoghesi

A New Renaissance

Zoroaster wants to lose nothing of humanity's past, and wants
to throw everything into the crucible.   (NIETZSCHE)

During the last decade, the adjective postmodern has made a journey of varying
success through the humanistic disciplines. Used systematically for the first time in
1971 by Ihab Hassan in relation to literature, it then made its way into the social
sciences, into semiology and philosophy. In architecture, the adjective postmodern
found fertile cultural ground, priming a process which started out from criticism and
historiography, and finally became the unifying label of a series of trends, theoretical
propositions and concrete experiences.

It is worth our while today to reflect upon the unforeseeable fortune of this word
in architecture, in order to try to clear up many misunderstandings, and to establish
just how useful it can be in relating parallel phenomena taking place in very different
areas. In the field of architecture, the term has been used to designate a plurality of
tendencies directed toward an escape from the crisis of the Modern Movement with
a radical refusal of its logic of development. In the last several decades, this
development had led to a chaotic labyrinth, or to the anachronistic attempt to
restore the orthodoxy of the golden age of functionalism: the age, of course, of the
Bauhaus and CIAM.

The postmodern has signalled, therefore, the way out of a movement that had for
some time stopped 'moving ahead', that had transformed itself into a gaudy bazaar
of inventions motivated only by personal ambition and by the alibi of technological
experimentation. The critics who first put into focus the vast and contradictory
phenomenon of an exit from orthodoxy tried to control it by putting it into

From Portoghesi, P., *Postmodern*, Rizzoli International Publications Inc., New York, 1983,
pp. 10–13, 68, 70.

traditional categories. They also tried to simplify it and make it more comprehensible; but in the end, the neutrality of a word like postmodern is tantamount to an absurd definition based on difference more than on identity. With regard to didactic simplification, the same critics finally surrendered to pluralism and complexity.

Charles Jencks, the most able of the announcers of this new show, proposed that its specificity can in fact be grasped, since it is the product of architects particularly mindful of the aspects of architecture understood as a language, as a means of communication:

> A Postmodern building is, if a short definition is needed, one which speaks on at least two levels at once: to other architects and a concerned minority who care about specifically architectural meanings, and to the public at large, or the local inhabitants, who care about other issues concerned with comfort, traditional building and a way of life. Thus Postmodern architecture looks hybrid and, if a visual definition is needed, rather like the front of a classic Greek temple. The latter is a geometric architecture of elegantly fluted columns below, and a riotous billboard of struggling giants above, a pediment painted in deep reds and blues. The architects can read the implicit metaphors and subtle meanings of the column drums, whereas the public can respond to the explicit metaphors and messages of the sculptors. Of course everyone responds somewhat to both codes of meaning, as they do in a Postmodern building, but certainly with different intensity and understanding, and it is this discontinuity in taste cultures which creates both the theoretical base and 'dual-coding' of Postmodernism. (From Charles Jencks, *The Language of Post-Modern Architecture*, London, Academy Editions, 1977)

This definition certainly covers the unifying aspect of many of the most significant works realized in the last decade which have overcome the ideological crisis of the Modern Movement. It fails, however, to satisfy the historical need of relating the shift carried out by architectural culture to the profound changes in society, and risks confining the phenomenon to an area completely within the private realm of the architect, therefore remaining more a psychological than a historical-critical definition. It is more correct, in my view, to try to get to the specificity of the phenomenon by revealing the substantial differences with modernity, from which it wishes to distinguish itself, in what are its most typical aspects. And since modernity coincides in Western architectural culture with the progressive rigorous detachment from everything traditional, it should be pointed out that, in the field of architecture, the postmodern means that explicit, conscious abolition of the dam carefully built around the pure language elaborated *in vitro* on the basis of the rationalist statute. This language is put into contact again with the universe of the architectural debate, with the entire historical series of its past experiences, with no more distinctions between the periods before or after the first industrial revolution. With the barrier torn down, old and new waters have mixed together. The resulting product is before our eyes, paradoxical and ambiguous but vital, a preparatory moment of something different that can only be imagined: reintegration in architecture of a vast quantity of values, layers, semitones, which the homologation of the International Style had unpardonably dispersed.

The return of architecture to the womb of its history has just begun, but the proportions of this operation are quite different from those which orthodox critics suppose. This reversion to history would always be a laboratory experiment if it were not also the most convincing answer given thus far by architectural culture to the profound transformations of society and culture, to the growth of a 'postmodern condition' following from the development of post-industrial society. To convince ourselves, a synthetic review of the historical symptoms of this condition should suffice.

The Age of Information

No technical revolution has thus far produced such great and lasting transformations as the quantification and elaboration of information, made possible by the new electronic technology. Our age has seen the world of the machine, with its working systems and its rhythms, miss the impact of novelty. It has watched a new artificial universe move ahead, composed of wires and circuits, which resemble more organic material than something really mechanical. Information and communication have therefore become terms of comparison with which to redefine and reinterpret the role of all disciplines. And at that moment when the semiotic aspect of architecture and that of the transmission of information, along with its productive and stylistic aspects, was put into focus, it was inevitable that the constrictive and utopian character of the revolution which took place beginning with the twenties, with the worldwide diffusion of the paradigms of the avant-garde, would be evident. In fact, renouncing the systems of conventions through which it had developed uninterruptedly, since the ancient world (the structural principle of the order, base, column, capital, trabeation, and so on), architecture had lost its specificity and had become, on the one hand, an autonomous figurative art, on the same level as painting, or, on the other hand, had reduced itself to pure material production.

Architecture, instead, seen in the area of the different civilization of man, reveals a much more complex nature and role. It is an instrument of the production and transmission of communicative models, which have for a particular society a value analogous to that of laws and other civil institutions, models whose roots lie in the appropriation and transformation of the places of the earth, and which have for centuries played the part of confirming and developing the identity of places (of cities) and of communities.

The result of the discovery of the sudden impoverishment produced in architecture by the adoption of technologies and morphologies separated from places and traditions has been the reemergence of architectonic archetypes as precious instruments of communication. These archetypes are elementary institutions of the language and practice of architecture that live on in the daily life and collective memory of man. These differ greatly depending on the places where we live and where our spatial experiences were formed. The postmodern in architecture can therefore be read overall as a reemergence of archetypes, or as a reintegration of architectonic conventions, and thus as a premise to the creation of an *architecture of communication*, an architecture of the image for a civilization of the image.

The Fall of Centered Systems

Another aspect of the postmodern condition is the progressive dismantling of the bases of the critical theory of bourgeois society. The sharp polarity of social classes, faith in the redeeming capabilities of the socialization of the means of production, and the analogy of the intricate processes of industrial society in capitalist and socialist countries have placed a profoundly changed reality on guard against the sterility of the dogmatisms and the incapability to explore, with the old tools of consecrated and sclerotic theories.

It should not surprise us that, together with the much more serious and proven ideological scaffolding, even the Modern Movement is in crisis: a variable and undefined container, within which quite different and often divergent phenomena were placed. This was an attempt to construct a linear function of architectural progress, in regard to which it would be possible at all times to distinguish good from evil, decree annexations and expulsions as in a political party. The Modern Movement proposed to change society for the better, avoiding (according to Le Corbusier) the revolution, or carrying it out, as the Russian Constructivists believed. Among its great tasks, the most important was that of teaching man to become modern, to change his way of life according to a model capable of avoiding waste. Today, this undertaking hardly seems valid for a colonialist program, while the real problem is one of understanding what postmodern man wants, and how he lives. He is not an animal to be programmed in a laboratory, but an already existing species which has almost reached maturity, while architects were still trying to realize their obsolete project of modernity.

The great intellectual work done in the past twenty years on the concept and structures of power has put another drifting mine beneath the fragile and suspect structure of the Modern Movement. Separating the idea of power from the relationships of work and property 'in which', as Alain Touraine has written, 'it seemed to be totally incarnated', even the role of the architectural avant-gardes has been able to be analyzed in different terms, recognizing its responsibilities and inadequacies, and putting in crisis the theory that stripped them of responsibility. They attributed all blame to the 'design of capital'.

The history of architecture of the past thirty years could, therefore, be written as the history of a 'way out' of the Modern Movement according to a direction already experimented by the masters in the last years of their lives, at the beginning of the fifties.

The crisis of theoretical legitimation, which Jean-François Lyotard calls the 'scarce credibility of the great *Récits*', and the fact that today we must confront the problem of the meaning 'without having the possibility of responding with the hope of the emancipation of Mankind, as in the school of the Enlightenment, of the Spirit, as in the school of German Idealism, or of the Proletariat, by means of the establishment of a transparent society', has unhinged the fundamental principles of architectural modernity, consisting of a series of equations which have never been verified except through insignificant small samples. These are the equations: useful = beautiful, structural truth = esthetic prestige, and the dogmatic assertions of the functionalist statute: 'form follows function', 'architecture must coincide with construction', 'ornament is crime', and so on. The truth of architecture as a simple coincidence of appearance and substance contradicts what is greatest and most lasting among the architectural institutions, from the Greek temple to the cathedral; and even what the Modern Movement built under the banner of truth often has its worth in an 'appearance' that has little to do with constructive truth. The great moral tale that hoped to grasp the human aspect of architecture, theorizing its function and 'sincerity', by this time has the distant prestige of a fable.

In place of faith in the great centered designs, and the anxious pursuits of salvation, the postmodern condition is gradually substituting the concreteness of small circumstantiated struggles with its precise objectives capable of having a great effect because they change systems of relations.

The Crisis of Resources and the City–Country Relationship

The postmodern condition has put into crisis even that discipline that the Modern Movement had placed beside architecture, as a theoretical guarantee of its socialization: city planning understood as the science of territorial transformations. From the time when city planning, abandoning the tradition of nineteenth-century urban rhetoric, had become that strange mixture of ineffectual sociological analyses and implacable zoning, the city seemed to have lost the very principle of its reproduction, growing from the addition of fatty or cancerous tissue, lacking essential urban features, as in the great peripheral areas.

The most obvious symptom of the change in direction of architectural research was a return to the study of the city as a complex phenomenon in which building typologies play a role comparable to that of institutions, and profoundly condition the production and change of the urban face. The analytical study of the city has skipped over the functionalist logic of the building block, reproposing instead the theme of the continuity of the urban fabric, and of the fundamental importance of enclosed spaces, actual component cells of the urban environment. The study of collective behavior divided the criterion of the dismemberment of the urban body into its monofunctioning parts, the standard which informs ideal cities, proposed as models by the masters of modern architecture.

The energy crisis, on the other hand, and the crisis of the governability of the great metropolitan administrations, has focused once again on the problem of the alternatives to the indefinite growth of the large cities, and on the necessity of correcting the relationship of exploitation still characterizing the city in relation

to small centers and the region. The great myth of the double equation city =
progress, development = well-being has given way to the theory of limit and of
controlled development. With regard to a postmodern urbanism, an institutional
reformism is beginning to be considered that would give new competitive strength
to smaller centers through federative initiatives (in Italy, a process of this kind is
going on in the Vallo di Diano, under the aegis of Socialist administrators). Ecological
problems and the energy crisis have led to the self-criticism of the acritical propensity
toward the new technologies that have substituted old ones, often with no advantage
whatsoever for the life span of the product, the absorption of manpower and esthetic
quality. A change of direction is inevitable if we do not want further to aggravate
economic and social problems. To realize the importance of these programs, it is
sufficient to reflect upon the fact that the energy consumption of a plastic panel is
twenty times that needed for the construction of a brick wall of the same area, or
that the progressive disappearance of certain trades because of the abandonment of
certain techniques would render us, for a lack of skilled workers, unable to restore
historic monuments and ancient cities, whose integral preservation seems to have
been, at least on paper, one of the great cultural conquests of our time.

The truth is that the postmodern condition has reversed the theoretical scaffolding
of so-called modernity. Those who are amazed that, among the most apparent
results of the new culture in its infancy, there is also a certain superficial feeling for
a 'return to the antique', seem to forget that in every serious mixture, the artificial
order of chronology is one of the first structures to be discussed and then dismissed.
Just as grandchildren often resemble their grandparents, and certain features of the
family reappear after centuries, the world now emerging is searching freely in
memory, because it knows how to find its own 'difference' in the removed repetition
and utilization of the entire past. Recently in Japan, sailboats have been built whose
sails are maneuvered not by hundreds of sailors, but by complicated and extremely
fast electronic devices. These ships, equipped also with conventional engines, allow
for a great saving in fuel. Postmodern architecture, whose naive manifestations of
a precocious childhood we see today, will probably resemble these ships that have
brought the imaginary even into the world of the machine.

The Crisis of the City

The metropolis leads toward the megalopolis, which leads sooner or later to the
necropolis. The prophetic journey which Mumford talked about thirty years ago has
not yet taken place, but continues to terrorize us. Every so often, the mechanism
of the big cities seems to jam irreparably, and the ghost of urban agony comes back
to haunt our dreams. Then, a balance, albeit precarious, is recomposed, as in a
spell. Some scheme is devised, and what seemed very near begins to move away
again.

The last of the great ghosts, the administrative and political ungovernability of
large urban systems, is also being redimensioned. Some years ago, New York

reported its economic bankruptcy. Cairo, Naples, and Rome have administrative balances that are hardly reassuring; but in the end, a corrective is found and the rendering of accounts deferred. In reality, it seems that a colossal regulator of watts guarantees the survival of this 'splendidly' ill institution called the large city.

Its fanatics insist that this is opportune and providential, because the preservation and development of human civilization are inseparably tied to the city. Should the city disintegrate, the narrow-minded and conservative spirit of the small town would suddenly arrest the prodigious critical vigor that generated the modern world. The big city is where exchanges, meetings, opportunities for intellectual growth and scientific research take place, where social tensions and intellectual ferment are created and constantly changed. While it does not necessarily grant happiness and serenity, the city guarantees that intense, rich and complex life 'that is worth living'.

What are the true and false elements of this rhetoric of urban greatness according to which quantity would be miraculously transformed into quality, and difficulties would become stimuli for the life of the intellect? We could begin to give some answers to this question, since the mythological phase of the modern world is ending. Every day, we witness the collapse and changes of the great central systems with which we deluded ourselves that everything could be explained.

The large city is the child of the great political institutions, beginning with the advent of capitalism, of the great productive organizations that benefit from physical contiguity, because in this manner the mechanism of the market and of competition is mirrored most directly in the urban fabric. The large city is essentially a city-factory, a city-workshop, where a gigantic invisible assembly line compels everyone to repeat daily both the ceremony of work, and an infinite series of useless acts. Slow and discontinuous vehicular traffic, periodically grinding to a maddening halt, and then gradually decongested into the still of the night, is the eloquent symbol of the sacrifices that must be made so that we can enjoy the privileges of its function as a great devourer of human time and a great machine of waste. What will become of this institution which has derived force from its illness, and which continues, like a siren, to attract its distant admirers with false promises? There is no doubt that the myth of infinite development (hypothesized in the sixties when the generalization of urban systems like that of Tokyo were considered) is in difficulty. The myth-antidote of zero growth was also invented. The salvation of the large city lies in its controlled growth and its ties with the surrounding territory. But it also lies, paradoxically, in a complete alternative that would make disadvantages accessible to a wider range of people and progressively weaken its force of attraction.

It is clear, now more than ever, that even for the large cities, egotism is a double-edged weapon. The concentration of public facilities, cultural institutions, places for recreation and scientific elaboration has given the metropolis the glory of two centuries, but in the long run it could have bad surprises in store. The cure for the sick metropolis lies perhaps in the potential of the smaller city, in the rediscovery of its competitive role in the field of culture and production. This new possibility has come up recently, with the generalization of the means of mass communication that increase the demand for services and collective institutions, precisely because the ruling culture of the big city makes its standards accessible at the level of the image and desire.

Post-industrial society (if we can advance a hypothesis) will no longer need great convulsive concentrations and *villes tentaculaires*, just as modern industry no longer needs cathedrals of work. Small cities will once again play a role not only in the consumption and passive reception of the culture of the metropolis, but also in autonomous creation and valid interlocution. The small centers, where a great part of the world's population still lives, will be able to find a competitive role in their refound autonomous identity, and in the process of federation which will permit them to develop sufficient force to give the new territory community structures similar to urban ones. A process of this type, the union of nineteen neighboring towns into a single town of 'urban force', is taking place in Italy south of Salerno in the Vallo di Diano, through the initiative of the enlightened administrator Gerardo Ritorto. I have made a technical contribution to the development of this interesting hypothesis of a discontinuous city.

It is believed that post-industrial society will be completely free from totalitarian temptations. The postmodern culture which arises from the new human condition produced by this society ought to defeat on another level even urban totalitarianism, separating the positive values of the big city from its negative connotations that have shaped a relationship of exploitation and alienating hegemony between the culture of the city and that of the region. For Italy, it would be the rediscovery of a very old calling. The old Italy of the courts could become the polycentric Italy of the 'small city'.

Part Six

Politics

Introduction

In the modern world – that is, since the eighteenth century – the discourse of politics is founded upon one problematic relation: the relation between the Subject of consciousness and its Object. From this relation all else follows, for what is at stake in it is the variety of ways in which humanity engages its environment. A conservative politics is one in which some Subjects arrogate to themselves the right to regard not only an inanimate environment as an Object over which they may hold sway, but also other human beings as legitimate Objects over whom they hold power. Such power consolidates the Identity of the dominant Subject in this state of affairs. An emancipatory politics is one in which this situation is addressed by an overt attention to alterity as such. In a radical politics, the Subject realises her or his identity through two different means: first, she or he acknowledges that identity is predicated upon the Other, i.e. upon other Subjects of consciousness; secondly, she or he questions the relation of dominance between consciousness and the inhuman environment. The name for the first of these radical positions is Marxism; that of the second, post-Marxism or postmodern Marxism.

The entire debate in the postmodern on the issue of politics really stems from within the discourse of Marxism itself, a discourse which is acknowledged – even by a conservative thinking which frequently steals and abuses its categories – to be the most thoroughgoing explanation of politics currently available. This is so even at a moment when, in the wake of events in Eastern Europe in 1989, certain conservatives such as Francis Fukuyama are announcing, in neo-Hegelian fashion, the 'end of history' (an announcement which, of course, is to some extent a rerun of the 'end of ideology' proclamations of Daniel Bell and others in the 1950s). The so-called 'inevitability' of capitalism in these conservative positions not only acknowledges Marx's analysis but also in fact strives to learn from Marx in the interests of an increased capitalist efficiency.

The most vigorous and varied political thought in the twentieth century has, however, come from the emancipatory political drive, in which the issue of democracy has given place to that of freedom. 'Democracy', after all, is a term so abused as to have become trivial; and the effect of this in the conservative world has been not only to reduce freedom but also to erode the substance of democracy precisely in those states where the word is increasingly claimed as a description of the political state of affairs: democracy now means increasingly the freedom to make a small hieroglyphic mark on a piece of paper on some twenty occasions in a normal human lifetime. This would not be so bad if the hieroglyphic mark made some substantive political difference, but increasingly this is not the case in the so-called 'democracies'. In the light of this, freedom becomes a much more pressing issue. Freedom has been articulated in various ways: in the existentialist terms of Sartre; in the postcolonialist terms of Said, Amin, Fanon and others; in the enormous range of feminist discourses which have placed the questions of gender and sexuality at the core of contemporary political debate; in the Green attitude which alerts us to the fact that the environment, the Object itself, has been victimised by the human Subject; and so on in an ever-increasing variety of ways.

In the question of the relation between Subject of consciousness and its Objectified environment, Marx made one fundamental move: he located the human body, the labouring human body, as the mediator between the two potentially disparate realms. Feminism has stringently modified this by indicating that this body is not itself neutral, but gendered. The structure of exploitation which is inscribed in capitalist economics had already made it clear that not all bodies were treated equitably, of course; and it is from this that a specific class consciousness and class struggle can develop. But what happens when efficiency, the key term for capitalist production, enables the reduction of labour? What happens when technological developments reduce the amount of employment possible in a social formation? And what happens when structural unemployment is itself developed as a central plank of conservative political ideology? These questions are among those which have initiated the postmodern political debate.

Richard Rorty comes at these questions from a philosophical position grounded in the American pragmatist tradition. In the piece included here, he makes a fundamental distinction between a 'foundational' and an 'anti-foundational' political philosophy; and he strives to hold a position which takes the best from both. The result is that he argues for a 'solidarity' instead of a class consciousness, and for a solidarity devoid of any ahistorical philosophical or ethical back-up. He describes this as 'postmodernist bourgeois liberalism', though to many people it looks very like an excuse for a quietistic acceptance that, as he has said elsewhere, 'there is no alternative to capitalism', or that the rich North Atlantic 'democracies' have established not a 'true' politics but a 'pragmatically acceptable' politics. Such pragmatism is, in fact, at the root of many of the neo-conservative political stances which claim to derive from a postmodern attitude.

Rorty's postmodern distrust of metanarratives, derived from Lyotard, is self-contradictory, argues Ernesto Laclau: the prescription to abandon foundationalist philosophy is itself foundational. Laclau suggests that it is better to consider the postmodern as a moment of 'weakening' (such as we have seen in Lyotard and Vattimo), which is perhaps a perfect counter to Rortyan 'solidarity'. Learning from a number of recent – and sometimes conflicting – developments broadly within Marxism, and especially from Gramsci, Laclau advocates a less monolithic attitude to political struggle than that presupposed by a Marxist–Leninist tradition which is solidly founded on class. The 'weakening' produces a pluralistic attitude in which, increasingly, the Subject is not considered as a unified and identifiable entity within one specific power configuration or within one specific relation to the environment; rather, the Subject is here increasingly seen to be traversed by all manner of different power configurations (those of gender, sexuality, race and nationality being only among the most obvious). Class is seen here as one determinant among many in the construction of political locatedness for the Subject, whose freedom or emancipation depends on a less monolithic struggle against a single, identifiable force of oppression, and more upon a diversity of struggles and strategies.

André Gorz, once a member of the editorial board of Sartre's journal *Les Temps modernes*, was vitally involved in the political struggles of 1968. In common with other activists, such as Bahro and Cohn-Bendit, however, Gorz began a significant political move 'from red to green'. In his reconsiderations of Marxism, one thing remains always central: the reduction of time spent in work in the human lifespan. The fundamental reorganisation of political life is now, for Gorz, a reorganisation of time. In classic Marxism, life is organised around, on the one hand, a 'centre' of work which is itself located in a solid urban forum of 'the city', and a 'periphery' of leisure relegated to the 'suburbs'; Gorz rethinks this, with a new 'centre' of 'free quality time' and a 'periphery' of work-time. In short, a politics founded upon a space-logic (central *polis*, sub-urban marginalised domesticity) is replaced by a politics based on a time-logic. Basic to this is a 'green' attitude to the environment, which argues for a less exploitative attitude to the world of nature. One problem with Marx, according to this view, is that he was really interested only in changing the power relations obtaining among Subjects, while taking for granted the continued exploitation of the Objective world. This is no longer sustainable, argues Gorz; and genuine political emancipation will not be possible until the erosion of such an exploitative attitude to the Other that is the natural environment. This is reminiscent to some extent of the attitude of Deleuze and Guattari in the late 1970s and early 1980s, for whom the eradication of fascism in the wide political world was to some extent predicated upon a similar eradication of the fascist attitude which lay covertly within any self-determining Subject. For Gorz, the question of emancipation and freedom is fundamentally tied in with an economy of time, in which the Subject will find a different manner of enfranchisement from that expected by classical Marxism.

Virilio has insisted on the relation of time to the political, most obviously in his work on speed and politics. The effect of speed is to change the status of political life and debate. If we remain locked within a space-logic of politics, then all argument is fundamentally hinged on one relation: overt appearance versus covert reality; and all analysis is based upon semiotics in the form of ideology critique. But, while this may hold good for earlier moments in political debate, it is no longer viable, for the arena of the political has shifted in our time. The fundamental political relation today, argues Virilio, is that between appearance and disappearance, and no longer between appearance and reality. The ancient idea of a political forum has been replaced by the screen, like a cinema screen, on which what is projected is but the shadow-play of a real which is in a constant state of disappearing. Political emancipation depends upon strategies for making the disappeared reappear, for evoking a presence of the real through its constantly threatened absence.

For Baudrillard, the real is also trammelled by its appearances and disappearances. At an early stage in his post-Marxist thinking, in *The Mirror of Production*, Baudrillard argued that Marx's fundamental political categories were themselves caught up in precisely the discourse of political economy which he wished to oppose, even to overthrow. Later, he arrived at the more general conclusion that all 'oppositional' thinking is always already negated by the structure of the entity which it wishes to oppose. 'Opposition', 'criticism', is nothing more than an inoculation of sorts which allows the dominant political power in a social formation further to strengthen itself. This breeds a political pessimism (though not necessarily a quietism, *contra* certain sloppy readings of selected parts of Baudrillard's writings). If politics is available today, then it is available first at the level of representations. But technology has so expanded and perfected the techniques of representing 'the real' that the very ontological status of the real itself has been called into question. Here there is room for a new politics. At the beginning of modern European philosophy, Descartes saw that his philosophical system was potentially thwarted and undone by one thing: the *malin génie*, an evil genius who was fundamentally in control of representations – even simulations – of the real. It is to this 'evil genius' that Baudrillard turns in his later work; and it offers a means of overcoming the 'winner loses' logic of the negation of opposition. If the fundamental question of the political is the relation between the Subject of consciousness and the 'Objectal' environment; and if all thinking from the point of view of the Subject is in some sense stymied or limited by this fundamental political structure, then, finally, there seems to be only one thing left to do. Impossible though it may seem, it is time to 'seduce' the *malin génie* by going over to the side of the Object. The world of Objects is and has been indifferent to the challenges posed to it by the Subject: as Baudrillard has it, the Object 'does not answer' to our demands. 'But, by disobeying laws and thwarting desire, it must answer secretly to some enigma. What is left but to go over to the side of this enigma?'

For some, the post-Marxist positions outlined in these articles will appear to be defeatist, even anti-Marxist; for others, it will appear that in their extreme questioning of the political there lies the most radical politics currently available, and that they therefore form a kind of political avant-garde (perhaps despite themselves) which will be as radical for the twenty-first century as Marx was for the twentieth.

24 □ *Postmodernist Bourgeois Liberalism*

Richard Rorty

Complaints about the social irresponsibility of the intellectuals typically concern the intellectual's tendency to marginalize herself, to move out from one community by interior identification of herself with some other community – for example, another country or historical period, an invisible college, or some alienated subgroup within the larger community. Such marginalization is, however, common to intellectuals and to miners. In the early days of the United Mine Workers its members rightly put no faith in the surrounding legal and political institutions and were loyal only to each other. In this respect they resembled the literary and artistic avant-garde between the wars.

It is not clear that those who thus marginalize themselves can be criticized for social irresponsibility. One cannot be irresponsible toward a community of which one does not think of oneself as a member. Otherwise runaway slaves and tunnelers under the Berlin Wall would be irresponsible. If such criticism were to make sense there would have to be a supercommunity one *had* to identify with – humanity as such. Then one could appeal to the needs of that community when breaking with one's family or tribe or nation, and such groups could appeal to the same thing when criticizing the irresponsibility of those who break away. Some people believe that there is such a community. These are the people who think there are such things as intrinsic human dignity, intrinsic human rights, and an ahistorical distinction between the demands of morality and those of prudence. Call these people 'Kantians'. They are opposed by people who say that 'humanity' is a biological rather than a moral notion, that there is no human dignity that is not derivative from the dignity of some specific community, and no appeal beyond the relative merits of various actual or proposed communities to impartial criteria which will help us weigh those merits. Call these people 'Hegelians'. Much of contemporary social philosophy in the English-speaking world is a three-cornered debate between Kantians (like John Rawls and Ronald Dworkin) who want to keep an ahistorical morality–prudence distinction as a buttress for the institutions and practices of the

From *Journal of Philosophy*, LXXX, 10 (1983), 583–9.

surviving democracies, those (like the post-Marxist philosophical left in Europe, Roberto Unger, and Alasdair MacIntyre) who want to abandon these institutions both because they presuppose a discredited philosophy and for other, more concrete, reasons, and those (like Michael Oakeshott and John Dewey) who want to preserve the institutions while abandoning their traditional Kantian backup. These last two positions take over Hegel's criticism of Kant's conception of moral agency, while either naturalizing or junking the rest of Hegel.

If the Hegelians are right, then there are no ahistorical criteria for deciding when it is or is not a responsible act to desert a community, any more than for deciding when to change lovers or professions. The Hegelians see nothing to be responsible to except persons and actual or possible historical communities; so they view the Kantians' use of 'social responsibility' as misleading. For that use suggests not the genuine contrast between, for example, Antigone's loyalties to Thebes and to her brother, or Alcibiades' loyalties to Athens and to Persia, but an illusory contrast between loyalty to a person or a historical community and to something 'higher' than either. It suggests that there is a point of view that abstracts from any historical community and adjudicates the rights of communities *vis-à-vis* those of individuals.

Kantians tend to accuse of social irresponsibility those who doubt that there is such a point of view. So when Michael Walzer says that 'A given society is just if its substantive life is lived in ... a way faithful to the shared understandings of the members', Dworkin calls this view 'relativism'. 'Justice', Dworkin retorts, 'cannot be left to convention and anecdote.' Such Kantian complaints can be defended using the Hegelian's own tactics, by noting that the very American society which Walzer wishes to commend and to reform is one whose self-image is bound up with the Kantian vocabulary of 'inalienable rights' and 'the dignity of man'. Hegelian defenders of liberal institutions are in the position of defending, on the basis of solidarity alone, a society which has traditionally asked to be based on something more than mere solidarity. Kantian criticism of the tradition that runs from Hegel through Marx and Nietzsche, a tradition which insists on thinking of morality as the interest of a historically conditioned community rather than 'the common interest of humanity', often insists that such a philosophical outlook is – if one values liberal practices and institutions – irresponsible. Such criticism rests on a prediction that such practices and institutions will not survive the removal of the traditional Kantian buttresses, buttresses which include an account of 'rationality' and 'morality' as transcultural and ahistorical.

I shall call the Hegelian attempt to defend the institutions and practices of the rich North Atlantic democracies without using such buttresses 'postmodernist bourgeois liberalism'. I call it 'bourgeois' to emphasize that most of the people I am talking about would have no quarrel with the Marxist claim that a lot of those institutions and practices are possible and justifiable only in certain historical, and especially economic, conditions. I want to contrast bourgeois liberalism, the attempt to fulfill the hopes of the North Atlantic bourgeoisie, with philosophical liberalism, a collection of Kantian principles thought to justify us in having those hopes.

Hegelians think that these principles are useful for *summarizing* these hopes, but not for justifying them (a view Rawls himself verges upon in his Dewey Lectures). I use 'postmodernist' in a sense given to this term by Jean-François Lyotard, who says that the postmodern attitude is that of 'distrust of metanarratives', narratives which describe or predict the activities of such entities as the noumenal self or the Absolute Spirit or the Proletariat. These metanarratives are stories which purport to justify loyalty to, or breaks with, certain contemporary communities, but which are neither historical narratives about what these or other communities have done in the past nor scenarios about what they might do in the future.

'Postmodernist bourgeois liberalism' sounds oxymoronic. This is partly because, for local and perhaps transitory reasons, the majority of those who think of themselves as beyond metaphysics and metanarratives also think of themselves as having opted out of the bourgeoisie. But partly it is because it is hard to disentangle bourgeois liberal institutions from the vocabulary that these institutions inherited from the Enlightenment – e.g. the eighteenth-century vocabulary of natural rights, which judges, and constitutional lawyers such as Dworkin, must use *ex officiis*. This vocabulary is built around a distinction between morality and prudence. In what follows I want to show how this vocabulary, and in particular this distinction, might be reinterpreted to suit the needs of us postmodernist bourgeois liberals. I hope thereby to suggest how such liberals might convince our society that loyalty to itself is morality enough, and that such loyalty no longer needs an ahistorical backup. I think they should try to clear themselves of charges of irresponsibility by convincing our society that it need be responsible only to its own traditions, and not to the moral law as well.

The crucial move in this reinterpretation is to think of the moral self, the embodiment of rationality, not as one of Rawls's original choosers, somebody who can distinguish her *self* from her talents and interests and views about the good, but as a network of beliefs, desires, and emotions with nothing behind it – no substrate behind the attributes. For purposes of moral and political deliberation and conversation, a person just *is* that network, as for purposes of ballistics she is a point-mass, or for purposes of chemistry a linkage of molecules. She is a network that is constantly reweaving itself in the usual Quinean manner – that is to say, not by reference to general criteria (e.g. 'rules of meaning' or 'moral principles') but in the hit-or-miss way in which cells readjust themselves to meet the pressures of the environment. On a Quinean view, rational behavior is just adaptive behavior of a sort which roughly parallels the behavior, in similar circumstances, of the other members of some relevant community. Irrationality, in both physics and ethics, is a matter of behavior that leads one to abandon, or be stripped of, membership in some such community. For some purposes this adaptive behavior is aptly described as 'learning' or 'computing' or 'redistribution of electrical charges in neural tissue', and for others as 'deliberation' or 'choice'. None of these vocabularies is privileged over against another.

What plays the role of 'human dignity' on this view of the self? The answer is well expressed by Michael Sandel, who says that we cannot regard ourselves as Kantian subjects 'capable of constituting meaning on our own', as Rawlsian choosers,

> without great cost to those loyalties and convictions whose moral force consists partly
> in the fact that living by them is inseparable from understanding ourselves as the
> particular people we are – as members of this family or community or nation or people,
> as bearers of this history, as sons and daughters of that revolution, as citizens of this
> republic.[1]

I would argue that the moral force of such loyalties and convictions consists *wholly* in this fact, and that nothing else has *any* moral force. There is no 'ground' for such loyalties and convictions save the fact that the beliefs and desires and emotions which buttress them overlap those of lots of other members of the group with which we identify for purposes of moral or political deliberations, and the further fact that these are *distinctive* features of that group, features which it uses to construct its self-image through contrasts with other groups. This means that the naturalized Hegelian analogue of 'intrinsic human dignity' is the comparative dignity of a group with which a person identifies herself. Nations or churches or movements are, on this view, shining historical examples not because they reflect rays emanating from a higher source, but because of contrast-effects – comparisons with other, worse communities. Persons have dignity not as an interior luminescence, but because they share in such contrast-effects. It is a corollary of this view that the moral justification of the institutions and practices of one's group – e.g. of the contemporary bourgeoisie – is mostly a matter of historical narratives (including scenarios about what is likely to happen in certain future contingencies), rather than of philosophical metanarratives. The principal backup for historiography is not philosophy but the arts, which serve to develop and modify a group's self-image by, for example, apotheosizing its heroes, diabolizing its enemies, mounting dialogues among its members, and refocusing its attention.

A further corollary is that the morality–prudence distinction now appears as a distinction between appeals to two parts of the network that is the self – parts separated by blurry and constantly shifting boundaries. One part consists of those beliefs and desires and emotions which overlap with those of most other members of some community with which, for purposes of deliberation, she identifies herself, and which contrast with those of most members of other communities with which hers contrasts itself. A person appeals to morality rather than prudence when she appeals to this overlapping, shared part of herself, those beliefs and desires and emotions which permit her to say 'WE do not do this sort of thing'. Morality is, as Wilfrid Sellars has said, a matter of 'we-intentions'. Most moral dilemmas are thus reflections of the fact that most of us identify with a number of different communities and are equally reluctant to marginalize ourselves in relation to any of them. This diversity of identifications increases with education, just as the number of communities with which a person may identify increases with civilization.

Intra-societal tensions, of the sort which Dworkin rightly says mark our pluralistic society, are rarely resolved by appeals to general principles of the sort Dworkin thinks necessary. More frequently they are resolved by appeals to what he calls 'convention and anecdote'. The political discourse of the democracies, at its best, is the exchange of what Wittgenstein called 'reminders for a particular purpose' – anecdotes about the past effects of various practices and predictions of what will happen if, or unless, some of these are altered. The moral deliberations of the postmodernist bourgeois liberal consists largely in this same sort of discourse, avoiding the formulation of general principles except where the situation may require this particular tactic – as when one writes a constitution, or rules for young children to memorize. It is useful to remember that this view of moral and political deliberation was a commonplace among American intellectuals in the days when Dewey – a postmodernist before his time – was the reigning American philosopher, days when 'legal realism' was thought of as desirable pragmatism rather than unprincipled subjectivism.

It is also useful to reflect on why this tolerance for anecdote was replaced by a reattachment to principles. Part of the explanation, I think, is that most American intellectuals in Dewey's day still thought their country was a shining historical example. They identified with it easily. The largest single reason for their loss of identification was the Vietnam War. The War caused some intellectuals to marginalize themselves entirely. Others attempted to rehabilitate Kantian notions in order to say, with Chomsky, that the War not merely betrayed America's hopes and interests and self-image, but was *immoral*, one which we had had no *right* to engage in in the first place.

Dewey would have thought such attempts at further self-castigation pointless. They may have served a useful cathartic purpose, but their long-run effect has been to separate the intellectuals from the moral consensus of the nation rather than to alter that consensus. Further, Dewey's naturalized Hegelianism has more overlap with the belief-systems of the communities we rich North American bourgeois need to talk with than does a naturalized Kantianism. So a reversion to the Deweyan outlook might leave us in a better position to carry on whatever conversation between nations may still be possible, as well as leaving American intellectuals in a better position to converse with their fellow citizens.

I shall end by taking up two objections to what I have been saying. The first objection is that on my view a child found wandering in the woods, the remnant of a slaughtered nation whose temples have been razed and whose books have been burned, has no share in human dignity. This is indeed a consequence, but it does not follow that she may be treated like an animal. For it is part of the tradition of *our* community that the human stranger from whom all dignity has been stripped is to be taken in, to be reclothed with dignity. This Jewish and Christian element in our tradition is gratefully invoked by free-loading atheists like myself, who would like to let differences like that between the Kantian and the Hegelian remain 'merely philosophical'. The existence of human rights, in the sense in which it is at issue in this meta-ethical debate, has as much or as little relevance to our treatment of such a child as the question of the existence of God. I think both have equally little relevance.

The second objection is that what I have been calling 'postmodernism' is better named 'relativism', and that relativism is self-refuting. Relativism certainly is self-refuting, but there is a difference between saying that every community is as good as every other and saying that we have to work out from the networks we are, from the communities with which we presently identify. Postmodernism is no more relativistic than Hilary Putnam's suggestion that we stop trying for a 'God's-eye view' and realize that 'We can only hope to produce a more rational conception of rationality or a better conception of morality if we operate from within our tradition.'[2] The view that every tradition is as rational or as moral as every other could be held only by a god, someone who had no need to use (but only to mention) the terms 'rational' or 'moral', because she had no need to inquire or deliberate. Such a being would have escaped from history and conversation into contemplation and metanarrative. To accuse postmodernism of relativism is to try to put a metanarrative in the postmodernist's mouth. One will do this if one identifies 'holding a philosophical position' with having a metanarrative available. If we insist on such a definition of 'philosophy', then postmodernism is post-philosophical. But it would be better to change the definition.[3]

Notes

1. *Liberalism and the Limits of Justice*, Cambridge University Press, New York, 1982, p. 179. Sandel's remarkable book argues masterfully that Rawls cannot naturalize Kant and still retain the meta-ethical authority of Kantian 'practical reason'.
2. *Reason, Truth and History*, Cambridge University Press, New York, 1981, p. 216.
3. I discuss such redefinition in the Introduction to *Consequences of Pragmatism*, University of Minnesota Press, Minneapolis, 1982, and the issue of relativism in 'Habermas and Lyotard on postmodernity', forthcoming in *Praxis International*, and in 'Solidarité ou objectivité?', forthcoming in *Critique*.

25 □ *Politics and the Limits of Modernity*

Ernesto Laclau

The theme of postmodernity, which first appeared within aesthetics, has been displaced to ever wider areas until it has become the new horizon of our cultural, philosophical, and political experience. In the latter realm, to which I shall here limit my analysis, postmodernity has advanced by means of two converging intellectual operations whose complex interweavings and juxtapositions have, however, also contributed to a large extent to obscuring the problems at hand. Both operations share, without doubt, one characteristic: the attempt to establish *boundaries*, that is to say, to separate an ensemble of historical features and phenomena (postmodern) from others also appertaining to the past and that can be grouped under the rubric of modernity. In both cases the boundaries of modernity are established in radically different ways. The first announces a weakening of the metaphysical and rationalist pretensions of modernity, by way of challenging the *foundational* status of certain narratives. The second challenges not the ontological status of narrative as such, but rather the current validity of *certain* narratives: those that Lyotard has called metanarratives [*méta-récits*], which unified the totality of the historical experience of modernity (including science as one of its essential elements) within the project of global, human emancipation.

In what follows, I shall consider the status of metanarratives and offer as basic theses: (1) that there has been a radical change in the thought and culture of the past few decades (concerning which there would be no inconvenience in considering it as the entry to a sort of postmodernity), which, however, passes neither through a crisis nor, much less, to an abandonment of metanarratives; (2) that the very idea of the abandonment of metanarratives is logically contradictory, for it reproduces within postmodern discourse the 'logic of foundations' that supposedly characterized modernity; and (3) that the decisive change relates to the new status of the discursive and the new language-games practiced around narratives – of all sorts, metanarratives included. The very idea of a boundary between modernity and

From Ross, A. (ed.), *Universal Abandon?*, University of Minnesota Press, Minneapolis/ Edinburgh University Press, Edinburgh, 1988, 1989, pp. 63–82.

postmodernity marked by the outmodedness of metanarratives presupposes a theoretical discourse in which the *end* of something is thinkable, which is to say, transparent and intellectually graspable. What does it mean for something to 'end'? It may be conceived, in a teleological sense, as the attainment of its highest form; in a dialectical sense, as its transformation into its contrary; in the movement of the eternal return, as a moment in the periodic becoming of forms; or as an annihilation that manifests its radical contingency. This is to say that a discourse is required that can conceive and construct the separation – even temporal separation – of two entities. Merely to proclaim the end of something is an empty gesture.

Even worse, the uncritical introduction of the category *end* into a discourse, to substitute an effective 'making an end' for the voluntarist transparency of a simply announced and postulated end, means to smuggle back in what was to have been jettisoned. This can happen in two ways. First, insofar as something ends, something radically different must commence. In such a case, it is impossible to avoid the category of the 'new' and the idea of an innovative vanguard, which is precisely what the discourse of postmodernity purports to have left behind. On the other hand, to postulate the outmodedness of metanarratives (without taking into consideration what happens to other narrative species) is to achieve rather modest intellectual gains in comparison with the objectives sought. The logic of identity, of full presence, is simply displaced, fully intact, from the field of totality to the field of multiplicity of atomized narratives.

If there is a sense of postmodernity, that is, an ensemble of pre-theoretical references that establish certain 'family resemblances' among its diverse manifestations, this is suggested by the process of erosion and disintegration of such categories as 'foundation', 'new', 'identity', 'vanguard', and so on. What the 'situation of postmodernity' challenges is not so much the discrimination and choice between social and cultural identities but the status and logic of the construction of those identities. Consequently, drawing up the limits of modernity involves a more complex and evolving operation than merely setting boundaries. Postmodernity cannot be a simple *rejection* of modernity; rather, it involves a different modulation of its themes and categories, a greater proliferation of its language-games.

Some of these games, which avoid conceiving the tradition with which they play in terms of rejection or affirmation of the radical novelty of the present, have long been inscribed in the intellectual history of this century. What Heidegger has called the 'de-struction of the history of ontology' is an example:

> The answer (to the question of Being) is not properly conceived if what it asserts propositionally is just passed along, especially if it gets circulated as a free-floating result, so that we merely get informed about a 'stand point' which may perhaps differ from the way this has hitherto been treated. Whether the answer is a 'new' one remains quite a superficial problem and is of no importance. Its positive character must lie in its being *ancient* enough for us to learn to conceive the possibilities which the 'ancients' have made ready for us.[1]

This excludes the possibility of a simple rejection. Instead, it attempts to trace the genealogy of the present, dissolve the apparent obviousness of certain categories that are the trivialized and hardened sedimentations of tradition, and in this way bring to view the original problem to which they constitute a response. So, too, in Heidegger:

> If the question of Being is to have its own history made transparent, then this hardened tradition must be loosened up, and the concealments which it has brought about must be dissolved. We understand this task as one in which by taking *the question of Being as our clue*, we are to *destroy* the traditional content of ancient ontology until we arrive at those primordial experiences in which we achieved our first ways of determining the nature of Being – the ways which have guided us ever since.[2]

This same argument can be extended to the most diverse theoretical discourses. Consider, for example, the category of 'class' within Marxism. Central to the series of recent exchanges are the following questions: Is it classes or social movements that constitute the fundamental agents of historical change in advanced industrial societies? Or, is the working class in the process of disappearing? But these questions are quite secondary because, whatever answers they elicit, they *presuppose* what is fundamental: the obviousness and transparency of the category 'class'. The 'destruction' of the history of Marxism, in Heidegger's sense, involves showing that a category such as 'class', far from being obvious, is already a synthesis of determinations, a particular response to a more primary question of social agency. Because the contemporary situation poses this problem again in much more complex terms than were available to Marx, it is necessary to understand his response as a partial and limited synthesis, while appreciating more clearly the original sense of his questions. The sense of an intellectual intervention emerges only when it is possible to reconstitute the system of questions that it seeks to answer. On the other hand, when these questions are taken as simply obvious, their sense is obscured, if not entirely lost. It is precisely the limitation of the responses that keeps alive the sense of a question.

In sketching out the limits of modernity, we must be agreed on what, in modernity, is being put to the test. If we question the specific values of the social/political/intellectual project that began globally with the Enlightenment, the narrative of its crisis requires the affirmation of *other* values; this, however, does not change the ontological status of the category of *value* as such. In this regard, it is important to point out that the critics of modernity have not even tried to introduce different values. When the theorists of the eighteenth century are presented as the initiators of a project of 'mastery' that would eventually lead to Auschwitz, it is forgotten that Auschwitz was repudiated by a set of values that, in large part, also stem from the eighteenth century. So, too, when criticism is directed at the category of totality implicit in metanarratives, only the possibility of reuniting the partial narratives into a global emancipatory narrative comes under fire; the category of 'narrative' itself is left completely unchallenged. I would like to argue that it is precisely the *ontological status* of the central categories of the discourses of modernity, and not their *content*, that is at stake; that the erosion of this status is expressed through the 'postmodern' sensibility; and that this erosion, far from being a negative phenomenon, represents an enormous amplification of the content and operability of the values of modernity, making it possible to ground them on foundations much more solid than those of the Enlightenment project (and its various positivist or Hegelian–Marxist reformulations).

Language and Reality

Postmodernity does not imply a *change* in the values of Enlightenment modernity but rather a particular weakening of their absolutist character. It is therefore necessary to delimit an analytic terrain from whose standpoint this weakening is thinkable and definable. This terrain is neither arbitrary nor freely accessible to the imagination, but on the contrary it is the historical sedimentation of a set of traditions whose common denominator is the collapse of the immediacy of the *given*. We may thus propose that the intellectual history of the twentieth century was constituted on the basis of three illusions of immediacy (the referent, the phenomenon, and the sign) that gave rise to the three intellectual traditions of analytical philosophy, phenomenology, and structuralism. The crisis of that illusion of immediacy did not, however, result solely from the abandonment of those categories but rather from a weakening of their aspirations to constitute full presences and from the ensuing proliferation of language-games which it was possible to develop around them. This crisis of the absolutist pretensions of 'the immediate' is a fitting starting point for engaging those intellectual operations that characterize the specific 'weakening' we call postmodernity. Each of these three intellectual traditions might serve as an equally valid point of departure for our analysis; in what follows, however, I shall base my argument on the crisis in structuralism.

As is well known, structuralism was constituted around the new centrality it accorded to the linguistic model. If we want to concentrate on the crisis of 'immediacy', which originally pretended to characterize the notion of the sign, we should concentrate not so much on the invasion of new ontic areas by the linguistic model but on the internal transformation of the linguistic model itself. The crisis consisted precisely in the increasing difficulty of defining the limits of language, or, more accurately, of defining the specific identity of the linguistic object.

In this respect, I could mention three fundamental stages in the structuralist tradition. The first is associated with Saussure, who, as is well known, tried to locate the specific object of linguistics in what he called *langue*, an abstraction from the ensemble of language phenomena based on a set of oppositions and definitions, the most important of which are: *langue/parole*, signifier/signified, syntagm/paradigm. The two basic principles that oversaw the constitution of the linguistic object were the propositions that there are no positive terms in language, only differences, and that language is form, not substance. Both principles were central to the category of *value*, which acquired increasing importance *vis-à-vis signification* in the subsequent evolution of the structuralist tradition.

The increasing refinement of linguistic formalism soon led, however, to an understanding that Saussurean theory was based on a set of ambiguities that could only be covered over by recourse to principles that contradicted its basic postulates. Take the distinction between signifier and signified: if language is all form and not substance, and if there is a perfect isomorphism between the order of the signifier and that of the signified, how is it possible to establish the difference between the two? Saussure could only do so by the recourse to the idea of substance, phonic in one case, conceptual in the other. As for the distinction between *langue* and *parole* – between language as collective 'treasure' and its use by each individual speaker – this distinction can be maintained *only* if one assumes a subject exterior to the linguistic system. Consequently, one of the fundamental oppositions of this system was required to be externally defined, thus confining linguistic formalism within a new limit. Beyond this point it was impossible to posit a 'linguistics of discourse', if by discourse we mean a linguistic unit greater than the sentence. Saussure had spoken of semiology as a general science of signs in social life, but so long as *langue* remained anchored in the materiality of the *linguistic* sign, such a project could not proceed beyond a vaguely metaphorical and programmatic level.

From this point on, post-Saussurean structuralism emphasized linguistic formalism in its bid to transcend the ambiguities and inconsistencies of Saussure's own work. This, then, is the second phase, in which Hjelmslev, for example, broke with the strict isomorphism between the order of the signifier and the order of the signified by defining units smaller than the sign, whose distinctive features are no longer isomorphic. In this manner, he was able to establish the difference between the two orders on purely formal grounds. Furthermore, the critique that had been taking place, of the Cartesianism inherent in the category of the subject, made it possible progressively to show that the linguistic interventions of individual speakers reveal patterns and regularities conceivable only as *systems of differences*. This enabled the linguistic model to be expanded to the field of discourse.

There was, however, one further development. Once linguistic formalism had radically eradicated substance, there was no way of distinguishing between those systems of differential positions proper to speech and the 'extralinguistic' or 'extradiscursive' actions to which they are linked, for both speech and actions are differential positions within operations of much larger scope. But if this development expanded the value range of the 'linguistic model', the linguistic *object* tended to lose its specificity. In this second moment of the radicalization of structuralism, the stable character of the relation between signifier and the signified had not, however, been questioned; only the structural isomorphism between the two had been broken. The boundaries of linguistics had been expanded, but the immediacy and the characteristic of full presence of its objects were only reaffirmed.

When the presence and self-evidence of these objects have faded, we can detect the transition to a third moment, which, following a certain tradition, we can denominate poststructuralism. At issue now was the fixed link between signifier and signified. The quasi-Cartesian transparency that structural formalism had established between the purely relational identities of the linguistic system served only to make them more *vulnerable* to any new system of relations. In other words, as the ideal conditions of closure were defined more precisely, it was increasingly more difficult to hold to the *closed* character of the system. From this point the radical questioning of the immediacy and transparency of the sign takes place, the sundry variants of which are well known: the critique of the denotation/connotation distinction in the later Barthes, the affirmation of the primacy of the signifier and the increasing centrality of the 'real' *vis-à-vis* the symbolic in Lacan, the emphasis on the constitutive character of *difference*, and the critique of the metaphysics of presence in Derrida.

The crisis of the immediacy of the sign appears to be dominated by a double movement: while the signified was ever less closed within itself and could be defined only in relation to a specific context, the limits of that context were increasingly less well defined. In effect, the very logic of limit was increasingly more difficult to define. For Hegel, for example, the perception of a limit was the perception of what is beyond it; the limit, then, lies within the conceivable. Structuralism's radical relationalism would thus be subsumable under the category of the infinite regress. This point could be generalized: the most diverse forms of contemporary thought are permeated by the relational character of identities in conjunction with the impossibility of intellectual mastery over the context. Consider the various contortions of Husserl's ego/splits, and his efforts to affirm the transcendental constitutivity of the subject: the weakening of the distinction between semantics and pragmatics in Wittgensteinian and post-Wittgenstenian philosophy; the character of Kuhn's paradigms; the unresolved problems in the transition from *épistémès* to *dispositifs* in Foucault; the pragmatic turn of dogmaless empiricism in Quine. Some of these examples, especially Husserl's, are attempts to break the impasse by means of an essentialist reaffirmation of closure. However, in the majority of cases, the realization of the openness of context has been the point of departure for a radical anti-essentialist critique.

Let us turn our attention, at this point, to the various dimensions opened up by the unfixed character of the signifier/signified relation, that is, of all identity. In the first place, its effect is polysemic: if a plurality of signifieds is joined in an unstable fashion to certain signifiers, the necessary result is the introduction of equivocality (in the Aristotelian sense). But if one can affirm that this instability does not depend entirely on the equivocality of the signifier but on the contexts in which the signifier is used, it is no longer a question of *equivocality* but of *ambiguity* and *unfixity*, in the strict sense of the terms. For example, when I say 'down the hill' or 'the soft down on his cheek',[3] the term *down* is equivocal: its meaning varies in relation to different contexts, although in each context its meaning is perfectly clear. On the other hand, if I speak about 'democracy' in the political context of Western Europe during the Cold War years, the ambiguity of the term proceeds from the context itself, which is constituted to some extent by the simultaneous presence of communist and anticommunist discourses. The term, therefore, is radically ambiguous and not simply polysemous. It is not a matter of its meaning one thing in communist discourse and another in anticommunist discourse; this, of course, may happen, but if that were the sole distinguishing circumstance, we would be left with a plurality of perfectly well-defined contexts and, consequently, with a case of simple equivocalness. Something very different, however, takes place: since both discourses are antagonistic and yet operate largely in the same argumentative context, there is a loosening of the relational systems that constitute the identity of the term. Thus, the term becomes a floating signifier. This radical ambiguity, which subverts the fixity of the sign, is precisely what gives the context its openness.

Three consequences follow from the above. First, that the concept of discourse is not linguistic but prior to the distinction between the linguistic and extralinguistic. If I am building a wall and I tell someone 'hand me a brick' and then place it on the wall, my first act is linguistic and the second is behavioral, but it is easy to perceive that they are both connected as part of a total operation, namely, the construction of the wall. This relational moment within the total operation is neither linguistic nor extralinguistic, for it includes both types of actions. If, on the other hand, we think about it positively, the concepts that apprehend it must be prior to the linguistic/extralinguistic distinction. This instance of ground is called discourse and is therefore coterminous with the 'social'. Because every social action has a *meaning*, it is constituted in the form of discursive sequences that articulate linguistic and extralinguistic elements.[4]

A second consequence is that the relational character of discourse is precisely what permits the generalization of the linguistic model within the ensemble of social relations. It is not that reality is language, but that the increasing formalization of the linguistic system brought about the definition of a set of relational logics that embrace more than the linguistic narrowly defined. The act of placing a brick on a wall is not linguistic, but *its relation* to the linguistic act of previously asking for the brick is a particular discursive relation: a syntagmatic combination of the two acts. The relational logics of the social widen considerably, which opens up the path toward a new conceptualization of objectivity.

The third consequence clearly derives from the two previous ones. The radical relationalism of social identities increases their vulnerability to new relations and introduces within them the effects of ambiguity to which we referred above.

These three consequences give us a framework that makes possible an approximation to the postmodern experience. If something has characterized the discourses of modernity, it is their pretension intellectually to dominate the foundation of the social, to give a rational context to the notion of the totality of history, and to base in the latter the project of a global human emancipation. As such, they have been discourses about essences and fully present identities based in one way or another upon the myth of a transparent society. Postmodernity, on the contrary, begins when this fully present identity is threatened by an ungraspable exterior that introduces a dimension of opacity and pragmatism into the pretended immediacy and transparency of its categories. This gives rise to an unbreachable abyss between the real (in the Lacanian sense) and concepts, thus weakening the absolutist pretensions of the latter. It should be stressed that this 'weakening' does not in any way negate the contents of the project of modernity; it shows only the radical vulnerability of those contents to a plurality of contexts that redefine them in an unpredictable way. Once this vulnerability is accepted in all its radicality, what does not necessarily follow is either the abandonment of the emancipatory values or a generalized skepticism concerning them, but rather, on the contrary, the awareness of the complex strategic-discursive operations implied by their affirmation and defense.

The narration of the beginnings of postmodernity – as with all beginnings – involves a multiple genealogy. In the next section, I shall attempt to trace this in relation to a particular tradition – Marxism – which constituted both one of the highest points of the emancipatory narratives of modernity and one of their first crises. Whence the emergence of a post-Marxism or a postmodern Marxism resulting from the new relational contexts in which the categories of classical Marxism were involved. Subject to increasing tensions, these categories became involved in newer and ever more complex language-games.

Capitalism, Uneven Development, and Hegemony

Let us clarify the sense of our genealogical question; the narrative that is being sought does not attempt to establish the *causes* of a certain process, if by causes we mean that which possesses all the internal virtualities that bring about an effect. If that were the case, we would have simply inscribed the past anew onto the rationalistic transparency of a conceptually graspable foundation. On the contrary, it is rather a question of narrating the *dissolution* of a foundation, thus revealing the radical contingency of the categories linked to that foundation. My intention is *revelatory* rather than *explanatory*.

I shall begin with a central tenet of Marxism: that capitalism exists only by dint of the constant transformation of the means of production and the increasing dissolution of preexisting social relations. The history of capitalism, therefore, is, on the one hand, the history of the progressive destruction of the social relations generated by it and, on the other, the history of its border with social forms exterior to it. Actually, it is a question of two borders that the very logic of capitalism must constantly re-create and redefine. Such a situation engenders two conceptual alternatives: either the movement of these borders is a process of contingent struggle whose outcome is largely indeterminate, or it is History brought to a predetermined and predeterminable end by a cunning Reason, which works on the contradictions of that History. It is clear that a philosophy of history can *only* be formulated along the lines of the second alternative. And there is little doubt that classical Marxism followed those lines. Suffice it to mention the preface to *A Contribution to the Critique of Political Economy*.[5]

Let us consider this latter alternative in relation to the radically relational character of identity discussed above. If the limits of the system can be subverted by a reality exterior to it, then, insofar as every identity is relational, the new relations of exteriority cannot but transform the identities. Identities can remain stable only in a closed system. Is there any compatibility, then, between the idea of historical agents – particularly the working class – as identities defined within the capitalist system, and the fact that the system always acts upon a reality exterior to it? Yes, if one accepts the solution put forth by classical Marxism: that the relation of exteriority can be *internally* defined, since every exterior relation is destined *a priori* to succumb as a result of capitalist expansion. The internal logic of capital thus comes to constitute the rational substrate of History, and the advent of socialism is thought to be made possible only by the results of the *internal* contradictions of capitalism.

If this were all, little would be left to say and the attempts to trace within Marxist discourses the genealogy of a post-Marxism would be doomed to failure. But this is not the whole story. In fact, emergent within Marxism are diverse discourses in which the relation between the 'internal' and the 'external' has become increasingly complex and has begun to deconstruct the categories of classical Marxism. The language-games played around these categories became ever more difficult and risky: 'classes', for example, were conceived as constituted by relational complexes quite removed from those originally attributed to them.

The history of Marxism has met with several such nodal moments of ambiguity and discusive proliferation. However, those phenomena grouped under the rubric of 'uneven and combined development' must be singled out for special consideration because of the variety and centrality of the effects they have produced. In a recently published book,[6] I have described the basic lines of the emergence and expansion of this concept of uneven and combined development, and so I shall only summarize its distinctive features here. At the beginning, this concept attempted only to characterize an exceptional context. The Russian bourgeoisie, having entered history belatedly and consequently having been rendered incapable of taking on the democratic tasks of overthrowing Czarist absolutism, gave way to the working class, who assumed these tasks. But the tasks 'proper' to the working class are socialist and not democratic. Therefore, how does one define the 'exceptionality' of one class taking over another class's tasks? The *name* given to this taking over was 'hegemony', but the *nature* of the relation it implied was far from being clear. Was the relation between the working class and the democratic tasks it took on *internal* or *external* to its nature as class? And what do we make of the fact that this uneven development soon ceased to have an exceptional character? The social upheavals proper to the age of imperialism necessitated ever more complex articulatory practices as a result of their operation in ever less orthodox historical contexts. Trotsky came to understand uneven and combined development as the historical law of our era. But what, then, is *normal* development supposed to be?

At this point I can return to some of the points made earlier. Every (social or other type of) identity is relational and vulnerable to the subversion of any exteriority. This implies that the combination of tasks proper to uneven development cannot but modify the nature of the social agents that enact them. Such was clearly the case in the emergence, during the era of popular fronts, of such entities as the 'masses', the 'national', the 'popular', etc., excluded from Marxist discourse in the heyday of the Second International. But this also implied, necessarily, that the suturing, foundational, and metaphysical value of classist categories had been radically questioned. That is, if classist identities are subverted by an exteriority, by new relational and articulatory contexts, they cannot be the *foundation* of History. The pragmatism and the contingency pass from the task to the agents, and the ground of possibility of a philosophy of History is dissolved.

This radical questioning of the logic of foundations is precisely the weakening effect that I and my colleague Chantal Mouffe found to be intrinsic to postmodern experience. And by exploring those points in the Marxist tradition in which the weakening effect operates, we can trace the genealogy of a post-Marxism. Let's look at two examples: Sorel and Gramsci. Sorel was clear on two issues: that the logic of capitalist development did not move in the direction that Marx predicated, and that the participation of the working class in the democratic political system led to its integration within that system. The first process weakened the logic of capital as the foundation of History; the second produced the same effect of weakening by showing that the social identity of the working class was vulnerable to the new system of relations by virtue of that class's very political participation. Sorel's response to this is well known: on the one hand, he posited a theory of myth that implied a radical relationalism, for only violence and the total severance of relations between the working class and the political system permitted a proletarian identity; and on the other, the absolute rejection of the underlying rationality of History, insofar as social relations assume structural coherence only when patterned by myth.

Gramsci presents us with an identical relationalism that leads, however, to the opposite solution. Sorel rejected all relations of exteriority and proposed a pristine proletarian identity. Gramsci, on the contrary, fully explored the multiplicity of relational ensembles which developed in the Italy of his time, thus systematically expanding the field of hegemonic relations, but as a result of that he had to acknowledge that the political subjects were not the classes but what he denominated as collective wills. Where Sorel saw all participation within the political system as a loss of identity, Gramsci conceived of hegemonic articulations as a process of creating identities. Both however, posited the same relational, and ultimately ungrounded, character of identities.

If we situate these two examples in a broader historical perspective, the direction our genealogical exploration should take is more easily discerned. The systematic discovery of discursive areas in the Marxist tradition saw the emergence of new entities and categories that, rather than prolong the basic concepts of classical Marxism through their cumulative enrichment, added a logically unintegratable *supplement* to them, in the manner of what Derrida has called the 'logic of supplementarity' – that hingelike discursive play that renders opposition ambiguous. I do not think it is an exaggeration to argue that the fundamental terminological additions to Marxism, from Lenin to Gramsci, constitute supplements in this very sense. The genealogy of Marxism, then, coincides with the deconstruction of its myth of origins.

This myth is continually nourished by a multitude of operations that tend to conceal its fissures. These operations find their crudest form in the glorious and invincible Marxism–Leninism *à la* Soviet, but it at least has the virtue of being visible, in the conspicuous clumsiness of the bureaucrat; the *trahison des clercs* shows a greater sophistication, which operates, however, in the service of concealment. All of Lukács's sophistication is reduced to mediations that make the highest forms of 'bourgeois' culture compatible with a transparent notion of class not much different from that held by a member of the Soviet Academy of Science. More recently, a highly capable group of German theorists wasted a great deal of their time, as well as that of their readers, in the alchemistic quest of trying to derive the concept of the State from the concept of Capital. When it comes to *the last instance*, the convictions of the 'refined' materialist are not much different from those of the vulgar materialist. What all this means is that the history of Marxism loses its plurality; the language-games within that history and its relation to our period are defined and codified beforehand. Marxism is accepted or rejected *in toto*; Marx's texts are not read as one reads texts by Freud, Hegel, or Plato, that is, by questioning them from the perspective of our own problems and present situation.

Rather, a final revelation is awaited that will allow us to distance ourselves from the reality we live and to inhabit a different history, an illusory one to be sure. But when we take up our current problems, our engagement with them is merely impressionistic and pragmatic. Most frequently, the ultimate act of servility and faith in the unity of Marxism is to abandon it completely; but this serves only to maintain the myth of its coherence and unity.

This attitude has become so generalized that the preceding arguments probably sound a bit outdated. This indifference to the Marxist tradition, however, leads to an important loss as regards the constitution of a radical politics. In the first place, there is an impoverishment of the tradition. If the isolated struggles cannot be inserted within a wider horizon that 'totalizes' an ensemble of an experience, the result is the impossibility of constructing a radical imaginary. Furthermore, an abstract, nondeconstructive rejection of a tradition in no way implies going beyond it. This brings us back to our original problem: to affirm the end of something means nothing unless we specify the form in which it ends. Both Spinoza's philosophy and Hitlerism have historically come to an *end* in some sense, but the different forms in which we conceive their end and closure impinge upon us, with respect to not only how we determine our relation to the past but also how we define our present.

Let us return to our arguments concerning the destruction of a tradition, in the Heideggerian sense. To set the limits of an answer is to re-create the original meaning of the question. To set the historical limits of Marxism is to reestablish a living dialogue with that tradition, to endow it with a certain contemporaneity against the *timelessness* that its orthodox defenders attribute to it. In this sense, 'post-Marxism' is not an 'ex-Marxism', for it entails an active involvement in its history and in the discussion of its categories. But this involvement does not imply a dogmatic affirmation of its unity and coherence; rather, it requires specification of its plurality. By tracing our current problems within the Marxist tradition – in the writings of Luxemburg, Bauer, Sorel, or Gramsci, in which many violently repressed intuitions brought about deconstructive effects – it becomes possible to construct a discourse that can creatively appropriate the past. Historical amnesia is a recipe for parochialism at best. At worst it leads to the appropriation of one's struggles by antagonistic discourses.

Here, however, it is necessary to be more precise: if we are to *reconstruct* radical tradition (because this is precisely what this is about), not as a necessary departure from a point of origin, but as the genealogy of the present, it is clear that Marxism cannot be its only point of reference. The plurality of current social struggles, emerging in a radically different and more complex world than could have been conceived in the nineteenth century, entails the necessity of breaking with the provincial myth of the 'universal class'. If one can talk about universality, it is only in the sense of the relative centralities constructed hegemonically and pragmatically. The struggles of the working class, of women, gays, marginal populations, Third World masses, must result in the construction of their own reappropriations of tradition through their specific genealogical efforts. This means, of course, that there is no *a priori* centrality determined at the level of structure, simply because there is no rational foundation of History. The only 'rationality' that History might possess is the relative rationality given to it by the struggles and the concrete pragmatic-hegemonic constructions. Sorel's and Gramsci's basic intuitions ought to be radically developed with this in mind. Only thus, by lowering the ontological pretensions of Marxist categories and treating them not as the ground of History but as pragmatic and limited syntheses of a historical reality that subverts and surpasses them, will it be possible to entertain their current validity. This puts us squarely within the discussion around postmodernity from the point of view of Marxism. Two central problems are at stake. The first is that of the consequences of the collapse of the discourse of foundation from the point of view of a radical political discourse: does not this collapse lead to political nihilism, to the impossibility of giving a foundation to the political practice and critique? The second refers to the unity of the emancipatory project as conceived by the Enlightenment: does not the plurality and dispersion of the current social struggles imply its necessary abandonment as a global project?

The Process of Arguing and Common Sense

The collapse of the myth of foundations deprives History and society of an ultimate meaning, of an absolute point of departure for political reasoning in the sense of a Cartesian *cogito*. In classical ontological terms, this means that the social is groundless; if we accept the relational character of all identity, the ideal conditions of closure for a system are never achieved and therefore all identity is more or less a floating signifier. This lack of closure modifies the nature and importance of political argument in two important senses. In the first place, if an ultimate ground is posited, political argument would consist in *discovering* the action of a reality external to the argument itself. If, however, there is no ultimate ground, political argument increases in importance because, through the conviction that it can contribute, it itself *constructs*, to a certain extent, the social reality. Society can then be understood as a vast argumentative texture through which people construct their own reality.[7]

However, in a second sense, this transition from argument as discovery to argument as social construction entails a necessary modification of the *type of argument*. On the one hand, if we could take as a point of departure a foundation of the social operating as *cogito*, the argument would be of a logical or algorithmic type insofar as it would constitute a forum of judgment beyond appeal. Without such a forum, however, the argument would have the tendency to prove the *verisimilitude* of an argument rather than its truth, thus becoming pragmatic and open-ended. This brings us back to the Aristotelian notion of *phronesis*. Let us suppose that we are trying to determine if an enemy is to attack by land or by sea. Recourse to an algorithm would be to no avail; we could, however, reason that one possibility is *more likely* than the other. This greater likelihood is, in turn, determined by other arguments used on other occasions. The ensemble of arguments constitutes the texture of a group's *common sense*. And this common sense, extended in time, is what constitutes a *tradition* (of struggle, of exercise of power, etc.). Now, since this tradition is by definition open-ended – that is, ungrounded in any ultimate algorithmic certainty – it is responsive to the diverse argumentative practices that take place in society. One argument answers another, but in this process of counterargumentation, the argument itself – that is, its own identity – is itself modified in one way or another.

Here is the basis for our answer to the first question. Abandonment of the myth of foundations does not lead to nihilism, just as uncertainty as to how an enemy will attack does not lead to passivity. It leads, rather, to a proliferation of discursive interventions and arguments that are necessary, because there is no extradiscursive reality that discourse might simply reflect. Inasmuch as argument and discourse constitute the social, their open-ended character becomes the source of a greater activism and a more radical libertarianism. Humankind, having always bowed to external forces – God, Nature, the necessary laws of History – can now, at the threshold of postmodernity, consider itself for the first time the creator and constructor of its own history. The dissolution of the myth of foundations – and the concomitant dissolution of the category 'subject' – further radicalizes the emancipatory possibilities offered by the Enlightenment and Marxism.

Another objection could be raised to this withdrawal of foundations: wouldn't this eliminate any motivation for action? Are we not then in the situation, evoked by Sartre, of a chooser with no motive to choose? This, however, is not a valid objection, for the lack of foundations leads only to the affirmation that 'human' as such is an empty entity, but social agents are never 'humans' in general. On the contrary, social agents appear in concrete situations and are constituted by precise and limited discursive networks. In this sense, lack of grounding does not abolish the meaning of their acts; it only affirms their limits, their finitude, and their historicity.

Global Emancipation and Empty Signifiers

I shall now take up the second problem of whether the dispersion and plurality of social struggles dissolve the global character of the emancipatory project. To be sure, one cannot smuggle in the unity and totality of a project once one has rejected its foundation. But is unity of foundation the only form of totalizing practice in society? Are there not also totalizing effects on the level of what we have called pragmatic hegemonic practices? Remember that any identity is ambiguous insofar as it is unable to constitute itself as a precise difference within a closed totality. As such, it becomes a floating signifier whose degree of emptiness depends on the distance that separates it from its fixedness to a specific signified. (Earlier, we used 'democracy' as an example of such a signifier.) This degree of fixity of a signifier varies in inverse proportion to the extent of its circulation in a given discursive formation. The ambiguity of the signifier 'democracy' is a direct consequence of its discursive centrality; only those signifiers around which important social practices take place are subject to this systematic effect of ambiguity. (The same argument could be made for the 'imprecision' of populist symbols.)

In reality, effective ambiguity does not arise only from the attempts to fix signifiers to antagonistic discourses, although this latter case is more interesting to us. It may have a multiplicity of sources, and it can be ascribed to the phenomenon of symbolic representation. A signifier is emptied when it is disengaged from a particular signified and comes to symbolize a long chain of equivalent signifieds. This displacement and expansion of the signifying function constitute the symbol.

The relationship between a foundation and what it founds is quite different from a symbolic representation and that which is symbolized. In foundational logic there is a necessary, determining relation between the founding agency and the founded entity; in symbolic representation, on the other hand, no such internal motivation exists and the chain of equivalent signifieds can be extended indefinitely. The former is a relation of delimitation and determination, i.e. fixation. The latter is an open-ended horizon.

It is the contraposition between foundation and horizon that I think enables us to understand the change in the ontological status of emancipatory discourses and, in general, of metanarratives, in the transition from modernity to postmodernity. A formation that is unified or totalized in relation to a horizon is a formation without foundation; it constitutes itself as a unity only as it delimits itself from that which it negates. The discourses of equality and rights, for example, need not rely on a common human essence as their foundation; it suffices to posit an egalitarian logic whose limits of operation are given by the concrete argumentative practices existing in a society. A horizon, then, is an empty locus, a point in which society symbolizes its very groundlessness, in which concrete argumentative practices operate over a backdrop of radical freedom, or radical contingency. The dissolution of the myth of foundations does not dissolve the phantom of its own absence. This absence is – at least in the last third of the nineteenth century – the condition of possibility for affirming the historical validity of our projects and their radical metaphysical contingency. This double insertion constitutes the horizon of postmodern freedom, as well as the specific metanarrative of our age.

Notes

Where full details are available in the Bibliography, references contain only essential information.

1. Martin Heidegger, *Being and Time*, transl. John Macquarrie and Edward Robinson, Basil Blackwell, Oxford, 1985, p. 40.
2. *Ibid.*, p. 44.
3. The example is from J. Lyons, *Introduction to Theoretical Linguistics*, Cambridge University Press, Cambridge, 1968, p. 69.
4. It would not be correct to argue, given the functional character of the discursive, that every discursive sequence presupposes language; this is no doubt true, but language in turn also presupposes vocal cords. Thus, rather than define the abstract conditions of existence of something, we should define the structural totality in which these conditions are articulated.
5. That there are, here and there, hints of a different perspective in Marx's work is undeniable; for example, the well-known letter to Vera Zasulich on the possibilities opened up by the Russian peasant communes. But they were only hints; there can be no doubt that his thinking moved in the opposite direction.
6. Ernesto Laclau and Chantal Mouffe, *Hegemony and Socialist Strategy: Towards a radical democratic politics*, 1985.
7. As I said above, this argumentative fabric is not solely verbal; it is also interlaced with nonverbal actions to which it gives rise. Thus, every nonverbal action has meaning, and, reciprocally, every verbal argument has a performative dimension.

26 □ *The Condition of Post-Marxist Man*

André Gorz

With the specialization of jobs, the division of labour has made it possible for vast amounts of knowledge to be employed across the whole of society. The speed with which technology has advanced, the power of the productive machinery and the wealth of the industrialized nations are all a product of this process.

But each individual is master of only a minute fraction of the expanding wealth of knowledge employed. The culture of work has fragmented into thousands of tiny areas of specialized know-how and has thus been cut off from the culture of everyday life. Occupational skills provide neither the references nor the criteria which would enable people to give meaning to the world, direct its course of events and find their own direction within it. De-centred from themselves by the one-dimensional nature of their jobs and know-how, their physical existences subjected to violence, they are forced to live in an environment which is becoming steadily more dislocated and fragmented, victims of megatechnological aggression. This world, which cannot be integrated by lived experience, has nothing of a life-world; rather, it is experienced as the life-world's painful absence. Everyday life has splintered into isolated pockets of time and space, a succession of excessive, aggressive demands, dead periods and periods of routine activity. This fragmentation, which is so resistant to a lived experience of integration, is reflected in a (non-)culture of everyday life, made up of thrills, transitory fashions, spectacular entertainment and fragments of news.

History has thus dismembered what Marx's vision made whole. Marx predicted that the domination of Nature by science would enable individuals to develop a totality of capabilities *within* their work, and that thanks to this '*richest development of the individual*', '*the free self-realization of individuality*' would become a need whose satisfaction would be sought and found outside work, thanks to the 'general reduction of the necessary labour of society to a minimum'.[1]

This reduction to a minimum is already in progress: industrial societies produce increasing amounts of wealth with decreasing amounts of labour. Yet they have not

From Gorz, A., *Critique of Economic Reason*, Verso, London, 1988, pp. 91–103.

created a culture of work which, having 'fully' expanded the individuals' abilities, would allow them to develop 'freely' during their disposable time – through voluntary co-operation, scientific, artistic, educational and political activities, and so on. There is no 'social subject' culturally or politically capable of forcing through a redistribution of labour which would allow everyone to earn their living by working, yet allow them to work less and less and at the same time receive an increasing income representing their share of the increasing socially produced wealth.

Such a redistribution is, however, the only way of giving meaning to the decrease in the volume of socially necessary work. It is the only way to prevent the disintegration of society and the division of the working population itself into a number of occupational elites on the one hand, and a mass of unemployed or casually employed people on the other, and an even greater number of indefinitely interchangeable and replaceable workers in industry and, more especially, industrialized and computerized services, sandwiched between the two. It is the only way, by reducing the amount everyone works, to make skilled jobs accessible to a greater number of people; to enable those who so desire to acquire new skills and qualifications at any stage in their lives; to reduce the polarizing effect work has on the way of life, compensatory needs and personality (or depersonalization) of each individual.

Indeed, as the periods of disposable time become longer, non-working time can become something other than the obverse of working time: something other than time for rest, relaxation and recuperation; or for activities secondary and complementary to working life; or idleness – which is but the obverse of compulsory hetero-determined wage slavery; or entertainment – the counterpart of a work which, by its monotony, is anaesthetizing and exhausting. As disposable time increases, it becomes both possible and necessary to find other activities and relations to structure it, in which individuals develop their faculties in other ways, acquire other skills and lead a different sort of life. It is then possible for our jobs and workplaces to cease to be our only sources of identity and the only spaces in which socialization is possible; and for the sphere of non-work to cease to be the sphere of private life and consumerism. It becomes possible for new relations of co-operation, communication and exchange to be forged in this free time and for a new societal and cultural space, composed of autonomous activities with freely chosen aims, to be opened up. There is, then, a possible evolution towards a new relation between working time and disposable time finally reversing the present situation: it allows for autonomous activities to become more important than working life, the sphere of freedom more important than the sphere of necessity. The way we organize the time we spend living need no longer be dictated by the time we spend working; on the contrary, work must come to occupy a subordinate place within the life plan of the individual.[2]

Individuals will, then, be much more exacting about the nature, content, goals and organization of their work. They will no longer accept stupefying work or subjection to oppressive surveillance and hierarchical structures. Liberation *from* work will have produced liberation *within* work, without as much as transforming work (as Marx predicted) into free self-activity with goals of its own. In a complex society, heteronomy cannot be abolished completely, to be replaced by autonomy. It is possible, however, for tasks performed within the sphere of heteronomy itself to be reskilled, restructured and diversified – notably (though not exclusively) by allowing individuals to *self-manage their working time* – in such a way as to increase the degree of *autonomy within heteronomy*. It would be wrong, therefore, to imagine there is a clear-cut separation between autonomous activities and heteronomous work, the realm of freedom and the realm of necessity. The former does indeed have repercussions on the latter, but can never subsume it entirely.[3]

This vision of a society of liberated time, or what the German Left refers to as a 'society of culture' [*Kulturgesellschaft*] by comparison with the 'work-based society' [*Arbeitgesellschaft*], is consonant with the *ethical content* (the 'free self-realization of individuality') of the Marxian utopia. Yet there are nevertheless a number of important philosophical and political differences between the two.

Marx believed the full development of individual capacities would accompany the full development of productive forces and lead necessarily to a *revolution* (in the philosophical sense) on two levels simultaneously:

1. Individuals who were fully developed *within* their work would take control of the latter in order to assert themselves as *de jure* subjects of what they already possessed *de facto*. In other words, the freedom historical development had *given* them, in the form of a set of capacities, would take possession of itself by means of *reflexive revolution*, that is, by the subject positing itself as such. This is the meaning of the distinction Marx makes between the *full* development of *individuals* and the *free* self-realization of *individualities* in what he terms 'higher activities', activities he locates in 'disposable time'.

2. Marx sees this reflexive – and, strictly speaking, existential – revolution, through which freedom (individual existence endowed with the means of achieving autonomy) becomes an end itself, as one side of a historical dialectic whose other side is the necessity for economic revolution. As the amount of necessary labour diminishes, 'labour in the direct form [ceases] to be the great well-spring of wealth, labour time ceases and must cease to be its measure, and hence exchange value [must cease to be the measure of] use value. ... With that, production based on exchange value breaks down' and the 'free development of individualities', and the 'reduction of the necessary labour of society to a minimum' become the goal.[4]

In other words, economic rationality (and not just capitalist rationality) has gone as far as it can. It has never had any end-goal other than the most efficient possible use of available means and the most efficient possible organization of systems of means. It is an essentially instrumental form of rationality, whose end-goal is the rational functioning of systems of means, for the purpose of accumulating means (by profit-making) which will provide for even more efficient systems of resources. Its means are thus its ends and its ends are means towards other means. Economic rationality economizes the 'factors of production' – essentially time and labour – in order to re-employ them 'elsewhere in the economy', with the aim of saving time and labour, which are, in their turn, to be re-employed elsewhere. Economic rationality saves labour in pursuit of an ever-vanishing end-goal which is always out of reach, and this end-goal is never the liberation of time itself, that is, the extension of the time we have for living. The function of leisure itself is to 'create jobs', to be useful for commodity production and profitable investment.

Now, with the full development of the productive forces, this dynamic of accumulation ceases to be workable. Instrumental rationality is thrown into crisis and its fundamental irrationality becomes patent. The crisis can only be resolved by applying a new form of rationality to savings in labour, a form of rationality consistent with the only objective which can give these savings any meaning: that of making time available for these 'higher activities' which are their own ends unto themselves, at one with the movement of life itself. Such activities are no longer ones which must be rationalized so they take up less time. On the contrary, spending time doing them, not saving time, becomes the objective. The activity is its own end; it *serves* no other purpose.

It is thus as if the crisis of economic rationality were the vacant site of another form of rationality *which will give meaning to the whole of the development that precedes it*. And this other rationality is, in Marx, none other than the rationality of fully developed individuals generated by the full development of the forces of production, who take reflexive possession of themselves in order to become the subjects of what they are, that is, in order to adopt as their goal the free self-realization of their individuality. According to Marx, material development thus engenders at once its own crisis and the historical subject who will be capable of overcoming it by revealing the meaning of the contradiction concealed within this development.

Liberation *within* work is, for Marx and Marxists, particularly those in workers' organizations, the necessary prerequisite for liberation *from* work; for it is through liberation *within* work that the subject capable of desiring liberation *from* work and of giving it a meaning will be born. Hence the supreme importance Marxist authors attribute to reprofessionalized multiskilled workers, responsible for 'sovereign' and complex tasks. They have a tendency to view these workers as the historical subjects of a potential reappropriation both of the productive forces *and* of the development of the individual by the individual her- or himself.

Now this is obviously an unsustainable utopia. Even Marx's own works reveal a gross contradiction between his theory and his exceptionally astute phenomenological descriptions of the relation of worker to machinery: the alienation of the worker from the means of labour, from the product and from the knowledge embodied in the machine. Nothing in this description justifies the theory of 'attractive labour' or the appropriation (appropriability) of the totality of productive forces as a result of workers developing a totality of capabilities; and this is true for his early writings as much as for *Grundrisse* and *Capital*.

Curiously enough the same is true, as we have seen, of Kern and Schumann. Their research indicates a tendency towards restructuring and reprofessionalizing the tasks of a small minority of industrial workers, but this reprofessionalization does not justify the authors' theory of 'sovereign' workers with fully developed faculties. On the contrary, Kern and Schumann's monographs reveal that *the degree of autonomy within heteronomy* enjoyed by the workers *is what they have to struggle for*, just as the recognition of skills – the source of the workers' power in production – has always been something workers had to fight for.[5]

However, if this is the case, if liberation *within* work (which is always partial and relative) is at stake in the workers' struggle, this means *the development of the forces of production does not of itself bring about either this liberation or its historical and social subject*. In other words, individuals do not struggle for this liberation, and the full development of their faculties associated with it, because of what they are already *but because of what they aspire to be and have not become* or not yet become. And the question of why they aspire to achieve free, autonomous self-realization will not be answered as long as it is seen from the perspective adopted by Marx. For him, this question simply did not arise because his philosophy (or anti-philosophy) took the form of an inverse Hegelianism: he saw history as the process through which meaning took possession of the real, this meaning being not spirit, as it was for Hegel, but the fully developed individual becoming the master of Nature and of the process by which Nature was mastered – this individual being none other than the Universal Proletarian.[6]

This utopia is dead: whether we take Kronstadt 1920, Moscow 1928, 1930, 1935 or 1937, Berlin 1933, Treblinka 1943, Hiroshima 1945, Paris 1968, or any other date as the signal of its demise. History might end in nuclear winter, or a global Chernobyl or Bhopal; it might unfold by continually reinforcing the domination of individuals by increasingly powerful means of dominating Nature; or by developing increasingly barbaric forms of violence against the growing mass of those who have been excluded, both within the industrialized world and outside it. If we avoid all this, it will not be because history *has* a different meaning but because we will have succeeded in investing it with one. If, thanks to the liberation of time, the full development of productive forces leads to economic rationality (and its crisis) being transcended and individualities being freely developed, it will not be because this is the meaning of history but because we will have made history take on this meaning.

Everything about our freedom hangs in the balance, including that freedom itself. The condition of post-Marxist Man is that the meaning Marx read in historical development remains for us the only meaning that development can have, yet we must pursue this meaning *independently of the existence of a social class capable of realizing it*. In other words, the only non-economic, post-economic goals capable of giving meaning and value to savings in time and labour are ones individuals must discover within themselves. No historical necessity imposes on us the reflexive revolution which the defining of these goals implies. The political will capable of realizing them has no pre-existent social base and cannot rest on any particular class interest or any past, present or future tradition or norm. This political will and the moral aspirations that inform it can only draw upon themselves: their existence presupposes and will have to demonstrate *the autonomy of ethics* and *the autonomy of politics*.

It is in this sense that I propose to read the programme for the reconstruction of a European Left set out in Peter Glotz's *Manifest*.[7] The analysis which serves as his point of departure appears to be a kind of counterpoint to the *Communist Manifesto*: the third industrial revolution destroys traditional bonds of solidarity, blurs the dividing lines between classes, breaks down social and family ties and keeps propelling society towards individualization [*Individualisierungsschub*]. This may imply 'a new social mobility of isolation, a growth of opportunities or the destruction of any possibility of community, a possible liberation from the many constraints that derive from work or the family or everyday culture, but also the danger of a withdrawal from social life, the destruction of solidarity':

> The electronic civilization will eliminate millions of jobs ... but at the same time, it could bring savings not only in work but also in raw materials, energy and capital. It offers us an opportunity to go beyond a system which produces for the sake of producing, to consign to machines the unpleasant, low-status jobs and to obtain for individuals growing amounts of *disposable time*. The workers, whose lives today are determined by the rhythm of work and for whom free time is hardly more than time for 'reproduction' of their labour power, for recuperation and for entertainment, could become to an unprecedented degree sovereign masters of their own lives (and time) without having first to go through a bloody process of revolution and counter-revolution, which would give rise to such hatred that constraints would necessarily have to be maintained.[8]

However, political action cannot count on any homogeneous social base to 'force technology to give birth to such a utopia', nor, more importantly, on any large and powerful social base such as the working class represented in the age of mass production and mass workers. Those sectors in which the great size of the workforce corresponded to the economic, or even strategic, importance of the production – the political and union bastions of the traditional Left – are all in decline: mining, the steel industry, shipbuilding and the heavy industries associated with it. The key sectors in the third industrial revolution employ relatively small workforces, with a high percentage of technical and clerical staff, with no tradition of trade-union association or affiliation to a particular political party. 'The new technologies and their intelligent application do not lead to the revolutionary union of the pauperized working masses but to the segmentation and division of the workers into quasi-classes which, in accordance with the diversity of their interests, act in a highly differentiated fashion.'

Political action can only be successful if it is able to:

> create 'majorities' by bringing together groups which have no definite social anchorage.
> ... Admittedly, work will remain an important field of activity exerting its influence on
> the formation of individual identities. But increasingly powerful influences are suddenly
> emerging from other quarters. ... The question arises: will the European labour
> movement be able to maintain its influence in the centres of production and will it be
> able to extend this to the spheres of reproduction and the world of 'leisure'? Will there
> be a European Left capable of *assigning social goals* to the innovation process?[9]

The task is clear, but 'the situation is not rosy: the Left will have to put together
a coalition which brings the greatest possible number of the strong [that is, chiefly
members of what I have called the 'elite of workers'] together in solidarity with the
weak, against their own interests. For strict materialists who see interests as more
determining than ideals, the task is a paradoxical one and yet it is our task today.'[10]
It presupposes a 'highly convincing project and unshakeable audacity'.[11] It requires,
in other words, a cultural project, a vision of the future, which – as the socialist
project did – transforms moral demands and the *need to give meaning to the future*
into political energy.

This amounts to saying that the autonomy of the political is the necessary
condition for political action. The latter can no longer be based on the interests of
electoral clienteles, if we are to avoid a 'Balkanization' of political life which will
further accelerate the decomposition of society. It calls for a project of society which
transcends the sectionalization of interests because it is borne by a vision – a 'utopia'
– capable of giving *meaning* to the third industrial revolution, that is, a purpose
and an orientation born of hope. Now a political project which transcends
conflicting interests by setting societal goals (and not just social ones) necessarily
carries a high degree of moral content. This is not to say that politics and morality
coincide here, but that the necessary autonomy of the political presupposes the
autonomy of the ethical imperative if it is to call upon it.

As will have become clear, this ethical imperative – the free self-realization of
individualities through activities which have no economic rationality – does not
coincide with any form of work or trade pursuing an economic end. The subjects
embodying this imperative are not created by socially necessary production or the
peripheral activities essential to material production. Almost all trades and forms of
labour presuppose a form of specialization which, while not necessarily being either
narrow or stupefying, thwarts rather than fosters the full intellectual, physical,
aesthetic, emotional, relational and moral development of the individual.

Nevertheless, the element of autonomy within heteronomy which a growing
percentage of occupations entail is sufficient for existential autonomy to be seen as
a *possibility that is thwarted* by the way society is organized. The limited autonomy
work and modes of socialization offer individuals is sufficient to make a growing
number of them aware of their potential and *of the limits of the autonomy conceded
from them*. These limits have lost their legitimacy: they cannot be justified by the

urgency of our material needs nor by the cohesion of our disintegrating society. On the contrary, lived forms of community relations, solidarity, mutual aid and voluntary co-operation only exist on the margins of this social system and its type of rationality, thanks to the autonomous and distinterested initiatives of freely associating individuals. Similarly, many of our vital needs – unpolluted air and water, areas preserved from industrial development, foodstuffs free from chemical adulteration, non-violent care and so on – can only assert themselves by opposing the rationality of the system, in an unequal and often violent struggle against the 'functionaries' of the state/industrial megamachine.

Both limited autonomy within work on the one hand, and on the other the disintegration of society, which makes us look for alternative modes of socialization and community integration, lead to individualization and the withdrawal of individuals into the sphere of non-work activities and life outside the system. The withdrawal from political parties, trade unions and the other cumbersome organizations which seek to monopolize 'public affairs' is one aspect of this movement towards individualization. The other is the growth in popularity of religious, charitable, associative and alternative – in short, disinterested – activities.

> The desire for autonomy finds its expression in criticism of and opposition to all forms of non-legitimized hetero-determination and, at the same time, in a willingness to participate in self-organized forms of life and labour; in forms of behaviour in which other people are treated as partners, not subordinates; in the priority given to quality of life over material success and a career; and in a growing awareness of the fragility of the natural foundation of life on Earth.

Thus concludes a report by the SPD's Commission on Fundamental Values.[12]

The commission bases its findings on the results of surveys which have put the same questions to representative samples of waged workers over the past twenty years. These surveys reveal that a rapidly growing percentage of employees (about half the present number, as opposed to 29 per cent in 1962), especially those under thirty (nearly two-thirds, as opposed to 39 per cent in 1962) attach greater importance to their non-working activities than to their paid jobs. However, 80 per cent of them think their working conditions have improved in the last ten years; nearly half (but more than half the young people interviewed) consider their work 'interesting' but do not think it should dominate their lives.

Surveys in Scandinavia and Britain have made similar findings, in particular those conducted by R. E. Lane, who observes: 'One life-satisfaction study reveals that satisfaction with non-working activities contributes more to variables in the Index of Well-Being than any other item in the Account',[13] and F. Block and L. Hirschhorn, who note: 'The more time people spend outside of the paid labour force, before, after and during a work career, the more they find that work is no longer a sufficient focus for organizing their lives.'[14] Consumption and the money which makes it possible, Lane goes on to say, only have a tenuous link with the things that make people happy: autonomy, self-esteem, a happy family life, the absence of conflicts in life outside work, friendship. In other words, quality of life depends on the intensity of human bonds and cultural exchanges, relations built on friendship, love, brother- and sisterhood and mutual aid, and not on the intensity of commodity relations.[15] But this also implies that *sociological categories can no longer explain individual behaviour and motivations*. Sociology – and this is the implication of the British studies quoted above – has reached its limits. It is the autonomy of individuals which sets these limits. This nascent, as yet insecure autonomy, coveted and threatened by the cultural industries and leisure moguls, constitutes the empty space in which a renewed Left's societal project will have to be rooted, if the Left wants to remain in existence.[16]

In brief, the functionalization and technicization of work have shattered the unity of life and work. Even before the present crisis worsened, work had ceased to ensure a sufficient degree of social integration. The progressive reduction in the amount of socially necessary work available has accentuated this process and aggravated the disintegration of society. Whether it takes the form of unemployment, marginalization and lack of job security, or of a general reduction in working hours, the crisis of the work-based society (that is, based on work in the economic sense of the word) forces individuals to look outside work for sources of identity and social belonging, possibilities of achieving personal fulfilment, and activities with a purpose which enable them to acquire self-esteem and the esteem of others.

Work is set to become one activity among a number of others, of equal or greater importance. The ethic of the free self-realization of individualities, which Marx believed would be the result of a decreasingly exacting, increasingly stimulating working life, today requires individuals not to identify themselves with their work but to become more detached from it; to develop other interests and situate their paid work, their occupation, within a multidimensional vision of their existence and of society. Activities performed for economic ends are to constitute only one dimension of existence and to become less and less important.

This is precisely the direction in which the aspirations of a significant number of people are moving. The crisis of the political parties – and the rise in popularity the churches and humanitarian associations are currently enjoying – stem initially from the former's inability to offer a practical and cultural outlet for these aspirations in which their political expression could be anchored. The crisis facing political parties is not primarily a crisis *of* the political but an indication that *the political space has been left vacant* by the organizations and apparatuses that behave primarily as machines for governing through a state apparatus which it is their ambition to control. By contrast, the political is primarily located where all nascent political forces placed it in periods of ongoing change: the labour movement itself, its trade unions and political parties, grew out of cultural and mutual aid associations, that is, out of study and self-education aimed at countering the dominant ideas and culture; out of forms of life and self-organization which foreshadowed possible alternatives to the dominant way of life and social organization: a 'concrete utopia'.

Peter Glotz formulates this pre-eminence of the cultural in times of social upheaval well when he writes: 'How is the Left to achieve cultural hegemony as a preliminary to achieving political power? How is it to form from the initially growing diversity of individual political critiques a small number of ideas which people will accept, retain and assimilate as personal convictions?'[17]

A new utopia is needed if we are to safeguard what the ethical content of the socialist utopia provided: the utopia of a society of free time. The emancipation of individuals, their full development, the restructuring of society, are all to be achieved through the liberation *from* work. A reduction in working hours will allow individuals to discover a new sense of security, a new distancing from the 'necessities of life' and a form of existential autonomy which will encourage them to demand more autonomy *within* their work, political control of its objectives and a social space in which they can engage in voluntary and self-organized activities.

It is important to identify the ontological foundations of a society of free time more precisely. Why, indeed, opt for a reduction in working hours? Why use at least parts of our liberated time to take over certain service activities currently provided by public or commercial bodies, on a voluntary, self-organized, co-operative basis? Why not instead turn the activities people somehow or other traditionally did for themselves into professional, paid ones? Why not get professional specialists in childminding and mothering to look after our children right from the moment they are born; professional employees in the tourist, culture and leisure industries to look after our ever-younger pensioners; professional home-helps to look after the aged; professional comforters and consolers to look after the dying? Why not adopt Alfred Sauvy's proposal and draw up an inventory of all our needs and potential demands, give them cash value and create jobs capable of satisfying them? Would this not provide virtually inexhaustible 'sources of employment'? Are not the possibilities of increasing our needs and, consequently, the potential growth of commercial exchanges and employment, unlimited? Why not admit that work done in the domestic sphere (the so-called sphere of reproduction) is socially useful, provide a wage for it and, as Barry Jones has proposed, view housewives as part of the labour force and housework as employment in the 'primary sector', essentially concerned with the endless satisfaction of endlessly recurring needs (for example, the provision of food and amusement, tasks related to sexual activity, etc.)?[18]

The answer to these questions is not to be found purely in political decisions or social and economic expediency; no more than in the values of the pre-modern tradition from which Reason was to liberate as by making us adopt those solutions which were most rational and most expedient. Rational in respect of what ends? Are there not, above and beyond inherited values and practical expediency, other types of rationality – indeed, limits to all possible types of rationalization and socialization – consonant with the ontological multidimensionality of existence?

Notes

1. Karl Marx, *Grundrisse*, Harmondsworth, 1973, pp. 541, 611, 706.
2. On this topic, see Oskar Negt, *Lebendige Arbeit, enteignete Zeit*, Frankfurt am Main, 1984, pp. 167, 178; and Peter Glotz, *Manifest für eine neue europäische Linke*, Berlin, 1985, pp. 54, 92.
3. Cf. André Gorz. *Farewell to the Working Class*, 1982, pp. 94, 102–4 and 107–9, where I follow Adret (*Travailler deux heures par jour*, Paris, 1977) and, more especially, Charly Boyadjian, in emphasizing this fact – which runs counter to the argument certain hasty readers have attributed to me, according to which there would be a clear-cut opposition between the two spheres.
4. Marx, pp. 705–6.
5. On this topic, see the excellent and still relevant article by Antonio Lettieri, secretary of the CGIL, 'Factory and school', in André Gorz, ed., *The Division of Labour*, Hassocks, 1976.
6. Cf. Gorz, *Farewell to the Working Class*, ch. 1, in which this analysis is set out in detail.
7. Glotz, *Manifest* passim.
8. *Ibid.*, pp. 34–5.
9. *Ibid.*, pp. 35–6.
10. *Ibid.*, p. 37.
11. *Ibid.*, p. 44.
12. Erhard Eppler (ed.), *Grundwerte für ein neues Godesberger Programm*, Reinbek bei Hamburg, 1984, ch. 5, particularly pp. 111–26.
13. R. E. Lane, 'Market and the satisfaction of human wants', *Journal of Ecnomic Issues*, 12 (1977), 815.
14. F. Block and L. Hirschhorn, 'New productive forces and the contradictions of contemporary capitalism: A post-industrial perspective', *Theory and Society*, 7 (1979), 373. These quotations are taken from the remarkable essay by Claus Offe 'Arbeit als soziologische Schlüsselkategorie?', in *'Arbeitsgesellschaft': Strukturprobleme und Zukunftsperspektiven*, Frankfurt/New York, 1984.
15. All this, of course, runs counter to the idea that the corresponding activities must be professionalized and commercialized in order to 'create jobs'.
16. This is the essence of Alain Touraine's research and the reason why this research is located at the frontiers of sociology, in an area ignored by political parties.
17. Glotz, *Die Arbeit der Zuspitzung*, Berlin, 1984, p. 7.
18. Barry Jones, *Sleepers, Wake! Technology and the Future of Work*, Melbourne and Oxford, 1983, pp. 51–2.

27 □ *Toward a Principle of Evil*

Jean Baudrillard

Do these fatal strategies exist? It does not appear that I have described them, nor even touched upon them. The power of the real over the imagination is so great that such a hypothesis appears to be no more than a dream. Where do you get the stories you tell about the object? Objectivity is the opposite of fatality. The object is real, and the real is subject to laws, and that is that.

There it is: faced with a delirious world, only the ultimatum of realism will do. Which means that if you wish to escape the world's insanity, you must sacrifice all of its charm as well. By increasing its delirium, the world has raised the stakes of the sacrifice, blackmailed by reality. Today, in order to survive, illusion no longer works; one must draw nearer to the nullity of the real.

There is perhaps one, and only one, fatal strategy: theory. And undoubtedly the only difference between a banal theory and a fatal theory is that in the former the subject always believes itself to be more clever than the object, while in the latter the object is always taken to be more clever, more cynical, more ingenious than the subject, which it awaits at every turn. The metamorphoses, tactics, and strategies of the object exceed the subject's understanding. The object is neither the subject's double nor his or her repression; neither the subject's fantasy nor hallucination; neither the subject's mirror nor reflection: but it has its own strategy. It withholds one of the rules of the game which is inaccessible to the subject, not because it is deeply mysterious, but because it is endlessly ironic.

An objective irony watches over us, it is the object's fulfillment without regard for the subject, nor for its alienation. In the alienation phase, subjective irony is triumphant. Here the subject constitutes an unsolvable challenge to the blind world that surrounds him. Subjective irony, ironic subjectivity, is the finest manifestation of a universe of prohibition, of Law and of desire. The subject's power derives from a promise of fulfillment, whereas the realm of the object is characterized by what is fulfilled, and for that reason it is a realm we cannot escape.

From Poster, M. (ed.), *Selected Writings*, Polity Press, Cambridge/Stanford University Press, Stanford, CA, 1958, pp. 198–206.

We confuse the fatal with the resurgence of the repressed (desire as that which is inescapable), but the order of fatality is antithetical to that of repression. It is not desire that we cannot escape, but the ironic presence of the object, its indifference, and its indifferent interconnections, its challenge, its seduction, its violation of the symbolic order (therefore of the subject's unconscious as well, if it had one). In short, it is the principle of Evil we cannot escape.

The object disobeys our metaphysics, which has always attempted to distill the Good and filter Evil. The object is translucent to Evil. This is why it appears, maliciously and diabolically, to be so voluntarily cooperative, and to bend willingly, like nature, to whatever law we may impose, thus violating all legislation. When I refer to the object, and to its fundamental duplicity, I am referring to all of us and to our social and political order. The whole problem of voluntary servitude is to be reexamined in this light, not to resolve it, but to anticipate the enigma; obedience is, in effect, a banal strategy, which need not be explained, for it secretly contains, every obedience secretly contains, a disobedience fatal to the symbolic order.

Herein lies the principle of Evil, not in some mystical agency or transcendence, but as a concealment of the symbolic order, the abduction, rape, concealment and ironic corruption of the symbolic order. It is in this way that the object is translucent to the principle of Evil: as opposed to the subject, it is a bad conductor of the symbolic order, yet a good conductor of the fatal, that is, of pure objectivity, sovereign and irreconcilable, immanent and enigmatic.

Moreover, Evil is not what is interesting; it is the spiraling of the worst that is interesting. The principle of Evil is indeed reflected in the subject's misfortune, in his or her mirror, but the object desires to be worst, it claims the worst. This represents a more radical negativity, which means, if all things eventually violate the symbolic order, that everything will have been diverted at its origin.

Prior to being produced, the world was seduced. A strange precession, which today still weighs heavily on all reality. The world was contradicted at its origin: it is therefore impossible ever to verify it. Negativity, whether historical or subjective, is nothing: the original diversion is truly diabolical, even in thought.

The vertigo of simulation, the Luciferian rapture in the eccentricity of the origin and the end, contrasts with the Utopia of the Last Judgement, the complement of original baptism. Which is why gods can only live and hide in the inhuman, in objects and beasts, in the realm of silence and objective stupefaction, and not in the human realm, that of language and subjective stupefaction. A human-god is an absurdity. A god who throws off the ironic mask of the inhuman, who abandons the bestial metaphor and the objective metamorphosis where, in silence, it embodied the principle of Evil, providing itself a soul and a face, simultaneously assumes the hypocrisy of human psychology.

We must be just as respectful of the inhuman as certain cultures, which we have therefore labeled fatalistic. We condemn them without further recourse because they obtained their commandments on the side of the inhuman, from the stars or the animal god, from constellations or a divinity without image. A divinity without image – what a grand idea. Nothing could be more opposed to our modern and technical iconolatry.

Metaphysics allows only the good radiations to filter through; it wants to make the world a mirror of the subject (having himself or herself passed the mirror stage), a world of forms distinct from its double, from its shadow, from its image: that is the principle of Good. Here the object is always the fetish, the false, the *feticho*, the factitious, the delusion – all that embodies the abominable integration of a thing and its magical and artificial double, and which no religion of the transparent or of the mirror will ever come to resolve: this is the principle of Evil.

When I speak of the object and of its fatal strategies I am speaking of a person and of his or her inhuman strategies. For example, a human being can find a much deeper boredom while on vacation than in daily life – boredom intensified by the fact that it contains all the elements of happiness and recreation. The important point is that vacation is predestined to boredom, along with the bitter and triumphant premonition of being unable to escape it. How can one imagine that people would repudiate their everyday life in search of an alternative? On the contrary, they make it their destiny: by intensifying it in the appearances of the contrary; by submerging themselves to the point of ecstasy; and by fixating monotony in an even greater one. Super-banality is the equivalent of fatality.

If we do not understand this, we will understand nothing of this collective stupefaction, even though it is a grand act of transcendence. I am not joking: people are not looking to amuse themselves, they seek a fatal diversion. Not matter how boring, the important thing is to increase boredom; such an increase is salvation, it is ecstasy. It can be the ecstatic amplification of just about anything. It may be the increase of oppression or abjection that acts as the liberating ecstasy of abjection, just as the absolute commodity is the liberating form of commodity. This is the only solution to the problem of 'voluntary servitude', and moreover, this is the only form of liberation: the amplification of negative conditions. All forms that tend to advertise a miraculous freedom are nothing but revolutionary homilies. The logic of liberation, essentially, is heard only by a few, and for the most part, a fatal logic prevails.

This will to spectacle and illusion, in contrast to every will to knowledge and power, is another form of fundamental cynicism. It is alive in the hearts of people, but haunts just as well the processes of events. In the raw event, in objective information, and in the most secret acts and thoughts, there is something like a drive to revert to the spectacle, or to climax on stage instead of producing oneself originally. To manifest one's being is necessary; to be enraptured is absolutely vital.

Things only occur under these extreme circumstances; that is, not under the constraint of representation, but through the magic of their effect – only here do they appear ingenious, and offer themselves the luxury of existence. Although we maintain that nature is indifferent, and it is certainly so to the passions and enterprises of people, perhaps it isn't when it makes a spectacle of itself in natural catastrophes. Catastrophe is a parable(?), which is there to signify this passion of passions, a simulating passion, a seductive passion, a diverting passion, where things are only meaningful when transfigured by illusion, by derision, by a staging that is in no way representational; only meaningful in their exceptional form, in their eccentricity, in the will to scorn their causes and extinguish themselves in their effects, and particularly in their form of disappearance. Moralists of all times have strictly condemned this exceptional form, because things here cynically divert from their origin and their end, in a distant echo of the original sin.

Nevertheless, this eccentricity is what protects us from the real, and from its disastrous consequences. The fact that things extinguish themselves in the spectacle, in a magical and artificial fetishization, is a distortion serious thinkers will always combat, under the Utopian banner of expunging the world in order to deliver it exact, intact, and authentic on the day of the Last Judgement. But this is perhaps the lesser evil, since God knows where the unleashing of meaning will lead when it refuses to produce itself as appearance.

Even revolution can take place only if there is the possibility of spectacle; what people of goodwill deplore is that the media have put an end to the real event. But if we take the example of the nuclear threat, it may be that its distillation in the simulated panic of our daily life, in the spectacular obsessions and thrills that feed our fear, and not the balance of terror (there is no strategic guarantee in deterrence, nor is there, in fact, any instinct of self-preservation), is what protects us from nuclear confrontation. What protects us is that in nuclear war the event is likely to eliminate the possibility of the spectacle. *This is why it will not take place.* For humanity can accept physical annihilation, but cannot agree to sacrifice the spectacle (unless it can find a spectator in another world). The drive to spectacle is more powerful than the instinct of preservation, and it is on the former that we must rely. [1]

If the morality of things is in their sacrosanct use of value, then long live the immorality of the atom and of weapons so that even they are subject to the ultimate and cynical terms of the spectacle! Hail the secret rule of the game whereby all things disobey the symbolic law! What will save us is neither the rational principle nor use value, but the immoral principle of the spectacle, the ironic principle of Evil.

To become absorbed in this second outcome is a sort of passion, a sort of fatal will. Likewise, no life can be conceived without the existence of a second chance. A purpose in life can only be ascertained by the strong certainty of a necessary return, sooner or later, of certain moments or faces that once appeared, like the resurrection of bodies, but without a Last Judgement. They will return, they have only temporarily disappeared from the horizon of our life, whose trajectory, specifically diverted by these events, curves sufficiently, and unconsciously, to provide them with the opportunity for a second existence, or a final return. Only then will they have truly lived. Only then will they have been won or lost.

From a certain time, these second events constitute the very guidelines of life, where things thus no longer occur by chance. It is the first event that occurs by chance, having no meaning in itself and losing itself in the banal night of experience. Only by redoubling itself does it become an actual event, thereby attaining the character of a day of reckoning – like a sign that would only be valid redoubled by its ascendant. The sign itself is indifferent; redoubled it becomes ineluctable.

Once certain life events have had their second chance, when the cycle has returned them once, and only once, then that life is completed. If a life is not given the opportunity of a second chance, it is finished before it has begun.

The fatal is there somewhere. In this sense, ancient heresies were right. Everyone has the right to a second birth, the real one, and everyone is predestined, not by astral decree, but rather by an internal predestination, one that is imminent in our own lives: the necessary return of certain events. This is why, once chance is abolished, the Last Judgement is unnecessary.

This is why the theory of predestination is infinitely superior to the theory of the freedom of the soul. Since, if one eliminates from life only that which is destined, but not predestined, everything that occurs only once is accidental, whereas that which is accomplished a second time becomes fatal. Predestination provides life with the intensity of these second events, which appear to have the depth of a previous life.

A first encounter has neither form nor meaning, it is always tainted by misunderstanding and banality. Fatality only comes after, by the present undertakings of a previous life. And, in this instance, there is a kind of will and energy, which no one knows anything about, and which is not the resurgence of a hidden order, not at all. It is in the full light of day that certain things come to their designated dead end.

If the stars would rise and set in any order, even the sky would be meaningless. Their recurrent trajectory makes the sky eventful. And the recurrence of certain fatal episodes makes life eventful.

Consequently, if the object is ingenious, if the object is fatal, what is to be done?

Does the ironic art of disappearance succeed the art of survival? The subject has always dreamed of disappearance: it is the converse of his or her dream of totalization; yet the one has never been able to suppress the other – quite the opposite. This failure currently arouses more subtle passions.

Is the insistent desire of fatal strategies thus at the heart of banal strategies?

Nothing can insure us against fatality, much less provide us with a strategy. Also, the conjunction of the two terms is paradoxical: how can there be fate if there is strategy? But precisely: the enigma is that fate is at the heart of every strategy; this is what emerges as a fatal strategy at the heart of most banal strategies. It is the object whose fate would be a strategy – like the rule of some other game. In fact, the object mocks the laws we decorate it with. It agrees to appear in our calculations as a sarcastic variable and to let the equations verify themselves. But no one knows the rules of the game, the conditions under which one accepts to play, and these may change all of a sudden.

No one knows what a strategy is. There are not enough means in the world to have the ends at our disposal. Thus no one is capable of articulating a final process. God himself is forced to tinker [*bricoler*]. What is interesting is the inexorable logical process that emerges whereby the object plays the very game we want it to play, and in a way it doubles the ante. By outbidding the strategic constraints we have imposed on it, the object institutes a strategy without finality, a 'dynamic' strategy that thwarts the subject's strategy; a fatal strategy, since the subject succumbs to the transgression of his own objectives.

We are accomplice to the object's excess of finality (it may be the excess of meaning, and thus the inability to decipher a single word, which is so effective at signaling us). Every strategy we invent is in the hope that it will unfold unexpectedly. We invent the real in the hope of seeing it unfold as a great ruse. From every object we seek a blind response that will disrupt our projects. From strategy we expect control, but from seduction we hope for surprise.

Seduction is fatal. It is the effect of a sovereign object which re-creates within us the original disturbance and seeks to surprise us. Fatality in turn is seductive, like the discovery of an unknown rule of the game. Discovering a rule of the game is wonderful and it compensates in advance for the most bitter losses.

Hence the phenomenon of wit. If I seek a fatal progression in language I confront the witticism, which is itself the dénouement of language that is immanent in language (this is the fatal: the same sign overseeing the crystallization and the solution of a life, the intricacies and the dénouement of an event). In language that has become pure object, irony (in Freud's *Jokes and their Relation to the Unconscious*) is the objective form of this dénouement. As in *Jokes*, redoubling and outbidding are always a spiritual form of dénouement.

Everything must unfold in the fatal and spiritual mode, just as everything was entangled in the beginning by an original diversion.

Even predestination is a form of the ironic diversion of fate, but then so too is chance. What is the point of turning chance into an objective process, since it is an ironic process? Of course it exists, but in contrast to everything scientific; it exists as the irony of risk, even at the level of the molecule. And of course fatality exists as well, simultaneously – there is no paradox here. The difference is that the irony of fate is greater than the irony of chance, which makes it more tragic and more seductive.

It is true that there is an obscure and difficult side to this: to pass on the side of the object, to take the side of the object. One must look for another rule, another axiomatic: there is nothing mystical here, no otherworldly delirium of a subjectivity entrapped and fleeing forward in a descriptive paroxysm. Simply to outline this other logic, to unfold these other strategies, to leave the field open for objective irony, is also a challenge, possibly absurd, and one which runs the risk of what it describes – but the risk is to be taken: hypothesizing the fatal strategy can only be fatal as well.

If there is morality, it is also caught in the eccentric cycle of its effects, it is itself hypermorality, just as the real is hyperreal. This is no longer moral stasis, but moral ecstasy. It is in itself a special effect.

Lévi-Strauss once claimed that the symbolic order had withdrawn to the benefit of history. Today, says Canetti, even history has retreated. What is left then but to pass over to the side of the object, to its affected and eccentric effects, to its fatal effects (fatality is merely the absolute freedom of effects)? Semiorrhage.

These days when all critical radicalism has become pointless, when all negativity is resolved in a world that pretends to be fulfilled, when critical thought has found in socialism a secondary home, when the effect of desire has long since gone, what is left but to return things to their enigmatic ground zero? The enigma has been inverted, however: previously it was the Sphinx who put to man the question about man, one which Oedipus is thought to have resolved, one which all of us thought we resolved. Today it is man who puts to the Sphinx, to the inhuman, the question of the inhuman, of the fatal, of the world's indifference to our endeavors and to objective laws. The object (the Sphinx) is more subtle and does not answer. But, by disobeying laws and thwarting desire, it must answer secretly to some enigma. What is left but to go over to the side of this enigma?

Everything finally boils down to this: let us for once hypothesize that there is a fatal and enigmatic bias in the order of things.

In any case there is something stupid about our present situation. There is something stupid in the raw event, to which destiny, if it exists, cannot help but be sensitive. There is something stupid in the current forms of truth and objectivity, from which a superior irony must give us leave. Everything is expiated in one way or another. Everything proceeds in one way or another. Truth only complicates things.

And if the Last Judgement consists, as everyone knows, in saving and eternalizing one moment of life, and only one, for each of us, with whom do we share this ironic end?

Note

1. Of course this is no longer the same spectacle situationists denounced as the height of alienation and the ultimate strategy of capital. It would instead be the opposite, for it is the case here of the victorious strategy of the object, its mode of diversion, and not of being diverted. This is much closer to the enchantment [*féerie*] of commodities described by Baudelaire.

Part Seven

Feminism

Introduction

According to one reading of Baudrillard, feminism, as an opposition to patriarchy, would be precisely the 'inoculation' upon which masculinism thrives and continues to sustain itself. If this is the case, then perhaps the most radical thing possible for feminism would be for women to adopt the position of the Object via seduction, thereby seducing masculinism and the patriarchal male towards such an 'objectal' condition. Clearly, for many feminists, such a suggestion is nothing less than outrageous, yet it does serve the purpose of indicating how austere and severe the question of postmodernism might be for feminism. For many, the theory and practice of feminism has been a means precisely of extending the successes and critiquing the failures of a Marxist discourse of liberation; and to this extent, feminism has opened various ways out of the deadlock of much Marxist thinking – just as postmodernism has also done. But feminism and postmodernism are not always easy allies, as the essays gathered here show.

One highly influential strand in contemporary feminism is that initially advanced by Julia Kristeva, who rebelled in her work against the monolithic and totalising procedures of formalist 'theory', turning instead to the historical practicalities and 'accidents' of the 'speaking Subject' and away from the system of linguistics. The totalising impetus of the system of linguistics itself – systematicity or, perhaps better, 'theory' – is seen as part of the masculinist framework which disables the possibility of a genuine feminist emancipation. To the extent that such thinking has had an enormous influence, so feminism can be seen as having already attained to the 'anti-foundationalist' strand so common among advocates of postmodernist philosophy in general. Yet if one is to be anti-foundational here, then the foundation of a politics or of a general life-practice based upon the differences of gender, and upon the social inflection of those differences, also begins to be lost. Feminism, in adopting the postmodern position readily, might also thereby deconstruct and indeed even eradicate itself, sawing the branch or pedestal upon which it sits precisely at the moment when it has managed, finally, to seize the saw in the first place.

It is precisely in this ground that Morris's piece included here makes its argument. Fundamentally, what has happened is that the discourse of postmodernism has itself been constructed upon a foundation which has systematically excluded women. As a result, feminism is now invited to situate itself 'in relation to' an already existing postmodernism. But by rehabilitating the founding work of feminism in the area of cultural debate, it becomes possible to reverse these priorities and to frame

postmodernism within a larger debate, the debate around feminism. The effect of
this would be to transform the postmodern debate. Morris is careful to indicate that
such transformation is not 'sufficient to, or coextensive with' the necessary tasks of
feminist struggle; simply, it is a vital part of such struggle, and one which enables
feminism to be heard, and not simply to be accommodated within an already
existing masculinism – or within a silently gendered postmodernism.

In recent times a certain tendency has emerged in some cultural discourse to argue
that feminism has been successful, that the basic advances have been made, and that
therefore the struggle – like the political struggle in general – is 'over': the so-called
'end of history' is deemed to include the 'end of women's history' as well. Many
would dispute this, in the same way as they might dispute the fact that the work
of 'modernity' is also complete; yet within feminism, the argument that much
remains to be done and that the struggle continues in as necessary a manner as ever
before does not necessarily go hand in hand with argument for the continuation of
philosophical modernity.

Feminists, at least since the work of Irigaray, have been suspicious of a 'universal
reason', for they have been made aware that rationality can itself be gendered in such
a way as silently to exclude women from the field of 'reasonable' behaviour. Further,
feminism has often been made profoundly aware of the difficulties of attaining to
the position of a historical Subject, either as the Subject of historical agency or even
as the Subject of consciousness. Given these states of affairs, feminism might
welcome certain aspects of a postmodern philosophy, suspicious of universals,
problematising the Subject, as an attack being made on a different front from that
engaged directly by feminism. The incipient 'pluralism' of postmodernism, however,
is not necessarily an ally, as Lovibond indicates here. In her stringent analysis of
what is at stake in such pluralism, Lovibond outlines the terms of a dilemma for
postmodernism in regard to its relation to feminism: 'either it can concede the
necessity, in terms of the aims of feminism, of "turning the world upside down" ...
thereby opening a door once again to the Enlightenment idea of a total
reconstruction of society on rational lines', or it can reject such an idea, 'thereby
licensing the cynical thought that, here as elsewhere, "who will do what to whom
under the new pluralism is depressingly predictable"'.

Fraser and Nicholson also ponder the sometimes fraught relations between
feminism and an interloping postmodernism. For them, a specific task is the
reconciliation of an ostensibly logically respectable philosophical position (of an
incredulity towards metanarratives) with a political demand for the necessity of
grounded action (the 'social-critical power of feminism'). Against Lyotard, they take
the line that it is not necessary to give up on the analysis of social macrostructures
even at a moment when one doubts a 'universal' history. It is perfectly possible to
be 'theoretical' while attending to the local. Here, a certain pragmatism appears, and
with it an acknowledgement of fallibility. Once again, there is a vigorous struggle
to retain the possibility of action under the form of a kind of 'weakening'.

Jardine's argument, in the chapter from *Gynesis* included here, is one which
fundamentally considers the postmodern in terms of a rethinking of modernity:

specifically, she opens the way to analysis of the intricate relations among the ideological triad truth–modernity–woman, organised around a key question of the status of 'experience', whose demise in twentieth-century philosophy is double-edged for feminism. The current rethinking of empiricism within postmodernising discourse is itself here properly situated within already existing feminist questions and debates.

The pieces collected here are testimony to the statement by Fraser and Nicholson that 'Feminism and postmodernism have emerged as two of the most important political-cultural currents of the last decade'; their interrelations will continue that situation for decades to come.

28 □ *Feminism, Reading,*
Postmodernism

Meaghan Morris

Some time in the early 1970s, a Women's Film Festival in Sydney tried to screen Nelly Kaplan's film *La Fiancée du pirate* (*A Very Curious Girl*, 1969). It was not a great success. One reel turned out to be unsubtitled and, if I remember rightly, the reels were screened out of order. At the time, this seemed like an omen against the use in feminist cinema of large narrative structures – then in question, in theory, as being somehow intrinsically 'male'. As images of a women's truth, eloquent in any order, the festival documentaries and expressive experimental shorts proved more resistant to accidents of context than Kaplan's tightly organized fiction.

Nevertheless, Kaplan's film made a profound impression on many women in the audience, and I have never forgotten it. I have also never been able to see it again – so it has acquired in my memory the abstraction of a multipurpose myth. It was certainly a fable. Kaplan's 'fiancée' lived on the edge of a village with her goods and chattels, her goat, and her bit of high-tech – a tape recorder. She makes money from men, and from cleaning. In town, the villagers spurn her and fear her because of her reputation and her sharp, insolent tongue. But in her house, the village men confide in her, depend on her, trust her (while allowing increasingly vicious attacks on her establishment). But she has saved their money, and with her recorder she has saved their words. One day she leaves: and as she sets off on the road, she leaves behind a village listening in horror not to the voice of the curious girl, but to its own most intimate secrets and confessions – playing loudly, in public, for all to hear.

As an allegory of vengeance and liberation, *La Fiancée du pirate* could be read as an improvement on another text popular in the enthusiastically uncompromising ambience of the early women's movement – the Brecht–Weill song from *The Threepenny Opera*, 'Pirate Jenny'. As a cleaning-woman's dream of being recognized as a pirate queen, possessing a secret knowledge that will give her the power to humiliate and destroy everyone who has ever humiliated her, 'Pirate Jenny' was often savoured straight as a bloodthirsty declaration of feminist utopian desires. But it maintains an ambivalent edge. 'Pirate Jenny' is Polly's song, an embedded

From Morris, M., *The Pirate's Fiancée*, Verso, London, 1988, pp. 1–23.

fiction of a fantasy, and she sings it at her wedding to MacHeath. Polly presents 'Pirate Jenny' as an 'imitation' of another woman posed as distant from herself. Jenny lives in a squalor that Polly pretends to transcend; Polly has actually married her bandit, while Jenny's is always about to arrive. But Polly's dream of action, just like Jenny's, is limited to waiting and watching till her ship comes in – commanded by a masculine saviour. Even her act of mimesis as Jenny is severely restricted. At the end of the song, Mac publicly praises Polly's 'art' to the other men – but then tells her in an undertone, 'I don't like you play-acting; let's not have any more of it'. [1]

Kaplan's narrative did away with the pirate, as well as with the heroine's oppressors. It also substituted, for Jenny's grim vision of having everyone massacred, a much more subtle form of poetic – and pragmatic – justice. The village society is undone by the broadcast of its own presuppositions, and the village economy is wrecked by an intensification of its own exploitative logic.

Kaplan's fiancée doesn't dream of waiting for her hero to arrive on stage in a moment of revolutionary rapture. She makes do herself by acting critically upon her everyday conditions of existence – to transform her position within them. She is not reduced to silence after her own 'play-acting'. Instead of performing another woman, she plays herself; then shifts from performer to director when she 'stages', by borrowing and quoting in an altered context, the voices of her former masters. It is their everyday conduct that is now framed as 'play-acting' – and after the performance there can't be any more of it in quite the same old way.

It was only some years after seeing *La Fiancée du pirate* that it became possible for me to think about Kaplan's achievement in quite those terms. At the time, the discussion was mainly about 'images of women', 'distribution of gender roles', and 'reflection of class position'. Those terms worked very well for debating the logic of the fiction, but by eluding (at least as we used them) the question of the practice of narration, they encouraged a hasty jump to debating (not for the first time in the history of modern aesthetics) whether such 'fiction' was generally *desirable*. However, work by feminist writers engaging with these issues, and with the history of aesthetics, soon provided a framework in which Kaplan's film could be read not only as a fable of political action, but as a political act of transforming fables (a song from *The Threepenny Opera*, but also a store of legends about witches, wicked women and outcast girls). For example, this passage from Anne Freadman's analysis of George Sand's *Indiana* in 'Sandpaper':

My major methodological presupposition will be that any text is a rewriting of the field or fields of its own emergence, that to write, to read, or to speak is first of all to turn other texts into discursive material, displacing the enunciative position from which those materials have been propounded. I mean that 'use' can always do something a little different from merely repeating 'usage'. In an attempt to do something towards specifying 'women's writing', I shall suppose that it is in the business of transforming discursive material that, in its untransformed state, leaves a woman no place from which to speak, or nothing to say. [2]

Freadman goes on to suggest that 'the production of a speaking-position, with respect to discursive material that is both given and foreign' can be studied by a 'feminist formalism'. Her own paper, in turn, can be read in this way. For example, by analysing the novel *Indiana* as a set of rhetorical and generic strategies rewriting the material of two discourses – the story of Don Juan, and the myth of the Muse – Freadman is able to produce a position from which the 'George Sand' of the history books ('prolix and repetitive when she is not just telling a good story, and when she is, a downright embarrassment to the modernist critic')[3] can be rewritten for a feminist literary *history*.

So she too transforms two discourses: one an essentialist theory of 'women's writing', the other a polemic against 'formalism'. The former, insisting on biological authorship as a source of meanings, threatens to leave a feminist *formalist* with nothing to say. If we reject 'femininity' as an *a priori* of feminist criticism, then 'how (it may well be asked) could feminist criticism select a corpus of women's writing?'[4] Freadman's response is to say that the woman writer *is* a given – but a given in (and by) discourse. 'I can read that discourse, and rewrite it.' This move in turn allows Freadman to transform an opposition between 'history' and 'form' that might leave a *feminist* formalist no place from which to speak. Since her rewriting of 'George Sand' as a discursive object involves a history of transformations produced in 'social conditions of some specificity', then Freadman's formalism could not be opposed to a political practice of reading and writing. On the contrary it would be one of the enabling conditions for such a practice. It is a way of writing a political history, as well as a theory, of how changes may take place in particular circumstances.

'Formalism' is still (like 'fiancée') a discomfiting term,[5] never easily disentangled from memories of the history of its uses. Many theorists now prefer to avoid it, rather than rewrite it, confining it to the museum of dead terms sometimes revisited by those renewing their own speaking-position as always already 'beyond'. In beginning this introduction by rereading a film and an essay that have been important to my work over several years, it would perhaps be easier now to situate both of them in the field of postmodernism, and in recent debates about appropriation, strategies of quotation, revision, mimicry, and, for that matter, of image and discourse *piracy* (or, more recently, 'poaching').

Indeed, in reading over again those texts that not only made me want to write about them, but changed the ways that I wanted to read, it occurred to me that much the same move of relocation 'in' postmodernism could easily be imposed on the project of Michèle Le Doeuff's *L'Imaginaire philosophique*. Le Doeuff's essays develop a number of themes about femininity, pleasure and power, the politics of 'style', the limitations of *philosophical* Reason, the work of figuration in discourse, the function of Other-ness in meta-discourse, and the complexity[6] of historical relations between a philosophical imaginary and popular culture – themes that have become key reference-points for 'postmodernism' insofar as that term defines a place for making generalizations about the stakes of otherwise disparate debates.

L'Imaginaire philosophique also develops a theory of quotation (and a practice of reading differences between particular acts of quoting) that moves away from the mourning and melancholia associated with quotation by Susan Sontag (for the context of photography) and Jean Baudrillard (in his myth of the simulacrum).[7] Her intricate analyses of how the act of referring to a previous 'image' can *work* in philosophy to formulate, solve or banish problems can then provide the more useful methodological precedent for thinking about much insistently lively contemporary art and commercial cinema. And her own practice of essay writing can be read as a transformation of the specific discourses she addresses in criticism – a subtle transformation, but one no less substantial than those performances of a 'feminine' writing in whose play she declines to participate.

But if it would be easy to re-present Le Doeuff's work in this way to produce a postmodern image, it is not so easy to say what would be gained by ignoring the specificity of its moves between the history of philosophy on the one hand, and the discourses of feminism on the other. It is her critical analysis of the function of images in both of them, and between them, that makes the politics of her writing make sense.

In the same way, it is significant for me that the precision of Anne Freadman's project is matched by few of the non-'formalist' theories of a strategic rewriting of cultural materials (from pop analyses of bricolage and recoding to Jean-François Lyotard's revision of the theory of language-games) that have been so influential in recent years. One problem now emerging as a result is that as the *terms* of such analyses become commodified to the point of becoming dated ('strategy', 'bricolage' and 'recoding' have the aura of the remainder sale about them now, too old to surprise, too new to seduce ...), they offer little resistance to the wearing effects of overuse. When any and every text can be read indifferently as another instance of 'strategic rewriting', another illustration of an established general principle, something more (and something more specific) is needed to argue how and why a particular event of rewriting might matter.

In this context, it is worth revisiting Barthes's comment in *Mythologies* 'that a little formalism turns one away from History, but that a lot brings one back to it'.[8] The history I want to return to here is one in which the question of rewriting 'discourses' emerges from a political critique of the social positioning of women. Just as a transformation of the meaning of a woman's 'play-acting' occurs in Kaplan's fiction as a solution to a local experience of sexual and class oppression (*and* as an alternative to the melancholy romance of Pirate Jenny's dream), so too, I think, does Freadman's feminist formalism depend on the political projects of the women's movement for its insistence that we say what *kinds* of discursive changes will matter, why, and for whom. In this way, the notion of a 'textual strategy' cannot become a sort of free-floating aesthetic ideal, interchangeable with any other general concept of action or a vague thematics of 'doing something'. On the contrary: 'strategy' here is a value that not only refers to and derives from the political discourses of feminism, but remains open to revision *by* them.

So rather than resituate *La Fiancée du pirate* and 'Sandpaper' in relation to postmodernism, I prefer initially to make a framework of introduction by relating them to each other like this: both can be read as 'formalist' practices in Freadman's sense; both are in the business of transforming discursive material that otherwise 'leaves a woman no place from which to speak, or nothing to say'. Both therefore actively assume that the movement of women to a position of power in discourse is a political necessity, and a *practical* problem.

It doesn't follow that I think their methods and interests are the same. It doesn't follow that, in making connections between a narrative film about a village outcast and an academic essay about reading women's writing, I would then rush on to an analogy between prostitutes, witches and academic feminist critics, or conflate a film or an essay with the social conditions that they may refer to or discuss. And it dosen't follow for one moment that I consider the activity of 'transforming discursive material' as sufficient to, or coextensive with, the tasks of feminist political struggle now or in the future.

But it does follow that I think such activity is part of that struggle and, more strongly, that it can be one of the enabling conditions for realizing, securing and renewing its wider political projects.

These qualifications are necessary, I think, because at a time of inflationary rhetoric about the importance of 'cultural' studies and criticism, it becomes all too easy in reaction to go back to 'basics' and declare that work on women's writing, after all, has nothing to say – and no place in politics.

Most of the essays in this volume [*The Pirate's Fiancée*] were written as an effort to produce a speaking-position in a particular political, critical and publishing context. Some, like the essays on Mary Daly, Jean Baudrillard and *Crocodile Dundee*, dealt with discourses tending to deny *all* critics (even feminist ones for Daly, feminists in particular for Baudrillard and Paul Hogan) a place from which to speak, or the possibility of having something to say. In each case, I have tried not simply a find a way to 'answer back', but to read the texts in question sympathetically in order to understand them *as* criticisms of those answers that my feminism might automatically provide, and so to use them to question my own assumptions and practices in the process of reading theirs.

Some essays were written directly in response to work which is explicitly concerned with the positioning of women, and with thinking about subjectivity, modes of address, and reference, in particular historical contexts. Since these preoccupations are often now considered to be the signs of an academic 'feminist theory', I want to stress here the art works of Lynn Silverman and Richard Dunn. Both artists ask us to consider our relationship to the images each provides of subjectivity not as a source of meanings, or as an object of quests, but as an elusive *reference-point*. Silverman's boots, recurring from image to image across the bottom of the bottom line, introduce the trace of a history in the mythic space of the so-called 'timeless land' of the (white) Australian interior.[9] Dunn's formal portraits construct a set of stylized positions – of which the most intriguing, for me, remains the image of the young woman (a fiancée, perhaps) from the far right of the series, gazing through fire at a story of her own positioning in that place. Each artist asks us to analyse the process of representation both arriving at and departing from that elusive reference-point – and allows us then to transform it by imagining a story in turn.

Finally, other essays pursued a feminist analysis of contemporary writing which, from Howard Felperin to Roland Barthes, Susan Sontag and Jean-François Lyotard, attempts to debate presumed general dilemmas about critical 'speaking' today. Sometimes the feminism of the essays is an explicit and polemical position. Sometimes it operates implicitly, as a set of theoretical and political assumptions about the questions that criticism might ask. In some of the more recent essays a 'feminist speaking-position' is framed as today defining a recognizable genre in criticism, which may in turn begin to impose new difficulties for the further work of (feminist) women.

In none of these essays, however, is the production of a speaking-position understood as a matter of inventing a 'personal voice' for '*me*'. None of them is presented as an instance of a subjective or 'reader' response. On the contrary, I think that producing a 'position' is a problem of rhetoric, of developing enunciative strategies (or ways of 'play-acting', in MacHeath's sense) precisely in relation to the cultural and social conventions that make speaking difficult or impossible for *women*.

To stress a relation to those conventions is to say that I think it is important to think of the 'production of a speaking-position' *as* a matter of strategies of reference,[10] rather than simply of 'the subject' or even 'subjectivity'. Several essays in this volume explore that argument further. One of the reasons that I think it worth pursuing is that in the uncertainty and confusion that attends speculation about the relations between semiotics, Marxism, feminism and politics, the one polemical position that for me has proved itself quite useless is that which insists on retaining 'in the last instance' an empiricist conception of '*the* referent' as 'the thing', as privileged synecdoche of 'the real (material) world'.[11] It may be useless for its own political purposes: few other theories of reference are quite so rhetorically vulnerable to the mega-empiricism of a Jean Baudrillard discovering, on a trip to Disneyland or on a quick run through some meta-*vérité* TV or high-tech Japanese videos, that 'the referent', and therefore 'reality', is dead.

The only other comment I wish to make to situate the essays that follow [in *The Pirate's Fiancée*] is that most of them were written for fun, or as a 'leisure' occupation. Fun, of course, can incorporate any number of reasons for writing something – enthusiasm, amusement, admiration, a sense of a challenge to learn, but also concern, irritation, anxiety or bemusement, a desire to confront something bothersome.

From 1978 to 1985, I worked primarily as a film reviewer for newspapers (the *Sydney Morning Herald*, and then *The Australian Financial Review*). While I also often taught part-time in several art and media colleges, the arduous physical and intellectual conditions of a job in which I might see up to a dozen films a week, and have to find 'something to say' about most of them, meant that while I have always understood mass-media work as an ideological practice involving acts of theorization, the activity of thinking and writing about *theories* that might inform my practice had to be cherished as a hobby.

This experience has influenced my work in a number of ways. I became as interested in addressing the theoretical debates that circulate in and as popular culture as I am in academically situated theoretical work *about* popular culture. In the process, maintaining the distinction I've just reiterated between the 'popular' and the 'academic' became increasingly awkward for any purposes of generalization. I make it again here only in order to say that I think some theories in wide circulation (like the 'gut reaction' theory of criticism [...] or the big-cinema theory of mass pleasure [...]) are still insufficiently addressed by academic work. The basic premises of each are so much in conflict that the former is simply dismissed as 'wrong', or ignored as *non*-theoretical. Yet serious engagement with popular culture must eventually accept to take issue with it and in it, as well as about it, and I think this means writing seriously about popular theories as well as (or even rather than) writing 'popular' spin-offs from academic theories.

However, many of the essays in this volume [*The Pirate's Fiancée*] were initially written *for*, if not 'from', an academic context. Others were not; but in neither case did the kind of critical response that helps any writer to shift her position (or change her mind) necessarily come from the imaginary addressee I may have inscribed as I wrote them. Perhaps the most demanding and useful criticism an intellectual can receive comes from the kind of 'mixed' public to be encountered at events organized on thematic or political, rather than purely professional, principles. So the experience of moving between a number of different social sites of debate and discussion about cultural politics has also left me very cautious about some aspects of recent attempts to come to terms with the limitations and specificities of 'academic' practice.

On the one hand, Foucault's notion of the 'specific intellectual', for example, has been particularly useful both in allowing institutional struggles to occupy a field of 'everyday life' rather than being relegated to an 'ivory tower' divorced from a 'real world', and in making it possible to criticize the moment in which a theory 'mistakes the liberal academy as the collective subject of a universally useful knowledge'.[12] Feminism has both profited from, and helped to produce, this kind of reconceptualization of academic politics. On the other hand, something slightly different seems to be happening when it becomes possible to claim, as Paul Smith does in an essay in *Men in Feminism*, that poststructuralist feminist theory 'however "feminist" it may be, and howsoever "feminist" is construed – *does not exist outside the academy*' (my emphasis).[13] Smith stresses in a note that he is referring only to what is known 'in the academic vernacular as feminist theory (the structuralist/poststructualist variety)'.

But I wonder – whose academic vernacular? Many feminist theorists involved in an academic practice (Mary Daly comes immediately to mind, but one might find any number in various disciplines) would be astonished and annoyed to find their work either categorized as poststructuralist or consigned to nonexistence. Furthermore, this 'vernacular' equation between a reified 'poststructuralism' and an equally reified 'theory' is not confined to the academy. As one of the means by which any part of a field of activity promotes itself as coextensive with the whole, the term 'theory' can be used in precisely that shorthand way (at least in my cultural context) by administrators and curators and bureaucrats in the visual and performing arts, by journalists, by film-makers ...

One must be passionately careful here, precisely because to state that a given activity has 'no existence' outside one's own immediate sphere of operations is to accept and reinforce as absolute, rather than to challenge and transform, prevailing *local* conventions about the available places from which people (and in this case, feminists) can be allowed to be saying something. If we extend the realm of the 'academy' to include a whole range of activities shuttling between pedagogical institutions and the culture industries, then we are no longer talking about the specificities and limitations of the former, but rather using a vaguely expansive metonym of 'the institution' to blur away a number of questions about *class* and cultural practice in specific sites today. We are, once again, universalizing the 'academy' (and in the name of only one of its elements).

A response to this objection is that an incessant 'shuttling' (of personnel as well as of activities) into other social sites is precisely what characterizes a primary function of the academy in post-industrial societies. Modern academies no doubt have always done this: but as they come to act not only as training grounds for a future elite diaspora, but *also* as pre-unemployment waiting rooms or as anti-unemployment therapy and 'personal improvement' centres, their ideological role in *moving discourses around* becomes increasingly complex (in a way which varies considerably, too, from country to country). But it is precisely when we begin to come to terms with this development that it becomes impossible to claim that a given theoretical activity 'does not exist outside' the academy. This can only be true in an academy imagined as without students who do not proceed to become professors, or with students who remain untouched by their own working experiences.

Furthermore, this academy functions in a world without bookshops, without 'amateur' readers and writers of theoretical work, without theorizing artists, without those ambiguous 'art-world' figures (critics, and especially curators) who can frame artists' work as 'theoretical' whether they wish it so or not, without TV chat-shows and intellectual talking-heads, without interviews, without media jokes about semiotics and poststructuralism, without private reading groups, without public forums, without young film-school graduates making both small film-essays and big blockbusters, without other than academic audiences for any of these, or anyone anywhere to go on to make something different from them: it is a world without any 'dissemination' of ideas, and finally without the rampant commodification of thought and feeling that makes it possible to speak of 'Theory' – in a vernacular sense – as a practice, as a problem, as a genre, and as a 'zone' of possible contestation.

I take issue with Paul Smith's comment in such detail because it seems to be one of the more careful formulations of a myth of institutional and discursive *closure* which may emerge from the important academic attempt to 'know your limitations', in Clint Eastwood's phrase, but which sometimes ends (as I have seen it do in feminist discussion groups) with a self-lacerating and ultimately self-defeating lament by 'theorists' that we (or 'they') aren't doing something else – something, perhaps, with more *power* to change prevailing conditions of existence.

It's a reasonable anxiety. Without worrying about the disconnections and the failures of intellectual work, we cannot transform it politically. Yet one of the most important consequences of the notion of the 'specific intellectual' is not to translate 'specificity' as 'confinement', but rather to begin to accept firstly that work produced in an academic context (even the writings of Foucault, even poststructuralist feminist theory) can be used and rewritten in unpredictable ways (and various media) elsewhere: and secondly that this movement can run the other way: academic theorization can and should transform its practices by learning from the experiences, the concepts, and the methodologies developed by people in broader social and political movements.

The relationship between feminist theory and the various women's movements has operated historically in this two-way sense, and I would add that non-academically constituted feminist groups provided an excellent training ground in not deducing people's reading habits or their intellectual interests from their social occupations. It is perhaps true today that the emergence of modes of feminist theorizing inflected by 'poststructuralism' corresponds both to an intensified discussion *of* feminism in the academies, and to the development of a more complex and indirect relationship between that discussion, a range of broad political struggles involving women, and a rapidly changing, sometimes weakened, sense of 'feminism' as a social force. But at that point it becomes crucial not only to ask, as Michèle Le Doeuff does of the work of Simone de Beauvoir (or as I would still wish to ask of the work of Mary Daly), what is it that has allowed this practice of theory to 'dynamize' so many diverse women's movements?; but also to ask how social movements *now* can generate changes in (even poststructuralist) feminist theory, and in our practice of feminist politics.

A declaration that a certain kind of feminist theory does not exist outside a specific institutional space may function as a way of denying certain women a place from which to speak, but it does so haphazardly, by the kind of accident that befalls any generalization. I should like to conclude by considering a much more coherently motivated denial (in a structural, not an individual, sense of 'motivation') that occurs when it is stated that women have had nothing to say about a particular topic.

In a number of recent discussions of postmodernism, a sense of intrigue develops around a presumed absence – or withholding – of women's speech in relation to what has certainly become one of the boom discourses of the 1980s. Feminists in particular, in this intrigue, have had little or nothing to say about postmodernism.

This very curious *doxa* emerges from texts by male critics referring primarily to each other commenting on the rarity of women's speech.

In 1983, in a text commenting on his own 'remarkable oversight' in ignoring the question of sexual difference in his previous critical practice, Craig Owens noted 'the fact that few women have engaged in the modernism/postmodernism debate'.[14] In an essay first published the following year, Andreas Huyssen – warmly agreeing with Owens that feminist work in art, literature and criticism has been 'a measure of the vitality and energy' of postmodern culture – none the less found it 'somewhat baffling that feminist criticism has so far largely stayed away from the postmodernism debate which is considered not to be pertinent to feminist concerns'.[15]

Both of these critics stressed the complexity and importance of a feminist contribution to what *they*, in turn, wished to describe as a 'postmodern' culture. Owens in particular was careful to disclaim any desire to efface the specificity of feminist critique, and to insist that his own project was to consider the implications of an *intersection* of feminism and postmodernism.

More recently, however, Jonathan Arac stated baldly in his Introduction to *Postmodernism and Politics*:

> *almost no women have figured in the debate*, even though many analysts include current feminism among the features of postmodernity. Nancy Fraser's important feminist critique of Habermas ('What's Critical') stands nearly alone (see also Kristeva), although Craig Owens and Andrew Ross have effectively situated feminist work by women in relation to postmodernism.[16]

In the bibliography which concludes Arac's Introduction, very few women do figure beside Fraser and Kristeva: five, to be precise, out of more than seventy individual and collaborative authorial entries. One of the five is Virginia Woolf. Another is Hannah Arendt.[17] Any bibliography, it is true, must be exclusive. This one is, when it comes to gender, *very* exclusive.

The interesting question, I think, is not whether feminists have or have not written about postmodernism, or whether they should have (for despite the 'baffled' expectation, the hope, perhaps, of eventual *fiançailles*, there is no suggestion here that feminism in any sense *needs* postmodernism as complement or supplement).[18] My question is rather under what conditions women's work *can* 'figure' currently in such a debate. There is general agreement between the male critics I've cited that 'feminist work *by women*' can figure when appropriately framed ('effectively situated') by what has mainly been, apparently, a man's discourse. But by what criteria does feminist work by women come to figure, or *not* to figure, when it comes raw-edged, without a frame?

Common sense suggests that perhaps all that is meant by these remarks is that few women so far have written articles explicitly entitled 'Feminism and postmodernism'; or that few have written analyses focused on the standard (male) referents of present debate – Habermas, Lyotard, Rorty, Jameson, Huyssen, Foster, Owens, and so on. If we accept that this is true (or that many of the texts that fulfil these conditions are quite recent) then perhaps feminists have merely been busy doing other things. It would be hard to deny that in spite of its heavy (if lightly acknowledged) borrowings from feminist theory, its frequent celebrations of 'difference' and 'specificity', and its critiques of 'Enlightenment' paternalism, postmodernism as a publishing phenomenon has pulled off the peculiar feat of reconstituting an overwhelmingly male pantheon of proper names to function as ritual objects of academic exegesis and commentary. It would be easy to shrug away a presumed feminist noninvolvement with postmodernism as a wise avoidance by women of a singularly ponderous, phallo-centred conversation – and to point out, with Michèle Le Doeuff, that the position of faithful reader to the great male philosopher is one that women have good reason to approach with caution. Many feminist criticisms of theories of postmodernism have occurred, in fact, in passing, in the context of saying something else as well.

Yet the matter is not quite so simple. *If* it is true that few women have explicitly inscribed their work in relation to postmodernism (and I am sceptical of such claims, since they tend to present the limits and biases of our local reading habits as a satisfactory survey of the state of the world), it should also be true that only male writers who *do* so inscribe their work then come to 'figure' in the debate.

Yet in Arac's bibliography, we find numerous figures whose contribution could only strictly be described as formative, enabling and/or indirect: Adorno and Horkheimer, Derrida, Heidegger, Lacan, Foucault (not to mention Althusser, Perry Anderson, Lukács and Raymond Williams). Their work can only be part of a debate about postmodernism when 'effectively situated' in relation to it by subsequent commentary and citation. But a formative or indirect role in postmodernism has been willingly accorded, by men cited by Arac, to feminism. Why then, alongside the names of those men, do we not find references to (for example) the closely and critically associated work of Catherine Clément, Hélène Cixous, Luce Irigaray, Shoshana Felman, Jane Gallop, Sarah Kofman, Alice Jardine, Michèle Le Doueff, Gayatri Chakravorty Spivak, or Jacqueline Rose?

One could continue this line of questioning. For example, it might be argued that the 'enabling' male figures have at least explicitly theorized 'modernity', and so provide the bases for thinking postmodernity. But then not only would my brief list of women recur with even greater insistence, but it would need immediate expansion: Janet Bergstrom, Mary Anne Doane, Elizabeth Grosz, Barbara Johnson, Donna Haraway, Teresa de Lauretis, Angela McRobbie, Patricia Mellencamp, Tania Modleski, Nancy K. Miller, Naomi Schor, Kaja Silverman, Judith Williamson ... (many of whom have had, in fact, quite a bit to say about postmodernism). Furthermore, if the 'politics' in the conjuction of *Postmodernism and Politics* authorizes the figuring under that rubric of the work of a Perry Anderson – then surely we might also expect to find listed works by Nancy Hartsock, Carole Pateman, Juliet Mitchell or Chantal Mouffe?

At this point, however, it becomes difficult to keep restricting my own inquiries to the names of (mostly white and Western) women. In the first and last sentence of his introductory text, Arac invokes 'the world' as the context of criticism. So why would a bibliography of 'postmodernism and *politics*' today still privilege only the great names of Western Marxism and their American academic heirs – at the expense of new theorizations of politics and culture by writers differently placed in histories of racism and colonialism? Rasheed Araeen, Homi K. Bhabha, Eduardo Galeano, Henry Louis Gates Jr, Geeta Kapur, Trinh T. Minh-ha, Nelly Richard. ... After all, if postmodernism really has defined a useful sphere for political debate, it is because of the awareness it can foster that its 'world' is finally not so small, so clearly 'mapped'.

It is, as a Derridean might observe, all a matter of borderlines and frames. Any bibliography 'frames', as it defines, its field of representation. But the paradox of the frame does not prevent us from asking, in relation to any instance of framing, where and why a line is drawn. As John Frow has argued in *Marxism and Literary History*, the paradox of the frame is most useful precisely for framing a political project of working on 'the limits of reading'.

In reading the limits of Arac's bibliography, it becomes particularly difficult to determine the difference between an act of re-presenting a presupposed historical not-figuring of women in postmodernism debates, and an act of re-*producing* the not-figuring, not counting, of women's work, by 'simple' omission (writing it out of history, by writing its absence into history).

I have a similar difficulty with the more sensitive comments of Owens and Huyssen. Why do women artists and feminist theorists count *as* postmodernist (and as objects of commentary) for Owens, but not as 'engaging' in a debate? Doesn't this distinction return us precisely to that division between a (feminized) object-language and a (masculine) meta-language that feminist theory has taught us to question for its political function, rather than for its epistemological validity? How can Huyssen simply cite and confirm what Owens says, while conceding that crucial aspects of postmodernism now would be 'unthinkable'[19] without the impact of feminist thought?

After all, it is Huyssen himself who has stressed in his feminist reading of 'Mass culture as woman: Modernism's Other' that male authors' preoccupation with imaginary femininity 'can easily go hand in hand with the exclusion of real women from the literary enterprise'.[20] Following Huyssen, then, a 'male' postmodernism could be seen as renewing one of the inaugural gestures (in Lyotard's sense) of modernism: inscribing its 'bafflement' by an imaginary, 'absent', silent femininity, while erasing and silencing the work of real women in the history and practice of the theoretical enterprise.

Given the persistence of the figure of woman as mass culture (the irony of modernism), it is no accident that a debate about a presumed silence and absence of women has already taken place in relation to the work on popular culture that is in turn a component of postmodernism.[21] But the bafflement about women that besets both is also perhaps the latest version of the 'why have there been no great women artists (mathematicians, scientists ...)?' conundrum – a badly posed question that assumes a negative response to a previous question, which remains, by default, unasked and unexamined.

How can this happen again? Again, there are some obvious responses that feminists might make. We could say that 'feminist theory' has come to function in academic publishing as a limiting category to a certain extent. It's now too easy to assume that if a text is labelled 'feminist' theory, then it can't properly 'count' or 'figure' as anything else ('woman's sphere', again). We could adopt a complacent paranoia, and assume that the male pantheon of postmodernism is merely a twilight of the gods – the last ruse of the patriarchal University trying for power to fix the meaning, and contain the damage, of its own decline. Or we could claim – probably with some justice, if much brutality – that in spite of many rhetorical flourishes from men about their recognition and acceptance of feminism's 'contribution' to cultural and political theory, not very many men have really read extensively, or kept on reading, very many women's books and essays – particularly those published off the fast-track of prestige journals, or in strictly feminist contexts. The bottom line of any working bibliography is not, after all, a frame, but a practical prerequisite: you have to know it to use it.

The problem that interests me, however, is rather the difficulty that a feminist critic now faces in *saying* something about this – in trying to point out, let alone come to terms with, what seems to be a continued, repeated, basic *exclusion* of women's work from a highly invested field of intellectual and political endeavour. What woman writer wants to say, in 1987, that men still aren't reading feminist work?; that women are being 'left out again'?; thus running the risk of being suspected of talking about herself ('if she writes about women's experiences, especially the unpleasant ones, declare her hysterical or "confessional"').[22]

In addressing the myth of a postmodernism still waiting for its women we can find an example of a genre, as well as a discourse, which in its untransformed state leaves a woman no place from which to speak, or nothing to say. For by resorting to the device of listing 'excluded' women, women excluded for no obvious reason except that given by the discourse – their gender – I have positioned myself in a speech-genre all too familiar in everyday life, as well as in pantomime, cartoons, and sitcoms: the woman's complaint, or *nagging*. One of the defining generic rules of 'nagging' is unsuccessful repetition of the same statements. It is unsuccessful, because it blocks change: nagging is a mode of repetition which fails to produce the desired effects of difference that might allow the complaint to end. In this it is quite close to what Anne Freadman, in her analysis of *Indiana*, calls the lament: a 'powerless text'. (A conventional comic scenario goes: she nags, he stops listening, nothing changes, she nags.) Yet there is always a change of sorts implied by repetition: in this case, her 'place' in speech becomes, if not strictly nonexistent, then insufferable – leaving frenzy or silence as the only places left to go. It is an awesome genre, and I am not sure, I confess, how to transform it.

A traditional method has always been for the nagger somehow to lose interest, and so learn to change her subject (and her addressee). One possibility in this context is to follow up Dana Polan's suggestion that postmodernism is a 'machine for producing discourse'.[23] Polan argues that as the input to this machine begins to determine what it is possible to say in its name, so it becomes increasingly difficult to generate as output anything non-repetitive. Participants in a postmodernism debate are 'constrained' to refer back to previous input, and to take sides in familiar battles on a marked-out, well-trodden terrain ('Habermas v. Lyotard', for example). The solution to feminist complaint might then be a simple one – switch position from nagger to nagged, then switch off.

But assuming a calculated deafness to discussion about postmodernism is not much of a solution for feminist women. To choose to *accept* a given constraint is not to challenge, overcome or transform anything. Besides, one of the fascinating paradoxes of the postmodernism machine is precisely how difficult it can be to switch it off (or switch off to it). Many of its best operators (Lyotard and Baudrillard, for example) have tried, and failed. As a discourse which runs on a 'paradoxical concern with its own lateness', as Andrew Ross points out (in one of the few essays relating feminism to postmodernism without attributing silence to women),[24] postmodernism has so far proved compatible with, rather than vulnerable to, vast quantities of input about its obsolescence or imminent breakdown.

A different response worth making would be, it seems to me, to make a generically feminist gesture of reclaiming women's work, and women's names, as a context *in* which debates about postmodernism might further be considered, developed, transformed (or abandoned).

The bibliography of women's writing at the end of this introduction is put forward in that spirit. It does not propose to present – or to 'effectively situate' – feminist theory *as* 'postmodernist', and it certainly does not propose to salvage feminism *for* postmodernism. It does presuppose that since feminism has acted as one of the enabling conditions of discourse *about* postmodernism, it is therefore appropriate to use feminist work to frame discussions of postmodernism, and not the other way around. To make this gesture of changing frames is to propose at least one alternative to nagging – and to wasting time waiting and watching for imaginary acts of piracy.

Notes

Where full details are available in the main Bibliography, references contain only essential information.

1. Bertolt Brecht, *Collected Plays*, vol. 2, part 2, *The Threepenny Opera*, Act 1, Scene 2, London, 1979, p. 22.
2. Anne Freadman, 'Sandpaper', *Southern Review*, 16, 1 (1983), 162.
3. *Ibid.*, p. 172.
4. *Ibid.*, p. 172.
5. Freadman's 'use' of formalism here is rigorously differentiated from that of North

American New Criticism. For her, formalism is 'the study of forms, insofar as form is the enabling condition of signification' (and so, not opposed to 'content'). 'Form', in turn, is a theoretical object derived from, not preexisting, the practices of formalism; and, far from being 'restricted to describing the linguistic forms deployed in any text', formalist *theories* of text for Freadman are 'practices of differentiation which take as their criteria conventions or rule-governed strategies for the formation of texts'. She stresses that 'formalism must in general be characterised as the practice of differentiation. Since difference is the primary enabling condition of signification, it follows that formalism is not the principle of what has been called the "autonomous" text, since "difference" supposes a field of pertinent comparison. But it is the case that it takes as its domain of inquiry (and as its theoretical object) not the "individual text", but the text as individuated.' *Ibid.*, p. 161.

6. See in particular Michèle Le Doeuff, 'Pierre Roussel's chiasmas: From imagining knowledge to the learned imagination', *I&C*, 9 (1981/2), 39–70.

7. Both Sontag and (more indirectly) Baudrillard derive the terms of their *thematics* of quotation from Walter Benjamin's work *The Origin of German Tragic Drama*, London, 1977. Neither, however, retains much from the historical project – or situation – of the book.

8. Roland Barthes, *Mythologies*, London, 1972, p. 112.

9. See Eleanor Dark, *The Timeless Land*, Sydney, 1941.

10. See Anne Freadman, 'On being here and still doing it', in P. Botsman, C. Burns and P. Hutchings (eds), *The Foreign Bodies Papers*, Sydney, 1981; and the collection of essays, Anna Whiteside and Michael Issacharoff (eds), *On Referring in Literature*, Indiana, 1987.

11. For a more measured account of the difficulties entailed by this tendency in moments of the work of Terry Eagleton, see John Frow, *Marxism and Literary History*, Harvard, 1986, pp. 41–50.

12. David Bennett, 'Wrapping up postmodernism', *Textual Practice*, 1, 3 (1987), 259.

13. 'Feminist theory of this sort – and however "feminist" it may be, and howsoever "feminist" is construed – does not exist outside the academy and, more specifically, is in many ways not easily separable from the general "theory" that has worked its way into studies in the humanities over the last ten or twenty years.' Paul Smith, 'Men in feminism: Men and feminist theory', in Alice Jardine and Paul Smith (eds), *Men in Feminism*, New York and London, 1987, p. 34, p. 267, n. 2.

14. Craig Owens, 'Feminists and postmodernism', in Hal Foster (ed.), *The Anti-Aesthetic: Essays on postmodern culture*, Washington, 1983, p. 61.

15. Andreas Huyssen, *After the Great Divide: Modernism, mass culture, postmodernism*, Indiana, 1986, pp. 198–9.

16. Jonathan Arac (ed.), *Postmodernism and Politics*, Manchester, 1986, p. xi. [Emphasis mine.]

17. The others are Rosalind Coward (as co-author with John Ellis); Sally Hassan (as co-editor with Ihab Hassan); and Laura Kipnis, for one article.

18. For discussions of the problems of an intersection between feminism and post-modernism (and responses to Craig Owens's essay), see Barbara Creed, 'From here to modernity: Feminism and postmodernism', *Screen*, 1987, 47–67; and Elspeth Probyn, 'Bodies and anti-bodies: Feminism and the postmodern', *Cultural Studies*, 1, 3 (1987), 349–60.

19. *After the Great Divide*, p. 220.

20. *Ibid.*, p. 45.
21. See papers in Colin MacCabe (ed.), *High Theory/Low Culture: Analyzing popular television and film*, Manchester, 1986.
22. Joanna Russ, *How to Suppress Women's Writing*, London, 1983, p. 66.
23. Dana Polan, 'Postmodernism as machine', paper to the Australian Screen Studies Association, Sydney, December 1986.
24. Andrew Ross, 'Viennese waltzes', *Enclitic*, 8, 1–2 (1984), 76.

Bibliography

For the reasons discussed in the preceding essay, I have included in this bibliography only works signed or cosigned as written by women. Since it combines entries about feminism, theories of reading, and postmodernism, it is for practical reasons mostly limited to works I have drawn on in some way for the essays in this book. Essays published in anthologies are not listed separately under their authors' names.

Abel, Elizabeth (ed.), *Writing and Sexual Difference*, Brighton, 1982.
Allen, Judith and Grosz, Elizabeth (eds), *Feminism and the Body, Australian Feminist Studies*, no. 5, 1987.
Allen, Judith and Patton, Paul (eds), *Beyond Marxism? Interventions after Marx*, Sydney, 1983.
Atkinson, Ti-Grace, *Amazon Odyssey*, New York, 1974.
Bell, Diane, *Daughters of the Dreaming*, Melbourne, 1983.
Bergstrom, Janet, 'Enunciation and sexual difference (Part 1)', *Camera Obscura*, 3–4 (1979).
Bergstrom, Janet, 'Violence and enunciation', *Camera Obscura*, 8/9/10 (1982).
Bergstrom, Janet, 'Androids and androgyny', *Camera Obscura*, 15 (1986).
Bernstein, Cheryl, 'Performance as news: Notes on an intermedia guerilla art group', in Michel Benamou and Charles Caramello (eds), *Performance in Postmodern Culture*, Milwaukee, 1977.
Braidotti, Rosi, *Féminisme et philosophie: La philosophie contemporaine comme critique du pouvoir par rapport à la pensée féministe*, Université de Paris-1, 1981.
Brooke-Rose, Christine, *A Rhetoric of the Unreal*, Cambridge, 1981.
Brown, Denise Scott, Izenour, Steven and Venturi, Robert, *Learning from Las Vegas: The forgotten symbolism of architectural form*, Cambridge, MA and London, 1977.
Bruno, Giuliana, 'Postmodernism and *Blade Runner*', *October*, 41 (1987).
Bruss, Elizabeth W., *Beautiful Theories: The spectacle of discourse in contemporary crititicism*, Baltimore, MD, London, 1982.
Burchill, Louise, 'Either/or: Peripeteia of an alternative in Jean Baudrillard's *De la séduction*', in André Frankovits (ed.), *Seduced and Abandoned: The Baudrillard scene*, Sydney, 1984.
Cameron, Deborah, *Feminism and Linguistic Theory*, London, 1985.
Chow, Rey, 'Rereading mandarin ducks and butterflies: A response to the "postmodern" condition', *Cultural Critique*, 5 (1986–7).
Cixous, Hélène *et al.*, *La Venue à l'écriture*, Paris, 1977.
Clément, Catherine and Cixous, Hélène, *La Jeune Née*, Paris, 1975.
Clément, Catherine, *Miroirs du sujet*, Paris, 1975.

Clément, Catherine, *Les Fils de Freud sont fatigués*, Paris, 1978; *The Weary Sons of Freud*, London, 1987.

Clément, Catherine, *Vies et légendes de Jacques Lacan*, Paris, 1981; *The Lives and Legends of Jacques Lacan*, New York, 1983.

Collins, Felicity, 'A (sad) song of the body', *Screen*, 28, 1 (1987).

Cornillon, Susan Koppelman, *Images of Women in Fiction: Feminist perspectives*, Ohio, 1972.

Coventry, Virginia, *The Critical Distance: Work with photography/politics/writing*, Sydney, 1986.

Coward, Rosalind, *Female Desire*, London, 1984.

Coward, Rosalind, and Ellis, John, *Language and Materialism: Developments in semiology and the theory of the subject*, London, 1977.

Creed, Barbara, 'From here to modernity: Feminism and postmodernism', *Screen*, 28, 2 (1987).

Daly, Mary, *Beyond God the Father: Towards a philosophy of women's liberation*, Boston, MA, 1973.

Daly, Mary, *Gyn/Ecology: The metaethics of radical feminism*, Boston, MA, 1978.

Davidson, Robyn, *Tracks*, London, 1980.

Delphy, Christine, *The Main Enemy: A materialist analysis of women's oppression*, London, 1977.

Doane, Mary Ann, 'Woman's stake: Filming the female body,' *October*, 17 (1981).

Doane, Mary Ann, 'Film and the masquerade: Theorizing the female spectator', *Screen*, 23, 24 (1982).

Doane, Mary Ann, 'When the direction of the force acting on the body is changed: The moving image', *Wide Angle*, 7, 1–2 (1985).

Doane, Mary Ann, *The Desire to Desire: The woman's film of the 1940s*, Indiana, 1987.

Dubreuil-Blondin, Nicole, 'Feminism and modernism: Paradoxes', in Benjamin Buchloh *et al.* (eds), *Modernism and Modernity*, Nova Scotia, 1983.

Duras, Marguerite and Gauthier, Xavière, *Les Parleuses*, Paris, 1974.

Ecker, Gisela (ed.), *Feminist Aesthetics*, London, 1985.

Eisenstein, Hester and Jardine, Alice (eds), *The Future of Difference*, Boston, MA, 1980.

Ellmann, Mary, *Thinking About Women*, London, 1969.

Ewen, Elizabeth and Ewen, Stuart, *Channels of Desire: Mass images and the shaping of American consciousness*, New York, 1972.

Felman, Shoshana *La Folie et la chose littéraire*, Paris, 1978; *Writing and Madness*, Ithaca, NY, 1986.

Felman, Shoshana, (ed), *Literature and Psychoanalysis, the Question of Reading: Otherwise, Yale French Studies*, nos 55–6, 1977.

Felman, Shoshana, *Le Scandale du corps parlant: Don Juan avec Austin ou la séduction en deux langues*, Paris, 1980.

Ferguson, Frances, 'The nuclear sublime', *Diacritics*, 14, 2 (1984).

Fraser, Nancy, 'The French Derrideans: Politicizing deconstruction or deconstructing politics', *New German Critique*, 33 (1984).

Fraser, Nancy, 'What's critical about critical theory? The case of Habermas and gender', *New German Critique*, 35 (1985).

Freadman, Anne, 'On being here and still doing it', in P. Botsman, C. Burns and P. Hutchings (eds), *The Foreign Bodies Papers*, Sydney, 1981.

Freadman, Anne, 'Sandpaper', *Southern Review*, 16, 1 (1983).

Freadman, Anne, 'Riffaterra cognita: A late contribution to the "Formalism" debate', *SubStance*, 42 (1984).

Freadman, Anne, 'Reading the visual', *Framework*, 30–1 (1986).

Gaines, Jane, 'White privilege and looking relations: Race and gender in feminist film theory', *Cultural Critique*, 4 (1986).

Gallop, Jane, *Intersections: A reading of Sade with Bataille, Blanchot, and Klossowski*, Nebraska, 1981.

Gallop, Jane, *Feminism and Psychoanalysis: The daughter's seduction*, London, 1982.

Gallop, Jane, *Reading Lacan*, Ithaca, NY/London, 1985.

Gaudin, Collette *et al.*, *Feminist Readings: French texts/American contexts, Yale French Studies*, no. 62, 1981.

Gould, Carol C. and Wartofsky, Marx W. (eds), *Women and Philosophy: Toward a theory of liberation*, New York, 1976.

Gross, Elizabeth, 'Derrida, Irigaray and deconstruction', *Leftwright, Intervention*, 20, (1986).

Gross, Elizabeth, 'Irigaray and the divine', Local Consumption Occasional Paper 9, Sydney, 1986.

Grosz, Elizabeth, 'Every picture tells a story: Art and theory re-examined', in Gary Sangster (ed)., *Sighting References*, Sydney, 1987.

Grosz, Elizabeth, 'The "People of the Book": Representation and alterity in Emmanuel Levinas', *Art & Text*, 26 (1987).

Grosz, Elizabeth *et al.* (eds), *Futur*fall: Excursions into post-modernity*, Sydney, 1986.

Gunew, Sneja, 'Feminist criticism: Positions and questions', *Southern Review*, 16, 1, (1983).

Gunew, Sneja, and Reid, Ian, *Not the Whole Story*, Sydney, 1984.

Gusevich, Miriam, 'Purity and transgression: Reflections on the architectural avantgarde's rejection of kitsch', Working Paper, Center for Twentieth Century Studies, University of Wisconsin-Milwaukee, 1986.

Haraway, Donna, 'A manifesto for cyborgs: Science, technology and socialist feminism in the 1980s', *Socialist Review*, 80 (1985).

Hartsock, Nancy C. M., *Money, Sex, and Power: Toward a feminist historical materialism*, Boston, MA, 1985.

Hermann, Claudine, *Les Voleuses de langue*, Paris, 1976.

Hill, Ernestine, *The Great Australian Loneliness*, Melbourne, 1940.

Hutcheon, Linda, *Narcissistic Narrative: The metafictional paradox*, Ontario, 1980.

Hutcheon, Linda, 'A poetics of postmodernism', *Diacritics* 13, 4 (1983).

Hutcheon, Linda, *A Theory of Parody: The teachings of twentieth century art forms*, New York and London, 1985.

Hutcheon, Linda, 'Beginning to theorize postmodernism', *Textual Practice*, 1, 1 (1987).

Irigaray, Luce, *Speculum de l'autre femme*, Paris, 1974; *Speculum of the Other Woman*, Ithaca, NY, 1985.

Irigaray, Luce, *Ce sexe qui n'en est pas un*, Paris, 1977; *This Sex Which is Not One*, Ithaca, NY, 1985.

Jacobus, Mary (ed)., *Women Writing and Writing About Women*, London, 1979.

Jardine, Alice, *Gynesis: Configurations of woman and modernity*, Ithaca, NY/London, 1985.

Jardine, Alice and Smith, Paul, *Men in Feminism*, New York and London, 1987.

Jayamanne, Laleen and Rodrigo, Anna, 'To render the body ecstatic', *Fade to Black*, Sydney College of the Arts Occasional Publication, 1985.

Jayamanne, Laleen, Kapur, Geeta and Rainer, Yvonne, 'Discussing modernity, "Third World", and *The Man Who Envied Women*', *Art & Text*, 23/4 (1987).

Jennings, Kate, *Come to Me My Melancholy Baby*, Melbourne, 1975.

Johnson, Barbara, *The Critical Difference: Essays in the contemporary rhetoric of reading*, Baltimore, MD/London, 1980.

Johnson, Barbara, 'Thresholds of difference: Structures of address in Zora Neale Hurston', in Henry Louis Gates (ed.), *'Race', Writing, and Difference, Critical Inquiry*, 12, 1, (1985).

Johnston, Jill, *Gullilbles Travels*, New York/London, 1974.

Jones, Lyndal, 'Prediction piece #9', *Art & Text*, 9 (1983).

Kaplan, Cora, *Sea Changes: Culture and feminism*, London, 1986.

Kelly, Mary, 'Re-viewing modernist criticism', *Screen*, 22, 3 (1981).

Kofman, Sarah, *Nietzsche et la métaphore*, Paris, 1972.

Kofman, Sarah, *Comment s'en sortir?*, Paris, 1983.

Kofman, Sarah, *Un métier impossible*, Paris, 1983.

Kofman, Sarah, *L'Enigme de la femme*, Paris, 1980; *The Enigma of Woman*, Ithaca, NY, 1985.

Kramarae, Cheris and Treichler, Paula A., *A Feminist Dictionary*, Boston, MA/London/Henley, 1985.

Krauss, Rosalind E., *The Originality of the Avant-Garde and Other Modernist Myths*, Cambridge, MA/London, 1985.

Kristeva, Julia, *Desire in Language: A semiotic approach to literature and art*, Oxford, 1980.

Kristeva, Julia, *The Kristeva Reader*, ed. Toril Moi, Oxford, 1986.

de Lauretis, Teresa, *Alice Doesn't: Feminism, semiotics, cinema*, Indiana, 1984.

de Lauretis, Teresa, (ed.), *Feminist Studies/Critical Studies*, Indiana, 1986.

de Lauretis, Teresa, *Technologies of Gender: Essays on theory, film and fiction*, Indiana, 1987.

Lawson, Sylvia, *The Archibald Paradox: A strange case of authorship*, London/Sydney, 1983.

Le Doeuff, Michèle, 'Women and philosophy', *Radical Philosophy*, 17 (1977).

Le Doeuff, Michèle, 'Operative philosophy: Simone de Beauvoir and existentialism', *Governing the Present, I&C*, 6 (1979).

Le Doeuff, Michèle, *L'Imaginaire philosophique*, Paris, 1980.

Le Doeuff, Michèle, 'Pierre Roussel's chiasmas', *Life, Labour and Insecurity, I&C*, 9 (1981/2).

Lewitt, Vivienne Shark, 'Why Egyptian mods didn't bother to bleach their hair or more notes about parkas and combs', *Art & Text*, 3 (1981).

Lewitt, Vivienne Shark, 'The end of civilisation Part 2: Love among the ruins', *Art & Text*, 10 (1983).

Lippard, Lucy, *Changing: Essays in art criticism*, New York, 1971.

Lloyd, Genevieve, *The Man of Reason: 'Male' and 'female' in Western philosophy*, London, 1984.

Long, Elizabeth, 'Reading groups and the postmodern crisis of cultural authority', *Cultural Studies*, 1, 3 (1987).

McRobbie, Angela, 'Settling accounts with subcultures', *Screen Education*, 34 (1980).

McRobbie, Angela, 'The politics of feminist research: Between talk, text and action', *Feminist Review*, 12 (1982).

McRobbie, Angela, 'Strategies of vigilance, an interview with Gayatri Chakravorty Spivak', *Block*, 10 (1985).

McRobbie, Angela, 'Postmodernism and popular culture', *Postmodernism*, ICA Documents 4, London, 1986.

McRobbie, Angela and Nava, Mica (eds), *Gender and Generation*, London, 1984.

Marini, Marcelle, *Territoires du féminin avec Marguerite Duras*, Paris, 1977.

Marks, Elaine and de Courtivron (eds), *New French Feminisms*, Amherst, MA, 1980.

Mellencamp, Patricia, 'Film history and sexual economics', *Enclitic*, 7, 2 (1983).

Mellencamp, Patricia, 'Postmodern TV: Wegman and Smith', *Afterimage*, 13, 5 (1985).

Mellencamp, Patricia, 'Situation and simulation', *Screen*, 26, 2 (1985).

Mellencamp, Patricia, 'Uncanny feminism: The exquisite corpses of Cecilia Condit', *Framework*, 32/3 (1986).

Mellencamp, Patricia, 'Images of language and indiscreet dialogue – "The Man Who Envied Women"' *Screen*, 28, 2 (1987).

Mellencamp, Patricia, 'Last seen in the streets of modernism', Hawaiian Film Festival, publication forthcoming.

Miller, Nancy K. (ed), *The Poetics of Gender*, New York, 1986.

Millett, Kate, *Sexual Politics*, London, 1970.

Minh-ha, Trinh T., 'The plural void: Barthes and Asia', *SubStance*, 36 (1982).

Minh-ha, Trinh T. (ed)., *The Inappropriate/d Other*, Discourse, 8 (1986/7).

Mitchell, Juliet, *Woman's Estate*, London, 1971.

Mitchell, Juliet, *Psychoanalysis and Feminism*, London, 1974.

Mitchell, Juliet, and Oakley, Anne (eds), *The Rights and Wrongs of Women*, Harmondsworth, 1976.

Modleski, Tania, *Loving with a Vengeance: Mass-produced fantasies for women*, New York/London, 1982.

Modleski, Tania, 'Femininity as mas(s)querade: A feminist approach to mass culture', in Colin MacCabe (ed.), *High Theory/Low Culture*, Manchester, 1986.

Modleski, Tania (ed.), *Studies in Entertainment: Critical approaches to mass culture*, Indiana, 1986.

Moi, Toril, *Sexual/Textual Politics: Feminist literary theory*, London/New York, 1985.

Montrelay, Michèle, *L'Ombre et le nom, sur la féminité*, Paris, 1977.

Moore, Catriona and Muecke, Stephen, 'Racism and the representation of Aborigines in film', *Australian Cultural Studies*, 2, 1 (1984).

Morgan, Robin (ed.), *Sisterhood is Powerful*, New York, 1970.

Morgan, Robin, *Monster*, private printing, 1972.

Mouffe, Chantal, 'Radical democracy: Modern or postmodern', in Andrew Ross (ed.), *Universal Abandon? The politics of postmodernism*, Minnesota, 1988.

Mouffe, Chantal and Laclau, Ernesto, *Hegemony and Socialist Strategy: Towards a radical democratic politics*, London, 1985.

Mulvey, Laura, 'Visual pleasure and narrative cinema', *Screen*, 16, 3 (1975).

Pateman, Carole, *The Problem of Political Obligation*, Cambridge, 1985.

Pateman, Carole, and Gross, Elizabeth (eds), *Feminist Challenges: Social and political theory*, Sydney/London/Boston, MA, 1986.

Penley, Constance, 'The avant-garde and its imaginary', *Camera Obscura*, 2 (1977).

Penley, Constance, 'Time travel, primal scene, and the critical dystopia', *Camera Obscura*, 15 (1986).

Petro, Patrice, 'Mass culture and the feminine: The "place" of television in film studies', *Cinema Journal*, 25, 3 (1986).

Petro, Patrice, 'Modernity and mass culture in Weimar: Contours of a discourse on sexuality in early theories of perception and representation', *New German Critique*, 40 (1987).

Petro, Patrice, *Joyless Streets: Women and melodramatic representation in Weimar Germany*, Princeton, NJ, 1988.

Pratt, Mary Louise, 'Interpretive strategies/strategic interpretations: On Anglo-American reader-response criticism', in Jonathan Arac (ed.), *Post-modernism and Politics*, Manchester, 1986.

Probyn, Elizabeth, 'Bodies and anti-bodies: Feminism and the postmodern', *Cultural Studies*, 1, 3 (1987).

Rich, Adrienne, *Of Woman Born: Motherhood as experience and institution*, London, 1977.

Rich, Adrienne, *On Lies, Secrets and Silence: Selected prose 1966–1978*, London, 1980.

Richard, Nelly, 'Body without soul: On the mechanism of quotation in the pictorial materialism of Juan Davila', *Art & Text*, 12–13 (1984).

Richard, Nelly, 'Notes towards a critical re-evaluation of the critique of the avant-garde', *Art & Text*, 16 (1984).

Richard, Nelly, 'Love in quotes: On the painting of Juan Davila', in Paul Taylor (ed.), *Hysterical Tears: Juan Davila*, Melbourne, 1985.

Richard, Nelly, 'Margins and institutions: Art in Chile since 1973', *Art & Text*, 21 (1986).

Rose, Jacqueline, *Sexuality in the Field of Vision*, London, 1986.

van Rossum-Guyon, Françoise (ed.), *Ecriture, fémininité, féminisme, Revue des sciences humaines*, no. 168, 1977–8.

Rowbotham, Sheila, *Hidden from History*, London, 1974.

Russ, Joanna, *How to Suppress Women's Writing*, Austin, TX, 1983.

Schor, Naomi, *Breaking the Chain: Women, theory and French realist fiction*, Columbia, NY, 1985.

Schor, Naomi, *Reading in Detail: Aesthetics and the feminine*, New York/London, 1987.

Schor, Naomi and Majewski, Henry F. (eds), *Flaubert and Postmodernism*, Nebraska, 1984.

Showalter, Elaine, *A Literature of Their Own: British women novelists from Brontë to Lessing*, Princeton, NJ, 1977.

Showalter, Elaine (ed.), *The New Feminist Criticsm: Essays on women, literature, theory*, New York, 1985.

Silverman, Kaja, *The Subject of Semiotics*, New York/Oxford, 1983.

Smock, Anne, 'Learn to read, she said', *October*, 41 (1987).

Solanas, Valerie, *The S.C.U.M. Manifesto*, London, 1983.

Sontag, Susan, *Against Interpretation*, New York, 1966.

Sontag, Susan, *On Photography*, London, 1977.

Sontag, Susan, *I, etcetera*, London, 1979.

Sontag, Susan, *Under the Sign of Saturn*, New York, 1981.

Spivak, Gayatri Chakravorty, 'Displacement and the discourse of woman', in Mark Krupnick (ed.), *Displacement: Derrida and after*, Indiana, 1983.

Spivak, Gayatri Chakravorty, *In Other Worlds: Essays in cultural politics*, New York/London, 1987.

Stanton, Domna C. (ed.), *The Female Autograph*, New York, 1984.

Stein, Gertrude, *How Writing is Written*, Los Angeles, CA, 1974.

Stein, Gertrude, *How to Write*, Toronto/London, 1975.

Stern, Lesley, 'The body as evidence', *Screen*, 23, 5 (1982).

Suleiman, Susan Rubin, *Authoritarian Fictions: The ideological novel as a literary genre*, New York, 1983.

Suleiman, Susan Rubin (ed.), *The Female Body in Western Culture*, Cambridge, MA/London, 1986.

Whiteside, Anna and Issacharoff, Michael (eds), *On Referring in Literature*, Indiana, 1987.

Williamson, Judith, *Consuming Passions: The dynamics of popular culture*, London/New York, 1986.

Wilson, Elizabeth, *Adorned in Dreams: Fashion and modernity*, London, 1985.

Wolff, Janet, 'The invisible flaneuse: Women and the literature of modernity', *The Fate of Modernity, Theory Culture & Society*, 2, 3 (1985).

29 □ *Feminism and Postmodernism*

Sabina Lovibond

I

The term 'postmodernism' exerts an instant fascination. For it suggests that 'modernity' is, paradoxically, already in the past; and consequently that a new form of consciousness is called for, corresponding to new social conditions. But of course it does not tell us what the distinctive character of these new conditions, or of the accompanying consciousness, is supposed to be.

Expositions of postmodernism in the context of political and cultural theory often take as a negative point of reference the idea of 'Enlightenment'. In this paper, therefore, I propose to look at some recent examples of anti-Enlightenment polemic and to consider their meaning from a feminist point of view. I shall use as source material the writings of three well-known philosophers – Jean-François Lyotard, Alasdair MacIntyre and Richard Rorty.[1]

These writers are among the most forceful exponents of the arguments and values which constitute postmodernism within academic philosophy. Inevitably, then, my response to their work will also be a response to the bigger picture which I shall trace in it. But this does not mean that I believe the whole of postmodernism, even in its philosophical variant, to be wrapped up in the pages I have chosen for study: what follows is, in the first instance, an account of a specific bit of textual exploration.

My chosen texts undoubtedly show certain common preoccupations, of which perhaps the most striking is an aversion to the idea of *universality*. The Enlightenment pictured the human race as engaged in an effort towards universal moral and intellectual self-realisation, and so as the subject of a universal historical experience; it also postulated a universal human *reason* in terms of which social and political tendencies could be assessed as 'progressive' or otherwise (the goal of politics being defined as the realisation of reason in practice).[2] Postmodernism rejects this picture: that is to say, it rejects the doctrine of the unity of reason. It

From Boyne, R. and Rattansi, A. (eds), *Postmodernism and Society*, Macmillan Education, Basingstoke/St Martin's Press, New York, 1990, pp. 154–86.

refuses to conceive of humanity as a unitary subject striving towards the goal of perfect coherence (in its common stock of beliefs) or of perfect cohesion and stability (in its political practice).

All of our three philosophers illustrate, in their different ways, the postmodernist advocacy of pluralism in morals, politics and epistemology. All are struck by the thought that justification or 'legitimation' are *practices*, sustained in being by the disposition of particular, historical human communities to recognise this and not that as a good reason for doing or believing something; and all associate 'Enlightenment' with a drive to establish communication between these local canons of rationality and to make them answerable to a single standard. But this is just what postmodernist thinkers complain of, for they question the merit of consensus as a regulative ideal of discourse. The policy of working for it seems to them to be objectionable on two counts: firstly as being historically outmoded, and secondly as being misguided or sinister in its own right.

The first claim frequently appears in the shape of triumphalist comments on the defeat of revolutionary socialism in the West. MacIntyre, for example, singles out Marxism for special mention as an 'exhausted' political tradition.[3] In a similar vein, Lyotard argues that 'most people have lost the nostalgia for the lost narrative' (that is, for the idea of humanity as tending towards a condition of universal emancipation, the prospect of which endows the historical progress with meaning;[4] and he connects the declining influence of such 'grand narratives' with 'the redeployment of advanced liberal capitalism [after 1960] ... a renewal that has eliminated the communist alternative and valorized the individual enjoyment of goods and services'.[5]

The second claim, namely that the pursuit of ideal consensus is misguided, finds expression in arguments for a more accepting attitude towards the contingency and particularity of our 'language-games'. It is not that postmodernism subscribes to the view that whatever is, is sacrosanct: quite the reverse, in fact, in the case of Rorty and Lyotard, who prize innovation for its own sake. It does, however, deny that the replacement of one 'game' by another can be evaluated according to any absolute standard (e.g. as being 'progressive' or the reverse, in the sense fixed by a teleological view of history). The thought is that since history has no direction (or: since it is no longer possible to think of it as having a direction), any new configuration of language-games which we may succeed in substituting for the present one will be just as 'contingent' as its predecessor – it will be neither more nor less remote from 'realising [universal] reason in practice'.

It is not surprising, then, to discover in this literature a leaning towards non-teleological descriptions of discursive activity. Rorty wishes to transfer to *conversation* the prestige currently enjoyed by 'enquiry';[6] MacIntyre's reflections on morality lead him to the conclusion that *mythology*, the range of narrative archetypes through which a culture instructs its members in their own identity, is 'at the heart of things'.[7] Neither 'conversation' nor 'mythology' is naturally understood as aiming at a single, stable representation of reality, one which would deserve the name of 'truth' in something more than a contextual or provisional sense. And it is this negative feature which fits the terms in question for their role in expounding a 'postmodernism of the intellect'.

But the divorce of intellectual activity from the pursuit of ideal consensus is too important a theme to be entrusted to one or two happily chosen words. Rorty, as we shall see later, explicitly states that a form of life which no longer aspires towards a more-than-provisional truth will be better, on broad cultural grounds, than one which continues to do so; while Lyotard goes further and equates that aspiration with 'terror',[8] believing as he does that it leads inevitably to the suppression of diversity or 'difference'. He even calls for a 'war on totality' – a reassertion of the familiar liberal teaching that, while it may be a regrettable necessity to place constraints on liberty in the name of social order, one must not actively seek to bind together the multiplicity of thought and practice into a single 'moral organism' or 'significant whole'.[9]

The robust partisanship of these texts entitles us to think of 'postmodernism' as a *movement* defining itself by reference to, and in reaction against, modernity. There is, admittedly, no single way in which our three sources illustrate this reaction.[10] They are united, though, in their opposition to the Enlightenment demand that what exists should justify itself before a timeless 'tribunal of reason'. In their view, justification (or legitimation) is always local and context-relative; and the supersession of one local criterion of legitimacy by another is not to be seen as an approximation towards some ultimate criterion that would transcend all local bias, but at most as the outcome of self-questioning on the part of a particular tradition.

This view of legitimation is sometimes presented as the (more attractive) rival of a view called 'Platonism'. The 'Platonism' in question is defined by reference to just one doctrine taken from the historical Plato: the idea that *truth* goes beyond, or 'transcends', our current *criteria of truth*. A recurrent feature of postmodernist theory is the claim that Platonism in this sense is obsolete – that is, that it is no longer possible to believe in a transcendent truth against which the whole intellectual achievement of the human race to date could be measured and found wanting. And postmodernist scepticism about this conception of truth extends also to the distinctive method of inquiry which Plato envisaged as our means of access to genuine knowledge. It extends, in other words, to the idea of human thought as a *dialectical* process: one which would generate a positive result (a body of beliefs which was perfectly stable, because incapable of further correction) by way of the relentless application of a negative method (the method of hunting down and eliminating internal contradiction).

According to the dialectical view of knowledge, this positive result would mark the *end* of inquiry, the point at which thought would come to rest because there would be no possibility of further progress. But this prospect is no longer viewed with universal enthusiasm; it has become controversial. Thus we are invited to see it as a merit of postmodernist 'conversation' that (in contrast to dialectic) it aims, not at its own closure, but at its own continuation: it offers us the prospect of a limitless future enlivened at one point by episodes of agreement, at another by 'exciting and fruitful disagreement'.[11]

To the postmodern reappraisal of our dealings with the objective world, or with 'reality', there corresponds a striking development on the side of the moral and cognitive *subject*. Here too there is some historical justification for attaching the label 'Platonist' to the view against which postmodernism is in revolt. For in Plato's *Republic* the dialectical progress of theory towards perfect coherence is supposed to go hand in hand with an analogous tendency towards coherence in the mind of the inquirer. As the practice of dialectic strengthens my intellectual grasp of truth and goodness, so I am to picture myself advancing towards perfect mental integration: that is, towards a condition in which no sudden access of emotion, no previously unconsidered aspect of things, is able to disturb the ordering of my beliefs and values.

Ever since its invention, this ideal of integrated or 'centred' subjectivity has been linked with that of *personal freedom*. However, the freedom which it promises is not the merely negative state of exemption from external constraints – the 'liberty of spontaneity' which Hume, for example, maintained was the only sort we could intelligibly wish for. It is, rather, a 'positive liberty' arising from the proper internal organisation of the mind. Positive liberty (also known as 'autonomy') results from the achievement of a state of mind in which the decisions or commands issued by the *true* subject (the subject *qua* exemplar of ideal coherence and stability) cannot be overturned by recalcitrant impulses or 'passions'.[12] To be free in this sense is to be emancipated from the influence of beliefs and desires which our critical judgement condemns as irrational.

The logical conclusion of this line of argument is that freedom can be attributed without qualification only to those in whom the potential for reason has been fully realised – that is, only to a perfectly rational being. Others (and that means all of us, though we presumably fall short of the ideal in varying degrees) may enjoy a subjective feeling of freedom in our actions; but if we continue to develop intellectually we are destined, some day, to perceive (with hindsight) the relative unfreedom of our current patterns of behaviour.

We can set down as a further component of the Enlightenment outlook the hope of achieving positive liberty by shaking off all accidental (i.e. non-rational) constraints on the way we think and act. The classical 'centred subject' was free because he was no longer at the mercy of unpredictable bouts of passion or appetite; analogously, the modern one is free in virtue of his or her liberation from the influence of social forces which s/he does not understand, and so cannot resist. Communism, for example, encourages us to work towards freedom in this sense by gaining insight into the capitalist economic order and the ideology that goes with it; feminism, at least some of the time, has invited us (women) to search our behaviour and our inner lives for signs of adjustment to a woman-hating culture, so that we can gradually overcome the *self*-hatred induced by that adjustment. (This was the idea behind 'consciousness-raising'.)

The long march towards autonomy by way of the conquest of our own stupidity (or more accurately, by making ourselves less susceptible to external determination) can be summed up in the word 'transcendence'. In the moral and political context, as in the epistemological one, to 'transcend' is to go beyond. The pursuit of a fully integrated subjectivity takes the form of an attempt to rise above our present mental limitations.

This related idea of transcendence has also attracted hostile attention in recent years. The hostility comes partly from postmodernist critics of Enlightenment, who have rightly observed its connection with the idea of 'universal reason' (if I'm trying to rise above the limitations of a *local or partial* understanding of things, then presumably what I'm aiming at is a fully rounded, impartial or *universal* understanding). Thus MacIntyre speaks in positively patronising terms of that last word in Enlightenment-style moral autonomy, the Nietzschean *Übermensch* or 'man who transcends':[13] isolated, self-absorbed, 'wanting in respect of both relationships and activities', this individual clearly needs help from a psychiatric social worker.

Interestingly for our purposes, though, criticism of transcendence as a moral ideal has also begun to be heard in feminist quarters. It has been argued that, from the outset, Western philosophy has devised one scheme of imagery after another to convey, essentially, a single vision – that of *man*, the normal or complete representative of the species, standing out against a background of mere 'nature'; and that this background has consistently been symbolised by *woman* or femininity. Plato's guardians emerge from the womblike Cave of 'common sense' into the daylight of knowledge; Hegel's citizens attain maturity by leaving the obscure, private world of the family, of which Woman is the presiding genius. In short, the passage from nature to freedom, or from 'heteronomy' to autonomy, has been represented in terms of an escape by the male from the sheltered, feminine surroundings in which he begins his life.[14]

We have arrived at a point of apparent convergence between feminism and postmodernism – a common coolness towards one of the key elements in the Enlightenment ideal. It is time now to change tack and to consider, in the light of feminist concerns, how far these two tendencies might be able to enter into a friendly relationship.

II

One of the first thoughts likely to occur in the course of any historical reflection on feminism is that it is a typically *modern* movement. The emergence of sexual equality as a practical political goal can be seen as one element in the complex course of events by which *tradition* has given way, over a matter of centuries, to a way of life that is deeply *untraditional* – in fact, to 'modernity' in a semi-technical sense of the word (the sense in which it denotes a historical period).

'Modern' conditions are those created by technological progress and by the ever-expanding commerce of nations. They are the kind of conditions which uproot people from ancient communities and force them to negotiate their own survival in a capitalist 'free market'. A key text in the development of this idea of modernity is Marx and Engels's famous description of the chaos and anarchy of life under capitalism – a description offset, however, by their positive vision of the old economic order as pregnant with a new one. [15] According to this view, the 'collapse of all fixed, fast-frozen relations' creates the historic opportunity for humanity, represented in the first instance by the industrial working class, to seize control over its own collective existence through revolution. In classical Marxist terms, the urban proletariat has the necessary qualifications for this role because it is made up of *modern* human beings – men (and also, though problematically, women)[16] who have been forcibly emancipated from traditional ways of life, and so from the limited outlook of their peasant ancestors. It is thanks to the formation of such a class that the horror of modernity also contains a promise: *sooner or later, arbitrary authority will cease to exist.*

Anyone who is stirred by this promise is still, to that extent, within the Enlightenment habit of thought. Their response indicates sympathy with the Enlightenment refusal to attach any moral or intellectual force to tradition as such.

Now, it is difficult to see how one could count oneself a feminist and remain indifferent to the modernist promise of social reconstruction. From a female point of view, 'tradition' has (to put it mildly) an unenviable historical record. Yet it is in the area of sexual relations that 'traditional values' (marriage, home ownership, wholesome family life, etc.) are proving hardest to shift. Perhaps no other feature of the pre-modern scene has persisted so stubbornly as male dominance – the class system constructed on the basis of biological sexual difference; certainly the thought of a time when concepts such as 'wife' and 'husband', with all the moral atmosphere they evoke, will be as obsolete as 'villein' or 'lord of the manor' is apt to set off a landslide in the mind. Still, if we assess without prejudice the implications for gender (I mean, for masculinity and femininity as cultural constructs) of the 'modern' repudiation of unearned privilege, we may well conclude that this development is an integral part of the package; and if so, it will follow that feminists have at least as much reason as the rest of the world for regarding the 'project of modernity', at the present time, as incomplete. [17]

What, then, are we to make of suggestions that the project has run out of steam and that the moment has passed for remaking society on rational, egalitarian lines? It would be only natural for anyone placed at the sharp end of one or more of the existing power structures (gender, race, capitalist class ...) to feel a pang of disappointment at this news. But wouldn't it also be in order to feel *suspicion*? How can anyone ask me to say goodbye to 'emancipatory metanarratives' when my own emancipation is still such a patchy, hit-and-miss affair?

Let us focus again on the idea of 'universal reason', and on the recent questioning of this idea. Among feminists, we noticed, the questions have been prompted by a sense of the historical connection between *rationalist ideals* and the belief in a *hierarchical opposition of 'mind' and 'nature'* – the latter opposition in turn being associated with a contempt for 'immanence', finitude, and the muddle of embodied existence generally (the 'lead weights of becoming', as Plato put it). [18] On this analysis, the Enlightenment rhetoric of 'emancipation', 'autonomy' and the like is complicit in a fantasy of escape from the embodied condition;[19] as such, it feeds into one of the most notorious aberrations of European culture, and any philosophy which challenges it is likely to have considerable critical force.

Feminist theory is, in fact, deeply indebted to the efforts of philosophy over the last century and more to 'naturalise' epistemology, or in other words to represent the activity we call 'inquiry' as part of the natural history of human beings. For naturalist or materialist analyses[20] of the institutions of knowledge-production – schools, universities, the wider 'republic of letters' – have made it possible to expose the unequal part played by different social groups in determining standards of judgement. In this way they have revealed the ideological character of value-systems which have previously passed as objective or universally valid (consider, for example, the growth of scepticism about academic canons of 'greatness' in literature). Feminism can benefit as much as any other radical movement from the realisation that our ideas of personal, technical or artistic merit, or of intelligibility and cogency in argument, do not 'drop from the sky' but are mediated by an almost interminable process of social teaching and training.

These achievements seem to demonstrate the critical potential of a local or plural conception of 'reason', and so to underwrite its claim to the confidence of feminists. But before we jump to any conclusions, we had better look more closely at the ways in which postmodernist theory puts that conception to work. In the remainder of this paper, I shall introduce three themes which seem to me to qualify as distinctively postmodern; and in each case I shall suggest grounds for doubting whether postmodernism can be adopted by feminism as a theoretical ally. For ease of reference I shall attach labels to my three postmodernist themes: we can call them respectively 'dynamic pluralism', 'quiet pluralism' and 'pluralism of inclination'.

As we begin our survey, we should bear in mind that there is nothing in the communitarian insight *per se* (I mean, in the idea that standards of judgement are historically and culturally conditioned) which would explain postmodernist hostility to the version of ideal consensus. One might very well be impressed by the perspectival character of knowledge-claims, and yet still see inquiry as necessarily seeking to bring all 'perspectives' on reality into communication – to construct a body of thought, or a system of values, accessible indifferently from any starting-point. This, after all, is the 'cheerful hope' which has animated coherentist theories of knowledge from Plato to C. S. Peirce and beyond,[21] and it is by no means obvious that when such theories take a naturalist turn they are bound to renounce the Kantian postulate of a 'special interest of reason' in picturing reality as a single, unified system.[22] In fact, there is no reason in principle why a naturalist epistemology should not interpret in its own terms – namely, as referring to the regulative idea of a single, unified *human culture* – Kant's metaphor of the 'imaginary point', located beyond the limits of possible experience, upon which all lines of rational activity appear to converge.[23]

To call this point 'imaginary' is simply to record the irrelevance, from an epistemological point of view, of worries about when (if ever) we can actually expect to reach the goal of inquiry. Continuing for a moment in a Kantian vein, we can say that although theory (like morality) would no doubt be impossible if the relevant subjective 'maxims' had *no* general appeal to the mind, still theoretical effort (like moral effort) is essentially non-contractual: that is, you are not genuinely engaged in either if you make your contribution conditional on an assurance that all other contributions required to achieve the goal of the exercise will actually be forthcoming. We are therefore concerned here with the epistemic equivalent of an article of faith, a commitment to persist in the search for common ground with others: in fact, something which could not be relinquished on pain of sinking into 'hatred of reason and of humanity'.[24]

As soon as the rationalist conception of inquiry is represented as a matter of *policy*, however (an idea already implicit in Kant's talk of the 'interests' of reason), it becomes fair game for psychological interpretation: that is, it can be seen as expressive of a certain temperament or cast of mind. And it is on this psychological territory that the tendency I have called 'dynamic pluralism' issues its challenge. Lyotard is an appropriate case-study here, since his historical thesis about the eclipse of 'grand narratives' develops itself into a series of more or less explicit suggestions on the subject of postmodern mental health.

As we saw earlier, Lyotard believes that the Enlightenment ideal of a 'revisable consensus governing the entire corpus of language-games played by a community'[25] has lost its grip on the collective imagination. Nowadays, he thinks, the main motive to intellectual activity is the hope of benefiting from the 'performance capabilities' of a 'complex conceptual and material machinery', whose users, however, 'have at their disposal no metalanguage or metanarrative in which to formulate the final goal and correct use of that machinery'.[26] Under these conditions, the rationalist demand for *legitimation* of a putative bit of 'knowledge' has been superseded by a limitless quest for discursive novelty or 'paralogy';[27] consequently, any lingering conviction that thought has some overarching *purpose*, some destination where it could rest, must be viewed as a sign of imperfect adaptation to postmodernity. The authentically postmodern consciousness is experimental, combative, 'severe': it 'denies itself the solace of good forms, the consensus of a taste which would make it possible to share collectively the nostalgia for the unattainable'.[28]

Postmodernism then, according to Lyotard, is an extension of modernism in that each seeks to articulate the experience of a disorderly, directionless world – an experience compounded of pleasure and pain, conducted in the glare of high-tech extravagance which, like the Kantian sublime, stuns the imagination.[29] But the two positions differ as to what sort of consciousness would be equal to, or worthy of, such conditions. Modernism remains within the 'Enlightenment project' to the extent that it pictures the cognitive mastery of modernity as a step on the road to *ending* it (by collective reimposition of form on chaos, as in the Marxist theory of revolution;)[30] postmodernism, on the other hand, would have us plunge, romantically, into the maelstrom without making it our goal to emerge on *terra firma*.

How should feminist readers respond to the charge of 'nostalgia' as directed against rationalist ideals? In considering this question, we may find it helpful to

draw on historical evidence: that is, to look into the formation of the sensibility
expressed in the relevant postmodernist texts. Taking a hint from some respectful
comments of Lyotard's,[31] we can enter more fully into the anti-Enlightenment spirit
by way of the writings of Nietzsche – perhaps the sternest of all critics of 'idealism'
in general, in the sense of a disposition to compare the real world with an ideal one
and to find it wanting. It is this disposition which, in Nietzschean terms, constitutes
'nihilism' – the tendency which he portrays on a more institutive level as a sickness
transmitted to European civilization through the combined impact of Platonism and
Christianity. 'Interesting' as humanity may have become by virtue of this sickness,[32]
Nietzsche's own thought achieves world-historic significance (or so he claims) by
bringing us to the threshold of recovery, and of a passage into the 'second innocence'
of godlessness. But the 'godless' condition is not so easily attained as many self-
styled free-thinkers imagine. 'They are far from being *free* spirits,' Nietzsche
comments on the positivists of his own day, '*for they still have faith in truth*';
whereas a more resolute scepticism would rise to the discovery that 'man's truths
[are ultimately] only his *irrefutable* errors'.[33]

Nietzsche's critique of truth may seem at first sight to be addressed mainly to
adherents of a foundational epistemology on empiricist lines (i.e. to those who
believe that knowledge rests on a foundation of indubitable, because purely
experiential, propositions). Taking a broader view, however, we find that he is at
least equally devastating about an alternative way of 'having faith in truth', namely
that embodied in the practice of *dialectics* and (by implication) in modern
coherentist theories of knowledge. In fact, Nietzsche discerns in the method of
argument invented by Socrates and Plato the psychological key to all subsequent
manifestations of rationalism. For the Socratic habit of thought is one which
assumes the possibility, and desirability, of *eliminating conflict* through the gradual
convergence of all parties on a single, stable point of view. As such, it has always
had a plebeian taint – for the elimination of conflict, Nietzsche observes, is a goal
apt to appeal, above all, to those who can expect to be worsted in conflict: in other
words, to the weak:

> Wherever authority is still part of accepted usage and one does not 'give reasons' but
> commands, the dialectician is a kind of buffoon. ... One chooses dialectics only when
> one has no other expedient. ... Dialectics can be only a last-ditch weapon in the hands
> of those who have no other weapon left. ... That is why the Jews were dialecticians.[34]

Rationalism, in Nietzsche's view, remains true to its origin in the will-to-power
of the dispossessed: its lineage is betrayed by its wish to transpose conflict from the
arena of blows (or of showmanship) into that of rule-governed argument, where the
physical or social underdog has a hope of winning. This wish marks it out as a
natural ally of the democratic movements of the modern world. For the aim of these
movements is to subvert the social conditions which Nietzsche would regard as
necessary to the expression of a 'natural order of rank'; that is, they aim to eliminate
various sorts of class relationship, and hence various forms of exploitation or

dispossession. (In another idiom: they seek to characterise, ever more rigorously, a social order in which the willing participation of all rational persons can be expected – a 'kingdom of ends' with each traditional impediment to membership, whether in terms of class, religion, race or sex, successively provoking resistance and being swept away.) In short, then, truth as a regulative ideal is the creation of a socially inferior type of mind. It is the *ressentiment* of the rabble – their sinister genius for making the 'naturally good' feel bad about themselves – which gives rise to this ideal. For as soon as humanity allows itself to be caught up in the 'pursuit of truth', it slips into the way of defining intellectual *virtue* in terms of contrasting *vice* invented by the rabble as an instrument of psychological warfare against their 'betters': the vice of *contradicting oneself*, or of being committed (unwittingly, no doubt, but this only adds to the intimidatory power of the dialectical method) to the assertion of propositions related as 'P' and 'not-P'. (Notice the daring of Nietzsche's suggestion that self-contradiction is not a fault in any absolute or eternal sense: he insists that it was *human beings*, and a particular category of human beings at that, who hit upon coherence as a criterion of value in assessing thought-processes.)

Nietzsche, too, dreams of overcoming 'modernity' in all its anarchic ugliness. But, in his view, this will be achieved, not through a *realisation* of Enlightenment political ambitions, but through a *recovery* from the 'sickness' of Enlightenment ideals – truth, reason, morality (the modern successors to 'God'). Nietzsche concurs in drawing together under the heading of 'modernity' all the egalitarian tendencies of the last few centuries in Europe – liberalism, socialism and feminism alike. He sees feminism, in other words, as one component of the rationalist political programme. And in fact this is a view which many feminists can probably share.[35] It is a view which can be summed up by saying that feminism, at least in its utopian moods (as opposed to its angry and pugnacious ones, which of course are equally essential to it), aspires to *end the war between men and women* and to replace it with communicative transparency, or truthfulness.

Now, it is well known that any expression of moral revulsion against war is, for Nietzsche, a 'symptom of declining life';[36] but there is, perhaps, no branch of life in which rationalism and pacifism are more offensive to him than in that of sexuality.[37] The force of his conviction on this point suggests to Nietzsche an intimate, even a quasi-conceptual, connection between the idea of an *emancipation from reason*, on one hand, and that of an *end to feminism*, on the other. This connection is mediated by his concept of *virility*, the quality supposedly expressed in a love of 'danger, war and adventures' – a refusal 'to compromise, to be captured, reconciled and castrated'.[38]

We must understand this statement not only in its obvious, literal, sense but also in an epistemological one. In a world without truth – a world in which the contrast between 'reality' and 'appearance' has been abolished – the interpretation of experience is itself a field for invention, for *hazarding* one's own expressive gestures or acts without seeking for them the safety of confirmation (i.e. of incorporation into a shared and stable body of theory). The cognitive activity of a future, and better, humanity will involve not the suppression of individuality and sensuality (the 'false private self' of the coherentist regime), but rather their subordination to a commanding will.

> Henceforth, my dear philosophers, let us be on our guard against the dangerous old conceptual fiction that posited a 'pure will-less, painless, timeless knowing subject'; let us guard against the snares of such contradictory concepts as 'pure reason', 'absolute spirituality', 'knowledge in itself': these always demand that we should think of an eye that is completely unthinkable, an eye turned in no particular direction, in which the active and interpreting forces, through which alone seeing becomes seeing *something*, are supposed to be lacking; these always demand of the eye an absurdity and a nonsense. There is *only* a perspective seeing, *only* a perspective knowing; and the *more* affects we allow to speak about one thing, the *more* eyes, different eyes, we can use to observe one thing, the more complete will our 'concept' of this thing, our 'objectivity', be. But to eliminate the will altogether, to suspend each and every affect, supposing we were capable of this – what would that mean but to *castrate* the intellect?[39]

Consistently with the idea that to attempt an impersonal or 'selfless' view of reality would be to 'castrate' the intellect, Nietzsche elsewhere describes his work in general as 'hostile ... to the whole of European *feminism* (or idealism, if [we] prefer that word)',[40] and speaks of his 'faith that Europe will become more virile'.[41] 'Feminism', then, occurs in Nietzsche's writing not only as the name of a contemporary political movement (though of course he has a good deal to say about women's emancipation on the level of indignant commonplace),[42] but also as a shorthand term for the mental impotence implicit (or so he believes) in the bondage of thought to regulative ideals such as truth, reality and goodness. Thought is *emasculated*, Nietzsche argues, in so far as it consents to be 'drawn aloft' (*à la* Goethe) by the ever-receding goal of a perfectly stable condition in which it could find peace.

My motive in introducing Nietzsche into the discussion has not been purely negative. I have no wish to ridicule his account of the psychological meaning of epistemological and political rationalism – his interpretation of the rationalist enterprise in terms of a desire for the elimination of conflict and of arbitrary relations of command. I wish, simply, to suggest that we take seriously Nietzsche's own understanding of his work as a contribution to the overcoming of 'feminism'; and that we maintain, as feminists, a suitably critical attitude to the reappearance in contemporary philosophy of one of Nietzsche's central themes – that of the supersession of 'modernity' by a *harder*, less wimpish form of subjectivity.[43]

I must stress that to point out the phallic or 'masculine protest' character of Nietzsche's philosophy, and of postmodernist theory in its more overtly Nietzschean moods, is not meant to be a prelude to arguing that the values despised by this tradition deserve to be restored to a position of honour *because* they are 'feminine' and, as such, good. I do not mean to suggest that we should turn to Nietzsche for an understanding of what is 'feminine', any more than to other purveyors of the dominant ideology of gender. Instead, my suggestion is that in reading postmodernist theory we should be on the watch for signs of indulgence in a certain collective *fantasy* of masculine agency or identity. Turning upon the Nietzscheans their own preferred genealogical method, we might ask: *who* thinks it is so humiliating to be caught out in an attitude of 'nostalgia for lost unity', or of longing for a world of human subjects sufficiently 'centred' to speak to and understand one another?[44]

III

I have been arguing for a sceptical response to the kind of postmodernist position which I labelled 'dynamic pluralism'. This position, I have suggested, is informed by an irrationalism whose historical origin lies in reactionary distaste for modernist social movements, and specifically for the movement towards sexual equality. I turn now to the second of my three postmodernist themes, namely 'quiet pluralism'. Our concern here will be with the postmodern 'rediscovery' of the local and customary – a societal counterpart, perhaps, of the revival of vernacular architecture.

It may appear, at first glance, that there is a world of difference between Nietzsche's own vision of a radical renunciation of the 'Socratic' or truth-orientated way of life, and on the other hand the postmodernist proposal that we scrap the Enlightenment project of *absolute* legitimation (the attempt, for example, to create a society that could not be faulted by any rational being). And with this difference in view, it may be objected that the discovery of Nietzschean echoes in the rhetoric of postmodernist theory is of no more than marginal philosophical interest. For to read that theory as an updated Nietzscheanism (the objection will run) is to miss its central point. Postmodernism does not condemn the pursuit of truth or virtue within *local, self-contained* discursive communities – the quest for 'truth' as distinct from 'Truth', as Rorty might put it, or of 'virtue' as distinct from 'Virtue' (the latter meaning the excellence of a human being simply *qua* human and without reference to any particular social role). It reserves its criticism for the idea that we should evaluate the activity of each of these communities by a universal standard – that we should try to make them all 'commensurable'.

We must recognise that postmodernist theory freely concedes the ability of local 'language-games' – natural science, moral traditions, etc. – to reflect on themselves and to pass judgements of value on particular 'moves' made or contemplated by participants. (That is to say, they can ask – according to the concession – questions such as 'Is this a valid contribution to scientific theory?' or 'Is this sort of conduct consistent with the received moral ideals of our community?') Thus, for Lyotard, 'the striking feature of postmodern scientific knowledge is that the discourse on the rules that validate it is (explicitly) immanent to it',[45] while MacIntyre, anxious to stress that a revival of virtue-centred ethical theory need not be opposed to debate and innovation, claims that 'a healthy [moral] tradition is sustained by its own internal arguments and conflicts'.[46]

This concession is chiefly interesting, however, for the question it raises: how are we to draw any principled distinction between the *rejection of Enlightenment rationalism* and the *rejection of legitimation as such*? The concession is, after all, a very significant one; for having been told that intellectual traditions incorporate a capacity for critical reflection, we might well suppose that the forces of Enlightenment had captured the high ground in the current argument. If discursive communities are capable of self-criticism in principle, we might ask, then who is to dictate how far they shall take it? Won't there always be room for more, so long as *any* intelligible criticism can be addressed to the moral or cognitive order under which we live? And what is this limitless commitment to the dialectical revision of theory and practice, if not precisely the Enlightenment commitment to haul up everything in life before the tribunal of reason?[47]

The likely reply to this challenge is that, although postmodernism may indeed be at a loss for any formal, *a priori* way of determining how far critical reflection can go, there is no real cause for embarrassment here. For the question is, in any case, best understood in a practical, or existential, sense – that is, as just one among many questions calling for deliberate collective choice, and conspicuous only for its unusual generality. Rorty puts the point succinctly:

> The pragmatist [e.g. Rorty himself] is betting that what succeeds the 'scientific', positivist culture that the Enlightenment produced will be *better* ... [This successor culture would be one] in which neither the priests nor the physicists nor the poets nor the Party were thought of as a more 'rational' or more 'scientific' or 'deeper' than one another. ... There would still be hero worship in such a culture, but it would not be worship of heroes as children of the gods, as marked off from the rest of mankind by closeness to the immortal. It would simply be admiration of exceptional men and women who were very good at doing the quite diverse kinds of things they did.[48]

MacIntyre's complaint against what he calls 'liberal individualist modernity', and against the 'modern self' corresponding to it, also rests on cultural considerations. The distinguishing mark of this 'self' is that it stands in a purely external relation to the various roles it may, from time to time, take on; that is, none of the activities in which it may become involved enters so deeply into it that to be severed from it would undermine its integrity.[49] The price paid for this radical emancipation from tradition is illustrated, as we have seen, by the sad fate of the Nietzschean *Übermensch*, whom MacIntyre uses as a foil to set off the attractions of a revived Aristotelianism. And the practical implication of his own Aristotelian programme is that we should call a halt to the pursuit of moral and political 'transcendence' and 'devote ourselves to the construction of *local* forms of community within which civility and the intellectual and moral life can be sustained'.[50] As for Lyotard, we have already noticed his use of the word 'terror' to characterise the idea of inquiry as a unified dialectical process aiming, ultimately, at its own completion or closure.

But, despite the valuable reminder issued by postmodernism that there is no such thing as a 'pure reason' dissociated from any basis in local custom, I do not think feminists should be unduly impressed by the theory in this modified version either.

I think we have reason to be wary, not only of the unqualified Nietzschean vision of an *end* to legitimation, but also of the suggestion that it would somehow be 'better' if legitimation exercises were carried out in a self-consciously parochial spirit. For if feminism aspires to be something more than a reformist movement, then it is bound sooner or later to find itself calling the parish boundaries into question.

To unpack this metaphor a little: feminists need to know, and postmodernist theory fails to explain, how we can achieve a thoroughgoing revision of the *range* of social scripts, narrative archetypes, ways of life, ways of earning a living, etc., available to individual women and men. Consider, for example, such mind-boggling, yet urgently necessary undertakings as the global redistribution of wealth and resources, the reallocation of work and leisure, the prevention of war and environmental destruction. Well, no doubt we shall be told that there is something *passé* in the very habit of mind which can still frame this kind of classically humanist agenda, given the alleged 'exhaustion' of all our political traditions (MacIntyre) and the extinction of any shared 'nostalgia for the unattainable' (Lyotard). But, on the other hand, if there can be no systematic political approach to questions of wealth, power and labour, how can there be any effective challenge to a social order which distributes its benefits and burdens in a systematically unequal way between the sexes? Thus, although it is courteous of Rorty to include women along with men in the class of 'expert-rulers' who will replace the Platonic philosopher-rulers in his pragmatist utopia, it remains a mystery how we can hope to achieve an equal sexual division of power unless we are 'allowed' (by epistemology and political theory) to address the structural causes of existing sexual *inequality*. But this would mean an assault on every social norm or institution which rests on biologistic assumptions about male and female 'nature' – on everything in our familiar way of life which can be traced to the entrenched functionalist notion that what women are *for* is to reproduce and nurture the species. And this, in turn, is far from being the sort of programme that could coexist with a meek, non-interventionist attitude towards the current inventory of social 'roles' or specialised functions. So postmodernism seems to face a dilemma: either it can concede the necessity, in terms of the aims of feminism,[51] of 'turning the world upside down' in the way just outlined – thereby opening a door once again to the Enlightenment idea of a *total* reconstruction of society on rational lines; or it can dogmatically reaffirm the arguments already marshalled against that idea – thereby licensing the cynical thought that, here as elsewhere, 'who will do what to whom under the new pluralism is depressingly predictable'.[52]

MacIntyre's discussion contains plenty of evidence, at a more intuitive level, for the reactionary implications of the proposed return to customary ethics. It is not that his portrayal of 'mythology' as a source of moral insight and guidance is so very wide of the mark phenomenologically. Who would deny the communal character of the ideas on which we draw when we set about the imaginative construction of our own lives as meaningful and unified chains of events? To be sure, 'myth' in this sense provides us with a more vivid conception of our own experience, it leaves us less bored and more in control. But a closer look at the workings of the process is less than reassuring from the point of view of sexual politics. MacIntyre pictures it as follows:

> I can only answer the question 'What am I to do?' if I can answer the prior question 'Of what story or stories do I find myself a part?' We enter human society ... with one or more imputed characters – roles into which we have been drafted – and we have to learn what they are in order to be able to understand how others respond to us and how our responses to them are apt to be construed. It is through hearing stories about wicked stepmothers, lost children, good but misguided kings, wolves that suckle twin boys, youngest sons who receive no inheritance but must make their own way in the world, and eldest sons who waste their inheritance on riotous living and must go and live with the swine, that children learn or mislearn both what a child and what a parent is, what the cast of characters may be in the drama into which they have been born and what the ways of the world are.[53]

This passage, if seriously intended, conveys the suggestion that the cornerstones of our mythical repertoire are the Bible, Grimm's Fairy Tales, and the Greek and Latin classics; and if that were the case, all good liberals would be bound to ask themselves whether the female half of the population can reasonably be asked to piece itself together out of the semiotic fallout from these sources. (Is it a coincidence that the only female role in MacIntyre's long list, for a human being at any rate, is that of a 'wicked stepmother'?) But, of course, the reality is even harsher. For our *effective* mythology, the one which actually determines the customary ethics of the (post)modern world, invites us to interpret ourselves and our neighbours in terms of a rather more topical range of 'imputed characters': good mothers, bad mothers, ruthless career women, gorgeous (dumb) blondes, ordinary housewives, women who are *no better than they should be*, loony lesbian feminists covered with badges ... anyone who ever reads a newspaper or watches TV can continue the list.

We might wonder whether it is fair to place such a gloomy construction on the 'narrative' model of personal identity. Why should it not be possible to reclaim some of the available roles and turn them, in a spirit of subversion, towards progressive ends? Aren't most, or at any rate *some*, political cultures of the late twentieth century sufficiently variegated to supply alternative story-lines to people of a critical turn of mind (the tireless activist, etc.)?

But MacIntyre seems to have pre-empted this move. For, although he mentions the 'protestor' as one of the 'stock character[s] in the modern social drama',[54] he consigns this type (along with the 'aesthete' and the 'bureaucrat') to a kind of limbo inhabited by those who have staked their selfhood on an illusion. These distinctively modern social roles, he suggests, can confer only a pseudo-identity on their bearers, since they all draw in one way or another on moral fictions spawned by the Enlightenment; in regard to the 'protestor' the relevant fiction is that of *natural rights*,[55] the defence of which MacIntyre apparently sees as constitutive of oppositional politics. Any idea that 'protest' might generate a substantive conception of personal virtue, and hence a viable postmodern life-pattern, must therefore be abandoned.

No doubt it is correct to see feminism as standing in a predominantly negative relation to the culture from which it springs. To use MacIntyre's idiom, no feminist can be content with the range of 'life-stories' currently on offer to girls and women; on the other hand, if we set our faces against that particular set of mythological suggestions, this does not imply that we ought to look forward with any eagerness to some putative neo-Aristotelian regime of 'morality and civility'.[56] (In fact, the very words kindle an obscure desire to commit social mayhem.)

We are not, however, under any obligation to accept the hackneyed characterisation of radical politics in terms of 'protest'. We can point instead to a positive aim which feminism has in common with other movements of liberation – an aim which, paradoxically, qualifies these movements as more genuinely Aristotelian than MacIntyre himself. For they are all concerned with the specification and construction of a *life worthy of human beings*: the very question under which Aristotle himself takes that of the individual 'good life' to be subsumed.[57] Interestingly, this is the question at which MacIntyre baulks; or rather, his moral epistemology reverses the direction of Aristotle's by treating the individual enterprise as a source of insight into the collective one:

> In what does the unity of an individual life consist? The answer is that its unity is the unity of a narrative embodied in a single life. To ask 'What is the good for me?' is to ask how best I might live out that unity and bring it to completion. To ask 'What is the good for man?' is to ask what all answers to the former question must have in common.[58]

The effect of this reversal is to bar the way to political *theory* and to force the aspiring theorist back into the ideologically saturated field of 'mythology' – i.e. back to a choice between the various narrative archetypes furnished by existing society. Ironically, then, it turns out that despite his use of Nietzsche as an object lesson in the perils of rampant individualism, MacIntyre's motives are not so very different from Nietzsche's own – at any rate, in those relatively unmetaphysical moments when the latter is pondering the 'immense stupidity of modern ideas'.[59]

IV

Finally, it remains to consider the third of my postmodernist themes, the 'pluralism of inclination'. I offer this (admittedly rather makeshift) term as a means of conferring some positive character on a development which has already been mentioned under its negative aspect – namely, the reaction against rationalist ideals of positive liberty and of the fully integrated human subject.

It would be beyond the scope of this paper to review the arguments for picturing subjectivity in general as 'decentred' or 'in process': these arguments have, in any case, been clearly expounded for the benefit of Anglophone readers by linguistic, literary and cultural theorists.[60] Nor can I offer any general appraisal of the 'philosophy of desire' as a possible successor to the historical-materialist tradition (I mean, in inspiring resistance to agencies of political and social control). We can, however, take advantage of the fact that these strains of anti-Enlightenment thinking have already begun to make their mark on the kind of cultural commentary produced by British feminists and socialists.[61]

Feminism has always given a central importance to the politics of personal choice and taste, and it is therefore significant that over the last few years the movement has made large concessions, in its treatment of these matters, to the anti-rationalist mood of the times. Perhaps the most important trend has been a loss of confidence in the idea of *false consciousness*: in other words, in the thought that our spontaneous aesthetic and emotional responses might require criticism in the light of a feminist analysis of sexual relationships.

To reject 'false consciousness' is to take a large step towards abandoning the politics of Enlightenment modernism. For it means rejecting the view that personal autonomy is to be reached by way of a progressive transcendence of earlier, less adequate cognitive structures: in our case, the transcendence of less adequate levels of insight into the operation of male power.

Many feminist writers now seem to hold that we shall be better equipped to think about the politics of personal life if we put the Enlightenment behind us. Influential in this respect has been Elizabeth Wilson's book *Adorned in Dreams: Fashion and modernity* (1985), which deplores the 'rational dress' tendency within feminism and affirms 'fashion' as a (potentially) oppositional medium of expression:

> Socially determined we may be [writes Wilson], but we consistently search for crevices in culture that open to us moments of freedom. Precisely because fashion is at one level a game ... it can be played for pleasure.[62]

The same theme has been taken up by journalist Suzanne Moore, who has written in defence of women's glossy magazines:

> We are waking up to the importance of fantasy, pleasure and style, and to awareness that a politics that excludes them will never be truly popular. ... We cannot just pull pleasure into the correct ideological space through political intention alone. The idea that we ever could results from an air of moral elitism prevalent on the left and unwittingly absorbed by feminism.[63]

And more recently, Brenda Polan of *The Guardian* has mounted the following attack on feminists who reject standard notions of how women ought to look:

> The puritans whose criticism disturbs me most are women who are self-righteous in their espousal of the belief that lack of artifice equals virtue. Aggressive lack of artifice ... declares a refusal to please, to charm, to be easy on the eye. It is an awesome

arrogance; a declaration that no improvement is necessary, that the aesthetic consensus is mistaken and those subscribe to it fools. (25 August 1988)

In all these texts the idea of *pleasure* is prominent – either our own, or, in Polan's cruder version of the argument, the pleasure we give others (thereby justifying our own existence and, presumably, gaining something of the narcissistic satisfaction traditionally allowed to women). The word 'pleasure', at all events, is apt to be brought out with a flourish, as if it clinched the case for seeing progressive or creative possibilities in something previously viewed with suspicion. The suggestion is that feminists have harmed their cause, they have *put people off*, by their gratuitous asceticism about make-up, frilly knickers and the like. But this invites the objection: whoever wants to claim that conventional femininity, even at its most abject, cannot be *pleasurable* for women?[64] Not long ago, it would have been widely accepted as self-evident that if for example I find that buying new clothes helps me to stave off boredom or sadness, that is not an argument in favour of shopping but a starting-point for reflection on my otherwise unsatisfied needs. If this is no longer common ground among feminists, it's arguable that the change is indicative not so much of an advance in wisdom or humanity as of a recourse to the consolations of the powerless – or rather, the consolations of those who have more purchasing power than power to influence the course of their common life.

There is, of course, something right in postmodernist warnings against insisting too much on 'ideological soundness', whether from oneself or – still worse – from others. No doubt there are pitfalls here; arrogance and self-deception are the most obvious. It would be sensible, therefore, to concede that there is no future in trying to conform on theoretical grounds to a definition of pleasure which is hopelessly remote from our current capacities for actually enjoying life. But if we accept that changes in these capacities can be emancipating – that they hold out a prospect of repairing some of the damage done to us in turning us out as women – then we are already committed to the idea that how things stand with a person in respect of her powers of enjoyment is a matter for political evaluation. And in that case, the occasional moralism or 'moral elitism' of radical movements will have to be understood as a vice of excess, rather than as a symptom of fundamental wrong-headedness: the danger lies, in other words, not in wishing to bring our (felt, empirical) desires into line with our rational understanding, but in tackling the job in a ham-fisted way that is doomed to provoke disgust and reaction.

Again, the postmodernist celebration of pleasure sometimes wins a trick by appealing to the role of immediate feeling in subverting psychic order.[65] The idea of subjectivity as socially (or discursively) constructed, and thus as inherently fluid and provisional, opens up a world of possibilities here.[66] But if feminism disowns altogether the impulse to 'enlighten', it will be at a loss to speak the wish to make these possibilities real. Subjectivity can be as fluid as you please, but this insight – once decoupled from the feminist ambition to *reconstruct* sensibility in the interest of women – will no longer be of any specifically political interest. Its political significance lies in the implication that contrary to appearances (to the nightmarish uniformity, give or take routine variations in 'style', of the cultural representation of gender), we can remake ourselves as better – more autonomous, less pathetic – people: 'better' by our own present lights, of course, but that is simply a condition of engagement in cognitive activity. Did anyone expect feminist theory to wipe out overnight every trace of the mythology which is, sexually speaking, at the heart of things? And if not, isn't the present surge of enthusiasm for 'pleasure' really the sign of a terrible pessimism?[67]

The alternative to this kind of pessimism, I suggest, is that feminists should continue to think of their efforts as directed not simply towards various local political programmes, but ultimately towards a global one – the abolition of the sex class system, and of the forms of inner life that belong with it. This programme is 'global' not just in the sense that it addresses itself to every corner of the planet, but also in the sense that its aims eventually converge with those of all other egalitarian or liberationist movements. (It would be arbitrary to work for *sexual* equality unless one believed that human society was disfigured by inequality *as such*.)

If this is a convincing overall characterisation of feminism, it follows that the movement should persist in seeing itself as a component or offshoot of Enlightenment modernism, rather than as one more 'exciting' feature (or cluster of features) in a postmodern social landscape. What does *not* follow is that it would be desirable for the women's movement – either world-wide, or in any one country – to be kept in order by some central authority (the 'totalitarian' spectre which postmodernists, in common with old-fashioned Cold Warriors, are fond of invoking). If, for example, European and/or North American feminism is alleged by black women to share in the racism of the surrounding culture, then their complaint rightly creates a new political agenda – a new set of pointers towards the goal of a genuinely 'heterogeneous public life';[68] and this sort of development certainly makes the movement (empirically speaking) less unified than before. But it does not prejudice the *ideal* unity of feminism.[69] Instead, it calls attention to a certain respect in which feminism has fallen short of its own idealised self-image as an occupant of the 'universal standpoint' (in contrast, say, to the traditional – male-dominated – Left). It is not 'liberal guilt', or conscientiousness in the abstract, which gives accusations of racism their urgency: it is the background commitment of feminism to the elimination of (self-interested) cognitive distortion.

Notes

Where full details are available in the Bibliography, references contain only essential information.

1. Specifically, I shall draw on Lyotard, *The Postmodern Condition: A report on knowledge* (hereafter *PMC*); MacIntyre, *After Virtue: A study in moral theory*, 1981 (hereafter *AV*); Rorty, *Philosophy and the Mirror of Nature*, 1980 (hereafter *PhMN*) and 'Pragmatism and philosophy' in his *Consequences of Pragmatism*, 1982, reprinted

in Kenneth Baynes, James Bohman and Thomas McCarthy (eds), *After Philosophy: End or transformation?*, MIT Press, Cambridge, MA, 1987.

Obviously the attempt to capture any complex argument in a brief survey is liable to lead to some oversimplification, and in particular it should be noticed that Rorty in *PhMN* refers to the Enlightenment separation of science from theology and politics as 'our most precious cultural heritage' (p. 333). The main motive of his book, however, is to voice a 'hope that the cultural space left by the demise of epistemology [i.e. of the commitment to rendering all discourse commensurable] will not be filled' (p. 315), and this identifies him for our purposes as an anti-Enlightenment theorist.

The themes of *After Virtue* are developed further in MacIntyre's more recent book, *Whose Justice? Which Rationality?* University of Notre Dame Press, Notre Dame, IN, 1988.

2. For an expression of this kind of intellectual monism, cf. Kant, Preface to *The Metaphysical Principles of Right* (in *The Metaphysical Principles of Virtue*, transl. James Ellington, 1964, p. 5): 'inasmuch as there can be only one human reason, so likewise there cannot be many philosophies; that is, only one true system of philosophy based on principles is possible, however variously and often contradictorily men may have philosophized over one and the same proposition'.

3. *AV*, p. 244.

4. *PMC*, p. 41.

5. *Ibid.*, p. 38.

6. *PhMN*, p. 318.

7. *AV*, p. 201.

8. *PMC*, p. 82.

9. For 'moral organism', cf. F. H. Bradley, *Ethical Studies*, Oxford University Press, Oxford, 1962, p. 177; and for 'significant whole', cf. H. H. Joachim, *The Nature of Truth*, Greenwood Press, Westport, CT, 1906, republ. 1969, pp. 68 ff.

10. Lyotard, for example, sees in the postmodern experience the 'truth' of the modern one (the former, he says, is *part* of the latter and inherits from it the maxim that 'all that has been received ... must be suspected' (*PMC*, p. 79); MacIntyre's position by contrast seems more akin to that of postmodernists in the field of art and design, where the distinguishing mark of the school has been found in a certain relation to the past – a reappropriation of traditional forms of expression, combined, however, with a historical knowingness acquired in the passage through modernity (cf. Charles Jencks, *What is Postmodernism?*, 1986, Academy Editions, London, p. 18).

11. *PhMN*, p. 318.

12. For this characterisation of 'positive' and 'negative' liberty, cf. Isaiah Berlin, 'Two concepts of liberty', in his *Four Essays on Liberty*, Oxford University Press, Oxford, 1969.

13. *AV*, p. 239.

14. For this reading of *Republic* VII, cf. Luce Irigaray, *Speculum of the Other Woman*, transl. Gillian C. Gill, Cornell University Press, Ithaca, NY, 1985, pp. 243 ff.; and for a fuller reconstruction of the idea of masculinity as transcendence, cf. Genevieve Lloyd, *The Man of Reason: 'Male' and 'female' in Western philosophy*, University of Minnesota Press, Minneapolis, 1984.

15. Marx and Engels, 'Manifesto of the Communist Party', in Karl Marx, *The Revolutions of 1848: Political writings*, vol. I, ed. David Fernbach, Penguin/NLB, Harmondsworth,

1973, p. 70: 'Constant revolutionizing of the means of production, uninterrupted disturbance of all social conditions, everlasting uncertainty and agitation distinguish the bourgeois epoch from all earlier ones. All fixed, fast-frozen relations, with their train of ancient and venerable prejudices and opinions, are swept away, all new-formed ones become antiquated before they can ossify. All that is solid melts into air, all that is holy is profaned ...'

Marshall Berman pursues this analysis in depth in *All That is Solid Melts into Air: The experience of modernity*, Simon & Schuster, New York, 1982, ch. 2.

16. For a review of the problems here, cf. Alison M. Jaggar, *Feminist Politics and Human Nature*, Rowman & Allanheld, Lanham, MD, 1983, ch. 4. More polemical discussions of the shortcomings of orthodox Marxist approaches to the 'woman question' can be found in Christine Delphy, 'The main enemy', in her *Close to Home: A materialist analysis of women's oppression* (transl. and ed. Diana Leonard, Hutchinson, London, 1984) and in Heidi Hartmann, 'The unhappy marriage of Marxism and feminism: Towards a more progressive union', in Lydia Sargent (ed.), *The Unhappy Marriage of Marxism and Feminism: A debate on class and patriarchy*, Pluto Press, London, 1981.

17. See ch. 5 above.

18. *Republic* VII, 519ab.

19. The exposure of this fantasy has been one of the concerns of feminist writing on pornography: cf. Susan Griffin, *Pornography and Silence: Culture's revenge against nature*, Harper & Row, New York, 1981.

20. 'Naturalist or materialist': there exists in the theory of knowledge a spectrum of positions prompted by the failure of the Cartesian quest for certainty. At one end of the spectrum – the 'positivist' end, so to speak – we have, for example, W. V. Quine's vision of 'epistemology, or something like it, simply fall[ing] into place as a chapter of psychology and hence of natural science', and his programmatic statement that 'We are after an understanding of science as an institution or process in the world' (cf. 'Epistemology naturalized' in his *Ontological Relativity and Other Essays*, Columbia University Press, New York, 1969, pp. 82, 84); at the other, 'critical', end we have a variety of views which take the latter programme in a political sense and search out the hidden power relations underlying not only (natural) science, but everything else to which the honorific title of 'knowledge' is assigned. 'Epistemic naturalism' can function as an umbrella term covering this whole spectrum of positions; 'epistemic materialism' is probably best reserved for a subset of them, namely those which seek to apply the Marxist method of historical materialism to the processes in question. (But Marxism does not exhaust the subversive options, which indeed can no longer be summed up without residue under the heading of 'critique' – witness the work of Nietzsche and Foucault.)

21. For Peirce's position, cf. 'How to make our ideas clear', in his *Collected Papers*, vol. V, Harvard University Press, Cambridge, MA, 1934, p. 268: 'all the followers of science are animated by a cheerful hope that the process of investigation, if only pushed far enough, will give one certain solution to each question to which they apply it. ... This great hope is embodied in the conception of truth and reality.'

22. *Critique of Pure Reason*, A648/B676.

23. *Ibid.*, A644/B672.

24. Plato, *Phaedo* 89d.

25. PMC, p. 65.

26. *Ibid.*, p. 52.

27. *Ibid.*, pp. 65–6. This theme is echoed by Rorty's account of the motive forces of post-epistemological discourse, which includes a reference to 'individual men of genius who think of something new' (*PhMN*, p. 264).

28. *PMC*, p. 81.

29. *Ibid.*, p. 77; cf. Kant, *Critique of Aesthetic Judgement*, §23.

30. Cf. Perry Anderson, 'Modernity and revolution', *New Left Review*, 144, 113 – a passage which, incidentally, contains a useful corrective to the tendency to confuse *eliminating contradiction* with *suppressing difference*. (For a more extended reply to the charge that discourse aiming at (universal) truth necessarily seeks to 'unify coercively a multiplicity of standpoints', cf. Peter Dews, *Logics of Disintegration: Poststructuralist thought and the claims of critical theory*, 1987, pp. 220 ff.; the words quoted appear on p. 222.)

31. *PMC*, p. 39. For reasons of space I have omitted any discussion of Lyotard's conspicuous *divergence* from Nietzsche in claiming that 'justice as a value is neither outmoded nor suspect' (p. 66). I do not think this need prevent us from getting to grips with his overall argument, since the idea that justice ought to be salvaged receives very perfunctory attention in *PMC* in comparison with the idea that universality ought to be jettisoned.

32. Cf. Nietzsche, *The Genealogy of Morals*, Random House, New York, 1969 (hereafter *GM*), Essay II, §16.

33. *GM*, Essay III, §25 (transl. Walter Kauffmann, 1969); *The Gay Science*, Random House, New York, 1974 (hereafter *GS*), §265 (transl. Kauffmann, 1974).

34. *Twilight of the Idols*, 'The problem of Socrates', §6 (transl. R. J. Hollingdale, 1968), Penguin, Harmondsworth.

35. 'Many', not all: obviously this conception rides roughshod over the claims of a 'feminism of difference'. I believe that reflection on sexual difference can be both intellectually and politically enabling, but incline ultimately towards the view that 'Glorification of the feminine character implies the humiliation of all who bear it' (Theodor Adorno, *Minima Moralia*, 1974, p. 96). However, I cannot argue the point here.

36. Cf. *GM*, *loc. cit.* (Kauffmann, p. 154): 'A predominance of mandarins always means something is wrong; so do the advent of democracy, international courts in place of war, equal rights for women, the religion of pity, and whatever other symptoms of declining life there are.'

    This feature of his thought should be kept clearly in view over against reminders – however valid – that Nietzsche is not a crude prophet of aggression, nor his 'will to power' equivalent to bloodlust (cf. Gillian Rose, *Dialectic of Nihilism: Poststructuralism and law*, Blackwell, Oxford, 1984, pp. 200 ff). No doubt it was vulgar of the Italian Futurists to babble about 'war, the sole hygiene ...', but the fact remains that for Nietzsche it is, in the end, a sign of spiritual poverty to regard war, injury and exploitation as detracting from the perfection of the world.

37. F. Nietzsche, *Ecce Homo*, Random House, New York, 1969, 'Why I write such good books', §5, transl. Kauffmann: 'Has my definition of love been heard? It is the only one worthy of a philosophy. Love – in its means, war; at bottom, the deadly hatred of the sexes.'

38. *GS*, §377 (transl. Kauffmann).

39. *GM*, Essay III, §12 (transl. Kauffmann).

40. F. Nietzsche, *Daybreak*, Cambridge University Press, Cambridge, Preface, §4 (transl. Hollingdale, 1982).

41. *GS*, §362; and cf. *GM*, *Essay III ad fin.*, where the statement that 'morality will gradually perish now' refers to the same historical prospect.

42. Cf. F. Nietzsche, *Beyond Good and Evil*, Harmondsworth, Penguin, 1973, §§231–9.

43. In the neo-Nietzschean discourse of the present day, the theme of 'hostility to feminism' is, not surprisingly, repressed. But this repressed material has a way of returning in contexts where the Enlightenment project of legitimation is up for criticism. An example is supplied by Vincent Descombes, expounding the views of Lyotard in *Modern French Philosophy*, transl. L. Scott-Fox and J. M. Harding, Cambridge University Press, Cambridge, 1980, p. 182: 'in more general terms, no sooner do we become aware that truth is only the expression of a will to truth than we must face the fact that this "truth" betrays a timid rejection of the world in as much as it is not a "true world" (stable, ordered and just)'. Notice the taunt: a *timid* rejection! This is the same rhetoric by means of which Nietzsche seeks to put the Enlightenment on the defensive – a rhetoric which associates the truth-orientated habit of thought with 'castration' (in the psychoanalytic sense).

44. Certainly, the idea of the outsider or 'nomad' (the individual who gets by, morally speaking, without any home base) has its own pathos, and even – in a rationalist context – its own justification (we have to deny ourselves *false* comforts in order not to be diverted from the quest for *true* ones, i.e. for a better world). But as the badge of a self-constituting elite – a Nietzschean 'aristocracy of the spirit' – it is merely the flip side of the bourgeois order. The nomad is the 'other' of the reliable paterfamilias; he is the 'untamed' male who has escaped from the trap of domesticity (cf. Gilles Deleuze's 'terrible mothers, terrible sisters and wives': *Nietzsche and Philosophy*, Athlone Press, London, transl. Hugh Tomlinson, 1983, p. 187). This cultural cliché is beginning to attract some well-deserved feminist criticism: cf. Deborah Cameron and Elizabeth Frazer, *The Lust to Kill: A feminist investigation of sexual murder*, Oxford, Polity Press, 1987, esp. pp. 52–69; 155–62. (Barbara Ehrenreich's *The Hearts of Men: American dreams and the flight from commitment*, New York, Doubleday, 1983, also contains relevant material.)

45. *PMC*, p. 54.

46. *AV*, p. 242.

47. It is sometimes suggested that this kind of 'legitimation from within' could not serve to keep the Enlightenment project in being, since its internality to the discourse on which it operates prevents it from being a *genuine* legitimation at all. This seems to be the reasoning of Lyotard, who also says of (postmodern) science that it is '*incapable* of legitimating itself, as speculation assumed that it [science] could' (*PMC*, p. 40, emphasis added). But this comment would be entirely out of place, were it not for an (unexamined) assumption that any 'legitimation' worthy of the name requires access to an *absolutely* transcendent standard of validity, i.e. to something exempt from the finite and provisional character attaching to all human discourse. (A related assumption can be seen at work in the attempt to discredit Enlightenment modernism by attaching fetishistic capital letters to the regulative ideas it invokes: 'Reason', 'Truth', etc.)

48. 'Pragmatism and philosophy', in Baynes, Bohman and McCarthy, *After Philosophy*, pp. 55–6.

49. Cf. *AV*, p. 30.

50. *Ibid.*, p. 245; emphasis added.

51. And of course those of socialism too, though it seems desirable to streamline the argument here.
52. Cf. Cameron and Frazer, *The Lust to Kill*, p. 175. (In its original context this remark refers to a 'pluralism' of sexual practice.)
53. *AV*, p. 201.
54. *Ibid.*, p. 238.
55. *Ibid.*, pp. 68–9.
56. *Ibid.*, p. 244.
57. Aristotle, *Nicomachean Ethics*, I, 2 (ethics is a branch of politics).
58. *AV*, p. 203.
59. Cf. *Beyond Good and Evil*, §239; other relevant passages are *GS*, §356 and *Twilight of the Idols*, 'Expeditions ...', §39. MacIntyre is of course aware of the contentiousness of his all-things-considered portrayal of Nietzsche as an *Aufklärer*, but decides to brazen it out (*AV*, p. 241); however, in view of Nietzsche's clear perception of his own work as a logical development of the Kantian 'critique of reason', I am unconvinced that MacIntyre succeeds in locating any flaw in the self-consciousness of his (Nietzsche's) texts.
    As a postscript to the foregoing discussion, I can warmly endorse these words of Seyla Benhabib and Drucilla Cornell in their Introduction to Benhabib and Cornell (eds), *Feminism as Critique*, 1987, pp. 12–13: 'Despite many common elements in their critique of the liberal concept of the self, feminist and communitarian perspectives differ: whereas communitarians emphasize the situatedness of the disembedded self in a network of relations and narratives, feminists also begin with the situated self but view the *renegotiation* of our psychosexual identities, and their *autonomous reconstitution* by individuals as essential to women's and human liberation.'
60. Cf. for example Deborah Cameron, *Feminism and Linguistic Theory*, Macmillan, London, 1985, ch. 7; Toril Moi, *Sexual/Textual Politics: Feminist literary theory*, 1985, pp. 99 ff.; Jacqueline Rose, *Sexuality in the Field of Vision*, Verso, London, 1986, esp. Introduction; Chris Weedon, *Feminist Practice and Poststructuralist Theory*, Blackwell, Oxford, 1987, chs 4, 5.
61. For a non-feminist statement of the case against 'political correctness' in the sphere of taste, cf. Robert Elms in *New Socialist*, May 1986. Curiously, some of Elms's 'designer socialist' claims in this article have a very Platonist ring ('there is no divide between form and content, they are both a reflection of each other. Good things look good ...'); but in his mouth these claims are far from bearing a rationalist meaning, since Elms assumes, in defiance of any 'Platonist' tradition, that what *looks good* is more knowable than what *is good* – that, in fact, appearances outweigh theory in the making of political value-judgements.
62. Elizabeth Wilson, *Adorned in Dreams*, Virago, London, 1985, p. 244. Notice that in her chapter on 'Feminism and fashion' Wilson does not limit herself to a simple critique of puritanism, but closes with a strong prescriptive message: 'The progressive project is not to search for some aesthetically pleasing form of utilitarian dress, for that would be to abandon the medium; rather we *should* use dress to express and explore our more daring aspirations' (p. 247; emphasis added).
63. 'Permitted pleasures', in *Women's Review*, August 1986 (order of excerpts reversed).
64. Cf. Catharine A. MacKinnon's description of sexism as 'a political inequality that is

sexually enjoyed, if unequally so' (in her *Feminism Unmodified: Discourses on life and law*, Harvard University Press, Cambridge, MA, 1987, p. 7).

65. Moore ('Permitted pleasures') tells us that 'Femininity is not indelibly stamped on to us, but continually in a process of re-creating itself.' But this does not deter her from writing of 'the early seventies, [when] some women were desperately trying to have the right kind of sexual fantasy that didn't actually involve any of the things that make sex exciting'. Despite the playful tone, these words clearly imply that we *know what it is* that 'makes sex exciting'. Well, *do* we know? It is too easy to say that if you are interested in 'sex' then you can't help knowing. On one level that is no doubt true; but strategically, a more fruitful principle for feminists (and other opponents of patriarchy) would be to assume that we still have everything to learn.

66. These are the possibilities I once tried to capture in terms of Quine's notion of a 'pull toward objectivity': what this phrase suggests is that we can pull the other way, i.e. that there can be a conscious, politically motivated resistance to the processes of socialisation (cf. Sabina Lovibond, *Realism and Imagination in Ethics*, Blackwell, Oxford, 1983, pp. 58 ff., 194).

67. Terry Eagleton's words about the 'characteristic post-structuralist blend of pessimism and euphoria' ('Capitalism, modernism and postmodernism', 64) seem very much to the point as a comment on the politics of 'crevices' and 'moments'.

68. Cf. §4 of Iris Marion Young, 'Impartiality and the civil public: Some implications of feminist critiques of moral and political theory' in S. Benhabib and D. Cornell (eds), *Feminism as Critique*, Polity, Oxford, 1987. As should be clear by now, I am unpersuaded by the view of 'Enlightenment' which prompts Young's statement that 'we cannot envision such a renewal of public life as a recovery of Enlightenment ideals' (p. 73).

69. That is, it does not constitute an argument against conceiving of feminism as essentially a single movement (because constituted by a single aim – the aim of ending sexual oppression).

30 □ *Social Criticism without Philosophy: An encounter between feminism and postmodernism*

Nancy Fraser and Linda Nicholson

Feminism and postmodernism have emerged as two of the most important political-cultural currents of the last decade. So far, however, they have kept an uneasy distance from one another. Indeed, so great has been their mutual wariness that there have been remarkably few extended discussions of the relations between them (exceptions are: Flax, 1986; Harding, 1986a, 1986b; Haraway, 1983; Jardine, 1985; Lyotard, 1978; Owens, 1983).

Initial reticences aside, there are good reasons for exploring the relations between feminism and postmodernism. Both have offered deep and far-reaching criticisms of the 'institution of philosophy'. Both have elaborated critical perspectives on the relation of philosophy to the larger culture. And, most central to the concerns of this essay, both have sought to develop new paradigms of social criticism which do not rely on traditional philosophical underpinnings. Other differences notwithstanding, one could say that, during the last decade, feminists and postmodernists have worked independently on a common nexus of problems: they have tried to rethink the relation between philosophy and social criticism so as to develop paradigms of 'criticism without philosophy'.

On the other hand, the two tendencies have proceeded, so to speak, from opposite directions. Postmodernists have focused primarily on the philosophy side of the problem. They have begun by elaborating anti-foundational metaphilosophical perspectives and from there have gone to to draw conclusions about the shape and character of social criticism. For feminists, on the other hand, the question of philosophy has always been subordinate to an interest in social criticism. So they have begun by developing critical political perspectives and from there have gone on to draw conclusions about the status of philosophy. As a result of this difference in emphasis and direction, the two tendencies have ended up with complementary strengths and weaknesses. Postmodernists offer sophisticated and persuasive

From *Theory, Culture and Society*, 5, 2–3 (1988), 373–94.

criticisms of foundationalism and essentialism, but their conceptions of social criticism tend to be anaemic. Feminists offer robust conceptions of social criticism, but they tend, at times, to lapse into foundationalism and essentialism.

Thus, each of the two perspectives suggests some important criticisms of the other. A postmodernist reflection on feminist theory reveals disabling vestiges of essentialism, while a feminist reflection on postmodernism reveals androcentrism and political naivete.

It follows that an encounter between feminism and postmodernism will initially be a trading of criticisms. But there is no reason to suppose that this is where matters must end. In fact, each of these tendencies has much to learn from the other; each is in possession of valuable resources which can help remedy the deficiencies of the other. Thus, the ultimate stake of an encounter between feminism and postmodernism is the prospect of a perspective which integrates their respective strengths while eliminating their respective weaknesses. It is the prospect of a postmodernist feminism.

In what follows, we aim to contribute to the development of such a perspective by staging the initial, critical phase of the encounter. In section 1, we examine the ways in which one exemplary postmodernist, Jean-François Lyotard, has sought to derive new paradigms of social criticism from a critique of the institution of philosophy. We argue that the conception of social criticism so derived is too restricted to permit an adequate critical grasp of gender dominance and subordination. We identify some internal tensions in Lyotard's arguments; and we suggest some alternative formulations which could allow for more robust forms of criticism without sacrificing the commitment to anti-foundationalism. In section 2, we examine some representative genres of feminist social criticism. We argue that, in many cases, feminist critics continue tacitly to rely on the sorts of philosophical underpinnings which their own commitments, like those of postmodernists, ought, in principle, to rule out. And we identify some points at which such underpinnings could be abandoned without any sacrifice of social-critical force. Finally, in a brief conclusion, we consider the prospects for a postmodernist feminism. We discuss some requirements which constrain the development of such a perspective and we identify some pertinent conceptual resources and critical strategies.

I Postmodernism

Postmodernists seek, *inter alia*, to develop conceptions of social criticism which do not rely on traditional philosophical underpinnings. The typical starting point for their efforts is a reflection on the condition of philosophy today. Writers like Richard Rorty and Jean-François Lyotard begin by arguing that Philosophy with a capital 'P' is no longer a viable or credible enterprise. From here, they go on to claim that philosophy, and, by extension, theory more generally, can no longer function to *ground* politics and social criticism. With the demise of foundationalism comes the demise of the view that casts philosophy in the role of *founding* discourse *vis-à-vis* social criticism. That 'modern' conception must give way to a new 'postmodern' one in which criticism floats free of any universalist theoretical ground. No longer anchored philosophically, the very shape or character of social criticism changes; it becomes more pragmatic, *ad hoc*, contextual and local. And with this change comes a corresponding change in the social role and political function of intellectuals.

Thus, in the postmodern reflection on the relationship between philosophy and social criticism, the term 'philosophy' undergoes an explicit devaluation; it is cut down to size, if not eliminated altogether. Yet, even as this devaluation is argued explicitly, the term 'philosophy' retains an implicit structural privilege. It is the changed condition of philosophy which determines the changed characters of social criticism and of engaged intellectual practice. In the new postmodern equation, then, philosophy is the independent variable while social criticism and political practice are dependent variables. The view of theory which emerges is not determined by considering the needs of contemporary criticism and engagement. It is determined, rather, by considering the contemporary status of philosophy. As we hope to show, this way of proceeding has important consequences, not all of which are positive. Among the results is a certain underdescription and premature foreclosure of possibilities for social criticism and engaged intellectual practice. This limitation of postmodern thought will be apparent when we consider its results in the light of the needs of contemporary feminist theory and practice.

Let us consider as an example the postmodernism of Jean-François Lyotard, since it is genuinely exemplary of the larger tendency. Lyotard is one of the few social thinkers widely considered postmodern who actually uses the term; indeed, it was he himself who introduced it into current discussions of philosophy, politics, society and social theory. His book *The Postmodern Condition* has become the *locus classicus* for contemporary debates, and it reflects in an especially acute form the characteristic concerns and tensions of the movement (Lyotard, 1984a).

For Lyotard, postmodernism designates a general condition of contemporary Western civilization. The postmodern condition is one in which 'grand narratives of legitimation' are no longer credible. By 'grand narratives' he means, in the first instance, overarching philosophies of history like the Enlightenment story of the gradual but steady progress of reason and freedom, Hegel's dialectic of Spirit coming to know itself, and, most importantly, Marx's drama of the forward march of human productive capacities via class conflict culminating in proletarian revolution. For Lyotard, these 'metanarratives' instantiate a specifically modern approach to the problem of legitimation. Each situates first-order discursive practices of inquiry and politics within a broader totalizing metadiscourse which legitimates them. The metadiscourse narrates a story about the whole of human history which purports to guarantee that the 'pragmatics' of the modern sciences and of modern political processes, that is, the norms and rules which govern these practices, determining what counts as a warranted move within them, are themselves legitimate. The story guarantees that some sciences and some politics have the *right* pragmatics and, so, are the *right* practices.

We should not be misled by Lyotard's focus on narrative philosophies of history.

In his conception of legitimating metanarrative, the stress properly belongs on the 'meta' and not the 'narrative'. For what most interests him about the Enlightenment, Hegelian and Marxist stories is what they share with other, non-narrative forms of philosophy. Like ahistorical epistemologies and moral theories, they aim to show that specific first-order discursive practices are well-formed and capable of yielding true and just results. 'True' and 'just' here mean something more than results reached by adhering scrupulously to the constitutive rules of some given scientific and political games. They mean, rather, results which correspond to Truth and Justice as they really are in themselves independently of contingent, historical, social practices. Thus, in Lyotard's view, a metanarrative is meta in a very strong sense. It purports to be a privileged discourse capable of situating, characterizing and evaluating all other discourses, but not itself infected by the historicity and contingency which render first-order discourses potentially distorted and in need of legitimation.

In *The Postmodern Condition*, Lyotard argues that metanarratives, whether philosophies of history or non-narrative foundational philosophies, are merely modern and dépassé. We can no longer believe, he claims, in the availability of a privileged metadiscourse capable of capturing once and for all the truth of every first-order discourse. The claim to meta status does not stand up. A so-called metadiscourse is in fact simply one more discourse among others. It follows for Lyotard that legitimation, both epistemic and political, can no longer reside in philosophical metanarratives. Where, then, he asks, does legitimation reside in the postmodern era?

Much of *The Postmodern Condition* is devoted to sketching an answer to this question. The answer, in brief, is that in the postmodern era legitimation becomes plural, local and immanent. In this era, there will necessarily be many discourses of legitimation dispersed among the plurality of first-order discursive practices. For example, scientists no longer look to prescriptive philosophies of science to warrant their procedures of inquiry. Rather, they themselves problematize, modify and warrant the constitutive norms of their own practice even as they engage in it. Instead of hovering above, legitimation descends to the level of practice and becomes immanent in it. There are no special tribunals set apart from the sites where inquiry is practiced. Rather, practitioners assume responsibility for legitimizing their own practice.

Lyotard intimates that something similar is or should be happening with respect to political legitimation. We cannot have and do not need a single, overarching theory of justice. What is required, rather, is a 'justice of multiplicities' (Lyotard, 1984a; see also: Lyotard and Thébaud, 1987; Lyotard, 1984b). What Lyotard means by this is not wholly clear. On one level, he can be read as offering a normative vision in which the good society consists in a decentralized plurality of democratic, self-managing groups and institutions whose members problematize the norms of their practice and take responsibility for modifying them as situations require. But paradoxically, on another level, he can be read as ruling out the sort of larger-scale, normative political theorizing which, from a 'modern' perspective at least, would be required to legitimate such a vision. In any case, his justice of multiplicities conception precludes one familiar, and arguably essential, genre of political theory: identification and critique of macrostructures of inequality and injustice which cut across the boundaries separating relatively discrete practices and institutions. There is no place in Lyotard's universe for critique of pervasive axes of stratification, for critique of broad-based relations of dominance and subordination along lines like gender, race and class.

Lyotard's suspicion of the large extends to historical narrative and social theory as well. Here, his chief target is Marxism, the one metanarrative in France with enough lingering credibility to be worth arguing against. The problem with Marxism, in his view, is twofold. On the one hand, the Marxian story is too big, since it spans virtually the whole of human history. On the other hand, the Marxian story is too theoretical, since it relies on a *theory* of social practice and social relations which claims to *explain* historical change. At one level, Lyotard simply rejects the specifics of this theory. He claims that the Marxian conception of practice as production occludes the diversity and plurality of human practices. And the Marxian conception of capitalist society as a totality traversed by one major division and contradiction occludes the diversity and plurality of contemporary societal differences and oppositions. But Lyotard does not conclude that such deficiencies can and should be remedied by a better social theory. Rather, he rejects the project of social theory *tout court*.

Once again, Lyotard's position is ambiguous, since his rejection of social theory depends on a theoretical perspective of sorts of its own. He offers a 'postmodern' conception of sociality and social identity, a conception of what he calls 'the social bond'. What holds a society together, he claims, is not a common consciousness or institutional substructure. Rather, the social bond is a weave of crisscrossing threads of discursive practices, no single one of which runs continuously throughout the whole. Individuals are the nodes or 'posts' where such practices intersect and, so, they participate in many simultaneously. It follows that social identities are complex and heterogeneous. They cannot be mapped onto one another, nor onto the social totality. Indeed, strictly speaking, there is no social totality and *a fortiori* no possibility of a totalizing social theory.

Thus, Lyotard insists that the field of the social is heterogeneous and nontotalizable. As a result, he rules out the sort of critical social theory which employs general categories like gender, race and class. From his perspective, such categories are too reductive of the complexity of social identities to be useful. And there is apparently nothing to be gained, in his view, by situating an account of the fluidity and diversity of discursive practices in the context of a critical analysis of large-scale institutions and social structures.

Thus, Lyotard's postmodern conception of criticism without philosophy rules out several recognizable genres of social criticism. From the premise that criticism cannot be grounded by a foundationalist philosophical metanarrative, he infers the illegitimacy of large historical stories, normative theories of justice and social-theoretical accounts of macrostructures which institutionalize inequality. What, then, *does* postmodern social criticism look like?

Lyotard tries to fashion some new genres of social criticism from the discursive resources that remain. Chief among these is smallish, localized narrative. He seeks to vindicate such narrative against both modern totalizing metanarrative and the scientism that is hostile to all narrative. One genre of postmodern social criticism then, consists in relatively discrete, local stories about the emergence, transformation and disappearance of various discursive practices treated in isolation from one another. Such stories might resemble those told by Michel Foucault, though without the attempts to discern larger synchronic patterns and connections that Foucault (1979) sometimes made. And like Michael Walzer (1983), Lyotard seems to assume that practitioners would narrate such stories when seeking to persuade one another to modify the pragmatics or constitutive norms of their practice.

This genre of social criticism is not the whole postmodern story, however. For it casts critique as strictly local, *ad hoc* and ameliorative, thus supposing a political diagnosis according to which there are not large-scale, systemic problems which resist local, *ad hoc*, ameliorative initiatives. Yet Lyotard recognizes that postmodern society does contain at least one unfavourable structural tendency which requires a more coordinated response. This is the tendency to universalize instrumental reason, to subject *all* discursive practices indiscriminately to the single criterion of efficiency or 'performativity'. In Lyotard's view, this threatens the autonomy and integrity of science and politics, since these practices are not properly subordinated to performative standards. It would pervert and distort them, thereby destroying the diversity of discursive forms.

Thus, even as he argues explicitly against it, Lyotard posits the need for a genre of social criticism which transcends local mininarrative. And despite his strictures against large, totalizing stories, he narrates a fairly tall tale about a large-scale social trend. Moreover, the logic of this story, and of the genre of criticism to which it belongs, calls for judgements, which are not strictly practice-immanent. Lyotard's story presuppose the legitimacy and integrity of the scientific and political practices allegedly threatened by 'performativity'. It supposes that one can distinguish changes or developments which are *internal* to these practices from externally induced distortions. But this drives Lyotard to make normative judgements about the value and character of the threatened practices. These judgements are not strictly immanent in the practices judged. Rather, they are 'metapractical'.

Thus, Lyotard's view of postmodern social criticism is neither entirely self-consistent not entirely persuasive. He goes too quickly from the premise that Philosophy cannot ground social criticism to the conclusion that criticism itself must be local, *ad hoc* and non-theoretical. As a result, he throws out the baby of large historical narrative with the bathwater of philosophical metanarrative and the baby of social-theoretical analysis of large-scale inequalities with the bathwater of reductive Marxian class theory. Moreover, these allegedly illegitimate babies do not in fact remain excluded. They return like the repressed within the very genres of postmodern social criticism with which Lyotard intends to replace them.

We began this discussion by noting that postmodernists orient their reflections on the character of postmodern social criticism by the falling star of foundationalist philosophy. They posit that, with philosophy no longer able credibly to ground social criticism, criticism itself must be local, *ad hoc* and untheoretical. Thus, from the critique of foundationalism, they infer the illegitimacy of several genres of social criticism. For Lyotard, the illegitimate genres include large-scale historical narrative and social-theoretical analyses of pervasive relations of dominance and subordination. [1]

Suppose, however, one were to choose another starting point for reflecting on postfoundational social criticism. Suppose one began, not with the condition of Philosophy, but with the nature of the social object one wished to criticize. Suppose, further, that one defined that object as the subordination of women to and by men. Then, we submit, it would be apparent that many of the genres rejected by postmodernists are necessary for social criticism. For a phenomenon as pervasive and multifaceted as male dominance simply cannot be adequately grasped with the meagre critical resources to which they would limit us. On the contrary, effective criticism of this phenomenon requires an array of different methods and genres. It requires as a minimum large narratives about changes in social organization and ideology, empirical and social-theoretical analyses of macrostructures and institutions, interactionist analyses of the micro-politics of everyday life, critical-hermeneutical and institutional analyses of cultural production, historically and culturally specific sociologies of gender. ... The list could go on.

Clearly, not all of these approaches are local and 'untheoretical'. But all are nonetheless essential to feminist social criticism. Moreover, all can, in principle, be conceived in ways that do not take us back to foundationalism even though, as we argue in the next section, many feminists have so far not wholly succeeded in avoiding that trap.

2 Feminism

Feminists, like postmodernists, have sought to develop new paradigms of social criticism which do not rely on traditional philosophical underpinnings. They have criticized modern foundationalist epistemologies and moral and political theories, exposing the contingent, partial and historically situated character of what have passed in the mainstream for necessary, universal and ahistorical truths. And they have called into question the dominant philosophical project of seeking objectivity in the guise of a 'God's-eye view' which transcends any situation or perspective (see, for example, Harding and Hintikka, 1983).

However, if postmodernists have been drawn to such views by a concern with the status of philosophy, feminists have been led to them by the demands of political practice. This practical interest has saved feminist theory from many of the mistakes of postmodernism: women whose theorizing was to serve the struggle against sexism were not about to abandon powerful political tools merely as a result of intramural debates in professional philosophy.

Yet even as the imperatives of political practice have saved feminist theory from one set of difficulties, they have tended at times to incline it toward another. Practical imperatives have led some feminists to adopt modes of theorizing which resemble the sorts of philosophical metannarrative rightly criticized by postmodernists. To be sure, the feminist theories we have in mind here are not 'pure' metanarratives; they are not ahistorical normative theories about the transcultural nature of rationality or justice. Rather, they are very large social theories, theories of history, society, culture and psychology which claim, for example, to identify causes and/or constitute features of sexism that operate cross-culturally. Thus, these social theories purport to be empirical rather than philosophical. But, as we hope to show, they are actually 'quasi-metanarratives'. They tacitly presuppose some commonly held but unwarranted and essentialist assumptions about the nature of human beings and the conditions for social life. In addition, they assume methods and/or concepts which are uninflected by temporality or historicity and which therefore function *de facto* as permanent, neutral matrices for inquiry. Such theories, then, share some of the essentialist and ahistorical features of metanarratives: they are insufficiently attentive to historical and cultural diversity; and they falsely universalize features of the theorist's own era, society, culture, class, sexual orientation, and/or ethnic or racial group.

On the other hand, the practical exigencies inclining feminists to produce quasi-metanarratives have by no means held undisputed sway. Rather, they have had to coexist, often uneasily, with counterexigencies which have worked to opposite effect, for example, political pressures to acknowledge differences among women. In general, then, the recent history of feminist social theory reflects a tug of war between forces which have encouraged and forces which have discouraged metanarrative-like modes of theorizing. We can illustrate this dynamic by looking at a few important turning points in this history.

When, in the 1960s, women in the new left began to extend prior talk about 'women's rights' into the more encompassing discussion of 'women's liberation', they encountered the fear and hostility of their male comrades and the use of Marxist political theory as a support for these reactions. Many men of the new left argued that gender issues were secondary because subsumable under more basic modes of oppression, namely, class and race.

In response to this practical-political problem, radical feminists such as Shulamith Firestone (1970) resorted to an ingenious tactical manoeuvre: Firestone invoked biological differences between women and men to explain sexism. This enabled her to turn the tables on her Marxist comrades by claiming that gender conflict was the most basic form of human conflict and the source of all other forms, including class conflict. Here, Firestone drew on the pervasive tendency within modern culture to locate the roots of gender differences in biology. Her coup was to use biologism to establish the primacy of the struggle against male domination rather than to justify acquiescence to it.

The trick, of course, is problematic from a postmodernist perspective in that appeals to biology to explain social phenomena are essentialist and monocausal. They are essentialist insofar as they project onto all women and men qualities which develop under historically specific social conditions. They are monocausal insofar as they look to one set of characteristics, such as women's physiology or men's hormones, to explain women's oppression in all cultures. These problems are only compounded when appeals to biology are used in conjunction with the dubious claim that women's oppression is the cause of all other forms of oppression.

Moreover, as Marxists and feminist anthropologists began insisting in the early 1970s, appeals to biology do not allow us to understand the enormous diversity of forms which both gender and sexism assume in different cultures. And in fact, it was not long before most feminist social theorists came to appreciate that accounting for the diversity of the forms of sexism was as important as accounting for its depth and autonomy. Gayle Rubin (1975: 160) aptly described this dual requirement as the need to formulate theory which could account for the oppression of women in its 'endless variety and monotonous similarity'. How were feminists to develop a social theory adequate to both demands?

One approach which seemed promising was suggested by Michelle Zimbalist Rosaldo and other contributors to the influential 1974 anthropology collection *Woman, Culture and Society*. They argued that common to all known societies was some type of separation between a 'domestic sphere' and a 'public sphere', the former associated with women and the latter with men. Because in most societies to date women have spent a good part of their lives bearing and raising children, their lives have been more bound to 'the domestic sphere'. Men, on the other hand, have had both the time and the mobility to engage in those out-of-the-home activities which generate political structures. Thus, as Rosaldo (1974) argued, while in many societies women possess some or even a great deal of power, women's power is always viewed as illegitimate, disruptive and without authority.

This approach seemed to allow for both diversity and ubiquity in the manifestations of sexism. A very general identification of women with the domestic and of men with the extra-domestic could accommodate a great deal of cultural variation both in social structures and in gender roles. At the same time, it could make comprehensible the apparent ubiquity of the assumption of women's inferiority above and beyond such variation. This hypothesis was also compatible with the idea that the extent of women's oppression differed in different societies. It could explain such differences by correlating the extent of gender inequality in a society with the extent and rigidity of the separation between its domestic and public spheres. In short, the domestic/public theorists seemed to have generated an explanation capable of satisfying a variety of conflicting demands.

However, this explanation turned out to be problematic in ways reminiscent of Firestone's account. Although the theory focused on differences between men's and women's spheres of activity rather than on differences between men's and women's biology, it was essentialist and monocausal nonetheless. It posited the existence of a 'domestic sphere' in all societies and thereby assumed that women's activities were basically similar in content and significance across cultures. (An analogous assumption about men's activities lay behind the postulation of a universal 'public sphere'.) In effect, the theory falsely generalized to all societies a historically specific conjunction of properties: women's responsibility for early child-rearing, women's tendency to spend more time in the geographical space of the home, women's lesser participation in the affairs of the community, a cultural ascription of triviality to domestic work, and a cultural ascription of inferiority to women. The theory thus failed to appreciate that, while each individual property may be true of many societies, the conjunction is not true of most.[2]

One source of difficulty in these early feminist social theories was the presumption of an overly grandiose and totalizing conception of theory. Theory was understood as the search for the one key factor which would explain sexism cross-culturally and illuminate all of social life. In this sense, to theorize was by definition to produce a quasi-metanarrative.

Since the late 1970s, feminist social theorists have largely ceased speaking of biological determinants or a cross-cultural domestic/public separation. Many, moreover, have given up the assumption of monocausality. Nevertheless, some feminist social theorists have continued implicitly to suppose a quasi-metanarrative conception of theory. They have continued to theorize in terms of a putatively unitary, primary, culturally universal type of activity associated with women, generally an activity conceived as 'domestic' and located in 'the family'.

One influential example is the analysis of 'mothering' developed by Nancy Chodorow (1978). Setting herself to explain the internal, psychological, dynamics which have led many women willingly to reproduce social divisions associated with female inferiority, Chodorow posited a cross-cultural activity, mothering, as the relevant object of investigation. Her question thus became: how is mothering as a female-associated activity reproduced over time? How does mothering produce a new generation of women with the psychological inclination to mother and a new generation of men not so inclined? The answer she offered was in terms of 'gender identity': female mothering produces women whose deep sense of self is 'relational' and men whose deep sense of self is not.

Chodorow's theory has struck many feminists as a persuasive account of some apparently observable psychic differences between men and women. Yet the theory has clear metanarrative overtones. It posits the existence of a single activity, 'mothering', which, while differing in specifics in different societies, nevertheless constitutes enough of a natural kind to warrant one label. It stipulates that this basically unitary activity gives rise to two distinct sorts of deep selves, one relatively common across cultures to women, the other relatively common across cultures to men. And it claims that the difference thus generated between 'feminine and masculine gender identity' causes a variety of supposedly cross-cultural social phenomena, including the continuation of female mothering, male contempt for women and problems in heterosexual relationships.

From a postmodern perspective, all of these assumptions are problematic because essentialist. But the second one, concerning 'gender identity', warrants special scrutiny, given its political implications. Consider that Chodorow's use of the notion of gender identity presupposes three major premises. One is the psychoanalytic premise that everyone has a deep sense of self which is constituted in early childhood through one's interactions with one's primary parent and which remains relatively constant thereafter. Another is the premise that this 'deep self' differs significantly for men and for women but is roughly similar among women, on the one hand, and among men, on the other hand, both across cultures and within cultures across lines of class, race and ethnicity. The third premise is that this deep self colours everything one does; there are no actions, however trivial, which do not bear traces of one's masculine or feminine gender identity.

One can appreciate the political exigencies which made this conjunction of premises attractive. It gave scholarly substance to the idea of the pervasiveness of sexism. If masculinity and femininity constitute our basic and ever-present sense of self, then it is not surprising that the manifestations of sexism are systemic. Moreover, many feminists had already sensed that the concept of 'sex-role socialization', an idea Chodorow explicitly criticized, ignored the depth and intractability of male dominance. By implying that measures such as changing images in school textbooks or allowing boys to play with dolls would be sufficient to bring about equality between the sexes, this concept seemed to trivialize and co-opt the message of feminism. Finally, Chodorow's depth-psychological approach gave a scholarly sanction to the idea of sisterhood. It seemed to legitimate the claim that the ties which bind women are deep and substantively based.

Needless to say, we have no wish to quarrel with the claim of the depth and pervasiveness of sexism, nor with the idea of sisterhood. But we do wish to challenge Chodorow's way of legitimating them. The idea of a cross-cultural, deep sense of self, specified differently for women and men, becomes problematic when given any specific content. Chodorow states that women everywhere differ from men in their greater concern with 'relational interaction'. But what does she mean by this term? Certainly not any and every kind of human interaction, since men have often been more concerned than women with some kinds of interactions, for example, those which have to do with the aggrandizement of power and wealth. Of course, it is true that many women in modern Western societies have been expected to exhibit strong concern with those types of interactions associated with intimacy, friendship and love, interactions which dominate one meaning of the late-twentieth-century concept of 'relationship'. But surely this meaning presupposes a notion of private life specific to modern Western societies of the last two centuries. Is it possible that Chodorow's theory rests on an equivocation on the term 'relationship'?[3]

Equally troubling are the aporias this theory generates for political practice. While 'gender identity' gives substance to the idea of sisterhood, it does so at the cost of repressing differences among sisters. Although the theory allows for some differences among women of different classes, races, sexual orientations and ethnic groups, it construes these as subsidiary to more basic similarities. But it is precisely as a consequence of the request to understand such differences as secondary that many women have denied an allegiance to feminism.

We have dwelt at length on Chodorow because of the great influence her work has enjoyed. But she is not the only recent feminist social theorist who has constructed a quasi-metanarrative around a putatively cross-cultural female-associated activity. On the contrary, theorists like Ann Ferguson and Nancy Folbre (1981), Nancy Hartsock (1983) and Catharine MacKinnon (1982) have done something analogous with 'sex-affective production', 'reproduction' and 'sexuality' respectively. Each claims to have identified a basic kind of human practice found in all societies which has cross-cultural explanatory power. In each case, the practice in question is associated with a biological or quasi-biological need and is construed as functionally necessary to the reproduction of society. It is not the sort of thing, then, whose historical origins need be investigated.

The difficulty here is that categories like sexuality, mothering, reproduction and sex-affective production group together phenomena which are not necessarily conjoined in all societies, while separating off from one another phenomena which are not necessarily separated. As a matter of fact, it is doubtful whether these categories have any determinate cross-cultural content. Thus, for a theorist to use such categories to construct a universalistic social theory is to risk projecting the socially dominant conjunctions and dispersions of her own society onto others, thereby distorting important features of both. Social theorists would do better first to construct genealogies of the *categories* of sexuality, reproduction and mothering before assuming their universal significance.

Since around 1980, many feminist scholars have come to abandon the project of grand social theory. They have stopped looking for *the* causes of sexism and have turned to more concrete inquiry with more limited aims. One reason for this shift is the growing legitimacy of feminist scholarship. The institutionalization of Women's Studies in the US has meant a dramatic increase in the size of the community of feminist inquiries, a much greater division of scholarly labor and a large and growing fund of concrete information. As a result, feminist scholars have come to regard this enterprise more collectively, more like a puzzle whose various pieces are being filled in by many different people than a construction to be completed by a single grand theoretical stroke. In short, feminist scholarship has attained its maturity.

Even in this phase, however, traces of youthful quasi-metanarratives remain. Some theorists who have ceased looking for *the* causes of sexism still rely on essentialist categories like 'gender identity'. This is especially true of those scholars who have sought to develop 'gynocentric' alternatives to mainstream androcentric perspectives, but have not fully abandoned the universalist pretensions of the latter.

Consider, as an example, the work of Carol Gilligan (1982). Unlike most of the theorists we have considered so far, Gilligan has not sought to explain the origins or nature of cross-cultural sexism. Rather, she set herself the more limited task of exposing and redressing androcentric bias in the model of moral development of psychologist Lawrence Kohlberg. Thus, she argued that it is illegitimate to evaluate the moral development of women and girls by reference to a standard drawn exclusively from the experience of men and boys. And she proposed to examine women's moral discourse on its own terms in order to uncover its immanent standards of adequacy.

Gilligan's work has been rightly regarded as important and innovative. It challenged mainstream psychology's persistent occlusion of women's lives and experiences and its insistent but false claims to universality. Yet insofar as Gilligan's challenge involved the construction of an alternative 'feminine' model of moral development, her position was ambiguous. On the one hand, by providing a counterexample to Kohlberg's model, she cast doubt on the possibility of any single universalist developmental schema. On the other hand, by constructing a female countermodel, she invited the same charge of false generalization she had herself raised against Kohlberg, though now from other perspectives such as class, sexual orientation, race and ethnicity. Gilligan's (1982: 2) disclaimers notwithstanding, to the extent that she described women's moral development in terms of *a* different voice; to the extent that she did not specify which women, under which specific historical circumstances have spoken with the voice in question; and to the extent that she grounded her analysis in the explicitly cross-cultural framework of Nancy Chodorow, her model remained essentialist. It perpetuated in a newer, more localized fashion traces of previous, more grandiose quasi-metanarratives.

Thus, vestiges of essentialism have continued to plague feminist scholarship even despite the decline of grand theorizing. In many cases, including Gilligan's, this represents the continuing subterranean influence of those very mainstream modes of thought and inquiry with which feminists have wished to break.

On the other hand, the practice of feminist politics in the 1980s has generated a new set of pressures which have worked against metanarratives. In recent years, poor and working-class women, women of color and lesbians have finally won a wider hearing for their objections to feminist theories which fail to illuminate their lives and address their problems. They have exposed the earlier quasi-metanarratives, with their assumptions of universal female dependence and confinement to 'the domestic sphere', as false extrapolations from the experience of the white, middle-class, heterosexual women who dominated the beginnings of the second wave. For example, writers like Bell Hooks (1984), Gloria Joseph (1981), Audre Lord (1981), Maria Lugones and Elizabeth Spelman (1983; 1980–1) have unmasked the implicit reference to white Anglo women in many classic feminist texts; likewise, Adrienne Rich (1980) and Marilyn Frye (1983) have exposed the heterosexist bias of much mainstream feminist theory. Thus, as the class, sexual, racial and ethnic awareness of the movement has altered, so has the preferred conception of theory. It has become clear that quasi-metanarratives hamper rather than promote sisterhood, since they elide differences among women and among the forms of sexism to which different women are differentially subject. Likewise, it is increasingly apparent that such theories hinder alliances with other progressive movements, since they tend to occlude axes of domination other than gender. In sum, there is growing interest among feminists in modes of theorizing which are attentive to differences and to cultural and historical specificity.

In general, then, feminist scholarship of the 1980s evinces some conflicting tendencies. On the one hand, there is decreasing interest in grand social theories as scholarship has become more localized, issue-oriented and explicitly fallibilistic. On the other hand, essentialist vestiges persist in the continued use of ahistorical categories like 'gender identity' without reflection as to how, when and why such categories originated and were modified over time. This tension is symptomatically expressed in the current fascination, on the part of US feminists, with French psychoanalytic feminisms: the latter propositionally decry essentialism even as they performatively enact it (Cixous, 1981; Cixous and Clément, 1986; Irigaray, 1985a, 1985b; Kristeva, 1980, 1981; see also critical discussions by Jones, 1985; Moi, 1985). More generally, feminist scholarship has remained insufficiently attentive to the *theoretical* prerequisites of dealing with diversity, despite widespread commitment to accepting it politically.

By criticizing lingering essentialism in contemporary feminist theory, we hope to encourage such theory to become more consistently postmodern. This is not, however, to recommend merely *any* form of postmodernism. On the contrary, as we have shown, the version developed by Jean-François Lyotard offers a weak and inadequate conception of social criticism without philosophy. It rules out genres of criticism, such as large historical narrative and historically situated social theory, which feminists rightly regard as indispensable. But it does not follow from Lyotard's shortcomings that criticism without philosophy is in principle incompatible with criticism with social force. Rather, as we argue next, a robust, postmodern-feminist paradigm of social criticism without philosophy is possible.

3 Toward a Postmodern Feminism

How can we combine a postmodernist incredulity toward metanarratives with the social-critical power of feminism? How can we conceive a version of criticism without philosophy which is robust enough to handle the tough job of analyzing sexism in all its 'endless variety and monotonous similarity'?

A first step is to recognize, *contra* Lyotard, that postmodern critique need forswear neither large historical narratives nor analyses of societal macrostructures. This point is important for feminists, since sexism has a long history and is deeply and pervasively embedded in contemporary societies. Thus, postmodern feminists need not abandon the large theoretical tools needed to address large political problems. There is nothing inconsistent in the idea of postmodern theory.

However, if postmodern-feminist critique must remain 'theoretical', not just any kind of theory will do. Rather, theory here would be explicitly historical, attuned to the cultural specificity of different societies and periods, and to that of different groups within societies and periods. Thus, the categories of postmodern-feminist theory would be inflected by temporality, with historically specific institutional categories like 'the modern, restricted, male-headed, nuclear family' taking precedence over ahistorical, functionalist categories like 'reproduction' and 'mothering'. Where categories of the latter sort were not eschewed altogether, they would be genealogized, that is, framed by a historical narrative and rendered temporally and culturally specific.

Moreover, postmodern-feminist theory would be non-universalist. When its focus became cross-cultural or transepochal, its mode of attention would be comparativist rather than universalizing, attuned to changes and contrasts instead of to 'covering laws'. Finally, postmodern-feminist theory would dispense with the idea of a subject of history. It would replace unitary notions of 'woman' and 'feminine gender identity' with plural and complexly constructed conceptions of social identity, treating gender as one relevant strand among others, attending also to class, race, ethnicity, age and sexual orientation.

In general, postmodern-feminist theory would be pragmatic and fallibilistic. It would tailor its methods and categories to the specific task at hand, using multiple categories when appropriate and forswearing the metaphysical comfort of a single 'feminist method' or 'feminist epistemology'. In short, this theory would look more like a tapestry composed of threads of many different hues than one woven in a single color.

The most important advantage of this sort of theory would be its usefulness for contemporary feminist political practice. Such practice is increasingly a matter of alliances rather than one of unity around a universally shared interest or identity. It recognizes that the diversity of women's needs and experiences means that no single solution, on issues like child care, social security and housing, can be adequate for all. Thus, the underlying premise of this practice is that while some women share some common interests and face some common enemies, such commonalities are by no means universal; rather, they are interlaced with differences, even with conflicts. This, then, is a practice made up of a patchwork of overlapping alliances, not one circumscribable by an essential definition. One might best speak of it in the plural as the practice of 'feminisms'. In a sense, this practice is in advance of much contemporary feminist theory. It is already implicitly postmodern. It would find its most appropriate and useful theoretical expression in a postmodern-feminist form of critical inquiry. Such inquiry would be the theoretical counterpart of a broader, richer, more complex and mutilayered feminist solidarity, the sort of solidarity which is essential for overcoming the oppression of women in its 'endless variety and monotonous similarity'.

Notes

We are grateful for the helpful suggestions of many people, especially Jonathan Arac, Ann Ferguson, Marilyn Frye, Nancy Hartsock, Alison Jaggar, Berel Lang, Thomas McCarthy,

Karsten Struhl, Iris Young, Thomas Wartenburg and the members of SOFPHIA. We are also grateful for word-processing help from Marina Rosiene.

1. It should be noted that, for Lyotard, the choice of Philosophy as a starting point is itself determined by a metapolitical commitment, namely, to anti-totalitarianism. He assumes, erroneously in our view, that totalizing social and political theory necessarily eventuates in totalitarian societies. Thus, the 'practical intent' which subtends Lyotard's privileging of philosophy (and is in turn attenuated by the latter) is anti-Marxism. Whether it should also be characterized as 'neo-liberalism' is a question too complicated to be explored here.
2. These and related problems were soon apparent to many of the domestic/public theorists themselves. See Rosaldo's (1980) self-criticism. A more recent discussion, which points out the circularity of the theory, appears in Sylvia J. Yanagisako and Jane F. Collier (1988).
3. A similar ambiguity attends Chodorow's discussion of 'the family'. In response to critics who object that her psychoanalytic emphasis ignores social structures, Chodorow has rightly insisted that the family is itself a social structure, one frequently slighted in social explanations. Yet she generally does not discuss families as historically specific social institutions whose specific relations with other institutions can be analyzed. Rather, she tends to invoke 'the family' in a very abstract and general sense defined only as the locus of female mothering.

Bibliography

Chodorow, Nancy (1978) *The Reproduction of Mothering: Psychoanalysis and the sociology of gender*. Berkeley: University of California Press.

Cixous, Hélène (1981) 'The laugh of Medusa'. Translated by K. Cohen and P. Cohen in E. Marks and I. de Courtivron (eds), *New French Feminisms*. New York: Schocken Books.

Cixous, Hélène and Clément, Catherine (1986) *The Newly Born Woman*. Minneapolis: University of Minnesota Press.

Ferguson, Ann and Folbre, Nancy (1981) 'The unhappy marriage of patriarchy and capitalism', in L. Sargent (ed.), *Women and Revolution*. Boston, MA: South End Press.

Firestone, Shulamith (1970) *The Dialectic of Sex*. New York: Bantam.

Flax, Jane (1986) 'Gender as a social problem: In and for feminist theory'. *American Studies/Amerika Studien*, June.

Foucault, Michel (1979) *Discipline and Punish: The birth of the prison*. Translated by Alan Sheridan. New York: Vintage Books.

Frye, Marilyn (1983) *The Politics of Reality: Essays in feminist theory*. Trumansburg, NY: The Crossing Press.

Gilligan, Carol (1982) *In a Different Voice: Psychological theory and women's development*. Cambridge, MA: Harvard University Press.

Haraway, Donna (1983) 'A manifesto for cyborgs: Science, technology and socialist feminism in the 1980s'. *Socialist Review* 80: 65–107.

Harding, Sandra (1986a) *The Science Questin in Feminism*. Ithaca, NY: Cornell University Press.

Harding, Sandra (1986b) 'The instability of the analytical categories of feminist theory'. *Signs: Journal of Women in Culture and Society* 11(4): 645–64.

Harding, Sandra and Hintikka, Merrill B. (eds) (1983) *Discovering Reality: Feminist perspectives on epistemology, metaphysics, methodology and philosophy of science.* Dordrecht: D. Reidel.

Hartsock, Nancy (1983) *Money, Sex and Power: Toward a feminist historical materialism.* New York: Longman.

Hooks, Bell (1984) *Feminist Theory: From margin to center.* Boston, MA: South End Press.

Irigaray, Luce (1985a) *Speculum of the Other Woman.* Ithaca, NY: Cornell University Press.

Irigaray, Luce (1985b) *This Sex Which is Not One.* Ithaca, NY: Cornell University Press.

Jardine, Alice A. (1985) *Gynesis: Configurations of women and modernity.* Ithaca, NY: Cornell University Press.

Jones, Ann Rosalind (1985) 'Writing the body: Toward an understanding of l'écriture féminine', in E. Showalter (ed.), *The New Feminist Criticism: Essays on women, literature and theory.* New York: Pantheon Books.

Joseph, Gloria (1981) 'The incompatible menage à trois: Marxism, feminism and racism', in L. Sargent (ed.), *Women and Revolution.* Boston, MA: South End Press.

Kristeva, Julia (1980) *Desire in Language: A semiotic approach to literature and art*, L. S. Roudiez (ed.), New York: Columbia University Press.

Kristeva, Julia (1981) 'Women's time'. Translated by A. Jardine and H. Blake. *Signs: Journal of Women in Culture and Society* 7(1): 13–35.

Lord, Audre (1981) 'An open letter to Mary Daly', in C. Moraga and G. Anzaldua (eds), *This Bridge Called My Back: Writings by radical women of color.* Watertown, MA: Persephone Press.

Lugones, Maria C. and Spelman, Elizabeth V. (1983) 'Have we got a theory for you! Feminist theory, cultural imperialism and the demand for the women's voice'. *Hypatia, Women's Studies International Forum* 6(6): 578–81.

Lyotard, Jean-François (1978) 'Some of the things at stake in women's struggles'. Translated by D. J. Clarke, W. Woodhull and J. Mowitt. *Sub-Stance* 20.

Lyotard, Jean-François (1984a) *The Postmodern Condition: A report on knowledge.* Translated by G. Bennington and B. Massumi. Minneapolis: University of Minnesota Press.

Lyotard, Jean-François (1984b) 'The differend'. Translated by G. Van Den Abbeele. *Diacritics* Fall: 4–14.

Lyotard, Jean-François and Thébaud, Jean-Loup (1987) *Just Gaming.* Minneapolis: University of Minnesota Press.

MacKinnon, Catharine A. (1982) 'Feminism, Marxism, method, and the state: An agenda for theory'. *Signs: Journal of Women in Culture and Society* 7(3): 515–44.

Moi, Toril (1985) *Sexual/Textual Politics: Feminist literary theory.* London: Methuen.

Owens, Craig (1983) 'The discourse of others: Feminists and postmodernism', in H. Foster (ed.), *The Anti-Aesthetic: Essays on postmodern culture.* Port Townsend, WA: Bay Press.

Rich, Adrienne (1980) 'Compulsory heterosexuality and lesbian existence'. *Signs: Journal of Women in Culture and Society* 5(4): 631–60.

Rosaldo, Michelle Zimbalist (1974) 'Woman, culture and society: a theoretical overview', in M. Z. Rosaldo and L. Lamphere (eds), *Woman, Culture and Society.* Stanford, CA: Stanford University Press.

Rosaldo, Michelle Zimbalist (1980) 'The use and abuse of anthropology: Reflections on feminism and cross-cultural understanding'. *Signs: Journal of Women in Culture and Society* 5(3): 389–417.

Rubin, Gayle (1975) 'The traffic in women', in R. R. Reiter (ed.), *Toward an Anthropology of Women*. New York: Monthly Review Press.

Spelman, Elizabeth (1980–1) 'Theories of race and gender. The erasure of Black women'. *Quest* 5(4): 36–62.

Walzer, Michael (1983) *Spheres of Justice: A defense of pluralism and equality*. New York: Basic Books.

Yanagisako, Sylvia J. and Collier, Jane F. (1988) 'Toward a unified analysis of gender and kinship', in J. F. Collier and S. J. Yanagisako (eds), *Gender and Kinship: Toward a unified analysis*. Stanford, CA: Stanford University Press.

31 □ *The Demise of Experience: Fiction as stranger than truth?*

Alice Jardine

> A labyrinthian man never looks for the truth, but only for his Ariadne.
>
> NIETZSCHE

> Truth is not an unveiling which destroys the secret, but the revelation which does it justice.
>
> WALTER BENJAMIN

The ancient problem of the relationship between what in everyday language we call 'experience' of 'reality' and what we then decide to call 'knowledge' about it (let alone knowing the 'truth' about it) has resurfaced with a vengeance in the twentieth century. Radical critics of dominant Western culture have been urgently concerned, since at least the turn of the century, with the problem of how to continue criticism in a modern world where it is understood not only that what is being criticized is already an ideological, symbolic construction, but also that it is therefore already a lie. So then, where might be found the truth? From the arts, especially modernist and postmodernist fiction, to the philosophies, a deep dissatisfaction with science has led to a radical reevaluation of the relationships between what Walter Benjamin called 'direct, lived experience' [*Erlebnis*, 'shock'] as opposed to retrospective, 'privileged, inward experience' [*Erfahrung*, 'aura'].[1] That the relationship between the two is no longer obvious; that, in any case, it can no longer be seen as reflective, natural, or unmediated, is now certain. As Gilles Deleuze has explained, we are talking about an era of generalized anti-Platonism, where it is no longer only models and their copies that are put into play, privileged; but also the *simulacrum*, traditionally seen as false, bad, and ugly because it does not resemble enough the Original *or* its copies.

In fact, 'One defines modernity by the potency of the *simulacrum*.'[2] The power

From Jardine, A., *Gynesis: Configurations of woman and modernity*, Cornell University Press, Ithaca, NY, 1985, pp. 145–55.

and full implications of this statement are only slowly becoming more tangible to those still thinking in a psychologized and representational mode (and almost everyone is), especially with regard to their own experience. For example, media and computer technology are no longer so limited in scope: most of us can at least begin to glimpse the ways in which the components of 'our lives' have already been imagined, repeated, erased, spliced to other 'lives'; ways which are not only out of our own control, but under no One's control at all, except perhaps that of technology itself.

In French thought over the past thirty years, the question of exactly how 'experience', 'knowledge', and 'truth' are so out of kilter for modernity has not been swept aside as it has tended to be in Anglo-American theory.[3] The effort to rethink and experiment with the ways in which reality, as imaginary and symbolic construction, can today be experienced, known, and finally changed has been constant. This has entailed, for the most part, the attempt to move beyond mechanistic cause/effect theories based in reflection; this has been done by privileging different kinds of 'cultural cement': ideology, the unconscious, language and therefore writing. In effect, for many contemporary theorists and writers, to be radical in our culture may require new kinds of mental acrobatics: for example, to be radical may no longer be to work for the side that is 'right', speaks the 'truth', is most 'just'. It may in fact be to work rather for the *Pseudos*, for 'the highest power of falsehood';[4] it may be to opt for overwhelming falsehood, thereby confusing and finally destroying the oppressive system of representation which would have us believe not only in its subsystems of models (the real, the first) versus simulacra (the unreal, inauthentic), good versus bad, true versus false; but would also have us believe in a world ultimately obsessed with self-destruction.

It is, in fact, most likely obvious by now to the reader that, following our writers, lost in the folds of the fabricated and delegitimized narratives that surround us, disarmed of the *cogito* and the dialectics of representation, any question of 'truth' in and for modernity can only be a tentative one. It will therefore only concern us here to the extent that a certain definition of truth, based in a highly personal, naturalized 'reality', is not only intrinsic to but also the last line of defense for feminism as hermeneutic. Feminism, while infinite in its variations, is finally rooted in the belief that women's truth-in-experience-and-reality is and has always been different from men's and that it as well as its artifacts and productions have consequently been devalued and always already delegitimized in partriarchal culture. Feminists tend to see the fact that Man, men, are experiencing a form of delegitimation today either as a positive step toward demystifying the politics of male sexuality in patriarchy or as nothing other than another complex ruse of patriarchal reason. As with the other questions in this study, it is not certain that the choice is that clear-cut.

It is certainly not clear if we look closely at the writers in France rethinking truth-in-modernity. Their major battle, in the wake of Heidegger, Nietzsche, and Freud, has been to unravel the illusion that some kind of universal truth exists which can be proven by some so-called universal experience. This stand against the historically

solid alliance between truth and experience has been a stand against humanism –
a positive step for women in most ways, but with a twist. For these writers, truth,
therefore, can equal neither 'experience' nor 'reality' as those words have been
philosophically understood in the West since Plato – and therefore any discourse
rooting itself in either one is, in truth, an ancient, uselessly repetitive fiction.

The history of universal truth is the history of metaphysics and its attendant
definitions of the Good and the Moral: from Plato's *esse verum* to Aristotle's *eikos*;
from the theological *propositio* of the Middle Ages to Positivist *Logic*; from Hegel's
Absolute to the Phenomenological *Experience*. Heidegger, closest to the writers we
are concerned with, was to place major emphasis on this long, common history. His
best-known analysis of metaphysical truth as *Alētheia* (the unveiled), that of Plato's
myth of the cave, makes clear the continuity in Western definitions of the Truth:
the unveiling, bringing to light of that which had been lost, hidden, veiled, badly
'represented'. Truth in the West has always been defined as 'exactitude of
representation' in which 'man thinks everything according to "ideas" and
appreciates all reality according to values'.[5] The stripping of veils, the ascendant
'striptease toward the Idea', ordered by Man-in-command, is what Heidegger tells
us has led to the twentieth century's dominantly pragmatic, when not imperialistic,
posture toward knowledge, as well as to a conjunction between the movement
toward pure Idea and the 'ought to' of teleology, futurity, and obligation. According
to Heidegger, if we are to survive the twentieth century, Man can no longer be the
'opener of truth' but must find a way to become the opening *for* it. Heidegger will
eventually turn to the poets to find that 'way'.

Before Heidegger, Nietzsche and Freud had already spread enormous doubt about
our ability to reach Truth through the ascendancy of judgment. For Nietzsche, truth
is Man's oldest illusion. Even more important, why is it that Man has so frequently
desired the Truth? '*Why not rather* untruth? And uncertainty? Even ignorance?'[6]
The shock of recognition that Western Truth, and the Western desire for Truth,
have been a terrible error is what Nietzsche leaves for the twentieth century to gain
the hard way.

Freud regards truth, of course, as even more difficult to locate, untenable-as-
judgment, and it is in his work that truth finds its first concrete displacements, away
from experience, away from reality: 'It has not been possible to demonstrate in other
connections that the human intellect has a particularly fine flair for the truth. We
have rather found, on the contrary, that our intellect very easily goes astray without any warning, and that nothing is more easily believed by us than what, without
reference to the truth, comes to meet our wishful illusions.'[7] For psychoanalysis,
truth can consist only of parcels of 'truth' from the past which return to us
deformed, disconnected; they return from and through the unconscious into the
fictions of our present lives. If, therefore, psychoanalysis as a science is to have any
truth-value, it is from this recognition that we can have no access to the truths of
our illusions except through an understanding of the logic of the unconscious.

Truth as veiled. Truth as error. Truth as partial and delayed, as that which we
do not want to know. With those threads, the theorists of, and in, modernity began

to weave new intellectual patterns, searching for the potential spaces of a 'truth' that would be neither true nor false; for a 'truth' that would be *in-vrai-semblable*, implausible, improbable, incredible, thereby making *vrai-semblance* the code word for our metaphysical heritage.[8] While this project is certainly not foreign to twentieth-century Anglo-American explorations in logic (e.g. Bertrand Russell), it has found its most radical directions and support in post-existential France.

I shall not follow in detail the battles between Lacanian psychoanalysis and Nietzschean philosophies over the stakes and status of 'truth' for modernity.[9] But it is interesting to note those points on which psychoanalysis and philosophy in France would seem to agree: that (1) truth and falsehood have been and must continue to be taken out of opposition; (2) reality defined as representation can no longer play the major part in reformulating a new approach to 'truth' if we are to avoid the repetitious violence of moralistic thinking; (3) no one can *tell* the truth – at least not all of it; and finally, (4) henceforth, 'truth' can only be thought through that which subverts it; the 'real' for Lacan; '*écriture*' for Derrida; and the 'becoming of difference' for Deleuze.[10]

This series of doubt-full debates around the possible positions of 'truth' for modernity largely centers around the problem of 'fiction', both written and oral, even as this latter distinction is already being broken down.[11] The metaphysical opposition of fiction versus truth makes no more sense; but to call it nonsense only throws us back to another opposition. Is fiction (coded as such, as a written text) a key to truth? Or is any truth always already a fiction (written or otherwise)? This debate obviously has important consequences for any literary, cultural and political criticism concerned with how to situate texts as a force for change in the 'reality' of the world – especially since these texts have caught up with psychoanalysis and philosophy in France. For 'truth' is traditionally 'to be right'; in French, it is to have reason [*avoir raison*]. Traditionally, where reason is lost, things are wrong, insane. A cultural critic who judges a fiction as not true judges it as being beyond reason – which is all it ever set out to be in the traditional scheme of things. To judge a text as wrong, as not having reason, is not to disrupt anything, but is instead, in a terrible twist, to confirm the viability of the original metaphysical opposition.[12] Clearly, traditional acts of literary criticism based in this kind of judgment are henceforth seen to be caught in a strange, mutually congratulatory relationship with the text they are judging.[13]

In any case, according to our writers, the true can no longer be linked to traditional notions of experience-in-the-world, those notions having reached their highest point in Hegel's definition of experience as discourse *within* a subject-conscious-of-himself: '*Inasmuch as the new true object issues from it*, this *dialectical* movement which consciousness exercises on itself and which affects both its knowledge and its object, is precisely what is called *experience* [*Erfahrung*].'[14] Experience in this sense can only be an *appropriation* of the 'real', thus transforming it into 'reality' by and for the Cartesian Subject. The phenomenology of existentialism, for example, came to be seen in Europe as the last anthropological system of thought to have attempted to bridge the gap between the *percipio* and the *cogito*: the fact that we *live* in one world where we can see only 'fragments' while we *think* in another world according to the knowledge that we can obtain about the whole that we can never see. The phenomenologists attempted to found the *cogito* in the *percipio* in order to understand how meaning comes to be and then judge that meaning according to moral standards. But ultimately, that transcendental gesture accounts for their sole reliance on the ethic of *praxis*: the only possible truth *now* is that truth based in the living present – for *me* – in the immediacy of true experience.

It is clear that this 'me' around which the world turns was to become totally unacceptable to post-existential France. The concept of experience was radically displaced: 'experience' came to be thought of as that process which exceeds mastery, as the 'silence' of discourse, as that which disturbs the subject-present-to-itself.[15] The emphasis has been placed on that which continually undermines any credulity or belief based in experience-only-to-be-then-expressed-in-language: on ideology, desire, the unconscious, fiction as anti-knowledge. For the theorists of modernity, only an empiricist could believe that language expresses-without-loss-of-reality, that it can faithfully translate experience, that it makes no *difference*.

Empiricism – the 'science of experience' – is of course, that doctrine which holds that all knowledge originates in direct experience of what is commonly called reality, without theory, and undisturbed by language. That is, where language is superfluous to life.

Whatever the fundamentally empirical foundations of psychoanalysis in practice (that is, as based in vision), Lacan's entire 'return to Freud' was in reaction against empiricism: empiricism was seen by Lacan as being at the very roots of Anglo-American conservative, normative, recuperative psychologies (such as behaviorism). The only possible place for 'experience', according to Lacan, is in the experiential and experimental language of the 'analytical experience' as analogous to fiction.

The philosophers, however, did not find it quite so easy, or productive, to reject empiricism so quickly. In fact, empiricism is in some ways posited by them as a beginning from which to question philosophy most radically – as its opposite.

For example, in Derrida's work, experience has always equaled presence, transparency, egotism, meaning, and, therefore, violence.[16] Like any other metaphysical commonplace, however, experience cannot simply be done away with or denied, but must be used under erasure because of its relationship to the history of philosophy as a nonphilosophy, an anti-philosophy.[17] Empiricism is philosophically incapable of justifying itself: 'But this incapacitation, when resolutely assumed, contests the resolution and coherence of the logos (philosophy) at its root, instead of letting itself be questioned by the logos. Therefore, nothing can so profoundly *solicit* the Greek logos – philosophy – than this irruption of the totally-other; and nothing can to such an extent reawaken the logos to its origin as to its mortality, its other.'[18] As the Other of philosophy, empiricism constitutes a point of departure, exorbitant in its exteriority, for Derridean deconstruction –

until the very concept of empiricism itself begins to self-destruct. 'To *exceed* the metaphysical orb is an attempt to get out of the orbit [*orbita*], to think the entirety of the classical conceptual oppositions, particularly the one within which the value of empiricism is held. ... The opening of the question, the departure from the closure of a self-evidence, the putting into doubt of a system of oppositions, all these movements necessarily have the form of empiricism and of errancy. ... We must begin *wherever we are* ...'[19] Those moments when the Derridean strategy opens the text to so-called empirical events – biography, historical anecdotes, and so on – are, from their beginnings, the most radical moments the reader can experience in philosophy – the openings toward the writing that can begin to split open any closed philosophical system.

Like Derrida, Deleuze sees empiricism as an anti-philosophy. Unlike Derrida, however, Deleuze does not put empirical experience under erasure but, with a non-self-reflexively exorbitant leap, explodes it beyond any possible or at least any believable representation of 'reality': empiricism is not Deleuze's philosophical doctrine, but his ode to Anglo-American philosophy and literature. For him, empiricism operates against the concept of 'the principle', the principles of philosophy, through a insistence on 'life' and the ways it can force systems to their breaking point: 'if one sees something there which traverses life, but which thinking finds repugnant, in that case thinking must be forced to think it, to make of it thinking's point of hallucination, an experimentation which does violence to thinking ...'[20] It is ultimately Deleuze's 'escape lines' away from founding principles that provide new pathways for this necessary hallucination; new ways towards *becoming* – the only ways Deleuze would risk changing what *is* (philosophy).

Faced with this demise of 'conscious experience' in the world, the feminist reader will perhaps find some more questions.

She will most certainly welcome the demise of Truth – Man's Truth. She will agree that the dream of unveiling the Truth-in-its-entirety, so as to shine in its veracity, has turned into a nightmare (created by men); that, in fact, it is Man's *apocalypse* (etymologically to dis-cover, un-cover, to reveal the secret).[21] But, on the other hand, she will also understand that it is not enough to *oppose* Man's Truth; the very conceptual systems that have posited it must be undermined. And, finally, she will begin to recognize that many of those conceptual systems are intrinsic to feminist thinking whether or not openly declared: systems of defining the self, perception, judgment, and, therefore, morality.[22]

'Morality' is perhaps that which most stubbornly adheres to Truth-in-judgment. What is true is also good. What is false is bad. *Ethics* – the discipline devoted to deciding what is good and bad – will be one of the first *systems* to be rejected as an institution, after Freud and Nietzsche, by psychoanalysis and philosophy in France. For Lacan, psychoanalysis must become allergic to any form of ethics – for to indulge in morality (or in any form of social reformation) is to fall prey to (American) normalizing pedagogy.[23] For the philosophers, ethics is inseparable from the history of philosophy. Both Greek and Christian, ethics is the language of priests. If Deleuzians have for the most part avoided the problem, creating an ethic for every new occasion, Derrideans have recently been a bit more sensitive to the necessity of necessity: 'There is therefore a duty – or, if you wish, a duty is being decided upon, a duty which is *final* in every sense of the expression, the duty of the question, of the maintenance of the question of the ends, or the question of the end of philosophy. That is the answer.'[24] Given that *ethos* means *heim*, at home, as in Plato's cavern, the point may be not to to rush out of the cavern with everyone else, but rather to stay, to render it strange, uncanny – to develop an *ethos unheimlich* by questioning the writing on the walls of the cave itself.[25]

The *true*, then, is to be thought strangely by modernity, outside of the metaphysical categories of opposition – or between them. This approach involves, first and foremost, a relinquishing of mastery, indeed a valorization of nonmastery. And, as we know, a lack of mastery has, historically, always connoted the feminine.[26] Secondly, the *true*, to be isolated in those processes anterior to or, in some cases, beyond the Truth as produced by the *technē*, is that which can never be seen, which never presents itself as such but rather captures, points, withdraws, hides itself in its veils: and that *true* is seen as being 'woman' – the 'nontruth' or 'partial true' of Truth. Or, for others, 'woman' is precisely that element which disturbs even that presupposition (Truth as castrated).

Whatever the strange intricacies of these new wanderings through the demise of Truth-in-Experience, 'woman' is that element most *discursively present*. Julia Kristeva has called this new element in modernity a *vréel* –a kind of 'she-truth':

> We can today perceive, by listening to the discourses that speak to us as contemporaries as well as to the approaches which try to speak of the source and progression of those discourses, that the great upheaval of speaking beings today can be summarized in this way: the *truth* [*vérité*] which they are seeking (which they are trying to tell), is the *real* [*réel*] – 'Vréel' then. An obsessive fear since the beginning of time, this experience is becoming today, if not one of the masses, at least massive, weighty; even more so because no common code is there to neutralize it by justifying it. ... The ancient question returns: how to render the vréel more likely, more representable [*vraisemblable*]?[27]

The only way, of course, to render this 'vréel' *vraisemblable*, seemingly true, is to put it into discourse in new ways: hence the *gynesis* whose potential spaces we have had to outline so schematically here. The demise of the Subject, of the Dialectic, and of Truth has left modernity with a *void* that it is vaguely aware must be spoken differently and strangely: as woman, through gynesis.

What can be the feminist's response to these manifestations of gynesis and its strange body? Is not her first impulse to deny it? – to charge that these 'processes beyond representation' are but part of a new ruse invented by Man to avoid, once again, his own truth and experience? But, on the other hand, in order to demonstrate that, are we not just as obliged, as feminists, to put the signifier woman into circulation, ourselves to engage in gynesis? Whose ruse is it *then*? And whose *gynesis*?

It is too easy to put gynesis down to 'idealism' as somehow opposed to feminism, a true 'materialism'. As long as we do not explore the boundaries of and possible common spaces between modernity and feminism; as long as we do not recognize new kinds of artificial, symbolic constructions of the subject, representation, and (especially) experience, we will be engaging in what are ultimately conservative and dated polemics, not radical theory and practice. It becomes particularly tempting at times of extreme political crisis to abandon this challenge of our century and revert to a 'natural view of things': reality is what I see, hear, and touch. Nothing could be more reactionary – or pointless – in postmodern culture. As Jane Gallop has so succinctly put it, 'Belief in simple referentiality is not only unpoetic but also ultimately politically conservative, because it cannot recognize that the reality to which it appeals is a traditional ideological construction, whether one terms it phallomorphic, or metaphysical, or bourgeois, or something else. The politics of experience is inevitably a conservative politics for it cannot help but conserve traditional ideological constructs which are not recognized as such but are taken for the "real".'[28]

To question how thought-in-modernity and feminism itself may both be inscribing woman as the ultimate truth of and for modernity is, for the feminist today, to risk becoming entangled in her own apocalypse.

But then, that is a risk intrinsic to modernity itself – and I think it is a risk worth taking.

To do so, however, feminists must *take* the risk, must 'dive into the wreck' of Western culture rather than push it aside:

> We are, I am, you are
> by cowardice or courage
> the one who find our way
> back to this scene
> carrying a knife, a camera
> a book of myths
> in which
> our names do not appear.[29]

Notes

1. See in particular Benjamin's *Charles Baudelaire: A lyric poet in the era of high capitalism*, transl. Harry Zohn, New Left Books, London, 1973.
2. See Gilles Deleuze, 'Simulacre et philosophie antique', in *Logique du sens*, p. 306.
3. Marcelin Pleynet has put it this way: 'Our experience remains the captive of a knowledge which is no longer really our experience; our knowledge is embarrassed by an experience which has not yet become knowledge.' 'La levée de l'interprétation des signes', in *Art et littérature*, Editions du Seuil, Paris, 1977.
4. Deleuze, *Logique du sens*, p. 303
5. Martin Heidegger, 'La doctrine de Platon sur la vérité', in *Questions II*, pp. 143–4,

162. The reader will also want to refer to 'On the essence of truth' in *Existence and Being*; as well as to 'Logos' and 'Alētheia' in *Early Greek Thinking*, transl. David Farrell Krell and Frank A. Capuzzi, Harper & Row, New York, 1975.

6. Nietzsche, *Beyond Good and Evil*, transl. Helen Zimmern, Macmillan, New York, 1924, p. 5.

7. Freud, *Moses and Monotheism,* transl. James Strachey, Hogarth, London, 1974, p. 129.

8. From a psychoanalytic perspective, Jean-Michel Ribettes has maintained that *vraisemblance*, exactitude of representation, is also particularly *male*, belonging as it does to an obsessional rather than hysterical economy. 'Le phallus (Vrai/semblant/ vraisemblance du texte obsessionnel)', in *Folle vérité*, ed. Julia Kristeva, Editions du Seuil, Paris, 1979, pp. 116–70.

9. For an introduction to some of the questions involved, see Barbara Johnson's 'The frame of reference: Poe, Lacan, Derrida'. For an overview of the polemic between Lacan and Derrida, also see Spivak's introduction to Derrida, *Of Grammatology*, esp. pp. lxiii–lxvii.

10. On 'truth' in Lacan, one would want to look especially at his 'Au-delà du "Principe de réalité"' and 'La science et la vérité', in *Ecrits*; the opening pages of *Télévision*, Editions du Seuil, Paris, 1973; 'Radiophonie' (on the *semblant*), *Scilicet*, 2/3, Editions du Seuil, Paris, n.d.; and 'Le savoir et la vérité', in *Encore*. For an overview of the problems of *la vérité, la vraisemblance*, and *le semblant* in psychoanalysis, I have found the collection of essays in *Folle vérité* (ed. Kristeva) very useful. On the position of 'truth' in Derrida, besides 'The purveyor of truth', see especially *Positions*, transl. Alan Bass, pp. 111–13, n. 44; and *Spurs/Eperons*. In Deleuze, cf., e.g.: *Différence et répétition*, pp. 198–217; and *Nietzsche*, pp. 108–11.

    The contemporary polemic surrounding truth and fiction is obviously not limited to these writers. Cf., for example, Barthes's early *Critique et vérité*, Editions du Seuil, Paris, 1966.

11. The Derridean wearing-away of both the common and the uncommon distinctions between speech and writing owes much to Freud. The reader might want to refer to Naomi Schor, 'Le détail chez Freud', *Littérature*, 37 (1980) for a reading, in the wake of Derrida, of how, in Freud, the detail in a written text is seen as a disseminator of fiction while, orally, it is revelatory of truth.

12. To begin unraveling this problematic more slowly, one might start with Foucault and Derrida's polemic over Descartes: Foucault, *Madness and Civilization*, transl. Richard Howard, Mentor, New York, 1967; Derrida, 'Cognito and the history of madness', in *Writing and Difference*; Foucault, 'Mon corps, ce papier, ce feu', appendix to the second edition of *Folie et déraison*. Also of import is Shoshana Felman's *La Folie et la chose littéraire*, where insanity *is* the literary substance.

13. Anglo-American feminist criticism is particularly prone to distinctions between Truth and Falsehood, Right and Wrong, Sane and Insane – or Honesty and Dishonesty. For example: '*The Great Gatsby* is a dishonest book because the culture from which it derives and which it reflects is radically dishonest' (Fetterley, *The Resisting Reader*, p. 94).

14. Hegel, *Phenomenology of Spirit*, transl. A. V. Miller, Clarendon, Oxford, 1977, p. 55. The reader might want to refer to Heidegger, *Hegel's Concept of Experience*, Harper & Row, New York, 1970.

15. The reader has probably already recognized the presence here of Georges Bataille: see

L'Expérience intérieure, Gallimard, Paris, 1970–3. On Bataille's notion of experience, see Kristeva's 'L'expérience et la pratique', in *Polylogue*, and Derrida's 'From restricted to general economy', in *Writing and Difference*.

16. Cf. Derrida, *Writing and Difference*, pp. 132–3; 152; *Of Grammatology*, pp. 60–1; and *Positions*, transl. Alan Bass, p. 30.
17. Derrida, *Of Grammatology*, p. 60.
18. *Writing and Difference*, p. 152.
19. *Of Grammatology*, p. 162.
20. Deleuze and Parnet, *Dialogues*, pp. 68–72.
21. See Derrida on the 'Apocalypse': 'D'un ton apocalyptique adopté naguère en philosophie', in *Les Fins de l'homme*, pp. 445–87.
22. The relationship of feminism to moral and moralistic thinking has recently become the site of new feminist questions in France, especially through the work of the study group 'Le Sexisme Ordinaire' of *Les Temps modernes*. For an introduction to the problem, see the issue of *Les Cahiers du GRIF* 'Jouir', 26 (March 1983), esp. Françoise Petitot, 'Interdire', 89–92. That the question of feminism's relationship to traditional morality has not been adequately posed in this country is evidenced by internal splits in the women's movement over S/M, pornography, censorship, etc.
23. See, for example, 'La direction de la cure'. Lacan himself delayed the publication of his *Ethique de la psychoanalyse* (published in a 'pirate edition') for fear it would be positivized.
24. *Les Fins de l'homme*, p. 169.
25. *Ibid.*, p. 172.
26. Cf., for example, Gilbert and Gubar's *Madwoman in the Attic*, p. 10.
27. Kristeva, *Folle vérité*, p. 11. The neologism, *vréel*, suggests the words *vrai* (truth), *réel* (real) and *elle* (she).
28. Jane Gallop, '*Quand nos lèvres s'écrivent*: Irigaray's body politic', *Romantic Review*, 74, 1 (1983), 83.
29. From Adrienne Rich's 'Diving into the wreck', in *Diving into the Wreck, Poems 1971–1972*, W. W. Norton & Company, Inc., New York, 1973.

Part Eight

Periphery and Postmodernism

Introduction

That mode of thinking which would set up 'centre' against 'periphery' in a bipolar structural opposition is unremittingly modernist. It is also just such an opposition which enables the power relations in imperialism and colonialism. When the north-western tip of Europe designated itself as the centre of 'Enlightenment' in the eighteenth century, it did so in the secure knowledge that an 'unenlightened periphery' was thereby constructed; and the imperialist expansion that went hand in hand with the development of Enlightenment philosophy was not just a mercantile affair, for it also had a series of conceptual components. To be 'enlightened', by definition, is implicitly to construct an idea of oneself as a Subject-in-time; one has a present, characterised by light, which is distinguished from something dark *which is necessarily prior to* the moment of enlightenment. A specific model of historical narrative is thereby put in place. It is this narrative which is exported partly 'in return for' the mercantile exploitation of a world which is now deemed to be *in need of* colonisation. This situation also produces a 'world history', a single narrative which leads inexorably to a delineation of the condition of the imperialist powers as the most advanced (somewhat akin to Rorty's pragmatism, discussed above). The politics of imperialism and colonialism is thus a politics which is founded not just upon geography but also upon a series of temporal factors, and most significantly upon a question of 'speed': the coloniser posits herself or himself as 'advanced' – in advance of a colonised, who is thereby stigmatised as 'tardy' or 'underdeveloped'. The coloniser thus comes 'first', while the tardy colonised comes in as a poor second or, more usually these days, a 'Third' world.

This all presupposes that the various regions of the world are all directed towards the same 'developed' end, that they all figure in one univocal and unilinear history, the history of the colonising power. The postmodern, however, is deeply suspicious of such a 'universal history' or metanarrative, preferring attention to the heterogeneities of the 'local' over the homogeneous universal. In a certain sense, the discourse of postmodernism – although it is a discourse established in a Eurocentred 'First' world – is the discourse *of* the periphery, a discourse which imperialism had strenuously silenced but which is now made available. It alerts the erstwhile centre to the possibility that there is not one world, but rather many worlds all being lived at different speeds, according to different rhythms, producing contradictory histories. It disturbs the centre's notion that its own mode of comprehension of the world is satisfactory, for it releases a number of worlds which, strictly speaking, simply cannot be understood in the languages and discourse of the imperialist central power. It does what the periphery has always silently and powerlessly done: it decentres the centre.

Even if we were to consider the postmodern in its bland chronological sense, the question of the peripheral would arise. For if we were to advocate a postmodernism in certain cultures, we would be asking those cultures to move from their 'pre-modern' condition straight to postmodernism without the intervening problematic of modernism itself. It is, of course, precisely the discourse of modernism which makes the peripheral a poor tardy underdeveloped deviation of a normative 'modernised' centre in the first place. All the more vital, therefore – and perhaps especially for the world stigmatised as 'peripheral' – that the postmodern, as a necessary reconsideration of modernism itself, proceeds apace.

The essays gathered here address some of the pressing issues in this question. During indicates that – as Ngugi, for example, is profoundly aware – the question of language is at the core of a post-colonialist experience. During makes a distinction between post-colonised and post-coloniser: the former 'identify with the culture destroyed by imperialism and its tongue'; the latter 'cannot jettison the culture and tongues of the imperialist nations'. Often, of course, the tongue of the imperialist nation is one of the dominant tongues in the contemporary world economy, so it is all the more difficult to survive in that world if one shuns its tongue altogether. But this is precisely the postmodern problem: living 'between' the language of the oppressor and the occluded language of the indigene: how can one locate oneself as a linguistic or historical Subject at all? The problem here afflicting the victim of imperialism is the 'postmodern' one of a linguistic loss of foundations, with the concomitant problem of a loss of a system or theory of universal justice precisely at the moment when justice is most pressingly required and demanded.

Nelly Richard draws attention to the inappropriateness of a European philosophy of modernisation when it is transplanted into the terrain of Latin America. Benedict Anderson has argued that the concept of a national identity is intimately linked to the development of print culture; and Richard modifies this here in the suggestion that modernity itself is established with the dominance of print. The postmodern challenges the security of the supposedly univalent sign; but as Richard points out, this is what Latin American narratives themselves 'typically' do. The heterogeneity, plurality or contradictory nature of Latin American space (of a geography which is not simply national) produced the effect of postmodernism prior to its descriptions in European discourse. But it would be a mistake to accept this basic deconstruction of centre and periphery as the whole story; for then it would begin to appear that Latin American culture exists – conceptually, at least – as a justification of and legitimation of the European discourse on postmodernism. Richard indicates that a further stage, the rewriting of modernity itself, is required to avoid what would amount to a continuation of imperialism by deconstructive means.

Rey Chow extends this in an 'interruption' of Fredric Jameson's ascription of the term 'postmodern' to contemporary Chinese literature. Through a rereading of 'Mandarin Ducks and Butterflies', a term used to describe a broad genre of populist writing in a Chinese tradition, Chow draws attention to the numerous difficulties encountered in reading what we might refer to as an 'object culture' through the discourses of a 'subject culture': in short, problems deriving from ethnocentrism.

In all the pieces included in this section, the difficulties of reading 'across a border' are highlighted, indicating that although the postmodern may be internationalist, it is also necessarily regionalist, attentive to locality and to the heterogeneous discourses of location. 'Here, now': the postmodern as a question of geography analysed elsewhere by Harvey and Soja is here addressed in geocultural terms.

32 □ *Postmodernism or Post-colonialism Today*

Simon During

Construction of the concept 'postmodernity' proceeds today at a rapid pace. A welter of articles and books define, elaborate, celebrate and denounce this thing, the postmodern, whose very existence is matter for separate, energetic debate. Clearly interests are at stake, careers are being made. But this activity is finally produced by the concept itself, which being based on paradox, generates discussion. On the one hand, 'postmodernity' names the loss of critical distance in the world today, and on the other, it names the delegitimation of those categories by which a cultural centre or a socio-economic base might be identified. So writing about postmodernity implies its absence. If there is no critical distance under post-modernity, then how can there be distance enough for analysis of it to proceed? And if it is knowable only as decentred, then how can its essence be recognized at all? To be dispersed in this sense is no longer to take the form of an identifiable object. Such paradoxes, which resist closure, produce the deeply problematic object of their attention.

The most persuasive accounts of the postmodern are those – like Jameson's essay 'Postmodernism, or the cultural logic of late capitalism'[1] and like Lyotard's recent work – which remain sensitive to these paralogisms. It is for this reason that I shall be concerned with Jameson and Lyotard here. But, partly in order to escape capture by the paradoxes of postmodernity, my argument will proceed from three positions which counter the conceptual underpinnings of 'postmodernity'.

First, I propose, against Jameson, that postmodernity ought not to be conceived of as 'a cultural dominant'.[2] Next, I want to urge that it is just as rewarding to construe literary postmodernism as an enemy of postmodernity as to consider it as its expression and helpmeet. Thus in ethico-political terms postmodernist texts do not differ from modernist texts which are simultaneously enemies of, and moments in, modernity. (This is to take a different line from that of either liberals like Trilling or Western Marxists like the later Adorno, who see contemporary culture as characterized by the disappearance of adverserial possibilities.) And, third, I take the

From *Textual Practice*, 1, 1 (1987), 32–47.

position that if there is something that may be called postmodern thought, it too works in ways that cannot be regarded as a mere expression of an underlying postmodernity.

We can, rather brutally, characterize postmodern thought (the phrase is useful rather than happy) as that thought which refuses to turn the Other into the Same. Thus it provides a theoretical space for what postmodernity denies: otherness. Postmodern thought also recognizes, however, that the Other can never speak for itself *as* the Other. One should hesitate to call a discourse which revolves around these positions either for or against postmodernity, but it is certainly not simply consonant with it.

These propositions, none of which is either original or uncontentious, and all of which will be fleshed out below, allow me to mount my central thesis. This is that the concept postmodernity has been constructed in terms which more or less intentionally wipe out the possibility of post-colonial identity. Indeed, intention aside, the conceptual annihilation of the post-colonial condition is actually necessary to any argument which attempts to show that 'we' now live in postmodernity. For me, perhaps eccentrically, post-colonialism is regarded as the need, in nations or groups which have been victims of imperialism, to achieve an identity uncontaminated by universalist or Eurocentric concepts and images. Here the argument becomes complex, since post-colonialism constitutes one of those Others which might derive hope and legitimation from the first aspect of postmodern thought, its refusal to turn the Other into the Same. As such it is threatened by the second moment in postmodern thought.

If postmodernity is regarded as a condition which is dominant today, then the question immediately arises: what else is there? Jameson, for instance, does not cope with this question easily. He conceives of postmodernity as the culture produced by multinational capitalism: a totality which is the effect of another totality. All the cultural phenomena that Jameson refers to instantiate postmodernity. (In fact, he comes ultimately to think of it as so powerful as to be literally inconceivable, that is, as only to be thought of indirectly, as the sublime.) The only tool for analysing an emergence as immense and total as postmodernity is expressive causality. For a theorist as sophisticated as Jameson elsewhere shows himself to be, this represents a retrogressive, not to say a defeatist move.

Jameson inherits these problems. His Hegelian heritage enables him to think both of culture as a totality and of history as a succession of epochs. Indeed, current Marxist accounts of 'postmodernity' are articulated in terms that repeat earlier accounts of modern culture by the Hegelian Marxism of the Frankfurt School. In particular, Adorno's important late essay 'Cultural criticism and society' lies behind Jameson's text. Adorno came to see what he too called late capitalism as a condition in which the world is totally mediated by consciousness. In it, ideology is no longer false consciousness, and high culture becomes 'neutralized'.[3] Adorno also argues that the conceptual underpinning of both transcendental critique (critique from a position outside the phenomena under analysis) and immanent critique (critique from contradictions noted within) has disappeared as society has become reified.

But Adorno goes further than Jameson. He argues that the Marxist transformation of truth as correspondence into truth as praxis has been absorbed by capitalism as the hegemonic forces have turned pragmatic views of truth to their own ends. And, on the other hand, the counter-attempt to protect areas of culture from instrumental reason now fails because ideology itself has no instrumental function. It has dissolved into distraction, pleasure. Thus the world is now an 'open-air prison'; a place where, in the words of a 1937 essay by Marcuse, which feeds into Adorno's, 'men can feel themselves happy without being so at all'.[4]

Jameson's cultural pessimism, then, is already laid out by Adorno. However, Adorno refers not to postmodernity but to a formation that includes totalitarian and fascist culture. For instance, it is the totalitarian state which has aestheticized existence to the degree that poetry cannot be written after Auschwitz. That famous line does not mean, as is generally supposed, that Auschwitz is too terrible an experience to be written about; it means that writing under fascism and late capitalism has become too trivial to express real horror. The discourse in which Jameson constructs postmodernity was once used, in part, to denounce fascism. (Marcuse's essay would be another point of departure.) This matters, not because analysis of fascism is irrelevant to our culture, but because it allows us to wonder whether the categories of totality and dominance need to be rethought when we turn them to our own times.

Adorno also differs from Jameson when he imagines lines of flight from late capitalism. Jameson sees escape in a postmodern politics whose vocation would be to map the contemporary condition, which he believes to be, under current categories, unmappable. Clearly his own essay believes itself to be engaging in such a politics. Adorno sees escape in a kind of thought 'which strives solely to help the things themselves to that articulation from which they are otherwise cut off by prevailing language'.[5] In almost a liberal spirit, Adorno wishes to provide room for self-determination. True, he cannot offer self-articulation a programme, though the fierce insistence of 'no poetry after Auschwitz' does, rhetorically, free a space in the unfreedom which is our freedom. Jameson's weak call for new forms of mapping, with its emphasis on cognitive knowledge, just like his return to expressive causality, shows how trapped he is compared to Adorno. Perhaps this is so *because* Adorno has a stronger grasp of the contemporary disintegration of cognition, expression and reflection. For he calls not just for knowledge but for action.

Yet – and here we approach the crux of the matter – the weakest moment in Jameson's essay comes when, despite everything, he tries to think postmodernity dialectically. He asks himself how a positive view of its emergence can be taken, and how it permits the forward march of history. He turns to the 'internationalism' of postmodernity. Its progressive task is to realize the end of nationalism so desired by some socialisms. He adds: 'The disastrous realignment of socialist revolution with the older nationalisms (not only in South East Asia), whose results have necessarily aroused such serious recent Left reflection, can be adduced in support of this position.'[6] The strongest enemies of postmodernity appear at this weak point: the new post-colonial nationalisms. Indeed, one can be forgiven for thinking that Jameson is harnessing all the power inherent in images of totalitarianism to eradicate cultural difference in the old spirit of enlightened modernity. The reason why one cannot view postmodernity dialectically becomes apparent. As soon as one allows the notion of the 'positive' or 'progressive' to reappear in analysis, the object one has in view is not postmodernity but a stage on the historical journey to the light. And progress, as ever, must be defined by determinate negation – as not the retrogressive, not the residual, not the primitive, not the irrationalism of other cultures. One can say in general, then, that in order to name postmodernity as a cultural dominant expressing itself in postmodern artifacts Jameson has to assume the coming to power of neo-imperialism, and to inflect postmodernity positively he has, for a moment, to become complicit with it.[7]

How to think postmodernity otherwise? How not to read it as the sublime, a totality so powerful as to resist our older knowledge? It seems to me that one must proceed at once on two registers: one archaeological, the other genealogical. (These words are used here at some distance from Foucault.) Postmodernity must be seen as an effect of discrete cultural systems and not as a spirit or epoch, the advance guard of history. The features of postmodernity, which no one has described better than Jameson, are produced within a finite field of what might be called cultural machines: those texts, images, discourses, each formed within particular technologies or media, each with its own way of organizing the intervention on the real, and each with its mode of subject formation.

But postmodernity is known as postmodernity within a discourse which, as we have begun to see, has its own past. Thus to think postmodernity outside the totalizing categories of Western Marxism is to interpret the ideological effects of discrete cultural systems without assuming that these effects take the form of a whole. Is is also to reflect on the sources and history of the concepts one uses to describe such effects. There is always a liberating moment when one examines the genealogy of one's discourse. That discourse becomes itself not natural and inevitable but historical, provisional and open to change. In addition to these dual projects of archaeology and genealogy one must also think postmodernity diacritically. Given that 'post-' which rules its usage, it remains a notion which needs to be defined against modernity.

I cannot offer a full reading of what I have called a cultural system here, but let me show what I mean by looking briefly at Coppola's film *Apocalypse Now*. It is an especially good example because it reworks Conrad's modernist classic *Heart of Darkness*, and so allows an entry for diacritical analysis. In turn, *Heart of Darkness* is canonical just because it offers a critique of modernity by breaking down the terms in which European thought distinguished itself from the primitive. Thus if one supposes that postmodernity differs from modernity in the way it legitimates or delegitimates imperialism, or, more radically, if one suspects that the discourse of postmodernity is once again grounded on a denial of otherness, then one would expect *Apocalypse Now* to bear these hypotheses out.

Heart of Darkness shows that the otherness of the primitive is precisely 'our' otherness – where that 'our' indicates, however tentatively, a civilized Eurocentric community. As the title suggests, it is a direct inversion of Enlightenment universalism, which assumes all human beings to be equal in so far as they are led by the light of reason and no further. The valorization of Western reason and civilization becomes for Conrad a cloak for greed, destruction and, paradoxically, the return of irrationality because it allows men to suppose themselves gods. The story makes its point, however, in terms of an old mythic narrative: the voyage to the underground and back, with its known stages and climax. There is therefore a confidence that the culture can narrativize its reneging on enlightenment. The text also has its own positive ideological project. Marlow's voice grafts the discourse of 'the common man' on to that of the sensitive, alienated intellectual. In this way, negative universalism still works towards a consensus. Marlow also attempts, though vainly, to autonomize instrumental reason – vainly, because his work finally fulfils imperialist ends. Finally, the text presents one place in society that is protected from its own truths. Marlow, who knows that enlightenment is a form of barbarism, that the West's Other is the West itself, protects Western women from that truth by lying to them. 'The horror, the horror', Kurtz's last words, are never reported to his fiancée. She continues to believe that he dies with her name on his lips. But there is a twist here. Her values that require protection from the truth *are* the horror too, making Marlow's lie a truth.

Given this summary reading of Conrad's story, one could simply go on to read the film to mark the division between the modern and the postmodern. But the primary shift is one of media and technology, not of meaning. Conrad's tale is *written*: how to catch the voice in writing and which voice to catch are questions it is overtly anxious about. *Apocalypse Now* consists of sounds and images. (This obvious point has a somewhat less obvious corollary. The privileging of the play in writing in current thought is in itself an act of resistance to postmodern technology.) Furthermore, Conrad's novel is the product of a man writing alone at home, autonomously; it requires no investment, no collective enterprise, and thus no high circulation. Although it was written for *Blackwood's Magazine* – no journal being less a vehicle for elitist modernism – the sense that it has no real audience is constantly foregrounded in the story. It is as if the text's implied reader belongs to Kurtz's fiancée's social space, where the truth may not be borne. But Coppola's film, which requires an audience for material reasons, cannot draw any bounds to its audience at all; its implied reader is the abstract consumer, anyone at all.

Because the film is a product of advanced technology, it has quite a different place in the world from that of the novella. In particular, it dissolves the division between truth and lie from quite another direction. Take the scene where Willard – the Marlow figure – first encounters the air cavalry. He jumps out of a helicopter into a blur of violence, noise and danger, in a scene whose production values are so strong that the film seems less the representation of a representation of battle than a recording of actual fighting itself. Suddenly a voice shouts: 'Look like you're fighting!' This is not the entry of postmodern self-referentiality. We soon realize that what we are seeing is, in part, the representation of a representation of a representation: the troops are fighting on and for the television cameras which are gradually panned into sight. Is all this totally fake, then – a mock battle for the folks back home watching the news? No: neither fake nor genuine, or fake *and* genuine. 'Real' bodies litter the ground. The fusion of theatre and war, war as theatre, is a product of modern communications technology and quite foreign to Conrad's moral sense that a lie may tell the truth.

In fact, not only is war theatre, but film is war. If we read (as good consumers) Eleanor Coppola's bestselling account of life on location, we realize that these stunningly realistic battle scenes were made possible by Coppola's hiring arms and equipment from the Filipino army.[8] During shooting these were periodically borrowed back by the army to fight real insurgents in the mountains. And the film set itself was under guard because of fears that it would be attacked for its supplies. The film is enabled by acts of neo-imperialist war: it cannot disengage itself from what it represents. The collapse of distinctions here between making films and making war is not primarily a cultural fact or a theme, but an outcome of specific material conditions. Its effects remain ideological, however: this particular system induces theories of the loss of distance between the image and the imaged.

The derealizing of the world is also an implicit theme of the film. Willard's eyes are constantly shown registering disbelief that the events he witnesses make up reality. But the naive response to this – 'Better than Disneyland', as one of the soldiers puts it – is inadequate. What the film makes clear is that Vietnam is 'irreal' because principles of intelligibility by which to experience it are missing. In Conrad these principles were narrativity on the one hand, and the unity of the subjective consciousness on the other. Marlow's story and the unity of his response make experiences of imperialist Africa, which he also knows to be unreal and unbelievable, ultimately meaningful. These categories do not work in the film, partly for technical reasons. Shots of Willard's eyes have to do much of the work of presenting subjective response. Yet they can never of themselves show how he interprets what he sees. Even sequences which move metonymically from an expression of disbelief to scenes of horror can only foreground the gap between each shot. The interaction between subjective consciousness and the outer world fails when subjects become visual objects: eyes, mouths, bodies. One might argue that the voice-over could do the work instead, bringing the events into the unity of a sovereign subject's response to them. The disjunction between image and sound in the film prevents that. Willard's voice-over, unlike Marlow's, is not in itself the means *both* of representing events *and* of interpreting them subjectively. In the film the representing function is given over to the camera, blocking control of representation by subjectivity. Thus the autonomy of the bourgeois subject, which depends not only on a clear division of self and world but on a means by which the self can absorb the world, comes apart in film. Here we encounter a moment in the system whose effect is the postmodern sense of the death of the psychological subject and the end of expression.

The film begins with a Doors song entitled 'The End' on the soundtrack as Willard undergoes a nervous breakdown. This breakdown is expressive, but of nothing.

After all, nothing has happened to him as yet. The scene seems to be an initial exorcizing of the possibility of expression: after this his only emotion – if emotion it is – is disbelief. But the first scene works against narrative: at the beginning is the end. At the beginning is a horror signifying nothing – or everything – just as at the end. The grounds for the dismantling of narrative progress can, however, be located more precisely. Conrad's narrative is a journey away from light to darkness and back to light as darkness. It requires a world with a boundary between civilization and savagery, even if those distinctions ultimately vanish. Such a difference exists in the film only as quotation. Willard, like Marlow, travels up a river by boat, but messages to him are always in front of him. Helicopters and jets fly above him towards his destination. The form of his journey is unmotivated; it seems a Conradian echo. Because there is no outside to the technology of war, a teleological narrative exists as no more than nostalgia.

Second, the Conradian climaxes which do occur – Kurtz saying 'The horror, the horror' – do so as citation. Just as technology is there before the individual (even Kurtz's compound has a radio), Conrad's text is always there before the film itself. This symmetry is much less than an equivalence, however. Coppola is using Conrad's narrative to tell the truth about Vietnam, but in the attempt we are left with historical incongruity and a mere monumentalization of modernism. Kurtz quotes Eliot; he is reading Frazer and Weston; he delivers a Nietzschean tirade on greatness as the capacity to bear the suffering of others. Though he is described as a genius, all this can never add up to charisma. It is the standard matter of a liberal arts education. His true distinction in the film's own terms is his efficiency, his refusal to play the hypocritical game of army bureaucrats. But in having him killed they do not play their own game either – so there is no final difference here. Ultimately, efficiency rules everywhere. The values of honour, truth and work for work's sake, which Conrad upholds as he reveals their limits, have disappeared along with the autonomous subject and work of art.

Finally, there is the question of cultural reproduction. In Conrad's text the story is told to a shadowy 'us' and not the fiancée. Coppola's Kurtz is obsessed with getting his truth told to his son; he entrusts that task to Willard before committing suicide. He and Willard think his truth is unrepresentable, sublime. 'I worry that you might not understand what I have had to be,' he tells Willard. Yet the impossibility of representing Kurtz is not the sublime impossibility of making the boundless conceivable; it is the trivial impossibility of making the secondhand firsthand. Kurtz's greatness is a requirement of narrative climax and intelligibility; it is not in him. A strange consequence emerges: if there is nothing great to tell, if the categories of intelligibility collapse, then it looks as if the culture might not reproduce itself historically. The age of history may disappear into history. Here we catch sight of the way in which postmodernity consumes history, in the sense of nullifying it. It remains an effect rather than an expression or theme.

Yet the failure to reproduce will not happen in silence. After all, Kurtz is on the screen for us all to see. Conrad believed his message to be so dangerous that it might really not have hearers. Coppola's film, which tells us that it bears an image so dangerous as to resist comprehension, requires that the unreproducible be shown everywhere. The true message is that nothing now is unreproducible; it is just that cultural reproduction has divorced itself from cultural values.

These remarks do not make up a full reading of the film, but they offer enough for us to see that it functions as a system creating *effects* of postmodernity within a quite specific technological, economic and ideological frame, rather than an *instance* of that octopus 'postmodernity' or even 'multinational capitalism'. What seems most deeply entrenched in these effects is the encroachment of Western power and technology upon the Third World. The destruction of narrativity is an effect of that power's being able to reach anywhere. The film itself becomes war within the frame of neo-imperialism.

At this point it is worth recalling a final difference between Conrad and Coppola. The original inhabitants of Africa are represented in Conrad's text. It is true that they are falsely presented as cannibals, but they play a role that allows the West to know itself as Other to itself. The Vietnamese enemy are nowhere in Coppola's movie. The film achieves its sense of total irreality by wiping them out of the screen. If the discourse of postmodernity characterizes the postmodern as that which knows no Other, then in this film that Other is eliminated by fiat. If there were an enemy available for representation, perhaps then there would be narrative rather than just citation. In the failure to concede Third World nationalism a right to existence, what is revealed is that will to totality and failure of imagination we have already found in Jameson. This seems more than coincidence. Is there, after all, a secret key with which to unlock postmodernity? If so, can it be found in those who come not to denounce the postmodern like Jameson, nor in that which produces effects of postmodernity, but in that very postmodern thought which is totality's enemy?

For Lyotard, postmodernity is a condition of knowledge at least as much as an epoch. It is a moment within and behind modernity, conceived of again much in the spirit of Marcuse and Adorno. Instead of proposing a history centred on the development of the capitalist mode of production, he thinks of modernity as a process of social rationalization. In his first account of the topic, *The Postmodern Condition*, this process is conceived of negatively: the modern is marked by the emergence of instrumental reason. In modernity, criteria of what he calls 'performaticity' overcome appeals to tradition or metaphysical truth. What counts is not why an act is done or why a thought is thought, but how efficiently and to what immediate end. Applied science is the home of instrumental reason, which (as research) gradually comes to be the standard against which all knowledge is measured.

This development has discursive consequences: cognitive utterances which can be verified and permit control over nature are privileged over those which cannot. But ultimately science cannot validate itself; only its services to power, its instrumentality, permit it to cast a spell of 'self-legitimacy'. The recognition of the failure of science's claim to self-legitimation spells the end for the grand narratives of human emancipation and philosophical speculation. Their collapse reveals a fragmented set of discursive formations and practices. The postmodern just accepts that science itself must act in terms of prescriptives, and cannot validate itself. It must be tolerant of paralogism, seeking no solace from the fragmentation and incommensurability of discourses. And in *The Postmodern Condition*, though not in Lyotard's later work, narrative knowledge takes the place of science as the preferred order.

Lyotard's most recent book, *Le Différend*, though not directly concerned with postmodernism, examines both the oral consequences and the philosophical grounds of discursive heterogeneity.[9] The paradigm for a *différend* is a case in which two parties in dispute cannot articulate their cause in the same idiom. He distinguishes an injury [*un dommage*] from an injustice [*un tort*]. In an injustice, the injury is not judged according to the litigant's own criteria of validity, so that the litigant (who then becomes a victim) is in effect silenced. This juridical paradigm is not limited to the courts. The privileging of descriptive statements over prescriptive ones is a *différend* which occurs within end–means rationality; the West places the colonized peoples in a *différend*; capitalism, with its ties to universality, creates a *différend*; for the specific, the unexchangeable, and so on.

For Lyotard, in a Cartesian spirit, what exists beyond doubt is the phrase or phrase event. But each phrase occurs as a *différend*: to link one phrase to another is to commit an injustice to possible genres which the first phrase might obligate. Once the nothingness between phrase events is bridged in the interest of a use, as it must be, a *différend* already exists. Thus Lyotard is able to say, 'politics is a matter of linkage between phrases' and is constituted within the 'civil war of language with itself'.[10] Here the Wittgensteinian sense that the limits of language are the limits of the world grasps hands with Derrida's proposition, in his remarks on Lévi-Strauss, that 'violence is writing'.[11] The groundlessness of language, its edging out on to nothing, its character as a mere *event*, the fact that it does not exist as a unity declaring its own linkages to itself, all enable the possibility of disagreement, of cultural difference, of violence, as well as the mirage of self-identity.

Unlike Wittgenstein and Derrida, Lyotard returns from these transcendental claims to history. The result disappoints at least as much as it promises. Because language is not a unity, because it necessarily sets *différends* into play, those meta-genres of discourse which claimed to cover all other genres of discourse (speculation) or which promised an end to injustice (narratives of human emancipation) are ungroundable. Philosophy alone is not responsible for their devalidation, however; they die in history. In modern history it becomes impossible to ignore certain cultural *différends*. These *différends* are recognized in the feelings signalled by the silences around certain proper names: Auschwitz is the example he uses most often. No genre of discourse presents itself which would permit a litigant to appeal for justice against the wrong Auschwitz connotes. This silence spells the end of the *grands récits* of Occidental emancipation and speculation which were the secular cover of Western cultural imperialism. Beyond it, no hope of a bridge between heterogeneous discourses survives. One must accept the *différend*.

From the other side, capitalism itself works to undo the force of the order of discourse. In capitalism, money, rather than language, instals exchangeability as the dominant relation between objects in the world. But money is also stored time and security – one might add, stored pleasure. Thus capitalism disburdens itself from notions such as humanity and progress which underpin high-cultural imperialism. But it also discounts the formations which resist these ideas: in particular, nationalism and philosophic deliberation. Ultimately, for Lyotard, capitalism even implies the end of effective political institutions. The play of exchange, the production of money as security, will delegitimate the discursive presuppositions of institutions too. In fact Lyotard's derationalized capitalism is close to Jameson's multinational capitalism, and, like Jameson, Lyotard sees post-colonial nationalism as not just archaic but dangerous. Post-colonial nationalism articulates itself in the 'narrative mythic'[12] which constructs an immutable cultural origin; it neutralizes the phrase as event, and it projects a 'home' in which difference is suspended; its greatest modern exemplar is Nazism. Thus it too is countered in those names surrounded by silence, pain and, finally, deliberation. Deliberation no doubt leads back to to the phrase event, and, if one is not to conspire in the concealment of a *différend*, one must punctuate the ebb and flow of phrases only by '*Arrive-t-il?*'

There is here the hope that the breakdown of legitimations for cultural imperialism will free the world both from the spell of instrumental reason and from the nostalgia for mythic origins. It is as if postmodernity would today be the play of post-colonialisms set free not only from the requirement of universality embedded in emancipation, but also from the hunger for identity implicit in narrative as myth. Lyotard aims to clear a space for maximizing the potential of articulation within all idioms. The problem is not just the universalism of Lyotard's own Cartesian approach. Nothing very much in the book softens the shock of the transition from '*Auschwitz*' to '*Arrive-t-il?*' This last seems a slight result for the promise implicit in his vision of discursive heterogeneity.

For Lyotard, Auschwitz is not only a name with a halo of silence; it produces a particular emotion, signalling a *différend*. Within what context does the binding of this emotion to the name occur? The events at Auschwitz do not come into the world with feelings attached to them as if by nature. Let us think of another name, one which has as little feeling attached to it as any for Western philosophy: New Zealand. This is the country that Maoris call Aotearoa. When one recalls this, one recalls the massacres, the deaths by introduced diseases, the destruction of a culture and a society which the name New Zealand silences. It is Lyotard's virtue to recognize that mere cognition of these matters can never be enough. How can we account for the difference between the respective silences around the names New Zealand and Auschwitz? One might say, of course, that Auschwitz happened to *us*, whereas New Zealand did not. That, however, would be to assume that we know who we are extradiscursively – by blood; and it is another of Lyotard's virtues that he does not want to concede that either. One might point to a qualitative difference – but how can we measure the loss of a culture against the loss of lives?

Auschwitz resonates for us, not because we are who we are genetically, but because memories of it are constantly circulated orally and in writing. New Zealand's history, on the other hand, is told within a different rhetoric and is barely circulated even inside the country itself. The emotions attached to Auschwitz are attached to language; they remain analytically inseparable from the discourse that produces them. The difference between affect and language begins only when one asks 'Does one have a right to a feeling?' It seems clear that one has a right to articulate the injuries one feels. It is less clear that one has a right to feel feelings as injuries in the first place. In philosophy this question rarely arises because it is generally assumed that an injury is simply felt as an injury, in a way that a bird is not simply seen as a bird. Lyotard does not address himself to the question of the transmission of either language or emotion. If the phrase event is the beginning and end of deliberation, it does not follow that it comes into the world merely bordered by nothingness. It comes transmitted, always already in the history that it makes possible. If philosophy cannot confront the phrase as transmitted, then again that marks a philosophical limit.

What one misses from Lyotard is any sense that a phrase occurs in, or in the gaps of, a particular language. Indeed, on one breathtaking occasion he declares succinctly: 'all *langue* is translatable'.[13] If he were to accept that the question of what is and what is not translatable across languages is interminably debatable, then he would have to accept once again that the limits of specificity within his own frame are not found in the phrase itself. To observe that phrases happen within a particular language is to note a kind other than the phrase: the language the phrase is in. And for philosophical deliberation to confront a particular language at the point where presuppositions end would also and again be to to confront a socio-cultural order inseparable from linguistic diversity. This order cannot be covered by the phrase and its linkages. In its flight from categories of totality, Lyotard's linguistic turn evades the one totality – so-called 'natural' language – which it cannot reduce or ignore *on its own terms*. It is precisely to this totality that post-colonialism today appeals.

The post-colonial desire is the desire of decolonized communities for an identity. It belongs to that programme of self-determination which Adorno, unlike Jameson, could envisage. Obviously it is closely connected to nationalism, for those communities are often, though not always, nations. In both literature and politics the post-colonial drive towards identity centres around language, partly because in postmodernity identity is barely available elsewhere. For the post-colonial to speak or write in the imperial tongues is to call forth a problem of identity, to be thrown into mimicry and ambivalence. The question of language for post-colonialism is political, cultural and literary, not in the transcendental sense that the phrase as *différend* enables politics, but in the material sense that a choice of language is a choice of identity.

The link between post-colonialism and language has a history. In his recent book *Imagined Communities*, Benedict Anderson has argued that nationalism has always been grounded in Babel. That is to say, nationalism is a product of what he calls 'print-capitalism'. He writes: 'the convergence of capitalism and print technology on the fatal diversity of human languages created the possibility of a new form of imagined community which in its basic morphology set the stage for the modern nation.'[14] One does not have to accept the faculty psychology hidden in the phrase 'imagined community' to take the point. Nationalism emerges when some languages get into print and are transmitted through books allowing subjects to identify themselves as members of the community of readers implied by these books.

Let us take Anderson's history further. Of all the works that created the new print languages, none had more authority than the sacred books. A whiff of heresy attaches itself to the story at this point. The sacred books, as vehicles of God's word, cannot be translated. No doubt, when God reveals himself in natural language, transposition of a kind has already taken place, but the human language becomes divine through the breath of God's voice, the trace of his hand. To deliver the Bible (or the Koran) to *any* demotic language is not just to allow nationalism to overpower the old church, but for meaning to precede form, for communication to precede revelation – is to admit, in fact, the arbitrariness of the sign.

Anderson does not make a further argument which seems to me inescapable. Once the sign becomes arbitrary, once divine self-revelation becomes transferable across secular languages, then not only may national identities attach to the print language, but language itself no longer permits of any proper identity. If one language can be translated into another, if there is no such thing as a dead language, what untranslatable residue remains to be the property solely of those who speak it; its form, which cannot be communicated in – as one says – any other form? Yet an identity granted in terms of the signifier (which I use, as it is often used, as a figure for form as such) is an identity that necessarily cannot be communicated. It would seem to be written into the fate of nationalism as print-capitalism that national identity is conferred in the form of its own death warrant. Indeed, there are moments in our culture where an unquenchable nationalist pathos confronts its own mortality: one thinks of Hölderlin's poetry.

The appeal to what is unexchangeable in language is especially tempting under capitalism, which deals with things and words for their exchange value. In the classic formulations of nationalism – Fichte's *Addresses to the German Nation*, for instance – national identity is based on both language (the home of culture) and soil. When a post-colonial nationalist like the Kenyan novelist Ngugi, living under multinational capitalism, looks at the soil, he sees it as a means of production, and means of production do not articulate identities; indeed, where they can be owned, they are often owned by foreigners. This leaves him language and, within language, culture. (One might note that for decolonized nations the other great ground for

nationalist pathos – war – has little place. Most post-colonial nations and tribes
have a history of defeat by imperialist powers. Freedom is often the enemy's gift.)

Pre-colonial language shelters all the particularity elided over by colonial
stereotyping, by modernist valorization of the primitive and by anthropology. In
return, as identical to itself, national language excludes the web of contacts, the play
of sameness and difference, which weave one society into another. It does so in
having the advantage that it is not unique. The number of languages available to
be spoken is infinite; the economy of Babel is not restricted. And yet language is not
identical to itself, and in translation a residue is always left behind.

Ngugi, who places language at the heart of his post-colonialism, was arrested for
co-writing plays in Gikuyu, although no doubt his crime was also to aid Gikuyu's
transformation into a print language. It is clear that he is not troubled by the sense
that an identity given in print language is given as a death warrant. Thus, when he,
or someone like him, enters a novel by a post-colonial writer who is disturbed by
such questions, the mode of encounter is predictable. Near the beginning of Salman
Rushie's novel *Shame*, the narrator is interrupted by such a speaker, disputing his
authority to tell the tale.

> *Outsider! Trespasser! You have no right to this subject!* ... I know: nobody ever
> arrested mc. Nor are they ever likely to. *Poacher! Pirate! We reject your authority. We
> know you, with your foreign language wrapped around you like a flag: speaking about
> us in your forked tongue, what can you tell but lies?* I reply with more questions: Is
> history to be considered the property of the participants solely? In what courts are such
> claims staked, what boundary commissions map out the territories?
>   Can only the dead speak? [15]

This is a dialogue across the bar which internally divides the post-colonial. The
divide separates what one can call the post-colonized from the post-colonizers.
The post-colonized identify with the culture destroyed by imperialism and its
tongue; the post-colonizers, if they do not identify with imperialism, at least cannot
jettison the culture and tongues of the imperialist nations. Of course there is not
always a choice here. For many ex-colonies the native tongue is the world tongue
– English. This is not just true for Australia and Canada, say, as it was once for
the United States. It is also true for West Indians as well as for many Maoris and
Aboriginals. Indeed, there exists a largely unrecognized but crucial difference in the
various post-colonial nations. A country like Australia has almost no possibility of
entry into the post-colonized condition, though its neighbour New Zealand, where
Maoris constitute a large minority, does. New Zealand retains a language, a store
of proper names, memories of a pre-colonial culture, which seductively figure
identity. I have no doubt that the very name New Zealand, and its *différend*, will
pass one day, the nation coming to call itself Aotearoa. What one encounters here
is a politics of language which rests not on the power within language, the power
of rhetoric, but on the power behind language. From the side of the post-colonizer,

a return to difference is projected. But, from the side of postmodernity, English (multinational capitalism's tongue) will museumify those pre-colonial languages which have attached themselves to print and the image so belatedly.

Rushdie's dialogue between the post-colonized and the post-colonizer takes place in a language which is not quite transatlantic English. For instance, the position of the adverb in the phrase 'Is history to be considered the property of the participants solely?' marks a tone at the slightest of removes from that English. But its difference may not be invested with nationalist pathos. It remains too close to what is not different but the norm, the language of world power. The sense that Indian, New Zealand, Australian or Irish English is not as different from transatlantic English as French is from English, let alone as different as Maori or Gikuyu, figures the post-colonizer's emptiness. 'Can only the dead speak?' Rushdie elliptically asks, hinting, among other things, at the powerlessness of the pre-colonial tongues and at the death warrant involved in finding an identity through fallen languages, of which his own has fallen furthest.

Rushdie answers the post-colonized challenge in terms of the *différend*. The narrator inquires: 'In what courts are such claims staked?' Now it is he, whose side is not quite that of the oppressed, who appears as victim. He cannot find a place for justice, nor plainly articulate his case, partly because he speaks neither the language of the international market nor a post-colonized language. What he is charged with is what he inherited. If Rushdie, as a post-colonizer, speaks from a place in contemporary history where a *différend* is dramatically foregrounded, then Lyotard's retreat into transcendental philosophy, his mysticism of selected proper names, his preference for experiment, have a strong competitor. If Jameson cannot fully distance himself from the sublimity and internationalism of what we can call image-capitalism, then that is perhaps because he has not listened carefully enough to those voices which talk of the *différend* on its borders.

To consider the *Apocalypse Now* system alongside *Shame* is chastening. The problem is not one of varieties of postmodernism. Rushdie's work is sometimes called postmodern, but it certainly does not reflect postmodernity. *Shame*'s purpose is to reconnect shame – that epic, indeed pre-capitalist, emotion the Greeks called *aidos* – to the recent history of Pakistan. In redirecting shame, the novel calls upon a violence, both feminine and monstrous, which does not, like that of *Apocalypse Now*, reach a climax from the very beginning. *Shame* imagines an unlocalizable, inexpressive, ethically proper violence we never see in *Apocalypse Now*. Indeed, the novel as a whole works in precisely the opposite direction to Coppola's movie. History is not derealized, affect is not atomized into intensity, narrative triumphs, other cultures are not confined within Occidental myth, nor outside the Western screen. So we can say that, when confronted by his post-colonized accuser, Rushdie is startled into an articulation of the problematic of the *différend*, but when faced with modern Pakistan, he acts as accuser in turn. Here his novel remains connected to those concepts of justice and reason that totalizing denouncers of our postmodernity assure us are in their safekeeping.

Notes

Where full details are available in the Bibliography, references contain only essential information.

1. See ch. 4 above.
2. *Ibid.*, p. 64.
3. Theodor Adorno, 'Cultural criticism and society', in *Prisms*, transl. Samuel and Shierry Weber, Neville Spearman, London, 1967, p. 34.
4. Herbert Marcuse, 'The affirmative character of culture', in *Negations: Essays in critical theory*, transl. Jeremy J. Shapiro, Allen Lane, London, 1968, p. 122.
5. Adorno, p. 29.
6. Jameson, p. 88.
7. This article was written before Jameson's essay 'On magic realism in film' (*Critical Inquiry*, 23 [1986], 301–25) appeared. It represents a departure from the 'cultural logic' piece because it does not allow that post-colonial films differ from postmodern artifacts in ways that offer promise. But from my point of view the essay remains based on doubtful assumptions, i.e.:

   1. Certain 'First World' films (nostalgia films) still *instantiate* postmodernity.
   2. Post-colonial films are more realist than 'First World' films because they are produced in conditions not totally dominated by late capitalism.
   3. Post-colonial films are also postmodern in that they exemplify 'denarrativization' and a 'reduction to the body', both of which 'libidinize' cultural residues.

   However suggestive an account which moves from these theses may be, it continues to rely on expressive causality and reflection theory; it still assumes that the 'postmodern' and 'realism' are textual features, not effects, or constituted by discourse on texts; and finally it does not allow for the particular mode of ethico-political debate and intervention which takes place only and precisely in post-colonial nations. There is a danger that the post-colonial here becomes both something like Europe before 1848 for Lukács *and* a site saturated by the progressive materialism of postmodernity, rather than a field of forces which postmodern thought must analyse without idealization or condescension.

8. See Eleanor Coppola, *Notes*, Pocket Books, New York, 1979, p. 9.
9. For what follows, see Jean-Françoise Lyotard, *Le Différend*, 1983.
10. *Ibid.*, p. 204.
11. Jacques Derrida, *Of Grammatology*, transl. Gayatri Chakravorty Spivak, Johns Hopkins University Press, Baltimore, London, 1976, p. 135.
12. Lyotard, p. 219.
13. *Ibid.*, p. 226.
14. Benedict Anderson, *Imagined Communities: Reflections on the origin and spread of nationalism*, Verso, London, 1983, ch. 3, 'The origins of national consciousness', p. 49. For further material on this topic, see John Edwards, *Language, Society and Identity*, Basil Blackwell, Oxford, 1985, 'Language and nationalism'.
15. Salman Rushdie, *Shame*, Vintage Books, New York, 1984, p. 23.

33 □ *Postmodernism and Periphery*

Nelly Richard

The Universalizing Model of Modernity

It is well known that modernity (historical, philosophical, political, economic and cultural) generates its principles from a threefold wish for unity. The Enlightenment ideals on which it is founded define modernity in terms of rationalization, as an 'advance' in cognitive and instrumental reason. This produces particular categories and systems through which historical development and social evolution are conceptualized, based on the notion of progress as the guideline of a universalist project. It also assumes the objective consciousness of an absolute meta-subject. The principles of modernity generate specific representations of society by means of bureaucratic and technological networks which incorporate institutional practices into an overall scheme. The spread of a 'civilizing' modernity is linked to a model of industrial progress and in this way it is part and parcel of the expansion of multinational capitalism and its logic of the marketplace, centred on the metropolis and its control of economic exchanges.

This threefold foundation of modernity's universalism suffices to show the link to the totalizing tendency of a hegemonic culture bent on producing and reproducing a consensus around the models of truth and consumption which it proposes. With regard to its economic programme and its cultural organization, this concept of modernity represents an effort to synthesize its progressive and emancipatory ideals into a globalizing, integrative vision of the individual's place in history and society. It rests on the assumption that there exists a legitimate centre – a unique and superior position from which to establish control and to determine hierarchies.

Traditionally, this position has been the privilege of Western patriarchal culture, whose representational apparatus has been the source of those homogenizing categories which apply to both language and identity:

As recent analyses of the 'enunciative' apparatus of visual representation – its poles of

From *Third Text*, 2 (1987–8), 6–12.

emission and reception – confirm, the representational systems of the West admit only one vision – that of the constitutive male subject – or, rather, they posit the subject of representation as absolutely centred, unitary, masculine.[1]

They suppress any notion of 'difference' which might challenge the dominant model of subjectivity. All the extensions of the idea of modernity work towards confirming the position of privilege, and to this end negate any particular or localized expression which could possibly interfere with the fiction of universality.

Transferred to the geographical and socio-cultural map of economic and communicational exchanges, this fiction operates to control the adaptation to given models and so to standardize all identifying procedures. Any deviation from the norm is classified as an obstacle or brake to the dynamic of international distribution and consumption. Thus modernity conceives of the province or periphery as being out of step or backward. Consequently, this situation has to be overcome by means of absorption into the rationality of expansion proposed by the metropolis.

Colonization and Cultural Reproduction

What does contact with the international procedures and rhetoric of modernity imply for the province/periphery?

From the outset, modernization in Latin America unfolded as a process of Europeanization. All the models to be imitated and consumed (industrial and economic organization, political structures, social behaviour, artistic values) were based on European prototypes. The construction of history in terms of progress and linear temporality is doubly inappropriate when applied to Latin America. It is alien to the stratifications of Latin American experience because it cannot accommodate the discontinuities of a history marked by a multiplicity of pasts laid down like sediments in hybrid and fragmented memories. The ideology of the 'New' as constructed in the discourses of modernity is founded on an idea of time which follows a sequence and rhythm that is completely foreign to Latin America. This is because the diachronic triggers articulating the logic of its periodicity do not have any equivalent in the clashing juxtaposition of the heterogeneous and intermittent processes which coexist in our subcontinent. The gap between images or symbols of 'progress' or 'rupture' which are constantly proposed as revelations of the 'New', and the fragility of the Latin American social and cultural environment that cannot usefully integrate these notions of modernity, produces an experience of continuous disassociation. This is particularly true if one is searching for a coherent system by identifying that which is 'one's own'. In the field of culture – of art, literature and the history of ideas – this dependent and imitative relation to European modernism as transmitted through local elites has created a particular instance of the centre–periphery relationship: that of 'reproduction'.

This model of reproduction is founded on what might be termed the constitutive evidence of Latin America: its relation to Europe and its belonging to the hegemonic world of the West from the time when it became part of world history. From this viewpoint, Latin American thought and culture have been obliged, from colonial days, to reproduce those of Europe, to develop as a periphery of that other 'universe' which, by dint of successive conquests, became one of the themes of its history ...

One of the aspects which illustrates this is the role of the enlightened elites or intellectuals, a defined group within Latin American society which, since independence, has been the expresser of foreign currents of thought.[2]

Thus, when references from the metropolis are brought to bear on the Latin American context, they become the objects of a process of cultural mimesis. This turns them into parodies or caricatures which lack their own operational dynamic because they either do not fit the context or are rejected by it. The application of this type of model becomes wholly cosmetic, since it is employed to forge an illusory identity, a fictional version of 'one's own identity' in terms of 'the other's desire'. As a consequence, processes of identification produce substitutes in the form of series of imported masks.

In the frequent periods during which the elites deny any Latin American cultural reality, the consequent lack of any underlying theoretical practice (identity) comes to be filled with problems, categories, and value judgements formulated elsewhere – in the metropolis. ... At a symbolic level, this contradiction is resolved by mimesis: a repetition of someone else's gesture, which entails the promotion of the pseudo-appropriation of that gesture's values: so a representation is made, and even lived out, of being what one is not. ... Mimesis because the gesture is represented without any awareness of its context: we copy the imported image without knowing about how it originally came into being, and also without any great concern as to whether or not it happened to be relevant to our own reality.[3]

The international model offers sham opportunities which are adopted as 'responses' to questions which have not as yet even been formulated by the new context in which they are placed. This means that signs are rendered meaningless and inoperative, since the mechanisms for a recontextualization that would endow them with a critical function are totally lacking. These signs have not been digested and reformulated according to the contradictions which would complicate their insertion into the socio-cultural arena which so far simply legitimates their international prestige. As long as imported theories and cultural movements remain divorced from the opposition of forces which are the only means of lending specific importance and historical density to the signs produced in Latin American cultures, they act as little more than orthopaedic aides within the contexts of those cultures. Characteristically, this kind of production exhausts itself in mere formal repetitions or 'doctrinal mannerism'. It produces pseudo-theories which are disassociated from the intellectual struggle in which the original concepts and interpretations had to fight for supremacy. They are now no more than fetishes in what has become a merely ornamental construction.

Contradictions of Modernity from the Perspective of a Latin American Essence

Criticisms of modernity have come from a wide range of areas including the arts, literature, sociology and theology. These criticisms are based on differing cultural and ideological views of what constitutes a 'Latin American identity'. Certain tendencies within sociology and theology,[4] for example, put forward the view that modernity's homogenizing project destroys all memory of a birth-process which embodies a multiplicity of pasts which must be rescued from European historical reductionism, so that Latin America may finally achieve its true identity on the basis of its own experience of time. As a functionalist and secularizing proposal, modernity has not only erased all the ritual dimensions of a culture to which the philosophy of the logos is profoundly alien, but it has also suppressed that culture's 'Catholic substratum', a popular religiousness whose stock of symbols form an integral part of the Latin American 'ethos'. A symbolic upgrading of this ethos would provide the platform from which to combat the distorting effects of the international modernizing influence since 'our cultural synthesis is Latin American, of mixed race, and ritual'.[5] As far as art and literature are concerned, a whole current of thought about the alienating role of the idea of modernity as the purveyor of European fictions is grounded in a defence of Latin American culture as derived from authochthonous beginnings. This culture is linked to forms of identity – representations of 'oneself' usually equated with the 'indigenous' – that are taken to represent the authenticity of a 'pure' culture. This purity is defined by the myth of its origins which predate modernity and the contaminating expansion of the culture industry of multinational capitalism. This view – both essentialist and metaphysical – of what constitutes a Latin American identity is mythologized and turned into folklore in any number of ways: indigenism, nationalism, thirdworldism. It consists of several kinds of primitivism in which Latin American identity is equated with a predetermined and fixed identity. The rediscovery of this identity therefore involves a mythical, backward-looking return to the sources and produces a static view of origin (the indigenous substratum) and memory (the mixed-race past), turned into ritual and applied over the whole continent.

Even in the most up-to-date versions of this argument, the demands for a Latin American art or literature still conform to a dichotomy which usually posits essences against categories. These are drawn from the opposition between self (seen as internal identity) and the 'other' (identity from outside); for instance, the regional (seen as authentic) versus the international (seen as false), the past (the vernacular roots) versus the present (seen as the destruction of the binding sense of community), popular culture (as part of the tradition of belonging) versus a mass culture (as alienating communication), and so on. In this Manichaean scheme of things, modernity is found guilty of having destroyed the characteristics of a true Latin American identity through a conglomeration of influences which are invariably regarded as threats, falsifications, or travesties of the region's original and authentic nucleus of culture.

Modernity and Postmodernity

What rupture does so-called postmodernism imply in this set-up? Does postmodernist criticism, interpreted as a crisis in the assumptions behind modernity, in any way modify our reading of the role which the province has hitherto played on the map of international dependencies?

Modernity has always been intimately linked to the idea and practice of writing. The storage of knowledge in books generated meaning and fixed reference points: the book as history is also history as the book. Postmodernity, on the other hand, declares itself concerned not with the question of establishing meanings, but with the challenging of the very concept of any monological or univalent structure of signification. Instead it postulates the destabilization of meaning (as part of the crisis of reference and a resulting delegitimization of knowledge). Every utterance is submitted to a generalizing intertextuality in order to take apart and reassemble its fragments. Postmodernist deconstruction as open-ended signification not only has a bearing on the illusion that utterances possess a single, definitive meaning, but is also and primarily aimed at combating the supposition that culture and society – understood as texts – still follow a historically and politically determined direction. Postmodernism states that all privileged points of view have been annulled, along with the dominant position which allowed the establishment of hierarchies of interpretation. To what extent can such a critique of the unidimensionality of meaning, aimed at the hegemonic system established by a self-centred culture, offer new approaches which might help the process of decolonization? This is the fundamental question raised by postmodernism in the periphery.

Postmodernism introduces a highly ambiguous set of co-ordinates into the worn-out context of modernity which has programmed backwardness – the province – in order to reintegrate it more readily into its framework of global consumption.

At first sight, it might appear as if postmodernism reformulates the old dependencies (centre/periphery, progress/backwardness) in a way which creates a new hierarchy. For almost the first time, Latin America finds itself in a privileged position, in the vanguard of what is seen as novel. Even though it only finds itself in this position within a theoretical framework formulated elsewhere, Latin American cultural practices are deemed to have prefigured the model now approved and legitimized by the term 'postmodernism'. The very heterogeneity of the experiences which have created a Latin American space out of its multiple and hybrid pasts creates, at least on the surface, the very qualities of fragmentation and dispersion associated with the semantic erosion characteristic of the crisis of modernity and modernism as its cultural dominant.

However, just as it appears that for once the Latin American periphery might have achieved the distinction of being postmodernist *avant la lettre*, no sooner does it attain a synchronicity of forms with the international cultural discourses, than that very same postmodernism abolishes any privilege which such a position might offer. Postmodernism dismantles the distinction between centre and periphery, and in so doing nullifies its significance. There are many instances in postmodernist discourse aimed at convincing one of the obsolescence of the opposition centre/periphery, and of the inappropriateness of continuing to see ourselves as the victims of colonialism. The significance of these categories has disappeared, the argument goes, as has the distinction between model and copy due to the 'planetary spread' of technological culture; the mass media have obliterated the relation between original and reproduction.

> M. Periola, author of an original study on simulacra, notes that the planetary triumph of communications destroys any possible confrontation between models and the very idea of a secondary copy. This disappears in the dizzying reproduction of ways of life in places, times, and socio-cultural contexts which are totally different from those which gave rise to the originals, without this spread leading to any kind of unification but rather to a recognition of individual particularities.

and

> As its everyday use suggests, a copy is secondary to the original, depends on it, is less valuable, and so on. This viewpoint therefore belittles the whole of our continent's cultural efforts, and is at the root of the intellectual unease which is our theme. However, current European philosophy (Foucault, Derrida) is concerned to show that such hierarchies are unjustified. Why should it be true that what comes before is more valuable than what comes later, the model be worth more than the imitation, what is central be more important than the peripheral ...?[6]

Or again, the centre itself has become the periphery,[7] since it has become fragmented into dissident micro-territories which fracture it into constellations of voices and a plurality of meanings.

Postmodernism's first claim, then, is that it offers room within itself for our Latin American space. This is the 'decentred' space of the marginalized or peripheral subject faced with a crisis of centrality. It is adorned with the ciphers of plurality, heterogeneity and dissidence, confirming Lyotard's observation that postmodernism 'refines our awareness of difference'. The stress is placed on specificity and regionalism, social minorities and political projects which are local in scope, on surviving traditions and suppressed forms of knowledge.

The fact is, however, that no sooner are these differences – sexual, political, racial, cultural – posited and valued than they become subsumed into the meta-category of the 'undifferentiated' which means that all singularities immediately become indistinguishable and interchangeable in a new, sophisticated economy of 'sameness'. Postmodernism defends itself against the destabilizing threat of the 'other' by integrating it back into a framework which absorbs all differences and contradictions. The centre, though claiming to be in disintegration, still operates as a centre: filing away any divergencies into a system of codes whose meanings, both semantically and territorially, it continues to administer by exclusive right.

Postmodernist Collage and Latin American Identity

Although this mechanism of the 'thirdworldization of the metropolis' (a symptom of Eurocentrism's uneasy conscience) immediately resolves into a new trick of rhetoric which is easy enough to uncover, it is none the less tempting to see if any of the 'concessions' made by postmodernism to the periphery can be of any critical value to us.

If postmodernism is an admission, on the international level, that a culture and society which previously saw itself as universal is now bankrupt, then those expressions which, merely by being peripheral to this scheme, were condemned to be constantly excluded, have no reason to feel threatened by this collapse. Nor is it necessary for them to feel the degree of perplexity or anguish which accompanies the shattering of those dreams which have supported the illusion of a position of dominance. Latin Americans need not feel the weariness of belonging to a sated, over-consuming society, since their connection to that culture has invariably been one of dispossession. If the collapse of values of an entire historico-cultural construction known as modernity has dealt the dominant tradition of European thought such a hard blow, it is because that construction guaranteed its Eurocentric prerogatives. This is why there is such a narcissistic outcry at its loss. To what extent does this loss implicate Latin Americans, who have always been on the outside of the sphere of references and privileges? How far is it true that the destroying of illusions and the consequent weakening of a cultural identity whose tradition had been presented as the paradigm of authority can facilitate a more *uninhibited* review of the falsehoods and circular evidence on which its hypotheses of power were based?

By creating the possibility of a critical rereading of modernity, postmodernism offers us the chance to reconsider all that was 'left unsaid' and to inject its areas of opacity and resistance with the potential for new, as yet undiscovered, meanings. In the Latin American context, this review of modernity allows us, once again, to pose the question of our own identity, that of individuals born of and into the dialectic mixture of the different languages surrounding us, which have partially fused to produce a cultural identity experienced as a series of collisions. This identity can be understood as an unstable product of modernity's tropes which involves a continuous regrouping, distorting and transforming of imported models, according to the specific pressures pertaining to the critical reinsertion of these models into a local network. This active participation, which the individual at the periphery performs, emphasizes a creativity based almost exclusively on the reuse of previously existing materials which are available either as part of the Western tradition or, more recently, prefabricated by the international culture industry. Innovative responses to these materials are based on strategies of redetermining the use of fragments or remains in ways which differ from their original frame of reference.

Perhaps our Latin American identity, seen from the perspective of the postmodernist 'collage', is no more than a rhetorical exacerbation of the strategies of decentralization and readaptation. The periphery has always made its own mark on the series of statements emitted by the dominant culture and has recycled them in different contexts in such a way that the original systemizations are subverted, and their claim to universality is undermined.

translated from Spanish
by Nick Caistor

Notes

Where full details are available in the Bibliography, references contain only essential information.

1. Craig Owens, 'The discourse of others: Feminists and postmodernism', 1983, p. 58.
2. Bernardo Subercaseaux, 'La appropriaciación cultural en el pensamiento latinamericano', *CERC*, June 1987.
3. Christian Fernandez, 'Identidad cultural y arquitectura en Chile', Catàlogo *Chile Vive*, Madrid, January 1987.
4. Pedro Morande, *Cultura y Modernización en America Latina*, Universidad Catolica de Chile, 1984; see also his contribution to *Los debates sobre la modernidad y el futuro de America Latina*, ed. José Joaquín Brunner, Flasco, 1986.
5. Pedro Morande, *Cultura y Modernización en America Latina*.
6. Rosa Maria Ravera, 'Modernismo y Postmodernismo en la plástica argentina', *Revista de Estética*, 3, Buenos Aires; Roberto Schwarz, 'Nacional por Sustracción', *Punto de Vista*, 28, Buenos Aires.
7. 'Certainly, marginality is not now given as critical, for in effect the center has invaded the periphery and vice versa.' Hal Foster, *Recodings*, 1985.

34 □ Rereading Mandarin Ducks and Butterflies: A response to the 'postmodern' condition

Rey Chow

I

A crucial, though largely unnoticed, moment emerges in the current debates on postmodernism when the American Marxist critic Fredric Jameson refers to the as-yet untranslated works of a contemporary Taiwanese writer, Wang Wenxing (Wang Wenhsing), as 'postmodernist'. With that word Jameson means to include contemporary Chinese literature in a new culture which 'articulates the logic of a new global and multinational late capitalism', and which 'can no longer be considered a purely Western export but may be expected to characterize at least certain other local zones of reality around the capitalist world'.[1]

From the perspective of Chinese studies, it would seem necessary to consider this claim of postmodernism with a large degree of caution. That consideration would begin with a foregrounding of Jameson's hypothetical reconstruction of Chinese modernism. Significantly, Jameson positions Lao She's *Camel Xiangzi* (first serialized in 1936–7) as an 'earlier moment in modern Chinese literature'[2] with which to measure the mutations and critical concepts that are brought up in the more contemporary works. What results is a kind of schema which reorders modern Chinese literature into the categories of realism (Lao She), modernism (Wang Meng, a contemporary PRC writer), and postmodernism (Wang Wenxing). This reordering, whereby early Chinese modernism, being boldly summed up in the one work *Camel Xiangzi*, is equated with a sort of critical realism whose 'Chinese' uniqueness is said to reside in the interaction between two mutually decoding narrative paradigms, makes it possible for Jameson to describe the works in contemporary Chinese literature as 'breakthroughs into literary modernity', which apparently are shifting the focus of critical discussions to 'language itself and to the stylistic "techniques" of narrative'.[3]

From *Cultural Critique*, 5 (1986), 69–93.

To intervene in this 'postmodernist' schema of modern Chinese literary history is embarrassing because it inevitably involves pointing to the voluminous studies which have already been done on the subject of Chinese modernism[4] – embarrassing also because the discussions of language and stylistic 'techniques' of narrative date back at least to 1919, the year of the May Fourth Movement, which is the official landmark for the birth of Chinese modernism, a modernism whose main features included the controversial advocation of *baihua* (the vernacular) for literary writing and myriad experimentations with 'Western' literary forms. The case of the novelist and playwright Lao She, in this light, is especially ironic, since his narrative methods have always been associated with traditional storytelling which is not upheld as representative of 'Chinese modernism'. For instance, in his studies of modern Chinese literature, the Czech sinologist Jarosloav Prušek interestingly argues that Lao She is an 'artistic failure' whenever he departs from stories of individuals and puts social problems in the foreground.[5]

What the name 'Lao She' calls to mind – though this is not the place to enter into Lao She's works here – is in fact a traditionalism which is irreducibly present in the history of modern Chinese literature but which Chinese modernism in its pro-Western tendencies has always wanted to suppress. What I would like to present in the rest of this essay is therefore a cultural critique within a cultural critique: a critical response to postmodernism as 'global culture' is possible only with a rewriting of modern Chinese literary history from within.

II

Modern Chinese literary history, as it is presented in the West, has, until fairly recently, been dominated by the May Fourth Movement and the cultural revolution that clusters around its memory. 'May Fourth' is now generally understood not only as the day in 1919 when students in Beijing protested against the Chinese government's self-compromising policies toward Japan and triggered a series of uprisings throughout the country, but as the entire period in early-twentieth-century China in which Chinese people of different social classes, all inspired by patriotic sentiments, were eager to revaluate tradition in the light of science and democracy and to build a 'new nation'.[6] In literature, the term 'May Fourth' signifies the call for a reformed practice of writing that was to be based on *baihua*, the vernacular.[7] Following the debates among May Fourth intellectuals such as Hu Shi, Chen Duxiu, Zheng Zhenduo, and Mao Dun on the need to create an 'improved' people's language and literature, writers of the period experimented with a variety of 'novel' forms that took their inspiration from Western romanticism, naturalism, realism, and pragmatism. Thus the process of cultural purification, which was ostentatiously iconoclastic, was instigated with the 'West' as 'theory' and 'technology'. Chinese culture itself, meanwhile, increasingly turned into some kind of primitive raw material which, being decadent and 'cannibalistic', was urgently awaiting enlightenment. There was not a better indication of this cultural ferment than the frequency with which the word 'new' [*xin*] appeared as a sign of change: 'new youth', 'new fiction', 'new literature', 'new woman', 'new times', 'new China', and so on. This desire for the new quickly acquired the force of an ideological imperative that successfully rationalized China's contact with the West. In one of his discussions of the May Fourth Movement as a Chinese cultural revolution, Hu Shi concludes: 'Without the benefit of an intimate contact with the civilization of the West, there could not be the Chinese Renaissance.'[8] In the word 'benefit', the Chinese predicament of the twentieth century is concisely summed up. According to the arguments of cultural revolutionaries like Hu Shi, the new or the modern is not only absolutely necessary but also good. And it is good because it comes from the West. The breakdown of traditional Chinese culture is thus self-imposed as much as it is coerced through foreign domination. We must now view the eagerness of May Fourth leaders like Hu Shi as the sign of desperation among a particular class which was traditionally appointed the guardian of its society, and which conceded perhaps too naively to seeing China's problems in terms of its 'inferiority' to the West. The open and willing espousal that resulted, the espousal of the Western as the 'new' and the 'modern', and thus the 'civilized' [*wenming*], meant the beginning of a long process of cultural imperialism that was to last beyond China's subsequent retrieval of her leased territories and official concessions.

But if the modernization of Chinese literature has been part and parcel of imperialism, the condemnation of which has become an ethical platitude in the late twentieth century, the subtle ramifications of imperialism are most actively with us today in the form of established cultural history, where residual[9] material specificities are smoothed over for the sake of 'major' landmarks which are held up as 'epochal' and thus representative. The May Fourth Movement, however contradictory and complex its developments might be, now stands in modern Chinese literary history as a primary event, a historic watershed between the old and new Chinas. As a topic which is amply researched within modern Chinese studies, the periodization 'May Fourth' thus exists as the synonym for 'modern Chinese literature': its problems function as signs of Chinese literature's 'modernity'; its theories and experiments testify to a Chinese literary 'modernism'. What such a periodization emphasizes is the alignment of Chinese literature to a 'world' status through 'modernity', while 'pre-modern' Chinese literature continues to remain in the esoteric realm of 'sinology'.

The issues of 'modernity' and 'modernism' in Chinese literature, however, have to be rethought precisely because they are inextricably bound up with imperialism. Could 'modern' here be strictly the 'new'? Progress from Oriental primitivism to the enlightenment of Western science and democracy? Cultural renaissance? Or could it be the process whereby all such concepts are parochialized as they are confronted with a culture which seems persistently subversive of their rhythms of development? Could 'modernity' in China be in fact a depletion of the usefulness of forms both 'old' and 'new', because the old have lost their original relevance and the new have been applied from without?

As an approach to these problems, the culturally monumental status of May

Fourth literature as 'modern' Chinese literature must be resituated in its historical context. The May Fourth writers were in fact writing in competition with a large number of 'old school' novelists who, by adhering to more traditional styles, continued throughout the teens and twenties to produce an extremely popular type of fiction that apparently sought only to entertain the reading public without striving for new social visions. These writers are known in history as the 'Mandarin Duck and Butterfly School' [*yuanyang hudie pai*], and their writings, 'Mandarin Duck and Butterfly literature' [*yuanyang hudie pai wenxue*, abbreviated to 'Butterfly literature' in the following]. This hilarious name was first used to refer to Xü Zhenya's *Yü li hun (Jade Pear Spirit)*, an early bestseller published in 1912. Written skillfully in semi-classical parallel prose, Xü's novel is strewn with sentimental poems in which lovers are compared to pairs of mandarin ducks and butterflies. A related series of jokes and rumors among some writers of the period resulted in the use of 'Mandarin Duck and Butterfly' as a pejorative label for the authors of this type of sentimental love story. These writers included Xü, Li Dingyi, Wu Shuangre, and a few others. During the twenties, as the May Fourth Movement gathered momentum in the process of Westernizing Chinese letters, the label 'Mandarin Duck and Butterfly' was used generally to attack all types of old-style fiction that continued to enjoy popularity. 'Butterfly' fiction henceforth included not only the love stories that were written during its heyday, but also 'social' novels, 'detective' novels, 'knight-errant' novels, 'scandal' novels, 'ideal' or 'fantasy' novels, 'comic' novels, 'legendary' novels and others. This broader definition of the label remains the one adopted by Chinese Communist critics today, while non-Communist writings tend to adhere to its narrower definition as 'love stories' only.

In rereading Butterfly literature, the first thing we notice is that the phenomenal production and consumption of Butterfly stories in their time are in conspicuous contrast to the marginality of their reception in modern Chinese studies. That marginality must now be reassessed to form a complex background against which the status of May Fourth literature as Chinese modernism can be reexamined. On the other hand, although Butterfly literature has begun to arouse interests among scholars in recent years, those interests seem confined to two major types of approaches. The first such approach, which aims to discover intrinsically 'literary' excellences in certain works of Butterfly literature, aims also to restore them to the 'canon' of Chinese vernacular fiction. As such, works of Butterfly literature are interpreted as second- or third-rate successors to a long-established literary tradition, and are stripped of their historical significance as subversive popular cultural forms.[10] The second type of approach defines Butterfly literature as documents of sociological interest. Largely in accordance with the Communist Chinese imperative to 'restore' a 'people's tradition' through 'material' culture – a tradition which would henceforth 'scientifically' reprove the idealism of feudal, 'literate' China[11] – this approach 'excavates' Butterfly literature together with massive historical data obtained from field work and statistics. Here, what is characteristically bypassed is the opacity or constructedness of Butterfly stories themselves, which are reduced to more or less transparent 'reflections' of ideas.[12]

The inadequacies of both these types of approaches alert us to how the specificity of Butterfly literature can be excluded from sight through acts of restorative appropriation just as much as through downright dismissal. My concerns therefore include not only refuting the historical rejection of Butterfly fiction as 'inferior' literature through explications of Butterfly stories' 'intrinsic' merits, but also questioning the persuasive influences of those methods by which it is now reappropriated into the homogeneity of 'tradition', literary or socialist. In other words, the task in rereading Butterfly literature is twofold: to recollect Butterfly stories from historical oblivion, and to find in them a method to read against the critical discourses which so powerfully dominate modern Chinese literary history at present.

As a working hypothesis, I redefine the historical appearance of Butterfly fiction as a *feminization* of the predominant Confucian culture, in the double sense that moments of subversion that exist in this fiction are closely related to the inferior positions of women in Chinese society, and that such moments, because they are part of popular culture, continually disrupt and resist some of modern China's most 'serious' concerns (such as 'modernization') even as they gesture toward them. 'Feminization' as such refers not only to the questioning of female oppression, which was scripturally and socially reinforced in traditional China, but also to the processes whereby the clearcut empiricist dichotomy between oppression and emancipation, or between traditionalism and modernism as stable, definite perspectives, becomes impotent.

An example of such processes of feminization can be described through the formal structure of a significant Butterfly subgenre, the love story.

A subgenre which began with Wu Woyao's *Hen hai* (*Sea of Remorse* or *Sea of Woe*) (1908), the Butterfly love story is often alluded to in this manner: 'boy meets girl, boy and girl fall in love, boy and girl are separated by cruel fate, boy and girl die of broken heart'.[13] Accordingly, *Sea of Remorse* has been summarized as a story which 'depicts the rapid degeneration of a weak-willed youth and the belated attempts by his devoted fiancée to restore him to physical and moral health. He dies, nevertheless, and she bids her parents farewell to enter a nunnery.'[14]

This kind of interpretation, in other words, sees Butterfly literature on neutral but imprecise grounds, as stories about unfulfilled love relationships whereby the male and female characters equally share the narrative focus. However, the consistently ascribed 'balanced reciprocity of the romantic relationships between lovers'[15] fails to account for the asymmetrical structure of many of these stories, in which women characters take up the major part of the narrative space.[16] In Wu Woyao's work, for instance, the 'weak-willed youth' is not merely separated from his fiancée, but is absent from the narrative for most of the time; he is reunited with her in his physically and morally degenerate state only in the last twenty pages or so. Further, his conspicuous absence is brought about in the most improbable manner. Evacuating their village during the Boxer Rebellion, the engaged couple travel in a cart pulled by a mule; but as they are not yet married, the man decides to keep his fiancée from feeling embarrassed by walking beside the cart himself while she sits in it. When they are attacked by a group of bandits, the mule runs off in another direction in fright, thus separating the couple by literally removing the man from the scene. Obviously crude and ridiculous, this device of separation nonetheless illustrates how essential it is for the novelist to find a way to stage the woman alone. In the events that follow, we see her as the virtuous daughter and wife-to-be, taking care of her sick mother and trying to contact her lost fiancée under the most poverty-stricken circumstances. When he finally reappears, his degeneracy remains strangely unexplained. This absence of any persuasive sense of development in the male character once again highlights the sensitive moral perceptiveness in the woman: the male becomes a mere stage prop to the melodrama of female melancholy.

Rather than being reciprocal, then, relationships between men and women in Butterfly love stories often take place in the conspicuous absence or lack of participation of the women's beloved, who may be weak, sick, dead, far away, or a foreigner beyond the grips of Confucian culture. In being left alone to struggle with the traumas of life, women characters are seen willingly to resist personal desires or to give up their own lives in the names of chastity and morality. This asymmetrical or *sacrificial* structure calls to mind the Chinese *lie nü* ('virtuous women') tradition, which stresses obedience to unwritten as well as written laws regulating female behavior.[17] As such, these popular stories become writings which 'imitate' or 'continue' traditional patterns of oppression against women in the Chinese culture.

However, the sacrificial structures which so pervade any reading of the stories are mediated by the fragmentariness of the narratives themselves. If Butterfly love stories could indeed be read as narratives which continue, in fictional form, the *lie nü* genre, we would still need to ask the question why Butterfly authors and readers were so tirelessly *fascinated* with this subject of female melancholy. The male authors' unabashed attempts to focus their literary energies on the subject in a kind of writing which was rooted in traditional storytelling and despised by the pre-modern Chinese literati as 'small talk' [*xiaoshuo*] suggest the working of another set of concerns which are closely related to but not identical with the feminine one. Female melancholy, being inextricably associated with 'love', is at the same time the occasion for art and fiction, and thus aligned with the activities which are traditionally condemned as immoral if they are pursued in themselves for pure 'play'.

What is most striking stylistically about the Butterfly love stories is their sense of *excess* – a characteristic which they have inherited from Chinese vernacular fiction and which appears, on the one hand, as the utmost sentimental indulgence and, on the other, as extreme social entrapment. The manner of narration in these stories is thus often visibly split between a fascination with the spontaneity of love, which is depicted as a *discovery* by the man of his beloved's charm, *and* a concurrent reinforcement of the oppressiveness of the public world. As romantic images are juxtaposed against the most frightening and repulsive ones, or as the stylized language of traditional storytelling is juxtaposed against the improbable, trivial, and fantastical events, 'love' of 'sentiment' (i.e. the 'beautiful') does not so much compel sympathy and identification as it produces feelings of excess and contradiction. For the Chinese reader especially, love's extravagant, superfluous clashes with the 'public' do not so much evoke, contemplatively, a sense of truth about 'private' emotions as they dramatize the effects of emptiness associated with a particular affective tendency as 'fictional'.

This 'fictional' narrative structure, which is apparently *divided* between sensationalism and didacticism, between sentimental melodrama and the author's avowed moral intent, has the effect not of balance and control, but rather of a staging of mutually uncomprehending realities (such as Confucianism and Westernization, female chastity and liberation, country and city lives, etc.). Irreconcilably juxtaposed against one another, such extreme stylizations produce narratives that are violent not only because of their subject matter but, more important, because of their implicit undermining of what they themselves consciously uphold, i.e. a Confucian attitude toward female virtue. This violence, whose *theatricality* ultimately strips any single reality of its claim to full authenticity, is what can then be rethought as the feminizing of the Confucian culture through storytelling. It is a violence that requires us to read Butterfly narratives the way they read history, as disjunct fragments rather than as a cohesive whole.

Not surprisingly, therefore, the fragmentary modes of Butterfly stories have been consistently misinterpreted by even the most sensitive critics as signs of their inferiority, their *failure* to become good 'canonical' literature. To this extent, rereading Butterfly stories is not merely an exercise in learning about the mediated nature of fictional discourse, but is crucial for deconstructing institutionalized criticism's erudite and persuasive *mishandling* of popular cultural forms. Such mishandling consists in a progressive refusal to accept the subversiveness which is peculiar to Butterfly literature.

This subversiveness lies not so much in any potential of Butterfly stories to look 'out' to a world beyond the one in which they are situated as in the impossibility of their narrative mode, that is, in their attempts to force together two essentially incompatible forms of writing, storytelling, and the moral treatise. The fact that Butterfly stories, in spite of their pronounced didactic intent, are held suspect by Chinese critics left and right since the days of the May Fourth Movement, indicates that something is amiss in their 'didacticism': not that it is not there, but that it is out of place. Their didacticism is inconsistent with their lurid depictions of a macabre reality. Butterfly authors were also 'untrustworthy' as they shamelessly regarded their own work as play [*youxi wenzhang*], as a leisurely withdrawal into the ideological leftovers of a social and political world which was collapsing but which still constituted, in broken-up forms, the materiality of a people's lives. Their fiction lacks that urgent sense of a complete break with the past, and contradicts the revolutionary optimism of a liberated and enlightened China. But through them we see a very different kind of subversion at work, a subversion by repetition, exaggeration, and improbability – a subversion that is parodic, not tragic, in nature.

The fragmentary quality of these stories which demand irreconcilably split interpretations necessarily evokes a critical, and not simply appreciative, response. This critical response is not just the awareness of what social problems the stories 'reflect' or 'criticize', but how their modes of presentation and contradictions relate to the society which gives rise to those problems and which at the same time censors their representation in this particular form. As melodrama, Butterfly love stories invite disbelief by inflating to fantastical proportions the Confucian society's addictive ideologies and are therefore 'dangerous' for that society, which relies on its members' *serious* involvement with what they read, learn, and study. Butterfly stories' frank operation as mere play, entertainment, weekend pastime, and distraction from 'proper' national concerns also meant that they had to be exorcized not because of their subject matter (which is much more homespun than most May Fourth literature) but because of their deliberately fictional stance, their absolute incompatibility with the modern Chinese demands for 'reality', personal and social. Thus these stories live on as inexplicable dreams for enlightened Chinese minds, their images hauntingly familiar but rationally repressed.

Finally, the processes of feminization must also be understood in their interrelatedness with the newly urban conditions under which Butterfly literature was produced and consumed. A good illustration of such interrelatedness can be found in Xü Zhenya's *Jade Pear Spirit*. A story which tells of the unfulfilled love between a scholar-teacher and a widow whose son he is tutoring, *Jade Pear Spirit* strikes us immediately with a certain dislocation between its language and its subject matter, which results from the narrator's attempt to record the tedious content of sentimental love with the ornate 'four-six' prose style [*pian li*] of the dying scholar-official class. While the classical, erudite prose style had lost none of its beauty, it was used here for selling 'middlebrow' entertainment to a rapidly growing reading public in urban centers like Shanghai. This dislocation between arcaneness and mundaneness, between the elitism of learned writing and the accessibility of popular fiction, suggestively connects the Butterfly love story with a kind of signification whose emergence coincided with the emergence of the modernized Chinese city masses: the 'personal'. This is an age in China when romantic emotions, which had usually been hushed up because any public demonstration of strong feelings was considered embarrassing, were released to untried degrees of exuberance. [18] The most unutterable, most 'feminine' feelings were now endowed with a tremendous sense of aura and put on a par with the most heroic and patriotic, precisely because *all* sentiments were made lucidly 'available' for the first time through the mass practices of reading and writing, activities which used to belong exclusively to the highbrow scholarly world.

This sentimental liberation was not naive, however, but complex. In the increasingly commercialized atmosphere of treaty ports like Shanghai, the no-longer-shameful production of such 'feminized' significations went hand in hand with unprecedented 'waves' of consumption. [19] Emotions, proclaimed as the 'truths' of human kind, meanwhile turned into lucrative commodities which often came in serialized form in popular journals and newspaper columns and gave rise to unending desires in the booming book market. The most interesting aspect of such serialization is that it happily coincided with a traditional storytelling device which had its origins in a form of Buddhist sermon that was popular in the Tang Dynasty

(AD 618–907) and which many Butterfly writers still used. This device was an expression that had become identified with the traditional storyteller's mannerism in the 'linked-chapter' form [*zhang hui ti*]: 'If you wish to know what happens next, you are welcome to hear my next exposition.' Thus a modern commercial gimmick found its precursor fantastically, in an outmoded popular cultural practice.

The interplay between traditionalism and modernism in *Jade Pear Spirit* is evident in the physical withholding of sentimental desires, which is characterized by a consistent concealment of the lovers' bodies. Though living in the same household, Mengxia and Liniang rarely see each other; they have two nocturnal meetings throughout the entire work, only one of which is described in full (Chapter XVIII: 'Crying Face to Face'). In that chapter, they clear their misunderstandings brought on by Mr Li, who had tried to expose their affair, then go on to exchange poetry for the rest of the night amid sobbing and gazing at each other. This melodramatic physical *restraint* on the lovers' part, just like the melodramatic excessiveness of their poetic and moral expressions, is an important signifying gesture in itself. Without this fundamental *veiling* of the bodily aspect of love, the excitement of the scholarly sentimental world would be completely lost. Instead of physical intimacy, the lovers engage in an endless series of masquerades: letters, books left behind in the lover's room, lost handkerchiefs, photographs, flowers, the remainder of a burnt sheet of poetry, a lock of hair, inscriptions made with blood – all of which conjure up the presence of the beloved in broken, missing forms, as incomplete traces. This construction of 'love' as a fundamentally empty process, an artful play in which gestures could be continuously exchanged without any positive goal, is probably what unconsciously led to the rejection of Butterfly literature as 'dangerous' and 'harmful'. What is alarming for the morally concerned is not simply that such love is immoral – a point which is perhaps too obvious to the Confucian world-view to be belabored – but also that it is fictional and unrealizable. For Xü Zhenya, on the other hand, the whole artistic meaning of Mengxia and Liniang's affair would have collapsed if they had allowed their love to be consummated physically.

Love, but love withheld from physical exhaustion, is *Jade Pear Spirit*'s most crucial formal aspect. It is what ultimately explains the fragmented impression of the story: while the actual contact between the lovers is almost non-existent, there is always yet another letter or poem to be written with ever greater lucidity and abundance of emotion. The result of such 'playful', self-perpetuating displacement is that every happening in this sentimental world always seems too large or too small, too much or too little, but never coherent and together. In this sensitive registering of the fundamentally dislocated nature of desire is thus inscribed the dilemma of a China which was still feudal, Confucian, and demoralized, but which was also modernized, progressive, and enamored of 'new and foreign' things – including the idea of a liberated China – that were at once the source of fascination and frustration.

This attempt to resketch the genealogy of modern Chinese literature is by no means exhaustive. What I hope to have suggested through the brief discussion of Butterfly literature above is that Chinese modernism was taking a rather different path from what its periodization in accordance with Western historical developments has granted. The production of a self-consciously revolutionary, nationalistic literature in the May Fourth period is now seen against the concurrent production of popular narratives which are, however, repudiated as 'barbaric' by the Chinese and China scholars themselves. What results from resketching as such is not the glorification of Butterfly literature for its intrinsic 'literary values' or for its usefulness in terms of 'popular knowledge', but a reconstituted relation of contradiction, a relation that disembodies the unifying gesture of a modernist culture that is compelled to authenticate its own relevance first and foremost in global terms.

III

Another way to intervene in Jameson's appropriation of Chinese literature within the contemporary Western context is by reexamining some of the important moments in critical theory that have contributed to the sense of urgency surrounding the recent 'postmodernist' debates. If we return briefly to the now-popularized phrase of the 'metaphysics of presence', it seems possible to identify in the modern West an influential epistemic concern that has led up to the despairing impulses of the current 'postmodernism' – the concern with 'language' as a pre-given ontological condition. Deconstructing the scientific optimism of structuralism's fascination with 'systems', the early work of Jacques Derrida leaves us with '*différance*', the 'difference-as-deferment' which is said to characterize all linguistic activities and all cultural acts of identification. 'Presence' is thus always as much an illusion as it is a necessary presumption for human undertakings. But while *différance*, as writing *sous rature*, may be equated with the Nietzschean affirmation of joy – the joy of 'dissemination' without the obsessive returns to 'origins' – it has also given us the preordainment of 'Language' in the form of a prison-house, which may be glimpsed from explications of deconstruction such as the following: deconstruction is 'the strategy of using the *only available language* while not subscribing to its premises'. 'Language *bears within itself* the necessity of its own critique' [my emphasis].[20]

For a reader with some knowledge of the non-Western world, this readily prescribed monolithic presence of Language (as World and critique of that World) can only arouse the most fundamental suspicions. Not only must she point out once again, at the expense of being obvious, that the attentiveness to Language as such has its origins in the twentieth century in the writings of Ferdinand de Saussure, who in spite of acknowledging the existence of ideographic writing systems such as Chinese,[21] nonetheless bases his 'course in general linguistics' on the phonetic; she must also reiterate the interesting fact that for Saussure, 'the linguistic signifier ... is not phonic but incorporeal – constituted not by its material substance but by the differences that separate its sound-image from all others'.[22] For poststructuralism *à la* Derrida, the assertion of language as 'incorporeal' is crucial as a way to undo the 'metaphysics of presence' as phonocentrism of 'logocentrism'. But the deconstruction of speech itself as an instance of the 'always already written', which is in turn grounded in an 'incorporeal' linguistic signifier, returns us to Language as a faculty that is ever-present precisely because it is inaudible and invisible, neither a stream of air nor a stream of ink.

The poststructuralist definition of Language as the now-perceivable, now-immaterial play that is paradigmatic of all human activities is what underlies the recent debates on postmodernism. Let us take, for instance, Jean-François Lyotard's critique of Jürgen Habermas's defense of the 'project of modernity'. Habermas's arguments are made in terms of the Enlightenment spirit. In his essay 'Modernism versus postmodernism', which was written upon the receipt of the Adorno prize, Habermas defines postmodernism, with its 'neo-conservative' tendencies, as a repudiation of culture and therefore a false program. [23] For the culture of modernism to continue and be 'completed', Habermas argues that there is the need to establish 'unconstrained interaction' between the cognitive, moral-practical, and aesthetic spheres, and to find ways of linking expertise with everyday praxis. This interaction among the different spheres of life is then what constitutes 'communicative rationality'. What is of interest to us here is the typology of scientific versus narrative knowledge that Lyotard offers as a way of criticizing Habermas's denunciation of postmodernism. For Lyotard, postmodernism is not a break from modernism; it is rather the nascent state by which modernism was possible in the first place. By that, he means that it is only in the postmodern condition that the rationality of the modernist is fully unravelled for the first time. In the short essay 'Answering the question: What is postmodernism?', which is appended to his longer work, *The Postmodern Condition: A report on knowledge*, Lyotard traces that relation in terms of aesthetics back to the Kantian 'sublime', whereby representation is fundamentally a representation of the 'unpresentable':

> The sublime ... takes place ... when the imagination fails to present an object which might, if only in principle, come to match a concept. We have the Idea of the world (the totality of what is), but we do not have the capacity to show an example of it. We have the Idea of the simple (that which cannot be broken down, decomposed), but we cannot illustrate it with a sensible object which would be a 'case' of it. We can conceive the infinitely great, the infinitely powerful, but every presentation of an object destined to 'make visible' this absolute greatness or power appears to us painfully inadequate. Those are Ideas of which no presentation is possible. Therefore, they impart no knowledge about reality (experience); they also prevent the free union of the faculties which gives rise to the sentiment of the beautiful; and they prevent the formation and the stabilization of taste. They can be said to be unpresentable.
>
> I shall call modern the art which devotes its 'little technical expertise' [*son 'petit technique'*], as Diderot used to say, to present the fact that the unpresentable exists. [24]

The difference between modernist and postmodern culture is that, while the modernist puts forward the unpresentable as missing contents in good forms, which still allows for aesthetic pleasure and a collective sense of nostalgia, the postmodern would be

> that which, in the modern, puts forward the unpresentable in presentation itself; that which denies itself the solace of good forms, the consensus of a taste which would make it possible to share collectively the nostalgia for the unattainable; that which searches for new presentations, not in order to enjoy them but in order to impart a stronger sense of the unpresentable.[25]

Interestingly enough, the negative dialectical relation argued here between what can be conceived and what can be presented, a relation whereby the generation of 'forms' is always accompanied with an ever-present sense of the unpresentable, calls to mind fundamental aspects of traditional Chinese aesthetics, an aesthetics which has been deemed to reside in the 'power of emptiness'.[26] In classical Chinese literature, what is emphasized again and again is a similar principle that we can detect in the otherwise cryptic opening lines of the *Dao De Jing*:

> The way that can be spoken of
> Is not the constant way;
> The name that can be named
> Is not the constant name.[27]

This linguistic/aesthetic principle could alternately be described in this way:

> Not only can the message reach its destination without having to be fully spelled out, but it is precisely because it is not fully spelled out that it can reach its destination. In this sense, the 'blanks' in painting, the silences in poetry and music are active elements that bring a work to life.[28]

Classical Chinese aesthetics as such can be identified with a 'trampoline effect',[29] whereby the tightening of a spring means that its sudden release will launch infinite vaster spaces of the unseen. As a convention in poetry, for instance, we have the familiar image of the hermit-sage who remains invisible and whose truth is 'beyond words'.

This formula of 'less is more', which recurs throughout ancient Chinese linguistics and poetics, and which seems to have pervaded the 'Chinese common sense' with the power of an unquestioned, idiomatic *raison d'être*, offers us an unexpected perspective from which to approach Lyotard's theory of the 'unpresentable'. In his longer work, Lyotard elaborates on the 'unpresentable' in terms of the persistence of what he calls the 'narrative function' in the postmodern world. On its own terms, the critical import of the 'narrative function' is as follows. Modernist culture, with its scientific tendencies to seek legitimation as the means to reality, has consistently suppressed and marginalized 'narrative knowledge', which differs from scientific knowledge most significantly in that it does not demand the legitimation of itself as the only form of truth, and does not require the exclusion of the Other in order to come into being itself. The persistence of this 'narrative function' in spite of its marginalization by modernist culture leads Lyotard to conclude that the postmodern should be defined as 'an incredulity toward metanarratives', and postmodern (or narrative) knowledge as that which 'refines our sensitivity to differences and reinforces our ability to tolerate the incommensurable'. Lyotard ends his short essay with a set of pleading imperatives – 'Let us wage a war on totality; let us be witnesses to the unpresentable; let us activate the differences and save the honor of the name' – imperatives which are paralleled by the concluding allusion in the longer work to 'a politics that would respect both the desire for justice and the desire for the unknown'.[30]

In spite of his use of the word 'knowledge', the question that Lyotard's anti-rationalist model of narrative raises is that of art as subversive practice. The formulaic belief in narrative and art *per se* as alternative ways of 'knowing' that are distinct from the officially endorsed is especially problematical *vis-à-vis* the Chinese context, where writing had always developed as a *critical* activity (in the form of censorship) while being ostensibly a 'record' of moral reason. The inveterate didacticism that resulted, a didacticism which still remains one of the reasons why Chinese literature can be unpalatable to Western readers, points to the ineffectiveness of writing or 'art' whose critical capacity has been historically institutionalized and politically reinforced. Canonical Chinese modernism, as is indicated by May Fourth writers' frequent attacks on their favorite target, *wen yi zai dao* ('litrature as the embodiment of moral instruction'), arose originally as a reaction *against* this traditionally institutionalized practice of writing and art. As vernacular fiction (rather than drama or poetry) was emphatically promoted as part of the nation-building program and increasingly practiced by all writers, the agenda of the May Fourth Movement became palpably that of the 'autonomy' of literature, on which a respectable because independently 'aesthetic' truth was endowed. Ironically, however, the elevation of fictional writing to a level of aesthetic significance, an elevation which was influenced by Western learning and liberating in principle, returned the passionately rebellious May Fourth intellectuals to the traditional status of the Chinese literati who had always monopolized the 'aesthetic' or 'literary' as a different, learned realm, a realm that was 'superior' to the vulgar, womanly narratives of the lower classes. The difference is that while the 'aesthetic' used to be situated in 'Chinese' literary excellences (such as the dichotomous interplay between expression and silence), it was now relocated in the novelty of foreign forms. Accordingly, the ideological positioning of what were considered 'vulgar', 'womanly', or 'barbaric' narratives also shifted, from the simple 'lower classes' to the 'unenlightened natives' who continued to interpret reality through traditional Chinese storytelling.

Paradoxically, then our 'local' history of Butterfly narratives as narratives jointly produced by foreign imperialism and native scholastic elitism makes the pronouncement of a 'narrative function', which is in turn intimated as a 'central instance of the human mind',[31] highly irrelevant. Such a pronouncement is possible only in terms of a 'monolingual' world-view, which may at first appear opposite to what Lyotard proposes, namely, that the postmodern world is made up of *different* 'language-games'. But the diversity of language-games is tolerable apparently only because something more fundamental called 'Language' (in the Derridean sense), which is now redefined as 'narrative', is what exists primordially between individuals and the world or the 'unpresentable'. We seem to have come back once again to a certain fatalistic inevitability, presented here as a 'natural' presence – a 'function'. What the rereading of Butterfly literature as marginalized popular narratives shows us, instead, is that there are always more than one language and one narrative function: between us and the unpresentable are interlocking and unequal narratives, which are further mediated by histories of institutional or political suppression. The unpresentable is in this respect not simply the 'name' of difference to which we must all 'be witnesses', but clusters of irreducibly contending, culturally specific relations. Therefore, the 'unpresentable' does not necessarily lead us to the refinement of sensitivity or the reinforcement of tolerance – qualities which rather dangerously resemble the 'benign' strategies of certain colonialisms *after* the natives have been conquered – but more truthfully, to an alertness to the power politics in all human undertakings.

The problem that ultimately faces us in any process of rereading is the problem of theoretical reconstitution. The upsurge of interest in the 'unpresentable', which is currently assuming a great variety of forms in academia, suggests that what should concern us now is no longer simply the unpresentable itself, but, more alarmingly, how the unpresentable is put to use. Here, the generation of contradictory implications which are inalienable to the critiques of the West from within can be fully realized only through such critiques' confrontation with the non-Western world in its non-hegemonic positions. A typical instance of this is the rearrangement of the 'constellations' of thinking, which begins as a critique of Western metaphysics and proceeds by redemptive reinscriptions of the 'unpresentable' in history, by now a fully conventionalized practice within the confines of First World academic institutions. To testify to this, we need only point to the notable prominence, in recent years, of critical methods which share a certain emphasis on the marginal, the unknown, the autobiographical, and the institutionally suppressed. Within literary academia, at least, it would be honest to admit that this overwhelming enthusiasm for obscure, unpresentable 'truths' not infrequently coincides with the institutional requirements for the 'originality' of research: to try to say what was not said before turns more and more into 'looking for a new territory which no one else has discovered'. Academic scholarship itself thus becomes a continuous widening of spaces, with an ever-increasing quantity of interest-topics. The accompanying demystification of Western cultures logically leads to the search for 'alternative' perspectives outside the 'hegemonic' space of the 'First World'. It is in this light that the current emergence of the 'Third World' as a viable critical signifier must be understood.

The resultant explosion of hitherto unpresentable perspective is, of course, not necessarily democratic. If Western theory, as a self-conscious attempt to negotiate some form of reconciliation with what is always missing from its own present attention, has now identified the non-Western world as a 'resourceful' territory for investigation, then it is Western theory too which, in spite of its original liberating intentions, is complicitous with the historical 'First World' desire to use the non-West to supply its 'lack' in so many different ways. This 'lack' is often eulogized as the 'Other': as woman, primitive nature, spiritual beyond. In each case the non-West receives full credit as alternative *representational principle*, while the 'hegemonic' West continues to balance such acts of metaphysical generosity with the most pragmatic discriminations and miscomprehensions.

An example of this type of complicity, which is implied though unintended, is then furnished by Jameson's proclamation of postmodernism on the contemporary Chinese literary scene. While he accepts Lyotard's ahistorical affirmation of narrative, Jameson also wants to *politicize* the global crisis in narrative in the following way: the great master narratives have not disappeared but have been driven underground, in what he has elsewhere called 'the political unconscious'. For Jameson, therefore, it is not enough just to assert, as Lyotard does, the narrative *potential* of a scientific and technological world, because whatever change might be induced by the narrative potential would automatically be reabsorbed by the capitalist system itself. Cryptically, he concludes his foreword to the English translation of Lyotard's book by pointing to 'genuinely political action'[32] as a means to interrupt the monopolistic tendencies of capitalism.

For Jameson, the postmodern is thus defined in terms not of a narrative function, but of a practice of mapping, a metaphor to which he attaches great significance in his essay 'Postmodernism, or the cultural logic of late capitalism'.[33] In the essay, Jameson proposes a definition of the postmodern world as one in which the dissolution of the autonomy of culture has led to an explosion that has abolished critical distance altogether. The moment of truth in postmodernism is therefore 'an extraordinarily demoralizing and depressing original new global space',[34] where, ideally, a new thinking that unites catastrophe and progress would arise. The invention and projection of a global cognitive mapping, which would take place in the 'symbolic' between the individual and knowledge, and which would generate relations to a new Totality, are then what would give postmodernism the meaning of a *pedagogical political culture*. Jameson concludes this essay by suggesting that his 'symbolic' is a reformulation of the Lacanian 'symbolic' as an 'aesthetic' of cartography.[35] It would seem that this 'aesthetic' is Althusserian too – even though Jameson would not give the latter credit – in the sense that art is the space where Ideology is internally distanced from itself, made incomplete and thus transformed: a space which is yet distinct from Science.[36]

What is at stake here is not exactly the reinscription of postmodernism in the aesthetic, be it in the form of narrative 'difference', or of cartographical 'totality'. The question that keeps rearing its ugly head is that of history and, in this case, its related issue of ethnocentrism. If the debates on postmodernism in the West have arisen out of a dissatisfaction with history as teleology, then the same debates are unavoidably faced with history as infinite, ungraspable historicity. Is the cultural historian condemned to ethnocentrism, in that he or she either has to reduce the 'alien' to some culture-bound total vision, or else become utterly incapacitated by the ever-multiplying otherness of even his or her 'own' world?

A pressing, though perhaps not yet fully articulated, alternative seems to lie in the use of history as a continuous *confrontation* with precisely these two impossible ends of totality and difference. That confrontation, which would always proceed with skepticism, has to be distinguished from cynical rejection. My interruption of Jameson's attribution of postmodernism to contemporary Chinese literature would hopefully be understood in this light. If the path of Chinese modernism has been marked off from the West, in that it was born as a reaction to foreign imperialism, imbued with traditional didacticism and modernist nationalism that in turn produced a revolutionary literature and its barbaric Other of popular narratives, and eventually punctuated by socialism on the mainland and colonialist capitalism in places like Taiwan and Hong Kong, then the label of 'postmodernism', which is itself a culture-specific periodizing concept, would seem facile and misleading. Is it not possible that in this postmodern narrativization of the 'Third World', the 'new' territories discovered are once again becoming exotic signifiers that are continually being reconstituted within the one familiar signified of 'world history', rather than being recognized genuinely for what they are not? In the 'new' mapping of the world as 'postmodernist', is the postmodernist cultural historian attending to the unpresentable, or is he retrieving information for an older system – a metanarrative?

Perhaps the words of a China historian can be redelivered here in contest. Reflecting on the Communist Chinese eagerness to periodize Chinese history in accordance with the West, Joseph R. Levenson writes:

> Chinese history *on its own* developed in a way *not just its own*. This was the basic communist historical statement ... with equal weight on subject and predicate; these together established the equivalence of China and Europe.

> I think Mao should be turned on his head: Chinese history *not* on its own (in modern times, at least) developed in a way *just* its own.[37]

Notes

1. Fredric Jameson, 'Literary innovation and modes of production: A commentary', *Modern Chinese Literature* I, 1 (1984), 75, 76.
2. *Ibid.*, 67.
3. *Ibid.*, 72.
4. Sidestepping sources in Chinese, Japanese, other languages and a good deal in English, the reader may want to consult some of the following: Chow Tse-tsung, *The May Fourth Movement: Intellectual revolution in modern China*, Harvard University Press, Cambridge, MA, 1960; C.T. Hsia, *A History of Modern Chinese Fiction, 1917–1957*, Yale University Press, New Haven, CT, 1961; Bonnie S. McDougall, *The Introduction of Western Literary Theories into Modern China*, Centre for East Asian Cultural Studies,

Tokyo, 1971, *Modern Chinese Literature in the May Fourth Era*, ed. Merle Goldman, Harvard University Press, Cambridge, MA/London, 1977; Marián Gálik, *The Genesis of Modern Chinese Literary Criticism (1917–1930)* Veda, Bratislava, 1980; Jaroslav Průšek, *The Lyrical and the Epic: Studies of modern Chinese literature*, Indiana University Press, Bloomington, 1980, *The Chinese Novel at the Turn of the Century*, ed. Milena Dolezelová-Velingerová, University of Toronto Press, Toronto/Buffalo/ London, 1980.

5. Průšek, *The Lyrical and the Epic*, p. 223.

6. See Chow Tse-tsung, *The May Fourth Movement*.

7. The Chinese vernacular had always been a part of traditional fiction and other colloquial literary genres, but its use was officially advocated for the first time under the new cultural conditions closely associated with the May Fourth Movement. The two most quoted spokesmen for the use of *baihua* were Hu Shi and Chen Duxiu, both of whom wrote for *Xin Qingnian (New Youth)*, a magazine which began its publication in the 1910s and which was read mainly by Chinese students who had studied abroad and derived their ideas about revolution from an intellectual acquaintance with the West. See for instance Hu's '*Wenxue gailiang chuyi*' ('Some suggestions for the reform of Chinese literature'), *New Youth*, January 1917, and Chen's '*Wenxue geming lun*' ('On literary revolution'), *New Youth*, February 1917. These articles have been reprinted in *Zhongguo xin wenxue daxi (A Comprehensive Anthology of the New Literature of China)*, ed. Zhao Jiabi, *Wenxue yanjiu she*, Hong Kong, 1962, vol. 1, pp. 62–71; 72–5. They have also been translated in part into English: see for instance William T. de Bary *et al.*, *Sources of Chinese Tradition*, Columbia University Press, New York, pp. 818–29; Chow Tse-tsung, pp. 271–9.

8. Hu Shi, *The Chinese Renaissance*, Paragon Reprint Corp., New York, 1963; reprinted in *Republican China*, ed. Franz Schurmann and Orville Schell, Vintage Books, New York, 1967, p. 55.

9. I take this term from Raymond Williams's account of the 'dominant', the 'residual', and the 'emergent' as ways of defining different moments in an existing culture. Williams, *Marxism and Literature*, Oxford University Press, Oxford, 1977, pp. 121–7.

10. Examples of this approach could be found in *Renditions* 17 and 18 (1982), a special issue devoted to Butterfly literature. The entire issue and two additional essays are now published as *Chinese Middlebrow Fiction from the Ch'ing and Early Republican Eras*, ed. Liu Ts'un-yan, The Chinese University Press, Hong Kong, 1984.

11. I owe this insight into Communist Chinese history to the inimitable perceptiveness of Joseph R. Levenson. See, for instance, part two of his *Confucian China and Its Modern Fate*, vol. III, University of California Press, Berkeley/Los Angeles, 1965. For a good example of the programmatic idealization of a 'people's tradition' through culture, see Mao Zedong's 'Talks at the Yenan Forum on literature and art' in *Mao Tse-tung [Mao Zedong] on Literature and Art*, Foreign Language Press, Beijing, 1960, pp. 1–43. This imperative to restore the truth of history through material manifestations which are denounced as false and deluded in themselves is the guiding principle for two major anthologies of materials on Butterfly literature that have been published in the PRC: *Yuanyang hudie pai yanjiu ziliao* [Research materials on the Mandarin Duck and Butterfly School], ed. Wei Shaochang, Shanghai, 1962; reprinted Hong Kong, 1980; and *Yuanyang hudie pai wenxue ziliao* [Materials on Mandarin Duck and Butterfly literature], vols I and II, Fuzhou, 1984.

12. Unfortunately, the groundbreaking work of E. Perry Link, who has written the first book-length study of Butterfly literature in English, takes exactly this approach. See Link, *Mandarin Ducks and Butterflies: Popular fiction in early twentieth-century Chinese cities*, University of California Press, Berkeley/Los Angeles/London, 1981. A succinct account of this work is found in Link's essay 'Traditional-style popular urban fiction in the teens and twenties', in Merle Goldman, ed., pp. 327–50. Link's methods lead not exactly to the *avoidance* of textual problems, but to the unconscious adoption of a particular aesthetic terminology as the natural way of discussing those problems whenever they come up. Hence, the scientific rigor of his sociological approach is strangely accompanied by evaluative pronouncements such as 'genius', 'unusual gift', 'life-like', etc.

13. John Berninghausen and Ted Huters, 'Introductory essay', *Bulletin of Concerned Asian Scholars* 8, 1 (1976) 2.

14. C. T. Hsia, 'Hsü Chen-ya's Yü-li hun: An essay in literary history and criticism', *Renditions* 17 and 18 (1982), 216.

15. E. Perry Link, 'Introduction to Zhou Shou-juan's "We Shall Meet Again" and two denunciations of this type of story', *Bulletin of Concerned Asian Scholars* 8, 1 (1976), 14.

16. In his story of Wu Woyao's novel, Michael Egan correctly identifies this asymmetrical structure when he points out the much richer psychological depiction of Dihua, the heroine, without whose reaction the tale of her beloved's degeneration would be meaningless. Egan, 'Characterization in sea of woe', in *The Chinese Novel at the Turn of the Century*, pp. 165–76.

17. The *lie nü* tradition originated in the *Lie nü zhuan* (*Biographies of Women*), which was compiled by the historian Liu Xiang in the former Han Dynasty (202 BC–AD 24) and which lists over one hundred biographies of women, both 'good' and 'bad', from legendary times to the Han Dynasty. With the passage of time, the character lie (列), meaning 'series' or 'list' in the original title, was replaced by its homonym lie (烈), meaning 'virtuous'. This slippage of meanings was poignantly coincident with the increasingly powerful social and legal restrictions on women's behavior in ancient China. The *lie nü* 'ideology', which has since then become well known for applauding women's ability to sacrifice themselves, gave rise to a popular genre in which the 'courageous' deeds of women, especially those who committed suicide, were glorified. Apart from its adaptation in many folk stories, the genre's wide acceptance by the public can also be seen in its use in the 'local gazetteers', the semi-official histories of counties whereby women's suicides and life-long chastity were frequently recorded in vivid detail among the 'significant' events that made a particular county outstanding.

18. See the descriptions of this age in Leo Ou-fan Lee, *The Romantic Generation of Chinese Writers*, Harvard University Press, Cambridge, MA, 1973.

19. Both *Jade Pear Spirit* and its sequel, *Xuehong leishi* (*The Snow and the Swan: A lachrymose story*), are 'generally estimated to have reached a total circulation somewhere in the hundred thousands, including large-scale reprintings in Hong Kong and Singapore. Some have even estimated a total circulation of over a million, counting continued reprintings in the 1920s and later' (Link, *Mandarin Ducks and Butterflies*, p. 53).

20. Gayatri Chakravorty Spivak, 'Translator's preface', in Jacques Derrida, *Of Grammatology*, transl. Gayatri Spivak, The Johns Hopkins University Press, Baltimore/London, 1976, p. xviii.

21. *Course in General Linguistics*, ed. Charles Bally and Albert Sechehaye in collaboration with Albert Reidlinger, transl. Wade Baskin, Fontana/Collins, Glasgow, 1974, pp. 25–6:

> There are only two systems of writing:
> 1) In an ideographic system each word is represented by a single sign that is unrelated to the sounds of the word itself. Each written sign stands for a whole word and, consequently, for the idea expressed by the word. The classic example of an ideographic system of writing is Chinese.
> 2) The system commonly known as 'phonetic' tries to reproduce the succession of sounds that make up a word....
>
> To a Chinese, an ideogram and a spoken word are both symbols of an idea; to him writing is a second language, and if two words that have the same sound are used in conversation, he may resort to writing in order to express his thought. But in Chinese the mental substitution of the written word for the spoken word does not have the annoying consequences that it has in a phonetic system, for the substitution is absolute; the same graphic symbol can stand for words from different Chinese dialects.
> *I shall limit discussion to the phonetic system, and especially to the one used today, the system that stems from the Greek alphabet.* [my emphasis]

22. Saussure, pp. 118–19.
23. See Habermas, 'Modernity versus postmodernity', *New German Critique* 22 (1981), 3–15 (see pp. 98–109 above).
24. Jean-François Lyotard, *The Postmodern Condition: A report on knowledge*, transl. Geoff Bennington and Brian Massumi, University of Minnesota Press, Minneapolis, 1984, p. 78 (see p. 43 above).
25. Lyotard, p. 81 (see p. 46 above).
26. Simon Leys (Pierre Ryckmans), *The Burning Forest, Essays on Chinese Culture and Politics*, Holt, Rinehart & Winston, New York, 1986, pp. 29 ff.
27. Lao Tzu, *Tao Te Ching*, transl. D.C. Lau, Penguin Books, Baltimore, MD, 1963, p. 37.
28. Leys, p. 29.
29. *Ibid.*, p. 32.
30. Lyotard, pp. xxiv, xxv, 82, 67.
31. Jameson, 'Foreword' to Lyotard, p. xi.
32. *Ibid.*, p. xx.
33. See ch. 4 above.
34. *Ibid.*, p. 87.
35. *Ibid.*, p. 91.
36. See Louis Althusser, 'A letter on art in reply to André Daspre' and 'Cremonini, painter of the abstract', in *Lenin and Philosophy*, transl. Ben Brewster, New Left Books, New York/London, 1971, pp. 221–8, 229–42. See also 'The "Piccolo Teatro": Bertolazzi and Brecht', in *For Marx*, transl. Ben Brewster, New Left Books, London, 1977, pp. 129–52.
37. Levenson, *Confucian China and Its Modern Fate*, vol. III, pp. 49, 60.

☐ *Bibliography*

I have restricted the entries to the bibliography in the interests of making it manageable. The comprehensive inclusion of everything relevant would result in a volume of incalculable magnitude; and, as research in the field continues its rapid expansion, a fully 'comprehensive' bibliography would rapidly become obsolescent. The basic reason for selecting items for inclusion is that the list should be useful for further research: interested readers will find that, on consultation of the works listed, a more inclusive bibliography pertinent to their own interests will be generated.

Accordingly, I have made this bibliography with some basic principles in mind. First, only works of a general nature pertaining to the field have been included: essays, articles or books which relate the postmodern to the work of one artist have by and large been dropped, on the tacit understanding that they are more about the artist in question than they are about postmodernism. Secondly, I have omitted much of the philosophical history which shapes the concept of the postmodern, assuming that readers will quickly discover the importance of Kant, Nietzsche, Heidegger and others from the work reprinted in the substance of the present volume. Thirdly, I have also assumed that bibliographies of the work of certain more recent philosophers whose thought is pertinent (Derrida, Foucault, Blanchot, Irigaray, Kristeva, Bataille, etc.) are readily available elsewhere; where these writers are concerned, I have listed only those items which seem most directly focused on the issue of postmodernism.

Abbas, M. A., 'Photography/writing/postmodernism', *Minnesota Review*, n.s. 23 (1984), 91–111.

Adams, R. M. 'What was modernism?', *Hudson Review*, 31 (1978), 29–33.

Adorno, T. W., *Negative Dialectics*, Routledge & Kegan Paul, London, 1973.

Adorno, T. W., *Minima Moralia: Reflections from a damaged life*, transl. E. F. N. Jephcott, New Left Books, London, 1974.

Adorno, T. W., *Against Epistemology*, transl. Willis Domingo, Blackwell, Oxford, 1982.

Adorno, T. W., *Aesthetic Theory*, G. Adorno and R. Tiedemann (eds), transl. C. Lenhardt, Routledge & Kegan Paul, London, 1984.

Adorno, T. W. and Horkheimer, M., *Dialectic of Enlightenment*, transl. J. Cumming, Verso, London, 1986.

Agamben, G., *Idea della prosa*, Feltrinelli, Milan, 1985.

Agamben, G., *La communutà che viene*, Giulio Einaudi, Turin, 1990.

Agger, B., *The Decline of Discourse: Reading, writing, resistance in postmodern capitalism*, Falmer Press, Bristol, PA, 1990.

Akkerman, J. S., 'Why classicism? (Observations in postmodern architecture)', *Harvard Architecture*, 5 (1987), 78–9.

Allen, D. and Butterick, G., *Postmoderns: The new American poetry revised*, Grove Press, New York, 1982.

Allen, R., 'Critical theory and the paradox of modernist discourse', *Screen*, 28, 2 (1987), 69–85.

Alpert, B., 'Post-modern oral poetry', *Boundary 2*, 3 (1975), 665–82.

Alter, R., *Partial Magic: The novel as a self-conscious genre*, University of California Press, Berkeley/Los Angeles, 1975.

Altieri, C., 'From symbolist thought to immanence: The ground of postmodern American poetics', *Boundary 2*, 1, 3 (1973), 605–41.

Altieri, C., 'The postmodernism of David Antin's *Tuning*', *College English*, 48, 1 (1986), 9–25.

Altieri, C., *Quality and Act*, University of Massachusetts Press, Amherst, 1982.

Amin, S., *Le Développement inégal*, Minuit, Paris, 1973.

Anderson, P., 'Modernity and revolution', *New Left Review*, 144 (1984), 96–113.

André, L., 'The politics of postmodern photography', *Minnesota Review*, n.s. 23 (1984), 17–35.

Antin, D., 'Modernism and postmodernism: Approaching the present in American poetry', *Boundary 2*, 1, 1 (1972), 98–133.

Appignanesi, L., (ed.), *Postmodernism*, Free Association Books, London, 1989.

Arac, J., *Critical Genealogies: Historical situations for postmodern literary studies*, Columbia University Press, New York, 1987.

Arac, J., (ed.), *Postmodernism and Politics*, Manchester University Press, Manchester, 1986.

Aronowitz, S., *The Crisis in Historical Materialism*, Praeger, New York, 1981.

Aronowitz, S., 'Postmodernism and politics', in A. Ross (ed.), *Universal Abandon?*, Edinburgh University Press, Edinburgh, 1989, pp. 46–62.

Attali, J., *Noise: The political economy of music*, 1977; transl. B. Massumi, Manchester University Press, Manchester, 1985.

Auslander, P., 'Towards a concept of the political in postmodern theatre', *Theatre Journal*, 39, 1 (1987), 20–34.

Bachelard, G., *La Poétique de l'espace*, PUF, Paris, 1957.

Badiou, A., *Théorie du sujet*, Seuil, Paris, 1982.

Badiou, A., *L'être et l'événement*, Seuil, Paris, 1988.

Bahro, R., *The Alternative in Eastern Europe*, New Left Books, London, 1978.

Balsamo, A., 'Unwrapping the postmodern: A feminist glance', *Journal of Communication Inquiry*, 11 (1987), 64–72.

Balsamo, A., 'Reading cyborgs writing feminism', *Communication*, 10 (1988), 331–44.

Banes, S., *Terpsichore in Sneakers: Postmodern dance*, Wesleyan University Press, Middletown, CT, 1986.

Barilli, R., 'Una generazione postmoderna', *Il Verri*, 1–2, 7th series (1984), 15–55.

Barilli, R., *Icons of Postmodernism: The nuovi-nuovi artists*, Allemandi, Turin, 1986.

Barth, J., 'The literature of exhaustion', in M. Bradbury (ed.), *The Novel Today*, Fontana, Glasgow, 1977.

Barth, J., 'The literature of replenishment: Postmodernist fiction', *Atlantic Monthly*, 245, 1 (1980), 65–71.

Barzun, J., *Classic, Romantic and Modern*, Secker & Warburg, London, 1962.

Baudrillard, J., *Le Système des objets*, Gallimard, Paris, 1968.

Baudrillard, J., *La Société de consommation*, Gallimard, Paris, 1970.

Baudrillard, J., *Le Miroir de la production*, Casterman, Tournail, 1973; transl. M. Poster as *The Mirror of Production*, Telos Press, St Louis, MO, 1975.

Baudrillard, J., *L'Echange symbolique et la mort*, Gallimard, Paris, 1976.

Baudrillard, J., *L'Effet Beaubourg*, Galilée, Paris, 1977.

Baudrillard, J., *Oublier Faucault*, Galilée, Paris, 1977.

Baudrillard, J., *De la séduction*, Denoël, Paris, 1979.

Baudrillard, J., *Pour une critique de l'économie politique du signe*, Gallimard, Paris, 1972; transl. C. Levin as *For a Critique of the Political Economy of the Sign*, Telos Press, St Louis, MO, 1981.

Baudrillard, J., *Simulacres et simulation*, Galilée, Paris, 1981.

Baudrillard, J., *In the Shadow of the Silent Majorities*, transl. P. Foss, P. Patton and J. Johnston, Semiotext(e), New York, 1983.

Baudrillard, J., *Les Stratégies fatales*, Grasset, Paris, 1983.

Baudrillard, J., *La Gauche divine*, Grasset, Paris, 1985.

Baudrillard, J., *Amérique*, Grasset, Paris, 1986.

Baudrillard, J., *L'Autre par lui-même*, Galilée, Paris, 1987.

Baudrillard, J., *Cool Memories*, Galilée, Paris, 1987.

Baudrillard, J., *The Evil Demon of Images*, Power Institute Publications, Sydney, 1987.

Baudrillard, J., *Selected Writings*, ed. Mark Poster, Polity Press, Cambridge, 1988.

Bauman, Z., *Legislators and Interpreters*, Polity Press, Cambridge, 1987.

Bauman, Z., 'Is there a postmodern sociology?', *Theory, Culture & Society*, 5 (1988), 217–37.

Bauman, Z., *Modernity and the Holocaust*, Polity Press, Oxford, 1989.

Baykan, A., 'Women between fundamentalism and modernity', in B. S. Turner (ed.), *Theories of Modernity and Postmodernity*, Sage, London, 1990, pp. 136–46.

Beebe, M., 'What modernism was', *Journal of Modern Literature*, 3, 5 (1974), 1065–84.

Bell, D., *The Coming of Post-Industrial Society*, Basic Books, New York, 1973.

Bell, D., *The Cultural Contradictions of Capitalism*, Basic Books, New York, 1976.

Bell, D., 'Modernism and capitalism', *Partisan Review*, 46 (1978), 206–26.

Bénamou, M. and Caramello, C. (eds), *Performance in Postmodern Culture*, Coda Press, Madison, WI, 1977.

Benhabib, S., 'Epistemologies of postmodernism: A rejoinder to Jean-François Lyotard', *New German Critique*, 33 (1984), 103–26.

Benjamin, W., *Illuminations*, ed. H. Arendt, transl. H. Zohn, Fontana, Glasgow, 1973.

Benjamin, W., *The Origin of German Tragic Drama*, Verso, London, 1977.

Benjamin, W., *Understanding Brecht*, Verso, London, 1977.

Benjamin, W., *One-Way Street and Other Writings*, Verso, London, 1979.

Benjamin, W., *Charles Baudelaire*, transl. H. Zohn, Verso, London, 1983.

Bennington, G., *Lyotard: Writing the event*, Manchester University Press, Manchester, 1988.

Bergonzi, B. (ed.), *Innovations*, Macmillan, London, 1968.

Berman, M., *All That is Solid Melts into Air*, Verso, London, 1982.

Berman, R. A., 'The routinization of charismatic modernism and the problem of post-modernity', *Cultural Critique*, 5 (1987), 49–68.

Bernstein, R. J. (ed.), *Habermas and Modernity*, MIT Press, Cambridge, MA, 1985.

Bertens, H., 'The postmodern *Weltanschauung* and its relation with modernism: An introductory survey', in D. Fokkema and H. Bertens (eds), *Approaching Postmodernism*, John Benjamins, Amsterdam, 1986, pp. 9–51.

Betz, A., 'Commodity and modernity in Heine and Benjamin', *New German Critique*, 33 (1984), 179–88.

Beverley, J., 'The ideology of postmodern music', *Critical Quarterly*, 31 (1989).

Bhabha, H. K., 'Difference, discrimination and the discourse of colonialism', in F. Barker *et al.* (eds), *The Politics of Theory*, University of Essex, Colchester, 1983.

Bhaskar, R., *Scientific Realism and Human Emancipation*, Verso, London, 1986.

Blanchot, M., *L'Espace littéraire*, Gallimard, Paris, 1956.

Blanchot, M., *L'Entretien infini*, Gallimard, Paris, 1969.

Blanchot, M., *The Writing of the Disaster*, transl. A. Smock, University of Nebraska Press, Lincoln, 1986.

Blau, H., 'The remission of play', in I. and S. Hassan (eds), *Innovation/Renovation*, University of Wisconsin Press, Madison, 1983, 161–88.

Blau, H., *The Eye of Prey: Subversions of the postmodern*, Indiana University Press, Bloomington, 1987.

Bloch, E., 'Nonsynchronism and dialectics', *New German Critique*, 11 (1977), 22–38.

Bloch, E. *et al.*, *Aesthetics and Politics*, Verso, London, 1977.

Blocker, H. G., 'Autonomy, reference and post-modern art', *British Journal of Aesthetics*, 20, 3 (1980), 229–36.

Blumenberg, H., *The Legitimacy of the Modern Age*, transl. R. M. Wallace, MIT Press, Cambridge, MA, 1983.

Boulez, P., *Penser la musique aujourd'hui*, Gonthier, Paris, 1963.

Bourdieu, P., *Distinction*, transl. R. Nice, Routledge & Kegan Paul, London, 1984.

Bové, P., 'The ineluctability of difference: Scientific pluralism and the critical intelligence', in J. Arac (ed.), *Postmodernism and Politics*, Manchester University Press, Manchester, 1986, pp. 3–25.

Bové, P., *Intellectuals in Power: A genealogy of critical humanism*, Columbia University Press, New York, 1986.

Boyd-Bowman, S., 'Imaginary cinemathèques: The postmodern programmes of INA', *Screen*, 28, 2 (1987), 103–17.

Boyne, R. and Rattansi, A. (eds), *Postmodernism and Society*, Macmillan, London, 1990.

Bradbury, M. and MacFarlane, J. (eds), *Modernism*, Penguin, Harmondsworth, 1976.

Bryson, N., *Word and Image*, Cambridge University Press, Cambridge, 1981.

Buchloh, B. H. D., 'The primary colors for the second time: A paradigm repetition of the neo-avant-garde', *October*, 37 (1986), 41–52.

Buci-Glucksmann, C., *La Raison baroque*, Galilée, Paris, 1984.

Bürger, P., *Theory of the Avant-Garde*, 1974; transl. M. Shaw, Manchester University Press, Manchester, 1984.

Burgin, V., *Thinking Photography*, Macmillan, London, 1982.

Burgin, V., 'Some thoughts on outsiderism and postmodernism', *Block*, 11 (1985–6), 19–26; repr. in *The End of Art Theory*.

Burgin, V., *The End of Art Theory: Criticism and postmodernity*, Macmillan, London, 1986.

Butler, C., *After the Wake: An essay on the contemporary avant-garde*, Oxford University Press, Oxford, 1980.

Cage, J., *Silence*, Wesleyan University Press, Middletown, CT, 1961.

Calinescu, M., 'Avant-garde, neo-avant-garde, postmodernism: The culture of crisis', *Clio*, 4 (1975), 317–40.

Calinescu, M., *Faces of Modernity: Avant-garde, decadence, kitsch*, Indiana University Press, Bloomington, 1977.

Calinescu, M., 'From the one to the many: Pluralism in today's thought', in I. and S. Hassan (eds), *Innovation/Renovation*, University of Wisconsin Press, Madison, 1983, pp. 263–88.

Calinescu, M., 'Postmodernism and some paradoxes of periodization', in D. Fokkema and H. Bertens (eds), *Approaching Postmodernism*, John Benjamins, Amsterdam, 1986, pp. 239–54.

Calinescu, M., *Five Faces of Modernity: Modernism, avant-garde, decadence, kitsch, postmodernism*, Duke University Press, Durham, NC, 1987.

Calinescu, M. and Fokkema, D. (eds), *Exploring Postmodernism*, John Benjamins, Amsterdam, 1988.

Callinicos, A., 'Poststructuralism, postmodernism, postmarxism?', *Theory, Culture & Society*, 2, 3 (1985), 85–102.

Callinicos, A., *Against Postmodernism*, Macmillan, London, 1990.

Canguilhem, G., *The Normal and the Pathological*, transl. C. R. Fawcett in collaboration with R. S. Cohen, Zone Books, New York, 1991.

Carraveta, P. and Spedicato, P. (eds), *Postmoderno e letteratura*, Bompiani, Milan, 1984.

Carroll, D., *The Subject in Question: The languages of theory and the strategies of fiction*, University of Chicago Press, Chicago, 1982.

Carroll, D., *Paraesthetics*, Methuen, London, 1988.

Carroll, N., 'Air dancing', *Drama Review*, 19, 1 (1975), 5–12.

Cavell, S., *The Claim of Reason*, Oxford University Press, New York, 1979.

Chambers, I., 'Maps for the metropolis: A possible guide to the present', *Cultural Studies*, 1 (1987), 1–21.

Chefdor, M., Wachtel, A. and Quinones, R. (eds), *Modernism: Challenges and perspectives*, University of Illinois Press, Urbana, 1986.

Chow, R., 'Rereading Mandarin ducks and butterflies: A response to the "postmodern" condition', *Cultural Critique*, 5 (1987), 69–93.

Clark, T. J., *The Painting of Modern Life*, Thames & Hudson, London, 1984.

Clifford, J. and Marcus, G. E. (eds), *Writing Culture: The poetics and politics of ethnography*, University of California Press, Berkeley/Los Angeles, 1986.

Collins, J., 'Postmodernism and cultural practice: Redefining the parameters', *Screen*, 28, 2 (1987), 11–27.

Collins, M., *Towards Postmodernism: Design since 1851*, British Museum, London, 1987.

Connor, S., *Postmodernist Culture: An introduction to theories of the contemporary*, Blackwell, Oxford, 1990.

Conroy, M., *Modernism and Authority: Strategies of legitmation in Flaubert and Conrad*, Johns Hopkins University Press, Baltimore, MD, 1985.

Cook, D. and Kroker, A., *The Postmodern Scene: Excremental culture and hyper-aesthetics*, Macmillan, London, 1986.

Cork, R., *Vorticism and Abstract Art in the First Machine Age*, 2 vols, Gordon Fraser, London, 1976.

Couturier, M., *Representation and Performance in Postmodern Fiction*, Université Paul Valéry, Montpellier, 1983.

Cox, H., *Religion in the Secular City: Toward a postmodern theology*, Simon & Schuster, New York, 1984.

Creed, B., 'From here to modernity: Feminism and postmodernism', *Screen*, 28, 2 (1987), 47–68.

Crimp, D., 'Pictures', *October*, 8 (1979), 67–86.

Crimp, D., 'The photographic activity of postmodernism', *October*, 15 (1980), 91–101.

Crimp, D., 'The end of painting', *October*, 16 (1981), 69–86.

Crimp, D., 'On the museum's ruins', in H. Foster (ed.), *Postmodern Culture*, Pluto Press, London, 1983.

Crook, J. M., *The Dilemma of Style: Architectural ideas from the picturesque to the postmodern*, John Murray, London, 1987.

Crosby, A. W., *Ecological Imperialism*, Cambridge University Press, Cambridge, 1986.

Crowther, P., *The Kantian Sublime*, Oxford University Press, Oxford, 1989.

Dallmayr, F. R., 'Democracy and post-modernism', *Human Studies* 10, 1 (1987), 143–70.

Danto, A. C., *The Philosophical Disenfranchisement of Art*, Columbia University Press, New York, 1986.

Davidson, D., *Inquiries into Truth and Interpretation*, Oxford University Press, Oxford, 1984.

Davidson, M., 'Palimptexts: Postmodern poetry and the material text', *Genre*, 20 (1987), 307–27.

Davis, D., *Artculture: Essays on the postmodern*, Harper & Row, New York, 1977.

Davis, D., 'Late postmodern: the end of style?', *Art in America*, 75, 6 (1987), 15.

Davis, M., 'Urban renaissance and the spirit of postmodernism', *New Left Review*, 151 (1985), 106–13.

de Certeau, M., *The Practice of Everyday Life*, transl. S. Rendell, University of California Press, Berkeley/Los Angeles, 1984.

de Certeau, M., *Heterologies: Discourse on the Other*, transl. B. Massumi, Manchester University Press, Manchester, 1986.

de Lauretis, T., *Alice Doesn't: Feminism, semiotics, cinema*, Macmillan, London, 1984.

de Lauretis, T., *Technologies of Gender*, Indiana University Press, Bloomington, 1987.

Deane, S., *The French Revolution and Enlightenment in England 1789–1832*, Harvard University Press, Cambridge, MA, 1988.

Debord, G., *La Société du spectacle*, Buchet-Chastel, Paris, 1968; repr. Champ Libre, Paris, 1983.

Debord, G., *Comments on the Society of the Spectacle*, Verso, London, 1990.

Deleuze, G., *Empirisme et subjectivité*, PUF, Paris, 1953.

Deleuze, G., *Le bergsonisme*, PUF, Paris, 1966.

Deleuze, G., *Différence et répétition*, PUF, Paris, 1969.

Deleuze, G., *Logique du sens*, Minuit, Paris, 1969.

Deleuze, G., 'Faille et feux locaux', *Critique* (1970), 344–51.

Deleuze, G., 'Qu'est-ce que c'est, tes "machines désirantes" à toi?', *Les Temps modernes*, (1972), 854–6.

Deleuze, G., 'Pensée nomade', in *Nietzsche aujourd'hui*, vol. 1, Union générale d'éditions, 10/18, Paris, 1973, pp. 159–74.

Deleuze, G., 'Philosophie et minorité', *Critique*, 369 (1978), 154–5.

Deleuze, G., *Cinéma: 1*, Minuit, Paris, 1983.

Deleuze, G., 'Francis Bacon: Logic of sensation', *Flash Art*, 112 (1983), 8–16.

Deleuze, G., *Kant's Critical Philosophy*, transl. H. Tomlinson and B. Habberjam, University of Minnesota Press, Minneapolis, 1984.

Deleuze, G., *Cinéma: 2*, Minuit, Paris, 1985.

Deleuze, G., *Le Pli*, Minuit, Paris, 1988.

Deleuze, G. and Guattari, F., *Anti-Oedipus*, transl. R. Hurley, M. Seem and R. Lane, Athlone Press, London, 1984.

Deleuze, G. and Guattari, F., *A Thousand Plateaus*, transl. B. Massumi, University of Minnesota Press, Minneapolis, 1987.

Denzin, N. K., *Images of Postmodern Society*, Sage, London, 1991.

Derrida, J., *D'un ton apocalyptique adopté naguère en philosophie*, Galilée, Paris, 1983.

Derrida, J., *Writing and Difference*, transl. A. Bass, Routledge & Kegan Paul, London, 1978.

Derrida, J., *La Carte postale: de Socrate à Freud et au-delà*, Flammarion, Paris, 1980.

Derrida, J., *La Vérité en peinture*, Flammarion, Paris, 1978.

Descombes, V., *L'Inconscient malgré lui*, Minuit, Paris, 1977.

Descombes, V., *Le Même et l'autre*, Minuit, Paris, 1979.

Dews, P., 'The letter and the line: Discourse and its Other in Lyotard', *Diacritics*, 14, 3 (1984), 40–9.

Dews, P., *Logics of Disintegration: Poststructuralist thought and the claims of critical theory*, Verso, London, 1987.

D'Haen, T., 'Postmodernism in American fiction and art', in D. Fokkema and H. Bertens (eds), *Approaching Postmodernism*, John Benjamins, Amsterdam, 1986, pp. 211–31.

Dickens, D. and Fontana, A. (eds), *Postmodernism and Sociology*, University of Chicago Press, Chicago, 1990.

Dilnot, C., 'What is the postmodern?', *Art History*, 9, 2 (1986), 245–63.

Dobson, A., *Green Political Thought*, Harper Collins, London, 1990.

Docherty, T., 'Theory, enlightenment and violence: Postmodern hermeneutic as a comedy of errors', *Textual Practice*, 1, 2 (1987), 192–216.

Docherty, T., *After Theory: Postmodernism/postmarxism*, Routledge, London, 1990.

Doyle, N., 'Desiring dispersal: Politics and the postmodern', *Subjects/Objects*, 3 (1985), 166–79.

Dubois, C.-G., *Le Baroque: profondeurs de l'apparence*, Larousse, Paris, 1973.

Durand, R., 'Theatre/SIGNS/Performance: On some transformations of the theatrical and the theoretical', in I. and S. Hassan (eds), *Innovation/Renovation*, University of Wisconsin Press, Madison, 1983, pp. 211–24.

During, S., 'Postmodernism or post-colonialism today', *Textual Practice*, 1, 1 (1987), 32–47.

Eagleton, T., 'Capitalism, modernism and postmodernism', *New Left Review*, 152 (1985), 60–73, repr. in Eagleton, *Against the Grain*, Verso, London, 1986.

Eagleton, T., *The Ideology of the Aesthetic*, Blackwell, Oxford, 1990.

Ebert, T., 'The convergence of postmodern innovative fiction and science fiction', *Poetics Today*, 1 (1980), 91–104.

Eco, U., *Postscript to the Name of the Rose*, Harcourt Brace Jovanovich, New York, 1984.

Eco, U., 'A guide to the neo-television of the 1980s', *Framework*, 25 (1984), 18–25.

Eco, U., *Travels in Hyperreality*, transl. W. Weaver, Pan, London, 1987.

Emberley, J., 'The fashion apparatus and the deconstruction of postmodern subjectivity', *Canadian Journal of Political and Social Theory*, 11 (1987), 38–50.

Enzensberger, H. M., *The Consciousness Industry*, Seabury Press, New York, 1974.

Enzensberger, H. M., *Dreamers of the Absolute*, Radius, London, 1988.

Faurschou, G., 'Fashion and the cultural logic of postmodernity', *Canadian Journal of Political and Social Theory*, 11 (1987), 68–84.

Featherstone, M., *Consumer Culture and Postmodernism*, Sage, London, 1990.

Federman, R. (ed.), *Surfiction: Fiction now ... and tomorrow*, Swallow Press, Chicago, 1975; 2nd expanded edn, 1981.

Fekete, J. (ed.), *The Structural Allegory: Reconstructive encounters with the new French thought*, University of Minnesota Press, Minneapolis, 1984.

Fekete, J. (ed.), *Life After Postmodernism: Essays on value and culture*, Macmillan, London, 1988.

Ferry, L., *Homo Aestheticus*, Grasset, Paris, 1990.

Ferry, L. and Renault, A., *La Pensée 68*, Gallimard, Paris, 1985.

Feyerabend, P., *Against Method*, New Left Books, London, 1975.

Fiedler, L. A., 'The new mutants', *Partisan Review*, 32, 4 (1965), 505–25.

Fiedler, L. A., 'Cross the border – close that gap: Postmodernism', in M. Cunliffe (ed.), *American Literature since 1900*, Sphere Books, London, 1975, pp. 344–66.

Fischer, M. M. J., 'Ethnicity and the post-modern arts of memory', in J. Clifford and G. E. Marcus (eds), *Writing Culture*, University of California Press, Berkeley/Los Angeles, 1986, pp. 194–233.

Flax, J., 'Postmodernism and gender relations in feminist theory', *Signs*, 12 (1987), 621–43.

Fokkema, D., *Literary History, Modernism, and Postmodernism*, John Benjamins, Amsterdam, 1984.

Fokkema, D. and Bertens, H. (eds), *Approaching Postmodernism*, John Benjamins, Amsterdam, 1986.

Forte, J., 'Women's performance art: Feminism and postmodernism', *Theatre Journal*, 40 (1988), 217–35.

Foster, H., '(Post)modern polemics', *New German Critique*, 33 (1984), 67–78.

Foster, H. (ed.), *Postmodern Culture*, Pluto Press, London, 1983; also published under the title *The Anti-Aesthetic: Essays on postmodern culture*, Bay Press, Port Townsend, WA, 1983.

Foster, H., *Recodings: Art, Spectacle, Cultural Politics*, Bay Press, Port Townsend, WA, 1985.

Foucault, M., *The Archaeology of Knowledge*, transl. A. M. Sheridan Smith, Tavistock, London, 1974.

Frampton, K., 'Towards a critical regionalism: Six points for an architecture of resistance', in H. Foster (ed.), *Postmodern Culture*, Pluto Press, London, 1983, pp. 16–30.

Frampton, K., 'Reflections on postmodernism and architecture', *Cuadernos del Norte*, 8, 42 (1987), 54–7.

Frank, J., 'Spatial form in modern literature', *Sewanee Review*, 53 (1945), 221–40, 433–56, 643–53.

Frankovits, A. (ed.), *Seduced and Abandoned: The Baudrillard scene*, Semiotext(e), New York, 1984.

Fraser, N., 'The French Derrideans: Politicizing deconstruction or deconstructing politics', *New German Critique*, 33 (1984), 127–54.

Fraser, N., 'What's critical about critical theory? The case of Habermas and gender', *New German Critique*, 35 (1985), 97–131.

Fraser, N. and Nicholson, L., 'Social criticism without philosophy: An encounter between feminism and postmodernism', *Theory, Culture & Society*, 5, 2–3 (1988), 373–94.

Frege, G., *Translations from the Philosophical Writings of Gottlob Frege*, transl. and ed. M. Black and P. T. Geach, Blackwell, Oxford, 1952.

Frisby, D., *Fragments of Modernity*, Cambridge University Press, Cambridge, 1985.

Gablik, S., *Has Modernism Failed?*, Thames & Hudson, London, 1984.

Gallagher, C., 'The politics of culture and the debate over representation', *Representations*, 5 (1984), 115–47.

Gane, M., *Baudrillard's Bestiary: Baudrillard and culture*, Routledge, London, 1991.

Garber, F., 'Generating the subject: The images of Cindy Sherman', *Genre*, 20 (1987), 359–82.

Garvin, H. R. (ed.), *Romanticism, Modernism, Postmodernism*, Bucknell University Press, Lewisburg, PA, 1980.

Gass, W. H., *Fiction and the Figures of Life*, Knopf, New York, 1970.

Gay, P., *The Enlightenment*, 2 vols, Oxford University Press, Oxford, 1966.

Geras, N., 'Post-marxism?', *New Left Review*, 163 (1987), 40–82.

Giddens, A., 'Modernism and postmodernism', *New German Critique*, 22 (1981), 15–18.

Giddens, A., *A Contemporary Critique of Historical Materialism*, University of California Press, Berkeley/Los Angeles, 1981.

Giddens, A. and Turner, J. (eds), *Social Theory Today*, Stanford University Press, Stanford, CA, 1987.

Gilson, E., *Peinture et réalité*, Vrin, Paris, 1958.

Goodman, N., *The Structure of Appearance*, Bobbs-Merrill, New York, n.d.

Goodman, N., 'Routes of reference', *Critical Inquiry*, 8, 1 (1981), 121–32.

Gorz, A., *Farewell to the Working Class*, transl. M. Sonenscher, Pluto, London, 1982.

Graff, G., 'The myth of the postmodernist breakthrough', *TriQuarterly*, 26 (1973), 383–417; repr. in M. Bradbury (ed.), *The Novel Today*, Fontana, Glasgow, 1977.

Graff, G., 'Babbitt at the abyss: The social context of postmodern American fiction', *TriQuarterly*, 33 (1975), 305–37.

Graff, G., *Literature Against Itself: Literary ideas on modern society*, University of Chicago Press, Chicago, 1979.

Greenberg, C., 'Modernist painting', in Gregory Battcock (ed.), *The New Art*, Dutton, New York, 1966.

Greenberg, C., 'Avant-garde and kitsch', in G. Dorfles (ed.), *Kitsch*, Universe Books, New York, 1969.

Greenberg, C., 'Modern and postmodern', *Arts Magazine*, 54 (1980), 64–6.

Griffin, D. R., *The Reenchantment of Science: Postmodern proposals*, State University of New York Press, Albany, 1988.

Grossberg, L., 'The in-difference of television', *Screen*, 28, 2 (1987), 28–46.

Grossberg, L., 'The politics of music: American images and British articulations', *Canadian Journal of Political and Social Theory*, 11 (1987), 144–51.

Grossberg, L., 'Putting the pop back into postmodernism', in A. Ross (ed.), *Universal Abandon?*, Edinburgh University Press, Edinburgh, 1989, pp. 167–90.

Grosz, E. *et al.* (eds), *Futur*fall: Excursions into postmodernity*, Power Institute of Fine Art, Sydney, 1986.

Guattari, F., *Molecular Revolution*, transl. R. Sheed, Penguin, Harmondsworth, 1984.

Guilbaut, S., 'The new adventures of the avant-garde in America', *October*, 15 (1980), 61–78.

Habermas, J., *Legitimation Crisis*, transl. T. MacCarthy, Heinemann, London, 1976.

Habermas, J., *The Theory of Communicative Action*, 2 vols, transl. T. MacCarthy, Polity, Oxford, 1984.

Habermas, J., *The Philosophical Discourse of Modernity*, transl. F. G. Lawrence, MIT Press, Cambridge, MA, 1987.

Hafrey, L., 'The gilded cage: Postmodernism and beyond', *TriQuarterly*, 56 (1983), 126–36.

Harvey, D., *The Condition of Postmodernity*, Blackwell, Oxford, 1989.

Hassan, I., *The Literature of Silence*, Knopf, New York, 1967.

Hassan, I. (ed.), *Liberations: New essays on the humanities in revolution*, Wesleyan University Press, Middletown, CT, 1971.

Hassan, I., 'POSTmodernISM', *New Literary History*, 3, 1 (1971), 5–30.

Hassan, I., 'Abstractions', *Diacritics*, 2 (1975), 13–18.

Hassan, I., *Paracriticisms: Seven Speculations of the Times*, University of Illinois Press, Urbana, Chicago/London, 1975.

Hassan, I., 'The critic as innovator: The Tutzing Statement in x frames', *Amerikastudien*, 22 (1977), 47–63.

Hassan, I., *The Right Promethean Fire: Imagination, science, and cultural change*, University of Illinois Press, Urbana, 1980.

Hassan, I., *The Dismemberment of Orpheus: Toward a postmodern literature*, 2nd edn, University of Wisconsin Press, Madison, 1982.

Hassan, I., 'Desire and dissent in the postmodern age', *Kenyon Review*, 5 (1983), 1–18.

Hassan, I., 'Pluralism in postmodern perspective', *Critical Inquiry*, 12, 3 (1986), 503–20.

Hassan, I., *The Postmodern Turn: Essays in postmodern theory and culture*, Ohio State University Press, Columbus, 1987.

Hassan, I. and Hassan, S. (eds), *Innovation/Renovation: New perspectives on the humanities*, University of Wisconsin Press, Madison, 1986.

Haug, W.-F., *Critique of Commodity Aesthetics*, Polity Press, Cambridge, 1986.

Haug, W.-F., *Commodity Aesthetics, Ideology and Culture*, International General, New York and Bagnolet, 1987.

Hayman, D., 'Double Distancing: An attribute of the "post-modern" avant-garde', *Novel*, 12, 1 (1978), 33–47.

Heath, S., *The Nouveau Roman*, Elek, London, 1972.

Hebdige, D., *Subculture: The meaning of style*, Methuen, London, 1979.

Hebdige, D., 'A report on the Western front: Postmodernism and the "politics" of style', *Block*, 12 (1986–7), 4–26.

Hebdige, D., 'The impossible object: Towards a sociology of the sublime', *New Formations*, 1 (1987), 47–76.

Hebdige, D., *Hiding in the Light: On images and things*, Comedia, London, 1988.

Heidegger, M., *Being and Time*, transl. J. Macquarrie and E. Robinson, Blackwell, Oxford, 1967.

Heidegger, M., *Poetry, Language, Thought*, Harper Colophon, New York, 1971.

Heidegger, M., *The Question Concerning Technology*, Harper & Row, New York, 1977.

Hekman, S. J., *Gender and Knowledge*, Polity, Oxford, 1989.

Hjort, A. M., 'Quasi-Una-Amicizia: Adorno and philosophical postmodernism', *New Orleans Review*, 14, 1 (1987), 74–80.

Hoesterey, I., 'Die Moderne am Ende? Zu den ästhetischen Positionen von Jürgen Habermas und Clement Greenberg', *Zeitschrift für Ästhetik und allgemeine Kunstgewissenschaft*, 29, 1 (1984), 19–32.

Hoffman, F. J., 'William James and the modern literary consciousness', *Criticism*, 4 (1962), 1–13.

Hoffmann, G., 'Social criticism and the deformation of man: Satire, the grotesque and comic nihilism in the modern and postmodern American novel', *Amerikastudien*, 28 (1983), 141–203.

Hoffmann, G., 'The absurd and its forms of reduction in postmodern American fiction', in D. Fokkema and H. Bertens (eds), *Approaching Postmodernism*, John Benjamins, Amsterdam, 1986, pp. 185–210.

Hoffmann, G., Hornung, A. and Kunow, R., '"Modern", "postmodern", and "contemporary" as criteria for the analysis of twentieth-century literature', *Amerikastudien*, 22 (1977), 19–46.

Höhendahl, P. U., *The Institution of Criticism*, Cornell University Press, Ithaca, NY, 1982.

Honneth, A., 'An aversion against the universal: A commentary on Lyotard's *Postmodern Condition*', *Theory, Culture & Society*, 2, 3 (1985), 147–57.

Honneth, A., *Critique of Power: Reflective stages in a critical social theory*, transl. K. Baynes, MIT Press, Cambridge, MA, 1991.

Howe, I., 'Mass society and postmodern fiction', *Partisan Review*, 26, 3 (1959), 420–36.

Hughes, R., *The Shock of the New*, Knopf, New York, 1981.

Hutcheon, L., *Narcissistic Narrative: The metafictional paradox*, Wilfred Laurier University Press, Waterloo, ON, 1980.

Hutcheon, L., *A Theory of Parody: The teachings of twentieth-century art forms*, Methuen, London, 1985.

Hutcheon, L., 'Beginning to theorize postmodernism', *Textual Practice*, 1, 1 (1987), 10–31.

Hutcheon, L., 'The politics of postmodernism: Parody and history', *Cultural Critique*, 5 (1987), 179–207.

Hutcheon, L., *A Poetics of Postmodernism: History, theory, fiction*, Routledge, London, 1988.

Hutcheon, L., *The Politics of Postmodernism*, Routledge, London, 1989.

Huyssen, A., *After the Great Divide: Modernism, mass culture, postmodernism*, Macmillan, London, 1986.

Irigaray, L., *Speculum: de l'autre femme*, Minuit, Paris, 1974; transl. as *Speculum of the Other Woman*, G. C. Gill, Cornell University Press, Ithaca, NY, 1985.

Irigaray, L., *Ce Sexe qui n'en est pas un*, Minuit, Paris, 1977.

Jacobs, J., *Death and Life of Great American Cities*, Vintage Books, New York, 1961.

Jameson, F., *Fables of Aggression*, University of California Press, Berkeley/Los Angeles, 1979.

Jameson, F., *Marxism and Form*, Princeton University Press, Princeton, NJ, 1971.

Jameson, F., *Modernism and Imperialism*, Field Day, Derry, 1988.

Jameson, F., *The Ideologies of Theory*, 2 vols, Routledge, London, 1988.

Jameson, F., *Late Marxism*, Verso, London, 1990.

Jameson, F., *Postmodernism*, Verso, London, 1991.

Jameson, F., *Signatures of the Visible*, Routledge, London, 1991.

Jardine, A., *Gynesis: Configurations of woman and modernity*, Cornell University Press, Ithaca, NY, 1985.

Jefferson, A., *The Nouveau Roman and the Poetics of Fiction*, Cambridge University Press, Cambridge, 1980.

Jencks, C., *Le Corbusier and the Tragic View of Architecture*, Allen Lane, London, 1973.

Jencks, C., *The Language of Post-Modern Architecture*, Academy Editions, London, 1977.

Jencks, C., *Post-Modern Classicism: The new synthesis*, Academy Editions, London, 1980.

Jencks, C., *Late-Modern Architecture and Other Essays*, Academy Editions, London, 1980.

Jencks, C., *Architecture Today*, Abrams, New York, 1982.

Jencks, C., *What is Postmodernism*, Academy Editions, London 1986.

Jencks, C., *The Post-Avant-Garde: Painting in the 1980s*, Academy Editions, London, 1987.

Jencks, C., *Postmodernism*, Academy Editions, London, 1987.

Kafalenos, E., 'Fragments of a discourse on Roland Barthes and the postmodern mind', *Chicago Review*, 35 (1985), 72–94.

Kaite, B., '"Obsession" and desire: Fashion and the postmodern scene', *Canadian Journal of Political and Social Theory*, 11 (1987), 84–9.

Kamper, D. and Wulf, C. (eds), *Looking Back on the End of the World*, transl. D. Antal, Semiotext(e), New York, 1989.

Kant, I., *Critique of Judgement*, transl. J. C. Meredith, Oxford University Press, Oxford and London, 1952.

Kaplan, E. A., *Rocking Around the Clock: Music, television, postmodernism, and consumer culture*, Methuen, London, 1987.

Kaplan, E. A. (ed.), *Postmodernism and its Discontents*, Verso, London, 1988.

Kariel, H., *The Desperate Politics of Postmodernism*, University of Massachusetts Press, Amherst, 1989.

Kearney, R., 'Ethics and the postmodern imagination', *Thought*, 62 (1987), 39–58.

Kearney, R., *The Wake of Imagination*, Hutchinson, London, 1988.

Kearney, R. (ed.), *Across the Frontiers*, Wolfhound, Dublin, 1989.

Kellman, S. G., *The Self-Begetting Novel*, Macmillan, London, 1980.

Kellner, D., *Jean Baudrillard: From Marxism to postmodernism and beyond*, Polity Press, Oxford, 1988.

Kellner, D. (ed.), *Postmodernism/Jameson/Critique*, Maisonneuve Press, Washington, DC, 1989.

Kern, R., 'Composition as recognition: Robert Creeley and postmodern poetics', *Boundary 2*, 6, 3; 7, 1 (1978), 211–30.

Kipnis, L., 'Feminism: The political conscience of postmodernism?', in A. Ross (ed.), *Universal Abandon?*, Edinburgh University Press, Edinburgh, 1989, pp. 149–66.

Kirby, M., 'Post-modern dance issue: An introduction', *Drama Review*, 19, 1 (1975), 3–4.

Kiremidjian, G. D., 'The aesthetics of parody', *Journal of Aesthetics and Art Criticism*, 28, 2 (1969), 231–42.

Klinkowitz, J., *Literary Disruptions: The making of a post-contemporary American fiction*, 2nd edn, University of Illinois Press, Urbana, 1980.

Klinkowitz, J., *Literary Subversions: New American fiction and the practice of criticism*, Southern Illinois University Press, Carbondale, 1985.

Kofman, S., *Camera obscura: de l'idéologie*, Galilée, Paris, 1973.

Kofman, S., *Le Respect des femmes*, Galilée, Paris, 1982.

Kohler, M., '"Postmodernismus": Ein begriffsgeschichtlicher Überblick', *Amerikastudien*, 22, 1 (1977), 8–18.

Kramer, H., *The Age of the Avant-Garde*, Farrar, Straus & Giroux, New York, 1973.

Kramer, H., 'Postmodern: Art and culture in the 1980s', *The New Criterion*, 1, 1 (1982), 36–42.

Kramer, H., *The Revenge of the Philistines: Art and culture 1972–1984*, Free Press, New York, 1985.

Kramer, J. D., 'Can modernism survive George Rochberg?', *Critical Inquiry*, 11, 2 (1984), 341–54.

Krauss, R., 'Poststructuralism and the "paraliterary"', *October*, 13 (1980), 36–40.

Krauss, R., 'Sculpture in the expanded field', in H. Foster (ed.), *Postmodern Culture*, Pluto Press, London, 1983.

Krauss, R., *The Originality of the Avant-Garde and Other Modernist Myths*, MIT Press, London, 1985.

Kristeva, J., *Pouvoirs de l'horreur*, Seuil, Paris, 1980.

Kristeva, J., 'Postmodernism?', in H. R. Garvin (ed.), *Romanticism, Modernism, Postmodernism*, Bucknell University Press, Lewisburg, PA, 1980, pp. 136–41.

Kristeva, J., *Desire in Language*, transl. T. Gora, A. Jardine and L. S. Roudiez, Blackwell, Oxford, 1981.

Kroker, A., 'Baudrillard's Marx', *Theory, Culture & Society*, 2, 3 (1985), 69–83.

Kroker, A. and Cook, D., *The Postmodern Scene: Excremental culture and hyper-aesthetics*, Macmillan, London, 1988.

Kroker, A. and Kroker, M. (eds), *Body Invaders: Sexuality and the postmodern condition*, Macmillan, London, 1988.

Kuhn, T., *The Structure of Scientific Revolutions*, University of Chicago Press, Chicago, 1962.

Laclau, E., 'Politics and the limits of modernity', in A. Ross (ed.), *Universal Abandon?*, Edinburgh University Press, Edinburgh, 1989, pp. 63–82.

Laclau, E. and Mouffe, C., *Hegemony and Socialist Strategy: Towards a radical democratic politics*, Verso, London, 1985.

Lacoue-Labarthe, P., 'Talks', transl. C. Fynsk, *Diacritics*, 14, 3 (1984), 24–37.

Lacoue-Labarthe, P., *Heidegger, Art and Modernity*, Blackwell, Oxford, 1990.

Laffey, J. F., 'Cacophonic rites: Modernism and postmodernism', *Historical Reflections*, 14, 1 (1987), 1–32.

Lang, B., 'Postmodernism in philosophy: Nostalgia for the future, waiting for the past', *New Literary History*, 18, 1 (1986), 209–23.

Lash, S., 'Genealogy and the body: Foucault/Deleuze/Derrida', *Theory, Culture & Society*, 2, 2 (1984), 1–17.

Lash, S., 'Postmodernity and desire', *Theory and Society*, 14, 1 (1985), 1–33.

Lash, S., 'Postmodernism as humanism? Urban space and social theory', in B. S. Turner (ed.), *Theories of Modernity and Postmodernity*, Sage, London, 1990.

Lash, S., *Sociology of Postmodernism*, Routledge, London, 1990.

Lawson, H., *Reflexivity: The post-modern predicament*, Hutchinson, London, 1985.

Lazarus, N., 'Modernism and modernity: T. W. Adorno and contemporary white South African literature', *Cultural Critique*, 5 (1986–7), 131–55.

Lea, K., '"In the most highly developed societies": Lyotard and postmodernism', *Oxford Literary Review*, 9, 1–2 (1987), 86–104.

Lecercle, J.-J., *Philosophy Through the Looking-Glass*, Hutchinson, London, 1985.

Lecercle, J.-J., *The Violence of Language*, Routledge, London, 1991.

Le Doeuff, M., *Women and Philosophy*, Blackwell, Oxford, 1990.

Lefebvre, H., *The Production of Space*, transl. D. Nicholson-Smith, Blackwell, Oxford, 1991.

Lemaire, G.-G., 'Le Spectre du post-modernisme', *Le Monde du Dimanche*, 18 October 1981, xiv.

Lentricchia, F., *After the New Criticism*, University of Chicago Press, Chicago, 1980.

Lethen, H., 'Modernism cut in half: The exclusion of the Avant-Garde and the debate on postmodernism', in D. Fokkema and H. Bertens (eds), *Approaching Postmodernism*, John Benjamins, Amsterdam, 1986, pp. 233–8.

Levin, D. M., *The Opening of Vision: Nihilism and the postmodern situation*, Routledge, London, 1988.

Levinas, E., *The Levinas Reader*, ed. S. Hand, Blackwell, Oxford, 1989.

Lewis, W., *Time and Western Man*, Chatto & Windus, London, 1927.

Lindenberger, H., 'From opera to postmodernity: On genre, style, institutions', *Genre*, 20 (1987), 259–84.

Lipsitz, G., 'Cruising around the historical block: Postmodernism and popular music in East Los Angeles', *Cultural Critique*, 5 (1986–7), 155–77.

Lodge, D., *Working with Structuralism*, Routledge & Kegan Paul, London, 1981.

Lukes, S., 'Can a Marxist believe in human rights?', *Praxis International*, 1 (1982), 334–45.

Lumsden, C. J., 'The gene and the sign: Giving structure to postmodernity', *Semiotica*, 62 (1986), 191–206.

Lyotard, J.-F., *La Phénoménologie*, PUF, Paris, 1954.

Lyotard, J.-F., *Dérives à partir de Marx et Freud*, Union générale d'éditions, 10/18, Paris, 1970.

Lyotard, J.-F., *Discours, figure*, Klincksieck, Paris, 1971.

Lyotard, J.-F., *L'Economie libidinale*, Minuit, Paris, 1974.

Lyotard, J.-F., *Instructions païennes*, Galilée, Paris, 1977.

Lyotard, J.-F., *Rudiments païens*, Union générale d'éditions, Paris, 1977.

Lyotard, J.-F., 'One of the things at stake in women's struggles', *SubStance*, 20 (1978), 9–17.

Lyotard, J.-F., *La Condition postmoderne*, Minuit, Paris, 1979; transl. G. Bennington and B. Massumi as *The Postmodern Condition: A report on knowledge*, Manchester University Press, Manchester, 1984.

Lyotard, J.-F., *Le Mur du pacifique*, Galilée, Paris, 1979.

Lyotard, J.-F., *L'Assassinat de l'expérience par la peinture: Monory*, Le Castor Astral, Paris, 1984.

Lyotard, J.-F., *Le Différend*, Minuit, Paris, 1983; transl. G. van den Abbeele as *The Differend*, Manchester University Press, Manchester, 1990.

Lyotard, J.-F., *Le Tombeau de l'intellectuel*, Galilée, Paris, 1984.

Lyotard, J.-F., *L'Enthousiasme: la critique kantienne de l'histoire*, Galilée, Paris, 1986.

Lyotard, J.-F., *Le Postmoderne expliqué aux enfants*, Galilée, Paris, 1986.

Lyotard, J.-F., 'Sensus Communis', *Le Cahier du Collége International de Philosophie*, 3, Paris, 1987, 67–87.

Lyotard, J.-F., *Peregrinations*, Columbia University Press, New York, 1988.

Lyotard, J.-F., *L'Inhumain*, Galilée, Paris, 1988.

Lyotard, J.-F., *The Lyotard Reader*, ed. A. Benjamin, Blackwell, Oxford, 1989.

Lyotard, J.-F., *Leçons sur l'analytique du sublime*, Galilée, Paris, 1991.

Lyotard, J.-F. and Chaput, T., *Les Immatériaux*, Centre Georges Pompidou, Paris, 1985.

Lyotard, J.-F. and Monory, J., *Récits tremblants*, Galilée, Paris, 1977.

Lyotard, J.-F. and Rorty, R., 'Discussion', *Critique*, 41 (1985), 581–4.

Lyotard, J.-F. and Thébaud, J.-L., *Au juste*, Christian Bourgois, Paris, 1979; transl. W. Godzich as *Just Gaming*, Manchester University Press, Manchester, 1985.

Lyotard, J.-F. *et al.*, *La Faculté de juger*, Minuit, Paris, 1983.

Lyotard, J.-F. and Francken, R., *L'Histoire de Ruth*, Le Castor Asral, Paris, 1983.

McCaffery, L., *The Metafictional Muse*, University of Pittsburgh Press, Pittsburgh, 1982.

McCaffery, L. (ed.), *Postmodern Fiction: A bio-bibliography*, Greenwood Press, London, 1986.

MacCannel, D. and MacCannell, J. F., *The Time of the Sign: A semiotic interpretation of modern culture*, Indiana University Press, Bloomington, 1982.

McGowan, J. P., 'Postmodern dilemmas', *Southwest Review*, 72, 3 (1987), 357–76.

McHale, B., 'Writing about postmodern writing', *Poetics Today*, 3 (1982), 211–27.

McHale, B., *Postmodernist Fiction*, Methuen, London, 1987.

MacIntyre, A., *After Virtue: A study in moral theory*, Duckworth, London, 1981.

MacRobbie, A., 'Postmodernism and popular culture', in L. Appignanesi (ed.), *Postmodernism*, Free Association Books, London, 1986, pp. 54–7.

Malmgren, C. D., *Fictional Space in the Modernist and Postmodernist American Novel*, Bucknell University Press, Lewisburg, PA, 1985.

Mandel, E., *Late Capitalism*, Verso, London, 1975.

Marcuse, H., 'The Affirmative Character of Culture', in *Negations*, transl. J. J. Shapiro, Beacon Press, Boston, 1968.

Martin, W., *Recent Theories of Narrative*, Cornell University Press, Ithaca, NY, 1986.

Mazzaro, J., *Postmodern American Poetry*, University of Illinois Press, Urbana, 1980.

Megill, A., *Prophets of Extremity: Nietzsche, Heidegger, Foucault, Derrida*, University of California Press, Berkeley/Los Angeles, 1985.

Mellencamp, P., 'Images of language and indiscreet dialogue: "The man who envied women"', *Screen*, 28, 2 (1987), 87–101.

Melville, S., 'Notes on the reemergence of allegory, the forgetting of modernism the necessity of rhetoric and the conditions of publicity in art and criticism', *October*, 19 (1981), 55–92.

Melville, S., *Philosophy Beside Itself: On deconstruction and modernism*, Manchester University Press, Manchester, 1986.

Meschonnic, H., *Modernité Modernité*, Verdier, Lagrasse, 1988.

Mitchell, W. J. T. (ed.), *On Narrative*, University of Chicago Press, Chicago, 1981.

Mitchell, W. J. T. (ed.), *Against Theory: Literary studies and the new pragmatism*, University of Chicago Press, Chicago, 1985.

Mitchell, W. J. T., *Iconology*, University of Chicago Press, Chicago, 1986.

Modleski, T. (ed.), *Studies in Entertainment*, Indiana University Press, Bloomington, 1987.

Montag, W., 'What is at stake in the debate on postmodernism?', in E. A. Kaplan (ed.), *Postmodernism and its Discontents*, Verso, London, 1988, pp. 88–103.

Montefiore, A. (ed.), *Philosophy in France Today*, Cambridge University Press, Cambridge, 1983.

Morgan, R. P., 'On the analysis of recent music', *Critical Inquiry*, 4, 1 (1977), 33–53.

Morris, M., *The Pirate's Fiancée*, Verso, London, 1988.

Morrissette, B., 'Post-modern generative fiction: Novel and film', *Critical Inquiry*, 2 (1975), 253–62.

Moser, W., 'Mode-Moderne-Postmoderne', *Etudes françaises*, 20, 2 (1984), 29–48.

Mouffe, C., 'Radical democracy: Modern or postmodern?', in A. Ross (ed.), *Universal Abandon?*, Edinburgh University Press, Edinburgh, 1989, pp. 31–45.

Mulvey, L., 'Feminism, film and the avant-garde', in M. Jacobus (ed.), *Women Writing and Writing About Women*, Croom Helm, London, 1979, pp. 177–95.

Nägele, R., 'Modernism and postmodernism: The margins of articulation', *Studies in Twentieth-Century Literature*, 5 (1980), 5–25.

Nead, L., 'Feminism, art history and cultural politics', in A. L. Rees and F. Borzello (eds), *The New Art History*, Camden Press, London, 1986, pp. 120–4.

Negri, A., *Politics of Subversion*, Polity, Oxford, 1989.

Nelson, C. and Grossberg, L. (eds), *Marxism and the Interpretation of Culture*, University of Illinois Press, Urbana, 1988.

Newman, C., *The Post-Modern Aura: The act of fiction in an age of inflation*, Northwestern University Press, Evanston, IL, 1985.

Nichols, B., 'The work of culture in the age of cybernetic systems', *Screen*, 29, 1 (1988), 22–46.

Norberg-Schulz, C., *Existence, Space and Architecture*, Studio Vista, London, 1971.

Norris, C., *The Contest of Faculties: Philosophy and theory after deconstruction*, Methuen, London, 1985.

Norris, C., 'Against postmodernism: Derrida, Kant, and nuclear politics', *Paragraph*, 9 (1987), 1–30.

Norris, C., *What's Wrong with Postmodernism*, Harvester Wheatsheaf, Hemel Hempstead, 1990.

Nyman, M., 'Against intellectual complexity in music', *October*, 13 (1980), 81–9.

Oliva, A. B., 'The international trans-avant-garde', *Flash Art*, 104 (1982), 36–43.

O'Neill, J., 'Religion and postmodernism', *Theory, Culture & Society*, 5, 2–3 (1988), 225–39.

Onopa, R., 'The end of art as a spiritual project', *TriQuarterly*, 26 (1973), 363–82.

Owens, C., 'The allegorical impulse: Toward a theory of postmodernism, Pt 1', *October*, 12 (1980), 67–86.

Owens, C., 'The allegorical impulse: Toward a theory of postmodernism, Pt 2', *October*, 13 (1980), 59–80.

Owens, C., 'Representation, appropriation and power', *Art in America*, 70, 5 (1982), 9–21.

Owens, C., 'The discourse of others: Feminists and postmodernism', in H. Foster (ed.), *Postmodern Culture*, Pluto Press, London, 1983, pp. 57–82.

Palmer, R. E., 'Postmodernity and hermeneutics', *Boundary*, 2, 5, 2 (1977), 363–93.

Parker, A., 'Taking sides (on history): Derrida re-Marx', *Diacritics*, 11, 2 (1981), 57–73.

Paterson, J., 'Le Roman "postmoderne": mise au point et perspectives', *Canadian Review of Comparative Literature*, 13, 2 (1986), 238–55.

Pavel, T., *The Feud of Language*, Blackwell, Oxford, 1990.

Pavis, P., 'The classical heritage of modern drama: The case of postmodern theatre', *Modern Drama*, 29 (1986), 1–22.

Penley, C., 'The avant-garde and its imaginary', *Camera Obscura*, 2 (1977), 3–33.

Peper, J., 'Postmodernismus: Unitary sensibility?', *Amerikastudien*, 22, 1 (1977), 65–89.

Perloff, M., *Poetics of Indeterminacy: Rimbaud to Cage*, Princeton University Press, Princeton, NJ, 1981.

Perloff, M., *The Dance of the Intellect: Studies in the poetry of the Pound tradition*, Cambridge University Press, Cambridge, 1985.

Perloff, M., *The Futurist Moment: Avant-garde, avant-guerre and the language of rupture*, University of Chicago Press, Chicago, 1986.

Perloff, M., 'Music for words perhaps: Reading/hearing/seeing John Cage's *Roaratorio*', *Genre*, 20, 3–4 (1987), 427–62.

Phillipson, M., *Painting, Language and Modernity*, Routledge & Kegan Paul, London, 1985.

Pippin, R. M., *Modernity as a Philosophical Problem*, Blackwell, Oxford, 1991.

Platten, D., 'Postmodern engineering', *Civil Engineering*, 56, 6 (1986), 84–6.

'p.m.', *Bolo'Bolo*, Semiotext(e), New York, 1985.

Poggioli, R., *Theory of the Avant-Garde*, transl. G. Fitzgerald, Harvard University Press, Cambridge, MA, 1968.

Portoghesi, P., *Le inibizioni dell'archittetura moderna*, Laterza, Bari, 1974.

Portoghesi, P., *After Modern Architecture*, transl. M. Shore, Rizzoli, New York, 1982.

Portoghesi, P., *Postmodern: The architecture of the postindustrial society*, transl. E. Shapiro, Rizzoli, New York, 1983.

Potter, K., 'Robert Ashley and postmodernist opera', *Opera*, 38 (1987), 388–94.

Pullin, F., 'Landscapes of reality: The fiction of contemporary Afro-American women', in A. R. Lee (ed.), *Black Fiction: New Studies in the Afro-American Novel since 1945*, Vision Press, London, 1980, pp. 173–203.

Putnam, H., *Realism and Reason*, Cambridge University Press, Cambridge, 1983.

Rabinow, P., 'Representations are social facts: Modernity and postmodernity in anthropology', in J. Clifford and G. E. Marcus (eds), *Writing Culture*, University of California Press, Berkeley/Los Angeles, 1986, pp. 234–61.

Radhakrishnan, R., 'The post-modern event and the end of logocentrism', *Boundary 2*, 12, 1 (1983), 33–60.

Rajchman, J., 'Postmodernism in a nominalist frame: The emergence and diffusion of a cultural category', *Flash Art*, 137 (1987), 49–51.

Rajchman, J. and West, C. (eds), *Post-Analytic Philosophy*, Columbia University Press, New York, 1985.

Raulet, G., 'From modernity as one-way street to postmodernity as dead-end', *New German Critique*, 33 (1984), 155–78.

Rees, A. L. and Borzello, F. (eds), *The New Art History*, Camden Press, London, 1986.

Reiss, T. J., *The Discourse of Modernism*, Cornell University Press, Ithaca, NY, 1982.

Richard, N., 'Postmodernism and periphery', *Third Text*, 2 (1987–8), 5–12.

Richters, A., 'Modernity–postmodernity controversies: Habermas and Foucault', *Theory, Culture & Society*, 5, 4 (1988), 611–43.

Riffaterre, M., 'Intertextual representation: On mimesis as interpretive discourse', *Critical Inquiry*, 11, 1 (1984), 141–62.

Roberts, J., 'Postmodern television and the visual arts', *Screen*, 28, 2 (1987), 118–27.

Roberts, J., *Postmodernism, Politics and Art*, Manchester University Press, Manchester, 1990.

Robinson, L. S. and Vogel, L., 'Modernism and history', *New Literary History*, 3, 1 (1971), 177–99.

Rochberg, G., 'Can the arts survive modernism? (A discussion of the characteristics, history and legacy of modernism)', *Critical Inquiry*, 11, 2 (1984), 317–40.

Rorty, R., *Philosophy and the Mirror of Nature*, Blackwell, Oxford, 1980.

Rorty, R., *Consequences of Pragmatism*, Harvester, Brighton, 1982.

Rorty, R., 'Postmodernist bourgeois liberalism', *Journal of Philosophy*, 80 (1983), 583–9.

Rorty, R., 'Habermas and Lyotard on postmodernity', *Praxis International*, 4 (1984), 32–44.

Rorty, R., 'Le cosmopolitisme sans émancipation: en réponse à Jean-François Lyotard', *Critique*, 41 (May 1985), 569–80.

Rose, J., '*The Man Who Mistook His Wife for a Hat* or *A Wife is Like an Umbrella* – Fantasies of the modern and postmodern', in A. Ross (ed.), *Universal Abandon?*, Edinburgh University Press, Edinburgh, 1989, pp. 237–50.

Rose, M. A., *The Postmodern and the Postindustrial*, Cambridge University Press, Cambridge, 1991.

Rosen, S., *The Ancients and the Moderns: Rethinking modernity*, Yale University Press, New Haven, CT, 1989.

Rosenberg, H., *Discovering the Present: Three decades in art, culture, and politics*, University of Chicago Press, Chicago, 1973.

Ross, A. (ed.), *Universal Abandon?*, Edinburgh University Press, Edinburgh, 1988.

Ross, A., *No Respect*, Routledge, New York, 1989.

Ross, A., *Strange Weather*, Verso, London, 1992.

Rosset, C., *L'Objet singulier*, Minuit, Paris, 1979.

Russell, C., 'The vault of language: Self-reflective artifice in contemporary American fiction', *Modern Fiction Studies*, 20, 3 (1974), 349–59.

Russell, C., 'Individual voice in the collective discourse: Literary innovation in postmodern American fiction', *SubStance*, 27 (1980), 29–39.

Russell, C. (ed.), *The Avant-Garde Today: An international anthology*, University of Illinois Press, Urbana, 1981.

Russell, C., *Poets, Prophets and Revolutionaries: The literary avant-garde from Rimbaud through postmodernism*, Oxford University Press, Oxford, 1985.

Ryan, M., *Marxism and Deconstruction: A critical articulation*, Johns Hopkins University Press, Baltimore, MD, 1982.

Ryan, M., 'Postmodern politics', *Theory, Culture & Society*, 5, 2–3 (1988), 559–76.

Said, E., *Orientalism*, Routledge & Kegan Paul, London, 1978.

Said, E., *The World, The Text, The Critic*, Faber & Faber, London, 1983.

Sandler, I., 'Modernism, revisionism, pluralism, and postmodernism', *Art Journal*, 40 (1980), 345–7.

Sasso, G., *Tramonto di un mito. L'Idea di 'progresso' fra Ottocento e Novecento*, Il Mulino, Bologna, 1984.

Scherpe, K. R., 'Dramatization and de-dramatization of the end: The apocalyptic consciousness of modernity and post-modernity', *Cultural Critique*, 5 (1987), 95–129.

Schmid, H., 'Postmodernism in Russian drama: Vampilov, Amalrik, Aksenov', in D. Fokkema and H. Bertens (eds), *Approaching Postmodernism*, John Benjamins, Amsterdam, 1986, pp. 157–84.

Scholes, R., *Structural Fabulation: Fiction of the future*, University of Notre Dame Press, Notre Dame, IN, 1975.

Scholes, R., *Fabulation and Metafiction*, University of Illinois Press, Urbana, 1979.

Schulte-Sasse, J., 'Modernity and modernism, postmodernity and postmodernism: Framing the issue', *Cultural Critique*, 5 (1987), 5–22.

Schulte-Sasse, J., 'Imagination and modernity; or, the taming of the human mind', *Cultural Critique*, 5 (1986–7), 23–48.

Schusterman, R., 'Postmodernist aestheticism', *Theory, Culture & Society*, 5, 2–3 (1988), 337–56.

Sekula, A., 'Dismantling modernism, reinventing documentary (Notes on the politics of representation)', *Massachusetts Review*, 19, 4 (1978), 859–93.

Sharrett, C., 'Sustaining romanticism in postmodernist cinema: An interview with Syberborg', *Cinéaste*, 15, 3 (1987), 18–20.

Silverman, H. J. (ed.), *Philosophy and Non-Philosophy since Merleau-Ponty*, Routledge, London, 1988.

Silverman, H. J. (ed.), *Postmodernism: Philosophy and the arts*, Routledge, London, 1990.

Silverman, H. J. and Welton, D. (eds), *Postmodernism and Continental Philosophy*, State University of New York Press, Albany, 1988.

Simmel, G., *The Philosophy of Money*, Routledge & Kegan Paul, London, 1978.

Sloterdijk, P., 'Cynicism – the twilight of false consciousness', *New German Critique*, 33 (1984), 190–206; repr. from Sloterdijk, *Kritik der zynischen Vernunft*, 2 vols, Sukrkamp, Frankfurt, 1984.

Smyth, E. J. (ed.), *Postmodernism and Contemporary Fiction*, Batsford, London, 1991.

Soja, E., *Postmodern Geographies*, Verso, London, 1990.

Solomon-Godeau, A., 'Photography after art photography', in B. Wallis (ed.), *Art After Modernism: Rethinking representation*, David Godine, Boston, MA, 1984, pp. 74–85.

Solomon-Godeau, A., 'Winning the game when the rules have been changed: Art photography and postmodernism', *Screen*, 25, 6 (1984), 88–102.

Solomon-Godeau, A., 'Living with contradictions: Critical practices in the age of supply-side aesthetics', *Screen*, 28, 3 (1987), 2–22.

Sontag, S., *Against Interpretation and Other Essays*, Dell, New York, 1967.

Spanos, W. V., 'The detective at the boundary: Some notes on the postmodern literary imagination', *Boundary 2*, 1, 1 (1972), 147–68.

Spanos, W. V. (ed.), *Martin Heidegger and the Question of Literature: Toward a postmodern literary hermeneutics*, Indiana University Press, Bloomington, 1979.

Spivak, G., 'Revolutions that as yet have no model', *Diacritics*, 10, 4 (1980), 29–49.

Spivak, G., 'Three women's texts and a critique of imperialism', *Critical Inquiry*, 12, 1 (1985), 243–61.

Sprinker, M., *Imaginary Relations*, Verso, London, 1987.

Steiner, W. (ed.), *The Sign in Music and Literature*, University of Texas Press, Austin, 1981.

Steiner, W., 'Intertextuality in painting', *American Journal of Semiotics*, 3, 4 (1985), 57–67.

Stevick, P., 'Scheherezade runs out of plots, goes on talking: the king, puzzled, listens: An essay on new fiction', *TriQuarterly*, 26 (1973), 332–62.

Stevick, P., *Alternative Pleasures: Postrealist fiction and the tradition*, University of Illinois Press, Urbana, 1981.

Stratton, J., *Writing Sites: A genealogy of the postmodern world*, Harvester Wheatsheaf, Hemel Hempstead, 1991.

Suleiman, S. R., 'Naming a difference: Reflections on "modernism versus postmodernism"', in D. Fokkema and H. Bertens (eds), *Approaching Postmodernism*, John Benjamins, Amsterdam, 1986, pp. 255–70.

Tafuri, M., *La sfera e il labirinto*, 2nd edn, Giulio Einaudi, Turin, 1980.

Tagg, J., 'Postmodernism and the born-again avant-garde', *Block*, 11 (1985–6), 3–7.

Tanner, T., *City of Words: American fiction 1950–1970*, Harper & Row, New York, 1971.

Tarn, N., 'Fresh frozen fenix: Random notes on the sublime, the beautiful and the ugly in the postmodern era', *New Literary History*, 16 (1985), 417–26.

Taylor, M., *Erring: A postmodern a/theology*, University of Chicago Press, Chicago, 1984.

Thiher, A., *Words in Reflection: Modern language theory and postmodern fiction*, University of Chicago Press, Chicago, 1984.

Thurley, G., *Counter-Modernism in Current Critical Theory*, Macmillan, London, 1983.

Timms, E. and Collier, P. (eds), *Visions and Blueprints: Avant-garde culture and radical politics in early twentieth-century Europe*, Manchester University Press, Manchester, 1987.

Todd, R., 'The presence of postmodernism in British fiction: Aspects of style and selfhood', in D. Fokkema and H. Bertens (eds), *Approaching Postmodernism*, John Benjamins, Amsterdam, 1986, pp. 99–117.

Toulmin, S., 'The construal of reality: Criticism in modern and postmodern science', *Critical Inquiry*, 9, 1 (1982), 93–111.

Trachtenberg, S. (ed.), *The Postmodern Moment*, Greenwood Press, Westport, CT, 1985.

Turner, B. S. (ed.), *Theories of Modernity and Postmodernity*, Sage, London, 1990.

Tyler, S., 'Post-modern ethnography: From document of the occult to occult document', in J. Clifford and G. E. Marcus (eds), *Writing Culture*, University of California Press, Berkeley/Los Angeles, 1986, pp. 122–40.

Ulmer, G. L., *Applied Grammatology: Post(e)-pedagogy from Jacques Derrida to Joseph Beuys*, Johns Hopkins University Press, Baltimore, MD, 1985.

Ulmer, G., *Teletheory*, Routledge, London, 1989.

Urry, J., *The Tourist Gaze*, Sage, London, 1990.

Vattimo, G., *La fine della modernità: Nichilismo ed ermeneutica nella cultura post-moderna*, Garzanti, Milan, 1985; transl. J. R. Snyder as *The End of Modernity*, Polity Press, Oxford, 1988.

Vattimo, G. and Rovatti, P. A. (eds), *Il Pensiero debole*, Feltrinelli, Milan, 1983.

Venturi, R., *Complexity and Contradiction in Architecture*, 2nd edn, Museum of Modern Art, New York, 1972.

Venturi, R., Scott-Brown, D. and Izenour, S., *Learning from Las Vegas*, MIT Press, Cambridge, MA, 1977.

Virilio, P., *Vitesse et politique*, Galilée, Paris, 1977.

Virilio, P., *Defense populaire et luttes écologiques*, Galilée, Paris, 1978.

Virilio, P., *L'Espace critique*, Christian Bourgois, Paris, 1984.

Virilio, P., *L'Horizon négatif*, Galilée, Paris, 1984.

Virilio, P., *L'Inertie polaire*, Christian Bourgois, Paris, 1990.

Virilio, P. and Lotringer, S., *Pure War*, transl. Mark Polizotti, Semiotext(e), New York, 1988.

Wallis, B. (ed.), *Art After Modernism: Rethinking representation*, David Godine, Boston, MA, 1984.

Wasson, R., 'From priest to Prometheus: Culture and criticism in the post-modernist period', *Journal of Modern Literature*, 3, 5 (1974), 1188–202.

Waugh, P., *Metafiction: The theory and practice of self-conscious fiction*, Methuen, London, 1984.

Wellmer, A., *Zur Dialektik von Moderne und Postmoderne*, Frankfurt, 1985.

Wellmer, A., 'On the dialectic of modernism and postmodernism', *Praxis International*, 4, 1 (1985), 337–62.

White, A. and Stallybrass, P., *The Poetics and Politics of Transgression*, Methuen, London, 1986.

White, H., *Tropics of Discourse: Essays in cultural criticism*, Johns Hopkins University Press, Baltimore, MD, 1978.

White, H., 'The value of narrativity in the representation of reality', *Critical Inquiry*, 7, 1 (1980), 5–27.

White, H., 'The narrativization of real events', *Critical Inquiry*, 7, 4 (1981), 793–8.

White, H., 'Historical pluralism', *Critical Inquiry*, 12, 3 (1986), 480–93.

Widgery, D., 'Postmodern medicine', *British Medical Journal*, 298 (1989), 897.

Wikstrom, J. H., 'Moving into the postmodern world', *Journal of Forestry*, 85, 1 (1987), 65.

Wilde, A., *Horizons of Assent: Modernism, postmodernism, and the ironic imagination*, Johns Hopkins University Press, Baltimore, MD, 1981.

Wilson, E., *Adorned in Dreams: Fashion and modernity*, Virago, London, 1985.

Wolfe, T., *The Painted Word*, Bantam Books, New York, 1975.

Wolff, J., 'Postmodern theory and feminist art practice', in R. Boyne and A. Rattansi (eds), *Postmodernism and Society*, Macmillan, London, 1990, pp. 187–208.

Wolin, R., 'Modernism versus postmodernism', *Telos*, 62 (1984–5), 9–29.

Wollen, P., *Readings and Writings*, Verso, London, 1982.

Wyschogrod, E., *Saints and Postmodernism*, University of Chicago Press, Chicago, 1990.

Wyver, J., 'Television and postmodernism', in L. Appignanesi (ed.), *Postmodernism*, Free Association Books, London, 1986, pp. 52–4.

Xenos, N., *Scarcity and Modernity*, Routledge, London, 1989.

Young, R., *White Mythologies*, Routledge, London, 1990.

Yúdice, G., 'Marginality and the ethics of survival', in A. Ross (ed.), *Universal Abandon?*, Edinburgh University Press, Edinburgh, 1989, pp. 214–36.

Ziolkowski, T., 'Toward a post-modern aesthetics?', *Mosaic*, 2, 4 (1969), 112–19.

Žižek, S., *Looking Awry*, MIT Press, London, 1991.

Žižek, S., *For they know not what they do*, Verso, London, 1991.

Zukin, S., 'The postmodern debate over urban form', *Theory, Culture & Society*, 5, 2–3 (1988), 431–6.

Zurbrugg, N., 'Postmodernity, *métaphore manquée*, and the myth of the trans-avant-garde', *SubStance*, 48 (1986), 68–90.

☐ *Acknowledgements*

Grateful acknowledgement is made to the following sources for permission to reproduce material in this book previously published elsewhere. Every effort has been made to trace copyright holders, but if any have been inadvertently overlooked the publisher will be pleased to make the necessary arrangement at the first opportunity.

Jean-François Lyotard, 'Answering the Question: What is Postmodernism?', from *Innovation/Renovation*, eds Ihab Hassan and Sally Hassan, University of Wisconsin Press, 1983. English translation of this essay by Régis Durand copyright © 1983 by University of Wisconsin Press.

Jean-François Lyotard, 'Note on the Meaning of "Post-"', from *The Postmodern Explained: Correspondent 1982–1985* by Jean-François Lyotard, transl. Julian Pefanis and Morgan Thomas, University of Minnesota Press, 1992; and from *The Postmodern Explained to Children*, The Power Institute of Fine Arts, University of Sydney, 1986. From the original French edition *Le Postmoderne expliqué aux enfants*, Editions Galilée, 1986.

Passages from *Philosophical Discourse of Modernity*, transl. F. G. Lawrence, MIT Press, 1987. English language translation from Jürgen Habermas, 'The entry into Postmodernity: Nietzsche as a turning point', copyright © 1987, Massachusetts Institute of Technology.

Fredric Jameson, from *Postmodernism, or the cultural logic of late capitalism*, Duke University Press and Verso, 1991. Reprinted by permission.

Gianni Vattimo, from *The End of Modernity*, Basil Blackwell, 1988. English translation copyright © Polity Press, 1988. First published in Italian as *La fine della modernità* © Garzanti Editore s.p.a. 1985.

Arthur Kroker and David Cook, from *The Postmodern Scene*, Macmillan Education Ltd and St Martin's Press, 1988 © New World Perspectives, Culture Texts Series, 1986, 1988.

Zygmunt Bauman, from *Legislators and Interpreters*, Polity Press in association with Basil Blackwell, 1987. Copyright © Zygmunt Bauman, 1987.

Material from Ihab Hassan, *The Postmodern Turn: Essays in postmodern theory and culture*, is reprinted by permission. © 1987 by the Ohio State University Press. All rights reserved.

Reprinted from Sally Banes, *Terpsichore in Sneakers: Post-modern dance*, paperback with new introduction, © 1989 by Sally Banes, Wesleyan University Press. By permission of University Press of New England.

Reprinted from *October*, 15 (1980) by Douglas Crimp, 'The Photographic Activity of Postmodernism', by permission of The MIT Press, Cambridge, Massachusetts. Copyright © *October* and The MIT Press, 1980.

Paul Crowther, 'Postmodernism in the Visual Arts', from *Postmodernism and Society*, ed. Roy Boyne and Ali Rattansi, Macmillan Education Ltd and St Martin's Press, 1990. Copyright © Paul Crowther.

Jean Baudrillard, from *Evil Demon of Images*, The Power Institute of Fine Arts, University of Sydney, 1987. © Jean Baudrillard 1987. From *Simulations* by Jean Baudrillard, transl. Paul Foss, Paul Patton, Philip Beitchman, Semiotext(e), New York, 1983.

Umberto Eco, from *Travels in Hyperreality*, Picador, 1987, Pan Books Ltd © Gruppo Editoriale Fabbri-Bompiani, Sonzogno, Etas s.p.a., 1973, 1976, 1986. English translation © Harcourt Brace Jovanovich 1986 © Umberto Eco 1967, 1986.

Reprinted from *October*, 13 (1980) by Michael Nyman, 'Against Intellectual Complexity in Music', by permission of The MIT Press, Cambridge, Massachusetts. Copyright © *October* and The MIT Press, 1980.

Andreas Huyssen, 'The Search for Tradition: Avant-garde and postmodernism in the 1970s', from *After the Great Divide*, Indiana University Press, 1986 and The Macmillan Press Ltd, 1988. Originally published in *New German Critique*, 22 (Winter 1981) © Andreas Huyssen 1986.

Peter Bürger, from *Theory of the Avant-Garde*, transl. Michael Shaw, University of Minnesota Press and Manchester University Press, 1984. Copyright © 1984 by the University of Minnesota. All rights reserved. Translation based on the second edition of *Theorie der Avantgarde* © 1974, 1980 by Suhrkamp Verlag, Frankfurt, Germany.

Jean-François Lyotard, 'The Sublime and the Avant-Garde', from *The Lyotard Reader*, ed. Andrew Benjamin, Basil Blackwell, 1989. © Oxford University Press 1985. Reprinted from *Paragraph*, 6 (1985) by permission of Oxford University Press.

Achille Bonito Oliva, 'The International Trans-Avant-Garde', from *Flash Art*, 104 (October/November 1991).

Kenneth Frampton, 'Towards a Critical Regionalism: Six points for an architecture of resistance', from Hal Foster (ed.), *The Anti-Aesthetic: Essays on postmodern culture*, Port Townsend, WA: Bay Press, 1983 and Pluto Press Ltd, 1985 (under the title *Postmodern Culture*). Copyright © 1983 Bay Press.

Charles Jencks, from *Postmodernism*, Rizzoli International Publications, Inc., 1987 and Academy Editions, 1987. Copyright © 1987 Charles Jencks and Maggie Keswick. Text and illustrations reprinted by permission of the author.

Robert Venturi, Denise Scott-Brown and Steven Izenour, from *Learning from Las Vegas*, The MIT Press, Cambridge, Massachusetts, 1972. Copyright © The MIT Press, 1972. Text and illustrations reprinted by permission.

Paolo Portoghesi, from *Postmodern*, transl. Ellen Shapiro, Rizzoli International Publications, Inc., 1983.

514   *Acknowledgements*

Richard Rorty, 'Postmodernist Bourgeois Liberalism', from *The Journal of Philosophy*, LXXX, 10 (October 1983). © 1983 *The Journal of Philosophy*, Inc. Reprinted by permission of the *Journal* and the author.

Ernesto Laclau, 'Politics and the Limits of Modernity', from *Universal Abandon?* ed. Andrew Ross, University of Minnesota Press, 1988 and Edinburgh University Press, 1989. © 1988 by the Regents of the University of Minnesota.

André Gorz, from *Métamorphoses du travail*, English translation: *Critique of Economic Reason*, Verso, 1988.

Jean Baudrillard, 'Toward a Principle of Evil', transl. Jacques Mourrain, from *Jean Baudrillard: Selected Writings*, ed. Mark Poster, Polity Press and Stanford University Press, 1988. First published in *Fatal Strategies*. Reprinted by permission of Semiotext(e)/Autonomedia © Editions Grasset & Fasquelle, 1983.

Meaghan Morris, from *The Pirate's Fiancée*, Verso, 1988 © 1988 Meaghan Morris. Reprinted by permission of the author.

Sabina Lovibond, 'Feminism and Postmodernism', from *Postmodernism and Society*, eds Roy Boyne and Ali Rattansi, Macmillan Education Ltd and St Martin's Press, 1990 © Sabina Lovibond. Reprinted by permission.

Nancy Fraser and Linda Nicholson, 'Social Criticism without Philosophy', from *Theory, Culture & Society*, 5, 2–3 (1988) (special double issue on Postmodernism) © *Theory, Culture & Society* Ltd. Reprinted by permission of Sage Publications Ltd.

Reprinted from Alice A. Jardine, *Gynesis: Configurations of woman and modernity*. Copyright © 1985 by Cornell University Press. Used by permission of the publisher.

Simon During, 'Postmodernism or Post-colonialism Today', in *Textual Practice*, 1 (1987) © Methuen and Co. Ltd, 1987.

'Postmodernism and Periphery' by Nelly Richard; translated from Spanish by Nick Caistor, and published in *Third Text*, 2, Winter 1987/88.

Rey Chow, 'Rereading Mandarin Ducks and Butterflies: A response to the "postmodern" condition', in *Cultural Critique*, 5, Winter 1986 © 1986, *Cultural Critique*, Oxford University Press. Used with permission.

Index